JN174557

Studies in
the Humanities
12

A Grammar of Irabu
A Southern Ryukyuan Language
Michinori Shimoji

Kyushu University Press

All rights reserved. No part of this publication may be reproduced or transmitted in any form or any means, electronic or mechanical, including photocopying and recording, or by any information storage and retrieval system, without the written permission form the publisher.

Copyright © 2017 by Michinori Shimoji

Kyushu University Press
3–8–34–305, Momochihama Sawara-ku, Fukuoka-shi 814–0001, Japan

ISBN 978–4–7985–0195–6

Printed in Japan

For Mika

Preface

The present work is a slightly revised version of my PhD thesis submitted to the Australian National University in 2008. It is a descriptive grammar of Irabu Ryukyuan, a Southern Ryukyuan language spoken on Irabu Island, which is one of the Miyako Islands, Okinawa, Japan. Irabu is an endangered Japonic language, with approximately 2,000 elder native speakers. The present work serves as the first descriptive grammar of this language.

It is a shared concern among Japanese linguists that all the local languages in Japan (Ryukyuan, Ainu and the mainland dialects of Japanese) are in an imminent danger of extinction. Many linguists are eager to publish books or organise symposia in which they continuously warn that every dialect will die out soon and make a valiant proposal that someone must describe and document the endangered local languages before they die out. However, the proposal always sounds like dealing with someone else's problem. Who does 'someone' refer to? When will the proposed action start? And in what way? It seems to me that what we must do is *not* to keep publishing books with similar and abstract slogans about language endangerment again and again. What *we* must do *now* is to take an immediate action, and one important task among others is to write a comprehensive grammar of each endangered local language in Japan. I am fully aware that the present work is not at all an ideal example, but I am certain that the present work is one concrete action against the language endangerment in Japan.

The present work has been brought to fruition through the help and support of countless people. My deepest gratitude goes to the people on Irabu Island who taught me their language with patience, eagerness, and generousness: Kimiko Namihira, Setsuko Sugama, Kani Aguni, Koichi Taketomi, Hatsue Ameku, Hiroyasu Sawada, Chiko Shiokawa, Yukio Okuhama, Takeshi Tokuyama, Asako Shimoji, Miyo Karimata, and Yoshiko Kawamitsu. My fieldwork was also supported by many other people whose name I do not reveal here.

My deep thank also goes to my supervisors of the linguistics department of ANU, Emeritus Professor Andrew Pawley and Emeritus Professor Malcolm Ross, who gave me continuous support and encouragement, without which I would have never been able to complete the thesis and publish this book. Professor Nicholas Evans also helped me at various times, giving me a lot of insightful comments on early drafts of my thesis.

The present work has been refined through countless discussions and interactions with the following great researchers at various occasions: Professor Shigehisa Karimata, Professor Yukinori Takubo, Professor Nobuko Kibe, Professor Hirotake Matsumoto, Professor Akihiro Kaneda, Professor Satoshi Nishioka, Professor Shinsho Miyara, Dr. Rumiko Shinzato, Dr. Leon Serafim, Dr. Alexander Vovin, Dr. Wayne Lawrence, Dr. Jo Nakahara, Professor Daniel Long, Dr. Shinji Ogawa, Dr. Yuto Niinaga, Ms. Reiko Aso, Dr. Masahiro Yamada, Dr. Kayoko Shimoji, Dr. Thomas Pellard, Dr. Yuka Hayashi, Professor Shoichi Iwasaki, Professor Tsuyoshi Ono, Mr. Hiroyuki Nakama, Mr. Kenan Celik, Ms. Yulia Koloskova, Dr. Aleksandra Yorosz, Dr. Hayato Aoi, Dr. Natsuko Nakagawa, Dr. Satomi Matayoshi, Dr. Nana Toyama, Dr. Rihito Shirata, Dr. Hiromi Shigeno, Ms. Akiko Tokunaga, Dr. Gijs van der Lubbe, Dr. Christopher Davis, Professor Matthew Dryer, Professor Tasaku Tsunoda, Professor Masayoshi Shibatani, Professor Toshihide Nakayama, Professor Honoré Watanabe, Dr. Yusuke Hiratsuka, Dr. Soichiro Harada, Dr. Shiro Takeuchi, Dr. Michio Matsumaru, Dr. Kunihiko Kuroki, Dr. Noboru Yoshioka, Dr. Shiho Ebihara, Dr. Ayako Shiba, Dr. Shengkai Zhang, Dr. Yosuke Igarashi, Dr. Tatsuya Hirako, Dr. Tomohide Kinuhata, Professor Kiyoko Somiya, Professor Ritsuko Kikusawa and Dr. Masayuki Onishi.

Before I started my PhD study at ANU, I studied at Tokyo University of Foreign Studies (TUFS) as an MA student. Professor Shinjiro Kazama was my supervisor. His approach of linguistics, which is characterised by a fieldwork-based description of a lesser-known language in a cross-linguistic perspective, is exactly what I pursued in the present work. I would like to express my gratitude to him for his dedicated supervision during the two years of MA and for his continuous support and encouragement until now.

The publication of the present work has been made possible by the publication grant of Studies in the Humanities, Faculty of Humanities, Kyushu University. A deep thank goes to Ms. Yuki Okuno of Kyushu University Press. I would also like to express my gratitude to the two anonymous external examiners of the present work for publication. Of course, all errors and shortcomings are mine alone.

Last but not least, I am grateful to my family from the bottom of my heart. My wife, Mika, gave me strong and continuous support during the process of the revision of my thesis for publication. In fact, I would not have thought of publishing this grammar without her encouragement. My father, Junji, was an important consultant of this grammar. I am proud of being the writer of the grammar of his own language, which is seriously endangered.

M. S.
November, 2016
Listening to AC/DC's 'It's a long way to the top'

Table of contents

Preface ·· i

Chapter 1 The Irabu language and its speakers ·································· 1

1.1. Geography ··· 1

1.2. Genealogy ·· 2

1.3. Notes on the settlement and political history of the
       Rykuku Islands ·· 3

1.4. Sociolinguistic overview ·· 4
    1.4.1. The name of the language   4
    1.4.2. Dialects   4
    1.4.3. The number of speakers   6

1.5. Previous works on Irabu ·· 6
    1.5.1. Detailed grammars   7
    1.5.2. Grammatical sketches   7
    1.5.3. Works on specific topics   7
        1.5.3.1. Phonological studies   7
        1.5.3.2. Morphosyntactic studies   8
    1.5.4. Dictionaries, texts, and unpublished materials   8

1.6. A typological overview of Irabu ·· 9
    1.6.1. Phonology   9
    1.6.2. Morphosyntax   10

1.7. Method and data ··· 11

1.8. Organisation of this grammar ·· 12

Chapter 2 Phonology ·· **13**

2.1. Segmentation ··· 13
    2.1.1. Grammatical word   13

vi　　　　　　　　　　　　Table of contents

2.1.2. Phonological word　　14

2.2. Classes of phonemes ·· 15
 2.2.1. Consonants　　15
 2.2.2. Glides　　16
 2.2.3. Vowels　　16

2.3. Minimal or quasi-minimal contrasts ····································· 17
 2.3.1. Consonants (stops, fricatives, and resonants)　　17
 2.3.2. Glides　　17
 2.3.3. Vowels　　17

2.4. The structure of the root word ··· 17
 2.4.1. Word template　　18
 2.4.2. Nucleic resonants　　20
 2.4.3. Heavy structures　　20
 2.4.4. Examples of root word structures　　20
  2.4.4.1. Examples of words with an initial syllable only　　21
  2.4.4.2. Examples of words with an initial and a non-initial syllable, showing the structure of the initial syllable　　21
  2.4.4.3. Examples of words with an initial and a non-initial syllable, showing the structure of the non-initial syllable　　22
  2.4.4.4. Examples of words with a presyllable plus initial syllable　　23
  2.4.4.5. Examples of words consisting only of a presyllable (a syllabic resonant)　　23

2.5. Phonotactics of the word-plus ·· 24
 2.5.1. Four primary phonotactic constraints of the word(-plus)　　25
  2.5.1.1. Final C　　25
  2.5.1.2. Medial cluster　　25
  2.5.1.3. Cluster of non-resonants　　26
  2.5.1.4. Ban on /C.V/ sequence　　26
 2.5.2. Long vowels and diphthongs　　27
 2.5.3. Single onset of initial and non-initial syllables　　28
 2.5.4. Initial syllable onset cluster　　28
 2.5.5. Non-initial cluster　　28
  2.5.5.1. Geminates　　28
  2.5.5.2. Partial geminates (homorganic /n/ + C of any place of articulation)　　29

2.5.5.3. Non-geminates (resonant C_i + resonant/non-resonant C_j)   29

2.5.6. Presyllable plus initial syllable onset   30

2.5.6.1. Geminates   30

2.5.6.2. Partial geminates (homorganic /n(n)/ + C of any place of articulation)   31

2.5.6.3. Non-geminates   31

2.5.7. Frequecy-based account of root structures   31

2.5.8. Consonant allophony   33

2.6. Mora ·· 33

2.6.1. Definition   34

2.6.2. Minimal word   34

2.6.3. Length (quantity) contrast   35

2.6.3.1. Short vs. long   35

2.6.3.2. Non-geminate vs. geminate   36

2.7. Phonological alternation rules ································· 36

2.7.1. Sequential voicing   36

2.7.2. Geminate copy insertion rule   38

2.7.3. The /ï/-insertion rule   39

2.7.4. The /ï/-spreading rule   42

2.7.5. Resonant geminate reduction   43

2.7.6. Sequential nasal deletion   44

2.7.7. Morpheme-specific alternation rules   44

2.7.7.1. /j/-insertion for topic and accusative particles   44

2.7.7.2. /s/-to-/r/ assimilation   45

2.8. Miscellaneous segmental issues ·································· 45

2.8.1. Homorganic nasal clusters in roots   45

2.8.2. Non-nasal alveolar resonants /v/ and /ž/   46

2.8.3. The status of glides   47

2.8.3.1. General remarks   47

2.8.3.2. Advantages in assuming a complex CG   48

2.8.4. The phonemic analysis of long vowels   49

2.8.5. The problem of the long /ïï/   50

2.9. Prosody ·· 51

2.9.1. Prosodic patterns of root words   52

2.9.1.1. Prosodic patterns of W_2 52

2.9.1.2. Prosodic patterns of W_3 53

2.9.1.3. Prosodic patterns of W_4 and longer words   56

viii   Table of contents

2.9.1.4. Summary   57
2.9.2. Footing   58
    2.9.2.1. Definition of the foot   58
    2.9.2.2. Ternary footing   59
2.9.3. Tone assignment   62
    2.9.3.1. The Principle of Rhythmic Alternation   62
    2.9.3.2. The rule   63
    2.9.3.3. Summary   66
2.9.4. Phrasal mapping of the alternating rhythm   67

2.10. Phonological characteristics of compounds ·· 70
    2.10.1. Productive compounds   71
    2.10.2. Lexicalised compounds   73

Chapter 3 Descriptive preliminaries ··· 75

3.1. Phrase structure ··· 75
    3.1.1. Predicate phrase   75
        3.1.1.1. Verbal predicate   76
        3.1.1.2 Nominal predicate   77
    3.1.2. Nominal phrase   78

3.2. Word, affix and clitic ·· 79
    3.2.1. Morphological dependency   80
        3.2.1.1. Isolatability test   81
        3.2.1.2. Reordering test   81
        3.2.1.3. Combinability test   86
    3.2.2. Phonological dependency   87
        3.2.2.1. Overview   87
        3.2.2.2. External clitics   89
    3.2.3. Problematic cases   92
        3.2.3.1. Auxuliary verb   92
        3.2.3.2. Clitics of the bound-word type   93
        3.2.3.3. Clitics with a limited combinability with a
                 phonological host   94

3.3. Word classes ·· 96
    3.3.1. Nominals   96
    3.3.2. Adnominals   97
    3.3.3. Verbs   97
    3.3.4. Adjectives   97

3.3.5. Bound markers   99
   3.3.5.1. Argument markers   99
   3.3.5.2. Predicate markers   100
   3.3.5.3. Discourse markers   101
   3.3.5.4. Relative ordering within bound marker chains   102
3.3.6. Others   103
   3.3.6.1. Underived adverbs   103
   3.3.6.2. Derived adverbs   104
   3.3.6.3. Conjunctions   106
   3.3.6.4. Interjections   107

3.4. Grammatical relations ···· 108
  3.4.1. Subject   108
  3.4.2. Direct object   109
  3.4.3. Indirect object   110

3.5. Argument structure ···· 111
  3.5.1. Core, extended core, and peripheral arguments   111
  3.5.2. Core arguments   112
  3.5.3. Extended core arguments   113
   3.5.3.1. The verb 'become'   113
   3.5.3.2. The verb 'get hit by'   114
   3.5.3.3. The verb 'meet'   114
   3.5.3.4. Indirect object   115
  3.5.4. Peripheral arguments   116

3.6. Morphological typology ···· 117
  3.6.1. Affixation   117
  3.6.2. Compounding   118
   3.6.2.1. Structure   119
   3.6.2.2. The word (as opposed to phrasal) status of the
       compound   120
  3.6.3. Full reduplication   121

Chapter 4 The nominal phrase ···· **123**

4.1. The modifier ···· 124
  4.1.1. Modifier filled by NP   124
  4.1.2. Modifier filled by adnominal   125
  4.1.3. Modifier filled by other syntactic constructions   127
  4.1.4. The semantic characteristic of genitive   128

4.2. The head ⋯⋯⋯⋯⋯⋯⋯⋯⋯⋯⋯⋯⋯⋯⋯⋯⋯⋯⋯⋯ 129
  4.2.1. Formal nouns   130
    4.2.1.1. *tukja* 'time'   130
    4.2.1.2. *mai* 'front; before'   130
    4.2.1.3. *atu* 'back; after'   131
    4.2.1.4. *kutu* 'thing; fact'   131
    4.2.1.5. *tami* 'purpose; benefit'   132
    4.2.1.6. *jau* 'state'   132
    4.2.1.7. *njaa* 'manner'   133
    4.2.1.8. *su(u)*   133
  4.2.2. Headless structure   135
  4.2.3. Appositional structure   136

4.3. Case ⋯⋯⋯⋯⋯⋯⋯⋯⋯⋯⋯⋯⋯⋯⋯⋯⋯⋯⋯⋯⋯⋯ 137
  4.3.1. Basic system   138
  4.3.2. Nominative and genitive   141
  4.3.3. Accusative and partitive   143
    4.3.3.1. The distributional properties of Partitive =*a*   143
    4.3.3.2. Specificity and partitive   145
    4.3.3.3. Partitive in contexts other than narrative converbal clauses   146
    4.3.3.4. Partitive in narrative convernal clauses   146
    4.3.3.5. The function of partitive: a cross-linguistic perspective   148
    4.3.3.6. The two principles for partitive marking   149
    4.3.3.7. Revisiting specificity   150
    4.3.3.8. Allomorphy of partitive   152
    4.3.3.9. Accusative   153
  4.3.4. Dative and allative   154
    4.3.4.1. Time   155
    4.3.4.2. Possessor   155
    4.3.4.3. Experiencer   156
    4.3.4.4. Passive agent   156
    4.3.4.5. Result of change   157
    4.3.4.6. Location   157
    4.3.4.7. Causee agent   158
    4.3.4.8. Beneficiary   159
    4.3.4.9. Goal-Location and Goal   160
    4.3.4.10. Object of communication   162
  4.3.5. Instrumental =*sii*   162
  4.3.6. Associative =*tu*   163

Table of contents   xi

4.3.7. Comparative =*jarruu*   164
4.3.8. Ablative =*kara*   165
4.3.9. Limitative =*gami*   165
4.3.10. Absence of case marking   166
    4.3.10.1. Subject case marking and information structure   166
    4.3.10.2. Object case marking and information-structure   166
    4.3.10.3. Case ellipsis   167

Chapter 5 Morphology of nominals and adnominals ···················· **169**

5.1. Nominals and adnominals: overview ···························· 169
    5.1.1. The distribution in terms of NP structure   169
    5.1.2. Demonstratives   170

5.2. Subclassification of nominals ······························ 171
    5.2.1. Nouns   171
    5.2.2. Pronouns   172
       5.2.2.1. Personal pronouns and demonstrative pronouns   172
       5.2.2.2. Reformulating personal pronominal system:
           minimal-augment system   175
       5.2.2.3. Reflexive pronouns   177
    5.2.3. Numerals   179
    5.2.4. Interrogatives   183
       5.2.4.1. Basic forms   183
       5.2.4.2. Complex form: 'how'   185
       5.2.4.3. Complex form: 'why/how'   185
    5.2.5. Indefinites   185
    5.2.6. Non-pronominal demonstrative nominals   187
       5.2.6.1. Demonstrative locatives   187
       5.2.6.2. Demonstrative manner words   187

5.3. The internal structure of the nominal word ···················· 188
    5.3.1. Diminutive -*gama*   189
    5.3.2. Plural -*mmi*/-*ta, etc.*   189
    5.3.3. Approximative -*nagi*   190

5.4. Adnominals ······································· 191
    5.4.1. Demonstrative adnominals   191
    5.4.2. Other adnominals   191

xii   Table of contents

Chapter 6 Verb morphology **193**

6.1. Functional overview 193
    6.1.1. Verb inflection and finiteness   193
    6.1.2. Tense, mood, negation, voice, and aspect   193
        6.1.2.1. Tense, mood-modality, and negation   194
        6.1.2.2. Voice   195
        6.1.2.3. Aspect   195
    6.1.3. Inflection and clause combining   195

6.2. The structure of the verb word 196
    6.2.1. Stem class   197
    6.2.2. Thematic vowel (stem extension)   198
    6.2.3. Some notes on the thematic vowel analysis   199

6.3. Inflectional morphology 202
    6.3.1. Finite inflection   202
    6.3.2. Non-finite inflection   206
        6.3.2.1. Narrative converbs   206
        6.3.2.2. Other converbs   207
    6.3.3. Internal structure of inflectional endings   210
        6.3.3.1. Finite realis inflection as -(NEG)-TENSE-MOOD   210
        6.3.3.2. Finite inflection as -TENSE-MOOD$_{[NEG]}$ 210
    6.3.4. Morphophonemics of Class 2 athematic stems   211
        6.3.4.1. Stem-final stop lenition   211
        6.3.4.2. Class 2 stems ending in fricative and resonant   212
        6.3.4.3. Class 2 stems that end in /v/   213
        6.3.4.4. Class 2 stems with -*u* thematic vowel   213
        6.3.4.5. Morphophonemic nominalisation   214
    6.3.5. Irregular verbs   214
        6.3.5.1. Deictic directional verb 'come'   214
        6.3.5.2. Light verb *(a)s*- 'do'   215
        6.3.5.3. Negative verb *njaa*- 'not exist'   216
    6.3.6. Existential verb, state verb, and copula verb   217
        6.3.6.1. Existential verb   217
        6.3.6.2. Copula verb   218
        6.3.6.3. State verb   220

6.4. Derivational morphology 221
    6.4.1. Derivational affixes   221
        6.4.1.1. Causative -*sïmi, -as*   222

Table of contents   xiii

      6.4.1.2. Passive-malefactive-potential *-(r)ai*   223
      6.4.1.3. Honorific *-(s)ama(r)*   223
    6.4.2. Primary stem   224
      6.4.2.1. Compounds   225
      6.4.2.2. Serial verb construction (SVC)   226
      6.4.2.3. Auxiliary verb construction   228

  6.5. Citation form 230

Chapter 7 The predicate phrase **231**

  7.1. The structure of verbal predicate phrase 231
    7.1.1. Verb inflection within a VP   232
    7.1.2. Lexical verb and auxiliary verb   232
    7.1.3. Phrasal serial verb constructions   233
      7.1.3.1. Definition   233
      7.1.3.2. Typological characteristics of phrasal SVCs   235
    7.1.4. Phrasal auxiliary verb constructions   241
      7.1.4.1. Aspectual AVCs   241
      7.1.4.2. Benefactive AVCs   243
      7.1.4.3. Auxiliary ellipsis   243

  7.2. The structure of nominal predicate phrase 244
    7.2.1. Basic structure   244
    7.2.2. Secondary inflection   245

Chapter 8 Property concepts, adjectives, and other derivational
          processes **249**

  8.1. Property concept stems (PC stems) 249
    8.1.1. Property concept   249
    8.1.2. Morphosyntax of the PC stem   250
      8.1.2.1. Prototypical PC stems: (a–f)   252
      8.1.2.2. Less prototypical PC stems: (g–j)   254
      8.1.2.3. Less prototypical nominal stems: (k–m)   256
    8.1.3. Non-class-changing derivation by *-gi* 'seem; appear'
        257

  8.2. The adjective class 260
    8.2.1. Overview   260
      8.2.1.1. Morphology   260

8.2.1.2. Semantics   261
8.2.1.3. Syntax   261
8.2.2. Adjectives in NP structure   262
8.2.2.1. Highly restricted argument function   264
8.2.2.2. Skewed functional preference for the modifier NP function   264
8.2.2.3. Modificational constraint   265
8.2.3. Adjectives in VP structure   266
8.2.4. Adjectives derived from nominal stems   267
8.2.5. Summary   267

8.3. Deriving nominals, verbs, and adverbs ·· 268
8.3.1. State nominal derivation with -sa   268
8.3.2. PC adverb with -fï   270
8.3.3. PC verb with -ka(r)   270
8.3.3.1. Diachronic account of -ka(r)   271
8.3.3.2. The PC verb as a subclass of verb   272
8.3.4. Compound nominals derived from PC stems   277
8.3.4.1. Overview   277
8.3.4.2. Lexical head compounds   279
8.3.4.3. Dummy head compounds   280

8.4. Adjective, compound nominal, and PC verb: functional account ·· 283
8.4.1. Dummy head compound vs PC verb: predicative function   283
8.4.2. Adjective vs lexical head compound: attributive function   285
8.4.3. Adnominal clause vs adjective: syntactic attributive function   285

8.5. Class-changing derivation ··· 286
8.5.1. Noun-to-verb derivation (verbalisation)   286
8.5.2. Verb-to-noun derivation (nominalisation)   288
8.5.3. Verb-to-PC-stem derivation   289
8.5.3.1. 'wanting to' -busï   290
8.5.3.2. 'difficult to' -guri   291
8.5.2.3. 'easy to' -jasï   292

Chapter 9 Bound markers ··· **293**

9.1. Overview of bound markers ·· 293

Table of contents

9.2. Conjunction markers ·· 293
   9.2.1. Temporal =*kja(a)*   293
   9.2.2. 'So' conjunction =*(ss)iba*   294
   9.2.3. 'But' conjunction =*suga*   295

9.3. Modal markers ·· 296
   9.3.1. Dubitative =*bjaam*   296
   9.3.2. Dubitative 2 =*gagara*   297
   9.3.3. Hearsay =*ca* and =*tim(dara/dooi)*   298
   9.3.4. Uncertainty =*pazï*   300
   9.3.5. Addressive assertive =*su(u)da*   300
   9.3.6. Certainty =*dara*   302
   9.3.7. Emphatic =*doo(i)*   303
   9.3.8. Reserved emphatic =*saa*   304

9.4. Limiter markers ·· 305
   9.4.1. 'Too' quantifier =*mai*   305
   9.4.2. 'Only' quantifier =*tjaaki*   306
   9.4.3. 'Only' quantifier 2: =*bakaar*   307
   9.4.4. 'Nothing' quantifier =*cumma*   307
   9.4.5. 'Primarily' qualifier =*kara*   308
   9.4.6. Emphatic qualifier =*dumma*   308
   9.4.7. Contrastive =*gami*   309

9.5. Information-structure markers ·· 311
   9.5.1. Topic markers   312
      9.5.1.1. Object topic =*ba(a)*   312
      9.5.1.2. Non-object topic =*a*   313
   9.5.2. Focus markers   315
      9.5.2.1. Declarative focus =*du*   315
      9.5.2.2. Interrogative focus =*ru* and =*ga*   316

9.6. Discourse markers ··· 317
   9.6.1. Information-updater =*ju(u)*   317
   9.6.2. 'How about' =*da*   319
   9.6.3. Confirmative =*i*   319
   9.6.4. Emotional =*ra(a)*, =*sja(a)*   320
   9.6.5. Question =*ru*/=*ga*   321
   9.6.6. Question 2 =*e(e)*   321

xvi   Table of contents

Chapter 10 The simple sentence **323**

10.1. Speech acts and clause types 323
    10.1.1. Declarative clauses   323
    10.1.2. Interrogative clauses   326
    10.1.3. Imperative clauses   327
    10.1.4. Mismatches or ambiguous cases   327
        10.1.4.1. Polite command   327
        10.1.4.2. Rhetorical question   327
        10.1.4.3. Self question and clause types   328

10.2. Proper inclusion, equation, state, location, and possession 329
    10.2.1. Proper inclusion   329
    10.2.2. Equation   330
    10.2.3. State   331
    10.2.4. Location   332
    10.2.5. Possession   333

10.3. Negation 336
    10.3.1. Inflectional negation   336
    10.3.2. Negation of existential and state verbs   337
    10.3.3. Negation of PC verb   338

10.4. Valency changing 338
    10.4.1. Causative   339
        10.4.1.1. Morphological causative   339
        10.4.1.2. Lexical intransitive-transitive pairs   342
        10.4.1.3. Anticausative   343
    10.4.2. Passive   344
    10.4.3. Malefactive   347
    10.4.4. Reflexive   350

10.5. Tense, mood, and aspect 351
    10.5.1. Tense and mood   351
        10.5.1.1. Realis mood   352
        10.5.1.2. Irrealis mood   357
        10.5.1.3. The verb form unmarked for mood   360
        10.5.1.4. Relative tense   364
    10.5.2. Aspect   365
        10.5.2.1. Progressive   366
        10.5.2.2. Resultative   366
        10.5.2.3. Prospective   368

Table of contents   xvii

10.5.2.4. Perfect   371
10.5.2.5. Experiential   372
10.5.2.6. Habitual and iterative   372

Chapter 11 The complex sentence ·········· **375**

11.1. Overview of complex clause structures ·········· 375

11.2. Coordination ·········· 375
  11.2.1. Symmetrical coordination   376
  11.2.2. Asymmetrical coordination   376

11.3. Clause chaining ·········· 379

11.4. Subordination ·········· 381
  11.4.1. Adsentential subordination   382
    11.4.1.1. Temporal clauses with =*kja* 'when/while'   382
    11.4.1.2. Conditional clause   383
    11.4.1.3. Causal clause with converb 'because; if/when'   384
    11.4.1.4. Continuous clause -*gakaazï* 'whenever'   384
    11.4.1.5. Immediate anterior clause with -*tuu* 'as soon as'   384
    11.4.1.6. Aversive clause with -*zïm* 'lest'   385
  11.4.2. Adverbial subordination   385
    11.4.2.1. Simultaneous clause with -*ccjaaki* 'while'   385
    11.4.2.2. Purpose clause with -*ga* '(go) in order to'   386
  11.4.3. Adnominal subordination   387
    11.4.3.1. Overview   387
    11.4.3.2. The NP that can be relativised   388
    11.4.3.3. Relativisation of an NP from a complement clause   389
    11.4.3.4. Relativisation of an NP from an adjunct clause   390
    11.4.3.5. Relativisation of an NP from other kinds of complex clause   391
    11.4.3.6. Simple attribution   392
  11.4.4. Complementation   394
    11.4.4.1. Quotative complement   394
    11.4.4.2. Adnominal clause structure functioning like a complement   395

11.5. Focus construction (*kakarimusubi*) ·········· 396
  11.5.1. A brief note on *kakarimusubi*   396
  11.5.2. Focus marking   398
    11.5.2.1. Sentence-Focus   398

xviii Table of contents

11.5.2.2. Argument Focus   398
11.5.2.3. Predicate Focus   401
11.5.2.4. WH Focus   402
11.5.2.5. Contrastive Focus   403

11.6. Degree of dependency: Coordination, clause chaining,
      adsentential and adverbial subordination ·· 404
   11.6.1. Focus marking   404
   11.6.2. Restricted clause-internal topic marking   405
   11.6.3. Main clause illocutionary scope   407
      11.6.3.1. The scope of negation   407
      11.6.3.2 The scope of interrogation   408
   11.6.4. Restrictions on relativisation   410

Appendix ·· 411

Bibliography ·· 417

Subject Index ·· 429

Language Index ··· 433

Abbreviations

ABL:	ablative	CRTN:	certainty	PC:	property concept
ACC:	accusative	CSL:	causal CVB		
AD.ASR:	addressive assertive	CVB:	converb	PL:	plural
		DAT:	dative	POT:	potential
ADV:	adverb	DIM:	diminutive	PRF:	perfect
ALL:	allative	ECHO:	echo element	PRH:	prohibitive
ANT:	immediate anterior CVB	EMO:	emotional	PROG:	progressive
		EMP:	emphatic	PROS:	prospective
ANTC:	anticipated future	EXP:	experiential	PRT:	partitive
		FIL:	filler	PST:	past
APPR:	approximative	FOC:	focus	PUR:	purposive CVB
ASC:	associative	GEN:	genitive	RED:	reduplication
ASR:	assertive	HON:	honorific	Q:	question
AVLZ:	adverbialiser	HS:	hearsay	QT:	quotative
AVR:	aversive	IMP:	imperative	RFL:	reflexive
BEN:	benefactive	INST:	instrumental	RLS:	realis
CAUS:	causative	INT:	intentional	RSL:	resultative
CLF:	classifier	INTJ:	interjection	SG:	singular
CMP:	comparative	LMT:	limitative	SIM:	simultaneous CVB
CND:	conditional CVB	MAL:	malefactive		
		NRT:	narrative CVB	THM:	thematic vowel
CNF:	confirmative	NEG:	negative		
CNT:	contrastive	NLZ:	nominaliser	TOP:	topic
CNTN:	continuous	NOM:	nominative	UPDT:	information updater
COMP:	complementiser	NPST:	non-past		
		OBL:	obligative/ potential	VLZ:	verbaliser
COP:	copula			-:	affix boundary
COR:	corrective	ONM:	onomatopoeia	=:	clitic boundary
CRCM:	circumstantial CVB	OPT:	optative	+:	stem boundary
		PASS:	passive		

A Grammar of Irabu, a Southern Ryukyuan Language

Chapter 1
The Irabu language and its speakers

This chapter introduces the language described in this grammar, Irabu Ryukyuan (henceforth Irabu). The chapter gives information about the genealogical and geographical affiliations of the language together with the settlement and political history of the Rykukus. This chapter also addresses the sociolinguistic situation, literature review, and a brief sketch of important features of phonology and grammar, with a particular focus on typological characteristics.

1.1. Geography

Irabu is spoken on Irabu, which is one of the Sakishima Islands within the Ryukyu archipelago, an island chain situated in the extreme south of the Japan archipelago.

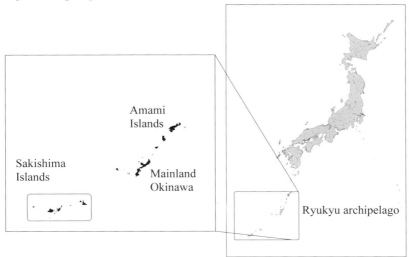

MAP 1   The Ryukyu archipelago

The Sakishima Islands consist of two groups: the Miyako Islands and the Yaeyama Islands. Irabu is the second largest island in the Miyako Islands (MAP 2).

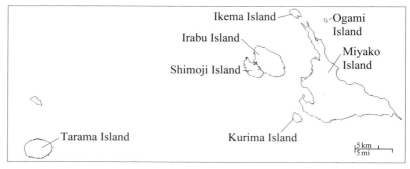

Map 2 The location of Irabu within the Miyako Islands[1]

Next to Irabu lies Shimoji, which has no permanent inhabitants and there is a very large airfield for training pilots and a small residential area of these pilots and associated people, surrounded by scattered fields of local people living in Irabu. However, this island used to be inhabited by Irabu people, and was called *macïnaka* [matsinaka] 'in-the-woods'. The previous importance of this island as a living place is evidenced in the fact that it is the setting of a lot of stories and legends (see Appendix (1)).

The distance between the Sakishima Islands and Mainland Okinawa is approximately 300 km, the greatest between any two adjacent islands in Japan. Moreover, this distance is the greatest between any two adjacent islands in the Western Pacific Rim (Kamchatka Peninsula through to Papua New Guinea, Uemura 1997: 319). As will be noted in the following section, this conspicuous geographic separation between the Sakishima Islands and Mainland Okinawa has significant consequences for the historical development of the languages of the Sakishima Islands.

1.2. Genealogy

Ryukyuan is a group of languages that forms a branch of the Japonic family, coordinate with Japanese.[2] Ryukyuan falls into two primary subgroups, Northern Ryukyuan and Southern Ryukyuan. These two subgroups in turn have a number of subdivisions. Figure 1–1 shows a genealogical classification of the Japonic family, where a detailed classification is made for the Miyako group based on Pellard (2009).

---

[1] The use of this map and Maps 3 and 4 below is by courtesy of Dr. Thomas Pellard.
[2] The term 'Japonic' is employed in diachronic studies such as Erickson (2003) and Serafim (2003), though a more traditional term would be Japanese (Osada 2003: 10).

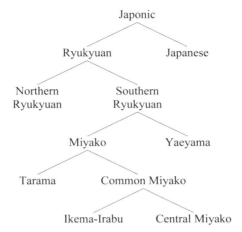

FIGURE 1–1. Genealogical classification of Ryukyuan (based on Pellard 2009)

Here I use the term 'language' to refer to the speech varieties listed in FIGURE 1–1, thus including Irabu, and 'dialect' to the subvarieties of each language. Dialectal variation in Irabu is discussed in §1.4.2.

Irabu belongs to the Miyako group, which first divides into Tarama and Common Miyako. Common Miyako then divides into the Ikema-Irabu subgroup and Central Miyako group (Pellard 2009). The Miyako group is defined by several lexical, phonological and morphological innovations that distinguish it from the other Southern Ryukyuan subgroups, e.g. the form of the limiter marker 'also; too' (=*mai* as opposed to =*n*; Pellard 2015: 19).

There is no mutual intelligibility between Japanese and Ryukyuan (Uemura 1997: 312). There is no mutual intelligibility between Northern and Southern Ryukyuan either (Uemura 1997: 313). Moreover, there is almost no mutual intelligibility between the Miyako group and the Yaeyama group of Southern Ryukyuan.

1.3. Notes on the settlement and political history of the Rykuku Islands

Early Japonic speakers from Mainland Japan are believed to have come southward to the north parts of the Ryukyu archipelago (Amami and Mainland Okinawa) sometime between the 2nd and 6th centuries (Uemura 1997). After that, particularly after the 8th century, there was no massive socio-cultural contact between the Ryukyu Islands and Mainland Japan until the 17th

4   Chapter 1

century, when the Ryukyu Islands were conquered by the Satsuma Domain
from Kyusyu, the southernmost large island of Japan.

Recent archaeological and anthropological studies have revealed that
there had been no major population movement from Okinawa to the
Sakishima Islands until the 13th century (Asato 1999).[3] Eventually the
Ryukyuan Dynasty, which had been established on Mainland Okinawa in
1429, colonised the Sakishimas, even though it is unclear how the actual
colonisation was carried out, and it is also unclear how massive the population movement was.

1.4. Sociolinguistic overview

1.4.1. The name of the language

The term 'Irabu' is a Japanese version of the local pronunciation *irav*
[iraʊ]. The noun *irav* simply designates the place name of the island. The
local people call their language by a nominal compound: *irav+(v)cï*
[iraʊ(ʊ)tsɨ] (Irabu+mouth). Thus in a strict sense this grammar should be 'A
Grammar of *Iravcï*'. However, I will continue to refer to Irabu rather than
irav or *iravcï*, because the term 'Irabu' has gained considerable currency in
Japan and even in the local society, and because 'Irabu' is now internation-
ally recognised as the standard name of the language (e.g. Grimes 1996).

1.4.2. Dialects

Based on differences in segmental phonology, four distinct dialects spoken
on Irabu are identified: (1) the Sawada-Nagahama dialect spoken in the
Sawada and Nagahama areas, (2) the Kuninaka dialect spoken in the Kuninaka area, (3) the Irabu-Nakachi dialect spoken in Irabu area and Nakachi
area, and (4) the Sarahama dialect spoken in the Sarahama area (MAP 3).
Genealogically, (4) belongs to Ikema (Motonaga 1982: 78), another Miyako Ryukyuan variety (FIGURE 1–1). In 1766 there was a massive migration
from Ikema to the Northern district of Irabu (Ooi 1984: 618–621) (MAP 4).

The following table briefly illustrates the differences among the three
dialects of Irabu in segmental phonology. For comparative purposes, I also
list the corresponding word forms in the Sarahama dialect.

---

[3] Until the 13th century, there must have been some indigenous people on the Sakishima Islands, who were decimated by the Ryukyuan newcomers, or gradually assimilated by them to
become Southern Ryukyuan speakers. The question of exactly who the indigenous people
were is controversial. Some researchers assert that they came from Indonesia or the Philip-
pines (Asato 1999; Kanaseki 1976). Linguistically speaking, all evidence is that Amami-Oki-
nawan and Southern Ryukyuan are in sister relationship, both branching off from Proto-Ryukyuan.

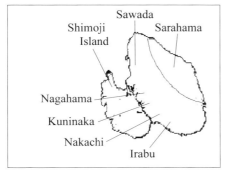 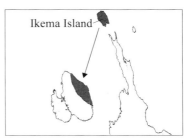

MAP 3   Irabu and its districts   MAP 4   Immigration to Sarahama

TABLE 1–1. The dialectal variation of Irabu

	Irabu			Ikema
	Sawada-Nagahama	Kuninaka	Irabu-Nakachi	Sarahama
'stick'	[bau]	[bau]	[boː]	[bau]
'needle'	[pal̺]	[pal̺]	[paẓ]	[hai]
'red'	[aka]	[aka]	[axa]	[aka]
'1PL'	[banti]	[bantʃi]	[banti]	[banti]

The major division within Irabu is between the Irabu-Nakachi dialect (IN) on one hand and the Sawada-Nagahama dialect (SN) and the Kuninaka dialect (K) on the other. First, the diphthong /au/ in SN and K corresponds to the long vowel /oː/ in IN. Second, the retroflex lateral [l̺] (written /r/ in phonemic orthography) in SN and K corresponds to the [z]-like approximant (or [z] with a less friction) [ẓ] in IN. Third, [k] within V_1 + k + V_2 (where V1 and V2 are /a/) in SN and K corresponds to [x] or [ʔ] in IN. The most conspicuous distinction between SN and K is that [ti] in SN corresponds to [tʃi] in K.

The higher-order distinction between the three dialects of Irabu and the Sarahama dialect is based on the fact that /p/ in all Irabu dialects corresponds to /h/ in the Sarahama dialect, and that [l̺]/[ẓ] in the Irabu dialects corresponds to /i/ in Ikema. There are also certain lexical differences among SN, K, and IN, especially between SN/K and IN. For example, 'in a hurry' is expressed by *pucci* in SN/K and *garamicci* in IN.

It is impossible at this stage to refer to a precise internal genealogical classification of Irabu, which is another matter than showing dialectal variation (isoglosses) as above. For a historical classification the proper question is which features are shared retentions from a proto language and

6   Chapter 1

which are shared innovations. The latter is difficult to answer at this stage, and I leave it for future research.

In terms of prosody, all dialects of Irabu have no lexical prosody, and have been referred to as 'accentless' dialects (Hirayama 1967). However, as will be demonstrated in §2.9 in this grammar, the Nagahama dialect has a rigid tonal pattern characterised by a regular alternation of tones (/H/ and toneless). Based on this feature, the Nagahama dialect can be distinguished from the Sawada dialect, which does not show this rigid tonal pattern.[4]

The focus in this grammar is exclusively on the Nagahama dialect, unless otherwise noted. In spite of all the phonetic/phonological differences noted above, the major grammatical aspects of each dialect are strikingly similar, and most of the morphosyntactic generalisations made in this grammar hold true or just require minor modifications for other dialects of Irabu. For example, as described in §4.3.3, there is non-canonical object marking in the Nagahama dialect, which is almost restricted to clause chaining constructions. This same generalisation largely holds true for the Nakachi dialect (Lawrence 2012).[5]

1.4.3. The number of speakers

There are about 5,623 people on Irabu in 2014. Considering that there were 6,660 people on Irabu according to the 2004 census, there has been an ongoing decrease of population.[6] The number of the population of the Nagahama area is 710.

However, the actual numbers of speakers are much lower than these figures. My fieldwork observations indicate that fluent speakers of Irabu and Sarahama are almost all over sixty years old. Given this, the estimated number of speakers of Nagahama Irabu is approximately 200–300.

1.5. Previous works on Irabu

In what follows I present a brief summary of published and unpublished works that deal with Irabu phonology and grammar. I also refer to works on other Miyako Ryukyuan varieties where necessary.

---

[4] This requires further research, however.
[5] On the other hand, there seem to be a lot of grammatical differences between Irabu and Ikema. For example, Irabu makes extensive use of reduplication of property concept stems (Chapter 8), but Ikema does not use this strategy (Hayashi 2013).
[6] http://www2.city.miyakojima.lg.jp/toukei_m_2014/ (last cited date: 01/09/2016)

1.5.1. Detailed grammars

There has been no descriptive grammar published for Irabu. There are two detailed grammars describing other varieties of Miyako: a grammar of Ogami (Pellard 2009) and a grammar of Ikema (Hayashi 2013), and both are unpublished PhD theses.

1.5.2. Grammatical sketches

There are two grammatical sketches of Irabu, one written in Japanese (Shimoji 2006) and the other in English (Shimoji 2011). Lawrence (2012) is a grammatical sketch of Southern Ryukyuan, where frequent reference is made to the Nakachi dialect of Irabu, and which addresses several important morphosyntactic features of Irabu that had not received attention in the literature (e.g. non-canonical object marking; see §4.3.3 in this grammar).

There are a number of grammatical sketches of other Miyako Ryukyuan varieties. Karimata (1997) and Izuyama (2002) describe Hirara, a dialect of Mainland Miyako. Hirayama (1967) gives a series of short grammatical sketches of Miyako Ryukyuan varieties including Irabu, especially noting basic verb and nominal morphology. Hayashi (2010) is a grammatical sketch of Ikema, a dialect that is in a sister relationship with Irabu. Kinuhata and Hayashi (2012) is a grammatical sketch of Karimata, a northern dialect of the mainland Miyako. The National Institute for Japanese Language and Linguistics (NINJAL) published a research report of their collaborative fieldwork on the Miyako island (Kibe, ed. 2012). It is a collection of papers on specific topics such as accent, verb conjugation, etc., together with a list of elicitation data and vocabulary data.

1.5.3. Works on specific topics

1.5.3.1. Phonological studies

Segmental phonology is a relatively well studied area in the literature of Irabu and other Miyako varieties, with several important contributions to segmental and supersegmental phonology. Four works exclusively refer to Irabu segmental phonology: Nakama (1983), Ryuukyuudaigaku Hoogenkenkyuu Kurabu (2005), Shimoji (2006, 2007). The following works deal with dialectal comparisons, referring to Irabu segmental phonology to varying degrees: Hirayama (1964), Hirayama, Ooshima, and Nakamoto (1966), and Hirayama (1967). Sawaki (2000) and a series of works by Karimata (1982, 1986, 2005, among others) address general characteristics of Miyako segmental phonology, and refer to Irabu phonology with a particular focus on syllable structure. Pellard (2007) is a useful summary of the theoretical issues of Miyako segmental phonology. Aoi (2010, 2012)

8   Chapter 1

discusses the phonetic and phonemic characterisation of what has been referred to as the 'central vowel' of Miyako (/ɨ/ and /ž/ in Irabu, see 1.6.1 below for a brief typological summary of this segment). This topic is one of
the most controversial issues of Miyako segmental phonology.

Supersegmental phonology has been much less studied, partly because
the prosody of Irabu has been viewed as what traditional dialectologists
call the 'collapsed system', a system which is claimed to display no lexical
prosody nor any rule-governed pattern (Hirayama 1964, Hirayama, Oshima, and Nakamoto 1966, Hirayama 1967). However, Shimoji (2009)
showed that Irabu prosody exhibits a highly principled and rule-governed
prosodic organisation although there is no lexical prosody. This discussion
will be given in Chapter 2 of this book.

1.5.3.2. Morphosyntactic studies

Compared with phonology, the grammatical aspects of Irabu and other Miyako Ryukyuan varieties have been much less studied. There are a number
of studies specifically dealing with Irabu, all of which are by the present
author except for Motonaga (1983), which deals with verb morphology and
dialectal variation. All the findings and discussions presented in the series
of works by the present author are found in the relevant sections of the
present work with in-line citations.

Turning to grammatical studies dealing with Miyako Ryukyuan in general, Nakama (1992) reports a cross-dialectal survey on Miyako Ryukyuan
morphology, with a particular focus on the historical comparison of Miyako Ryukyuan varieties. Motonaga (1978) and Karimata (2002) describe the
adjectival morphology of Miyako Ryukyuan in general. Nakasone (1976)
describes honorific expressions of Miyako Ryukyuan. Shimajiri (1983) describes case morphology in Miyako Ryukyuan (with a particular focus on
the Nohara dialect). Karimata (1999) is a study of the historical morphology of Miyako Ryukyuan verbs. Hayashi (2007) gives an analysis of the
tense-mood system of Ikema. Kawada, Hayashi, Iwasaki, and Ono (2008)
is a study of the discourse function of an interjection *mmja*, a word characteristic of Miyako Ryukyuan. Koloskova and Ohori (2008) is a typological
study of the adjectival system of Hirara, addressing various striking features of the adjectival system of this dialect (see Chapter 8 of this grammar
for the Irabu adjectival system).

1.5.4. Dictionaries, texts, and unpublished materials

Many dictionaries of Ryukyuan varieties have been published both by linguists and native speaker authors who are not linguists. All are bilingual

The Irabu language and its speakers   9

Ryukyuan-Japanese. Karimata (2004: 66) gives a list of the dictionaries published for Miyako and other Ryukyuan varieties. An extensive dictionary of the Nakachi dialect of Irabu was published by Sadayoshi Tomihama (2013), who is a native speaker of the Nakachi dialect. This dictionary includes a grammatical sketch by the author. There are a number of dictionaries of other Miyako Ryukyuan varieties, e.g. Shimoji (1979).

Some text materials, song lyrics and fieldnote data are available for Irabu. A series of text materials collected and transcribed by Nikolai A. Nevski (1971; 1998) is extremely important in that it records the speech of Irabu and other Miyako Ryukyuan varieties nearly one hundred years ago, and that it records the linguistic data with IPA symbols. In her PhD thesis, Yarosz (2015) gives a detailed phonological and grammatical analysis of Nevski's texts, and this work is particularly useful to see the difference between the older system and the current system of Miyako phonology and grammar. Sibata (1972) lists two conversational texts of Irabu. Nakasone (n.d. a–h) is a collection of his unpublished fieldnotes, which include a lot of information about Irabu phonology and grammar.

1.6. A typological overview of Irabu

1.6.1. Phonology

Irabu segmental phonology is typologically noteworthy in a number of respects. First, there are a lot of moraic consonants functioning either as syllabic consonants (e.g. /m.na/ [m̩na] 'shellfish', /n.za/ [n̩dza] 'where', etc.) or as part of onset (e.g. the first /f/ in /ffa/ [ffa] 'child'), and there are even words consisting only of moraic consonants (e.g. /mm/ [m̩ː] 'potato', /rr/ [l̩ː] 'enter', etc.). Second, a length distinction is made in consonants as well as in vowels (/m.na/ 'shellfish' vs. /mm.na/ 'all'). Third, two resonants, i.e. /ž/ which covers a range of sounds including [z]-like approximant ([z̧], and a [z] with less friction, and their voiceless counterparts) and the retroflex lateral allophone of /r/ ([l̢]) can serve as a nucleus of regular syllables, and can even carry certain (labial) onsets. (Thus we have such words as /bž.da/ [bz̧da] 'low' (CV.CV), /mžž/ [mz̧ː] 'flesh' (CVV), /prr.ma/ [pl̢ːma] 'daytime' (CVV.CV), /br.brr.gas.sa/ [bl̢bl̢ːgassa] 'alocasia odora' (CV.CVV. CVC.CV).

Prosodically, Irabu is a pitch language in which two tones, i.e. the marked High and the default Low (or zero) are distinguished. The tone system is not lexical but rhythmic, characterised by the alternation of the two tone features based on bi- or trimoraic foot structure within the phonological word. Thus a quadrimoraic phonological word has the metrical struc-

10   Chapter 1

ture $(\mu\mu)(\mu\mu)$, onto which tone is assigned $(\mu\mu)_H$ $(\mu\mu)_L$. The rhythmic tone assignment is explained as follows: one to three adjacent feet form a single higher rhythmic unit, or a foot group, in which the first foot is assigned High tone $((\mu\mu)_H$ $(\mu\mu)_L$ $(\mu\mu)_L)$. If a phonological word is extended by affixation and cliticlisation so that it contains four feet, then the foot group is broken down into two foot groups $(<(\mu\mu)_H$ $(\mu\mu)_L$ $><(\mu\mu)_H$ $(\mu\mu)_L$ $>)$. This break-down process is iteratively applied, so that a phonological word with twelve morae have three foot groups, with the prosodic pattern $<$(H) (L)$><$(H)(L)$><$(H)(L)$>$. This rhythmic organisation is precisely an instantiation of the Principle of Rhythmic Alternation (Selkirk 1984, Kubozono 1993). This kind of alternating rhythm is not commonly known in pitch languages, making Irabu particularly noteworthy in terms of prosodic typology.

1.6.2. Morphosyntax

Irabu is a verb-final language with a modifier-head order and a dependent-marking system. It prefers SV as an unmarked word order for intransitive clauses, and AOV as an unmarked word order for transitive clauses, and AEOV in the case of extended transitive clauses (where E(xtended core argument; see §3.5.1) represents an indirect object). However, since Irabu is a pro-drop language like Japanese, where a pragmatically recoverable argument or arguments may be unexpressed, it is extremely rare to find clauses with A, O, and E.

Irabu distinguishes eight word classes: nominals, verbs, adjectives, adnominals, adverbs, conjunctions, interjections and bound markers. A given property concept is expressed by a bound stem, from which an adjective, a nominal, a verb, or an adverb is formed. This flexibility in the formation of property concept words is typologically noteworthy, and Wetzer (1996) classifies such a flexible system as 'switch-adjectival' where a property concept may be encoded either nominally or verbally.

Irabu is largely characterised by agglutinative morphology, though verbs have a lot of morphophonemic alternations and portmanteau affixes. Affixation and cliticisation are exclusively suffixal and enclitic. There is no agreement morphology. In addition to affixation, there are also compounding and reduplication. I recorded some words consisting of as many as nine morphemes, as in *puri+munu+mmsa-kar-as-ai+u-i-ba* 'Because (I) am being made to behave like a crazy person' (get.mad+man+similar-VLZ-CAUS-PASS+PROG-THM-CSL).

Nominal morphology is only derivational, and the case relation is marked by a case marker whose syntactic host is an NP. Verb morphology

The Irabu language and its speakers   11

consists of both derivational and inflectional morphology. Inflection may be finite (inflecting for tense/mood/polarity) or non-finite (not inflecting for tense/mood but for dependency relations such as subordination).

The pronominal system (§5.2.2) displays a typologically recurrent problem of clusivity, i.e. the distinction between inclusive and exclusive, and its related problem of number (dual and plural). Irabu distinguishes between inclusive and exclusive for first person non-singular reference, with the problematic pronominal word *bafïtaa* 'me and you', which is, according to the person-number system, the first person dual inclusive. As Greenberg (1988) points out, this category is difficult to capture in the person-number system presupposed in the euro-centric view of language, but if we give up the person-number system and introduce the notions of combination (of persons) and group size (minimal-augment), it is possible to situate such a seemingly problematic form. The minimal-augment system is not common in Japonic or in Ryukyuan in general, but is rather common in other languages such as Austronesian languages (see Fillimonova 2005).

Irabu clauses display a nominative-accusative case system with some typologically interesting peculiarities: nominative case forms and genitive case forms are syncretised, and accusative case forms fall into the (unmarked) accusative =u and the partitive =a, the latter being a non-canonical object marker. Its exact function is still unclear, but one possible analysis is that it marks the imperfective aspect of the clause in which it occurs. As will be discussed in §4.3.3 and §11.3, the partitive is almost always restricted to occurring in a narrative converbal clause, whose aspectual value (perfective vs. imperfective) is unmarked in the verb form. The presented analysis is that the partitive helps disambiguate the aspectual distinction by occurring only in the imperfective narrative converbal clause. The aspect marking function of the non-canonical object marking reminds us of the partitive case in Finnish (Kiparsky 1998), but such a phenomenon has not been reported in Japonic.

Irabu and many other Ryukyuan varieties have a rich inventory of focus markers and topic markers, and a typologically remarkable syntactic construction, called *kakarimusubi* (literally governing-and-concordance) in Japanese linguistics, in which the presence of a focus marker within a clause restricts the choice of verb inflection. See §11.5 for more detail.

1.7. Method and data

This grammar is based on inductive generalisations made from text materials collected by the present author and deductive analyses based on elicited materials. Even though this grammar does not employ one particular theoretical model, it occasionally makes reference to theoretical issues where the Irabu fact deserves attention. For example, in §2.9 I note the Principle of Rhythmic Alternation suggested in generative phonology, as this principle is directly manifested in rhythmic alternation of tone features in Irabu, thus further supporting the universality of this principle, and demonstrating that this principle is not restricted to stress rhythm as previously assumed, but extensible to tonal rhythm as in Irabu.

The main data for this grammar were collected during two periods of fieldwork (six months in 2005–2006, six months in 2007). In the first spell of fieldwork I mostly focused on phonology, mainly because this area is one of the most difficult parts of Irabu. I also collected various text materials (seven hours in total). The second spell consisted of two kinds of tasks: one focused on making thorough transcriptions of selected texts (four hours of texts which have a good quality in length, cohesion, and cultural information, etc.) with the help of two consultants, Setsuko Sugama and Junji Shimoji, and the other on intense elicitations with various consultants including these two persons.

Twenty one native speakers of Irabu (nine males, twelve females; twelve speakers from Nagahama, six speakers from Sawada, two from Irabu, one from Kuninaka) gave text data and elicitation data, as well as helping me transcribe texts. All consultants were over sixty five years old, as it was very difficult to find younger consultants who are fluent enough to sustain a discourse in Irabu, to construct example sentences freely, and to give subtle grammaticality judgements in elicitation sessions.

1.8. Organisation of this grammar

This grammar consists of eleven chapters and a set of text materials as an appendix. In terms of their approach, the chapters fall into two major parts: Chapters 2 to 9 have a form-to-function orientation and Chapters 10 and 11 have a function-to-form orientation. In particular, each section of Chapter 10 commences with a particular functional-typological issue such as speech act, negation, voice, tense-aspect-mood, etc., which often crosscut different structures each of which is thoroughly described in Chapters 2 to 9.

Chapter 2

Phonology

Irabu phonology is characterised by rather complex syllable structures which are dependent on their position in words, gemination and length contrast sensitive to the notion mora, and a non-contrastive and rhythmic tone system where the High tone appears iteratively based on foot structure. Several major phonological rules are effectively described by referring to the underlying and the surface levels of the phonological system. Thus this chapter employs the following symbols for different representational levels:

- Square brackets '[ ]': phonetic representation
- Slashes '/ /': surface phonemic representation
- Double slashes '// //' underlying phonemic representation (where necessary)

2.1. Segmentation

A frequent reference will be made to the notion 'word' in describing both the phonology and the grammar. There are two kinds of word, i.e. grammatical word and phonological word. The grammatical word will be described in Chapter 3 in detail, and it is sufficient here to note the basic definition and terminology of the grammatical word and its related units, i.e. the affix, the clitic and the word-plus (a construction that consists of a word and a whole number of clitics).

2.1.1. Grammatical word

A grammatical word (henceforth simply 'word' unless an explicit distinction between a grammatical word and a phonological word is necessary) is an independent unit both in terms of morphology and phonology (See §3.2 for the notions of morphological and phonological dependency). As a morphologically independent unit, a word heads a phrase or functions as a member of a phrase (as a modifier, complement, auxiliary, etc.). A word may be a bare root or may be morphologically complex with compounding and/or affixation.

14   Chapter 2

A clitic is like a word in that it is morphologically independent, occurring as a member of phrase/clause structure. It usually occurs phrase-finally (e.g. a case marker) or clause-finally (e.g. a discourse marker), designating a grammatical feature of the phrase/clause they syntactically attach to. Unlike a word, a clitic is phonologically dependent, always occurring with its host word to which it is phonologically attached.

A word-plus (or *bunsetsu* 'syntagma' in traditional Japanese grammar) is a morphosyntactic unit that consists of a word and a whole number of clitics that attach to the host word. A phrase consists of one or more word(-plus)es. Below are illustrative examples of word and word-plus.

(2–1)   a. Word (root)
            jarabi
            child
            'child'
        b. Word (with affixes)
            jarabi-gama-mmi
            child-DIM-PL
            'little children'
        c. Word-plus
            jarabi-gama-mmi=kara=mai
            child-DIM-PL=from=even
            'even from little children'

An affix boundary and a clitic boundary are represented by a hyphen '-' and equal sign '=' respectively. Plus sign '+' represents a root boundary as in compounding and full reduplication (e.g. *biki+jarabi* 'male child'; *jarabii+jarabi* 'childish'). A word-plus is the orthographic word throughout this grammar.

2.1.2. Phonological word

A word-plus is in most cases a phonologically coherent unit, or a phonological word in terms of (1) syllable structure, (2) the applicability of phonological rules, and (3) prosody. Note that a word-plus, which consists of one or more morphologically independent units (a word and optionally clitic(s)), corresponds to a single phonological word. This is due to the fact that a clitic is not phonologically independent, and is always attached to the preceding host to constitute a phonological word (§3.2).

Most compound stems are separate phonological words in (1) and (3), and the compound structure will be described in §2.10 after introducing all

Phonology 15

these relevant phonological criteria for the phonological wordhood (§2.4, §2.5, §2.7, and §2.9). There are more complex cases where the different phonological criteria yield different phonological word boundaries. That is, certain affixes and clitics are separate phonological words in terms of (1) and (2) but not of (3), and certain phrases may be phonological words in terms of (3) but not of (1) and (2). These specific cases will be noted where necessary.

2.2. Classes of phonemes

Irabu phonemes can be divided into three classes based on their distribution in larger phonological structures and their behaviour in (morpho-) phonological processes: **Consonants**, **Glides**, and **Vowels**.

2.2.1. Consonants

TABLE 2–1 below shows the inventory of consonant phonemes. There are three phonemic places of articulation (labial, alveolar, velar(/glottal)) and three phonemic manners of articulation (stop, fricative, resonant).

TABLE 2–1. Inventory of consonant phonemes

		LABIAL	ALVEOLAR	VELAR/GLOTTAL
STOPS	voiceless	p	t	k
	voiced	b	d	g
Fricatives	voiceless	f	s, c	(h)
	voiced		z	
Resonants	nasal	m	n	
	approximant	v	ž	
	tap		r	

Note:
(A) Stops and fricatives have voice opposition.
(B) Resonants may be lengthened (e.g. /mna/ [mna] 'shellfish' vs. /mmna/ [m:na] 'all'), and the long consonants are phonemically treated as sequences of the identical consonant segments.
(C) /c/ [ts] and /z/ [dz] are phonemically classified as fricatives because of their phonotactic and morphophonemic behaviours. See below.
(D) Resonants may be syllabic. For example, a resonant is syllabic in a special type of syllable, or the presyllable (e.g. /m.ta/ [m̩ta] 'mud'; see §2.4.1).
(E) The phonetic symbol [z̞], the major allophone of /ž/, is meant to cover a range of sounds from [z] with less friction to a [z]-like approximant.
(F) The phoneme /r/ is pronounced as [ɾ] as an open syllable single onset, as in /kuri/ [kuɾi] 'this' (CV.CV), and [l] otherwise (e.g. /urir/ [uɾil] 'go down').

16   Chapter 2

Among the five fricative consonants, /h/ is not systemic: its lexical distribution is mostly restricted to non-native words, and it is the only phoneme
whose place of articulation does not form a natural class with other phonemes. The other 'regular' fricatives, /f/, /s/, /c/, and /z/, share the phonotactic pattern summarised below, which justifies classifying the phonetic
affricates phonemically as fricatives.

- Only fricatives can serve as the onset of /ɨ/ (§2.7.3).

2.2.2. Glides

Glide phonemes consist of /w/ and /j/. /j/ plays a major role in the syllable
G slot. /w/ is peripheral in Irabu phonology, occurring syllable-initially
only in the syllable /wa(V)/ (e.g. /wai.si/ [waiʃi] 'onomatopaeic expression', /ni.wa:/ [niwaː] 'garden'), and, only occasionally, between the stops
/k/ and /g/ and a vowel, e.g. /kwa:.si/ [kʷaːsɨ] 'snack'. The CG sequence
(e.g. /pj/ as in /pja:/ (CGVV) [pʲaː] 'early') is phonetically realised as a single palatalised phone (e.g. [pʲ]) rather than a consonant plus glide phone
([pj]). However, the justification for assuming a sequence CG as a phonemic representation rather than a single palatal consonant is noted in §2.8.3.

2.2.3. Vowels

The inventory of vowel phonemes is given in **TABLE 2–2** below.

TABLE 2–2. Inventory of vowel phonemes

	FRONT	CENTRAL	BACK
HIGH	i	ï	u
MID	(e)	(o)	
LOW		a	

(A) Long vowels are phonemically treated as sequences of the identical segments. See §2.8.4 for the validity of this analysis.

(B) Mid vowels are rare, only occurring in loanwords or in clitics such as the
question marker =e (§9.6.6). Long /ee/ and /oo/ are relatively more common, occurring in native roots such as /oo/ 'yes' (used when responding to
an elder person), /ee/ 'yes' (used otherwise), /ttee/ [ʔteː] 'then' as well as in
clitics /=dooi/ (emphatic; §9.3.7).

(C) /u/ is phonetically [ʊ] or [ʉ], i.e. a slightly lower and/or front version of cardinal [u]. Since these phonetic realisations are largely free variation, they
are simply represented as [u] henceforth.

(D) /ɨ/ only combine with fricative onsets. It is underlyingly absent, and is predictably inserted as an epenthetic segment to break up prohibited phonotactic patterns of word-plus (e.g. */st/, as in //sta// > /sïta/ [sïta] 'tongue';

Phonology   17

*/s/#, as in //pus// > /pusɨ/ [pusɨ] 'star'). See §2.7.3 for detail.

2.3. Minimal or quasi-minimal contrasts

Here I list minimal or quasi-minimal pairs for short segments.[1] Long segments are collectively noted in §2.6.3.1.

2.3.1. Consonants (stops, fricatives, and resonants)

- /p/ vs. /t/ vs. /k/: /pusɨ/ [pusɨ] 'star', /tusɨ/ [tusɨ] 'year', /kusɨ/ [kusɨ] 'belly'
- /p/ vs. /b/: /puu/ [puː] 'spike', /buu/ [buː] 'thread'
- /t/ vs. /d/: /tusɨ/ [tusɨ] 'year', /dusɨ/ [dusɨ] 'friend'
- /k/ vs. /g/: /kuu/ [kuː] 'powder', /guu/ [guː] 'cave'
- /f/ vs. /s/ vs. /z/: /fau/ [fau] 'eat', /sau/ [sau] 'pole', /zau/ [dzau] 'gate'
- /c/ vs. /z/: /aca/ [atsa] 'tomorrow', /aza/ [adza] 'elder brother'
- /p/ vs. /h/: /pira/ [piɾa] 'tailcutter', /hira/ [çiɾa] 'hey'
- /m/ vs. /n/: /kam/ [kam] 'god', /kan/ [kaŋ] 'crab'
- /v/ vs. /ž/ vs. /r/: /pav/ [pav] 'snake', /paž/ [paʐ] 'fly', /par/ [paɭ] 'needle'
- /r/ vs. /n/: /sira/ [ʃiɾa] 'after birth', /sina/ [ʃina] 'commodity'

2.3.2. Glides

- /j/ vs. /w/: /jaa/ [jaː] 'house', /waa/ [waː] 'pig'

2.3.3. Vowels

- /a/ vs. /i/ vs. /u/: /par/ [paɭ] 'needle', /pir/ [piɭ] 'garlic', /pur/ [puɭ] 'dig'
- /i/ vs. /e/: /=i/ [i] (confirmative), /=e/ [e] (question)
- /u/ vs. /o/: /kuma/ [kuma] 'here', /koma/ [koma] 'spinning top' (< Japanese)
- /a/ vs. /ɨ/: /sata/ [sata] 'sugar', /sɨta/ [sɨta] 'tongue'

2.4. The structure of the root word

In this section I give an overview of the syllable structure of the root word. The generalisations here mostly apply to morphologically complex words and word-pluses as well. This general syllable structure and phonotactic constraints serves as the definition of a phonological word in terms of syl-

---

[1] As will be described in §2.9 below, there is no lexically contrastive prosody in Irabu. Irabu has a foot-based rhythmic tone system where /H/ and /Ø/ (phonetically [L]) alternates.

18 Chapter 2

lable structure and phonotactics. That is, most word(-plus)es are phonological words in these respects. Some divergences are noted in §2.5.

2.4.1. Word template

For descriptive purposes it is convenient to divide the structure of root words into three portions, i.e. presyllable, initial syllable, and non-initial syllable(s):

(2–2)   WORD TEMPLATE
(presyllable +) initial syllable (+ non-initial syllable$_{1...n}$)

The term presyllable is meant to represent a minor syllable in terms of phonotactics and structure, which deserves a different descriptive treatment than ordinary syllables (initial syllable and non-initial syllable).

The following generalisations, followed by exceptions to them, obtain as to the structure of the root word:

(2–3)   A presyllable is a syllabic resonant (abbreviated as R):
   a. /m.ta/ [m̩ta] 'mud' (R.CV)
   b. /mm.ta/ [m̩ːta] 'k.o.tree' (RR.CV)
   c. /n.sï/ [n̩sɨ] 'north' (R.CV)
   d. /v.cca/ [ʋ̩ttsa] 'quail' (R.CCV)

(2–4)   An initial syllable has an optional onset and coda. The initial cluster CC must be a geminate voiceless fricative or resonant.
   a. ((C$_i$) C$_i$) (G) V$_1$ (V$_2$) (C$_{coda}$)
   b. /ma.cja/ [matʃa] 'little bird' (CV.CGV)
   c. /maa.da/ [maːda] 'very' (CVV.CV)
   d. /mai.cja/ [maitʃa] 'sleeve' (CVV.CGV)
   e. /maž/ [maẓ] 'rice' (CVC)
   f. /mma/ [mma] 'mother' (CCV)

(2–5)   A non-initial syllable has an obligatory onset and optional coda.
   a. C (G) V$_1$ (V$_2$) (C$_{coda}$) or G V$_1$ (V$_2$) (C$_{coda}$)
   b. /ma.ju/ [maju] 'cat' (CV.GV)
   c. /ni.sjai/ [niʃai] 'young man' (CV.CGV)
   d. /bu.dur/ [buduɭ] 'dance' (CV.CVC)

(2–6)   A presyllable + initial syllable produces consonant clusters R.C, RR.C, or in very rare cases R.CC, but not RR.CC in roots.
   a. /m.cï/ [m̩tsɨ] 'road' (R.CV)
   b. /nn.di/ [n̩ːdi] 'Yes' (RR.CV)
   c. /v.cca/ [ʋ̩ttsa] 'quail' (R.CCV)

Phonology

(2–7) In polysyllabic words, the structure of a final syllable is as for a non-initial syllable as in (2–5), i.e. with an obligatory onset and optional coda, except in cases where the final syllable is an initial syllable (as in disyllabic words consisting of a presyllable + an initial syllable). The final coda is a resonant.

    a. /pa.sam/ [pasam] 'clow' (CV.CVC)

    b. /gu.sjan/ [guʃaŋ] 'stick' (CV.CGVC)

    c. /ni.niv/ [ɲiɲiʋ] 'snooze' (CV.CVC)

    d. /ju.baž/ [jubaʐ] 'the act of visiting a woman's house at night' (GV.CVC)

    e. /ku.par/ [kupaɭ] 'stammerer'

    f. /n.kum/ [ŋkum] 'strain' (R.CVC)

(2–8) There are occasions when the nucleus of an ordinary syllable is filled by an alveolar non-nasal resonant /ʐ(ž)/ or /r(r)/, or a nucleic resonant (Rn). The onset is always a bilabial stop or nasal /p/, /b/ and /m/. See also §2.4.2 below.

    a. /pž.tu/ [pʂtu] 'man' (CRn.CV)

    b. /pžž/ [pʂ:] 'day' (CRnRn)

    c. /bž.da/ [bʐda] 'low' (CRn.CV)

    d. /ju.bžž/ [jubʐ:] 'suck' (GV.CRnRn)

    e. /mžž/ [mʐ:] 'flesh' (CRnRn)

    f. /prr.ma/ [pl̩:ma] 'daytime' (CRnRn.CV)

    g. /na.brr/ [nabl̩:] 'slippery' (CV.CRnRn)

    h. /mrr.na/ [ml̩:.na] 'green chive' (CRnRn.CV)

(2–9) Exceptions

    a. Exception to (2–2): though an initial syllable is obligatory by definition, a very few presyllable-only words do exist.

       i. /mm/ [m̩:] 'potato' (RR)

       ii. /žž/ [ʐ:] 'rice ball' (RR)

    b. Exception to (2–4): /t/ may be exceptionally geminated in initial clusters, though there are very few attested examples.

       i. /ttjaa/ [ʔttʲaː] 'then' (CCGVV)

       ii. /tti.gaa/ [ʔttigaː] 'then' (CCV.CVV)

    c. Exception to (2–5): there are very rare instances of /VV.V/ in roots, i.e. cases where the onset of the non-initial syllable is missing (such instances always involve /aa.i/ or /uu.i/).

       i. /aa.i/ [aːi] 'No' (VV.V)

       ii. /juu.i/ [juː.i] 'preparation' (GVV.V)

2.4.2. Nucleic resonants

Alveolar non-nasal resonants /ž(ž)/ and /r(r)/ may appear in V slots of initial syllables and of non-initial syllables, serving as nucleic resonants. The onset must be a labial, and mostly the labial stops /p/ and /b/, and only in rare cases the labial nasal /m/. This indicates that there is a tendency towards maximising the feature difference between the onset phoneme (labial and stop) and the nucleus phoneme (alveolar and resonant).

/ž(ž)/ Initial syllable
/pž.tu/ [pṣtu] 'man' CRn.CV
/pžž/ [pˢẓː] 'day' CRnRn
/bž.da/ [bẓda] 'low' CRn.CV
/bžž/ [bẓː] 'sit' CRnRn
/mžž/ [mẓː] 'flesh' CRnRn

Non-initial syllable
/su.ku.bž/ [sukubẓ] 'belt' CV.CV.CRn
/ka.bžž/ [kabẓː] 'paper' CV.CRnRn

/r(r)/ Initial syllable
/prr.ma/ [pl̩ːma] 'daytime' CRnRn.CV
/br.brr/ [bl̩.bl̩ː] 'alocasia odora' CRn.CRnRn
/mrr.na/ [ml̩ːna] 'green chive' CRnRn.CV

Non-initial syllable
/na.brr/ [nabl̩ː] 'slippery' CV.CRnRn

The tendency towards maximising feature difference also holds in presyllable plus initial syllable non-geminate clusters (such as /m.ta/ [m̩ta] 'mud' R.CV), where the cluster consists of a labial nasal resonant plus an alveolar non-resonant (see §2.5.6.3).

2.4.3. Heavy structures

Monosyllables of the super heavy structure $((C_i)C_i)(G)V_1V_2C_{coda}$ are rare in roots: among the attested words are /aur/ [aul̩] 'still', /saar/ [saːl̩] 'take (someone to somewhere)', /juuž/ [juːẓ] 'celebration', /daav/ [daːʋ] 'tool', etc. The 'fully-loaded' monosyllable $C_iC_iGV_1V_2C_{coda}$ is not attested in the root word. The codaless but otherwise fully-loaded monosyllable structure is attested though rare: $C_iC_iGV_1V_2$ (e.g. /ttjaa/ [ʔttʲaː] 'then').

2.4.4. Examples of root word structures

In this section I give some examples illustrating root word structure step by step. The focus is first on the initial syllable (§2.4.4.1 and §2.4.4.2), then non-initial syllable (§2.4.4.3), and finally the presyllable (§2.4.4.4 and §2.4.4.5). The phonotactic details involved in each structural position will be covered in depth in §2.5.

Phonology

2.4.4.1. Examples of words with an initial syllable only

Here, an onset consisting of a single C may be filled by a stop (**S**), fricative (**F**), or a resonant (**R**), while an onset of two consonants CC is filled by identical segments, either a fricative or a resonant (exceptionally a geminate stop cluster /tt/). The coda is a resonant.

	#	$((C_i)$	$C_i)$	(G)	V_1	(V_2)	(C_{coda})	#
		R	R				R	
		F	F					
		(S)	S					
/aa/ [aː] 'foxtail millet'					a	a		
/ai/ [ai] 'like that'					a	i		
/jaa/ [jaː] 'house'				j	a	a		
/am/ [am] 'net'					a		m	
/jam/ [jam] 'disease'				j	a		m	
/kam/ [kam] 'god'			k		a		m	
/maž/ [maẓ] 'rice'			m		a		ž	
/aur/ [auɭ] 'still'					a	u	r	
/pjar/ [pʲa/r] 'leave'			p	j	a		r	
/ffa/ [ffa] 'child'		f	f		a			
/ssam/ [ssam] 'lice'		s	s		a		m	
/ccir/ [ʔttʃiɭ] 'pipe'		c	c		i		r	
/ttjaa/ [ʔttʲaː] 'then'		t	t	j	a	a		
/mmja/ [mmʲa] 'well'		m	m	j	a			
/vva/ [ʋva] 'you'		v	v		a			
/žža/ [ẓza] 'father'		ž	ž		a			
/rra/ [ɭɭa] 'placenta'		r	r		a			
/pžž/ [pˢẓː] 'day'			p		ž	ž		

2.4.4.2. Examples of words with an initial and a non-initial syllable, showing the structure of the initial syllable

Here, it is noted that the set of consonants which may fill the coda of the word medial position is larger than for the word final coda (cf. §2.4.4.1). Word-medial codas allow fricatives and stops in addition to resonants. However, a coda fricative or stop must be identical with the onset of the following syllable.

22   Chapter 2

	#	((Cᵢ)	Cᵢ)	(G)	V₁	(V₂)	(C_coda)	$	Cᵢ ...
		R	R				R		
		F	F				F		
		(S)	S				S		
/an.na/ [anna] 'mother'					a		n		na
/aʋ.ʋa/ [avva] 'oil'					a		v		va
/ja.ma/ [jama] 'mountain'				j	a				ma
/ka.gi/ [kagi] 'beautiful'			k		a				gi
/kaa.gi/ [kaːgi] 'smell'			k		a	a			gi
/bat.ta/ [batta] 'armpit'			b		a		t		ta
/bas.si/ [baʃʃɨ] 'forget'			b		a		s		si
/pin.za/ [pindza] 'goat'			p		i		n		za
/kiʋ.sï/ [kiʋsɨ] 'haze'			k		i		v		sï
/mjaa.ku/ [mʲaːku] 'Miyako'			m	j	a	a			ku
/kjav.dai/ [kʲaʋdai] 'brother'			k	j	a		v		dai
/nna.ma/ [nnama] 'now'	n		n		a				ma
/pž.tu/ [pʂtu] 'man'			p		ž				tu

2.4.4.3. Examples of words with an initial and a non-initial syllable, showing the structure of the non-initial syllable

Here the focus is on the non-initial syllable (of the word-final position below). The onset of the non-initial syllable is obligatory (exceptions being
mentioned in (2–9c)), and it must be a single consonant (plus glide) or a
single glide.

	$	Cᵢ	(G)	V₁	(V₂)	(C_coda)	#
/mjaa.ku/ [mʲaːku] 'Miyako'	mjaa	k		u			
/an.na/ [anna] 'mother'	an	n		a			
/av.va/ [avva] 'oil'	av	v		a			
/kjav.dai/ [kʲaʋdai] 'brother'	kjav	d		a	i		
/juu.rja/ [juːrʲa] 'season'	juu	r	j	a			
/tun.bjan/ [tumbʲaŋ] 'k.o. vegetable'	tun	b	j	a			n
/ta.ja/ [taja] 'power'	ta		j	a			
/na.brr/ [nabḷː] 'slippery'	na	b		r	r		

The /nb/ found in roots, such as /tun.bjan/ [tumbʲaŋ] 'k.o. vegetable' should
not be analysed as /mb/, nor as reflecting a neutralisation of /n/ and /m/.
The /nb/ analysis is preferable in terms of the phonotactic patterns of nasal
consonant clusters (see §2.8.1). In morpheme boundaries, of course, /mb/
may occur (e.g. /kam/ 'god' + /=bjaam/ 'I wonder' > /kam.bjaam/ 'I wonder if it's a god')

Phonology

2.4.4.4. Examples of words with a presyllable plus initial syllable
Here, the consonant clusters R.C, RR.C (where the RR is a long resonant phoneme), or in vary rare cases R.CC, are attested.

	# (((R_i)	R_i)	$ (C_i)	C_i)	(G)	V_1	(V_2)	(C_coda)	#
		R	R	R	R			R	
				F	F				
					S				
/m.ta/ [m̥ta] 'mud'		m		t		a			
/m.su/ [m̥su] 'miso'		m		s		u			
/m.na/ [m̩na] 'shellfish'		m		n		a			
/v.ta/ [v̥ta] 'song'		v		t		a			
/v.cca/ [v̥ttsa] 'squirrel'		v	c	c		a			
/n.gja/ [ŋgʲa] 'spike'		ŋ		g	j	a			
/n.bir/ [mbil̩] 'stretch'		n		b		i		r	
/n.fi/ [ŋfi] 'warm'		n		f		ï			
/n.kum/ [ŋkum] 'strain'		n		k		u		m	
/mm.ta/ [m̩ːta] 'k.o. tree'		m	m		t		a		
/nn.di/ [n̩ːdi] 'yes'	n	n		d		i			
/nn.ku/ [ŋ̩ːku] 'pus'	n	n		k		u			

2.4.4.5. Examples of words consisting only of a presyllable (a syllabic resonant)
There are pre-syllable-only words. Most are derived by the resyllabification of the underlying //CC[V]// where the CC is a resonant geminate and the [V] is an unfilled nucleus, as in //žž// 'scold' which is usually followed by a vowel-initial affix to inflect, as in /žžan/ 'not scold', /žži/ '(you) scold' (imperative), etc. If the root with the form //CC[V]// occurs without an affix that begins in a vowel, the geminate onset is resyllabified for the resonants to be syllabic, or RR. See §2.7.5 for detail.

	# R_i	R_i #
/mm/ [m̩ː] 'potato'	m	m
/nn/ [n̩ː] 'yes'	n	n
/vv/ [v̩ː] 'sell' (//vv[V]// → resyllabification → /vv/)	v	v
/žž/ [z̩ː] 'scold' (//žž[V]// → resyllabification → /žž/)	ž	ž
/rr/ [l̩ː] 'go into' (//rr[V]// → resyllabification → //rr/)	r	r

2.5. Phonotactics of the word-plus

This section describes the phonotactics of the word-plus domain, taking morphologically complex structures into account, and noting the phonotactic differences between root structures and morphologically complex structures. As will be noted below, there are a number of phonotactic restrictions that hold in the domain of word-plus, indicating that the word-plus is a phonologically coherent domain. If we take that different phonological criteria (e.g. phonotactics, prosody, morpho-phonemic alternations, word minimality, etc.) yield different kinds of phonological word segmentations, we can define a phonological word in terms of phonotactics (or 'phonotactic word' in Hyman's 2006 terms) by the series of constraints and characteristics described in (2–10) to (2–16).

TABLE 2–3. Basic phonotactic schema (s: stops; f: fricatives; r: resonants)

#Presyllable	Initial syllable			Non-initial syllable$_{1...n}$#		
$((R_i) R_i)$	$((C_i) C_i)(G)V_1(V_2)$		(C_{coda})	$C (G)V_1(V_2)$	(C_{coda})...	(C_{coda})
R R	R R		R	R	R	R
	F F		F	F	F	
	(S) S		S	S	S	

(2–10) There are four primary phonotactic constraints that generally hold both in root words and polymorphemic word(-pluse)s. See §2.5.1.
a. Final coda must be a resonant.
b. Medial clusters are heterosyllabic C.C only.
c. The CC cluster of non-resonant consonants must be a geminate.
d. C.(G)V is impermissible, i.e. a non-initial syllable must carry onset C.

(2–11) V_1V_2 may be a long vowel or a (generally rising) diphthong. See §2.5.2.

(2–12) The single onset in an initial syllable can be filled by any consonant but /v/, /ž/, and /r/. See §2.5.3.

(2–13) Initial syllable onset clusters consist of geminates only, of any resonants or of fricatives other than /z/ and /h/ (also /t/ exceptionally). See §2.5.4.

(2–14) Non-initial clusters, i.e. coda plus onset clusters, are (a) geminates, (b) partial geminates (homorganic /n/ + C), or (c) restricted non-geminates. See §2.5.5.

Phonology 25

(2–15) Presyllable plus initial syllable onset clusters are generally of the type (b) and (c) above. See §2.5.6.

(2–16) Word initial geminates are more common than geminates across syllable boundaries. See §2.5.7.

As an initial approximation, it can be said that there is an overwhelming tendency for Irabu consonant clusters to be geminates or partial geminates (involving homorganic /n/ + C) in consonant clusters within/across syllables. This generalisation holds for Miyako Ryukyuan as a whole.

2.5.1. Four primary phonotactic constraints of the word(-plus)
2.5.1.1. Final C

The final coda of a word(-plus) must be a single resonant, except in very limited cases where an affix -*m* (realis mood) or a case marker =*n* (dative) attaches to a consonant-final host.

(2–17)   /pav/ 'snake' + =n (dat)   > /pavn/ 'to snake'
         /paž/ 'fly' + =n   > /pažn/ 'to fly'
         /mii-/ 'look' + /-r/ (non-past) + /-m/ (realis mood) > /miirm/ 'look:NPST.RLS'

Assuming that there is a phonological word in terms of phonotactics, these examples indicate that there is a phonological-word boundary between the stem and the affix/clitic.

2.5.1.2. Medial cluster

The medial consonant cluster in a word(-plus) is in principle restricted to a heterosyllabic C.C. However, a few affixes and clitics begin in CC or R.C, and these may give rise to such exceptional medial C.CC or C.R.C clusters.

(2–18)   -ccjaaki (simultaneous converb suffix)
         a. /tur-/ 'take' + /-ccjaaki/ → /tur.ccjaa.ki/ 'while taking' (CVC. CCGVV.CV)
         b. /jum-/ 'read' + /-ccjaaki/ → /jum.ccjaa.ki/ 'while reading' (GVC.CCGVV.CV)
         c. /kav/ 'buy' + /-ccjaaki/ → /kav.ccjaa.ki/ 'while buying' (CVC.CCGVV.CV)
(2–19)   =nkai (allative case marker)
         a. /paž/ 'fly' + /=nkai/ → /pažnkai/ 'to fly' (CVC.R.CVV)

26   Chapter 2

  b. /pav/ 'snake' + /=nkai/ → /pav.n.kai/ 'to snake' (CVC.
     R.CVV)
  c. /kan/ 'crab' + /=nkai/ → SND → /kan.kai/ 'to crab' (CVC.
     CVV)
  d. /kam/ 'god' + /=nkai/ → SND → /kam.kai/ 'to god' (CVC.
     CVV)

In (2–19c) and (2–19d), the exceptional medial C.R.C is avoided by the
sequential nasal deletion rule (SND above). See §2.7.6 for the detail of this
rule.

The above exceptional phonotactic patterns are explained by the assumption that such affixes and clitics are outside of the phonological word
domain defined in terms of syllable structure and phonotactics (i.e. the
phonotactic word). However, =nkai may be integrated into the preceding
host when it undergoes the sequential nasal deletion rule as in (2–19c, d).
But it must be emphasised here that =nkai is still a part of a phonological
word in terms of prosody (prosodic word). Thus, in Irabu, different criteria
yiled different phonological word segmentations and there is a mismatch
between a phonotactic word boundary on the one hand and a prosodic
word boundary.

2.5.1.3. Cluster of non-resonants
A consonant cluster of non-resonants must be geminate, both in root words
and morphologically complex word(-plus)es, and both in initial and medial
clusters.

2.5.1.4. Ban on /C.V/ sequence
A sequence consisting of a coda /C/ directly followed by a V is prohibited
in word(-plus)es. That is, a non-initial syllable must carry an onset C. If
affixation or cliticisation result in //C.V// sequence, a phonological rule operates to fix this ill-formed structure (//C.V// → /C$_i$.C$_i$V/, by the geminate
copy insertion rule; see §2.7.2). Whereas /C.V/ is impermissible, /C.GV/ is
permissible, indicating that /G/ aligns with /C/ rather than /V/ in terms of
this phonotactic constraint. As is shown below, comparative case /=jarruu/
may give rise to the /C.GV/ sequence.

  (2–20) /kan=jarruu/ [kaŋjaɭɭuː]
          crab=CMP
          'than a crab'
  (2–21) /mm=jarruu/ [mːjaɭɭuː]

Phonology 27

potato=CMP
'than a potato'

2.5.2. Long vowels and diphthongs

The table below shows the attested combinations of V_1 and V_2 in word(-plus)es. Diphthongs are mostly rising dipthongs. A falling dipthong /iu/ (phonetically [juː]) is exceptional in roots, but is rather common in morpheme boundaries. /ia/ [jaː] is not found in roots, and only occurs in morpheme boundaries.

TABLE 2–4. Long vowels and diphthongs

V_2	/a/	/u/	/i/	/ï/	(/e/)	(/o/)
V_1						
/a/	aa	au	ai			
/u/		uu	ui			
/i/	[[ia]]	[iu]	ii			
/ï/				ïï		
(/e/)					(ee)	
(/o/)						(oo)

Note: (x) x is rare in roots

[x] x is rare in roots, but common in morpheme boundaries

[[x]] x is not attested in roots, and only found in morpheme boundaries

With onset

/kaa/ [kaː] 'skin'
/nau/ [nau] 'what'
/kai/ [kai] 'like that'
/muu/ [muː] 'sea weed'
/kui/ [kui] 'voice'
/kuri=a/ [kuɾʲaː] 'this:TOP'
/kiusï/ [kʲuːsï] 'haze' (< /kivsï/ [kiʋsï])
/kuri=u/ [kuɾʲuː] 'this:ACC'
/kii/ [kiː] 'tree'
/sïï/ [sïː] 'nest'
/nauttee/ [nautteː] 'why'
/doo/ [doː] (emphatic)

Without onset (initial only)

/aa/ [aː] 'foxtail millet'
/au/ [au] 'blue'
/ai/ [ai] 'like that'
/u/ [uː] 'Hare'
/ui/ [ui] 'that'
Not attested
Not attested
Not attested
/ii/ [iː] 'stomach'
None by definition (see §2.8.5)[2]
/ee/ [eː] 'Yes' (informal)
/oo/ [oː] 'Yes' (formal)

---

[2] /sïï/ is underlyingly //ss//, a fricative geminate onset without a nucleus. It is subject to the predictable /ï/-insertion rule to derive /ssï/. It then undergoes the lengthening rule to meet the word minimality constraint, hence we get the surface /sïï/. See §2.8.5.

28   Chapter 2

2.5.3. Single onset of initial and non-initial syllables

All consonants but /v/, /ž/, /r/ may appear in the single onset of an initial syllable. All consonants but /v/ and /ž/ may appear in the single onset of non-initial syllables.

2.5.4. Initial syllable onset cluster

All resonants and fricatives other than /z/ and /h/ may be geminated. The cluster /tt/ is also found in a very limited number of words.

(2–22)   RESONANTS   FRICATIVES   STOP: /t/ only; rare
         /mmi/ [mmi] 'crowd'   /ffa/ [ffa] 'child'   /ttjaa/ [ʔttʲaː] 'then'
         /nnucɨ/ [nnutsɨ] 'life' /ssu/ [ssu] 'white'   /ttigaa/ [ʔttigaː] 'then'
         /vva/ [ʋva] '2SG'   /ccir/ [ʔttʃil] 'pipe'   /ttar/ [ʔttal] 'came'
         /žžu/ [ʐʐu] 'fish'   (/t-tar/ 'come-PST')
         /rra/ [ɭɭa] 'placenta'

2.5.5. Non-initial cluster

Non-initial clusters, i.e. clusters of coda plus onset across syllable boundaries (mostly C.C but may be C.CC or C.R.C in exceptional cases; §2.5.1.2), may be geminates (of any consonant other than voiced stop, voiced fricative, or /h/), partial geminates involving a homorganic nasal, phonemically /n/, plus another consonant (other than resonants), or non-geminates (a resonant plus (mostly) an alveolar consonant). Non-geminates are rare in root words.

2.5.5.1. Geminates
The examples below illustrate the possible non-initial geminates.

(2–23)   RESONANTS   FRICATIVES   STOPS
         /dum.ma/ [dumma]   /maf.fa/ [maffa]   /ip.pai/ [ippai]
         (onm.)   'pillow'   'many'
         /an.na/ [anna]   /umis.si/ [umiʃʃi]   /bat.ta/ [batta]
         'mother'   'funny'   'armpit'
         /av.va/ [avva] 'oil' /ac.ca/ [attsa]   /uk.ka/ [ukka]
                               'side'   'debt'
         /taž.žasɨ/ [tazzasɨ] (/fïz.za/ [fuddza] 'whale')
         'bind'
         /jur.ru/ [juɭɭu] '*jurru* fish'

The non-initial geminate /z.z/ seems to be on a diachronic path towards

Phonology

/c.c/. For example, while some very old speakers do distinguish /fïz.za/ [fuddza] 'whale' and /fïc.ca/ [futtsa] 'mouth' (topic),[3] many others do not distinguish them, pronouncing both as [futtsa]. This and the strong ban on voiced stop geminates indicate that there is a clear tendency in Irabu to disfavour phonemically voiced (i.e. non-resonant /b, d, g, z/) geminates. In association with this, /z.z/ in morpheme boundaries, as in /az=za/ (//az// 'taste' plus //=a// topic marker), involves neutralisation with /c.c/ [tts] in many speakers' speech, where the phonetic realisation of /z.z/ as well as /c.c/ is [tts], as in /az=za/ [attsa] (~ [addza]).

2.5.5.2. Partial geminates (homorganic /n/ + C of any place of articulation)
In roots as well as in morphologically complex words, /n/ can combine with a C of any place of articulation. [mp] or [mb] in roots is treated as /np/ or /nb/ (rather than /mp/ or /mb/) as suggested in /juunpuu/ [juːmpuː] 'firefly' and /unbu/ [umbu] 'carrying on one's back' below. This matter is taken up in §2.8.1.

(2–24) C: LABIAL   C: ALVEOLAR   C: VELAR/GLOTTAL
        /juun.puu/ [juːmpuː]   /pin.za/ [pindza]   /min.ku/[miŋku]
        'firefly'   'goat'   'deaf'
        /unbu/ [umbu]
        'carrying on one's back'

2.5.5.3. Non-geminates (resonant C_i + resonant/non-resonant C_j)
The examples in (2–25) are from root words or fossilised compounds, while those in (2–26) are from morphologically complex word(-plus)es. In roots, the overwhelming majority of examples involve a non-geminate cluster in which the second consonant is alveolar.

(2–25) /am.dir/ [amdiɭ] 'a fish-carrying bag' (< am 'net' + tir 'small bag')
        /kiv.sï/ [kiʋsɨ] 'haze' (~ /kiusï/ [kʲuːsɨ])
        /paž.gi/ [paʐgi] 'rash/swelling'
        /ur.zïn/ [uɭdzɨŋ] 'early summer season'
(2–26) /num/ [num] 'drink' + /-tar/ (past unmarked) > /num.tar/ 'drank'
        /iv/ [iʋ] 'heavy' + /-sa/ [sa] (state nominaliser) > /iv.sa/ 'heavi-

---

[3] Nakama (1983) also reports that his consultant (female; born in 1922) had a phonetic [ddz] in /fizza/ 'whale', implying that this phonemically contrasted with [tts]. My consultants who do have this voiced geminate, and who do distinguish it phonemically from voiceless [tts], were all over 80 years old at the time of research, i.e.in 2007.

ness'

/až/ [aẓ] 'say' + /=bjaam/ 'I wonder' > /až.bja:m/ 'I wonder if (s/
he) says'

/tur/ [tuɭ] 'bird' + /-nagi/ [nagi] (approximative) > /tur.na.gi/
'bird, and so on'

/tur/ + /=kara/ [kaɾa] (ablative) > /tur.ka.ra/ 'from bird'

As is shown in (2–25), in roots /v/ often lenites to /u/. I refer to this as
/v/-lenition. This occurs to avoid a consonant cluster within a root word.
Note that in (2–26) /iv/ does not cause this lenition.

2.5.6. Presyllable plus initial syllable onset
This type of cluster basically follows non-initial clusters in §2.5.5.3, except
that:

(2–27)   a. Geminates are rare in roots, and
         b. Non-geminates are rather common both in roots and morpho-
            logically complex words and word-pluses.

2.5.6.1. Geminates
The only kind of geminate in roots is the initial syllable onset of the $R.C_iC_i$
cluster (see (2–28) below). Geminates across presyllable and initial syllable
(i.e. $R_iR_i.C_iV$) are not found in roots. From the few attested examples of
type (2–28) a generalisation obtains that R is a labial resonant, and a geminate CC is alveolar.

(2–28)   /v.cca/ [ʊttsa] 'quail'
         /m.ssïï/ [m̩ssɨ:] 'miso soup' (which is a former compound
         //msu// 'miso' + //sïï// 'soup')

In morphologically complex word(-plus)es it is common to find both $R.C_i$
C_i clusters and $R_iR_i.C_iV$, but not $R_iR_i.C_iC_iV$.

(2–29)   //mc// 'road' + //=a// (topic) > /m.cca/ [m̩ttsa] 'road:TOP'
         (R.CCV)
         //nv// 'pull out' + //=a// > /n.vva/ [ŋ̩vva] 'pulling out:TOP'
         (R.CCV)
(2–30)   /mm/ [m̩:] 'potato' + /=mai/ [mai] 'too' > /mm.mai/ 'potato, too'
         (RR.CVV)
         /žž/ [ẓ:] 'rice ball' + /=a/ > /žž.ža/ 'rice ball:TOP' (RR.CV)

Phonology   31

/rr/ [l̩ː] 'enter' + /=ru/ [ɾu](question marker) > /rr.ru/'enter?'
(RR.CV)

2.5.6.2. Partial geminates (homorganic /n(n)/ + C of any place of articulation)

(2–31)   C: LABIAL   C: ALVEOLAR
         /n.bir/ [m̩bil̩] 'stretch'   /n.sï/ [n̩sɨ] 'north'
         /nn.bu/ [m̩ːbu] 'navel'   /nn.di/ [n̩ːdi] 'yes'
         C: VELAR/GLOTTAL
         /n.kair/ [ŋ̍kail̩] 'welcome'
         /nn.ku/ [ŋ̍ːku] 'pus'

2.5.6.3. Non-geminates
In root words (as shown in (2–32)), there is a tendency towards labial (and
in particular nasal) resonant plus an alveolar consonant.

(2–32)   LABIAL: /m/   (/v/: lenition is pervasive)
         /m.ta/ [m̩ta] 'mud'   /v.ta/ [ʋta]~/u.ta/ [uta] 'song'
         /m.su/ [m̩su] 'miso'   /v.da/ [ʋda]~/u.da/ [uda] 'thick;
                                      fat'
         /m.na/ [m̩na] 'shellfish'   /v.sï/ [ʋsɨ]~/u.sï/ [usɨ] 'rice
                                      mortar'
         /mm.ta/ [m̩ːta] 'a kind of tree' /v.cï/ [ʋcɨ]~/u.cï/ [utsɨ] 'intree'
         /mm.sa/ [m̩ːsa] 'similar'   /mm.na/ [m̩ːna] 'all'

/v/-lenition (/v/ > /u/) is pervasive in roots here. As in the case of medial
non-geminates (§2.5.5.3) this lenition is a cluster breaking strategy: the
cluster R.CV is broken down to V.CV (e.g. /v.ta/ > /u.ta/), where the presyllable R resolves into the initial syllable V. It is an emerging phonotactic
pattern, then, that in the presyllable plus initial onset clusters, the presyllable must be a nasal (short /m/ and /n/ or long /mm/ and /nn/), excluding the
possibility of the other labial resonant, i.e. /v/.

   The same generalization holds in morphologically complex word(-plus)
es, since an R.C cluster is always contained in the root part of morphologically complex word(-plus)es.

2.5.7. Frequecy-based account of root structures
TABLE 2–5 gives a statistical account of Irabu root word structure. This
shows that some structures are more frequently found than others, and so

32   Chapter 2

allows us to have a basic idea of what is the unmarked/marked structure/
phonotactic patterns. The database here is of 600 native roots (mostly nominal and adjectival, together with some zero affix verb forms.

TABLE 2–5. Frequently occurring root structures in 600 roots

RANK	STRUCTURE	TOKENS	EXAMPLE
1.	CV.CV	180	/pu.ni/ [puni] 'bone'
2.	CVV	66	/kaa/ [ka:] 'skin'; /kui/ [kui] 'voice'
3.	CV.CV.CV	54	/ka.ta.na/ [katana] 'knife'
4.	V.CV	40	/u.tu/ [utu] 'sound'
5.	CVC	38	/paž/ [paẓ] 'fly'
6.	R.CV	32	/n.za/ [ndza] 'where'; /m.su/ [m̩su] 'miso'
7.	CV.CVC	30	/pa.sam/ [pasam] 'scissors'
8.	GV.CV	16	/ju.da/ [juda] 'branch'
9.	CCV.CV	14	/nna.ma/ [nnama] 'now'
10.	CVC.CV	12	/kuv.va/ [kuvva] 'calf of leg'
	CCV	12	/mma/ [mma] 'mother'

The most important generalisations to emerge from this table are:

(2–33)   a. The most frequently occurring roots are di- or trisyllabic.
             Next come monosyllabic structures, of RANKS 2 (CVV), 5
             (CVC), and 10 (CCV).
         b. The most typical root structure is CV.CV with the open sylla-
             ble CV.
         c. Neither initial clusters nor medial clusters are common in the
             most frequently occurring root structures. Initial clusters are
             more common than non-initial clusters in roots.

In association with (2–33a), we will see in §2.6.2 that Irabu phonological
words must have at least two moras. Thus, the monosyllabic roots in RANKS
2, 5, and 10 have heavy syllable structures. The definition of mora is given
in §2.6.1.

     With regard to (2–33b), it is noted that the structure CV.CV.CV (RANK 3)
is also built from CV syllables, showing that CV syllables constitute the
most basic structural type in terms of frequency.

     With regard to (2–33c), it is noted that the presyllable plus initial onset
cluster R.CV (as found in RANK 6; 32 tokens) is slightly more frequent than
the initial syllable onset cluster CCV (as found in RANKS 9 and 10, accounting for 26 tokens in total), and there is no R.CGV or CCGV in the

Phonology

most frequently occurring patterns. Also, the root structures containing non-initial clusters are rather rare in the top ten list, only appearing at RANK 10.

2.5.8. Consonant allophony

Now that we have a clear picture of the structure of the word, we can summarise the allophonic variation of consonants, which is heavily dependent on syllable structure and the position of a syllable in a word.

TABLE 2–6. Consonant allophony (S: stops; F: fricatives; R: resonants)

		Presyllable		Initial (C)CV		Medial V(C)CV		Final C
		#RR#	#(R)R	#CCV	#CV	VC.CV	V.CV	VC#
S	/p/	*	*	*	[p]	[pp]	[p]	*
	/t/	*	*	([ʔtt])	[t]	[tt]	[t]	*
	/k/	*	*	*	[k]	[kk]	[k]	*
	/b/	*	*	*	[b]	*	[b]	*
	/d/	*	*	*	[d]	*	[d]	*
	/g/	*	*	*	[g]	*	[g]	*
F	/f/	*	*	[ff]	[f]	[ff]	[f]	*
	/s/	*	*	[ʃʃ/ss]	[s]	[ʃʃ/ss]	[ʃ/s]	*
	/c/	*	*	[ʔttʃ/ʔtts]	[tʃ/ts]	[ttʃ/tts]	[tʃ/ts]	*
	/z/	*	*	*	[dʒ/dz]	([ddz])	[dʒ/dz]	*
	(/h/)	*	*	*	([ç/h])	*	([ç/h])	*
R	/m/	[m̥ː]	[m̥(ː)]	[mm]	[m]	[mm],[mC]	[m]	[m]
	/n/	[n̥ː]	[N(ː)]	[nn]	[ɲ/n]	[ɲɲ/nn],[NC]	[ɲ/n]	[ŋ]
	/v/	[v̥ː]	[v̥(ː)]	[ʋv]	*	[vv], [ʋC]	*	[ʋ]
	/ž/	[z̥ː]	[z̥(ː)]	[z̥z]	*	[ʒʒ/zz], [z̥C]	*	[z̥]
	/r/	[l̥ː]	[l̥(ː)]	[ll]	*	[ll], [lC]	[ɾ]	[l]

Note: [N]: homorganic nasal; [x/y]: [x] before i /[y] elsewhere
(x): x is rare in roots
[xC]: x followed by a non-x consonant
*: non applicable (the phoneme cannot fill the slot marked by *)

2.6. Mora

This section introduces the phonological unit mora, which is important in describing segmental and supersegmental phenomena in Irabu.

34   Chapter 2

2.6.1. Definition
Moras are counted as follows:

IN A SYLLABLE						IN A PRESYLLABLE	
C_i	C_i	G	V_1	V_2	C_{coda}	R_i	R_i
μ	—	—	μ	μ	μ	μ	μ

2.6.2. Minimal word
A word is minimally bimoraic. Thus we have the following set of minimal words in terms of syllable structure:

Presyllable only
    RR: /mm/ [m̥ː] 'potato'
           /vv/ [v̥ː] 'sell'
           /žž/ [z̧ː] 'rice ball'
           /rr/ [l̩ː] 'enter'
Initial syllable only
    (C)(G)VV: /pjaa/ [pʲaː] 'early; fast'   /paa/ [paː] 'tooth'
               /jaa/ [jaː] 'home'   /aa/ [aː] 'foxtail millet'
    (C)(G)VC: /pjal̩/ [pʲal̩] 'leave'   /par/ [pal̩] 'needle'
               /jar/ [jal̩] 'spear'   /ar/ [al̩] 'exist'
    CC(G)V: /mmja/ [mmʲa] (emphasis) /mma/ [mma] 'mother'
Initial syllable plus non-initial syllable
    (C)(G)V.C(G)V: /ma.cja/ [matʃa] 'bird' /ma.ta/ [mata] 'and'
                    /ma.ju/ [maju] 'cat'
Presyllable plus initial syllable
    R.C(G)V: /m.cï/ [m̥tsɨ] 'road'
             /n.gja/ [ŋgʲa] 'spike'

There are a number of bimoraic roots which contain long vowels (e.g. /kaa/ 'river', /kii/ 'tree', /mii/ 'look', etc.). It is impossible to assume that they are underlyingly short and a rule augments them when they surface as words (e.g. //ka// → /kaa/, //ki// → /kii/, //mi// → /mii/, etc.), since many do not occur as the shorter forms in any environment and we cannot be sure if they are actually short underlyingly. Although a very few examples such as /kii/ 'tree' and /mii/ 'eye' have their short forms (as in /ffuki/ 'Kuroki tree', /mi-pana/ 'face'), all these examples are highly lexicalised and it would also be possible for /ffuki/ and /mipana/ to be simply analysed as monomorphemic roots. Thus, it is best to assume that the bimoraic roots with long vowels are all long underlyingly.

Phonology   35

It is important to note that a clitic does not count towards a bimoraic phonological word. Thus, it is impossible to find cases where a monomoraic word is followed by a clitic, with only one exception where the nominative case marker =ga is attached to the monomoraic form of the first person singular pronoun *ban* (§5.2.2.1). This combination results in an exceptional reduction on the part of *ban*, giving rise to *ba=ga*. Here, the word is not bimoraic.

In terms of minimality, then, a word rather than a word-plus is treated as a phonological word, which is defined as a phonological unit that is minimally bimoraic. A clitic is thus not simply part of a phonological word in this particular phenomenon. However, in most other respects, i.e. syllable structure/phonotactics (§2.4 and §2.5), phonological rules (§2.7 below), and prosody (§2.9), a word-plus is treated as a single phonological word, indicating that the word-plus is the most coherent phonological domain in the Irabu phonology.

2.6.3. Length (quantity) contrast
2.6.3.1. Short vs. long
As is illustrated below by minimal contrasts and quasi-minimal contrasts, there are both phonemically contrastive long vowels and consonants in roots. Long consonants are all resonants, and usually occur in presyllables (as noted in §2.4.2, however, /žž/ and /rr/ may appear in V slots in regular syllables).

Short vowel	Long vowel
/kagi/ [kagi] 'beautiful'	/kaagi/ [kaːgi] 'smell'
/kasi/ [kaʃi] 'a kind of local tree'	/kasii/ [kaʃiː] 'help'
/tur/ [tuɭ] 'bird'	/tuur/ [tuːɭ] 'cross'
/sïsï/ [sɨsɨ] 'grime'	/sïïsï/ [sɨːsɨ] 'meat'

Short consonant	Long consonant
/m.na/ [m̩na] 'shellfish'	/mm.na/ [m̩ːna] 'all'
/n.sï/ [n̩sɨ] 'north'	/nn.sa/ [n̩ːsa] 'dumb'

I have not found minimal or quasi-minimal contrasts of /e/ vs. /ee/ or /o/ vs. /oo/ in roots. In fact it is difficult to find /e/ and /o/ in Irabu in the first place. This is simply because the Proto-Ryukyuan */e/ and */o/ are reflected as /i/ and /u/ in Irabu, and so the mid vowels are scarce in the Irabu lexicon.

Nasal resonants /m/ and /n/ show a length contrast in roots as demon-

36   Chapter 2

strated above. On the other hand, non-nasal resonants in roots do not show
a length contrast, except in the cases where alveolar non-nasal resonants
appear in the regular syllable V slots.

2.6.3.2. Non-geminate vs. geminate

Irabu has geminate /C_iC_i(G)V/ in initial syllables and across syllable
boundaries. Non-geminate monomoraic /C(G)V/ and geminate bimoraic
/C_iC_i(G)V/ are phonemically contrastive. Thus initially /na.ma/ [nama]
'raw' and /nna.ma/ [nnama] 'now' are distinguished; likewise medially
/ba.si/ [baʃi] 'in between' and /bas.si/ [baʃʃi] 'forget' are distinguished.
Further examples of contrasts include:

Non-geminate	Geminate
/fau/ [fau] 'eat' CV	/ffau/ [ffau] 'child' (accusative) CCVV
/sa.gi/ [sagi] 'k.o.bird' CV.CV	/ssa.gi/ [ssagi] 'bridal' CCV.CV
/ci.bi/ [tʃïbi] 'hip' CV.CV	/ccir/ [ˀttʃil] 'pipe' CCVC
/maa.su/ [maːsu] 'salt' CVV.CV	/mmaa/ [mmaː] 'No' CCVV
/na.ma/ [nama] 'raw' CV.CV	/nna.ma/ [nnama] 'now' CCV.CV
/ba.ta/ [bata] 'stomach' CV.CV	/bat.ta/ [batta] 'armpit' CVC.CV
/ba.si/ [baʃi] 'edge' CV.CV	/bas.sir/ [baʃʃil] 'forget' CVC.CVC
/a.ca/ [atsa] 'tomorrow' V.CV	/ac.ca/ [attsa] 'side' VC.CV
/ga.ma/ [gama] 'cave' CV.CV	/gam.ma/ [gamma] (onom.) CVC.CV
/a.na/ [ana] 'hole' V.CV	/an.na/ [anna] 'mother' VC.CV

It is noted that two non-nasal resonants, /v/ and /ž/, must be geminated in
surface syllable onsets (as in /vva/ [ʋva] '2SG' and /žža/ [ʑʑa] 'father'),
and so do not show a length contrast in gemination at the surface level. As
will be noted in §2.7.2, these surface geminates are analysed underlyingly
as single moraic //C//, and an obligatory rule operates to produce the surface /vv/ and /žž/ from undelryingly moraic //v// and //ž// respectively (thus
//va// > /vva/, //ža// > /žža/ above).

2.7. Phonological alternation rules

This section notes major phonological alternation rules, which in most cases apply in roots and morphologically complex word(-plus)es, but not
across word(-plus)es.

2.7.1. Sequential voicing

In Japonic languages, there is a special morphophonological process that

Phonology

clearly distinguishes a compound from a phrase or from an affixed word. In Japanese linguistics this is called 'sequential voicing', which I also adopt in describing Irabu compounds. Thus in compounds, not in phrases, a non-word-initial stem of a compound may undergo sequential voicing in which a stem-initial voiceless onset consonant is replaced by its voiced counterpart. Note that in the fricative class /f/ lacks a phonemically voiced counterpart, and /f/ is replaced by /v/, which belongs to the resonant class. Also, either /s/ or /c/ is replaced by its phonemically voiced counterpart /z/.

(2–34) *mcï* 'road'+*fisa* 'grass' → *mcï+vsa* 'wandering'

mii- 'female'+*ffa* 'child' → *mii+vva* 'daughter'

uku- 'big'+*ssam* 'louse' → *uku+zzam* 'big louse'

(2–35) Voiceless   Voiced

/p/ *pjaar* 'hot season' → /b/ *nacï+bjaar* 'summer'
summer+hot.season

/t/ *tur* 'bird' → /d/ *uku+dur* 'big bird'
big+bird

/k/ *kan* 'crab' → /g/ *uku+gan* 'big crab'
big+crab

/f/ *ffa* 'child' → /v/ *biki+vva* 'son'
male+child

/s/ *sïma* 'island' → /z/ *imi+zïma* 'small island'
small+island

/c/ *cïn* 'clothes' → /z/ *jari+zïn* 'worn-out clothes'
worn.out+clothe

Sequential voicing is not obligatory and its occurrence cannot be precisely predicted. As a general tendency, the more conventional the combination of the compound stems is, the more likely it is to undergo sequential voicing, though this is not iron-clad, as seen in the examples above (*uku+dur* 'big bird', for example, is not considered to be a 'conventionalised' expression). However, we can tell in which context sequential voicing *never* occurs: if a potential target stem of sequential voicing already contains a non-initial syllable that carries a phonemically voiced onset (i.e. stops and fricatives), sequential voicing is blocked. For example, in *kazi* 'wind' the second syllable carries a phonemically voiced fricative onset /z/, and it never undergoes sequential voicing: *uku-* 'big' + *kazi* 'wind' > *uku+kazi* 'big wind' rather than **uku+gazi* (cf. *uku-* + *kan* 'crab' > *uku+gan* 'big crab'). This constraint is also found on sequential voicing in Japanese, and the constraint as noted above is known as Lyman's Law

38   Chapter 2

(Martin 1975; Sato 1989; Shibatani 1990; Ito and Mester 2003).

In a ternary compound, which is not uncommon in Irabu, the target stem of sequential voicing rule may be the second stem or the third, or both.

(2–36)   *biki+vva+zii* (< biki + ffa + sii)
          male+child+rock
          'a rock whose shape is like a male child'
(2–37)   *waa+kurusï+bžž* (< waa + kurusï + pžž)
          pig+killing+day
          'New year's eve'

2.7.2. Geminate copy insertion rule

This rule is sensitive to moraicity. As noted in §2.5.1.4, there is a strict constraint in the domain of word-plus that a moraic /C/ cannot directly precede a /V/ at the surface level. If morphological processes produce the prohibited pattern, the following phonological rule operates to avoid it.

(2–38)   Geminate copy insertion rule: if underlyingly moraic //C// and //V// are adjacent in a word-plus, then a geminate copy of //C// is inserted to produce a surface /C_iC_iV/.
          a. //va// '2sG'   →   /vva/ [ʋva] '2sG'
          b. //ava// 'oil'   →   /avva/ [avva] 'oil'
          c. //ža// 'father'   →   /žža/ [ẓza] 'father'
          d. //kam// 'god' + //=a//   →   /kam=ma/ [kamma] 'god:TOP'
             (topic)
          e. //sukubž// 'belt' + //=a//   →   /sukubž=ža/ [sukubzza]
             (topic)   'belt:TOP'
          f. //pus// 'star' + //=a//   →   /pus=sa/ [pussa] 'star:TOP'
             (topic)

(2–38a) to (2–38c) are roots, whose underlying forms contain an initial moraic //C// directly followed by //V//. Given the fact that the surface /v/ and /ž/ before a vowel are always geminated, and given the phonotactic constraint in Irabu that a moraic //C// cannot directly precede //V//, it is a reasonable assumption that an underlying structure //va// and //ža// (moraic //C// plus //V//) become /vva/ and /žža/ at the surface level, with an obligatory application of geminate copy insertion.

(2–38d) to (2–38f) illustrate morphophonemic processes. As defined above, the geminate copy insertion rule operates within a word-plus, but never occurs across word-pluses. Thus (2–39) below induces the geminate

Phonology   39

copy insertion rule, while in (2–40), where two word-pluses are adjacent, the rule does not operate.

(2–39)   Word-plus containing a clitic //=a// (topic)
         a. /kan=na/   b. /tur=ra/
            //kan =a//   //tur =a//
            crab =TOP   bird =TOP
            'crab:TOP'   'bird:TOP'

(2–40)   Adjacent words /kan/ 'crab' and /atar/ (copula)
         /uri=a   kan   a-tar/   (cf. */kan natar/)
         //uri =a   kan   a -tar//
         3SG =TOP   crab   COP-PST
         'It was a crab'

2.7.3. The /ï/-insertion rule

The high central vowel /ï/ cannot occur without a preceding onset and occurs only with fricative onsets, e.g. /fï.sa/ [fʉsa] (or [fʲsa]) 'plant', /sï.ta/ [sɨta] 'tongue', /cï.na/ [tsɨna] 'rope', /zï.mi.zï/ [dzɨmidzɨ] 'warm', /u.sï/ [usɨ]'cattle'.

The phoneme /ï/ is an epenthetic phoneme, which is uderlyingly absent and is predictably inserted through the /ï/-insertion rule, to keep the phonotactic well-formedness of a phonological word (§2.4, §2.5). Specifically, this occurs to avoid a nucleus-less fricative, i.e. a fricative-final coda (cf. §2.5.1.1) and a fricative+C non-geminate cluster (cf. §2.5.1.2). For example, as shown in (2–41a-d), a fricative-final coda is impermissible in a phonological word.

(2–41)   a. //tauf// 'tofu' > /taufï/
         b. //pus// 'star' > /pusï/
         c. //umac// 'fire' > /umacï/
         d. //muz// 'barley' > /muzï/

Likewise, a fricative+C is impermissible unless this cluster is a geminate, so that /ï/ is inserted to syllabify an otherwise impermissible sequence, as illustrated in (2–42).

(2–42)   a. //fsa// 'plant' > /fïsa/
         b. //sta// 'tongue' > /sïta/
         c. //cna// 'rope' > /cïna/
         d. //zmiz// 'worm' > /zïmizï/

40   Chapter 2

There are many pieces of evidence for the analysis that /i/ is best treated as being underlyingly absent, where the surface /Cï/ is underlyingly //C//. In what follows I note one major process which clearly depicts this. This process involves vowel-initial suffixes and clitics, such as the accusative case //=u//:

(2–43)   The morphophonemic rule of the accusative case //=u//
         a. If a nominal stem ends in a V_1V_2 other than a //Cïï// (C: /s, c,
            z/), //=u// is realised as /=ju/:
            //kaa// 'skin'   + //=u// > /kaa=ju/
            //kii// 'tree'   + //=u// > /kii=ju/
            //kuu// 'powder'   + //=u// > /kuu=ju/
            //kui// 'voice'   + //=u// > /kui=ju/
            //fïï// 'coming'   + //=u// > /fïï=ju/
         b. If a nominal stem ends in a consonant C, //=u// is realised as
            /=Cu/:
            //kam// 'god'   + //=u// > /kam=mu/
            //kan// 'crab'   + //=u// > kan=nu/
            //pav// 'snake'   + //=u// > /pav=vu/
            //paž// 'fly'   + //=u// > /paž=žu/
            //par// 'needle'   + //=u// > /par=ru/
         c. Otherwise //=u// is realised as /=u/:
            //pana// 'flower'   + //=u// > /pana=u/
            //sïï// 'nest'   + //=u// > /sïï=u/

(2–43b) is an instance where the geminate copy insertion rule (§2.7.2) applies. The behaviour of /Cïï/ is rather complicated, and we will discuss this in §2.8.5.

Our attention now turns to such nominal stems as /taufi/ [taufɯ] 'tofu', /pusï/ [pusɨ] 'star', /umacï/ [umatsɨ] 'fire', and /muzï/ [mudzɨ] 'barley', all of which end in surface /i/. If the /i/ were underlyingly present, i.e. the nominal stems were underlyingly vowel-final (//CV//#), then (2–43c) would apply and we would get something like */taufi=u/ [taufiɯ], /pusï=u/ [pusɨɯ], and so on. However, what happens is that we get the surface /tauf=fu/ [tauffɯ], /pus=su/ [pussɯ], /umac=cu/ [umattsɯ], and /muz=zu/ [muddzɯ] (~[muttsɯ]), indicating that the underlying forms of the above nominal stems are //tauf//, //pus//, //umac//, and //muz//, and that (2–43b) applies. The short vowel /i/ at the surface is underlyingly absent and the nominal stems listed here are underlyingly consonant-final (//C//#).

Thus, as illustrated below, /taufi/ is underlyingly //tauf//, and if it surfac-

es with //=u// the surface form is /tauf=fu/, with the application of the geminate copy insertion rule (GCI in (2–44)); if //tauf// surfaces with no clitici-
sation/affixation, then /ɨ/ is added word finally as a result of the application
of the /ɨ/-insertion rule.

(2–44)	Input	GCI	/ɨ/-Insertion	Output
	a. //tauf// + //=u// → /tauffu/ →		N/A	/tauffu/ [tauffu]
	b. //tauf// →	N/A	→ /taufi/	/taufi/ [taufɯ]

On the other hand, as is shown in (2–45a-d), when the underlying phonotactic structure is already well-formed, no insertion occurs. Note that in
(2–45d), /ɨ/ is inserted to syllabify *//fz//, not //zz//, the latter being already
well-formed.

(2–45)	Input	/ɨ/-copy insertion	Output
	a. //ffa// 'child' (CCV) →	N/A	/ffa/
	b. //ssam// 'louse' (CCVC) →	N/A	/ssam/
	c. //acca// 'side' (VC.CV) →	N/A	/acca/
	d. //fzza// 'whale' (*C.CCV) →	/fizza/ (CV.CCV)	/fizza/

The evidence that fricative geminates such as //ff// and //ss// in (2–45) do
not undergo the /ɨ/-insertion rule is seen not only in the phonetic fact that
[ɨ] is absent, but in morphophonemics as well. As was noted in §2.7.1, if
the sequential voicing rule applies to a non-initial stem of a compound
(e.g. the Stem 2 of Stem 1+ Stem 2), it undergoes the voicing of its initial
syllable onset. In (2–46a) below, the stem //fsa// undergoes sequential voicing rule, whereby the stem-initial syllable onset //f// is replaced by /v/ at
the surface level. This means that //fsa// is //f.sa//, and sequential voicing
rule applies to the syllable //f//. If //fsa// surfaces with no sequential voicing, then it must require the /ɨ/-insertion, since */f.sa/ is impermissible
(//f.sa// > /fɨ.sa/). On the other hand, in (2–46b), //ff// of the second stem is
treated as the stem-initial syllable onset, which is evidenced in the fact that
the //ff// as a whole undergoes sequential voicing rule (//ff// > /vv/). At the
underlying level, then, the onset of //ffa// is //ff// (i.e. //ffa// is underlyingly
syllabified as //CCV//, unlike //f.sa//).

(2–46) a. //imi// 'small' + //fsa// 'plant' > /imivsa/ 'small plant'
        b. //imi// + //ffa// 'child' > /imivva/ 'small child'

42   Chapter 2

2.7.4. The /ï/-spreading rule

This rule specifically targets a tautosyllabic fricative geminate onset //CC[V]// (where [V] is an unfilled nucleus) and applies after the /ï/-insertion rule operates. As an initial approximation, let us observe the verb root //ss[V]// 'know' (which surfaces as various inflected forms such as /ssan/ 'not know' (negative), /ssii/ 'know, and' (narrative converb), etc.) and the way its unmarked non-past form /sïï/ is derived[4].

(2–47) Input   /ï/-insertion   /ï/-spreading   Output
        //ss[V]// 'know' → /ssï/   →   /sïï/   /sïï/ [sɨː]

Here, the /ï/-spreading rule replaces the second segment of the geminate by /ï/, thus spreading of /ï/ backwards. This rule is interpreted as a strategy to gain sonority, as the unatestted structure */ssï/ would be low in sonority and is actually never found in roots.

(2–48) The /ï/-spreading rule: /CCï/ is changed into /Cïï/ by replacing the second C of the cluster by /ï/.

    Input   /ï/-insertion   /ï/-spreading   Output
    //ff// '(rain) fall' → /ffï/   →   /fïï/   /fïï/ [fʊː]
    //ss// 'know'   →   /ssï/   →   /sïï/   /sïï/ [sɨː]
    //cff// 'make'   →   /cïffï/   →   /cïfïï/   /cïfïï/ [tsɨfɨː]
    //pancc// 'bite'   →   /panccï/   →   /pancïï/   /pancïï/ [pantsɨː]

The question might arise why the /ï/-insertion rule does not insert /ï/ after each fricative, yielding /sïsï/ instead of /ssï/, for example. The answer lies in the nature of the /ï/-insertion rule, which is sensitive to the syllable structure of the input: a heterosyllabic fricative geminate cluster //C.C// (as in (2–49a, b) below) requires /ï/ to be inserted after each C, i.e. //C.C// → /Cï.Cï/, whereas a tautosyllabic fricative geminate cluster //CC[V]// (as in (2–49c, d)) requires /ï/ to be inserted after the second C alone, i.e. //CC[V]// → /CCï/. The fact that the tautosyllabic geminate //CC[V]// does not allow /ï/ to be inserted between the CC is independently justified by observing sequential voicing as mentioned in the preceding section.

(2–49)   Input   /ï/-insertion   /ï/-spreading   Output
        a. //s.s// 'grime'   → /sïsï/   →   N/A   /sïsï/
        b. //c.c// 'the moon' → /cïcï/   →   N/A   /cïcï/

---

[4] The analysis that the surface /Cïï/ (where C is fricative) is underlyingly //CC// is inspired by Takubo (2015), who describes the morphophonemics of Ikema.

	Phonology					43

    c. //ss// 'know'   →   /ssï/   →   /sïï/   /sïï/

    d. //cc// 'wear'   →   /ccï/   →   /cïï/   /cïï/

    e. //ff// '(rain) fall'   →   /ffï/   →   /fïï/   /fïï/

The derivation of the verb root //fk// (//C.C//) 'blow' to derive the unmarked non-past form /fïfï/ is worth discussing here. The /k/ of the root undergoes the stop lenition rule (§6.3.4.1) whereby the stop /k/ turns into /f/. After deriving /f.f/, the /ï/-insertion rule applies and we get the surface out put /fïfï/. Thus, the relative order of the relevant rules is presented below.

(2–50)   Input   stop lenition   /ï/-insertion   /ï/-spreading   Output

           //fk// →   /f.f/   → /fïfï/   → N/A   /fïfï/

2.7.5. Resonant geminate reduction

Some roots (especially verb roots) have a syllable-final geminate cluster underlyingly (//CC[V]// where [V] represents an unfilled nucleus, as in //cff// 'make', //ažž// 'say', //parr// 'go into', etc.). The resonant geminate cluster is avoided by deleting the second C of the geminate. The fricative geminate cluster is fixed by the /ï/-insertion rule and then the /ï/-spreading rule, as was noted in §2.7.3 and §2.7.4.

(2–51)   Resonant geminate reduction rule: the syllable-final geminate resonant cluster //CC[V]//) is avoided by deleting the second C of the CC to make the cluster a coda, as in (a) and (b) below, unless it results in the violation of word minimality, as in (c).

       a. //ažž// 'say' → /až/

       b. //parr// 'go into' → /par/

       c. //rr// 'enter' → /rr/ (non applicable)

In the case of (2–51c), a simple resyllabification occurs, whereby the second C now functions as a nucleus, since resonants may be nucleic (§2.4.4.5).

     In sum, the rule ordering of the resonant geminate reduction, /ï/-insertion and /ï/-spreading is illustrated in (2–52).

(2–52)   Input   RGR   /ï/-insertion   /ï/-spreading   Output

           //ažž// → /až/ → N/A   →   N/A   /až/ (VC)

           //parr// → /par/ → N/A   →   N/A   /par/ (CVC)

           //rr//   → N/A → N/A   →   N/A   /rr/ (RR)

//cff// → N/A → /cïffï/ → /cïfïï/ /cïfïï/ (CV.CVV)

2.7.6. Sequential nasal deletion

A sequence of moraic nasals (/mm/, /nn/, /mn/, /nm/) across morpheme boundaries undergoes the deletion of the second nasal.

(2–53) *kan* 'crab' + *-mmi* (plural) → *kan-mi*
kan + *=n* (dative) → *kan*
kan + *=nkai* (allative) → *kan=kai*
kam 'god' + *-mmi* → *kam-mi*
kam + *=n* → *kam*
kam + *=nkai* → *kamkai*

As noted in §2.5.1.2, the sequential nasal deletion rule never applies across two word-pluses (e.g. *uja=n#nkairair* (father=DAT#be.brought) 'be brought by my father'), so that the fact that it does apply to *=nkai* in (2–19) suggests that it is part of a phonological word in terms of this particular phonological rule.

2.7.7. Morpheme-specific alternation rules

2.7.7.1. /j/-insertion for topic and accusative particles

The topic marker //=a//, accusative pacticle //=u//, and partitive marker //=a// are subject to /j/ insertion (in addition to other predictable general phonological rules as noted above) when attaching to a host ending in VV (long vowel or diphthong).

(2–54) Topic //=a// (and partitive //=a//: these are homophonous)
//pana// 'nose' + //=a// → /pana=a/ [panaː] 'nose:TOP'
//kuri// 'this' + //=a// → /kuri=a/ [kurʲuː] 'this:TOP'
//tur// 'bird' + //=a// → /tur=ra/ [tuḷḷa] 'bird:TOP' (geminate copy insertion)
//kaa// 'skin' + //=a// → /kaa=ja/ [kaːja] 'skin:TOP' [/j/ insertion]/
/kui// 'voice' + //=a// → /kui=ja/ [kuija] 'voice:TOP' [/j/ insertion]
(2–55) Accusative //=u//
//pana// 'nose' + //=u// → /pana=u/ [panau] 'nose:ACC'
//kuri// 'this' + //=u// → /kuri=a/ [kurʲuː] 'this:ACC'
//tur// 'bird' + //=u// → /tur=ra/ [tuḷḷu] 'bird:ACC' (geminate copy insertion)

//kaa// 'skin' + //=u// → /kaa=ju/ [ka:ju] 'skin:ACC' [/j/ inser-
tion]
//kui// 'voice' + //=u// → /kui=ju/ [kuiju] 'voice:ACC' [/j/ inser-
tion]

2.7.7.2. /s/-to-/r/ assimilation

The formal noun *su(u)* 'thing; man; COMP' (§4.2.1.8) and diachronically
related forms (forms that derived from *su(u)*) undergo assimilation when
preceded by /r/.

(2–56) *kanamar=nu   cuu-kar-Ø   ruu=nu=du   icïban.*
        head=NOM   strong-VLZ-NPST   man=NOM=FOC   No.1
        'Those who are wise are the best.'

(2–57) *ba=a   ujaki-ka-tar=ruga=du,   nnama=a   jaa=mai*
        1SG=TOP   rich-VLZ-PST=but=FOC   now=TOP   house=even
        njaa-n.
        NEG-NPST
        'I used to be rich, but now I do not have even a house.' [=*suga*;
        §9.2.3]

(2–58) *kuri=a   midum   jar-Ø=ruuda.*
        3SG=TOP   woman   COP-NPST=AD.ASR
        'This is a woman, isn't she?' [=*su(u)da*; §9.3.5]

2.8. Miscellaneous segmental issues

2.8.1. Homorganic nasal clusters in roots

The phonemic treatment of phonetic partial geminates [m(:)p] and [m(:)b]
occurring in *root* words requires careful discussion. Irabu has both nasal
/m(:)/ and /n(:)/, both of which participate in a nasal plus consonant cluster.
Note that /n(:)C/ clusters are phonetically partial geminates, where the
place of articulation of homorganic /n/ assimilates to that of the following
C. Thus there emerge three analytical possibilities for [m(:)p] and [m(:)b],
of which the first is my current analysis: (**A**) the phonetic partial geminates
are analysed as /n(:)p/ and /n(:)b/, where the homorganic /n(:)/ is realised
as [m(:)]; (**B**) the phonetic partial geminates are analysed as /m(:)p/ and
/m(:)b/; and (**C**) there is neutralisation of /n(:)/ and /m(:)/ before [p]/[b].[5]
   The analysis (**A**) allows us to have the systematic phonotactic pattern

---

[5] Of course, if the [m(:)p] or [m(:)b] results from a morphological process, there emerges no
problem in identifying the underlying representation of these surface segments: //kam// 'god'
+ //pazï// 'maybe' > /kampazï/ '(That's) a god, perhaps.'

described in §2.5.5.2 and §2.5.5.3 (non-initial cluster C.C) and in §2.5.6 (presyllable plus initial onset (R)R.C). First, aside from phonetic [m(:)p] and [m(:)b], two generalisations obtain with regard to the above mentioned clusters in roots:

> **Generalisation 1.** /n(:)C/ partial geminate involves all places of articulation of C *but bilabial*.
>
> **Generalisation 2.** /m(:)C/ involves /m(:)/ + *alveolar* consonant.

Now, with regard to Analysis (**A**), i.e. if we assume that [m(:)p] and [m(:)b] represent phonemic /n(:)p/ and /n(:)b/, we can have a full set of places of articulation in /n(:)C/ partial geminates, making **Generalisation 1** complete. Also, we do not harm **Generalisation 2** for non-geminates.

If we alternatively take Analysis (**B**), i.e. if we assume that [m(:)p] and [m(:)b] are /m(:)p/ and /m(:)b/ respectively, then the odd gap still occurs in **Generalisation 1**, and we even harm **Generalisation 2**, where the odd exception appears in the combinations of /m(:)C/, where /m(:)/ combines with a labial, but otherwise it only combines with alveolar consonants.

Finally, Analysis (**C**) just keeps the status quo, with no positive effect on either Generalisation, since this analysis only says that [m(:)p] and [m(:)b] are phonemically ambiguous. Thus it is best to take Analysis (**A**) (resulting in positive effects on Generalisations 1 and 2), as opposed to (**B**) (resulting in negative effects on Generalisations 1 and 2) and (**C**) (with no positive effect on either).

2.8.2. Non-nasal alveolar resonants /v/ and /ž/

The non-nasal alveolar resonants /v/, /ž/ and /r/ show some peculiarities that are not found in nasal resonants.

First, they cannot occur in presyllables unless they are long. It is true that the resonant /v/ may appear if it is followed by an initial syllable, as in /v.cï/ [ʋtsɨ] (R.CV) 'inside', but short /ž/ and /r/ cannot fill the presyllable slot. Note also that the short /v/ in the presyllable shows instability, frequently undergoing lenition (e.g. /v.cï/ R.CV > /u.cï/ V.CV: see §2.5.6.3). Thus, the presyllable slot is not easily accessible to short non-nasal resonants.

Second, in the onset, /v/ and /ž/ only appear as a geminate, as in /vva/ 'you', /av.va/ 'oil', and so on, and this gemination is a result of a predictable rule, the geminate copy insertion rule (§2.7.2).

   (2–59)   //va// 'you' (//C.V//) → /vva/

Phonology

//ava// 'oil' (//VC.V//) → /avva/
//ža// 'father' (//C.V//) → /žža/
//paž// 'fly' + //=a// (topic) → /pažža/

2.8.3. The status of glides
2.8.3.1. General remarks
As is shown below, I treat labialised and palatal(ised) phones, i.e. [Cʷ] (e.g.
[kʷ]) and [Cʲ] (e.g. [pʲ] and [ʃ]), as two phoneme sequences (non-glide consonant plus /w/ or /j/), rather than single consonant unit-phonemes. Thus
[kʷ] is treated as /k/ plus /w/, while [pʲ] and [ʃ] are treated as /p/ plus /j/ and
/s/ plus /j/ respectively.

(2–60) GENERAL TREATMENT   EXAMPLE
        [Cʷ] > /C/ + /w/   [kʷaːsɨ] 'snack'   > /kwaa.sɨ/
                                                          CGVV.CV

        [Cʲ] > /C/ + /j/   [ʃaːka] 'late midnight' > /sjaa.ka/
                                                          CGVV.CV

The main reasons for assuming the complex CG are twofold. First, it allows a straightforward description of such morphological processes where
a sequence of C and G produces a phonetic [Cʷ] or [Cʲ] (e.g. stem-final C
plus suffix initial -G > C-G; as in /kak-/ [kak] 'write' + /-ja/ (agent nominal
suffix) > /kakja/ [kakʲa] (CV.CGV) 'writer'). Second, it minimises the consonant phoneme inventory. These two are addressed in the following section.

The labio-velar glide /Cw/ has a low functional load in Irabu. It is only
found in a handful of words and affixes. Attested examples are:

(2–61) a. /kwaasɨ/ [kʷaːsɨ] 'snack'
        b. /kwaarja/ [kʷaːɾʲa] (Place name)
        c. /ukwaasa/ [ukʷaːsa] 'many'
        d. /jakkwan/ [jakkʷaŋ] 'kettle'
        e. /jukwaara/ [jukʷaːɾa] 'side'
        f. /jukwaira/ [jukʷaiɾa] 'four times'
        g. /gwatsɨ/ [gʷatsɨ] 'month'
           (e.g. /sici-gwacɨ/ [ʃitʃigʷacɨ] '7-month: July').

In (2–61c) and (2–61e) /kw/ arguably reflects //u// + //a//: (2–61c) //uku//
'big' + //asa// '?'; (2–61e) //juku// 'side' + //ara// 'left-over'. Furthermore,
according to many speakers, (2–61c) to (2–61g) are in free variation with

48   Chapter 2

/ukaasa/, /jakkan/, /jukaara/, /jukaira/ and /gacï/ respectively, where /w/ is dropped. Thus the /Cw/ sequence is unstable, and so peripheral in Irabu phonology. The discussion that follows thus focuses on /Cj/.

2.8.3.2. Advantages in assuming a complex CG

At the phonetic level, Irabu has the full set of palatal(ised) phones corresponding to non-palatal(ised) phones which are the major allophones of the consonant phonemes. That is, a given non-palatal [C] (/C/) has its palatal counterpart [Cj]. The non-palatal and palatal phones contrast phonemically. Examples are listed below:

(2–62) Root-internal ((quasi) minimal contrasts are given)

    /paa/ [paː] 'tooth'   vs. /pjaa/ [pʲaː] 'old days'

    /unta/ [unta] 'frog'   vs. /untja/ [untʲa] '3PL'

    /ukugan/ [ukugaŋ] 'big crab' vs. /ukugjam/ [ukugʲam] 'millet'

    /sabi/ [sabi] 'rust'   vs. /sjabi/ [ʃabi] 'Shabi (name)'

    /ica/ [itsa] 'board'   vs. /icjagara/ [itʃagara] 'some-

                   how'

    /maaku/ [maːku] 'round' vs. /mjaaku/ [mʲaːku] 'Miyako

                   Island'

    /naa/ [naː] 'name'   vs. /njaan/ [ɲaːŋ] 'not exist'

(2–63) a. Root-final //Ci// plus clitic-initial //a// or //u// > /Cia/ [Cʲaː] or

     /Ciu/ [Cʲuː]

     //kuri// 'this' + //=a// (topic) > /kuri=a/ [kurʲaː] 'this' (topic)

     //nabi// 'pot' + //=u// (accusative) > /nabi=u/ [nabʲuː] 'pot'

     (accusative)

    b. Root-final //C// plus suffix–initial //j//

     //kak-// 'write' + //-ja// (agent nominal) > /kak-ja/ [kakʲa]

     'writer'

     //sadur-// 'search' + //-ja// > /sadur-ja/ [sadurʲa] 'searcher'

As is shown above, not all the phonetic palatals are necessarily phonemic. First, palatals of the type (2–63a) are morphophonological products, which are produced by the root-final //i// plus the clitic-initial //a// or //u//, giving rise to /ia/ or /iu/ (falling diphthong; phonetically [jaː] and [juː]). Second, the phonetic palatals of the type (2–63b) are produced by the root-final //C// plus the suffix–initial //-ja// (person nominaliser suffix), and it is for this morphological process that our complex /CG/ approach, i.e. the separation of /C/ and /j/ for phonetic palatals, works well.

  In this latter morphological process, the person nominaliser suffix //-ja//

Phonology   49

is typically attached to a verb root, as exemplified in (2–64) and (2–65) below. If it is attached to a root which ends in a vowel, as in (2–64), there is
no conspicuous morphophonological alternation observed (except in //i//
final roots, where //i// drops), displaying a fairly agglutinative pattern.

(2–64)   **Vowel-final root plus //-ja//**
         a. //fa-// 'eat' + //-ja// → /fa-ja/ [faja] 'person who eats (a lot)'
         b. //ubui-// 'memorise'+ //-ja// → /ubu-ja/ [ubuja] 'person who
            memorise well'
         c. //mii-// 'look' + //-ja// → /mi-ja/ [mija] 'person who stares a
            lot'
         d. //kagi// 'beautiful' + //-ja// → /kag-ja/ [kagʲa] 'beautiful per-
            son'

(2–65)   **Consonant-final root plus //-ja//**
         a. //kak-// 'write' + //-ja// → /kak-ja/ [kakʲa] 'writer'
            CVC-   CVC-GV
         b. //sadur-// 'search' + //-ja// → /sadur-ja/ [saduɾʲa] 'searcher'
            CVCVC-   CVCVC-GV
         c. //ss-// 'know' + //-ja// → /ss-ja/ [ʃʃa] 'a person who knows a
            CC-   CC-GV   lot'

(2–65) illustrates consonant-final roots plus //-ja//. Here, the suffix attaches
to a consonant which becomes the onset when the suffix is attached, and
the consonant and the //-ja// form a syllable whose onset is a single palatalised consonant [Cʲa]. As is suggested in (2–65), the most plausible phonemic analysis is to treat [Cʲa] as a phonemic sequence /C/+/j/: we do not
need to come up with any special morphophonological alternation for such
cases as (2–65), as the suffix //-ja// is agglutinatively attached to the root
ending in onset //C//. If we alternatively assume that the resulting [Cʲ] is
phonemically a single segment /Cj/, we would introduce an irregular
morphophonological rule for such examples as (2–65): the root-final consonant //C// is replaced by the surface /Cj/.

There is another obvious advantage in terms of the economy of phoneme
inventory. If we analysed each [Cʲ] as a single phoneme /Cj/, we would
double the consonant inventory, by having /Cj/ corresponding to each of
the 16 non-glide consonant phonemes in Irabu.

2.8.4. The phonemic analysis of long vowels

As was briefly noted in §2.2.3, I treat long vowels as sequences of the
identical short vowel phonemes, rather than as distinct phonemes. This

50 Chapter 2

analysis is supported by the discussion of the person nominaliser -*ja* in the preceding section. The key lies in the morphophonemic alternation of the vowel-final roots in (2–64). The simplest and most consistent analysis is to state that the root-fonal /i/ drops when -*ja* is attached (e.g. //ubui// 'memorise' + //-ja// → /ubu-ja/ 'a person who memorises well'). Note that in (2–64c), //mii// is subject to the same rule if we assume that /ii/ is a sequence of the short /i/, in such a way that the second /i/ drops (//mii// + //-ja// → /mi-ja/). Now, if we assumed that /ii/ is a distinct phoneme independent of /i/, we would have to add an ad-hoc rule that replaces the /ii/ by /i/ when //mii// is suffixed by //-ja//. A similar kind of morphophonemic alternation is found elsewhere in Irabu, as in the morphophonemics of the irrealis intentional suffix (§6.3.1).

Apart from the above reason for treating long vowels as sequences of identical short vowels, there is an obvious advantage in doing so: we can minimise the number of vowel phonemes.

2.8.5. The problem of the long /ïï/

In my description, the long /ïï/ is phonemically interpreted as the doubling of the phoneme /ï/. It occurs both in roots and morphophonemically derived forms, as in /sïï/ [sɨː] 'nest', /cïï/ [tsɨː] 'breast', /zïï/ [dzɨː] 'letter' (all roots) and in /fïï/ '(rain) fall' (unmarked non-past) (< //ff//), /pancïï/ 'bite' (unmarked non-past) (< //pancc//). The issue here is whether the /ïï/ in roots is underlyingly present or, as in the case of the morphophonemically derived forms, it is underlyingly absent and generated by rule. I take the latter analysis, for the reason to be discusses below.

As was briefly noted in §2.7.3, /ïï/ behaves differently from the other long vowels with respect to the morphophonemic alternation of //=a// (topic), //=a// (partitive) and //=u// (accusative). That is, whereas the other long vowels attract /j/-insertion before the above-mentioned forms, as illustrated in (2–66a, b, c) below, /ïï/ does not attract this morphophonemic alternation, as shown in (2–66d). This induces us to suspect that /ïï/ is not simply underlying as suggested in (2–66d) and that a different underlying representation is necessary for the words ending in /ïï/ at surface level.

(2–66) The applicability of /j/-insertion rule
 a. //suu// 'vegitable' + //=a// → /suu=ja/
 b. //sii// 'rock' + //=a// → /sii=ja/
 c. //saa// 'difference' + //=a// → /saa=ja/
 d. //sïï// 'nest' + //=a// → */sïï=ja/

Quite apart from this peculiarity of /ïï/ in terms of /j/-insertion, another obvious reason for not treating /ïï/ as underlying is that since the short /ï/ is not underlyingly present but inserted afterwords, the long /ïï/ must also be underlyingly absent. If we do claim that /ïï/ is underlying even when its short counterpart is not, we are claiming that the two are different phonemes, i.e. a short vowel and a long vowel are distinct phonemes, an analysis which goes against our current analysis. Noe that there is an independent motivation for treating long vowels as sequences of short vowels (§2.8.4). Thus, the most reasonable solution is to assume that /ïï/ is not underlying as in the case of /ï/, and to seek for ways to derive it by some rule.

In order to derive the surface /ïï/, it is possible to postulate the following underlying form to which the geminate copy insertion (GCI), the /ï/-insertion and the /ï/-spreading apply in this order, with the geminate copy insertion being non-applicable.

(2–67) Input   GCI   /ï/-insertion   /ï/-spreading
        //ss// 'nest' + //=a// → /ss.a/ → /ssï.a/   →   /sïï.a/
        Output
        /sïïa/

This analysis regards the underlying representation as a fricative geminate onset without a nucleus, just as in the case of the verb roots that have /ïï/. The //ss// in (2–67) and //=a// combine and we get /ss.a/, which is not subject to the geminate copy insertion rule since the second /s/ is an onset and is not moraic. The /ï/-insertion and the /ï/-spreading rule operate to yield the surface /sïï/.

The analyses is also applicable to all roots with /ïï/ at surface, such as /sïïsï/ [sɨːsɨ] 'flesh', /cïïzï/ [tsɨːdzɨ] 'spike', /mucïï/ [mutsɨː] 'rice cake'. To derive /sïïsï/, for example, the underlying form is analysed as //ss.s//, where the fricative geminate onset without its nucleus undergoes the /ï/-insertion and then the /ï/-spreading and the second single fricative segment undergoes the /ï/-insertion alone.

2.9. Prosody

Irabu lacks lexical prosody, or is an 'accentless' language (Hirayama 1964, 1967, Hirayama, Oshima, and Nakamoto 1966, Nakasone n.d (b)). However, Irabu shows a strikingly rigid prosodic organisation in terms of rhythmic structure. Irabu prosody has a hierarchical structure in which the most basic structure is mora structure, which is the tone-bearing unit and which

52   Chapter 2

is in turn the basis of bi- or trimoraic foot structure based on which tone is
assigned to produce rhythmic alternation of tones (High and toneless).

The phonological word in terms of prosody is the domain of this alternating tonal pattern. The phonological word thus defined in most cases
corresponds to a word-plus. However, it may be an entire phrase if certain
conditions are met (§2.9.4).

2.9.1. Prosodic patterns of root words

In this section I will demonstrate that Irabu words do not show lexically
contrastive tonal patterns. Below a word-plus of n morae is optionally abbreviated as W_n.

2.9.1.1. Prosodic patterns of W_2

The prosodic patterns of W_2 are listed in TABLE 2–7.

TABLE 2–7. Prosodic patterns of W_2

	Form	Gloss	Pitch pattern	Tonal pattern
a.	pa.na	'nose'	[HH] (or [HL])	/HH/
	ja.ma	'mountain'	[HH] (or [HL])	/HH/
	i.cu	'thread'	[HH] (or [HL])	/HH/
b.	kam	'god'	[HL]	/HH/
	kan	'crab'	[HL]	/HH/
	paž	'fly'	[HL]	/HH/
	pav	'snake'	[HL]	/HH/
	par	'needle'	[HL]	/HH/
c.	mii	'eye'	[HH] (or [HL])	/HH/
	naa	'name'	[HH] (or [HL])	/HH/
	sïï	'nest'	[HH] (or [HL])	/HH/
d.	kai	'that way'	[HH] (or [HL])	/HH/
	nau	'what'	[HH] (or [HL])	/HH/
	kui	'voice'	[HH] (or [HL])	/HH/

There are one or two surface pitch patterns in each W_2 (which are indicated
by '[ ]'), and there is one phonological tonal representation (indicated by
'/ /') set up from the pitch pattern(s). The tone-bearing unit is the mora, and
there are two surface pitches [H] and [L].

The coda consonant in word(-plus) final position is obligatorily lowered.
Otherwise, the presence or absence of lowering of the final mora seems to
be a matter of free variation, though lowering typically does *not* take place.
Note here that the second member of a long vowel or a diphthong behaves

Phonology   53

like a light syllable with regard to final lowering.

TONAL PATTERN	FINAL SYLLABLE	FINAL LOWERING	PITCH PATTERN
/HH/	C#	+	[HL]
	Otherwise	±	[HH] (or [HL])

As mentioned above, final lowering is not inherent in the lexical property of each word that undergoes this lowering. Final lowering occurs either
at the end of a word or of an entire word-plus, and this is induced when the
word(-plus)-final mora is a coda. When such a word as *mii* 'eye' (typically
[HH] with no final lowering in a citation form) is followed by the dative
case marker =*n*, we get the word-plus *miin* [HHL], where the word-plus-
final /n/ is lowered as a result of final lowering, since the word-plus ends in
a coda. When such a word as *par* 'needle' ([HL] with an obligatory final
lowering in a citation form) is followed by the dative case marker, we get
parn [HHL], where the word-plus-final /n/, not the word-final /r/, is subject
to final lowering. When *par* is followed by another case marker =*nu* (nominative) we get the word-plus *parnu*, where final lowering is typically absent ([HHH]), since the word-plus does not end in a coda. The first person
singular pronoun is *ban*, with the pitch pattern [HL] in citation. However, if
ban is followed by nominative =*ga*, the resulting word-plus is *ba=ga* (/n/ is
irregularly deleted by a minor rule), and it is typically pronounced as [HH],
as *ba=ga* lacks a coda.

   With regard to other examples than those ending with a coda, it is not
possible to predict exactly when final lowering takes place, as it is in free
variation with its absence; however, lowering is possible only if the word
in question comes finally: *pana* is pronounced as [HH] (or [HL]) in citation, but *pana=nu* is typically pronounced as [HHH] where no final lowering occurs on the host word *pana*, as it is in the middle of a word-plus.

   Thus we can assume that a W_2 has an underlying tonal pattern /HH/,
which may be realised as [HL] if final lowering, which targets the final
mora of a word(-plus), applies.

2.9.1.2. Prosodic patterns of W_3
We now turn to W_3. Although it is still uncontroversial to analyse W_3 as
showing an invariable tonal pattern, the situation is somewhat more complicated. In TABLE 2–8 below I list the prosodic patterns of W_3.

54   Chapter 2

TABLE 2–8. Prosodic patterns of W_3

	Form	Gloss	Pitch pattern		Tonal pattern
a.	*ka.ta.na*	'knife'	[HHH]	(or [LHL])	/HHH/
	ja.ra.bi	'child'	[HHH]	(or [LHL])	/HHH/
	žža.ra	'tail cutter'	[HHH]	(or [LHL])	/HHH/
b.	*bu.dur*	'dance'	[LHL]	(or [HHL])	/HHH/
	pi.sir	'lunch'	[LHL]	(or [HHL])	/HHH/
	mi.dum	'woman'	[LHL]	(or [HHL])	/HHH/
c.	*pa.sïï*	'bridge'	[LHL]	(or [HHL])	/HHH/
	n.gii	'root of sweet potato'	[LHL]	(or [HHL])	/HHH/
	ka.tai	'in-law'	[LHL]	(or [HHL])	/HHH/
d.	*juuž*	'celebration'	[HHL]		/HHH/
	pjaar	'summer'	[HHL]		/HHH/
	daav	'tool'	[HHL]		/HHH/
e.	*av.va*	'oil'	[HHH]	(or [HHL])	/HHH/
	an.na	'mother'	[HHH]	(or [HHL])	/HHH/
	jur.ru	'k.o.fish'	[HHH]	(or [HHL])	/HHH/
f.	*kaa.gi*	'smell'	[HHH]	(or [HHL])	/HHH/
	kai.na	'arm'	[HHH]	(or [HHL])	/HHH/
g.	*mm.na*	'all'	[HHH]	(or [HHL])	/HHH/
	nn.sa	'dumb'	[HHH]	(or [HHL])	/HHH/

A number of generalisations can be made about these patterns.

- Unlike W_2, final lowering is regularly seen if a word in a citation form ends in any kind of heavy syllable: the lowered mora may be a coda, the second member of a long vowel or of a diphthong. See (b) to (d). Otherwise, as shown in (a) and (e–g), final lowering is possible but not typical.
- There is initial lowering, whereby the initial mora of a word is L-pitched. This is possible if a word begins in a $(C_i)(C_i)(G)V$, i.e. if the initial mora is a light syllable or a geminate initial C (see *žža.ra* in (a)), or a light presyllable (see *n.gii* in (c)). All other initial heavy syllables are never subject to initial lowering (see (d), (e), (f), and (g)). As is noted below, initial lowering is optional, and is heavily dependent on the presence or absence of final lowering within the same word.
- Initial lowering is present only if final lowering is present within the same word (thus [LHH] is unattested in my database). In (b) and (c) in which the initial syllable is a light syllable or a light presyllable (and

Phonology

thus may be subject to initial lowering) and in which final lowering is obligatory, the typical pitch pattern is [LHL], where both final and initial lowering are present. On the other hand, the parenthesised [HHL] in these examples, where there is only final lowering, is atypical but possible. Thus it seems that a phonetically 'angular' contour is preferred.

Tonal pattern	Initial lowering	Final lowering	Pitch pattern
/HHH/	+	+	[LHL]
	−	+	[HHL]
	−	−	[HHH]
	+	−	*[LHH]

- In (d), there is a regular final lowering as it ends in a coda, but there is no initial lowering since the initial syllable is not $(C_i)(C_i)(G)V$ or a light R, and therefore initial lowering is blocked.
- In (e), (f), and (g), final lowering is not typical, as the final mora is a light syllable; however, even if final lowering occurs, initial lowering is still blocked since the initial syllable here is not $(C_i)(C_i)(G)V$ or a light presyllable.
- In (a) final lowering is not typical, as the final mora is a light syllable. When final lowering does occur in these examples, initial lowering becomes possible. The pattern [HHL] (only with final lowering) is also possible in (a), but it is almost absent in my database, and I do not consider this to be a productively attested pattern, and do not list it in the table below.

In the surface pitch pattern [LHL], the final L pitch is slightly lower than the initial L pitch. Thus a more elaborate auditory approximation of the pitch pattern of (b) *budur* 'dance' is [-‾_] (as opposed to (d) *juuž* 'celebration' [‾ ‾_]), in which straight lines represent relative pitch height per mora.

As in the case of final lowering, initial lowering in W_3 is phonetic, influenced by the syllable structure of the initial syllable of a word, and by the presence or absence of final lowering, not by an inherent lexical tonal pattern of the word.

Thus, we can set up the underlying tonal pattern /HHH/ with exclusion of the final and initial lowering effects that can be assumed to be phonetic.

56 Chapter 2

2.9.1.3. Prosodic patterns of W$_4$ and longer words

In TABLE 2–9 below I list the prosodic patterns of W$_4$ and longer words. Irabu roots are mostly bi- or trimoraic and W$_4$ is not common in roots. It is even more difficult to find native roots of more than four moras, so that the list below includes a proper name of Japanese origin (W$_6$: *koozaburoo*), and western loans (W$_7$).

TABLE 2–9. Prosodic patterns of W$_4$ and longer words

Form	Gloss	Pitch pattern	Tonal pattern
W$_4$			
u.tu.ga.ja	'jaw'	[LHLL] (or [HHLL])	/HHLL/
a.kjaa.da	'merchant'	[LHLL] (or [HHLL])	/HHLL/
a.mair	'bulb'	[LHLL] (or [HHLL])	/HHLL/
a.pav.cï	'chatterer'	[LHLL] (or [HHLL])	/HHLL/
mmiv.cï	'chest'	[LHLL] (or [HHLL])	/HHLL/
n.kjaan	'old times'	[LHLL] (or [HHLL])	/HHLL/
kam.nar	'thunder'	[HHLL]	/HHLL/
kuu.mu.ja	'cockroach'	[HHLL]	/HHLL/
W$_5$			
ban.cï.ki.ra	'guava'	[HHLLL]	/HHLLL/
sï.mu.juuž	'ankle'	[LHLLL] (or [HHLLL])	/HHLLL/
W$_6$			
koo.za.bu.roo	'Kozaburo'	[HHLLLL]	/HHLLLL/
kuu.sjan.guu	'fist'	[HHLLLL]	/HHLLLL/
W$_7$			
oo.sï.to.ra.ri.a	'Australia'	[HHLLLLL]	/HHLLLLL/
fa.mi.rii.maa.to	'Family Mart'	[LHLLLLL] (or [HHLLLLL])	/HHLLLLL/

Western loans such as frequently used country names (e.g. *oosïtoraria* 'Australia' [HHLLLLL], *amerika* 'America' [LHLL]) and common concepts in daily use (e.g. *paama* 'perm' [HHH], *arubaito* 'part-time job (< German *Arbeit* via Japanese *arubaito*)' [LHLLL], *deisaabisï* [HHLLLL] 'day service', *famiriimaato* 'Family Mart (a convenience store)' [LHLLLLL]) seem to be well integrated into Irabu prosody, given that my consultants all produced these words with the same prosodic patterns.

Unlike W$_2$ and W$_3$, these longer words have a regular falling pitch between the second and the third moras without respect to syllable structure, i.e. without respect to whether the second mora and the third mora of a word are tauto-syllabic or not. This is exemplified in W$_4$ above. Also, this medial falling pitch is observed without respect to whether the word in

Phonology 57

question comes finally or is followed by a clitic. This medial falling pitch after the second mora in W_4 and longer words seems to be fairly widespread in other Miyako Ryukyuan varieties as well (e.g. Hirara; see Hirayama 1967). The underlying /L/ is toneless (i.e. unmarked for /H/), that is, Irabu tone system is privative (this will be discussed in §2.9.3).

In addition to medial falling pitch there is initial lowering as observed in W_3. This is only observed in the initial mora when the initial syllable is a light syllable, a $C_iC_i(G)V$, or a light presyllable. There is no final lowering as the words here underlyingly end in /L/. The fact that initial lowering may occur in absence of final lowering suggests that initial lowering is induced by the simple fact that a word ends in L pitch (which may be phonetic, as in W_3, or phonological, as in W_4 and longer words). As in the case of W_3, we can see a preference for a phonetically 'angular' contour in these longer words. As the parenthesised patterns above suggest, initial lowering may be absent (e.g. *utugaja* 'jaw' [HHLL]), but this is not typical, just as in the case of W_3.

The final L pitch is lower than the initial L pitch that results from initial lowering. Also, in a sequence of L-pitched moras, a gradual lowering is observed toward word final position, before arriving at a level low after two or three moras. Thus more elaborate auditory approximations of the pitch patterns of *kam.nar* 'thunder' ([HHLL]) and *sï.mu.juuž* 'ankle' (typically [LHLLL]) are [‾ ‾-_] and [-‾-_ _] respectively.

2.9.1.4. Summary

As described in the sections above, Irabu root words do not show lexically contrastive prosodic patterns, so that a given W_n shows an invariable underlying tonal pattern. For example, all W_4 invariably show the /HHLL/ pattern. This is true across word classes (i.e. W_4 is pronounced with /HHLL/ without respect to whether it is a noun, a verb, an adverb, etc. For example, in addition to a nominal W_4, a verb *patarafï* 'work' and an adjective *aparagi* 'beautiful' have the same tonal pattern /HHLL/.

In sum, it is possible to set up the following underlying tonal patterns of the root words, without respect to word class. These tonal patterns are of course subject to various intonational modifications.

(2–68) a. W_2: /HH/
        b. W_3: /HHH/
        c. W_{4-7}: /HHLL(L...)/

Irabu prosody is described by two independent (ordered) processes: (a) footing on the segmental structure and (b) tone assignment to this foot structure. I first introduce foot structure and footing principles in §2.9.2, then proceed to introduce a tone assignment rule for the existing foot structure in §2.9.3.

2.9.2. Footing
2.9.2.1. Definition of the foot

The notion foot in Irabu is defined as the bimoraic or trimoraic constituent that serves as the domain of tone assignment, as schematically shown in (2–69) below, where tone is associated with the foot structure on the segmental tier.[6] The domain of footing is the word(-plus). Binary footing (μμ) goes from left to right iteratively, except for two special cases to be explained in the following section, where ternary footing (μμμ) may occur.

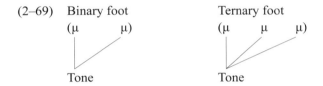

(2–69)   Binary foot   Ternary foot
         (μ   μ)   (μ   μ   μ)

         Tone   Tone

Thus the following association patterns of tone are impermissible.

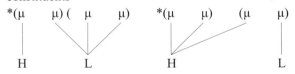

(2–70)   Impermissible tonal configuration: tone is associated across constituents
         *(μ   μ) (μ   μ)   *(μ   μ)   (μ   μ)

         H   L   H   L

The word minimality is now interpreted in terms of foot structure: a word must contain at least one foot (otherwise it is impossible to assign tone), a cross-linguistically recurrent constraint on foot structure and word structure (McCarthy and Prince 1995).

Now it is possible to describe the root words in (2–71) below as having the underlying foot structures shown to the right of each word, with tone assigned per foot. Henceforth, (2–69) above will be represented as (μμ)$_T$ or (μμμ)$_T$, as illustrated in (2–71) (e.g. W$_5$ has (μμ)$_H$ (μμμ)$_L$, which means that

---

[6] Thus the Irabu foot is precisely the tonal foot suggested by Leben (1997) and in his other works thereafter (Leben 2002, 2003).

Phonology

H tone is associated with the two moras of the first foot, and L tone is associated with the three moras of the second foot, rendering /(HH)(LLL)/.

(2–71)   Tonal pattern Foot structure
    a. W$_2$: *pana* 'nose'   /HH/ $(\mu\mu)_H$
    b. W$_3$: *katana* 'knife'   /HHH/ $(\mu\mu\mu)_H$
    c. W$_4$: *utugaja* 'jaw'   /HHLL/ $(\mu\mu)_H (\mu\mu)_L$
    d. W$_5$: *bancïkira* 'guava'   /HHLLL/ $(\mu\mu)_H (\mu\mu\mu)_L$
    e. W$_6$: *koozaburoo* 'Kozaburo'   /HHLLLL/ $(\mu\mu)_H (\mu\mu)_L (\mu\mu)_L$
    f. W$_7$: *oosïtoraria* 'Australia' /HHLLLLL/ $(\mu\mu)_H (\mu\mu)_L (\mu\mu\mu)_L$

2.9.2.2. Ternary footing

If the word(-plus) has an odd number of moras, the exhaustive binary footing from left to right naturally results in one stray mora finally. Ternary footing assigns a tone to the stray mora. This is exactly what is shown in (2–71) above.

Ternary footing results from an additional morphological factor: polymoraic affixes and clitics always commence their own footing, i.e. the left boundary of a polymoraic form always coincides with the left boundary of a foot (a few exceptions will be noted below). Thus if a root has an odd number of moras and precedes a bimoraic form, as in (2–72a) to (2–72c) below (W$_3$ + bimoraic form = W$_5$) and in (2–73a) to (2–73c) below (W$_7$ + bimoraic form = W$_9$), the root receives ternary footing rather than leaving one stray medially (i.e. (ii) in each example is impermissible):

(2–72) a. *katana-nagi*   b. *katana=mai*
       knife-and.so.on   knife=too
       'knife, and so on'   'knife, too'
       i. (katana)$_H$ (nagi)$_L$ i. (katana)$_H$ (mai)$_L$
       *ii. (kata)na(nagi)   *ii. (kata)na(nagi)
    c. *katana=bjaam*
       knife=I.wonder
       'wonder if it's a knife'
       i. (katana)$_H$ (bjaam)$_L$
       *ii. (kata)na(bjaam)
(2–73) a. *oosïtoraria-nagi*   b. *oosïtoraria=mai*
       Australia-and.so.on   Australia=too
       'Australia, and so on'   'Australia, too'
       i. (oo)$_H$ (sïto)$_L$(raria)$_H$ (nagi)$_L$ i. (oo)$_H$ (sïto)$_L$(raria)$_H$ (mai)$_L$
       *ii. (oo)(sïto)(rari)a (nagi)   *ii. (oo) (sïto)(rari)a (mai)

60 Chapter 2

　　c. *oosïtoraria=bjaam*
　　　Australia=I.wonder
　　　'wonder if it's Australia'
　　　i. (oo)$_H$(sïto)$_L$(raria)$_H$ (bjaam)$_L$
　　　*ii. (oo)(sïto)(rari)a(bjaam)

However, monomoraic affixes and clitics do not necessarily come at the left boundary of a foot. That is, they do not obligatorily commence a foot, but are simply treated as part of the preceding host, to which the default footing applies (bimoraic footing from left to right with an optional final ternary footing). For example, a W$_2$ *pana* 'nose' + *=u* (accusative) give rise to a W$_3$ (panau)$_H$ with no special footing. Likewise, a W$_3$ *katana* 'knife' + *=u* give rise to a W$_4$ (kata)$_H$ (nau)$_L$ with no special footing. W$_7$ *oosïtoraria* 'Australia' + *=u* give rise to (oo)$_H$ (sïto)$_L$ (rari)$_H$ (au)$_L$, with no special footing. If the default footing does allow monomoraic affixes and clitics to commence a foot, they do so accordingly (e.g. *pana* 'nose' + *=u* (accusative) + *=du* (focus) > (pana)(udu), where =u happens to commence a foot).

(2–74) contains examples where the accusative case marker *=u* is in the middle of a word-plus. In these, the monomoraic *=u* is treated as part of the host for the footing purpose, but the clitics *=kara* and *=mai* commence their own footing since they are bimoraic. With respect to *=mai* in (2–74), its immediately preceding host containing *=u* undergoes ternary footing since this host has an odd number of moras.

(2–74)　a. *bancïkira=u=mai*　　　b. *bancïkira=kara=u=mai*
　　　　　guava=ACC=too　　　　　　guava=from=ACC=too
　　　　　'from guava:ACC'　　　　　'from guava:ACC, too'
　　　　　(ban)$_H$ (cïki)$_L$(rau)$_H$ (mai)$_L$　　(ban)$_H$ (cïkira)$_L$(karau)$_H$ (mai)$_L$

A sequence of two monomoraic clitics such as *=u=du* (accusative + focus) below is simply treated as part of the host, to which the default footing applies. Compare (2–75a) and (2–75b) with (2–72a, b) and (2–73a, b) above respectively.

(2–75)　a. *katana=u=du*　　　b. *oosïtoraria=u=du*
　　　　　knife=ACC=FOC　　　　　Australia=ACC=FOC
　　　　　'knife:ACC:FOC'　　　　　'Australia:ACC:FOC'
　　　　　(kata)$_H$ (naudu)$_L$　　　(oo)$_H$ (sïto)$_L$ (rari)$_H$ (audu)$_L$

Some morphemes have both monomoraic and bimoraic allomorphs, and

Phonology 61

this difference is reflected in footing. For example, quotative //=ti// has the variant /=tii/, which always commences its own footing, and /=ti/, which does not.

(2–76) a. *katana=tii*
        knife=QT
        'knife:QT'
        (katana)$_H$ (tii)$_L$

                                   b. *katana=ti*
                                     knife=QT
                                     'knife:QT'
                                     (kata)$_H$ (nati)$_L$

(2–77) a. *oosïtoraria=tii*
        Australia=QT
        'Australia:QT'
        (oo)$_H$ (sïto)$_L$(raria)$_H$ (tii)$_L$

                                     b. *oosïtoraria=ti*
                                     Australia=QT
                                     'Australia:QT'
                                     (oo)$_H$ (sïto)$_L$(rari)$_H$ (ati)$_L$

Likewise, the plural affix //-mmi// has two allomorphs, /-mmi/ and /-mi/. If a stem ends in /m/, the latter is frequently chosen (as a result of the sequential nasal deletion rule, §2.7.6), though the former may also be chosen as a less preferred option. The difference is reflected in footing.

(2–78) a. *midum-mmi*
        woman-PL
        'women'
        (midum)$_H$ (mmi)$_L$

                                     b. *midum-mi*
                                     woman-PL
                                     'women'
                                     (midu)$_H$ (mmi)$_L$

A few polymoraic verbal affixes are exceptional in footing, as they do not always commence a foot, and thus resemble monomoraic morphemes in this regard. Such verbal affixes are: *-rai* (passive) and *-tigaa* (conditional converb). Unlike other polymoraic affixes that always start their own footing (e.g. causative *-sïmi* in (2–79a) and past unmarked *-tar* in (2–80a)), these exceptional affixes do not commence a foot unless the default footing allows them to do so, and so do not induce ternary footing on the part of the host. Thus we get (2–79b ii) and (2–80b ii) rather than (2–79b i) and (2–80b i).

(2–79) a. *nkai-sïmi-tar=pazï*
            pick.up-CAUS-PST=maybe
            'may have told (someone) to pick up'
            (nkai)$_H$ (sïmi)$_L$ (tar)$_H$ (pazï)$_L$
       b. *nkai-rai-tar=pazï*
            pick.up-PASS-PST=maybe
            'may have been picked up'

62   Chapter 2

            *i. (nkai)$_H$ (rai)$_L$ (tar)$_H$ (pazï)$_L$
            ii. (nka)$_H$ (irai)$_L$ (tar)$_H$ (pazï)$_L$
(2–80) a. *nkai-tar*   b. *nkai-tigaa*
           pick.up-PST   pick.up-CVB.CND
           'picked up (someone)'   'if (x) picks up (someone),'
           (nkai)$_H$ (tar)$_L$ *i. (nkai)$_H$ (tigaa)$_L$
                                           ii. (nka)$_H$ (iti)$_L$ (gaa)$_L$

To sum up this and the preceding sections, there is a restriction on the
distribution of tones so that tone assignment is conditioned by bi- or trimoraic constituency, or foot structure. Footing is sensitive to morphological
structure, so that polymoraic forms commence their own footing with just a
few exceptions.

2.9.3. Tone assignment
In this section I introduce a tone assignment rule on the pre-existing foot
structure produced by the above mentioned strategies.

2.9.3.1. The Principle of Rhythmic Alternation
Tone assignment in Irabu prosody is an instantiation of a cross-linguistically recurrent principle of alternating rhythm ('Principle of Rhythmic Alternation' (henceforth PRA); Selkirk 1984). The PRA states that 'between two
successive strong beats there intervenes at least one and at most two weak
beats' (p. 12). That is, there is a strong tendency for binary organisation of
linguistic rhythm, which may allow a variation in which 'one may encoun-
ter ternary beats (a strong accompanied by a sequence of two weaks), but
quaternary groups seem to be felt as two binary' (*ibid*). Let us schematically show the above statement as follows (where 's' represents a strong beat,
and 'w' represents a weak beat in Selkirk's terms; a square indicates a
rhythmic group):

    $\boxed{\text{s w (w)}}$

    $\boxed{\text{s w}}$ $\boxed{\text{s w}}$ but not *$\boxed{\text{s w w w}}$

Note that the PRA refers to 'strong' and 'weak' since Selkirk's focus was
on stress languages. However, as will be shown later, this can be restated
with more general terms, i.e. 'marked' (H) and 'unmarked' (L, i.e. toneless)
prosodic features, whereby we can refer to the PRA in the Irabu case.

2.9.3.2. The rule

The following rule set is postulated for Irabu prosody, where the rule set applies to the word(-plus) unless in certain special cases to be noted in §2.9.4.

(2–81) Tone assignment rulea.
   a. Group one to three adjacent feet into a single 'foot group' (indicated by a square in (2–82a-c) below).
   b. If a foot group is going to contain a sequence of four feet within it (e.g. when a foot is added to (2–82c) to create (2–82d)), regroup the quaternary feet into two foot groups (as in (2–82d)).
   c. Assign /H/ to the left-most foot of each foot group.

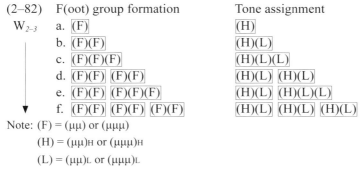

(2–82) F(oot) group formation   Tone assignment
W$_{2-3}$
   a. (F)   (H)
   b. (F)(F)   (H)(L)
   c. (F)(F)(F)   (H)(L)(L)
   d. (F)(F) (F)(F)   (H)(L) (H)(L)
   e. (F)(F) (F)(F)(F)   (H)(L) (H)(L)(L)
   f. (F)(F) (F)(F) (F)(F)   (H)(L) (H)(L) (H)(L)

Note: (F) = (μμ) or (μμμ)
      (H) = (μμ)H or (μμμ)H
      (L) = (μμ)L or (μμμ)L

Rule (2–81b) is iteratively applicable, as shown in (2–82e) and (2–82f), where the addition of a foot to the second foot group of (2–82e) induces its division into two foot groups in (2–82f), forming three foot groups in total.

The set of examples in (2–83) below is a complete set of examples where *kan* 'crab' is progressively derived into longer word-pluses, from W$_2$ (one foot, illustrating (2–82a)) to W$_{12}$ (six feet, illustrating (2–82f)). Note that monomoraic =*nu* (nominative) and =*du* (focus) are treated as part of the host.

(2–83) Note: -*gama* (diminutive), -*mmi* (plural), -*nagi* (approximative 'etc.') =*nu* (nominative), =*kara* (ablative), =*du* (focus), =*mai* 'too'

W$_2$	*kan* 'crab'	(kan)$_H$
W$_3$	*kan=nu*	(kannu)$_H$
W$_4$	*kan-gama*	(kan)$_H$ (gama)$_L$
W$_5$	*kan-gama=nu*	(kan)$_H$ (gamanu)$_L$

64 Chapter 2

W$_6$ *kan-gama-mmi*   (kan)$_H$ (gama)$_L$ (mmi)$_L$
W$_7$ *kan-gama-mmi=nu*   (kan)$_H$ (gama)$_L$ (mminu)$_L$
W$_8$ *kan-gama-mmi-nagi*   (kan)$_H$ (gama)$_L$ (mmi)$_H$ (nagi)$_L$
W$_9$ *kan-gama-mmi-nagi=nu*   (kan)$_H$ (gama)$_L$ (mmi)$_H$ (naginu)$_L$
W$_{10}$ *kan-gama-mmi-nagi=kara*   (kan)$_H$ (gama)$_L$ (mmi)$_H$ (nagi)$_L$ (kara)$_L$
W$_{11}$ *kan-gama-mmi-nagi=kara=du*

(kan)$_H$ (gama)$_L$ (mmi)$_H$ (nagi)$_L$ (karadu)$_L$

W$_{12}$ *kan-gama-mmi-nagi=kara=mai*

(kan)$_H$ (gama)$_L$ (mmi)$_H$ (nagi)$_L$ (kara)$_H$ (mai)$_L$

Further examples follow. Examples (2–84) to (2–89) illustrate the tonal patterning of nominal word(-plus)es, and (2–90) to (2–93) illustrate the tonal patterning of verb word(-plus)es.

(2–84) a. W$_2$: *pav* 'snake'   (pav)$_H$
        b. W$_4$: *pav* + *-gama*   (pav)$_H$ (gama)$_L$
        c. W$_6$: *pav* + *-gama* + *=kara*   (pav)$_H$ (gama)$_L$ (kara)$_L$
        d. W$_8$: *pav* + *-gama* + *=kara*+ *=mai*

(pav)$_H$ (gama)$_L$ (kara)$_H$ (mai)$_L$

Note: *-gama* (diminutive), *=kara* (ablative), *=mai* 'too'

(2–85) a. W$_3$: *jarabi* 'child'   (jarabi)$_H$
        b. W$_5$: *jarabi* + *-gama*   (jarabi)$_H$ (gama)$_L$
        c. W$_7$: *jarabi* + *-gama* + *=kara*

(jarabi)$_H$ (gama)$_L$ (kara)$_L$

        d. W$_9$: *jarabi* + *-gama* + *=kara* + *=mai*

(jarabi)$_H$ (gama)$_L$ (kara)$_H$ (mai)$_L$

In (2–85) above there is ternary footing on the part of the host *jarabi*.

(2–86) a. W$_4$: *akjaada* 'merchant'   (akja)$_H$ (ada)$_L$
        b. W$_6$: *akjaada* + *-gama*   (akja)$_H$ (ada)$_L$ (gama)$_L$
        c. W$_8$: *akjaada* + *-gama* + *=kara*

(akja)$_H$ (ada)$_L$ (gama)$_H$ (kara)$_L$

        d. W$_{10}$: *akjaada* + *-gama* + *=kara* + *=mai*

(akja)$_H$ (ada)$_L$ (gama)$_H$ (kara)$_L$ (mai)$_L$

(2–87) a. W$_5$: *bancïkira* 'guava'   (ban)$_H$ (cïkira)$_L$
        b. W$_7$: *bancïkira* + *-gama*   (ban)$_H$ (cïkira)$_L$ (gama)$_L$
        c. W$_9$: *bancïkira* + *-gama* + *=kara*

(ban)$_H$ (cïkira)$_L$ (gama)$_H$ (kara)$_L$

        d. W$_{11}$: *bancïkira* + *-gama* + *=kara* + *=mai*

Phonology   65

$(ban)_H (c\ddot{i}kira)_L (gama)_H (kara)_L (mai)_L$

In (2–87) above there is ternary footing on the part of the host *bancïkira*.

(2–88) a. W_6: *koozaburoo* 'Kozaburo' $(koo)_H (zabu)_L (roo)_L$
        b. W_8: *koozaburoo + -gama* $(koo)_H (zabu)_L (roo)_H (gama)_L$
        c. W_{10}: *koozaburoo + -gama + =kara*
                    $(koo)_H (zabu)_L (roo)_H (gama)_L (kara)_L$
        d. W_{12}: *koozaburoo + -gama + =kara + =mai*
                    $(koo)_H (zabu)_L (roo)_H (gama)_L (kara)_H (mai)_L$

(2–89) a. W_7: *famiriimaato* 'Family Mart' $(fami)_H (rii)_L (maato)_L$
        b. W_9: *famiriimaato + -gama* $(fami)_H (rii)_L (maato)_H (gama)_L$
        c. W_{11}: *famiriimaato + -gama + =kara*
                    $(fami)_H (rii)_L (maato)_H (gama)_L (kara)_L$
        d. W_{13}: *famiriimaato + -gama + =kara + =mai*
                    $(fami)_H (rii)_L (maato)_H (gama)_L (kara)_H (mai)_L$

In (2–89) above there is ternary footing on the part of the host *famiriimaa-to*.

(2–90) a. W_2: *tur-* 'take' $(tur)_H$
        b. W_3: *tur- + -as* $(turas\ddot{i})_H$
        c. W_4: *tur- + -as + -rai* $(tura)_H (sai)_L$
        d. W_6: *tur- + -as + -rai + -tar* $(tura)_H (sai)_L (tar)_L$
        e. W_8: *tur- + -as + -rai + -tar + =pazï*
                    $(tura)_H (sai)_L (tar)_H (paz\ddot{i})_L$
        f. W_{11}: *tur- + -as + -rai + -tar + =pazï + =dooi*
                    $(tura)_H (sai)_L (tar)_H (paz\ddot{i})_L (dooi)_L$
        Note: *-as* (causative), *-rai* (passive), *-tar* (past unmarked),
              =pazï 'maybe', *=dooi* (emphatic)

(2–91) a. W_3: *barau-* 'laugh' $(barau)_H$
        b. W_4: *barau- + -as* $(bara)_H (as\ddot{i})_L$
        c. W_5: *barau- + -as + -rai* $(bara)_H (asai)_L$
        d. W_7: *barau- + -as + -rai + -tar* $(bara)_H (asai)_L (tar)_L$
        e. W_9: *barau- + -as + -rai + -tar + =pazï*
                    $(bara)_H (asai)_L (tar)_H (paz\ddot{i})_L$
        f. W_{12}: *barau- + -as + -rai + -tar + =pazï + =dooi*
                    $(bara)_H (asai)_L (tar)_H (paz\ddot{i})_L (dooi)_L$

In (2–91) above, the stem-final /u/ is deleted unless the stem is word-final.

66   Chapter 2

(2–92)   a. W_4: *patarak-* 'work'   (pata)$_H$ (rafi)$_L$
            b. W_5: *patarak-* + *-as*   (pata)$_H$ (rakasï)$_L$
            c. W_6: *patarak-* + *-as* + *-rai*   (pata)$_H$ (raka)$_L$(sai)$_L$
            d. W_8: *patarak-* + *-as* + *-rai* + *-tar*   (pata)$_H$ (raka)$_L$(sai)$_H$ (tar)$_L$
            e. W_{10}: *patarak-* + *-as* + *-rai* + *-tar* + *=pazï*
                                         (pata)$_H$ (raka)$_L$ (sai)$_H$ (tar)$_L$ (pazï)$_L$
            f. W_{13}: *patarak-* + *-as* + *-rai* + *-tar* + *=pazï* + *=dooi*
                                         (pata)$_H$ (raka)$_L$ (sai)$_H$ (tar)$_L$ (pazï)$_H$ (dooi)$_L$

(2–93)   a. W_5: *ugunaar-* 'gather'   (ugu)$_H$ (naar)$_L$
            b. W_6: *ugunaar-* + *-as*   (ugu)$_H$ (naa)$_L$(rasï)$_L$
            c. W_7: *ugunaar-* + *-as* + *-rai*   (ugu)$_H$ (naa)$_L$(rasai)$_L$
            d. W_9: *ugunaar-* + *-as* + *-rai* + *-tar*   (ugu)$_H$ (naa)$_L$(rasai)$_H$ (tar)$_L$
            e. W_{11}: *ugunaar-* + *-as* + *-rai* + *-tar* + *=pazï*
                                       (ugu)$_H$ (naa)$_L$ (rasai)$_H$ (tar)$_L$ (pazï)$_L$
            f. W_{14}: *ugunaar-* + *-as* + *-rai* + *-tar* + *=pazï* + *=dooi*
                                       (ugu)$_H$ (naa)$_L$ (rasai)$_H$ (tar)$_L$ (pazï)$_H$ (dooi)$_L$

The passive suffix *-rai* is a bimoraic affix, whose onset /r/ is deleted when attaching to hosts ending in a consonant, as shown in the examples above. As was noted in §2.9.2.2, it behaves like a monomoraic affix, in that it does not necessarily commence a foot, i.e. is treated simply as part of the host to which the default footing applies. Thus in (2–91c) *baraasai* is parsed into (bara)(asai) rather than (baraa)(sai), and in (2–93d) *ugunaarasaitar* is parsed into (ugu)(naa)(rasai)(tar) rather than (ugu)(naara)(sai)(tar). On the other hand, a bimoraic form such as *-tar* consistently induces ternary footing on the part of its host if the host has an odd number of moras.

2.9.3.3. Summary

By assuming the PRA, we only need to refer to the specification of /H/. That is, we can simply state that in each foot group (which is automatically parsed by the PRA) /H/ is assigned to the first foot, and no further statement for /L/ is required. This means that in the Irabu language the H tone is marked and the L tone is default, with a privative system of /H/ vs. /Ø/ (Hyman 2001), in which rules specify the marked /H/ only, and the other feature is seen as an absence of the /H/ feature. The alternating tonal pattern is thus analysed as the presence of the marked prosodic feature /H/ at as regular intervals as possible in accordance with the PRA, rather than as the presence of a specific tonal melody such as /HL/. Thus the Irabu alternating tonal pattern is not as different as it first appears from the rhythmic alternation phenomena in stress languages in which stressed or 'strong'

Phonology   67

syllables (marked) and stressless or 'weak' syllables (unmarked) alternate.
The differences are that in Irabu the marked prosodic feature is tone rather
than stress and such a feature is borne by an entire foot rather than an indi-
vidual syllable.

2.9.4. Phrasal mapping of the alternating rhythm

Even though the tone assignment rule given in §2.9.3 *in principle* applies to
the word(-plus) domain, it may apply to an entire phrase if the first member of the phrase has only one foot. In the (a) examples of (2–94) to (2–97)
below, two nominal word(-plus)es form an NP. If the tone assignment rule
exactly applied to each word(-plus) the expected pattern should be (i),
where each member of a phrase (i.e. a word(-plus)) would constitute a single prosodic domain of tone assignment. However, what we actually get is
(ii), which demonstrates that an entire phrase is a single prosodic domain
of the tone assignment. Compare the (a) examples with the (b) examples,
where the first member of a phrase consists of more than one foot the
phrasal mapping of tone assignment does not occur, and each word(-plus)
remains the domain of tone assignment.

(2–94) a. *ba=ga*   *ffa-gama*
           1SG=GEN   child-DIM
           'my little child'
           *i. (baga)$_H$ (ffa)$_H$(gama)$_L$
           ii. (baga)$_H$ (ffa)$_L$(gama)$_L$
        b. *koozaburoo=ga*   *ffa-gama*
           Kozaburo=GEN   child-DIM
           'Kozaburo's little child'
           (koo)$_H$(zabu)$_L$(rooga)$_L$ (ffa)$_H$(gama)$_L$

(2–95) a. *ba=ga*   *ffa-gama-mmi*
           1SG=GEN   child-DIM-PL
           'my little children'
           *i. (baga)$_H$ (ffa)$_H$(gama)$_L$(mmi)$_L$
           ii. (baga)$_H$ (ffa)$_L$(gama)$_H$(mmi)$_L$
        b. *koozaburoo=ga*   *ffa-gama-mmi*
           Kozaburo=GEN   child-DIM-PL
           'Kozaburo's little children'
           (koo)$_H$(zabu)$_L$ (rooga)$_L$(ffa)$_H$(gama)$_L$(mmi)$_L$

(2–96) a. *ba=ga*   *kjavdai=mai*
           1SG=GEN   sibling=too
           'my sibling, too'

68 Chapter 2

       *i. (baga)$_H$ (kjav)$_H$ (dai)$_L$ (mai)$_L$
        ii. (baga)$_H$ (kjav)$_L$ (dai)$_H$ (mai)$_L$
    b. *koozaburoo=ga*   *kjavdai=mai*
       Kozaburo=GEN   sibling=too
       'Kozaburo's sibling, too'
       (koo)$_H$ (zabu)$_L$ (rooga)$_L$ (kjav)$_H$ (dai)$_L$ (mai)$_L$
(2–97) a. *ba=ga*   *bancïkira=mai*
       1SG=GEN   guava=too
       'My guava, too'
       *i. (baga)$_H$ (ban)$_H$ (cïkira)$_L$ (mai)$_L$
        ii. (baga)$_H$ (ban)$_L$ (cïkira)$_H$ (mai)$_L$
    b. *koozaburoo=ga*   *bancïkira=mai*
       Kozaburo=GEN   guava=too
       'Kozaburo's guava, too'
       (koo)$_H$ (zabu)$_L$ (rooga)$_L$ (ban)$_H$ (cïkira)$_L$ (mai)$_L$

Phrasal mapping applies if any mono-foot word is the first member of an NP, such as *vva=ga* (2SG=GEN) 'your', *kai=ga* (3SG=GEN) 'his/her', *pžtu=nu* (man=GEN) 'someone's', *unu* 'that', etc. Below are examples with a trimoraic foot word-plus *naa=ga* 'one's own (reflexive pronoun)' as the first member of an NP.

(2–98) *naa=ga*   *ffa-gama*
        RFL=GEN   child-DIM
        'one's own little child'
    *a. (naaga)$_H$ (ffa)$_H$(gama)$_L$
     b. (naaga)$_H$ (ffa)$_L$(gama)$_L$
(2–99) *naa=ga*   *ffa-gama-mmi*
        RFL=GEN   child-DIM-PL
        'one's own little children'
    *a. (naaga)$_H$ (ffa)$_H$(gama)$_L$(mmi)$_L$
     b. (naaga)$_H$ (ffa)$_L$ (gama)$_H$ (mmi)$_L$
(2–100) *naa=ga*   *kjavdai=mai*
        RFL=GEN   sibling=too
        'one's own sibling, too'
    *a. (naaga)$_H$ (kjav)$_H$ (dai)$_L$ (mai)$_L$
     b. (naaga)$_H$ (kjav)$_L$ (dai)$_H$ (mai)$_L$
(2–101) *naa=ga*   *bancïkira=mai*
        RFL=GEN   guava=too
        'one's own guava, too'

Phonology   69

    *a. (naaga)_H   (ban)_H (cïkira)_L (mai)_L
     b. (naaga)_H   (ban)_L (cïkira)_H (mai)_L

The phrase may also be a VP. As is shown below, the VP (main verb +
auxiliary verb + modal marker) in each example forms a single prosodic
domain to which the tone assignment rule applies, rendering the pattern
(b).

(2–102)   *mii-Ø*   *fii-tar=pazï.*
          look-NRT   BEN-PST=maybe
          '(S/he) may have watched (something) (for someone).'
              *a. (mii)_H   (fii)_H (tar)_L (pazï)_L
               b. (mii)_H   (fii)_L (tar)_H (pazï)_L
(2–103)   *jum-i–i*   *fii-tar=pazï.*
          read-THM-NRT   BEN-PST=maybe
          '(s/he) may have read (a book) (for someone).'
              *a. (jumii)_H   (fii)_H (tar)_L (pazï)_L
               b. (jumii)_H   (fii)_L (tar)_H (pazï)_L
(2–104)   *jum-i–i*   *njaat-tar=pazï.*
          read-THM-NRT   PRF-PST=maybe
          '(S/he) may have finished reading.'
              *a. (jumii)_H   (njaat)_H (tar)_L (pazï)_L
               b. (jumii)_H   (njaat)_L (tar)_H (pazï)_L

Especially noteworthy in (2–102) to (2–104) above is the fact that the second member of a phrase in each example commences with L tone, a fact
which would not be expected if the tone assignment rule exactly applied to
each word(-plus).

Note that phrasal mapping occurs in tone assignment but not in foot
building: footing commences and ends in each word(-plus), not across two
word(-plus)es, as was defined in §2.9.2. Thus in a phrase like W1 + W2
below, we have the footing pattern (a) and not (b), the latter of which
would be possible if the W1+W2 as a whole were treated as a single domain of footing.

(2–105)   W1   W2
           μ   μ   μ   μ   μ   μ   μ
        a. (μ   μ   μ)   (μ   μ) (μ   μ)
       *b. (μ   μ) (μ   μ) (μ   μ   μ)

70   Chapter 2

This supports the view held in this thesis that footing is independent of (i.e. prior to) tone assignment.

Two juxtaposed word(-plus)es that do not form a phrase do not induce phrasal mapping of tone assignment. Thus in (2–106) below, the subject NP *baga* and the object NP *ffa-gama=u* do not form a single prosodic domain, even when the first word-plus *baga* is a mono-foot word-plus (cf. (2–94)).

(2–106)   *ba=ga*   *ffa-gama=u*   *žž-a-di*
          1SG=GEN   child-DIM=ACC   scold-THM-NPST.INT
          Subject   Direct object   Verb
          'I will scold my little child.'
          (baga)$_H$ (ffa)$_H$ (gamau)$_L$ (žžadi)$_H$
          <Prosodic domain>   <Prosodic domain>   <Prosodic domain>

Similarly, in (2–107) below, where the mono-foot word *jumii* is followed by *fiitar* (cf. (2–103)), the two verbs do not form a single VP but form distinct VPs (*jumii* is a chained clause head, and *fiitar* is a main clause head, thus (2–107) is a clause chaining structure). Thus each word(-plus) serves as distinct prosodic domain to which tone assignment applies.

(2–107)   *jum-i-i,*   *fii-tar=pazï.*
          read-THM-NRT   give-PST=maybe
          [chained clause]   [main clause]
          '(S/he) may have read (a book) and have given (it) (to someone).'
          (jumii)$_H$ (fii)$_H$ (tar)$_L$ (pazï)$_L$
          <Prosodic domain>   <Prosodic domain>

Thus phrasal mapping takes place only when two word(-plus)es form a single morphosyntactic phrase *and* the first member of the phrase is a mono-foot word(-plus).

In sum, the tone assignment rules defined in §2.9.3 may map onto either a word(-plus) or a phrase, the latter being restricted to certain special cases. On the other hand, footing is consistently per word(-plus), supporting the view that footing is assigned before tone assignment.

2.10. Phonological characteristics of compounds

The phonological characteristics of compounds are rather complex. This is

Phonology   71

due to the cross-linguistically common fact that grammatical word boundaries and phonological word boundaries do not coincide in compounds.

A compound is a single word-plus rather than a phrase (see §3.6.2.2 for
the justification for this view). We have noted throughout the sections
above that a word-plus is in most cases a single phonological word in terms
of (1) syllable structure, (2) phonological rules, and (3) prosody, with just a
very few restricted exceptions (phrasal mapping of prosody where an entire phrase becomes a single phonological word in terms of (3)).

However, a compound is an important exception to this generalisation,
in that each stem of a compound is in most cases treated as a separate phonological word in respect of the three criteria of (1), (2), and (3). Moreover,
with respect to (2), one specific rule, or sequential voicing (§2.7.1), treats a
whole compound word as a single phonological word, whereas all others
treat each stem as a phonological word, showing a complex (but cross-linguistically not uncommon) mapping pattern of phonological word boundaries. In what follows I first note cases where each compound stem usually
acts as a separate phonological word, then proceed to note unproblematic
cases where an entire compound is always treated as a phonological word
in all three respects.

2.10.1. Productive compounds

The first type of compound is called a productive compound, because it is
highly productive, showing a 'phrasal' character in terms of productivity
(but see §3.6.2.2 for the distinction between a productive compound word
and a phrase). For example, (2–108) below demonstrates that the first stem
ffu 'black' can combine with various stems with a transparent meaning,
while (2–109) below demonstrates that the second stem *gii* 'tree' can combine with various stem, again with a transparent meaning.

(2–108) a. *ffu+karazï* b. *ffu+kabžž*   c. *ffu+dur*   d. *ffu+guruma*
            black+hair   black+paper   black+bird   black+car
            'black hair'   'black paper'   'black bird'   'black car'
(2–109) a. *ffu+gii*   b. *taka+gii*   c. *bžda+gii* d. *gazïpana+gii*
            black+tree   high+tree   low+tree   Gazïpana+tree
            'black tree'   'tall tree'   'short tree'   'Gazïpana tree'

In most cases, each stem in a productive compound is a separate phonological word. First, the word minimality applies to each stem rather than to
an entire compound, indicating that each stem is treated as a phonological
word in terms of minimality (which has to do with syllable structure).

72   Chapter 2

Also, as shown in (2–110a), /C.V/ sequence is possible in a productive compound, which is strictly prohibited within a phonological word domain and induces the geminate copy insertion rule to avoid this, as illustrated in (2–110b), where the same stem is affixed by the circumstantial verbaliser -as and the thematic -i and the narrative converbal suffix -i to form a single phonological word.

(2–110)   a. /kiban+anna/   b. /kiban-nas-i–i/
                poor+old.lady   poor-VLZ-THM-NRT
                'poor old lady'   'being poor'
                CV.CVC.VC.CV   CV.CVC.CVV

Finally, each stem is the domain of alternating rhythm, demonstrating that each stem is treated as a separate phonological word in terms of prosody. Also, if the first stem of a productive compound is a mono-foot stem, it becomes part of the second stem for the alternating rhythm, just as in the case of a phrase (§2.9.4). Thus in (2–111) below, the attested rhythmic pattern is (a), where the first stem is a mono-foot stem and becomes part of the second stem for rhythmic alternation (*agar+patiruma* is the single domain for rhythmic alternation), and the third stem, which commences a phonological word in terms of prosody, is likewise part of the fourth stem for rhythmic alternation. Pattern (b) would obtain if the entire compound were treated as a single domain for the rhythmic alternation, which is not the case.

(2–111)   *agar+patiruma+baka+aza*
               East+Hateruma+young+elder.brother
               'The young man of East Hateruma'
           a. (agar)$_H$ (pati)$_L$ (ruma)$_L$ (baka)$_H$ (aza)$_L$
          *b. (agar)$_H$ (pati)$_L$ (ruma)$_H$ (baka)$_L$ (aza)$_L$

A similar example is also found in a verb-verb stem sequence, or an agglutinative serial verb construction (§6.4.2.2). In (2–112) below, there is a prosodic boundary between the first stem *patarakasai* (containing affixes) and the second stem *pazïmitar*, each stem being the domain of rhythmic alternation. Again, the unattested (b) pattern would be expected if the entire verb series were treated as a single domain of rhythmic alternation, which is not the case.

(2–112)   *patarak-as-ai+pazïmi-tar.*

Phonology 73

work-CAUS-PASS+begin-PST
'(I) began to be forced to work'
a. (pata)$_H$ (raka)$_L$ (sai)$_L$ (pazïmi)$_H$ (tar)$_L$
b. (pata)$_H$ (raka)$_L$ (sai)$_H$ (pazïmi)$_L$ (tar)$_L$

One important phonological rule that treats a whole compound as a single phonological word is sequential voicing (§2.7.2). It causes the voiceless onset of the initial syllable of a non-initial stem of a compound to be voiced (e.g. *taka-* 'tall' + *kii* 'tree' > *taka+gii* 'tall tree'; *waa* 'pig' + *kurusï* 'killing' + *pžž* 'day' > *waa+kurusï+bžž* 'New Year's Eve'). As is clear from the above examples, this rule targets a non-initial stem of a compound word. On the assumption that a phonological word is the domain in which a phonological rule operates, the entire compound should be a phonological word in terms of this particular phonological rule. In other words, this rule marks the phonological-word-medial status of the stem that undergoes this allomorphy.

2.10.2. Lexicalised compounds

The second type of compound is rather rare, and highly lexicalised. Unlike productive compounds, a lexicalised compound exactly follows the general phonotactic pattern that characterise a phonological word, serves as the domain of major phonological rules, and is the domain of alternating rhythm. A typical example is /mi+pana/ in (2–113) and /ffuki/ in (2–114). These compounds are lexicalised in the sense that the meaning of each is not compositional. The compound /mipana/ has CVCVCV structure, which is one typical syllable structure of root words (§2.5.7, TABLE 2–5, Rank 3). Likewise /ffuki/ has CCVCV structure, which is also common in root words (Rank 9). Neither stem in each example undergoes the lengthening rule even when /mi/ in (2–113) and /ki/ in (2–114) are monomoraic (cf. (2–109)). That is, the entire compound words are treated as phonological words, to which the word minimality constraint applies. In each example the entire compound is parsed into a single ternary foot, to which /H/ is assigned.

(2–113)   /mi+pana/
eye+nose
'face' (not 'eye and nose')
a. CVCVCV
b. No lengthening rule on either stem
c. (mipana)$_H$

74   Chapter 2

(2–114)   /ffu+ki/
           black+tree
           'Kuroki tree' (not 'black tree'; cf (2–109a))
           a. CCV.CV
           b. No lengthening rule on either stem
           c. (ffuki)$_H$

Chapter 3

Descriptive preliminaries

This chapter introduces descriptive units and categories that will be pre-supposed in the subsequent grammatical description. In §3.1 phrase structure is overviewed. In §3.2 the notions word, clitic, and affix are defined. In §3.3 word classes are defined. In §3.4 grammatical relations are defined. In §3.5 three major argument types, i.e. core, extended core, and peripheral arguments, are introduced and defined. In §3.6 three major word formation processes are described, i.e. affixation, compounding, and full reduplication.

3.1. Phrase structure

In this section I introduce two phrase types, a predicate phrase and a nominal phrase. Detailed descriptions of each phrase type are given in Chapters 4 and 7, but it is necessary to give an overview of these structures here as they are basis for the definition of certain word classes.

3.1.1. Predicate phrase

A predicate phrase falls into two types as shown in (3–1) and (3–2) below. A verbal predicate phrase consists of a verb phrase (VP) and its comple-ment (if required).[1] A nominal predicate phrase consists of a nominal phrase (NP) and a copula verb which is only obligatory under certain con-ditions (which will be described in §3.1.1.2) and is left unstated elsewhere. In each type of phrase, the relative ordering of the constituents is largely fixed. In addition to the constituents specified here, there may occur a bound marker (e.g. focus marker) that may be attached to a given constitu-ent.

(3–1)   Predicate phrase 1: verbal predicate
         (VP complement+) [lexical verb (+auxiliary verb/lexical verb 2)]$_{VP}$

(3–2)   Predicate phrase 2: nominal predicate

---

[1] The notion of VP here is different from the generative notion of VP, where a verb and its complements are all within the VP domain.

76   Chapter 3

NP (+copula verb)

3.1.1.1. Verbal predicate

A lexical verb is the only obligatory component, which primarily determines the argument structure of the entire predicate. Thus the minimal
predicate phrase is exemplified as follows, where there is a single lexical
verb *ur* 'exist' in the predicate phrase.

(3–3) *pžtu=nu=du*   *ur-Ø.*
       man=NOM=FOC   exist-NPST
       '(There) is a man.'

An auxiliary verb is a verb that functions as an aspect marker or a benefactive marker ('do for the benefit of'). As is indicated in (3–1), this slot is
also filled by a verb that retains more semantic content than an auxiliary
verb (e.g. 'come'), or a second lexical verb. That is, Irabu has a serial verb
construction (Chapter 7). Either type of the second verb carries finite inflection in a complex VP (whereas the (first) lexical verb in a complex VP
obligatorily carries non-finite inflection). Thus in (3–4) below, the (a) example contains a simplex VP where the lexical verb *tumitar* 'looked for'
shows finite inflection (*-tar*, past unmarked), whereas the (b) example contains a complex VP where the same lexical verb inflects for a specific
non-finite verb form *tumi-i* (narrative converbal form), and the auxiliary
verb *u-* (progressive) carries the finite inflectional affix *-tar* on behalf of the
lexical verb. In the (c) example, the second verb slot is filled by a second
lexical verb *t-* 'come', which, like an auxiliary, carries finite verb inflection.

(3–4) a. *tuz=zu=du*   *tumi-tar.*
          wife=ACC=FOC   look.for-PST
          '(I) looked for a wife.'
       b. *tuz=zu*   *tumi-i=du*   *u-tar.*
          wife=ACC   look.for-NRT=FOC   PROG-PST
          '(I) was looking for a wife.'
       c. *tuz=zu*   *tumi-i=du*   *t-tar.*
          wife=ACC   look.for-NRT=FOC   come-PST
          '(I) brought a wife.' [lit. (I) looked for a wife and came back
          (with her).]

A VP complement is required in the following three construction types:

Descriptive preliminaries   77

(1) the light verb construction (as shown in (3–5) and (3–6)), where the lexical verb is filled by the light verb *(a)sï* 'do', (2) the state verb construction (3–7), where the lexical verb is filled by the state verb *ar* 'be (in a state)', and (3) the 'become' verb construction (3–8), where the lexical verb is *nar* 'become'. In each example, the complement is a derived adverb (§3.3.6.2).

(3–5) *kunur=ra*   *taka=u=baa*   *juu*   *mii=du*
       these.days=TOP   hawk=ACC=TOP   very   looking=FOC
       sï-Ø.
       do-NPST
       'These days (I) see hawks many times.' [lit. these days I do looking at hawks.]

(3–6) *pžtu=u*   *mii+mii*   *as-i+ur-Ø.*[2]
       man=ACC   RED+looking   do-THM+PROG-NPST
       '(He is always) staring at persons.' [lit. He is always doing staring.]

(3–7) *kari=a*   *taka-fï=du*   *ar-Ø.*
       3sg=TOP   tall-AVLZ=FOC   be-NPST
       'He is tall.' [lit. he is in a tall state.]

(3–8) *kari=a*   *taka-fï=du*   *nar-kutu.*
       3sg=TOP   tall-AVLZ=FOC   be-OBL
       'He will become tall.' [lit. he will become in a tall state.]

3.1.1.2. Nominal predicate

A nominal predicate phrase consists of an NP as a predicate head, followed by a copula verb, which is obligatorily absent when certain conditions are met (see below).

(3–9) a. *kari=a*   *sinsii=du*   *a-tar.*
          3SG=TOP   teacher=FOC   COP-PST
          'He was a teacher.'
       b. *kari=a*   *sinsii.*
          3SG=TOP   teacher
          'He is a teacher.'

The copular verb is necessary when at least one of the following conditions

---

[2] The complement of the light verb *(a)sï* 'do' is a (reduplicated) verb stem. When the complement is a reduplicated verb stem, the light verb may be the bimoiraic form *asï*.

78   Chapter 3

is met: (1) in past tense, (2) when negated, (3) when a conjunction marker
follows a predicate NP, and (4) when focus is marked on the predicate NP
(as shown in (3–9a)). When all of these features are absent, the copular
verb must be absent.

(3–10)   *kari=a*   *sinsii*   *a-ta-m.*
         3SG=TOP   teacher   COP-PST-RLS
         'He was a teacher.' [past tense]

(3–11)   *kari=a*   *sinsii*   *ar-a-n.*
         3SG=TOP   teacher   COP-NEG-NPST
         'He was a teacher.' [negation]

(3–12)   *kari=a*   *sinsii*   *jar=ruga,*
         3SG=TOP   teacher   COP-NPST-RLS=but
         jana+pžtu=dooi.
         evil+man=EMP
         'He is a teacher, but (he is) evil.' [conjunction marker attach-
         ment]

(3–13)   *kari=a*   *sinsii=du*   *ar-Ø=ri.*
         3SG=TOP   teacher=FOC   COP-NPST=CNF
         'He is a teacher, isn't he?' [focus marking on the predicate NP]

(3–14)   *kari=a*   *sinsii=du*   *jar-Ø.*
         3SG=TOP   teacher=FOC   COP-NPST=CNF
         'He is a teacher, isn't he?' [*jar* is more preferred than *ar*]

(3–15)   *kari=a*   *sinsii.*
         3SG=TOP   teacher
         'He is a teacher.'

As will be described in §6.3.6.2, the copula verb has an allomorph *jar*,
which is obligatorily required when (a) the copula verb appears in a non-
main clause and (b) the predicate head NP is not focused, as in (3–12). On
the other hand, *jar* may also appear when the NP is focused in non-past
tense in a main clause, as in (3–14), even though it is not obligatory. The
tendency here is that if there is no marker following the copula, as in (3–
14), *jar* is more preferred.

3.1.2. Nominal phrase

A nominal phrase (NP) is a syntactic constituent that functions as an argument of a verb or a predicate head of a nominal predicate phrase. NP structure is schematised as (modifier+) head, to which a case marker is attached
to form an extended NP (Chapter 4). Case is obligatory unless it functions

Descriptive preliminaries   79

as a predicate head. However, there may be case ellipsis in subject and direct object (§4.3.10). The modifier slot may be filled by an NP itself in a
recursive manner (where the case marker attaching to the NP is a genitive
case marker), as shown in (3–16) and (3–17), or by an adnominal word, as
shown in (3–18). It may also be filled by an adnominal clause, as shown in
(3–19).

(3–16) *vva=ga*   *jaa=n*   *asïb-a-di.*
        2SG=GEN   house=ACC   play-THM-INT
        'Let's play at your house' [[simplex NP+case]$_{modifier}$ + head +
        case]

(3–17) *vva=ga*   *jaa=nu*   *naka=n*   *asïb-a-di.*
        2SG=GEN   house=GEN   inside=DAT   play-THM-INT
        'Let's play inside of your house' [[complex NP +case]$_{modifier}$ +
        head + case]

(3–18) *kanu*   *jaa=n*   *asïb-a-di.*
        that   house=DAT   play-THM-INT
        'Let's play at that house' [[adnm w]$_{modifier}$ + head + case]

(3–19) *ba=ga*   *agu=nu*   *ur-Ø*   *jaa=n*
        1SG=GEN   friend=GEN   exist-NPST   house=DAT
        asïb-a-di.
        play-THM-INT
        'Let's play at a house where my friend lives.' [[adnm c]$_{modifier}$ +
        head + case]

A head is obligatory in principle, but there does exist a headless adnominal clause structure (§4.2.2).

(3–20) *nafï-tar=ra*   *taru=ga?*
        cry-PST=TOP   who=Q
        'Who cried?' [lit. Who was (the person who) cried?]

3.2. Word, affix and clitic

Words, affixes and clitics are defined in terms of morphological and phonological dependency, as summarised in TABLE 3–1 below. As noted in
§2.10.1, a compound consists of two or more roots each of which constitutes a phonological word (thus phonologically independent) but is part of
a grammatical word (thus morphologically dependent).

80   Chapter 3

TABLE 3–1. Word, clitic and affix in terms of morphological and phonological
            dependency

		Phonologically	
		Independent	Dependent
Morphologically	Independent	Word	Clitic
	Dependent	Compound stem	Affix

There are no prefixes or proclitics in Irabu, so that a word always commences with a root. When discussing the distinction between affixes and
clitics, we are concerned with which morpheme is a suffix and which morpheme is an enclitic within a sequence of morphemes beginning with a
root.

When discussing clitics and affixes, it is necessary to distinguish between a morphosyntactic host and a phonological host. A morphosyntactic
host is the constituent to which a unit is attached and over which it has semantic scope, e.g. an NP, a clause, etc., whereas a phonological host is an
element with which the unit forms a phonological word, e.g. the last word-
plus within an NP. The morphosyntactic host of a case marker is an NP,
whereas its phonological host is the head noun. The morphosyntactic host
of a nominal suffix such as plural -mmi is the noun stem, while its phonological host is also the noun stem.

3.2.1. Morphological dependency

A unit is morphologically independent if it is a syntactic unit that constructs a phrase or a clause. Words and clitics are morphologically independent since the position of a word or a clitic in a sentence is described in
terms of phrase structure or clause structure, which is characterised by potential reordering and recursiveness. By contrast, the distribution of the internal members of a word (roots and affixes), which are morphologically
dependent, is described in terms of a morphological template, which is
characterised by its fixed and non-recursive ordering of the internal members.

There are three useful tests for morphological dependency that resul
from the above-mentioned characteristics of words/clitics and affixes: (1)
isolatability test, which examines whether the unit in question may constitute an utterance on its own, (2) reordering test, which examines whether
or not the unit in question occurs in a domain in which the components are
recordable, and (3) combinability test, which examines the degree of restriction on the type of host with which a unit combines. (1) is useful in
distinguishing words (and larger units) from the smaller units (clitics and

Descriptive preliminaries   81

affixes), though some words are immune to this test (e.g. conjunction words and adnominal words). (2) is useful in distinguishing between words and clitics on the one hand and affixes on the other, though this test is diffi-cult to apply to certain clitics and affixes, so (3) becomes useful in distin-guishing between such clitics and affixes that are immune to the reordering test.

TABLE 3–2. The suggested tests for morphological dependency

	Morphological dependency			Phonologically dependency (see §3.2.2)
	Isolatability test	Reordering test	Combinability test	
Prototypical words	+	+	+	+
Prototypical clitics	-	+	+	-
Prototypical affixes	-	-	-	-

NB: '+' indicates that the test reveals morphological/phonological independence of the unit in question.

3.2.1.1. Isolatability test

A unit which may constitute an utterance should be morphologically inde-pendent. This test distinguishes words (and larger units) from other smaller units (clitics, bound roots and affixes). It is difficult to argue for isolatablity for some words, such as adnominals (e.g. *unu* 'that'), conjunctions (e.g. *ttjaa* 'then') and auxiliary verbs (e.g the progressive *ur*), which are syntac-tically bound, i.e. always occur with other elements to constitute a full-fledged phrase or clause. So, this test is useful only for words that may function as heads of phrases such as nouns, verbs, adjectives and interjec-tions. Adnominals and conjunctions will be justified as morphologically independent in terms of the reordering test (§3.2.1.2), whereas auxiliary verbs will be discussed in §3.2.3.1.

3.2.1.2. Reordering test

This test is based on the assumption that the internal ordering of a phrase or a clause (the order of each word/clitic in a phrase/clause) is more flexi-ble than the internal ordering of a word (the order of a root and affixes). As an initial approximation, let us observe (3–21) below, where there are a string of nine morphemes that constitute an NP.

(3–21)	*unu*	*asïb-i-u-tar*	*biki+vva-gama-mmi*
	that	play-THM-PROG-PST	male+child-DIM-PL
	1	2–3–4–5	6–7–8–9

Modifier   Modifier   Head
'the sons (who) are playing'

The nine morphemes are segmented into three words, i.e. the adnominal word *unu* (1), the verb *asïb-i-u-tar* (2–3–4–5) and the noun *biki-vva-gama-mmi* (6–7–8–9). The first two words, which are the modifiers of the NP headed by the noun *bikivvagamammi*, can be reordered as follows.

(3–22) *asïb-i-u-tar*   *unu*   *biki+vva-gama-mmi*
        play-THM-PROG-PST   that   male+child-DIM-PL
        2–3–4–5   1   6–7–8–9
        'the sons (who) were playing'

The phrase structure of NP (see Chapter 4) allows reordering of modifiers as long as each modifier in question directly modifies the head noun. On the other hand, there is strong restriction that the head slot must come finally. However, since reordering is possible for the two modifiers, the head noun is also proven to be outside of the morphological domain: if the head noun were a part of the morphological template, the reordering of the preceding elements would be impossible. That is, (3–22) consists of three words.

By contrast, the internal members of the noun *bikivvagamammi* (6–7–8–9) and the verb *asïbiutar* (2–3–4–5) cannot in any way be reordered, as nouns and verbs have their fixed templates that define their internal structures (see Chapters 5 and 6 respectively). The strings 2–5 (asïv-tar) and 6–7–9 (biki-vva-mmi) are possible, but note here that these different patterns do not involve reordering but the skipping of particular morphological slots, i.e. 2–(3)–(4)–5 and 6–7–(8)–9, where the bracketed slots are skipped in the formation of the new words in question. Thus, the templates are still fixed.

It is less straightforward to distinguish between clitics and affixes with regard to the reordering test. Since clitics mostly occur phrase-finally, their position is fixed at the final slot of a phrase[3]. Thus, a clitic ([D] in (3–23a)) might first appear to be like an affix that occurs word-finally ([D] in (3–23b)). However, a clitic is different from an affix in that, as in the case of the head noun in an NP as we discussed above, a clitic may often allow the

---

[3] In this respect, most clitics in Irabu are of the 'phrasal affix' type in Bickel and Nichols' (2007) typology, showing an inflectional-affix-like distributional pattern, and there are very few clitics of the 'bound word' type (which are simply phonologically reduced versions of a full word and whose distribution is similar to that of words) in Bickel and Nichols' typology.

Descriptive preliminaries   83

preceding elements (i.e. the words which constitute the phrase to which a clitic is attached, schematised in [A][B][C]) to be reordered, while an affix never does.

(3–23)   a. Clitic in a phrase structure: [A][B][C]=[**D**] → [C][B][A]=[**D**]
         b. Affix in a word structure: [A–B–C–**D**] → never reorderable

In short, if the preceding elements of a unit in question may be reordered, then it is a clitic rather than an affix. The reverse situation of clitics is found in conjunction words, which only occur clause-initially. Even though their morphological independence is not justifiable in terms of the isolatability test, they are still claimed to be morphologically independent since the subsequent elements may be reordered, as in:

(3–24)   *ttjaa   unu   asïb-i-ur-Ø*   *jarabi=u   jurab-i.*
         then   that   play-THM-PROG-NPST   child=ACC   call-IMP
         'Now call that child who is playing.'
(3–25)   *ttjaa   asïb-i-ur-Ø*   *unu   jarabi=u   jurab-i.*
         then   play-THM-PROG-NPST   that   child=ACC   call-IMP
         'Now call that child who is playing.'

The conjunction word *ttjaa* 'then' above is justified as morphologically independent, although they cannot constitute an independent utterance on their own.

Let us now turn to the distinction between affixes and clitics. To justify the claim summarised in (3–23), let us observe the difference between the nominal suffix *-mmi* (plural) and the case marker clitic *=kara* (ablative 'from') in the following examples, where the NP which consist of two conjoined nouns by the associative case marker *=tu* 'and; with'. The NP consists of three morphosyntactically independent units (which are bracketed below), i.e. the noun *bikidum*, the associative case marker *=tu* and the noun *midum-gama-mmi*.

(3–26)   *[bikidum]=[tu]*   *[midum-gama-mmi]*
         man=ASC   woman-DIM-PL
         'A man and little girls'

The three units can be reordered as in (3–27), since the associative NP *A=tu B* may be reordered as *B=tu A*.

(3–27)   *[midum-gama-mmi]=[tu]*   *[bikidum]*

84   Chapter 3

woman-DIM-PL=ASC   man
'little girls and a man'

Here, the two series of suffixes -*gama-mmi* must be moved together with
the noun stem when the latter is moved, since the syntactic rule of reordering can only reorder the three morphologically independent units, not their
internal parts.

The following example might first appear to be a case where the the final
suffix -*mmi* (which surfaces as -*mi* as a result of the deletion of the first
nasal; see §2.7.6) remains at phrase-final position as against (3–26).

(3–28)   *midum-gama=tu*   *bikidum-mi*
          woman-DIM=ASC   man-PL
          'a little girl and men'

There are two possible analyses for (3–26) and (3–28).

(3–29)   a. [bikidum]=[tu] [midum-gama]=[mi] → [midum-gama]=[tu]
             [bikidum]=[mi]
          b. [midum-gama]=[tu] [bikidum-mi]

According to the frist analysis (3–29a), the first three 'morphogically independent' elements constitute an NP and are reordered, and the suffix -*mmi*
scopes over the entire phrase with the semantic interpretation 'little girls
and men', which is an incorrect interpretation. The plural suffix scopes
over the stem *bikidum* alone, as the translation of (3–28) shows. If the semantic interpretation 'little girls and men' is intended, the following construction must be used, where the suffix attaches to each noun stem.

(3–30)   *midum-gama-mmi=tu*   *bikidum-mi*
          woman-DIM-PL=ASC   man-PL
          'little girls and men'

Thus, the suffix -*mmi* is stem-specific, occurring with the noun stem as its
phonological as well as morphological host, as is shown schematically in
(3–29b). The same holds true for -*gama*. The two nominal affixes occur
according to the fixed template root-(DIM)-(PL), and if a noun is moved,
the suffixes are also moved together, with the internal order being fixed.

By contrast, the ablative case marker =*kara* in (3–31) is claimed to occur
phrase-finally and not word-finally.

Descriptive preliminaries 85

(3–31) *[bikidum]=[tu]*   *[midum-gama]=[kara]*
        man=ASC   woman-DIM=ABL
        'from a man and a little girl'

Compare *=kara* in (3–31) and *-mmi* in (3–26), both of which occur in the same place in a sequence of five morphemes. However, unlike the plural *-mmi*, *=kara* never moves together with the noun when the noun is moved before *=tu*, since it is pinned down to the phrase-final position. The preceding NP may be reordered, as in (3–32).

(3–32) *[midum-gama]=[tu]*   *[bikidum]=[kara]*
        woman-DIM=ASC   man=ABL
        'from a little girl and a man'

The observed facts allow us to assume that *=kara* is morphologically independent, with the preceding three elements being reorderable.

All argument markers (case markers, limiter markers, information-structure markers) and most predicate markers (modal markers and discourse markers) are deemed morphologically independent with respect to the reordering test, since they can attach to a associative NP whose internal members are reorderable, even though they themselves are fixed at phrase-final position.

Conversely, most affixes are justified as morphologically dependent with respect to the reordering test, in the sense that they are never reordered themselves nor allow the reordering of the preceding elements, since they occur in a fixed template. The only problem is found in verbal inflectional affixes and conjunction markers. See §3.2.3.3 for the issue of conjunction markers. To illustrate the problematic nature of verbal inflectional affixes, let us first examine the following examples, both of which are auxiliary verb constructions (§7.1.4 for Irabu AVCs).

(3–33) *mii*   *fii-tar.*
        look.NRT   BEN-PST
        1   2–3
        'looked (for someone's benefit)'
(3–34) *fii*   *mii-tar.*
        give.NRT   EXP-PST
        2   1–3
        'tried giving'

86 Chapter 3

Here, the morphemes 1 and 2 appear to be reorderable before -*tar* if we compare the two examples. Is it possible to argue, as we did for the nominal suffix -*mmi*, that the past suffix is attached to the second verb stem and not an entire phrease? In the case of -*mmi*, this argument is easily justifiable based on the fact that the semantic scope of -*mmi* is only limited to the noun stem to which it is phonologically attached. However, the inflectional affix -*tar* clearly scopes over an entire verb phrase. The same kind of problem occurs for most other verbal inflectional affixes as well.

However, it is still argued that verbal inflectional affixes are distinct from clitics and words in that the former are morphologically dependent, morphologically as well as phonologically bound to the stem to which they attach. The morphological dependence surfaces when we pay attention to the third test for morphological dependency, the combinability test. The test reveals their conspicuously low degree of freedom with respect to the phonological host with which they occur. That is, they only occur with verb stems.

3.2.1.3. Combinability test

This test is based on the assumption that the distribution at a syntactic level allows the syntactic elements, i.e. clitics (and words), to occur with a much wider range of hosts than affixes, given that the host of a clitic is whatever word closes off the phrase to which the clitic is syntactically attached. For example, the case marker =*u* (accusative) is syntactically attached to an NP only, but without respect to whether the phonological host is a nominal word (3–35) or the verb of an adnominal clause in the headless structure (3–36).

(3–35) *[kai=ga   ssagi=u   asï-tar   kutu]=u=du*
        3SG=NOM   bridal=ACC   do-PST   fact=ACC=FOC
        cïfi-tar.
        hear-PST
        '(I) heard the fact that he got married.'

(3–36) *[kai=ga   ssagi=u   asï-tar]=ru=du   cïfi-tar.*
        3SG=NOM   bridal=ACC   do-PST=ACC=FOC   hear-PST
        '(I) heard (the news that) he did a bridal.'

The focus marker =*du* shows an even freer combinability. Its syntactic host may be an argument NP, an adjunct, a subordinate clause, or (part of) a predicate phrase, etc.

Descriptive preliminaries   87

(3–37)   *pav=nu=du*   *juu*   *idi-i*   *t-tar.*
          snake=NOM=FOC   very   exit-NRT   come-PST
          'SNAKES came out very (frequently).' [syntactic host: subject
          argument]

(3–38)   *pav=nu*   *juu=du*   *idi-i*   *t-tar.*
          snake=NOM   very=FOC   exit-NRT   come-PST
          'Snakes came out VERY (FREQUENTLY)' [syntactic host:
          predicate adjunct]

(3–39)   *pav=nu*   *juu*   *idi-i=du*   *t-tar.*
          snake=NOM   very   exit-NRT=FOC   come-PST
          'Snakes CAME OUT very (frequently).' [syntactic host: lexical
          verb of a VP]

(3–40)   *pav=nu*   *idi-i*   *t-ta=iba=du,*
          snake=NOM   exit-NRT   come-PST=so=FOC
          uturusï-ka-tar.
          fearful-VLZ-PST
          'Snakes came out, so (it) was fearful.' [syntactic host: adverbial
          clause]

The distribution at a morphological level, on the other hand, restricts an affix to occurring with a limited set of elements, since the affix in question is placed according to a fixed template. The plural suffix -*mmi*, for example, occurs according to the noun word template Noun root (-DIM)(-PL), so it only occurs with a nominal stem (bare root) or a complex nominal stem extended by the diminutive suffix -*gama*. The same generalization holds true for verbal affixes, which only occur with a verbal stem, and other kinds of affixes. In other words, affixes are stem-specific.

3.2.2. Phonological dependency

3.2.2.1. Overview

The phonologically independent status of words and compound roots is seen in the fact that it may constitute an independent phonological word. As noted in §2.1.2, there are three criteria for defining the phonological word (i.e. phonotactic, morpho-phonological and prosodic), but for brevity let us take the prosodic criterion here, as this criterion is always applicable for any kind of word, affix or clitic or their combination. A phonological word is the domain of HL alternation (§2.9).

HL alternation requires its domain to be footed before tone is assigned, the domain must consist of one or more feet, to which the tone assignment rule applies. Thus, for an element to be phonologically independent, it must satisfy the minimality constraint (which says that it must have at least one foot, or two morae) and it must also serve as an independent domain in which the tone assignment occurs. Therefore, if an element is monomoraic, it is necessarily phonologically dependent. If an element is bimoraic or longer, then the next question is whether it serves as an independent domain of HL alternation. Only words and roots in compounds are phonologically independent (see §2.10.1 for compounds and their phonological characteristics). Clitics and affixes are phonologically dependent either because they are monomoraic (e.g. the nominative case marker =*ga*) or because they cannot be an independent domain of tone assignment even though they are polymoraic (e.g. the ablative case marker =*kara*).

Even though clitics are phonologically dependent, the dependency is not homogeneous and needs a careful examination. Before going further, let us introduce the units phonological word (PW) and clitic group (CG) for the ease of the subsequent discussion (see the schematic structure in (3–41) below).

(3–41)

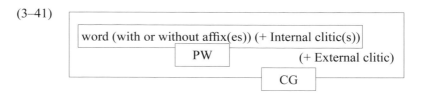

As mentioned above, a phonological word is a phonologically coherent domain, and it usually corresponds to a word-plus, which consists of a word and a whole number of clitics. However, this statement is rather simplified. As indicated in (3–41), there are two kinds of clitic: clitics that are fully integrated into the host PW, or internal clitics, and clitics that are treated as a sort of 'extra' elements, not integrated into the phonological word domain, even though they cannot stand as PWs on their own. I call the latter external clitics. Thus, if a word-plus only contains internal clitics, then it corresponds to a phonological word, but if a word-plus contains one or more external clitics, then it corresponds to a clitic group. The term 'clitic group' is taken from the theory of the prosodic hieararchy suggested by Selkirk (1984) and Nespor and Vogel (1986).

The clitics we examined in §2.9 were all internal clitics, which are fully integrated into the host phonological word in terms of foot building and/or tone assignment. That is, they do not necessarily come at the left edge of the footing domain, nor do they serve as an independent domain for tone assignment. In §2.9, it was noted that foot building does not refer to the

Descriptive preliminaries

distinction between (internal) clitics and affixes, to the extent that any monomoraic morph is treated as a part of the preceding host for the purpose of footing, and any polymoraic morph is treated as a distinct domain of footing. Internal clitics and affixes show an identical behaviour in tone assignment as well, in that they are always treated as internal members of a phonological word.

By contrast, as will be discussed in the following section, external clitics behave differently from words on the one hand, and from Internal clitics and affixes on the other. They differ from words in that they do not constitute phonological words on their own. They also differ from internal clitics and affixes in that the former are never integrated into the host phonological word.

3.2.2.2. External clitics

The following three bound markers are analysed as external clitics: the information-updater =ju (A=ju '(not B) but A'; §9.6.1), hearsay =ca (§9.3.3) and confirmative =i(i) (§9.6.3). The confirmative may be lengthened (e.g. =i → =ii), which indicates that its phonological dependency fluctuates between the more phonologically dependent monomoraic form (which violates the minimality constraint) and more independent bimoraic form (which satisfies the minimality constraint).

The bound markers =ju and =ca are identified as external clitics because of their peculiar behaviours of foot building, where they do not become a part of the preceding host for footing. This becomes clear when they are compared with internal clitics and affixes, as shown in Table 3–3, where the case markers =ga and =nu and the plural affixes -du and -ta are treated equally in terms of prosodic organisation.

TABLE 3–3. Phonological dependency of internal clitic and affix

Underlying form	Foot building	Tone assignment	Pitch shape of PW
(a) vva '2SG' + =ga (NOM)	(vvaga)	(H)	[HHH]
(b) vva '2SG' + -du (PL)	(vvadu)	(H)	[HHH]
(c) imsja 'fisherman' + =nu (NOM)	(im)(sjanu)	(H)(L)	[HHLL]
(d) imsja 'fisherman' + -ta (PL)	(im)(sjata)	(H)(L)	[HHLL]

In (a) and (b), the second person pronoun vva takes the nominative case marker =ga (which is an internal clitic) and the plural suffix -du respectively. In (c) and (d), the noun imsja 'fisherman' takes the nominative case marker =nu (which is again an internal clitic) and the plural suffix -ta re-

90   Chapter 3

spectively. As is usual in bound monomoraic morphs, these bound morphemes are integrated in the host for the purpose of footing, yielding a trimoraic foot in (a–b) and two bimoraic feet in (c–d). Then tone is assigned
according to the existing foot structure.

The situation is different when the same hosts are followed by external
clitics. In (3–42), the second person pronoun *vva* is cliticised by the external clitics *=ju* and *=ca* both being outside of the footing domain, thus caus-
ing a bimoraic foot in each case.

(3–42)   Underlying form   Foot structure
          a. *vva* '2SG' + *=ju*   (vva) ju
          b. *vva* '2SG' + *=ca*   (vva) ca

Tone is assigned by rule, as shown in (3–43) below. The H-toned foot in
each example is realised as [HL] rather than the expected [HH], and the
external clitic that attaches to the host is pronounced with a slightly higher
pitch than the [L] of the host, or with a rise-fall contour (and phonetically
with a slightly longer duration). The tonal characteristic of the external clitic is independent of the HL alternation, and is determined by the sentential
intonation.

(3–43)   Underlying   Foot   Tone   Pitch shape
          form   building   assignment   of PW
          a. *vva* '2SG' + *=ju*   (vva) ju   (H) ju   [HL] ju
          b. *vva* '2SG' + *=ca*   (vva) ca   (H) ca   [HL] ca

In (3–44), the noun *imsja* 'fisherman' is cliticised by the external clitics
=ju and *=ca*.

(3–44)   Underlying form   Foot   Tone   Pitch shape
                                       building   assignment   of PW
          a. *imsja* 'fisherman' + *=ju* (imsja) ju (H) ju   [HHL] ju
          b. *imsja* 'fisherman' + *=ca* (imsja) ca (H) ca   [HHL] ca

Again, both clitics are outside of the footing domain, yielding a trimoraic
foot in each case rather than two bimoraic feet as in the case of TABLE
3–3(c). The H-toned foot in each case of (3–44) is phonetically realised as
[HHL] with the final mora being lowered, and the external clitics are pronounced with a slightly higher pitch than the [L] of the host.

When the last foot of the host is /L/ as in (3–45) below, external clitics

Descriptive preliminaries 91

do not affect the pitch of the final foot of the host. Still, they are pronounced with a higher pitch than the final foot of the host, just as in the case of the above examples, demonstrating that their pitch realisation is independent of the tone assignment of the host.

(3–45)
Underlying form	Foot building	Tone assignment	Pitch shape of PW
a. *aparagi* 'beautiful' + =*ju*	(apa)(ragi)ju	(H)(L)ju	[HHLL]ju
b. *aparagi* 'beautiful' + =*ca*	(apa)(ragi)ca	(H)(L)ca	[HHLL]ca

The phonological behaviours of the bound markers allow us to assume that the information-updater =*ju* and hearsay =*ca* are attached *after* the footing and tone assignment apply to the host, i.e. after a phonological word is formed. That is, these clitics occur at the level of what we call CG (Clitic Group). The pitch lowering of the final mora of the host is a rule that applies to the CG. In summary, (3–46) is the ordering of rules that apply to a PW and a CG with regard to the attachment of the external clitics =*ju* and =*ca* (EC below).

(3–46)   Reformulation of External clitic attachment

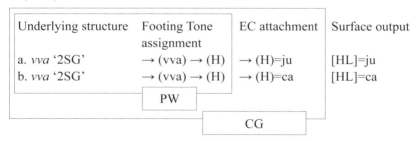

Like the information-updater =*ju* and hearsay =*ca* above, the confirmative =*i* is not integrated into the host in terms of footing. This is clearly seen in (3–47b), where the surface form *imsja*=*i* (the host midum + the clitic =*i*) does not constitute two-foot structure *(im)(sjai).

(3–47)   Attachment of =*i*
Underlying structure	Footing	Tone assignment	EC attachment	Surface output
a. *vva* '2SG'	(vva)	(H)	(H)=i	[HH]=i
b. *imsja* 'fisherman'	(imsja)	(H)	(H)=i	[HHH]=i

92   Chapter 3

c. *aparagi* 'beautiful' (apa)(ragi) (H)(L)   (H)(L)=i   [HHLL]=i

Unlike the other two bound markers, the confirmative =*i* never causes the
final mora of the host to be lowered, which indicates that =*i* is more independent in terms of prosody than the other two markers, since there is no
prosodic interaction between the host and the clitic. This observation is
further supported by another fact that the confirmative =*i* is often realised
as the bimoraic *ii*. The bimoraic form can be used as a complete utterance
without any preceding element (e.g. as a short response to the addressee)
with the high pitch [HH]. The former feature indicates that the bimoraic *ii*
is a morphologically independent unit in terms of the isolatability test
(§3.2.1.1). The latter feature indicates that it is an independent phonological word. That is, the confirmative =*i* has two variants, the external clitic =*i*
and the word *ii*.

(3–48)   Phonological dependency
         more dependent   least dependent
         internal clitics   <   external clitics   <   word
                                     =*i*   *ii*

3.2.3. Problematic cases

The above criteria for words, affixes and clitics mostly work well to identify a word, an affix, or a clitic in a given string of morphemes. However,
there are a few cases that need to be examined more carefully. One compli-
cating factor in distinguishing between a word, clitic and affix is the diachronic process of grammaticalisation, where a word gradually changes to
a clitic and eventually to an affix. Many constructions are in the middle of
this grammaticalisation pathway, making it difficult, or pointless, to give a
solid distinction between a word, a clitic and an affix.

3.2.3.1. Auxuliary verb

A typical example of grammticalisation is found in the Auxiliary Verb
Construction (§7.1.4). The AVC is schematised as Lexical verb +Auxiliary
verb. The three suggested criteria for morphological dependency indicate
that the auxiliary verb is like an affix. First, it must co-occur with the lexical verb. Second, the internal order is much more fixed than that of an NP,
and no reordering is possible for the two components. Third, the auxiliary
verb shows a high degree of selectional restriction with respect to its preceding element, requiring the auxiliary to be preceded by a verb (lexical
verb element) alone.

Descriptive preliminaries 93

The auxiliary may still be said to be morphologically independent, based on the fact that the sequence Lexical verb +Auxiliary verb may be broken up by the insertion of the focus marker, which is independently justified as a morphologically independent unit (in terms of the reordering test and the combinability test). Since the sequence A–B is broken up by a morphologically independent unit [C], the sequence A–B cannot be a morphological template *[A–B], and it is reasonable to assume that the sequence comprises two morphologically independent units [A][B], to which the insertion of [C] may occur.

(3–49) *zin=nu*   *[muc-i-i]*   *[ur-Ø].*
        money=ACC1   carry-THM-NRT   PROG-NPST
                          [Lexical verb]   [Auxiliary verb]
        "He has money."

(3–50) *zin=nu*   *[muc-i-i]=du*   *[ur-Ø].*
        money=ACC1   carry-THM-NRT=FOC   PROG-NPST
                          [Lexical verb]=Focus marker [Auxiliary verb]
        "He has money."

Interestingly, if the focus marker is not present in the sequence Lexical verb +Auxiliary verb, the sequence may often become a single compound word with the narrative converbal affix being deleted ('word-phrase alternation', see §6.4.2.3 for detail).

(3–51) *zin=nu*   *[muc-i+ur-Ø].*
        money=ACC1   carry-THM+PROG-NPST
                              [Lexical verb+Auxiliary verb]

        "He has money."

Thus, we are looking at an ongoing grammaticalisation process where the source structure consists of the lexical verb and the auxiliary verb as morphologically independent units as in (3–49) and the target structure consists of the same components which has lost morphological independence (3–51). The situation where the focus marker can be inserted between the two units is somewhere in the middle of the grammaticalisation path.

3.2.3.2. Clitics of the bound-word type
Even though most clitics in Irabu are of the 'phrasal affix' type in Bickel and Nichols' (2007) typology, showing an inflectiona-affix-like distributional pattern, there are a very few cases where a word is simply phonolog-

94   Chapter 3

ically reduced and becomes cliticised, showing a word-like distributional
pattern. This kind of clitic is called 'bound word' type in Bickel and Nichols' typology and 'simple clitics' in Zwicky's (1977) theory of clitic.

The first person singular pronoun is underlyingly *ban*, which is a word.
However, when it is followed by the nominative marker =*ga*, it becomes a
bound form *ba*=, an exceptionally proclicised to the nominative marker
=*ga*, as in *ba=ga jaa* 'our house'.

As is illustrated in (3–52a), the light verb designating 'do' has two variants, the free word form with *as*- and the bound word form with *s*-. The
distributional pattern of the bound form is exactly the same for the free
word with *as*-, as the former fills the lexical verb slot of a VP (3–52b), just
like a free word counterpart (3–52a).

(3–52)   a. *kair+kair*   *as-i-i=du*   *ur-Ø.*
             RED+turn.round   do-THM-NRT=FOC   PROG-NPST
             '(He) is turning round a lot.'
         b. *kair+kair=s-i-i=du*   *ur-Ø.*
             RED+turn.round=do-THM-NRT=FOC   PROG-NPST
             '(He) is turning round a lot.'

3.2.3.3. Clitics with a limited combinability with a phonological host
There are a few clitics that combine with only one type of phonological
host. They are conjunction markers (§9.2), such as =*suga* 'but' in (3–53a)
below (/s/ is assimilated to /r/ when preceded by /r/), and a modal marker=
su(u)da (§9.3.5). The distribution of these markers first appears to be like
that of affixes, in that the phonological host of the markers is a verb only. If
the conjunction marker =suga is attached to a nominal predicate, as in (3–
53b), a copula verb is obligatorily present, to which the marker is attached.

(3–53)   a. *ffa=nu*   *nak-i+u-tar=ruga,*   *nau=mai*
             child=NOM   cry-THM+PROG-PST=but   what=even
             as-irai-t-tar.
             do-POT-NEG.-PST
             '(My) child was crying, but (I) couldn't do anything.'
         b. *kari=a*   *sinsii*   *jar-Ø=ruga,*   *nau=mai*
             3SG=TOP   teacher   COP-NPST=but   what=even
             ss-a-n-Ø.
             know-THM-NEG-NPST
             'He is a teacher, but (he) does not know anything.'

Descriptive preliminaries 95

This restriction on the phonological host in the case of these markers is in sharp contrast to the case of other predicate markers like modal markers (§9.3) and discourse markers (§9.6). As illustrated in (3–54) below, the modal marker =*ca* (hearsay) may be phonologically attached to either a verb (a) or a predicate nominal (b), since its syntactic host is simply a predicate phrase.

(3–54) a. *ffa=nu*   *nak-i+u-tar=ca*
            child=NOM   cry-THM+PROG-PST=HS
            '(My) child was crying, they say.'
        b. *kari=a*   *sinsii=ca.*
            3SG=TOP   teacher=HS
            'He is a teacher, they say.'

Thus, the comparison with modal markers call into question the analysis that conjunction markers like =*suga* 'but' are clitics.

Diachronically speaking, we are again looking at an ongoing grammaticalisation process whereby a former word is becoming an affix. As noted in detail in each section of conjunction markers (§9.2) and in §9.3.5, most of these forms were formal nouns, i.e. head nouns of NPs modified by an adnominal clause (e.g. /su/ in =*suga* 'but' came from the bound word *suu*; see §4.2.1.8). Thus, it is natural for them to combine only with the verb word, since the adnominal clause must end in a verb (a copula verb in the case of nominal predicate). These morphemes are synchronically not analysable as the head of an NP since they do not carry case. These morphemes have lost their nominal feature in present Irabu, but its diachronic characteristic as NP head is still found in the restricted combinability with the phonological host. The conjunction marker =*(ss)iba* 'so' (§9.2.2) is still problematic, since its historical source is unknown.[4] So, it is impossible to argue that the syntactic host of the marker is a phrase or a clause like other conjunction markers.

---

[4] This might be the causal converbal form of the bound verb *s-* 'do' (§3.2.3.2). In Irabu, the verb 'do' may be used as a speech verb 'say', and the construction consisting of the clause + =*ssiba* might historically be the complement clause + the speech verb. If this is true, the reason why =*ssiba* only combine with a verb word is obvious: if the predicate of the subordinate clause is a nominal predicate, the copula verb is necessary. In this case, then, we can maintain that =*ssiba* has a phrasal scope, scoping over an entire predicate, either nominal or verbal.

96   Chapter 3

3.3. Word classes

Morphologically independent forms, i.e. words and clitics, are classified
into several word classes according to their syntactic functions in phrases/
clauses and/or their morphological shape.

Irabu has five major word classes, nominals, verbs, adjectives, adnominals and bound markers (e.g. case markers and modal markers). The suggested criteria for word class assignment are listed in (3–55), which are either syntactic (A, B, E) or morphological (C, D). The 'Others' are negatively
defined as those parts-of-speech that do not satisfy any of the criteria, and
this catch-all category falls into three subdivisions (adverbs, conjunctions,
and interjections).

(3–55) Criteria for word class assignment
        (A) Heads an NP
        (B) Directly fills the dependent slot of an NP
        (C) Inflects
        (D) Is a reduplicated form with the input-stem-final phoneme
             lengthened
        (E) Occurs phrase- or clause-finally to mark grammatical
             functions

TABLE 3–4. Word classes: distinctive criteria

	(A)	(B)	(C)	(D)	(E)
Nominal	+	-	-	-	-
Adnominal	-	+	-	-	-
Verb	-	-	+	-	-
Adjective	+	-	-	+	-
Bound marker	-	-	-	-	+
Others	-	-	-	-	-

3.3.1. Nominals

A nominal is a word that can only head an NP. There is another word class,
or adjective, that may head an NP (§3.3.4), but a nominal and an adjective
may be unambiguously distinguished by the morphological criterion (D),
and by the fact that an adjective may also appear in a VP. Since a nominal
exclusively heads an NP, if a nominal is to modify another nominal in an
NP, it must first head an NP, which then fills the modifier slot of a larger
NP recursively (§3.1.2).

There are six major subclasses of nominals: nouns, pronouns (personal,

Descriptive preliminaries   97

demonstrative, reflexive), numerals, interrogatives, indefinites and non-pronominal demonstratives (Chapter 5). Thus demonstratives are distributed across two nominal subclasses. Furthermore, as noted in §3.3.2 below, there is a class of demonstratives that belongs to the adnominal word class (adnominal demonstrative).

3.3.2. Adnominals

An adnominal is a word that only serves as modifier of an NP. Thus an adnominal cannot function as an argument or a predicate head of a nominal predicate. And since it does not head an NP, it never carries case when functioning as a modifier of an NP (In the examples below an adnominal is underlined).

(3–56)   a. <u>unu</u>   jaa=n=du   asuv-tar.
             that   house=DAT=FOC   play-PST
             '(I) played at that house.'
         b. <u>daizïna</u>   jarabi=du   jar-Ø.
             great   child=FOC   COP-NPST
             '(He) is an awesome child.'

The list of adnominals is given below. As seen, the native adnominals are all demonstratives. *daizïna* 'great' is a recent loan from Japanese (Karimata 2002).

TABLE 3–5. Adnominals

Demonstrative	kunu	'this'
	unu	'that (medial)'
	kanu	'that (distal)'
Japanese loan	daizïna	'great; awful'

3.3.3. Verbs

A verb is a word that inflects. Inflection is marked verb-finally (e.g. *mii-tar* (look-PST) 'looked', *mii-di* (look-INT) 'will look', and so on). Inflectional categories vary depending on whether a verb is a finite verb (inflecting for tense and/or mood) or a non-finite verb (inflecting for neither). Negative polarity may be inflectional in either type of verb form. Verb morphology is described in Chapter 6.

3.3.4. Adjectives

An adjective is a word that is created by the reduplication of a property

98 Chapter 3

concept stem (PC stem) where the final phoneme of the input stem is lengthened by one mora. In addition, a few noun stems such as those in (3–58) can also be input stems of adjectives (see also Motonaga 1978 and Karimata 2002).

	Input stem		Output word
(3–57)	PC stem	>	Adjective
	taka- 'high'		*takaa+taka*
	'high'*kiban-* 'poor'		*kibann+kiban* 'poor'
	pjaa- 'fast'		*pjaaa+pjaa* 'fast'
(3–58)	Noun stem	>	Adjective
	avva 'oil'		*avvaa+avva* 'oily'
	jarabi 'child'		*jarabii+jarabi* 'childish'

The morphological definition here is iron-clad, i.e. we can identify an adjective without ambiguity by this criterion.

There is no class of adjective phrases. Rather, as shown in TABLE 3–6, adjectives are 'parasitic' on NP structure and on VP structure, able to appear in either, even though they show a clear preference to occur in NPs (§8.2.3). That is, the adjective class aligns with nominals in terms of syntax. In particular, an adjective primarily functions as head of an NP that fills the modifier slot of a larger NP (as shown in (3–59) below). That is, an attributive function is typical (Chapter 8). Note that the NP headed by the adjective in (3–59) carries genitive case, just as in the case of an NP headed by a nominal word (3–60). Also, as will be fully described in Chapter 8, an NP headed by an adjective can be modified by an adnominal (3–61), a word that only fills the modifier slot of an NP, even though it is less preferred than when an NP is headed by a nominal.

(3–59)	*ujakii+ujaki=nu*	*pžtu=tu*	*kibann+kiban=nu*	*pžtu*
	RED+rich=GEN	man=ASC	RED+poor=GEN	man
	'A rich man and a poor man'			
(3–60)	*irav=nu*	*pžtu=tu*	*pžsara=nu*	*pžtu*
	Irabu=GEN	man=ASC	Hirara=GEN	man
	'A man from Irabu and a man from Hirara.'			
(3–61)	*daizïna*	*ujakii+ujaki=nu*	*pžtu*	
	great	RED+rich=GEN	man	
	'very rich man.'			

Descriptive preliminaries 99

TABLE 3–6. Nominal, verb, and adjective in phrase structure

	In NP structure	In VP structure
Nominal	+	-
Adjective	+	+
Verb	-	+

3.3.5. Bound markers

Bound markers are clitics that occur phrase- or clause-finally, marking the grammatical functions of the phrase or clause to which they are syntactically attached. Bound markers are further subclassified into (a) argument markers, (b) predicate markers and (c) discourse markers.

3.3.5.1. Argument markers

Argument markers comprise case markers, limiter markers and information-structure markers. They all mark the grammatical function of NPs, even though the latter two may occur with a limited kind of adjuncts.

Case markers occur with argument NPs. See §4.3 for detail. Limitter markers consist of quantifier markers (e.g. =*mai* 'too') and qualifier markers (e.g. contrastive/emphasis =*gami*). See §9.4 for detail.

(3–62)   *mm=mu=mai*   *nii+fau-Ø.*
         potato=ACC=too   boil+eat-NPST
         '(I) boil-and-eat potatoes, too.'

(3–63)   *vva=ga*   *ah-u-ba=gami=du*   *zau-kar-Ø.*
         2SG=NOM   do-THM-CND=CNT=FOC   good-VLZ-PST
         'If you do (it), (that's) fine.'

Information-structure markers comprise topic markers and focus markers (§9.5). They may apply to a range of different syntactic constituents. The syntactic host may be a coordinate clause or a clausal element (an argument, a (clausal) adjunct, or a predicate). When a verbal predicate (§3.1.1.1) serves as a syntactic host, a topic/focus marker may attach to either a complement or the VP, as shown in (3–64). When the VP is marked by a topic or a focus, it must have a complex structure (V1+V2), and the topic/focus marker attaches to the first part of the VP.

(3–64)   a. *kuri=a*   *taka-fi=du*   *nar-i-i*
            3SG=TOP   high-AVLZ=FOC   become-THM-NRT
                             VP complement=FOC   [V1

         ur-Ø.

PROG-NPST
V2]$_{VP}$
'This has (gradually) become high.'

b. *kuri=a*   *taka-fï*   *nar-i-i=du*
   3SG=TOP   high-AVLZ   become-THM-NRT=FOC
                VP complement   [V1=FOC

   ur-Ø.
   PROG-NPST
   V2]$_{VP}$
   'This has (gradually) become high.'

Likewise, when a nominal predicate (§3.1.1.2) serves as a syntactic host, it must have a complex structure (NP + copula), and the topic/focus marker is attached to the NP.

(3–65)   *kuri=a*   *imsja=du*   *a-tar.*
          3SG=TOP   fisherman=FOC   COP-PST
                  NP=FOC   copula
          'This (guy) was a fisherman.'

3.3.5.2. Predicate markers

Predicate markers mark the grammatical categories that pertain to the predicate, such as dependency (coordination and subordination) and modality.

A conjunction marker (§9.2) marks coordination. A conjunction marker requires the copula verb when attaching to a nominal predicate. That is, its phonological host must be a verbal word-plus. In relation to this, as shown below, the 'so' conjunction marker *=(ss)iba* has a reduced allomorph *=iba*, which also triggers an irregular allomorphy on the part of the host (the past unmarked suffix *-tar* > *-ta*), indicating an affix-like morphological bonding (see §3.2.3.3).

(3–66)   a. *kuumuja=nu*   *u-ta=iba=du,*   *uturusï+munu*
            cockroach=NOM   exist-PST=so=FOC   fearful+thing
            a-ta-m.
            COP-PST-RLS
            '(There) was a cockroach, so (it) was fearful.'

       b. *giin=du*   *a-ta=iba=du,*   *daizïna*
            congressman=FOC   COP-PST=so=FOC   great
            ujaki+pžtu=dooi.
            rich+man=EMP

'(He) was a congressman, so (he) is a very rich man'

Modal markers (§9.3) mark the modality of the predicate, such as the certainty modal marker =*dara*. Except for =*su(u)da* (§9.3.5), modal markers do not require a copula verb, and may be directly attached to a predicate nominal, demonstrating that they syntactically attach to a predicate (whether it be a verbal or nominal), rather than attaching morphologically to a verb stem.

(3–67) *kan=nu=du*   *ur-Ø=dara.*
         crab=NOM=FOC   exist-NPST=CRTN
         '(There) is a crab.'

(3–68) *uri=a*   *parumna=dara.*
         3SG=TOP   snail=CRTN
         'It is a snail.'

3.3.5.3. Discourse markers

Discourse markers (§9.6) mark various discourse-related functions such as confirmation, correction, etc. Discourse markers are distinct from argument and predicate markers in that the former is attached to any constituent rather than a specific morphosyntactic unit such as a predicate or an argument/adjunct. The confirmative =*i* is a typical discourse marker, occurring with almost any utterance unit, as illustrated below.

(3–69) *nubir=gami=a*   *[mma+munu*   *a-ta-m]=mi.*
         nubir.plant=EMP=TOP   tasty+thing   exist-PST-RLS=CNF
         '*Nubir* plant [was tasty], eh?' [matrix predicate]

(3–70) *[uri=u]=i,*   *im=nu*   *mizï=sii*   *arav-Ø.*
         3SG=ACC=CNF   sea=GEN   water=INST   wash-NPST
         '(When you got a seaweed, you) wash [it], you see, with sea water.' [direct object argument]

(3–71) *[kuma=nu*   *nii=ju*   *kir-i-i]=i,*
         this.place=GEN   root=ACC   cut-THM-NRT=CNF
         kaa=ju=du   *piccjafï-Ø.*
         skin=ACC=FOC   tear.off-NPST
         '[(You) cut a root here], you see, and tear off the skin of the root.' [sentential adjunct: non-finite adsentential adjunct clause]

(3–72) *[butu=u*   *sïn-tar=ruga=du]=i,*   *pataki=mai*
         husband=TOP   die-PST=but=FOC=CNF   field=too
         a-ta-m.

102   Chapter 3

exist-PST-RLS
'(My) husband died, but (there) was (still) a field.' [coordinate
clause]

3.3.5.4. Relative ordering within bound marker chains
Bound markers can co-occur, forming a chain of bound markers. Thus in
(3–73) below, the conjunction marker =*iba* 'so' is followed by the limiter
marker =*gami* (contrastive), which is in turn followed by the focus marker
=*du* and the discourse marker marker =*i*.

(3–73)   *banti=a*   *kuu-ka-ta=iba=gami=du=i,*
         1PL=TOP   poor-VLZ-PST=so=CNT=FOC=CNF
         kookoo=mai   *idah-a-t-tar=dooi.*
         high.school=even   let.go-THM-NEG-NPST=EMP
         'We were poor, so (our family) didn't let me go to high school.'

Their relative ordering within the chain mostly reflects restrictions on their
co-occurrence with a given type of host (i.e. the higher degree of restriction a bound marker shows, the nearer to the host it comes). As is shown in
TABLE 3–7 below, all conjunction markers behave similarly, requiring their
phonological host to be verbal. Other bound markers have at least two
kinds of phonological host, and this characteristic is a major criterion for
distinguishing clitics from most affixes (§3.2.1.2). In the table, the phonological hosts listed are not exhaustive but distinctive (e.g. the adjective
word-plus is excluded here). In particular, limiter markers, topic/focus
markers, and discourse markers are distinguished from each other by their
(in)ability to be attached to a word-plus containing a PC adverb (§8.3.2), a
word-plus containing an underived adverb (§3.3.6.1), and an adnominal
word-plus (§5.4, see also below).

TABLE 3–7. Bound markers and their phonological hosts

	Verb word-plus	Nominal word-plus	Other word-plus		
			PC adv	Un.adv	Adn
Conjunction marker	*				
Modal marker	*	*			
Limiter marker	*	*	*		
Information-structure marker	*	*	*	*	
Discourse marker	*	*	*	*	*

Descriptive preliminaries   103

Basically, an adnominal word does not carry any bound marker when it occurs in an NP. Unlike a noun, it does not carry the genitive marker as it directly fills the modifier slot of an NP (whereas a noun does so indirectly, by first heading an NP, which then carries the genitive marker). However, a discourse marker can phonologically attach to any constituent of a clause including the modifier of an NP. In (3–74) below, the confirmative marker =*i* 'eh?; you know' (§9.6.4) is attached to the adnominal *kanu* 'that' and the head noun with the accusative marker.

(3–74) *kanu=i,*   *jaa=ju=i,*   *vv-m=ti=du*
        that=CNF   house=ACC=CNF   sell-NPST-RLS=FOC
        as-i+ur-Ø.
        do-THM+PROG-NPST
        '(That guy) is going to sell that house.'

Conjunction markers are only attached to a verb, so it precedes any other kind of bound markers. Modal markers and limiter markers do not appear in the same slot. Both these markers precede topic/focus markers, and finally discourse markers close off a chain of bound markers.

3.3.6. Others

This catch-all category is a set of words that do not satisfy any of criteria (A) to (E). They do not share any morphological or syntactic features. It is possible to divide this category into several subcategories depending on their syntactic distribution: underived adverbs, derived adverbs, conjunctions, interjections, and edge markers.

3.3.6.1. Underived adverbs

An underived adverb is a word that serves as a predicate adjunct, directly modifying a predicate (mostly a verbal predicate, but certain nominal predicates may be modified by an underived adverb; §8.2.2.3 and §8.3.4).[5] There are just a small number of underived adverbs in Irabu, most of which are adverbial quantifiers.

(3–75) *cïnuu=ja*   *saki-gama=u*   *juu=du*   *num-tar.*
        yesterday=TOP   sake-DIM=ACC   a.lot=FOC   drink-PST
        'Yesterday (I) drank sake a lot.'

---

[5] Sentential adjuncts such as temporal modifiers *cïnu* 'yesterday' are encoded by nouns such as time nouns (§5.2.1).

104   Chapter 3

(3–76) *mazïmunu-mmi=a*   <u>*ati*</u>   *uturusï-ka-i-ba=i...*
        devil-PL=TOP   very   fearful-VLZ-THM-CSL=CNF
        'devils are very fearful, so, you know...'

(3–77) *ba=a*   *mmja*   <u>*maadaa*</u>   *ss-ai-n=dooi.*
        1SG=TOP   INTJ   not.very   know-POT-NEG=EMP
        'I don't know (that) well.'

Below is a list of adverb roots that are frequently used in natural discourse. Adverb roots that are suspected to be recent loans from Japanese (e.g. *taigai* 'normally' < Japanese *taigai*) are excluded. As is shown, *maada* has its negative form *maadaa*, which can be analysed as *maada* + =*a* (topic marker), given that in negative constructions in general, topic marking is almost obligatory (§9.5.1.2).

TABLE 3–8. Adverb roots

Form	Gloss	Related form (if any)
juu	very; frequently	
ati	very	
maada	very	*maadaa* 'not very'
murtu	almost	
mmja(*hi*)	more	
aur	only	
sugu	immediately	

3.3.6.2. Derived adverbs

A derived adverb is a word that functions as (1) a predicate adjunct just like an underived adverb, or (2) a VP complement in a verbal predicate phrase (§3.1.1.1). There are three kinds of word form in this class depending on the stem from which the word is derived: PC adverb, zero-converted verbal stem, and verbal reduplication.

A PC adverb is derived from a PC stem (§3.3.4; §8.1). It may function either as (1) or (2). As a predicate adjunct, the PC adverb in (3–78) can be omitted, since it is not part of the predicate phrase. Also, its position may not be contiguous with the predicate. On the other hand, as a VP complement the PC adverbs in (3–79) cannot be omitted, and is contiguous with the other predicate components.

(3–78) As a predicate modifier
        taka-fï=du   *tuv-tar.*
        high-AVLZ=FOC   fly-PST

Descriptive preliminaries   105

'(He) jumped high'

(3–79)   As a VP complement

     a. *taka-fï=du*   *a-tar.*
        high-AVLZ=FOC   be-NPST
        '(He) was (in a) tall (state).'

     b. *taka-fï=du*   *nar-tar.*
        high-AVLZ=FOC   become-PST
        '(He) became tall.'

(3–79a) is a state verb construction, where the state verb 'be' (§6.3.6.3) requires an adverb derived from a PC stem. See also §8.3.3.1 for the relationship between this state verb construction and another construction involving PC stems.

A zero-converted verbal stem is a bound word, and only serves as (2). The complement-taking verb is the light verb *sï* (§6.3.5.2). The zero conversion takes place to accommodate focus marking on the verb stem. When the focus marker is attached to a predicate, it cannot directly attach to a stem or an affix within a verb word. Thus zero conversion takes place to extract a verb stem from a verb word and put it into the VP complement slot (as a derived adverb word). The undocked inflection of the original verb (*-tar* below) is attached to the light verb, which is cliticised to the preceding component of the verb phrase.

(3–80)   *mii-tar.*   →   *mii=du=sï-tar.*
        look-PST   look=FOC=do-PST
        VP   VP comp=FOC=VP
        'looked'   'did looking.'

Reduplicated verbal forms are also derived adverbs, but their syntactic status is somewhat difficult to analyse. It mostly functions as a VP complement, as shown in (3–81) below, and can be treated as a derived adverb in this regard. However, in a number of instances they can terminate a sentence (3–82), encoding habitual aspect, but unlike verbs cannot carry any verb inflection, failing to satisfy the criterion for the verb word class. Thus reduplicated verbal forms seem to be intermediate between verb and derived adverb (VP complement).

(3–81)   *tu-i+cc-i-i*   *fau+fau=s-i-i,*
        take-THM+come-THM-NRT   RED+eat=do-THM-NRT
        ai=du   *asï-tar*

106 Chapter 3

that.way=FOC do-PST

'Bringing (the food), eating, (we) would do like that (in those days).'

(3–82) *unagaduu=nu   tami=tii   asï+asï.*
oneself=GEN benefit=QT RED+do

'(He) would do (i.e. say) "(That's) our own benefit".'

3.3.6.3. Conjunctions

A conjunction is a word that appears clause-initially and marks an inter-clausal relation. In example (3–83) the two clauses are connected by the conjunctive *ttjaa* 'then; if so' which is put at the initial position of the second clause.

(3–83) *kuma=a   punicï-ka-i-ba,*
this.place=TOP   rocky-VLZ-THM-CSL
nivv-ai-n-Ø=nju.
sleep-POT-NEG-NPST=UPDT

'This place is so rocky that I cannot sleep (here).'

ttjaa   ba=ga   uma=n=na   nivv-a-di.
then   1SG=NOM   that.place=DAT=TOP   sleep-THM-INT

'Then I'll sleep there.'

TABLE 3–9 is a list of conjunction roots. As is shown, *aidu* appears to contain =*du* (focus). However, there is evidence that =*du* is not functioning as a focus marker here: there may occur another focus marker within the same clause, and it would be odd if both were treated as focus markers, since a focus marker appears only once within the same clause. Thus I treat *aidu* as a single conjunction morpheme. Likewise, *assiba* and *assuga* can be decomposited into the light verb *asï* + the conjunction marker =*ssiba* (§9.2.2). However, I treat them as single morphemes since the *asï* here does not inflect.

TABLE 3–9. Conjunction roots

Form	Gloss	Related form (if any)
aidu	And then,	*ai* 'that way' + =*du* (focus)
mata	And,	
ttjaa	(If so) then,	
asi	Well; then; by the way;	imperative form of *asï* 'do'
assiba	So,	*asï* 'do' + =*iba* 'so'
assuga	But,	*asï* 'do' + =*suga* 'but'

Descriptive preliminaries 107

3.3.6.4. Interjections

An interjection is a word that (1) constitutes an utterance by itself, as illustrated in (3–84), and (2) must be followed by a quotative marker =ti(i) if it is embedded into another clause, it, as shown in (3–85).

(3–84) *gammja!*   *vva=ru*   *a-tar=ru!?*
       oh.my.god   2SG=FOC   COP-PST=Q
       'Oh my god! Was (it) you!?'

(3–85) *kari=a*   *gammja=tii*   *až-tar=ca.*
       3SG=TOP   oh.my.god=QT say-PST=HS
       'S/he said, "Oh my god!"'

Onomatopoeic words are classified as interjections in these two regards.

(3–86) *dumma,*   *dumma=ti,*   *ai=nu*   *utu=u*
       ONM   ONM=QT   like.that=GEN sound=ACC
       cïk-i-i...
       hear-THM-NRT
       '*Dumma! dumma!* Hearing such a sound...'

(3–87) *doofi=ti*   *uti-i=i,*   *tooriike=n*
       ONM=QT   drop-NRT=CNF tooriike=DAT
       nar-tar=ca.
       become-PST=HS
       '(The ground) collapsed (with the sound like *doofi*), (the collapsed area) became (what we now call) *tooriike*.'

TABLE 3–10. Interjection roots (non-onomatopoeic)

Form	Gloss	Related form (if any)
hai	'Hey!'	
hira	'You see?'	
ahaa	'I see...'	
agai	(when surprised; impressed)	*agaitandi!*
ugui	(when surprised)	
mmja	(when upset; afraid)	*mmja* (discourse marker; Chapter 9)
(a)gammja	(when highly upset; afraid)	
tandi	I'm sorry!	*tandi* 'begging' (nominal root)
tandigaatandi	'Thank you!'	
ttaaree	'No way!'	
ugutaajubaa	'It's ruined!'	

108   Chapter 3

TABLE 3–11. Interjection roots (onomatopoeic)

Form	Gloss
guffa	sound of stabbing, hitting, etc.
zaffa	sound of falling down
zavva	sound of falling down
dumma	sound of light striking
bamma	sound of severe striking
doofï	sound of collapsing (of building, etc.)
bžžbžž	sound of crying
kjaakjaa	sound of noisy situation
pacipaci	sound of fire burning
putuputu	sound of rain spotting; state of shivering

3.4. Grammatical relations

In this section I define subject, direct object, and indirect object. Irabu lacks cross-reference morphology that would serve as strong evidence for subject and/or direct object relation in many languages. However, as will be shown in the sections below, there are several syntactic tests that allow us to identify these two grammatical relations. On the other hand, as is typical cross-linguistically (cf. Comrie 1981; Payne 1997), the evidence for 'indirect object' as a grammatical relation is weak, as it is identified not by a syntactic characteristic but by a semantic role and a morphological case. I will not include it as a grammatical relation.

3.4.1. Subject

The grammatical relation subject is defined as an NP that shows the following two syntactic characteristics.

(A) HONORIFIC CONTROL
(B) REFLEXIVE CONTROL

In terms of (A), only the subject NP triggers honorification (the suffix -(s) *ama* on verb; §6.4.1.3). Thus in (3–88), the subject NP *sinsii* 'teacher' triggers honorification. Likewise, in (3–89) the honorific controller must be the subject NP *siitummi* 'students' even when such an interpretation is pragmatically odd.

(3–88)   *sinsii=nu*   *siitu-mmi=u=du*   *jurab-i-i*
            teacher=NOM   student-PL=ACC=FOC   call-THM-NRT

Descriptive preliminaries 109

ur-ama-r.
PROG-HON-NPST
'The teacher is calling the students.'

(3–89) *siitu-mmi=nu*   *sinsii=ju=du*   *jurab-i-i*
        student-PL=NOM   teacher=ACC=FOC   call-THM-NRT

        ur-ama-r.
        PROG-HON-NPST
        'The students are calling the teacher.'

The reflexive controller is also a subject NP. In (3–90) below, this re-quires the interpretation (a) rather than (b), even when it is (b) that is prag-matically natural. This suggests that reflexive control is an abstract and purely syntactic phenomenon, only explainable in terms of the grammati-cal relation subject.

(3–90) *žžkuja=a*   *ujaki+sjuu=kara*   *naa=ga*
        beggar=TOP   rich+old.man=ABL   RFL=GEN

        zin=nu=du   *žži-tar.*
        money=ACC=FOC   get-PST

        (a) 'From the rich man, the beggar got his (i.e. the beggar's) money'

        *(b) 'From the rich man, the beggar got his (i.e. the rich man's) money'

Even though a subject NP is normally assigned nominative case, case marking cannot be used to define subject (or direct object, which is defined in the following section), since there are non-canonically-marked subjects and objects (§3.5.2). That is, strictly speaking, grammatical relation and case marking are mutually independent.

3.4.2. Direct object
Direct object is a grammatical relation in which the following characteris-tics cluster:

(A) PASSIVE SUBJECT: direct object may become subject in a passivised clause.

(B) SPECIAL TOPIC MARKING: only a direct object may be marked by a special topic marker *=ba(a)*, as opposed to a general (non-direct-ob-ject) topic *=a* (§9.5.1.1)

110   Chapter 3

Direct object is less easy to define than subject, as the availability of criterion (A) is heavily dependent on the transitivity of a verb. For example, in
the following transitive clause, the NP *hon* 'book' cannot be passivised.

(3–91)   *hon=nu=baa*   *jum-ta-m.*
         book=ACC=TOP   read-PST-RLS
         '(I) read the book.'
         **hon=na*   *jum-ai-ta-m.*
         book=TOP   read-PASS-PST-RLS
         [intended meaning] 'The book was read'

Also, passivisation is not the defining property of direct object, since an
indirect object may also be passivised (see the next section).

A more reliable criterion is (B). The NP *hon* above satisfies criterion (B),
as shown in the above example. Moreover, (B) is not applicable to indirect
objects as will be noted in the next section. The NP that satisfies criterion
(A) always satisfies criterion (B). However, since =ba cannot follow partitive =a (§4.3.3.8), the feature (B) may be related to morphological case
rather than grammatical relation.

3.4.3. Indirect object
There is no syntactic behaviour that justifies the postulation of indirect object as a grammatical relation. Rather, indirect object is defined with case
marking and semantic role: indirect object is a dative-marked or allative-marked NP that encodes recipient, goal, or in a causative, causee
agent.

(3–92)   *ukka=u=mai*   *tur-a-da,*   *ui=n*
         debt=ACC=even   take-THM-NEG.NRT   3SG=DAT
         fii-tar=ca.
         give-PST=HS
         '(He) did not take the debt, but gave (it) to him.'
(3–93)   *fini=kara=du*   *pžsara=nkai*   *kuruma=u*
         ship=ABL=FOC   Hirara=ALL   car=ACC
         ufïï-kutu.
         send-NPST.OBL
         '(I) am supposed to send a car to Hirara (place name) by ship.'
(3–94)   *nara=a*   *ah-u-da,*   *pžtu=nkai=du*
         RFL=TOP   do-THM-NEG.NRT   man=ALL=FOC
         sïgutu=u   *as-ïmi-tar=ca.*

Descriptive preliminaries   111

work=ACC   do-CAUS-PST=HS
'(It is said that he) did not do (the work), but told others to do the job.'

As noted in §3.4.2, an indirect object of a clause may be turned into the subject in a passivised clause. Thus, from the main clause of (3–94) above (i.e. *pžtu=nkai=du sïgutu=u as-ïmi-tar=ca*), it is possible to get the following passive sentence where the underlying indirect object is rearranged as the subject.

(3–95)   *pžtu=nu*   *sïgutu=u*   *as-ïmi-rai-tar=ca.*
         man=NOM   work=ACC   do-CAUS-PASS-PST=HS
         'A man was made to do a work, they say.' [cf. (3–94)]

3.5. Argument structure

3.5.1. Core, extended core, and peripheral arguments

In the layering of the clauses, a distinction is made between core arguments (S/A, O), extended core arguments (or 'extension to core'; E), and peripheral arguments (cf. Dixon 1994: 122–124; Dixon and Aikhenvald 2000: 3). As Irabu is a nominative-accusative language, it is unnecessary to distinguish between S and A, and I will instead refer to S/A. Core arguments are part of the argument structure of the verb and bear a grammatical relation to the verb (contributing to syntactic valence as well as semantic valence; Payne 1997: 170). Extended core arguments are also part of the argument structure of the verb but do not bear a grammatical relation to the verb (only contributing to semantic valence); peripheral arguments are not part of the argument structure of the verb (i.e. not required by the inherent meaning of the verb) and do not bear a grammatical relation to the verb.

TABLE 3–12. Core, extended core, and peripheral arguments

	Core	Extended core	Peripheral
	S/A, O	E	
Part of the argument structure	+	+	-
Grammatical relation	+	-	-
	subject	theme of 'become'	locative, etc.
	direct object	indirect object, etc.	

112   Chapter 3

TABLE 3–13. Transitivity and valency

Transitivity	Argument structure		
Intransitive	S		
Extended intransitive	S		E
Transitive	A	O	
Extended transitive	A	O	E
Syntactic valence	+	+	-
Semantic valence	+	+	+

3.5.2. Core arguments

Typically, nominative case is used for marking a subject NP, and accusative case for marking a direct object NP, as illustrated in (3–96). Usually, however, a subject NP is marked by the topic marker =a (or =u), which replaces the nominative case (3–97).

(3–96) *maju=nu*   *jumunu=u=du*   *tur-tar.*
        cat=NOM   mouse=ACC=FOC   catch-PST
        'A cat caught a mouse.'

(3–97) *maju=u*   *jumunu=u=du*   *tur-tar.*
        cat=TOP   mouse=ACC=FOC   catch-PST
        'The cat caught a mouse.'

There are two non-canonical constructions. One is the dative subject construction, as illustrated in (3–98), and the other is the partitive construction, as illustrated in (3–99).

(3–98) <u>*vva=n=na*</u>   *pžtu=nkai*   *naa=ga*   *tuz=zu=ba*
        2SG$_i$=DAT=TOP   man=ALL   RFL$_i$=GEN   wife=ACC=TOP
        fii-rai-r-m=mu?
        give-POT-NPST-RLS=Q
        'Can <u>you</u> give others your own wife?' [dative subject: controlling reflexive]

(3–99) <u>*budur=ra*</u>   *mii-Ø,*   *kagi+munu=i,*
        dance=PRT   look-NRT   beautiful(+thing)=CNF
        aparagi+munu=i=tii,   *uccja=du*   *a-tar.*
        beautiful(+thing)=CNF=QT   that.much=FOC   COP-PST
        'Watching <u>a dance</u>, (I thought like) "(It's) beautiful"; (it) was like that.'

The dative marking on subject is always triggered by the potential suffix

Descriptive preliminaries   113

-*(r)ai* on the verb, as shown in (3–98) above. Alternatively, the subject may be marked by nominative (which is replaced by the topic marker =*a* if the latter is present):

(3–100) *vva=a*   *pžtu=nkai*   *naa=ga*   *tuz=zu=ba*
         2SG$_i$=TOP   man=ALL   RFL$_i$=GEN   wife=ACC=TOP
         fii-rai-r-m=mu?
         give-POT-NPST-RLS=Q
         'Can <u>you</u> give others your own wife?' [dative subject: controlling reflexive]

The partitive marking on direct object mostly takes place in clause chaining constructions, as illustrated in (3–99) above (where the chained clause is marked by the narrative converb inflection). The partitive is almost always restricted to occurring in a narrative converbal clause, whose aspectual value (perfective vs. imperfective) is unmarked in the verb form. As will be noted in §4.3.3, the partitive helps disambiguate the aspectual distinction by occurring only in the imperfective narrative converbal clause.

3.5.3. Extended core arguments

Extended core arguments may appear both in intransitive and transitive clauses, constituting extended subtypes of each clause. In an extended intransitive clause, the E argument is required by such verbs as *nar* 'become', *atar* 'get hit by', and *av* 'meet'. In an extended transitive clause, the E argument is an indirect object NP. In either clause type, the E argument is dative-marked as an unmarked choice. In an extended transitive clause, however, the E argument may alternatively be marked by allative, which entails a physical movement of a patient to a recipient/goal.

3.5.3.1. The verb 'become'
The verb designating 'become' may be intransitive or extended intransitive, in that its semantically required element (i.e. the theme role) may be an E argument NP, which is not part of a predicate, or a VP complement, which is part of a predicate (§3.3.6.2). Thus from this verb either an extended intransitive clause or an intransitive clause is constructed.[6]

---

[6] The light verb *(a)sï* is similar in this regard: it may take an O argument, constructing a transitive clause, or a VP complement (§3.3.6.2), constructing an intransitive clause. Thus *budur=ru=du asï* '(I) do a dance' is a transitive clause where a noun *budur* 'dance' is a direct object NP, marked by accusative =*ru*. On the other hand, the light verb construction *budur=*

114   Chapter 3

(3–101) *kari=a*   *sinsii=n=du*   *nar-tar.*
         3SG=TOP   teacher=DAT=FOC   become-PST
         'He became a teacher.' [Extended intransitive containing an E
         argument]

(3–102) *kari=a*   *aparagi-fï=du*   *nar-tar.*
         3SG=TOP   beautiful-AVLZ=FOC   become-PST
         'He became beautiful' [Intransitive containing a VP comple-
         ment]

3.5.3.2. The verb 'get hit by'
The verb *atar* 'get hit by' requires two semantic arguments, (1) the one
who gets hit and (2) the thing that hits him. The former is coded as an S
argument, and the latter as an E argument (underlined).

(3–103) *tama=n*   *atar-i-i,*   *sïn-i-i*
         bullet=DAT   get.hit.by-THM-NRT   die-THM-NRT
         njaa-n.
         PRF-NPST
         '(He) got hit by a bullet, and has died.'

This dative-marked NP cannot be seen as a direct object, since it cannot be
passivised, or cannot be topic-marked by *=ba(a)* (§3.4.2). If it is topic-marked, it is marked by non-object topic *=a*.

(3–104) *tama=n=na*   *atar-tar=ruga,*
         bullet=DAT=TOP   get.hit.by-PST=but
         sïn-a-t-tar.
         die-THM-NEG-NPST
         '(He) got hit by a bullet, but did not die.' [topic: contrastive
         reading]

3.5.3.3. The verb 'meet'
The verb *av* 'meet' requires two semantic arguments, (1) the one who
meets someone, and (2) the one who is met by him. The (1) is coded as an
S argument, and the (2) as an E argument (underlined).

(3–105) *ssjugacï=tii*   *ik-i-i,*   *ujaku-mmi=n*

---

du=sï (where the verb root *budur* '(to) dance' is zero-converted to serve as a VP complement)
is an intransitive clause.

Obon.festival=QT	go-THM-NRT	relative-PL=DAT

av-Ø=dara.
meet-NPST=CRTN
'When it comes to the Obon festival, (we) go (to the relatives'
place) and meet the relatives.'

This dative-marked NP cannot be seen as a direct object, since it cannot be passivised, or cannot be topic-marked by =*ba*(*a*) (§3.4.2). If it is topic-marked, then it is marked by non-object topic =*a*.

(3–106) *ujaku-mmi=n=na*   *a-a-t-ta-m.*
          relative-PL=DAT=TOP   meet-THM-NEG-PST-RLS
          'As for the relatives, (I) didn't meet (them).'

3.5.3.4. Indirect object

In an extended transitive clause, the E argument is an indirect object NP, and is marked by dative case as the unmarked choice. However, it may be marked by allative case if the speaker focuses on, or emphasises the fact that the event described involves movement of the patient/theme towards the recipient/goal (§4.3.4). The transitive verbs that take an E argument are *fiir* 'give', *ufïï* 'send', and verbs derived from transitive verbs by morphological causative.

(3–107) a. *ba=a*   *kai=n=du*   *zin=nu*   *fii-tar.*
              1SG=TOP   3SG=DAT=FOC   money=ACC   give-PST
              'I gave him/her money.' [unmarked choice: dative marking]
          b. *ba=a*   *kai=nkai=du*   *zin=nu*   *fii-tar.*
              1SG=TOP   3SG=ALL=FOC   money=ACC   give-PST
              'I gave him/her money.' [marked: movement of the theme is
              emphasised]

(3–108) a. *ba=a*   *sinsii=n*   *nengazjoo=ju=du*
              1SG=TOP   teacher=DAT   new.year.card=ACC=FOC
              ufïï-tar.
              send-PST
              'I sent a New Year card to (my) teacher.' [unmarked choice:
              dative   marking]
          b. *ba=a*   *sinsii=nkai*   *nengazjoo=ju=du*
              1SG=TOP   teacher=ALL   new.year.card=ACC=FOC
              ufïï-tar.
              send-PST

116 Chapter 3

'I sent a new year card to (my) teacher.' [marked: movement
of the theme   is emphasised]

(3–109) *ba=a*   *kai=n=du*   *pisïr=ru*
1SG=TOP   3SG=DAT=FOC   lunch=ACC
cïff-asï-tar.
make-CAUS-PST
'I made him prepare lunch.'

3.5.4. Peripheral arguments

Peripheral arguments encode various optional semantic roles such as instrument (3–110), spatial-temporal limit (3–111), accompaniment (3–112),
locative (3–113), goal (3–114), and source (3–115).

(3–110) *karï=a*   *fïcï=sii*   *icu=u*   *kir-tar.*
3SG=TOP   mouth=INST   thread=ACC   cut-PST
'S/he cut thread with his/her mouth.' [instrumental][7]

(3–111) *aca=gami*   *ur-i.*
tomorrow=LMT   exist-IMP
'Stay until tomorrow.' [limit]

(3–112) *agu-mmi=tu*   *asuv-tar.*
friend-PL=ASC   play-PST
'(I) played with friends.' [accompaniment]

(3–113) *ba=a*   *uma=n*   *žžu=u*   *cïï-ta-m.*
1SG=TOP   that.place=DAT   fish=ACC   catch-PST-RLS
'I got fish at that place.' [locative]

(3–114) *gakkoo=nkai=du*   *ifï-tar.*
school=ALL=FOC   go-PST
'(He) went to school.' [goal]

(3–115) *im=kara*   *sïdasï+kazi=nu*   *idi-i*   *fïï-Ø.*
sea=ABL   cool+wind=NOM   come.out-NRT   come-NPST
'Cool wind comes through from the sea.' [source]

It is sometimes difficult to draw a clear line between an E argument,
which is an NP whose referent is part of the argument structure of the verb,
and a peripheral argument, whose referent is not part of the argument
structure of the verb, given that this distinction is semantic. For example,

---

[7] In Irabu, the instrumental subject construction (e.g. 'The teeth cut the thread' or 'The key
opened the door') is not allowed. Rather, the verbs *kir* 'cut' and *akir* 'open' require an agent
and a patient/theme, which are coded as an A argument and an O argument respectively (in
active voice).

Descriptive preliminaries 117

the deictic directional verb *ifi* 'go' in (3–114) might be argued to have its goal argument NP as part of the argument structure, and the verb *idii* 'come out' in (3–115) might also be argued to have its source argument NP as part of the argument structure.

However, what is important is the fact that in terms of *syntactic* valence, E arguments and peripheral arguments are not part of the syntactic valence of the verb, and that in terms of *semantic* valence, there is a continuum between prototypical peripheral arguments (such as an instrumental NP (3–110)) and prototypical core arguments, and along this continuum lie the arguments which are more or less relevant to the event that a verb describes. Among such intermediate cases, there are NPs that are, as an unmarked choice, coded as dative NPs, which I refer to an E argument.[8] I limit the use of the E argument only insofar as such a notion is useful in describing valency (changing) phenomena. For example, it is clear that the theme argument of the verb 'become' must be stated in a semantically well-formed sentence. Thus it cannot be simply grouped under the 'peripheral argument' on the basis of the fact that it does not bear a grammatical relation, as it is semantically required. Thus I introduce the notion E argument to explicate this distinction. Also, the causee agent is better characterised as an E argument rather than simply as a peripheral argument, as this formulation allows us to generalise that the causative operation is to increase (semantic) valence.

3.6. Morphological typology

A word may consist minimally of a root, but may be morphologically complex. There are three major types of processes that produce morphologically complex structures: affixation (§3.6.1), compounding (§3.6.2) and full reduplication (§3.6.3). Affixation is attachment of a non-root bound morpheme within a word, whereas compounding and full reduplication involves two (or more) roots, where reduplication consists of $root_i$ + $root_i$, and compounding consists of $root_i$ + $root_j$.

3.6.1. Affixation
Affixation in Irabu is suffixation. Even though there are a few cases in which a verb appears to contain a prefix-like element, e.g. *pic-* 'off' in *pic-*

---

[8] This narrow definition of an E argument is cross-linguistically plausible as well. For example, Dixon and Aikhenvald (2000: 3) argue that extended intransitives and extended transitives are greatly outnumbered by plain intransitives and transitives. Also, they generalise that an E argument is dative-marked (if such a case is available).

118   Chapter 3

cjafï 'tear apart' and *pic-cïï* 'pluck away', the prefix-like element is highly lexicalized and has no productive use. Thus *pic-* above is only observed in the above-mentioned words. Diachronically, such prefix-like elements must have developed from compound stems (e.g. *pic-* can be traced back to a verb stem whose contemporary form is *pžk-*).

On the other hand, there are a few cases in which a compound stem shows prefix-like characteristics, though it is argued that they are stems rather than affixes. For example, *mi-* 'female' is always bound and always appears before another stem, thus looks like a prefix only in these regards. However, there is evidence that *mi-* is a compound stem: it is always lengthened to satisfy the minimality constraint (*mi-* + *uttu* 'younger sibling' > *mii+uttu* 'younger sister').[9] The obligatory lengthening is observed in each stem of a productive compound (§2.10) but is never found in affixes.

3.6.2. Compounding

Compounding is a morphological process whereby two (or more) roots are connected to form a single word stem. In many cases a compound is made up of two roots, though longer compounds as shown below are also well attested in free texts in my data. Examples (3–119) and (3–120a, b) have clause-like syntax in the compound structure, as if it were a structure consisting of an adnominal clause and a head nominal, though, as will be shown in §3.6.2.2, it is easy to distinguish between a compound word and a phrase.

(3–116)   *uku+bata+giin+sinsii*
              big+belly+congress.man+gentleman
              'Mr. big belly congress man'

(3–117)   *umukutu+nkjaan+banasï*
              implicational+old.days+talk
              'implicational folktale'

(3–118)   *agar+patiruma+baka+aza*
              east+Hateruma+young+big.brother
              'The Brother East Hateruma' [legendary person]

(3–119)   *juu+fau+busï*
              dinner+eating+star
              'the star that is observed in evening'

(3–120)   a. *waa+kurusï+bžž*

---

[9] There is a fossilized compound *mi-* + *-dum* 'person' > *mi+dum* 'woman'. This is not treated as a compound since the second stem is not used in other contexts, i.e. is only used when combining with *mi-* 'female' or *biki-* 'male'. I treat *midum* and *bikidum* as single morphemes.

Descriptive preliminaries 119

pig+killing+day
'New Year's Eve'
b. *asi+idi+pžtu*
sweat+coming.out+man
'person who tends to have a lot of sweat'

In what follows I mostly focus on more frequently observed two-root compounds and their general characteristics.

3.6.2.1. Structure

The possible patterns for two-root compounds are listed below, where lower case n, v, and pc represent nominal, verb, and PC roots respectively, and the upper case N, V, and PC represent derived nominal, verbal, and PC stems respectively. Of the logically possible nine combinations, two are unattested: pc-v and v-pc. The verb root must be converted into a nominal stem when followed by a nominal root, as is indicated by v > N (see §6.3.4.5 for this morphophonemics).

(3–121)

Root 1	Root 2	Stem	Example	Frequency
n	n	N	*midum+vva* woman+child 'daughter'	High
n	v >N	N	*munu+kacï* thing+writing 'writing'	High
v >N	n	N	*pataracï+munu* working+man 'hard worker'	High
v	v	V	*jum+pazïmi-r* read+start-NPST 'start to read'	High
pc	n	N	*aparagi+midum* beautiful+woman 'beautiful woman'	High
n	pc	PC	*cïmu+daka* heart+high 'difficult (person)'	Low

120   Chapter 3

pc   pc   PC   *uku+naga*   Low
                                     big+long
                                     'big and long'

3.6.2.2. The word (as opposed to phrasal) status of the compound

As noted in §2.10, there are two kinds of compound: (1) productive compounds and (2) lexicalised compounds. Most compounds are of type (1), with a compositional semantic structure and derived by a highly productive process of word formation. In productive compounds, each stem is a phonological word. This type of compound is exemplified in (3–122) to (3–124) below. On the other hand, as is illustrated in (3–125), there are just a few compounds which are lexicalized in meaning and are derived from an unproductive word formation process, and an entire compound behaves as a phonological word.

(3–122) a. *biki+kjavdai*   b. *biki+uttu*   c. *biki+vva*
             male+sibling   male+younger.sibling   male+child
             'brother'   'younger brother'   'son'
(3–123) a. *uku+pžtu*   b. *uku+jaa*   c. *uku+gan*
             big+man   big+house   big+crab
             'big man'   'big house'   'big crab'
(3–124) a. *mi+gaa*   b. *sïba+gaa*   c. *mim+gaa*
             eye+skin   lip+skin   ear+skin
             'eye ridge'   'skin around lips'   'earlap'
(3–125) a. *mi+pana*   b. *irav+cï*   c. *aka+ccir*
             eye+nose   Irabu+mouth   red+pipe
             'face'   'the Irabu language'   'angry person'

All compounds are distinguished from phrases by the potential presence of sequential voicing (§2.7.1). Furthermore, a given compound, whether it be a productive or lexicalised one, cannot be broken up by the insertion of another word, whereas a phrase can.

To avoid circularity, let us use the adnominal *unu* 'that (medial)', which is independently justifiable as a word (see §3.2.1.2 for justification). Now, if a constituent A+B is an NP, it is possible for an adnominal word to be inserted between A and B, as in:

(3–126) *banti=ga*   *jaa*   >   *banti=ga*   *unu*   *jaa*
             1PL=GEN   house   1PL=GEN   that   house

Descriptive preliminaries   121

'our house'   'that house of ours'

On the other hand, if A+B constitute a compound, then the insertion is disallowed, as in:

(3–127)   *uku+jaa*   >   *uku- *unu* -jaa
              big+house   big- that -house
              'big house'   'that big house' [intended meaning]

Here, if the stem *uku-* 'big' is reduplicated to become an adjective (i.e. if the compound is transformed into an NP), the insertion becomes possible, as in:

(3–128)   *ukuu+uku=nu*   *unu*   *jaa*
              RED+big=GEN   that   house
              'that big house'

In (3–120a) we observed that the compound *waa+kurusï+bžž* (pig+killing+day) 'New Year's Eve' shows a clause-like syntax within the compound. Here, the final stem undergoes sequential voicing (*pžž* > *bžž*), thus the construct is clearly a compound. Also, no word can intervene between the two boundaries between the three stems. If it is actually turned into a phrase, then the insertion of a word becomes possible (or, the insertion of a word turns it into a phrase):

(3–129)   a. *waa=ju*   *kurusï-Ø*   *pžž*
                pig=ACC   kill-NPST   day
                'The day when (one) kills a pig.' [NOT New Year's eve]
           b. *waa=ju*   *kurusï-Ø*   *unu*   *pžž*
                pig=ACC   kill-NPST   that   day
                'That day when (one) kills a pig.' [NOT New Year's eve]

Note that *waa* now carries accusative case, as it is a direct object NP, and that the sequential voicing is absent in the final stem *pžž*, which is now a head nominal word of an NP. Also, since it is a phrase, its semantics is compositional, unlike its compound counterpart *waa+kurusï+bžž* 'New Year's eve'.

3.6.3. Full reduplication

Reduplication in Irabu is mostly full reduplication. There are just a few examples of partial reduplication: *niv* 'sleep' > *ni-niv* 'snooze', *maar* 'around (n)' > *ma-maar* 'around (n)'. These attested examples indicate that the partial reduplication targets the stem-initial mora, rather than the stem-initial syllable (**niv-niv* or **maar-maar*).

There are two major types of full reduplication: PC stem reduplication, which creates an adjective (3–130), and verbal reduplication, which creates an adverb (3–131). These two can be distinguished by the fact that in PC stem reduplication the final phoneme of the input stem is lengthened by one mora.

(3–130) PC stem reduplication

Input stem	Output word
taka-	*takaa+taka* 'high'
pjaa-	*pjaaa+pjaa* 'fast'
zau-	*zauu+zau* 'good'
kiban-	*kibann+kiban* 'poor'
mm-	*mmm-mm* 'similar'

(3–131) Verbal reduplication

Input stem	Output word
asï- 'do'	*asï+asï* 'do iteratively; do as a custom'
mii- 'look'	*mii+mii* 'stare'
kair- 'turn round'	kair+kair 'turn round iteratively'
vv- 'sell'	*vv+vv* 'sell iteratively: sell as a custom'

Chapter 4

The nominal phrase

This chapter sets out to describe the syntactic structure and function of nominal phrases (NPs).[1] An NP consists of a phrasal modifier and a head, which is followed by a case marker as an extension to an NP. The head is the minimal NP. Thus we recognise an extended NP structure consisting of an NP + case marker. NPs function either as clausal modifier (argument), clausal head (nominal predicate), or as phrasal modifier (i.e. as a genitive-marked NP), as exemplified below.

(4–1) *naa=ga*   *ffa=u=mai=du*   *saar-i-i*
       oneself=GEN   child=ACC=too=FOC   take-THM-NRT
       ifi-tar.
       go-PST
       '(They) took their own child, too.' [NP as direct object]

(4–2) *kaun*   *pžtu=u*   *mmja*   *mazïmunu=dooi*
       that   man=TOP   INTJ   monster=EMP
       'That person is in fact a monster.' [NP as nominal predicate]

(4–3) *naa=ga*   *ffa=nu*   *naa=ju=mai*
       oneself=GEN   child=GEN   name=ACC=even
       ss-a-da...
       know-THM-NEG.NRT
       'Not knowing his own child's name...' [NP as phrasal modifier]

The extended NP structure is schematised in terms of its functional slots in (4–4) below. The head is obligatory, though there is a headless adnominal clause structure where the head slot is empty (§4.2.2). The modifier is optional. The head and the modifier constitute the core of the NP, and is followed by its extension, i.e. case.

(4–4) (Modifier)   Head   =Case

---

[1] The structure and subclass of nominal will be dealt with in Chapter 5. I discuss the nominal phrase first because the subclassification of nominal in Irabu is defined in relation to NP structure, and the structure of a nominal word is in turn dependent on the subclass of nominal, whereas NP structure can be defined without reference to subclasses of nominal.

124 Chapter 4

The occurrence and choice of the case marker vary, depending on the syntactic function of the NP (see below). Case is obligatory unless an NP functions as nominal predicate, or unless there is case ellipsis (§4.3.10.3), which may occur with core argument NPs (subject and direct object).

At a clause-level, an extended NP in an argument slot may be further followed by various limiter markers such as the additive quantifier =*mai* 'too' and/or information-structure markers such as the focus marker =*du*, as is illustrated in (4–1). Also, an extended NP as predicate may be followed by predicate markers (e.g. =*dooi* (emphasis) in (4–2)). These bound markers will be described in Chapter 9.

4.1. The modifier

The modifier of an NP may be filled by an NP itself (including an NP headed by an adjective), an adnominal (clause), or other limited constructions.

4.1.1. Modifier filled by NP

The modifier NP carries a genitive case marker as its extension, without respect to whether the modifier is a noun, pronoun, interrogative, indefinite, or numeral (see Chapter 5 for a detailed description of subclasses of nominals). The semantic relationship between the modifier NP and the head is not limited to possession, but includes whole-part relation, attribution, and number specification (where the modifier NP is a headed by a numeral word). Some representative examples follow.

(4–5) a. *vva=ga*   *ffa*
   2SG=GEN   child
   'your child' [possession: modifier as a pronoun]

  b. *taru=nu*   *ffa?*
   who=GEN   child
   'Whose child?' [possession: modifier as an interrogative]

  c. *taugagara=nu* *ffa*
   someone=GEN child
   'someone's child' [possession: modifier as an indefinite]

(4–6) *vva=ga*   *jaa*
  2SG=GEN   house
  'your house' [possession]

(4–7) *kii=nu*   *juda*
  tree=GEN   branch
  'Tree's branch' [whole-part relation]

The nominal phrase   125

(4–8)   irav=nu   pžtu
        Irabu=GEN   man
        'A man from Irabu' [attributive]
(4–9)   vva=ga   panasï
        2SG=GEN   talk
        'your talk' or 'a talk about you' [attributive or 'about' relation]
(4–10) giin=nu   zjunji+sinsii
        congressman=GEN   Junji+gentleman
        'Mr. Junji, a congressman' [appositional]
(4–11) mž-taar=nu   pžtu
        three-CLF.HUMAN=GEN   man
        'three men' [number specification]

As is shown in (4–5) and (4–6), there is no formal distinction between alienable and inalienable possession in Irabu. General attributive modification in which the modifying NP describes an unidentified NP by attributing some property on it, as in 'a man from Irabu', 'a foreign person', and so on, is encoded more often by compounding, which also accounts for the bulk of property concept modification as in *imi+gan* 'small+crab: a small crab' (§8.3.4). Thus (4–8) is preferably restated as *irav+pžtu* 'Irabu man'.

Along with the fact that a modifier NP may be headed by a numeral word (which is a subclass of nominal in Irabu; see §5.2.3), it is noted that a modifier NP may be headed by an adjective (§8.2). Thus, as exemplified in (4–12) below, an adjective as a modifier NP carries genitive case, as in the case of other modifier NPs as noted above.[2]

(4–12) takaa+taka=nu   pžtu=nu=du   ur-Ø.
        RED+high=GEN   man=NOM=FOC   exist-NPST
        '(There) is a tall man.'

4.1.2. Modifier filled by adnominal

The modifier slot may be filled by an adnominal word (§3.3.2; §5.4) or an adnominal clause (§11.4.3). See §3.3.2 for cases where an adnominal word fills the modifier slot. As a clausal equivalent of an adnominal word, an adnominal clause does not carry any case when filling the modifier slot, just like an adnominal word.

Under the term 'adnominal clause' are subsumed both relative clauses, where an argument within an adnominal clause is grammatically related to

---

[2] See §4.1.4 for a discussion in favour of the analysis that an adjective really heads an NP.

126   Chapter 4

an NP head (i.e. relativised), and other kinds of 'simple attributive' clause,
where no argument within an adnominal clause is grammatically related to
the head. As will be discussed shortly, the distinction between these two
clause types is not fundamental in Irabu grammar. Thus I continue to refer
to the single category 'adnominal clause'.

Structurally, an adnominal clause cannot carry genitive case, but the
predicate verb of the adnominal clause must inflect for the finite unmarked
form (§6.3.1).

(4–13)   *sïn-tar*   *pžtu=nu*   *paka=kara*   *idi-i*   *fï-Ø*.
         die-PST   man=NOM   grave=ABL   exit-NRT   come-NPST
         'A man (who) died will come out of the grave.' [S relativized]

(4–14)   *unu*   *kiban+pžtu=nu*   *nara-asï-tar*   *munu,*
         that   poor+man=NOM   learn-CAUS-PST   thing
         uri=u   *nara-a-dakaa*   *nau=n=mai=du*
         that=ACC   learn-THM-NEG.CND   what=DAT=even=FOC
         nar-i+ufï-Ø=pazï.   *kari=a.*
         become-THM+PRF-NPST=maybe   3SG=TOP
         'The thing (that) that person taught, if (he) hadn't learnt it, (he)
         would have become whatever (bad person he would become),
         maybe.' [O relativized]

(4–15)   *žžu=u*   *jafï-Ø*   *kaagi=nu=du*   *fï-Ø*.
         fish=ACC   burn-NPST   smell=NOM=FOC   come-NPST
         '(There) comes a smell (that) (someone) burns fish.' [simple
         attributive]

(4–16)   *ami* *fï-Ø*   *tukja=n=na*   *bannja=nkai*   *par-kutu.*
         rain   fall-NPST   time=DAT=TOP   field.hut=ALL   leave-OBL
         'In case it rains, (we) are supposed to go to the field hut.' [simple
         attributive]

The syntactic distinction between relative clause and non-relative simple
attributive clause is not fundamental in Irabu grammar. That is, in Irabu
adnominal clauses, whether the head of the NP modified by an adnominal
clause has a role in the clause is not a relevant strategy in encoding the
modificational relationship between the adnominal clause and the head,
and the two elements (adnominal clause and the head) are simply juxtaposed, and much is left to inference. See §11.4.3 for a more detailed discussion to support this claim that there is no categorical distinction between a simple attributive clause and a relative clause. In this grammar,
therefore, both kinds of clause are loosely subsumed under the term 'ad-

The nominal phrase   127

nominal clause'.

4.1.3. Modifier filled by other syntactic constructions
There are expressions where constructions other than an NP or an adnominal clause fill the NP modifier slot. Here, the quotative nominalizing marker =ti(i) serves as an important means to put various sorts of construction into the modifier slot. That is, these constructions are turned into NPs by quotation embedding. The constructions with =ti(i) carry genitive case just as normal NPs do.

(4–17) *nau=ti=nu*   *munu=u=ga*   *bannja=ti*
        what=QT=GEN   thing=ACC=FOC   field.hut=QT
        až-Ø=ga?
        say-NPST=FOC
        'What kind of thing (do you) refer to as *bannja*?'

(4–18) *taru=nu*   *ah-u-ba=mai*   *zjaubu=ti=nu*
        who=NOM   do-THM-CND=even   alright=QT=GEN
        munu=dara.
        thing=EMP
        '(This) is like a thing that anyone can do.'

Another very common example involving quotative =ti(i) is a structure in which the NP modifier is filled by a property concept stem followed by =ti(i):

(4–19) *ujakii=ti=nu*   *pžtu*   *mjaaku+pžtu,*
        rich=QT=GEN   man   Miyako+man
        kibann=ti=nu   *pžtu*   *irav+pžtu*   *a-tar=ca.*
        poor=QT=GEN   man   Irabu+man   COP-PST=HS
        '(Of the two) the rich was a man from Miyako, (while) the poor was a man from Irabu.'

As will be fully accounted for in §8.1, property concept stems are bound forms that cannot head a phrase, and require various word formation processes to become an adjective, a nominal, a verb, or an adverb. In addition to these, as was illustrated in (4–19), the quotation strategy may be employed, by which otherwise bound property concept stems are put into the NP modifier slot with the help of the embedding function of =ti(i) (see §11.4.4.1 for quotative constructions). Note that property concept stems here involve a morphophonemic lengthening of the root-final mora (*ujaki*

128   Chapter 4

>*ujakii, kiban* > *kibann*).

4.1.4. The semantic characteristic of genitive

As noted in §4.1.1, in addition to possession, Irabu genitive marks general attribution (4–8, 4–9), number specification (4–11), and adjectival attribution (4–12).[3] So, the question might be raised whether this modifier marker is really a genitive case marker, which usually marks a possessor NP. Some would argue that it is a different kind of modifying marker, like *de* in Chinese and *ng* in Philippine languages, which occurs between most modifiers of nouns and the noun (or a sequence of NPs). This alternative analysis would let us avoid the typologically unusual situation where an adjective heads an NP, a situation that naturally results from the genitive case analysis (i.e. since an adjective carries a case marker, it should head an NP).[4]

However, there are two independent arguments for analysing Irabu genitive as such, and against the alternative analysis suggested above.

First, there is strong evidence that the genitive marker should be treated as a case marker. In Irabu, the genitive marker has two forms =*ga* and =*nu*, either of which is chosen based on the semantic property of the head of the NP to which it is attached (see below), and the same set of forms is found in nominative case.

(4–20)   a. *vva=ga*   *uttu=ga=du*   *asï-tar.*
             2SG=GEN   younger.sibling=NOM=FOC   do-PST
             '(It was) Your younger sibling (who) did (it).'
         b. *irav=nu*   *im=nu=du*   *icïban.*
             Irabu=GEN   sea=NOM=FOC   best
             'The sea of Irabu is the best.'

The crucial issue here is that what I treat as the nominative case marker and the genitive case marker are arguably analysable as the same morpheme, and that it is inappropriate to treat one as a linker (a non-case-marking, modifier-marking morpheme) and the other as a case marker. Rather, both are simply a single case marker. One strong piece of evidence for the same morpheme analysis is that the set of forms in both nominative and genitive follows the identical alternation pattern: generally speaking, a pronoun, a proper name, a kinship term, and a definite human common noun are marked with =*ga*, whereas the others are marked with =*nu* (see

---

[3] And this is true for the genitive case of Japonic languages in general.
[4] This alternative solution was suggested by an anonymous reviewer of the original thesis.

The nominal phrase 129

§4.3.2 for detail). Even though the existing typological wisdom cannot capture the Irabu phenomenon properly, the Irabu case system treats an NP that serves as a phrasal dependent (i.e. NP modifier) and a primary clausal dependent (i.e. subject in this nominative-accusative language) as a single group, and marks them with the same case. I distinguish the phrasal dependent marker and the clausal dependent marker by calling the former genitive case marker and the latter nominative case marker, following the generally accepted conventions in linguistic typology, but I do not want to consider them to be different morphemes.[5]

A second reason to stick to my genitive case analysis as opposed to the linker analysis is that the adjective class in Irabu is in fact highly nominal in nature (as is usual in many languages), so that it is not disquieting to assume that it may head an NP in the first place. As noted in §3.3.4, the adjective class can be distinguished both from nominals and from verbs by the morphological criterion of reduplication of a bound PC stem or a nominal stem (*taka-* 'high' > *takaa+taka* 'high'; jarabi 'child' > *jarabii+jarabi* 'childish'). An adjective thus defined is syntactically 'parasitic', occurring in NP structure or in VP structure (see §3.3.4). However, its occurrence in a VP is highly limited both in function and in frequency, and an adjective most typically occurs in NP structure (see §8.2.2). Furthermore, an adjective may carry the diminutive affix *-gama* (§8.2.1.1), which is a nominal derivational affix (§5.3.1). Given these, then, it is quite clear that the adjective class in Irabu aligns with nominals morphosyntactically. This highly nominal nature of the adjective class would be blurred if we introduced an ad-hoc category called 'linker' only to avoid the seemingly odd situation that an adjective heads an NP. In fact, this situation is harmonious with the nominal features of the adjective class as noted above, and should be described explicitly.

4.2. The head

The head is filled by a minimal NP (the nominal word) or an internally complex NP. A head nominal may be any subclass of nominal.

Even though there is no peculiar NP structure depending on the type of

---

[5] As an anonymous reviewer rightly points out, treating the nominative =*nu*/=*ga* and the genitive =*nu*/=*ga* as separate morphemes is like treating the object case after the verb and the object case after the preposition as separate cases in English, an analysis that would confuse the form and the syntactic function associated with the form. In dealing with the nominative and the genitive in Irabu, it is emphasised that they are not separate morphemes and that the same case form marks two different syntactic functions of an NP.

130   Chapter 4

the head, there are three cases that deserve special attention with regard to
the syntax of NP: (1) a formal noun head, (2) a headless NP, and (3) an appositional structure in which an NP consists of the modifier + complex NP
head with the two slots being semantically appositional.

4.2.1. Formal nouns

A formal noun is a nominal with an abstract meaning which is the syntactic
head of an NP containing an adnominal clause. The noun has a special
grammatical function, a function similar to a complementiser ('that' in English) or a conjunctive marker ('when', etc.). Although such nouns are on a
diachronic pathway toward becoming clitics, many of them are still also in
use as words. The degree of grammaticalisation varies depending on the
transparency of their lexical meaning (which is in turn related to how productively the form in question is used as a nominal) and on their phonological dependency (§3.2.2). In what follows I first describe free formal
nouns, then a bound formal noun.

4.2.1.1. *tukja* 'time'
This noun literally expresses 'time' (4–21), but when it serves as a head of
an NP modified by an adnominal clause (4–22), it functions like conjunctive 'when' (see §9.2.1 for a true conjunctive *=kja(a)* 'when').

(4–21) *sjensoo=nu   tukja=n=na   nausi=ga   ffa-mmi=u*
       war=GEN   time=DAT=TOP   how=FOC   child-PL=ACC
       sudati-tar=ga?
       grow-PST=Q
       'In the time of war, how (did you) grow children?'

(4–22) *sjensuu=nu   cuu-fï   nar-Ø   tukja=n=na*
       war=NOM   strong-AVLZ   become-NPST   time=DAT=TOP
       taiwan=kai=ja   ik-ah-a-t-ta-m=mu?
       Taiwan=ALL=TOP   go-CAUS-THM-NEG-PST-RLS=Q
       'When the war became severe, (did the government) not make
       (people) move to Taiwan?'

4.2.1.2. *mai* 'front; before'
This noun literally expresses 'front' (4–23), but when it serves as a head of
an NP modified by an adnominal clause, it functions like conjunctive 'before' (4–24).

(4–23) *vva=ga   jaa=nu   mai=n   pžtu=nu=du*

The nominal phrase   131

    2SG=GEN   house=GEN   front=DAT   man=NOM=FOC
    u-tar.
    exist-PST
    'In front of your house, (there) was a man.'

(4–24)   *cïfi-Ø*   *mai=n=du*   *denwa*   *ah-u-di.*
        arrive-NPST   before=DAT=FOC   phone   do-THM-INT
        'Before (I) arrive, (I) will make a call.'

4.2.1.3. *atu* 'back; after'

This noun literally expresses 'back; after' (4–25), but when it serves as a head of an NP modified by an adnominal clause, it functions like conjunctive 'after' (4–26).

(4–25)   *sjensoo=nu*   *atu=n=na*   *haikjuu=ja*
        war=GEN   after=DAT=TOP   rationing=TOP
        njaa-t-tar?
        not.exist-NEG-PST
        'After the war, wasn't (there) rationing?'

(4–26)   *agu=nu*   *pjar-tar*   *atu=n=na*
        friend=NOM   leave-PST   after=DAT=TOP
        sabicï-kar-Ø=ruda.
        lonely-VLZ-NPST=AD.ASR
        'After (your) friend has left, (you) feel lonely, don't you?'

4.2.1.4. *kutu* 'thing; fact'

This noun literally expresses 'thing' (4–27), but when it serves as a head of an NP modified by an adnominal clause, it functions like the English complementiser '(the fact) that' (4–28).

(4–27)   *ai=nu*   *kutu=u=gami=a*   *bassi-i*
        that.way=GEN   thing=ACC=LMT=TOP   forget-NRT
        njaa-n.
        PRF-NPST
        '(I) have forgot the things like that.'

(4–28)   *tuz=zu*   *muc-i+ur-Ø=kutu=u=mai*
        wife=ACC   have-THM+PROG-NPST=COMP=ACC=even
        bassi-i=du   *ur-Ø.*
        forget-NRT=FOC   PROG-NPST
        '(He) has forgot even the fact that (he) has a wife.'

132   Chapter 4

4.2.1.5. *tami* 'purpose; benefit'

This noun literally expresses 'purpose' or 'benefit' (4–29), but when it
serves as a head of an NP modified by an adnominal clause, it is often followed by dative case =*n*, and functions like a purposive adverbial clause
conjunction 'in order to' (4–30).

(4–29) *vva=ga*   *tami=n=du*
         2SG=GEN   benefit=DAT=FOC
         patarak-i+ur-Ø=ca.
         work-THM+PROG-NPST=HS
         '(He said he) works for your benefit.'

(4–30) *daigaku=nkai*   *gookaku*   *asï-Ø*   *tami=n*
         University=ALL   pass   do-NPST   purpose=DAT
         jobikoo=tii=mai   *ik-asï-Ø.*   *taka+dai=dooi.*
         prep.school=QT=too   go-CAUS-NPST costly+price=EMP
         'In order that (she) will pass (entrance examination of) the uni-
         versity, (her parents) make her go to prep-school. (That's) cost-
         ly.'

4.2.1.6. *jau* 'state'

This noun has the abstract meaning 'state', and I have not been able to find
an example in which *jau* is used in other constructions than an adnominal
clause. Furthermore, it is always followed by the dative case, and functions
as a subordinating conjunctive encoding 'so that; in order (for someone)
to'.

(4–31) *mazïmunu=nu*   *parr-i-i*
         evil.spirit=NOM   go-THM-NRT
         kuu-n-Ø=jau=n
         come-NEG-NPST=state=DAT
         maasu   *rri-i*   *zau=n=du*   *nci-r=dara.*
         salt   put-NRT   gate=DAT=FOC   put-NPST=EMP
         'So as not for the evil spirit to come, (we) put salt (into a bucket
         of water), and put (the bucket) in front of the gate.'

The fact that *jau* is not used as a noun nor does it combine with different
case markers suggests that the morpheme is becoming more and more like
a conjunction rather than a nominal.

The nominal phrase   133

4.2.1.7. *njaa* 'manner'

njaa has the meaning 'a way; a manner', and mostly occurs with the dative marker =*n*.

(4–32) vva=ga   njaa=n=na   as-irai-n-Ø=suga.
        2SG=GEN   manner=DAT=TOP   do-POT-NEG-NPST=but
        '(I) cannot do like you, though.' [lit. (I) cannot do in your way.]

When *njaa* heads an NP modified by an adnominal clause, it functions as a subordinating conjunctive 'in the way; as'.

(4–33) ba=ga   asï-Ø   njaa=n   vva=mai   as-i.
        1SG=NOM   do-NPST   manner=DAT   2SG=too   do-IMP
        'Do (that) as I do.'

4.2.1.8. *su(u)*

This noun is a bound word (§3.2.3.2), designating a non-referential or mass entity 'thing, man, that which, those which, one who, those who, etc'.[6] As a bound word it must attach to the preceding element, but it functions like a free word in that it heads an NP. Note that *su(u)* is realised as *ru(u)* when following /r/ (§2.7.7.2).

(4–34) taja=nu   ar-Ø   ruu=nu=du   masï.
        strength=NOM   exist-NPST   men=NOM=FOC   better
        'Those who are strong are better.'

(4–35) sïn-i-i   par-Ø   ruu   mmja
        die-THM-NRT   leave-NPST   men   INTJ
        son=saa=i.
        no.profit=R.EMP=CNF
        'Those who died out, you know, get no profit.'

(4–36) sacï=n   fau-tar   ru=kara   kama=nkai
        earlier=DAT   eat-PST   men=ABL   that.place=ALL
        ik-i.
        go-IMP
        'Those who have eaten earlier should go there.'

It is clear from the above examples that *su(u)* is a nominal as it heads the

---

[6] *su(u)* in Irabu has cognates in Northern Ryukyuan and in some Japanese varieties, with similar semantic and syntactic characteristics (Shinzato 2011)

NP. In fact, the bound noun can be replaced by another free nominal word. Compare, for example, (4–34) with the following, where the head NP is filled by a free word *pžtu* 'man':

(4–37) *taja=nu*   *ar-Ø*   *pžtu=nu=du*   *masï.*
        strength=NOM   exist-NPST   man=NOM=FOC   better
        'A man who is strong is better.'

In addition to the fact that *su(u)* cannot stand alone, there is a prosodic characteristic such that the final grammatical word of an adnominal clause predicate + *su(u)* is treated as a single domain of the alternating rhythm, i.e. as a single phonological word. Thus there are examples where the final foot of the predicate-final grammatical word is H-toned, as in *patarak-ai-r=ruu* (work-POT-NPST=man) 'those who can work' > (pata)_H (raka)_L (ir)_H (ruu) _L, a pattern which would never occur if each of the two were a separate domain of the alternating rhythm (since the alternating rhythm must end in /L/ in each prosodic domain; §2.9.3.2).

su(u) can function as head of an adnominal clause which is no longer seen as modifying the head, due to a semantic abstraction of the ostensible head *su(u)*. Here, *su(u)* designates 'fact' or something like the English complementiser 'that'.

(4–38) *pisir=ru*   *fau-Ø*   *su=u*   *jami-ru.*
        lunch=ACC   eat-NPST   COMP=ACC   stop-IMP
        'Stop eating lunch.'

su(u) also functions as a modal marker. This is a grammaticalisation process in which the former NP head *su(u)* has been reanalysed as a post-predicate modifier clitic. Thus in (4–39) below *su(u)* functions as modal marker meaning 'seem (that)'.

(4–39) *pžtu=nu*   *jaa=nu*   *suija-gama=n*
        man=GEN   house=GEN   balcony-DIM=DAT
        ik-i-i   *mmna*
        go-THM-NRT   all
        par-ri+uk-i+ar-Ø=ruu.
        leave-THM+PRF-THM+RSL-NPST=seem
        'It seemed that (they) had gone to the balcony of someone's house, and had all entered (under the balcony).'

The nominal phrase   135

Likewise, the conjunctive marker =suga 'but' (§9.2.3) possibly reflects su(u) and =ga (archaic conjunctive 'but'?), but =suga is always contiguous and no other element can intervene. Synchronically, I treat =suga as a single morpheme functioning as a conjunctive.

(4–40) ffa=nu   nak-i+u-tar=ruga=du
        child=NOM   cry-THM+PROG-PST=but=FOC
        cïk-ai-n-Ø   firi-as-i-i=du
        hear-POT-NEG-NPST   pretension-VLZ-THM-NRT=FOC
        u-tar.
        PROG-PST
        '(My) child was crying, but (I) was pretending not to hear.'

4.2.2. Headless structure

There is a headless adnominal clause structure in Irabu. A headless adnominal clause structure is syntactically analysed as a structure in which the head is omitted (the omitted head is indicated by [x] below). The omitted head can easily be pragmatically recovered. The predicate verb of the adnominal clause serves as the phonological host of the case marker, whose syntactic host is an NP, however.

(4–41) jaa=ju   ficï-Ø[x]=n=na   nausi=ga
        house=ACC   build-NPST=DAT=TOP   how=FOC
        mimai-asï-tar?
        compliment-VLZ-PST
        'In [the time] (when one) built a house, how did (you) do compliments (i.e. sending food and money to help the person who is building the house)?
(4–42) vva=ga   tur-asï-tar[x]=ru=du
        2SG=NOM   take-CAUS-PST=ACC=FOC
        jum-i+ur-Ø.
        read-THM+PROG-NPST
        '(I) am reading [the book] you let (me) take.'

Note that in (4–42) accusative //=u// is realised as /ru/ due to Geminate copy insertion (in which the final C of the predicate verb is copied onto the onset of //=u//; §2.7.2), which never occurs across two phonological words.

Some headless structures are more like clausal nominalisations where the adnominal clause has no clear semantic head. However, this is due to

136   Chapter 4

the fact that the omitted head is a formal noun (§4.2.1). The omitted formal noun is recoverable as either *kutu* 'fact' (§4.2.1.4) or *su(u)* (§4.2.1.8).

(4–43) *munu=u*   *kafï-Ø=fa*   *mucïkasï-munu.*
        thing=ACC   write-NPST=TOP   difficult-thing
        'Writing is a difficult thing.'

(4–44) *kanu   ubaa=nu*   *sïn-tar=ru=du*   *cïfï-tar.*
        that   old.woman=NOM   die-PST=ACC=FOC   hear-PST
        '(I) heard (that) the old woman died.'

4.2.3. Appositional structure

When *su(u)* (cf. §4.2.1.8) fills the head slot of an NP, this NP can occur in an appositional structure as exemplified below, where a modifier NP and a complex head (which is itself composed of a [adnominal clause]$_{modifier}$ + head) are semantically appositional:

(4–45) *pana=nu*   *ssu-kar-Ø*   *ruu=nu=du*
        flower=GEN   white-VLZ-NPST   things=NOM=FOC
        kagi-kar-Ø.
        beautiful-VLZ-NPST
        'Flowers, white ones, are beautiful.'

In (4–46) below, the surface (highest-order) phrase structure of (4–45) is shown at 'NP layer 1', where *pana* is a minimal NP that fills the modifier slot, carrying genitive case as an extension, and *ssukar ruu* is a complex head, and the entire NP *pana=nu ssukar ruu* is followed by case *=nu* as an extension, which is further followed by the information structure marker *=du* (focus). The complex head at NP layer 1 is recursively analysed as the modifier adnominal clause *ssukar* and the head *ruu* at NP layer 2.

(4–46)   *pana=nu*   *ssukar*   *ruu*   *=nu*   *=du*
        NP layer 2:   [Mod]   [Head]
        NP layer 1:   [Mod]   [Head]   Case

The apposition holds between the modifier and the head at NP Layer 1. As noted in §4.2.1.8, the semantic value of *su(u)* is abstract, designating 'thing' or 'man', so the head of NP layer 1 designates 'white thing'. The referent of 'thing' is specified by the apposite modifier *pana=nu* 'flower', so that the entire meaning of the highest-order NP is 'a flower as a white thing; a white flower'.

The nominal phrase   137

Similar examples follow, in which the structural schema is as shown in (4–46).

(4–47) *bikidum-m̃i=nu   uu-kar-Ø*   *ruu=nu*   *jaa=nu*
male-PL=GEN   big-VLZ-NPST   men=NOM   house=GEN
naugara=nkai   *un=nu=baa*   *nuusi-i...*
FIL=ALL   devil=ACC=TOP   lift-NRT
'Men, <u>big ones</u>, lift the devil on the thing-you-imagine of the house, and...'

(4–48) *herumetto=nu*   *pžkki+ar-Ø*   *ru=u*
helmet=GEN   hollow+RSL-NPST   thing=ACC
muc-i-i   *avva=nu*
take-THM-NRT   oil=NOM
cïk-i+u-i-ba=i,   *uri=u*
become.caked-THM+PROG-THM-CSL=eh   that=ACC
sugu   *guusï=tii*   *arav-Ø*
EMP   ONM=QT   wash-THM-NRT
'(I) took <u>a helmet, one which is hollowed</u>, you know it is caked with oil, so (I) washed it (with onomatopoeic expression).'

The examples above and other attested examples in my data suggest that the adnominal clauses in the appositional construction have stative rather than active predicates. Thus in the examples above the adnominal clause verb is an existential verb or a property concept verb (§8.3.3), or a verb containing a resultative aspect marker (a suffixed version of an existential verb).

4.3. Case

A case relation is formally encoded by a case marker, which attaches to the final morpheme of an NP, forming an extended NP structure. Case marks either clausal dependency (between the predicate and the argument NP that is governed by the predicate) or phrasal dependency (between the head of NP and the modifier).

As defined in §3.5 there are core, extended core, and peripheral arguments. The case system for core arguments is of the nominative-accusative type, in which intransitive subject NP and transitive subject NP have the same case-marking, while transitive direct object NP has a different case-marking. Case ellipsis in core arguments does occur but is very limited unlike colloquial Japanese (§4.3.10). I do not treat ellipted case as a

138   Chapter 4

'zero case form' but simply as ellipsis, since the absence of an overt case form (either nominative or accusative) is not a regular means of expressing nominative or accusative case, and it does not specify one and only one case relation (i.e. ellipsis may indicate nominative or accusative).

4.3.1. Basic system

Irabu is a nominative-accusative language in which S/A and O are obligatorily marked, with the nominative case marker of S/A (=ga/=nu) and the accusative case marker of O (=u). There is non-canonical object marking, whereby O is marked by the partitive rather than the default accusative. The alignment pattern does not vary in any syntactic context, even though topic marking replaces the case marking of S/A (see §4.3.10.1 and 4.3.10.2 for a discussion of the interaction between case marking and information-structure).

The S/A marking is either =ga or =nu (cognates of =ga and =no in Japanese respectively), and the differential subject marking is largely based on the animacy of S/A. The form =ga is used when S/A is higher in the animacy hierarchy (only human: a pronoun or an address noun like a proper name or a (elder) kinship term, a restricted set of human nouns such as sinsii 'teacher') whereas =nu is used elsewhere. See §4.3.2 for detail.

The O marking is either =u (accusative, default) or =a (partitive, non-canonical), and the differential marking is roughly explained in terms of the aspect (perfective vs. imperfective) of the clause in which the O occurs. The non-canonical =a occurs mostly in a sequential converbal clause (which is similar in function to the –te clause in SJ) with imperfective aspect. See §4.3.3 for detail.

There are argument case markers (nominative, accusative, partitive, dative, allative, ablative, instrumental, associative, limitative, comparative) and a genitive case marker (§4.1.1). Nominative, accusative, partitive and dative code core argument NPs, though dative-marked core arguments are highly constrained (occurring only in the dative subject constructions). The dative may also, along with the allative, mark an (extended) core argument. The other argument case forms mark peripheral arguments.

The nominal phrase 139

TABLE 4–1. Basic case frames (excluding dative subject)

Intransitive	S_{NOM}
Extended intransitive	$S_{NOM} + E_{DAT}$
Transitive	$A_{NOM} + O_{ACC/PRT}$
Extended transitive	$A_{NOM} + O_{ACC} + E_{DAT/ALL}$
(NP modifier	$ModNP_{GEN} + Head)$

(4–49) *pžtu=nu=du*　　　　　*fïï-Ø.*
　　　　man=NOM=FOC　　　come-NPST
　　　　'a man comes over.' [Intransitive]

(4–50) *vva=a*　　　*sinsii=n*　　　　*nar-i.*
　　　　2SG=TOP　　teacher=DAT　　become-IMP=QT
　　　　'You become a teacher.' [Extended intransitive]

(4–51) *pžtu-kiv=nu*　　　　　　　*pžtu=nu*　　　　*junaitama=u*
　　　　one-CLF:HOUSE=GEN　　man=NOM　　mermaid=ACC
　　　　tu-i+cc-i-i...
　　　　take-THM+come-THM-NRT
　　　　'A man of one household caught a mermaid, and...' [Transitive:
　　　　accusative O]

(4–52) *saz=za*　　　kavv-i-i　　　　*uma=n=du*
　　　　towel=PRT　　wear-THM-NRT　　there=DAT=FOC
　　　　bizi+ur-Ø.
　　　　sit+PROG-NPST
　　　　'Wearing a towel (on his head), (he) is sitting.' [Transitive: par-
　　　　titive O]

(4–53) *unu pžtu-mmi=n*　　*aagu=u=du*　　　*nara-asï-tar=ca.*
　　　　that man-PL=DAT　　song=ACC=FOC　　learn-CAUS-PST=HS
　　　　'(She) taught those guys songs.' [Extended transitive: dative
　　　　indirect object]

(4–54) *samsin=mai*　　*pžk-i-i,*
　　　　Sanshin=too　　play-THM-NRT
　　　　aagu=u=mai　　　　*agu+dusï-mmi=nkai*
　　　　song=ACC=too　　friend+friend-PL=ALL
　　　　cïk-as-i-i,　　　　　*ai-jas-i-i=du*
　　　　listen-CAUS-THM-NRT　　that.way-VLZ-THM-NRT=FOC
　　　　asuv-tar.
　　　　play-PST
　　　　'Playing the Sanshin guitar, and letting my close friends listen
　　　　to songs, (we) would play like that.' [Extended transitive: alla-
　　　　tive indirect object]

140   Chapter 4

Even though case markers primarily function as case markers, two case forms that mark peripheral arguments can appear *after* another case form, functioning as limiter markers, whose function is to modify an (case-marked) argument or an adjunct, marking quantification and qualification (§9.4). Thus =*kara* (ablative) and =*gami* (limitative) can mark either a peripheral argument as a case marker (4–55a, b), or a case-marked argument NP as a limiter marker (4–56a, b).

(4–55)   a. *vva=a*   *jamatu=kara=ru*   *t-tar?*
            2SG=TOP   Japan.mainland=ABL=FOC   come-PST
            'Did you come from Mainland Japan?'
         b. *uma=gami*   *ik-i-i*   *kuu-di.*
            that.place=LIM   go-THM-NRT   come-INT
            'How about going as far as that place (and then) coming back?'
(4–56)   a. *sïgutu=u=kara*   *ass-u.*
            work=ACC=PRM   do-INT
            'Let's do the work first.' [=*kara* encoding primacy ('first; primarily')]
         b. *banti=n=gami=a*   *asi-rai=du*   *sï-Ø*
            1PL=DAT=CNT=TOP   do-POT=FOC   do-NPST
            'We can do (that).' [=*gami* encoding contrast]

In summary, the interrelationship between the (argument) case markers and their functions can be configured as shown in TABLES 4–2 and 4–3 below.

TABLE 4–2. Case forms and their functions: Sort by form

Name	form	Function	Function (as a limiter)
NOMinative	=*ga*/=*nu*	S/A	
GENitive	=*ga*/=*nu*	NP modifier	
ACCusative	=*u*	O (default)	
PaRTitive	=*a*	O (non-canonical)	
DATive	=*n*	S/A, E, locative, etc.	
ALLative	=*nkai*	(E); goal	
INSTrumental	=*sii*	instrument	
ASsoCiative	=*tu*	associated motion	
CoMParative	=*jarruu*	comparative 'than'	
ABLative	=*kara*	source; path	PRiMacy 'primarily'
LIMitative	=*gami*	limit ('as far as')	CoNTrastive

The nominal phrase   141

TABLE 4–3. Case forms and their functions: Sort by function

Function \ Form	NOM	ACC	PRT	DAT	ALL	INST	ASC	CMP	ABL	LMT
Case										
Core argument	*	*	*	(*)						
Extended core				*	(*)					
Peripheral				*	*	*	*	*	*	*
Limiter									*	*

4.3.2. Nominative and genitive

A single pair of case forms (=ga and =nu; see below for the choice between these) marks both subject NPs and phrasal modifier NPs. I call the =ga/=nu that marks subject NPs nominative case, and the =ga/=nu that marks phrasal modifier NPs genitive case (see §4.1.4 for a more detailed discussion). Thus in (4–57) and (4–58) below ba=ga (1SG=ga) may be either 'I' or 'my'.

(4–57) ba=ga   ffa-gama=u=du   žž-a-di
        1SG=GEN   child=ACC=FOC   scold-THM-INT
        '(I) will scold my little child' [=ga as genitive] See (2–92) in
        §2.9.4.

(4–58) ba=ga   ffa-gama=u=du   žž-a-di.
        1SG=NOM   child-DIM=ACC=FOC   scold-THM-INT
        'I will scold (my) little child' [=ga as nominative] See (2–104)
        in §2.9.4.

As briefly mentioned above, both nominative and genitive have two variant forms, =ga as noted above, and =nu as exemplified below.

(4–59) pžtu=nu   ffa=u=du   jurav-tar.
        man=NOM   child=ACC=FOC   call-PST
        'A man called (his/her) child' [=nu as nominative]

(4–60) pžtu=nu   ffa=u=du   jurav-tar.
        man=GEN   child=ACC=FOC   call-PST
        '(someone) called a man's child' [=nu as genitive]

The alternation of =ga and =nu in both nominative and genitive is in accordance with the hierarchy as suggested below.

142   Chapter 4

TABLE 4–4. ga (G)/nu (N) alternation of nominative-genitive

	NPs with pronominal function					no pronominal function
	pronouns	proper names	kinship for elders	social status terms	numerals	Others
nominative	G	G	G	G	G	N
genitive	G	G	G	GN	N	N

Typologically, this hierarchy is basically analogous to the Animacy Hierarchy (Silverstein 1976) or Topic-worthiness hierarchy (Payne 1997), in which nominals are hierarchically arranged: pronouns (1 > 2 > 3), human proper names, kinship terms, and other nouns (definite > indefinite). But in Irabu, this hierarchy works primarily in terms of the opposition *pronoun vs. non-pronoun*: the alternation of =*ga* and =*nu* is dependent primarily on whether a given nominal is integrated into personal pronominal system. That is, as will be explained in the following paragraph, there are certain nouns that are used in place of pronouns in Irabu, such as proper names, kinship terms for elders (e.g. *uja* 'father'; *ani* 'elder sister') and a restricted set of social status terms (e.g. *sinsii* 'teacher'; *soncjoo* 'mayor'), and they are marked by =*ga* when they are used in place of personal/demonstrative pronouns, as in *sinsii=ga ffa=a umukutukam=mi.* '(addressing teacher) your child is smart, teacher.' Such nouns may be marked by =*nu* when they are not used pronominally, as in *sinsii=nu ffa=a umukutukar kutu=nu uukam.* '(in general) a teacher's child tends to be smart'.

The difference between the nominative alternation and the genitive alternation is found in social status terms and numerals: the nominative invariably opts for =*ga* for both kinds of nouns, whereas the genitive opts for =*ga* or =*nu* for social status terms and =*nu* for numerals, with a wider distribution of =*nu* over =*ga*.

This integration of certain nouns into the personal pronominal system, or avoidance of personal or demonstrative pronouns in favour of kinship terms and social status terms comes from an Irabu cultural norm. If the speaker refers to the addressee or some non-speech participant with a pronoun, then the relationship between the former and the latter will be one of equal or higher-to-lower social relationship, as between friends, or between a parent and his/her child, an elder sibling and his/her younger sibling, a teacher and his/her pupil, etc. If the speaker is lower in social status than the addressee/third person referent, then the latter is referred to by kinship/social status terms or by proper names with a proper honorific stem such as *sinsii* 'teacher', as in *Kiigin-sinsii* 'Teacher Keigen').

The nominal phrase   143

Numerals may be marked either by =*ga* or by =*nu*, depending on their
syntactic function. On the one hand, a numeral may modify a newly introduced referent. The numeral in such a use is marked by =*nu*.

(4–61) *ju-taar=nu*   *pžtu=nu=du*
        four-CLF.HUMAN=GEN   man=NOM=FOC
        maar-i+u-tar.
        wander-THM+PROG-PST
        '(There were) four persons walking around.'

On the other hand, a numeral can often function anaphorically, serving as
head of an argument NP. Here, =*ga* is employed to mark the numeral.

(4–62) *ssibara,*   *maibara,*   *satubžtu=nu*   a-tar=ca,
        north   south   neighbour=NOM   exist-PST=HS
        fïta-kiv.   *pžtu-kiv=ga*   *im=nu*
        two-CLF.HOUSE   one-CLF.HOUSE=NOM   sea=GEN
        acca   *ja-i-ba...*
        side   COP-THM-CSL
        'There lived two households, north and south. Because one
        (was) near the sea...'

4.3.3. Accusative and partitive
There are two case forms that mark direct object: the accusative =*u* (an
unmarked choice for a direct object NP) and the partitive =*a* (a marked
choice). Since the partitive is a marked choice and the accusative has no
restriction, I focus on the criteria for the choice of the partitive, which can
appear environments where the partitive cannot appear. The accusative will
be briefly described in §4.3.3.7.

4.3.3.1. The distributional properties of Partitive =*a*
Whereas there is no restriction on the occurrence of accusative O, there are
two strong and one weak restrictions on the occurrence of partitive O.

(4–63)   Restrictions on Irabu partitive marking
         a. Strong restriction: The partitive occurs mostly in narrative
            converbal clauses.
         b. Strong restriction: The partitive occurs mostly in imperfec-
            tive clauses.
         c. Weak tendency: The partitive tends to occur with non-specif-

144 Chapter 4

ic Os.

The restriction of partitive marking to narrative converbal clauses is pervasive to all the dialects of Irabu (Lawrence 2012 for the Nakachi dialect), and is also found to varying degrees in Miyako Ryukyuan in general. While in Gusukube non-canonical O marking appears to be restricted to narrative converbal clauses just as in the case of Irabu (Mika Sakai, p.c.), Hirara (Koloskova 2007) and Ikema (Hayashi 2013) allow non-canonical marking to occur in other clause contexts, even though there is a clear tendency for it to occur in narrative converbal clauses. The other restriction that pertains to aspect has not been discussed in the literature of the non-canonical object marking in Miyako, but as will be discussed below, this feature is crucial in understanding the function of the partitive in Irabu. The weak tendency towards low referential Os has been noted in Koloskova (2007) for her description of Hirara, but as will be noted in §4.3.3.2, this does not seem to be a very strong restriction in the case of Irabu.

TABLE 4–5 shows the distribution of the partitive in ten narrative texts (10,066 words). In (a), the numbers here demonstrate clearly that, whereas the accusative (ACC) occurs in a wide range of clauses, the partitive (PRT) is primarily restricted to narrative converbal clause (94%). The other 6% of PRT clearly constitute marginal uses of the partitive. In (b), among all tokens of narrative converbal clauses in which the accusative (ACC) occurs, perfective use is slightly outnumbered by imperfective uses (which include circumstantial, iterative, habitual, etc.). By contrast, among all instances of the partitive (PRT) that occurred in the narrative converbal clause, 90% occurred in clauses that have imperfective aspect.

TABLE 4–5. ACC vs. PRT

(a) Distribution

Clause type (categorized by predicate head)	ACC	PRT
Narrative converbal clause	56(22%)	46(94%)
Converbal clause (other)	28(11%)	1(2%)
Clause headed by adnominal form	125 (50%)	1(2%)
Clause headed by independent realis form	17 (7%)	0(0%)
Clause headed by independent irrealis imperative form	8 (3%)	1(2%)
Clause headed by other independent irrealis form	7(3%)	0(0%)
Verb-less (with O stranded)	8 (3%)	0(0%)
Total	249	49

The nominal phrase 145

(b) Aspect in narrative converbal clauses

	ACC	PRT
Perfective	23(41%)	2(4%)
Imperfective	29(52%)	41(90%)
Ambiguous	4(7%)	3(7%)
Total	56	46

Before leaving this section, it should be emphasized that the biased distribution of the partitive in (a) does not reflect the relative frequency of the narrative converbal clause itself. In my text database, by far the most frequently observed clause types are those headed by an adnominal form. Indeed, the distribution of the ordinary accusative in the text actually parallels this overall distributional pattern.

4.3.3.2. Specificity and partitive
An analysis of our text data reveals no conspicuously skewed distributional pattern with respect to the definiteness scale, even though there is a weak tendency for the partitive to mark non-specific objects: definite/specific nouns (including pronouns and proper names, N=13) make up 27% of the nouns marked partitively, indefinite/specific nouns (N=3) 6%, and indefinite non-specific nouns (N= 33) 67%. The following example contains a pronominal O marked with the partitive, even though pronouns occur at the top of the definiteness scale.

(4–64) ba=ga   ffa-gama-mmi,   pai=kara   cc-i-i,
        1SG=GEN   child-DIM-PL   field=ABL   come-THM-NRT
        [uri=a   mii],   nacï+tuur-i-i=du
        that=PRT   look.NRT   cry+keep.on-THM-NRT=FOC
        u-tar.
        PROG-PST
        '(I was thinking about) my children; (I) returned from the field,
        and looking at them, (I) was crying over and over again.'

Here, the bracketed narrative converbal clause contains the demonstrative *uri* 'that (i.e. 'my children')', which is definite and specific, and is even human. It is impossible therefore to claim that there is a direct relationship between low referential status of O and occurrence of partitive marking. The text-count only suggests a relatively high frequency of non-specific Os in the partitive case, but this is not sufficient to show that referential status is the determining factor for partitive marking. As will be discussed in

146   Chapter 4

§4.3.3.6, this weak tendency for partitive Os to be low in prominence should be regarded as a side effect of the imperfective aspect that induces the occurrence of the partitive marking.

4.3.3.3. Partitive in contexts other than narrative converbal clauses
The following examples are the very few attested examples of partitive marking found in clauses other than the narrative converbal clause. Note that all these involve the imperfective aspect, in that there is no clear end-point in the events described in the clause in which the partitive occurs.

(4–65) Conditional converbal clause (in brackets)
      [bura=a   *mak-i-i*   *u-tigaa]*   *unu*
      band=PRT   wear-THM-NRT   PROG-CND   that
      suncjuu=ja=i,   *kaee=tti*   *gusjan=na*   *nci-i,*
      mayor=TOP=eh   ONM=QT   stick=PRT   put-CVB.NRT
      tii-gama   *kacmi-i*   *cc-i-i,*
      hand-DIM   get-CVB.NRT   come-THM-NRT
      zjautu=n=tii   *fïzï-gama=u=mai*   *mjaanai=i,*
      nice=DAT=QT   sleeve-DIM=ACC=too   fix.NRT=eh
      'The mayor wore a band, and, leaning his stick against the wall, he would take (my) hand and fix up (my) sleeves to make (me) look nicer.'

(4–66) Adnominal clause (in brackets)
      [jaa=ja   *njaa-n]*   *su=u*
      house=PRT   not.exist-NPST   person=TOP
      ukukazifïcï-nagi=n=mai   *ik-i-i...*
      typhoon-APRX=DAT=too   go-NRT
      'Those who did not have their own houses left in the middle of the typhoon...'

(4–67) Finite main clause (imperative)
      vva=mai   *hoogen=na*   *azz-i.*
      2SG=too   vernacular=PRT   say-IMP
      'Speak the Irabu language like us.'

4.3.3.4. Partitive in narrative convernal clauses
The optimal environment for the occurrence of partitive marking is in a narrative converbal clause that has imperfective aspect, a situation that ac-counts for most of the occurrences of partitive marking. Example (4–68) illustrates partitive marking occurring in a narrative converbal clause, where the bracketed converbal clause (Event 1) and the main clause (Event

The nominal phrase   147

2) together constitute a single iterative macro-event. Thus, Event 1 is imperfective since this event has no clear endpoint and the two events occur in a back-and-forth fasion.

(4–68) *[miz=za*   *fim-i-i]*   *waagi=nkai*
        water=PRT   get-THM-NRT   upward=ALL
                           Event 1

        nuur-i-i   *fïï-Ø?*
        climb-THM-NRT   come-NPST
                                  Event 2

        '(Did people) used to get water (down there) and come upward (over and over)?'

In (4–69) below, the clause is a manner adverbial clause that denotes an event (Event 1) temporally overlapping with the event denoted by the clause that follows (Event 2).

(4–69) *[paz=za*   *nbi-i]*   *bizi+u-tigaa*
        leg=PRT   stretch-NRT   sit+PROG-CND
                          Event 1   Event 2

        daizïna   *munu=tii*   *kangair=dara.*
        awful   thing=QT   think.NPST=CRTN

        'If (you) sit stretching (your) legs, (people) would think (it's) awful.'

In (4–70), the event of watching the dance in the narrative converbal clause is imperfective in aspect, as evidenced by the fact that it persists during the occurrence of the event in the main clause (the act of thinking about the dance) and modifies its meaning. The first event, in other words, functions as a circumstantial or simultaneous event that overlaps with the main clause event, the two events together constituting a macro-event.

(4–70) *[budur=ra*   *mii]*   *agai*   *kagi-munu=i*
        dance=PRT   watch.NRT   INTJ   nice-thing=TAG
                          Event 1

        aparagi-munu=i=ti   *umuv-tar.*
        beautiful-thing=eh=QT   think-PST
                                        Event 2

        'Watching the dance, (I) thought like, "Wow, (it's) nice, beautiful!"'

148   Chapter 4

4.3.3.5. The function of partitive: a cross-linguistic perspective

The term 'partitive' is emplpoyed in the present work since the non-canon-ical object marker =a has a function similar to the partitive case in Finnish. Finnish is a notorious example of a language system where case morpholo-gy may encode aspect (De Hoop 1992, Krifka 1992, Kiparsky 1998, Haspelmath 2001, Aissen 2003, Fischer 2005, Malchukov and De Hoop 2011), and Fischer (2005) argues that the aspectual function of case mor-phology 'apparently [are] due to the lack of an aspectual and a determiner system.'

The following pair of examples (taken from Malchukov and De Hoop 2011: 35) illustrate the aspectual function of case in Finnish, where there is a choice for marking O between partitive case -*a* and accusative -*n*.

(4–71)   *Anne*   rakensi   *talo-a.*
         Anne   built   house-PRT
         'Anne was building a/the house.'
(4–72)   *Anne*   rakensi   *talo-n.*
         Anne   built   house-ACC
         'Anne built a/the house.'

In the literature on Finnish partitive marking, there is agreement that parti-tive case has two basic functions: aspectual function and NP-related (i.e. referential) function (Kiparsky 1998). Note that in Finnish accusative ver-sus partitive marking is a more reliable indicator of aspect than referential status of O, a fact that is evident from the free translations of the examples above. This has led many linguists to conclude that Finnish case marking of O primarily encodes aspect (Kiparsky 1998, Aissen 2003, Fischer 2005). Fischer (2005) argues that the referential and aspectual functions of case morphology 'apparently [are] due to the lack of an aspectual and a deter-miner system.'

Turning to Irabu, I argue that Irabu has a similar system in which the partitive marking of O primarily functions to encode imperfective aspect. The aspectual function of partitive is crucially related to the fact that parti-tive marking is limited to the narrative converbal clause. I argue that this syntactic restriction is due to the fact that narrative converbs conflate the aspectual distinction between the perfective-narrative meaning and the im-perfective-modificational meaning (§6.3.2.1, §11.3). That is, just as in the case of Finnish, the potential ambiguity of aspect (either due to the un-availability of aspect morphology, as in Finnish, or to the conflation of the narrative vs. modificational meanings in the narrative converbal clause, as

The nominal phrase   149

in Irabu) leads to a bifunctionality in case morphology. Thus, distributional peculiarities of the Irabu partitive may be straightforwardly explained by mechanisms independently proposed for other languages.

4.3.3.6. The two principles for partitive marking
To explain our observation that partitive marking occurs most frequently in imperfective clauses, on the one hand, and that it is restricted to narrative converbal clauses, on the other, I propose the following pair of rules that predict and constrais the occurrence of partitive marking in Irabu.

(4–73)   a. Basic function of partitive: The partitive case marker functions to encode imperfective aspect.
         b. Principle of economy: The partitive O occurs only where necessary, i.e. if there is no other means available for explicitly marking imperfectivity.

In principle, the basic function (a) predicts that partitive case is assigned to *all* imperfective clauses, but the principle of economy (b), by which avoidance of redundancy is taken as the norm, restricts partitive marking to occurrence in clauses that lack aspectual marking, i.e. in narrative converbal clauses.

The principle (b) can be demonstrated in a number of ways. First, let us consider (4–74), where the aspect of the bracketed narrative converbal clause is ambiguous in the absence of context.

(4–74)   *[mm=mu   tumi-i]=du   ifi-tar.*
         potato=ACC   search.for-NRT=FOC   go-PST
         a. '(I) went while looking for potatoes.' (imperfective reading)
         b. '(I) looked for potatoes (at some place), then went (to somewhere else).' (perfective reading)

Now if accusative *u* is replaced by partitive *a*, this sentence can only be interpreted as in (4–74a), with the partitive marking serving to resolve the ambiguity. If the ambiguity is resolved through other means such as morphological marking of aspect on the verb, partitive marking does not occur, as it would be redundant. This is illustrated in (4–75), where the same meaning as (4–74a) is expressed by the simultaneous converb without partitive marking.

(4–75)   *mm=mu(/*=ma)   tumi-ccjaaki=du   ifi-tar.*

potato=ACC(/*=PRT)   search.for-SIM=FOC   go-PST
'(I) went while looking for potatoes.'

In (4–75), the verb inflection *-ccjaaki* (simultaneous converb) indicates that the act of searching for potatoes is simultaneous with the act of going. Aspect is in this case morphologically encoded on the verb.

Another fact that supports (4–73b) is that the partitive does not occur in an progressive aspectual AVC (§7.1.4.1), which developed from the combination of a narrative converbal clause plus existential verb. In some dialects such as Ikema (Hayashi 2010: 180), the partitive occurs in matrix clauses with the AVC, as well as in narrative converbal clauses. This might seem natural, given the distributional tendency for the partitive to occur in narrative converbal clauses. However, in Irabu the partitive is *not* found in the AVC (an exception for this is (4–65), where the conditional clause has the progressive AVC as its predicate). Elicitation reveals that examples such as the following are not accepted.

(4–76)   **mm=ma*   *tumi-i=du*   *u-tar.*
           potato=PRT   search.for-NRT   PROG-PST
           '(I) was looking for potatoes.'

This seemingly puzzling distributional fact is naturally explained by an appeal to the principle of economy. That is, since the AVC is clearly imperfective due to the presence of the progressive auxiliary, the partitive is not needed in this case to mark imperfective aspect.

A similar constraint on case marking and aspect is found in Russian, where the choice for O is between accusative and genitive. The genitive case, which is associated with imperfective aspect, is blocked if the verb morphology explicitly marks imperfective aspect, a situation that likewise can be explained in terms of avoidance of redundancy (De Hoop and Malchukov 2007: 1653). Thus, principle of economy does not seem to be language-particular, but is based on a cross-linguistic tendency to avoid redundancy in encoding meaning.

4.3.3.7. Revisiting specificity

If we assume that imperfective aspect is the determining factor for predicting the occurrence of partitive marking, it is readily possible to correlate partitive marking with the observed weak (but not perfect) tendency towards non-specific O. For example, if a telic verb like *pur* 'dig' is interpreted as imperfective (i.e., as an unbounded, incomplete process) in some way

The nominal phrase   151

or another, the action of digging cannot be exhaustive, and the patient cannot therefore be exhaustively affected. This imperfective construal is possible if, among other things, the referent of O is non-specific, with no specific quantity subject to the act of digging (See Kiparsky 1998 for a similar
discussion of the partitive case in Finnish). This situation is illustrated in
(4–77).

(4–77)   *mm=ma*   *pur-ii=du*   *uma+kuma*
         potato=PRT   dig-NRT=FOC   here+there
         maar-i+ur-Ø.
         wander-THM+PROG-NPST
         'Digging potatoes (here and there), (I) went.'

In (4–77), what is being dug is an unspecified quantity of potatoes that are
planted here and there. If the referent of O here were specific, such as 'the
potato' or 'the potatoes planted in that particular field', an imperfective
construal would be impossible. The same holds for (4–78), where the action denoted by the narrative converb occurs iteratively, so that the patient
in that clause (*ukuzii* 'rocks') cannot be construed as a specific set of rocks
in a specific place.

(4–78)   *uku-zii=ja*   *kais-i-i*   *kan=nu*
         big-stone=PRT   turn.over-THM-NRT   crab=ACC
         tur-Ø.
         catch.NPST
         'Turning over rocks (those guys) caught crabs.'

If the demonstrative *uma=nu* 'of that place' is added to *ukuzii* 'rock' in (4–
79) to delimit its specific reference, the accusative becomes acceptable in
place of the partitive, as shown in (4–79), something confirmed by all of
the subjects in our study.

(4–79)   *uma=nu*   *uku-zii=ju=baa*   *kais-i-i*
         there=GEN   big-stone=ACC   turn.over-THM-NRT
         kan=nu   *tur-Ø.*
         crab=ACC   catch.NPST
         '(They) turned over the rock over there, and caught crabs.'

There is thus a clear interface between imperfective meaning and
non-specificity on the one hand, and between perfective reading and refer-

152   Chapter 4

entiality on the other. This interface is something commonly observed
cross-linguistically (Langacker 1987, Abraham 1997, Fischer 2003), although it is not always active, as one can easily think of imperfective
events that involve specific sets of patients. For example, the action of
turning over a specific rock can be incomplete if it is in progress, such as
when the rock is held in a half-overturned position as in (4–80).

(4–80)   *uma=nu*   *uku-zii=ja*   *kais-i-i*
         there=GEN   big-stone=PRT   turn.over-THM-NRT
         kan=nu   *tur-Ø.*
         crab=ACC   catch.NPST
         '(They) turned over the rock over there, and caught crabs.'

I conclude therefore that the weak tendency observed in our data toward
non-specific O's with partitive marking is partially (though not necessarily)
due to the effect of the imperfective aspect of the clause in which they occur.

4.3.3.8. Allomorphy of partitive

Before leaving the discussion of the partitive, it is necessary to note the
fact that partitive =*a* is homophonous with topic marker =*a*. The allomorphy is identical in these two morphemes.

TABLE 4–6. Topic marker and the partitive marker: allomorphy

	CVV_	C_	Cu_	Elsewhere
TOP =*a*	=*ja*	=*Ca*	=*u*	=*a*
PRT =*a*	=*ja*	=*Ca*	=*u*	=*a*

Given this identical morphophonemic behavior, the question arises
whether they have developed historically from the same morpheme, which
later split into a topic marker on the one hand and an object marker on the
other. However, there is another hypothesis about the historical origin of
the partitive. If we look at neighbouring dialects of Miyako, such as Karimata, there is a non-canonical object marker =*ba*, whose distributional
pattern is very much like that of the partitive =*a* in Irabu, occurring mostly
in narrative converbal clauses. Interestingly, the =*ba* as a non-canonical
object marker and the partitive =*a* show a complementary distribution in
Miyako dialects. Thus, it is a reasonable hypothesis that the =*ba* is reflected as =*a* in certain Miyako dialects such as Irabu, Ikema and Hirara. The
problem of this hypothesis is that Irabu has the object topic =*ba*. We need

The nominal phrase   153

to clarify the historical relationship between the non-canonical =*ba* in Miyako dialects and the object topic =*ba* in Irabu. It might be the case that the latter is a later borrowing in Irabu and some other Miyako dialects.

Apart from the diachronic treatment of the topic =*a* and the partitive =*a*, there are strong grounds for them to be treated as distinct morphemes synchronically (a similar argument is given in Koloskova 2007: 288 for Hirara). First, the two morphemes have very different, in fact opposite, functions. Whereas the topic marker =*a* marks a sentential topic or a contrasted element and typically occurs in a main clause, the partitive *a* marks elements that are little topic-worthy (e.g. inanimate and non-specific referents) and almost always occurs in a subordinate clause. Second, there is a complementary distribution in topic marking whereby the topical object is uniquely marked by =*ba* and all other topical NPs are marked by =*a*.

4.3.3.9. Accusative

The accusative case marker =*u* occurs much more frequently than the partitive (see Table 4–5 above), and is not restricted to occurring in specific environments like the partitive. Thus it may occur whether the object NP and the verb is adjacent or not, whether the object NP occurs in a chained clause or not, or whether the object is non-referential or not.

(4–81) a. *kari=a   tuz=zu   tum-i+a-Ø-m.*
  3SG=TOP   wife=ACC   search-THM+RSL-NPST-RLS
  'He has searched (i.e. has got) a wife.' [O and V are adjacent]

 b. *kari=a   tuz=zu=du   tum-i+ar-Ø.*
  3SG=TOP   wife=ACC=FOC   search-THM+RSL-NPST
  'He has searched (i.e. has got) a wife.' [O and V are not adjacent]

(4–82) a. *[kari=u=ba   kurus-i-i],*
  3SG=ACC=TOP   kill-THM-NRT
  sïn-ah-a-Ø=tti   irav=nkai   t-tar=ca.
  die-CAUS-THM-INT=QT   Irabu=ALL   come-PST=HS
  '(He thought) "(I'll) kill him, make him die!", (and he) came to Irabu.'
  [O in a chained clause]

 b. *kari=u=ba   kurus-a-di=tii*
  3SG=ACC=TOP   kill-THM-INT=QT
  irav=nkai   t-tar=ca.
  Irabu=ALL   come-PST=HS
  '(He thought) "(I'll) kill him!", (and he) came to Irabu.'

154   Chapter 4

[O not in a chained clause]
(4–83) a. *ba=a*   *manzjuu=ju=du*   *juu*   *fau-Ø.*
           1SG=TOP   papaya=ACC=FOC   very   eat-NPST
           'I often eat papayas.' [O is non-referential]

        b. *ba=a*   *unu*   *manzjuu=ju=du*   *fa-a-di.*
           1SG=TOP   that   papaya=ACC=FOC   eat-THM-INT
           'I will eat that papaya.' [O is referential]

4.3.4. Dative and allative

Dative case and allative case are marked by =*n* and =*nkai*, respectively.
There is good reason to deal with these two case markers together. First,
their functional range is similar, in that both may mark extended core arguments (indirect object, etc.) and peripheral arguments (goal, etc.), though
dative case is additionally used to mark subject in the dative subject construction (§3.5.2). Second, the same extended core argument, specifically
the indirect object, may be marked by either form, with a certain slight semantic difference.

TABLE 4–7 summarises various usages of the two case markers according to two broad categories: location-oriented and direction-oriented. The
location-oriented usages do not involve any physical or mental direction
and the NP marked by the dative or allative is construed as, broadly speaking, the locus of the event. On the other hand, The direction-oriented usages involve the physical or mental direction and the NP marked by the dative or allative is construed as the direction/goal of the event.

TABLE 4–7. Dative and allative: functional distribution

	Location-oriented								Direction-oriented		
	Time	Possessor	Experiencer	Passive agent	Result of change	Location	Causee agent	Benefactee	Goal-Location	Goal	Object of communication
Dative	+	+	+	+	+	+	+	+	(+)	-	-
Allative	-	-	-	-	(+)	(+)	(+)	(+)	+	+	+

As is clear from the table, the dative marking is the only option for many
location-oriented usages, whereas the allative marking is preferred or is the

The nominal phrase

only option for some direction-oriented usages. For the other (intermediate) usages both markers are possible though the dative marking seems more preferred.

4.3.4.1. Time

The dative marker is used to encode the time of the event being described in the sentence.

(4–84) *kanimega=a*　　　　*kuzu=n=du*　　　　　*ffa=u*
　　　　Kanimega=TOP　　　last.year=DAT=FOC　　child=ACC
　　　　nasï-tar.
　　　　bear-PST
　　　　'Kanimega bore a child last year.'

(4–85) *san-zi=n*　　　　　*mata*　　*kuu-Ø.*
　　　　three-CLF.TIME　　again　　come-IMP
　　　　'Come again on three.'

(4–86) *ui=mai*　　*ar-i-i=ru*　　　　　　　*u-tar?*
　　　　that=too　　exist-THM-NRT=FOC　　　PROG-PST
　　　　ifïsa=n=na.
　　　　war=DAT=TOP
　　　　'Was there such a thing, during the war?'

(4–87) *juž=žu*　　　　*fau-Ø=n=na*　　　　　*panas=su=ba*
　　　　dinner=ACC　　eat-NPST=DAT=TOP　　chatting=ACC=TOP
　　　　ah-u-n-Ø.
　　　　do-THM-NEG-NPST
　　　　'One (should) not chat when eating dinner.'

Note that in (4–87) the dative is directly attached to the adnominal clause without the head noun (a headless structure, §4.2.2).

4.3.4.2. Possessor

The possessor may be encoded by the dative in the existential construction. The construction without the dative marking, as in (4–89) is also common.

(4–88) *kanimega=n=na*　　　*zin=na*　　　*njaa-n-Ø.*
　　　　Kanimega=DAT=TOP　　money=TOP　　not.exist-NEG-NPST
　　　　'Kanimega does not have money.'

(4–89) *kanimega=a*　　*zin=na*　　*njaa-n-Ø.*
　　　　Kanimega=TOP　　money=TOP　　not.exist-NEG-NPST
　　　　'Kanimega does not have money.'

156 Chapter 4

4.3.4.3. Experiencer

The experiencer of the potential form of the verb is marked by the dative.

(4–90) *nara=n=na*   *kuu-rai-n-Ø=ti*   *až-tar=ca.*
REF=DAT=TOP   come-POT-NEG-NPST=QT   say-PST=HS
'(She) said, 'I cannot come.''

(4–91) *sinsii=n=na*   *nkjagi-rai-n-Ø=pazï.*
teacher=DAT=TOP   eat.HON-POT-NEG-NPST=perhaps
'You would not be able to eat (such a miserable food of us),
Mister.' [dative subject]

The first and second person pronouns are likely to be left unmarked, as in
(4–93), though the dative marking is also grammatical (4–92). For the other pronouns and lexical nouns, the dative marking is almost obligatory, as
in (4–90) and (4–91).

(4–92) *ban=Ø=na*   *ai=nu*   *kutu=u=baa*
1SG=DAT=TOP   that.way=GEN   thing=ACC=TOP
as-irai-n-Ø=nju.
do-POT-NEG-NPST=UPDT
'I cannot do such a thing'. [Dative marking; =n → =Ø as a result
of the sequential nasal deletion; §2.7.6]

(4–93) *ba=a*   *ai=nu*   *kutu=u=baa*
1SG=TOP   that.way=GEN   thing=ACC=TOP
as-irai-n-Ø=nju.
do-POT-NEG-NPST=UPDT
'I cannot do such a thing.' [no dative marking]

4.3.4.4. Passive agent

The agent in the passive construction is marked by the dative.

(4–94) *kari=a*   *mmja*   *uku+saba=n*   *fa-ai-i*
3SG=TOP   FIL   big+shark=DAT   eat-PASS-NRT
naugara=ca.
whatever=HS
'He was eaten by the big shark, and, you know.'

See §10.4.2 for a detailed account of the syntactic and functional characteristics of the passive construction.

The nominal phrase   157

4.3.4.5. Result of change

The verb 'become' takes the dative-marked E argument (§3.5.3). The result of the 'become' event is metaphorically construed as the location (goal) of the change-of-state event. Thus, it is understandable for the E argument of the verb 'become' to take the dative.

(4–95) *kari=a*   *sinsii=n=du*   *nar-tar.*
        3SG=TOP   teacher=DAT=FOC   become-PST
        'He has become a teacher.'

Since the change-of-state event involves the phase in which the entity has not yet changed (source) and the phase in which the entity has become something else (goal), there is some directionality involved in the event. Even though I could not find in my text corpus an example where the verb 'become' takes the allative-marked E argument, elicitation revealed that it is not ungrammatical, though consultants prefer to use the dative.

4.3.4.6. Location

The location is indicated by the dative by default.

(4–96) *gakkoo=n=du*   *sïm=mu*   *narav-tar.*
        school=DAT=FOC   charcoal=ACC   learn-PST
        'I studied at school.'[7]

(4–97) *mizï-gama=n*   *ara-i-i=du*   *mm=mu=mai*
        water-DIM=DAT   wash-THM-NRT=FOC   potato=ACC=too
        nii+fau-Ø.
        boil+eat-NPST
        '(we) would boin and eat potatoes, etc., by washing them in the water (of a pond).'

In (4–97), the noun *mizïgama* 'water' is indicated by the dative since it is interpreted as the locus of the washing (e.g. a pond). If the speaker intends the action of washing potatoes with running water (running from a tap), then the instrumental case is used instead.

(4–98) *mizï-gama=sii*   *ara-i-i=du*   *mm=mu=mai*
        water-DIM=INS   wash-THM-NRT=FOC   potato=ACC=too
        nii+fau-Ø.

---

[7] The expression *sïm=mu narav* is an idiom that means 'to study'.

158 Chapter 4

boil+eat-NPST

'(we) would boin and eat potatoes, etc., by washing them with water.'

The allative may be used for the location marking in a very limited environment. The allative may be used if the location of the event and the location of the subject at the time of the utterance are different. The condition is a necessary condition, and I could not find the sufficient condition that predicts the occurrence of the allative. In the following pair of examples, the allative may be used for (4–99) since the example satisfies the condition. In (4–100) the dative must be used, since the condition is not satisfied.

(4–99)   *gakkoo=n/=nkai*   *asïb-a-di.*
         school=DAT/=ALL   play-THM-INT
         '(I) will play at school.'

(4–100) *kuma=n/*=nkai*   *asïb-a-di.*
         here=DAT/*=ALL   play-THM-INT
         '(I) will play here.'

The directional meaning is evident in an example like (4–100), where the subject moves to the location which is encoded by the NP marked by the allative. If we assume that the core meaning of the allative is that of directionality (goal), the use of the allative in (4–100) is understandable.

4.3.4.7. Causee agent

The cause agent in the causative construction is syntactically encoded as the indirect object, and it usually opts for the dative case. As is shown in (4–101), the underlying agent of an underived verb *pžk-* 'pull out' becomes the causee, which is encoded as indirect object (*jarabi-mmi* 'children').

(4–101) *jarabi-mmi=n*   *akavdi=nu*   *mm-gama=u*
         child-PL=DAT   red.arm=GEN   potato-DIM=ACC
         pžk-as-i-i=du,   *nara=a*
         pull.out-CAUS-THM-NRT=FOC   oneself=TOP
         im=nkai   *ik-i-i,*   *suu=ju=mai*
         sea=ALL   go-THM-NRT   seaweed=ACC=too
         tur-Ø.
         take-NPST
         '(I) had children pull out red-armed potatoes (i.e. small and premature potatoes), whereas (I) myself go to the sea and take

The nominal phrase   159

seaweeds.'

However, it is also possible for a causee agent to be marked by the allative, though such an example is very rare. One of the few attested examples in which allative encodes indirect object in a causative is given below.

(4–102)   ba=a   maada=a   jum-ai-n-Ø=ssiba,
          1SG=TOP   very=TOP   read-POT-NEG-NPST=so.that
          kazï=nkai   jum-asï-tar.
          Kazu=ALL   read-CAUS-PST
          'I can't read well, so (I) had Kazu read (the letter).'

Most examples of allative-marked causees involve a situation where there
should be a more appropriate candidate who carries out the action of the
underived verb (e.g. in (4–102) above it should be the speaker) but for
some reason such a role has been passed to someone else (e.g. in (4–102)
above kazï). This means that there is some directionality involved in the
causative event: the movement of one candidate causee (as 'source') to another (as 'goal'), the latter being marked by the allative.

4.3.4.8. Beneficiary
The beneficiary is usually marked by the dative, but if the event actually
involves the physical movement of a thing to the beneficiary, then the allative may also be used. In (4–103), there is no physical movement of the
money, but there is only the movement of the ownership of the money. So,
the dative marking is obligatory.

(4–103)   ukka=u=mai   tur-a-da,   ui=n
          debt=ACC=too   take-THM-NEG.NRT   3SG=DAT
          fii-tar=ca.
          give-PST=HS
          '(He) didn't take the money back (from him), but gave the
          money.'

The benefactive verb fiir 'give' may designate the movement of ownership
as well as the physical movement, i.e. sending of something. If the allative
is used with the verb fiir 'give', then the event must involve the physical
movement (sending) of something to the beneficiary.

(4–104)   zin=nu=baa   ui=nkai   fii-tar=ca.

160   Chapter 4

money=ACC=TOP   3SG=ALL   give-PST=HS
'As for the money, (he) gave (it) to him.'

Conversely, if a verb always designates the physical giving/sending of
something, such as ufïï 'send', then the allative must be used instead.

(4–105) *zin=nu=baa*   *ui=nkai/*=n*   *ufïï-tar=ca.*
         money=ACC=TOP   3SG=ALL/*=DAT   give-PST=HS
         'As for the money, (he) sent (it) to him.'

The allative marking again designates the directionality, marking the allative-marked NP as the goal of the motion event.

4.3.4.9. Goal-Location and Goal
The three of the location-oriented and direction-oriented caegories, the location, the goal-location and the goal, can be distinguished from each other
in the following schema.

(4–106) Location: Existence
         Goal-Location: (Movement +) Existence
         Goal: Movement (+ Existence)

The location category (§4.3.4.6) only involves the existence of the referent
encoded as the subject of the sentence. The other two categories involve
two phases, i.e. (1) Movement phase, in which an entity moves to some
place, and (2) Existence phase, in which the success of the event results in
the existence of the entity being moved. The location category may be said
to lack the movement phase. This way of understanding allows us to make
the generalisation that the allative is used if and only if the event has the
movement phase, and the more the movement phase is focused, the more
likely the allative is to be used.
   As is indicated by the schema, the goal-location category focuses on the
existence phase, either because the movement phase is simply irrelevant or
because the success of the movement phase is implied.

(4–107) Goal-Location
         kii=n/?=nkai   *nuur-i-i=du*
         tree=DAT/?=ALL   climb-THM-NRT=FOC
         asïb-i+ur-Ø.
         play-THM+PROG-NPST

'(He) is playing on the tree' [lit. (He) climed on the tree and is playing]

Here, the movement phase of the action 'climb on the tree' is irrelevant.

The same verb may be used with the allative rather than the dative, as in this case the movement phase is relevant in the event being depicted.

(4–108) Goal
   maju=nu *kii=nkai/?=n* *nuur-i-i*   *ifï-Ø*
   cat=NOM tree=ALL/?=DAT climb-THM-NRT go-NPST
   'A cat is climing on the tree.'

The major directional verbs such as *ifï* 'go', *fï* 'come', etc., usually take the allative-marked NPs as their arguments. If these verbs designate the resuting state of the movement, i.e. the existence phase, by using the progressive auxiliary (which designates the resulting state for the verb *ifï*) then the use of the dative becomes more natural.

(4–109) Goal
   kari=a   *pžsara=nkai=du* *ifï-tar.*
   3SG=TOP Hirara=ALL=FOC go-PST
   'He has gone to Hirara.'
(4–110) Goal-Location
   kari=a   *pžsara=n/=nkai=du*
   3SG=TOP Hirara=DAT/=ALL=FOC
   ik-i+ur-Ø.
   go-THM+PROG-NPST
   'He went to (and is in) Hirara'

The directional verbs *par* 'leave' and *magar* 'turn' always take the allative-marked argument, indicating that they lexically require the goal argument. Actually, they are different from the vern *ifï* 'go' in that the existence phase is not included in their lexical meaning. That is, the resulting state of the action of leaving and turning is simply the completion of the movement phase, and does not include the subsequent existence phase as in the case of *ifï* 'go'.

(4–111) Goal
   kari=a   *pžsara=nkai=du* *par-i+ur-Ø.*
   3SG=TOP Hirara=ALL=FOC leave-THM+PROG-NPST

162   Chapter 4

'He has gone to Hirara.'

(4–112) Goal
         kuruma=a   *mcï=nkai=du*   *magar-i+ur-Ø.*
         car=TOP   right=ALL=FOC   turn-THM+PROG-NPST
         'The car has turned to the right.'

4.3.4.10. Object of communication

The object of the communicative event (i.e. the person who is being spoken to) is always coded by the allative NP. The object of the communicative event can be considered to have directionality in the sense that the
speech event is directed from the speaker to the interrocutor.

(4–113) *uja=a*   *taugagara=nkai=du*
         father=TOP   someone=ALL=FOC
         panas-sas-i+ur-Ø.
         speak-VLZ-THM+PROG-NPST
         'My father is speaking to someone.'

(4–114) *sinsii=nkai*   *ck-i-i*   *mii-di.*
         teacher=ALL   ask-THM-NRT   EXP-INT
         'Let's ask the teacher.'

In (4–114), the verb *ck-* has the volitional meaning 'ask', with the speech
event being directed from the speaker to the allative-marked *sinsii* 'teacher'. On the other hand, if the verb means 'hear', a non-volitional action
where the speaker receives information from the information source, then
the ablative *=kara* (§4.3.8) is used.

(4–115) *sinsii=kara=du*   *cfi-tar.*
         teacher=ALL   hear-PST
         '(I) heard from the teacher.'

4.3.5. Instrumental =sii

Instrumental case marks an instrument or a cause (peripheral argument).

(4–116) *fïzï=sii*   *jari+zïn=nu=baa*
         mouth=INST   worn.out+clothes=ACC=TOP
         sak-i-i=ju,   *ui=sii*   *sazï-nagi=mai*
         split.up-THM-NRT=EMP   that=INST   towel-APPR=too
         cïfïï-tar=dooi.
         make-PST=EMP

The nominal phrase   163

'(We) would split up worn out clothes with mouth (i.e. teeth), and (one) would make towels and so on from that (i.e. split cloths)' [instrument]

(4–117) *umacï=sii   akaras-i.*
fire=INST   light.up-IMP
'Light up with fire.' [instrument]

(4–118) *kanamar+jam=sii=du   nivv-i+ur-Ø.*
head+disease=INST=FOC   lie-THM+PROG-NPST
'(He) is lying with headache.' [cause]

It is possible for =*sii* to encode a means of transportation when subject is in control (e.g. as a driver), but not when subject is not in control (e.g. as a passenger). In the latter case, the ablative case =*kara* (§4.3.8) is used.

(4–119) *ba=a   kuruma=sii=du   ifi-tar.*
1SG=TOP   car=INST=FOC   go-PST
'I went by car.' [as a driver]

(4–120) *ba=a   kuruma=kara=du   ifi-tar.*
1SG=TOP   car=ABL=FOC   go-PST
'I went by car.' [as a passenger]

4.3.6. Associative =*tu*

Associative case has two different functions that involve two different structures. First, it connects two NPs into a single complex head (NP*₁*=*tu* NP*₂*), just like 'and' in English. In Irabu =*tu* is cliticised to the first (head of) NP. The second NP may also be marked by =*tu*, thus showing the structure NP*₁*=*tu* NP*₂*=*tu*, which is then followed by case. This double marking of the associative is common when the larger NP (i.e. NP*₁*=*tu* NP*₂*=*tu*) functions as a core argument (4–122) or the left dislocated element (4–123).

(4–121) *banti=tu   vvadu=u   agu+dusï   jar-Ø=ruda.*
1PL=ASC   2PL=TOP   friend+friend   COP-NPST=AD.ASR
'We and you are close friends, aren't us?'

(4–122) *naa=ga   ffa=tu   mama+ffa=tu=u*
oneself=GEN   child=ASC   step+child=ASC=ACC
im=nkai   saar-i-i   ifi-tar=ca.
sea=ALL   take-THM-NRT   go-PST=HS
'(She) took her own child and her stepchild to the sea.'

(4–123) *kui=tu   kui=tu   nzi=nu=ga   masï?*

164 Chapter 4

this=ASC   this=ASC   which=NOM=FOC   better
'(Of) this and this, which is better?'

A second function of =*tu* is to mark a peripheral argument encoding an associative role, analogous to 'with' in English.

(4–124)   *miju+sinsii-ta=tu*   *ucïnaa=nkai*   *ifï-tar.*
          Miyo+teacher-PL=ASC   Okinawa=ALL   go-PST
          banti=a=ju.
          1PL=TOP=EMP
          'We went to Okinawa with Teacher Miyo and others.'

(4–125)   *kunu*   *tuz=za*   *sïtabutu=tu*   *mmja*
          this   wife=TOP   bedfellow=ASC   INTJ
          maar-i-i   *ur-Ø=pazï=tii*
          wander-THM-NRT   PROG-NPST=maybe=QT
          umu-i-i...
          think-THM-NRT
          'This wife (of mine) is probably keeping company with a bed-fellow, thought (the husband)...'

4.3.7. Comparative =*jarruu*

=*jarruu* marks a peripheral argument encoding a comparative relation, roughly corresponding to 'than' in English.

(4–126)   *im=nu*   *munu=jarruu*   *pai=kara=nu*
          sea=GEN   thing=CMP   field=ABL=GEN
          munu=nu=du   *masï*
          thing=NOM=FOC   better
          'The things from field are better than the things of the sea.'

(4–127)   *aca=nu*   *usï=nu*   *mumu=jarruu*
          tomorrow=GEN   cattle=GEN   leg=CMP
          kjuu=nu   *macja=nu*   *mumu.*
          today=GEN   bird=GEN   leg
          'Rather than tomorrow's cattle's leg, today's bird's leg.' [i.e. immediate small profit is more valuable than uncertain bigger profit.]

This clitic developed from the copular *jar* + *suu* (§4.2.1.8), with /s/-to-/r/ assimilation unique to the formal noun *suu* (§2.7.7.2).

The nominal phrase   165

4.3.8. Ablative =*kara*

The case marker =*kara* functions either as an ablative case marker of a peripheral argument encoding source, beginning point, or path ('plorative'),
as in (4–128) to (4–131) below, or as a limiter encoding primacy, i.e. 'primarily; first; to begin with', as will be described in §9.4.5.

(4–128) *guu=nu*   *mii=kara*   *unu*   *pav=nu*   *idi-i*
         cave=GEN   inside=ABL   that   snake=NOM   exit-NRT
         cc-i-i,   *kanu*   *midum=mu=du*
         come-THM-NRT   that   woman=ACC=FOC
         saar-i-i   *ifi-tar=ca.*
         take-THM-NRT   go-PST=HS
         'From inside the cave, that snake came out, and took that
         woman away.' [source]

(4–129) *uri=u=baa*   *pžtu=kara=du*   *cïfi-tar=ri.*
         that=ACC=TOP   man=ABL=FOC   hear-PST=eh
         '(You) heard about that from someone, eh?' [source]

(4–130) *kjuu=kara*   *aca=gami*   *kakar-kutu*
         today=ABL   tomorrow=LMT   sustain-NPST.OBL
         ja-i-ba,   *ba=a*   *mmja*   *ik-ai-n-Ø.*
         COP-THM-CSL   1SG=TOP   INTJ   go-POT-NEG-NPST
         '(The job) will last from today to tomorrow, so I cannot go.'
         [beginning point]

(4–131) *mmi-gama=nu*   *ir=nu*   *mcï=kara*   *sugu*   *kunu*
         sea-DIM=GEN   west=GEN   road=ABL   now   this
         mazïmunu=nu=du   *kaju-i+ur-Ø=pazï.*
         evil.spirit=NOM=FOC   go-THM+PROG-NPST=maybe
         'Maybe through the road (which is) west to the sea, this evil
         spirit is going (to my house), perhaps.' [path]

4.3.9. Limitative =*gami*

The case marker =*gami* functions either as a limitative case marker of a
peripheral argument encoding limitation 'until; as far as', as is shown in
(4–132) and (4–133) below, or as a limiter encoding contrast (§9.4.7).

(4–132) *icinensjee=kara*   *cjuugakkoo=gami*   *zazaa=tti*
         freshman=ABL   junior.highschool=LMT   ONM=QT
         suru-i-i   *mmja*   *cjokugo=ti*
         gather-THM-NRT   INTJ   Imperial.speech=QT
         asï-ta-m.

166 Chapter 4

do-PST-RLS

'From freshmen (of elementary school) to (students of) junior high school, people gather and line up, and (the principal) read Imperial speech.'

(4–133) *icï=gami=mai*   *ganzuunar-ras-i-i*   *nagaiki*
when=LMT=even   good.health-VLZ-THM-NRT   long.live
ass-u=juu.
do-IMP=UPDT

'For all time (lit. Until whenever) keep good health and live long.'

4.3.10. Absence of case marking

As a topic-prominent rather than a subject-prominent language, Irabu case system is sensitive to information-structure. The topic-comment structure requires topic marking (=a) on the topic element, and the topic marking on S/A replaces the case marking for the core arguments (nominative =ga/=nu), while the topic marking on O follows the case-marked O by the dedicated object topic marker =ba (§9.5.1).

4.3.10.1. Subject case marking and information structure

The nominative case and certain limiter markers or the topic marker =a shows a paradigmatic relationship. Thus if a subject NP is marked by a limiter marker =mai 'too; even', =dumma (emphasis), or topic marker =a, nominative case is always absent.

(4–134) <u>*ba=a*</u>   *uri=u=baa*   *ss-i+u-Ø-m*
1SG=TOP   that=ACC=TOP   know-THM+PROG-NPST-RLS
'I know that, too.'

(4–135) *ban=mai*   *uri=u=baa*   *ss-i+u-Ø-m*
1SG=too   that=ACC=TOP   know-THM+PROG-NPST-RLS
'I know that, too.'

(4–136) <u>*ban=dumma*</u>   *uri=u=baa*
1SG=EMP   that=ACC=TOP
ss-i+u-Ø-m
know-THM+PROG-NPST-RLS
'I know that, too.'

4.3.10.2. Object case marking and information-structure

The accusative =u and the topic marker =ba shows a syntagmatic relationship, with the sequence =u=ba. However, the limiter marker =mai 'too'

The nominal phrase 167

may replace the accusative marker or follow it. The latter structure occurs if the object NP is focused. In the short dialogue below, the direct object NP in the speech of A is not case-marked, carrying the limiter marker =*mai* 'even' alone. However, in the speech of B the same direct object carries accusative case-marking. Note that focus marking can occur when case-marked object and =*mai* co-occur, but does not occur when case-ellipted object and =*mai* co-occur.

(4–137) A. *kuri=a*   *nau=mai*
             3SG=TOP   what=even
             ss-a-n-Ø=dara=i.
             know-THM-NEG-NPST=EMP=eh
             'This (woman) doesn't know anything, does she?'
          B. *gui!*   *kuri=a*   *nau=ju=mai=du*
             Wow   3SG=TOP   what=ACC=even=FOC
             ss-i+u-Ø-m!
             know-THM+PROG-NPST-RLS
             'Come on! This (woman) knows everything!'

4.3.10.3. Case ellipsis

As mentioned briefly in §4.3.1, Irabu is a nominative-accusative language in which S/A and O are obligatorily marked, with the nominative case marker of S/A (=*ga*/=*nu*) and the accusative case marker of O (=*u*). This system is similar to that of Japanese (the standard language), where S/A is marked by =*ga* and O is marked by =*o*. However, there is one conspicuous difference between the case marking system of Irabu and that of Japanese. In Japanese, especially its colloquial version, the overt case-marking is not at all obligatory. In fact, the overt case-marking of both arguments is extremely rare in natural discourse (Kazama 2015). By contrast, in Irabu natural discourse, both arguments *must* be overtly case-marked. The obligatory marking of both S/A and O is extremely rare in Japanese dialects, and it is Irabu and other Miyako Ryukyuan that serve as the only unambiguous example of this pattern. In elicitation, if the researcher constructs a sentence with one or both of the core arguments being left unmarked, the native speakers always correct the sentence to mark S, A and O.

However, in my text corpus, it is possible to find a very few examples of case ellipsis. According to the few attested examples of ellipsis, the generalisation can be made that case ellipsis is more likely to occur in O than S/A, and S than A. In fact, I have never encountered any example where the nominative case of A is ellipted either in natural discourse or in elicitation.

168 Chapter 4

(4–138) O > S > A

Also, case ellipsis seems more common in subordinate clauses than in main clauses.

(4–139) Subordinate clause > Main clause

In the following pair of examples, (a) illustrates the nominative case ellipsis in an adnominal clause with S, whereas (b) shows that the nominative case cannot be ellipted. This demonstrates that case ellipsis is more likely to occur in subordinate clauses than in main clauses.

(4–140) a. *ami   fïï-Ø   tukja=n=na   nau=ju=ga*
             rain   fall-NPST   time=DAT=TOP   what=ACC=FOC
             asï-kutu?
             do-OBL
             'What should (we) do (in the time) when the rain is falling?'
             [=nu is ellipted]
          b. *amï=nu   fïï-kutu.*
             rain=NOM   fall-OBL
             'It will rain.' [=nu cannot be ellipted]

In the following pair of examples, (a) illustrates the accusative case ellipsis in an adnominal clause. In (b), unlike (4–140b), the accusative case can be ellipted in the main clause, demonstrating that O is more likely to be ellipted than S.

(4–141) a. *žžu   fau-Ø   tukja=n=na   nausi=ga   asï-kutu?*
             fish   eat-NPST   time=DAT=TOP   how=FOC   do-OBL
             'What should (we) cook when we eat fish?'
          b. *žžu=u   fau-kutu.*
             fish=ACC   eat-OBL
             '(I) am supposed to eat fish (for today's lunch).'

Chapter 5
Morphology of nominals and adnominals

This chapter presents the subclassification and morphology of the nominal word class and the adnominal word class and their internal structures. As noted in Chapter 3, a nominal is a word that only heads an NP, serving syntactically as an argument, a predicate nominal, or the modifier of an NP in a recursive manner. Adnominals are a very small class. I deal with nominals and adnominals together in this chapter because they are defined in terms of NP structure.

Nominals fall into five subclasses based on their syntactic and semantic features. These are: pronouns, nouns, numerals, interrogatives, indefinites, and non-pronominal (manner and locative) demonstrative nominals. At this stage, one note is necessary about the fact that numerals and certain demonstratives are classified as nominals. They can serve as minimal NPs and demonstrate all of the three syntactic functions of NPs (arguments, predicates, or the modifier of NPs), though the argument function may be rarely attested (specifically, in demonstrative manner words). Even though not criterial for the nominal word class, unlike typical nominals such as nouns, it is not common for these nominals to be modified by another NP or an adnominal (clause).

5.1. Nominals and adnominals: overview

5.1.1. The distribution in terms of NP structure

Both nominals and adnominals occur in NP structure. As was noted in §3.3.1, a nominal is defined as a word that exclusively heads an NP. NP structure is recursive, and so an NP may be the modifier of another NP. Thus, the element filling the modifier slot of an NP in (5–1) is actually an NP itself. This is evidenced in the fact that it also carries the NP extension, i.e. case.

(5–1)   *agu=nu*   *jaa=n=du*   *asuv-tar.*
        friend=GEN   child=DAT   play-PST
        '(I) played at (my) friend's house.'

170   Chapter 5

Thus, *agu* in (5–1) is an NP, in the same sense that *agu=nu jaa* in (5–2) below is an NP. The difference is that *agu* in (5–1) is a minimal NP, whereas *agu=nu jaa* in (5–2) is a complex NP.

(5–2) *agu=nu*   *jaa=nu*   *mai=n=du*   *asuv-tar.*
       friend=GEN   house=GEN   front=DAT=FOC   play-PST
       '(I) played in front of (my) friend's house.'

On the other hand, adnominals, like *unu* in (5–3), only fill the modifier slot of an NP. They cannot be considered minimal NPs, since they do not *head* an NP. They do not carry case, the NP extension.

(5–3) *unu*   *jaa=n=du*   *asuv-tar.*
       that   house=DAT=FOC   play-PST
       '(I) played at that house.'

5.1.2. Demonstratives

Demonstrative is a functional category, not a word class, as some demonstratives are nominals and some are adnominals.

Demonstrative roots are bound morphemes from which are derived either pronouns or non-pronominal demonstratives, by attaching derivational affixes such as *-(r)i* (pronominaliser), *-ma* (locative), *-i* (manner), and *-nu* (adnominal). The demonstrative root formally distinguishes between proximate (close to both the speaker and the hearer), medial (close to the hearer), and distal (distant from both).

TABLE 5–1. Demonstrative root and derived forms

		PROXIMATE	MEDIAL	DISTAL
Pronoun	Singular	*ku-(r)i*	*u-(r)i*	*ka-(r)i*
	Plural	*ku-nukja/ku-ntja*	*u-nukja/u-ntja*	*ka-nukja/ka-ntja*
Locative		*ku-ma*	*u-ma*	*ka-ma*
Manner		*(ku-i)*	*a-i*	*ka-i*
Adnominal		*ku-nu*	*u-nu*	*ka-nu*

Demonstrative adnominals belong to the adnominal word class, whereas all other demonstratives belong to the nominal word class. Demonstrative pronouns are composed of a demonstrative root (*ku-* for proximate, *u-* for medial, and *ka-* for distal) and a demonstrative pronominaliser which further distinguishes singular and plural (see §5.2.2 for more detail). The parenthesised /r/ is retained when the following /i/ is followed by a vowel, as

Morphology of nominals and adnominals   171

in *ku(r)i* 'this' + *=a* (topic) > *kuria* [kuɾʲaː], or *ku(r)i* + *=u* (accusative) >
kuri=u [kuɾʲuː]. Otherwise /r/ is deleted, as in *ku(r)i* > *kui* 'this', *ku(r)i* + *=n*
(dative) > *kui=n*, especially in fast speech.

In addition to these frequently used demonstratives in which a demonstrative root is followed by a derivational affix to form a nominal or adnominal stem, there is a compounding strategy in which a demonstrative
root is directly followed by a nominal root to form a nominal word:

(5–4)   a. *ku+pagi*   b. *u+pagi*   c. *ka+pagi*
           this+bigness   that+bigness   that+bigness
           'this size'   'that size'   'that size'
(5–5)   a. *ku+daki*   b. *u+daki*   c. *ka+daki*
           this+state   that+state   that+state
           'like this'   'like that'   'like that'

Also, there are a few nominals (especially time nouns) which contain one
of the three demonstrative roots, as in <u>*kunur*</u> 'these days' (which apparently
contains the proximate demonstrative <u>root *ku-*</u>) and <u>*un*</u> 'those days' (which
apparently contains the medial demonstrative root *u-*). However, as these
examples show, such forms are not systematically combinable with the full
set of demonstrative roots, bur rather are lexicalised.

5.2. Subclassification of nominals

5.2.1. Nouns
A noun functions as an NP of any kind (i.e. argument, predicate, and modifier of a larger NP). A noun may consist of a root alone, as in *jarabi* 'child',
but may also be morphologically complex with various derivational affixa-
tions (as in *jarabi-gama-mmi* 'child-DIM-PL: little children') and/or compounding or reduplication (as in *biki+jarabi* 'male+child: boy'). The derivational morphology of nominals is described in §5.3.

(5–6)   *jarabi=nu=du*   *nak-i+ur-Ø.*
           child=NOM=FOC   cry-THM+PROG-NPST
           'A child is crying.' [subject argument NP]
(5–7)   *jarabi=u=du*   *jurav-tar.*
           child=ACC=FOC   call-PST
           '(x) called a child' [direct object argument NP]
(5–8)   *uri=a*   *jarabi=dara*
           3SG=TOP   child=CRTN

172   Chapter 5

'It's a child' [predicate NP]

(5–9) *jarabi=nu*   *cïn*
       child=GEN   clothes
       'A child's clothes' [the modifier of an NP]

Time nouns such as *aca* 'tomorrow', *cïnu* 'yesterday', *sïtumuti* 'morning', and *mainicï* 'everyday' can additionally function adverbially. As in the case of adverbs (b), these time nouns directly modify predicates without carrying case (a).

(5–10) a. *cïnu=du*   *asï-tar*
            yesterday=FOC   do-PST
            '(I) did (the job) yesterday.' [*cïnu* is a nominal]
        b. *juu=du*   *asï-tar.*
            very=FOC   do-PST
            '(I) did (the job) much.' [*juu* is an adverb]

(5–11) a. *sïtumuti=du*   *par-tar=ca.*
            morning=FOC   leave-PST=HS
            '(He) left (in the) morning, they say.' [*sïtumuti* is a nominal]
        b. *sïgu=du*   *par-tar=ca.*
            shortly=FOC   leave-PST=HS
            '(He) left shortly.' [*sïgu* is an adverb]

5.2.2. Pronouns

Pronouns are words that have little intrinsic meaning, referring to entities in the immediate physical or discourse context, and which normally functions as NPs without modifiers. They include personal pronouns, demonstrative pronouns, and reflexive pronouns. As was noted in §4.3.2, one systematic behaviour shared by pronouns is that they require *=ga* rather than *=nu* for nominative and genitive cases. Also, pronouns formally distinguish number for human referents.

When a pronoun heads an NP, a modifier does not normally occur, though it is possible for an adnominal clause to modify a pronoun, as in:

(5–12) [*vva=ga*   *ažž-i+u-tar]*   *kari=a=da?*
        2SG=NOM   say-THM+PROG-PST   3SG=TOP=how.about
        'What happened to that (guy) [who you were talking about]?'

5.2.2.1. Personal pronouns and demonstrative pronouns
Irabu is a language where personal pronouns exist only for first and second

Morphology of nominals and adnominals   173

persons, exemplifying Bhat's (2004: 134) 'two person' type. Functionally speaking, person reference in Irabu is a system where first and second person reference (speech participant reference) is marked by distinct forms that are used exclusively for person reference, or personal pronouns, while third person reference (speech non-participant reference) is obligatorily combined with demonstrative reference, formally coded by demonstrative pronouns.

TABLE 5–2. Personal and demonstrative pronouns in terms of function

	Person reference	Demonstrative reference	Form
1st person	+	−	Personal pronoun
2nd person	+	−	Personal pronoun
3rd person	+	+	Demonstrative pronoun

TABLE 5–3. Personal pronouns and demonstrative pronouns in terms of form

		Singular	Plural (root-PL)
1st person		*ba(n)*	*ban-ti* (exclusive) / *duu* (inclusive)
2nd person		*vva*	*vva-du*
3rd person	proximate	*ku-(r)i*	*ku-nukja/ku-ntja*
	medial	*u-(r)i*	*u-nukja/u-ntja*
	distal	*ka-(r)i*	*ka-nukja/ka-ntja*

As can be seen, personal and demonstrative pronouns distinguish number (singular vs. plural) for human referents. Thus the plural forms of the third person are used for human referents only, which is indicated by the broken lines (*-nukja* and *-ntja* are allomorphs with no semantic difference; probably **-nukja* > *-ntja* diachronically).

The first person forms deserve special attention in two respects. First, the singular form is irregularly bound (*ba-*) when followed by =*ga* (nominative or genitive) or =*a* (topic). When followed by =*u* (accusative), the first person singular form is realised as another bound stem *banu-*. Nakama (1992) reports that =*n* (dative) also requires this latter type of stem, giving rise to *banu=n*, which is also wide-spread across Miyako varieties, but I could not elicit the form or find it in the text data. Rather, dative is realised as simple *ban* (nasal$_1$+nasal$_2$ > nasal$_1$: sequential nasal deletion; §2.7.6).

(5–13)	*ba=ga*	*ffa*	cf.	*ban=kara*	*tur-tar*
	1SG=GEN	child		1SG=ABL	take-PST
	'My child'			'(x) took (something) from me'	
(5–14)	*ba=a*	*par-a-di.*			

174   Chapter 5

                   1SG=TOP   leave-THM-INT
                   'I will leave.'
                   [irregular]

(5–15)   *banu=u*   *mii-ru.*
            1SG=ACC   look-IMP
            'Look at me'
            [irregular]

(5–16)   *ban=Ø*   *munu=u*   *fii-ru.*
            1SG=DAT   thing=ACC   give-IMP
            'Give me something to me.' [sequential nasal deletion]

Second, the first person plural form *banti* is only used to encode 'us but not you' (i.e. exclusive implication). If one wants to express 'me/us and you' (inclusive), the noun *duu* 'body' is used instead. That *duu* is a noun rather than a pronoun is indicated by the fact that it carries nominative/genitive =*nu*, and does not contain a plural morpheme. From the functional point of view, however, I integrate *duu* into the personal pronominal system, in such a way that the first person plural category has a cross-linguistically common exclusive-inclusive distinction.

(5–17) a. *kuma=a*   *banti=ga*   *sïm-i+ur-Ø*
           this.place=TOP 1PL=NOM live-THM+PROG-NPST
           sïma.
           island
           'This is the land we live in' (e.g. speaking to a traveller)

       b. *kuma=a*   *duu=nu*   *sïm-i+ur-Ø*
           this.place=TOP body=NOM live-THM+PROG-NPST
           sïma.
           island
           'This is the land we live' (e.g. speaking to audience in the local congress)

(5–18) a. *banti=ga*   *ffa*
           1PL=GEN   child
           'Our child' (e.g. when introducing the child to someone)

       b. *duu=nu*   *ffa*
           body=GEN   child
           'Our child' (e.g. when speaking to the partner)

Morphology of nominals and adnominals

5.2.2.2. Reformulating personal pronominal system: minimal-augment system

The pronominal paradigm presented in TABLE 5–3 is a cross-linguistically common system in which person (1st, 2nd and possibly 3rd) and number (singular vs. plural) are distinguished. However, if we integrate one more form in the paradigm, then we have a very different picture of the Irabu personal pronominal system. The form is another inclusive word, *bafïtaa* 'me and you', which rarely occurs in discourse.

The word *bafïtaa* always refers to two people, 'me and (singular) you'. It must have been a compound, consisting of the first person root (which is *ban* in present Irabu) and the numeral 'two persons' (which is *fïtaar* in present Irabu). Elicitation revealed that the word can have a range of grammatical functions as illustrated below, though the instrumental function (5–19) is extremely common.

(5–19) *bafïtaa=sii*   *fai*   *mii-di.*
        me.and.you=INST   eat.NRT   EXP-INT
        'Let's eat together.'

(5–20) *bafïtaa=ja*   *mmja*   *kuma=n*   *ur-kutu.*
        me.and.you=TOP   FIL   together   exist-OBL
        'You and I have to stay here.'

(5–21) *bafïtaa=ju=baa*   *žž-a-n-Ø=pazï.*
        me.and.you=ACC=TOP   scold-THM-NEG-NPST=maybe
        '(They) will not scold me and you, I think.'

(5–22) *bafïtaa=ga*   *jaa=n=na*   *nau=mai*
        me.and.you=GEN   house=DAT=TOP   what=even
        njaa-n-Ø=ni.
        not.exist-NEG-NPST=CNF
        'There is nothing in our house, isn't there?'

Synchronically speaking, this form should be treated as a personal pronoun both in terms of function and form. With regard to its function, it refers to the speech act participants only, satisfying the definition of personal pronoun. With regard to form, it contains the first person pronominal root *ba-*, and it takes *=ga* when functioning as the genitive NP, unlike the numeral *fïtaar* 'two persons' which takes *=nu* when functioning as the genitive NP (§4.3.2). These two properties indicate that *bafïtaa* is a pronoun, not a numeral.

If this form is situated in the current number-person system in TABLE 5–3, it is analysed as the word that has the 'dual' number and the first per-

176   Chapter 5

TABLE 5–4. Personal pronominal system in terms of person and number

		Singular	Dual	Plural (root-PL)
1st person	exclusive	*ba(n)*		*ban-ti*
	inclusive		*bafïtaa*	*duu*
2nd person		*vva*		*vva-du*

son (inclusive) features. Together with the other inclusive word *duu* 'us (including you)', which should be analysed as the word with the plural number and the first person (inclusive) features, we would be able to have the following paradigm (which excludes the 3rd person demonstrative sub-paradigm).

This system is problematic, since there are three odd gaps in the paradigm. This does not mean, however, that the word *bafïtaa* should not be dealt with in the Irabu pronominal system. Rather, by giving up the current way of approaching the pronominal system, we can reach a very consistent and systematic paradigm that can handle all the pronominal words.

Instead of person, let us introduce the notion 'combination', i.e. the combination of speech participants, as is shown in the upper-most column of TABLE 5–5. The combinations are distinguished according to whether the speaker (1) and the hearer (2) are included (+) or excluded (−). We have four possible combinations, [+1, −2], [+1, +2], [−1, +2] and [−1, −2], with the last combination being the third person referents, which are encoded by the demonstratives as noted in the preceding section.

Instead of number, let us introduce the notion of group size: 'minimal' and 'augment', which are indicated in the left-most column of the table (−A: minimal or −augmented; +A: augmented). Note that the Irabu pronominal system has no leaky gap in the paradigm now. The most significant divergence from the person-number system is the treatment of the combination [+1, +2]. In terms of person, it is made up of two persons. In the suggested system, it constitutes a single group. In terms of number, it would be regarded as a marked number as against singular, since it involves two or more participants ('dual' or 'plural'). However, in the suggested system, it divides into the unmarked minimal group (which would correspond to 'dual') and the marked augmented group (which would correspond to 'plural').

Thus, the suggested minimal-augment system works better than the person-number system suggested in §5.2.2.1. The key is a rarely-occurring form *bafïtaa*, which is, according to the person-number system, the first person dual inclusive. As Greenberg (1988) points out, this category is difficult to capture in the person-number system presupposed in the euro-cen-

TABLE 5–5. Minimal-Augment system

	+1, −2	+1, +2	−1,+2
−A	ban	bafïtaa	vva
+A	banti	duu	vvadu

tric view of language, but if we give up the system and introduce the notions of combination (of persons) and group size, it is possible to situate such a seemingly problematic form. The minimal-augment system is not common in Japonic or in Ryukyuan in general, but is rather common in other languages such as Austronesian languages (see Fillimonova 2005 for a fuller discussion on the typology of minimal-augment, inclusive-exclusive, etc.).

The question arises as to which system (TABLE 5–3 and TABLE 5–5) should be adopted as the personal pronominal system of Irabu. This is dependent on whether we regard *bafïtaa* as a productively used form in contemporary Irabu. As mentioned, the word is very rare in natural discourse, and some speakers, especially the generations under their sixties, have no or limited command of this form. If we respect the older system where the word must have been more productively used, then the minimal-augment system should be adopted. If we respect the current system where the word is losing its productivity and is becoming archaic, then the paradigm set out in TABLE 5–3 should be adopted. In the subsequent description, I take the latter analysis, with the use of the terms 'singular/plural', 'first person/second persons' for personal pronouns. However, it should be emphasised that for those speakers who retain *bafïtaa*, the minimal-augment analysis should work.

5.2.2.3. Reflexive pronouns

Reflexive pronouns are *na(r)a* 'oneself' (singular) and *naa-du* 'selves' (plural). The parenthesised /r/ is deleted when *na(r)a* is followed by nominative/genitive =ga, as in *na(r)a + =ga > naa=ga*, or by the plural morpheme *-du* as shown above. If an NP is a subject and if another NP in the same clause is co-referential with it, a reflexive pronoun is substituted for the latter. This rule is obligatory in the case of third person pronouns but is optional in first and second persons (because the use of the first/second per-

178   Chapter 5

son pronouns for the co-referential NPs would not result in any ambiguity).

(5–23) 1st person subject > the same referent as a direct object
       ba=a   *kagami=n*   *nara=u=du*   *mii-tar.*
       1SG$_i$=TOP mirror=DAT RFL$_i$=ACC=FOC see-PST
       'I saw myself in a mirror.'
       Or *ba=a*   *kagami=n*   *banu=u=du*   *mii-tar.*
          1SG$_i$=TOP mirror=DAT 1SG$_i$=ACC=FOC see-PST

(5–24) 2nd person subject > the same referent as a direct object
       vva=a   *kagami=n*   *nara=u=ru*   *mii-tar?*
       2SG$_i$=TOP   mirror=DAT   RFL$_i$=ACC=FOC see-PST
       'Did you see yourself in a mirror?'
       Or *vva=a*   *kagami=n*   *vva=u=ru*   *mii-tar.*
          1SG$_i$=TOP mirror=DAT 2SG$_i$=ACC=FOC see-PST

(5–25) 3rd person subject > the same referent as a direct object
       kari=a   *kagami=n*   *nara=u=du*
       that.person$_i$=TOP mirror=DAT   RFL$_i$=ACC=FOC
       mii-tar.
       look-PST
       'S/he looked at himself/herself in the mirror.'
       cf. *kari=a*   *kagami=n* *kari=u=du*
             that.person$_i$=TOP mirror=DAT that.person$_j$=ACC=FOC
             mii-tar.
             look-PST
             'S/he looked at him/her in the mirror.'

na(r)a and *naadu* have one characteristic apparently not typical in reflexive pronouns cross-linguistically, i.e. as pronouns co-referential with subject 'in the same clause' (Schachter and Shopen 2007: 26). In quoted speech (typically in narratives), they can occur sentence-initially with no obvious reflexive controller (i.e. subject) present in the clause, as in (5–26) and (5–27) below. Such examples are typically accompanied by the hearsay marker =*ca* (§9.3.3) or the quotative marker =*tii* (§11.4.4.1) after the quoted portion.

(5–26) *nara=a*   *ik-a-di=ca.*
       RFL=TOP   go-THM-INT=HS
       '(X$_i$ says) "I$_i$'ll go".'

(5–27) *nara=u=ba*   *pus-i-i*   *nci+a-r=tii*

Morphology of nominals and adnominals   179

RFL=ACC=TOP   dry-THM-NRT   put+RSL-NPST=QT
'(Mermaid*i* said) "(they) dried me*i* on (the roof)"'

This 'sentence-initial reflexive' suggests that the reflexive controller is not necessarily an overt subject in the clause in which the reflexive pronoun appears, but the subject of a quotative expression that can be contextually recovered. For example, as is shown in the free translation of (5–26) and (5–27), it is possible to recover the clause 'X said', and the third person 'subject' X controls the reflexive.

Functionally speaking, the appearance of the 'sentence-initial reflexive' in quoted speech indicates the commencement of a quotation, and this is a helpful indicator especially because Irabu is an OV language where the actual quotation markers such as =*tii* come only after the quoted speech section.

5.2.3. Numerals

Numerals are made up of a numeral root and a classifier suffix. They can function as NPs, but most of their uses are adverbial, i.e. modifying predicates with no case (in generative grammar this would be called 'quantifier float'). The adverbial function is illustrated in (5–28) to (5–30):

(5–28) *pžtu=nu=du*   *mž-taar*   *kuma=n*
        man=NOM=FOC   three-CLF.HUMAN   this.place=DAT
        ur-Ø.
        exist-NPST
        'Persons, (with) three members, are here.'

(5–29) *pžtu=nu=du*   *kuma=n*   *mž-taar*
        man=NOM=FOC   this.place=DAT   three-CLF.HUMAN
        ur-Ø.
        exist-NPST
        'Persons are here (with) three members'

(5–30) *mž-taar*   *ur-Ø.*
        three-CLF.HUMAN   exist-NPST
        '(Persons) are here (with) three members'

Note in (5–30) that it is not possible to analyse the numeral as floating, as the head nominal from which the numeral should float (as in, say, *mž-taar=nu pžtu* 'three <u>persons</u>') is missing here. Rather, the examples above are better analysed as being used adverbially, one very common characteristic of nominals in Irabu.

180   Chapter 5

When used as an NP, a numeral either functions as the modifier of an NP
(as in (5–31) below), or as an argument NP (as in (5–32) to (5–36) below)
or a predicate NP (as in (5–37) below). It is very common for a numeral to
be modified by another NP, as shown in (5–35), or by an adnominal
(clause), as shown in (5–33) and (5–34). In (5–32), *mž-taar* 'three persons'
and *fi-taar* 'two persons' function anaphorically just like pronouns. As was
noted in §4.3.2, whereas in the NP modifier function numerals opt for genitive *=nu* rather than *=ga*, in the subject function they take the nominative
=ga rather than *=nu*.

(5–31) *mž-taar=nu*   *pžtu*
        three-CLF.HUMAN=GEN   man
        'Three persons'

(5–32) *mž-taar=ga*   *kuma=n,*
        three-CLF.HUMAN=NOM   this.place=DAT
        fitaar=ga   *kama=n*   *u-ta-m.*
        two-CLF.HUMAN=NOM   that.place=DAT   exist -PST-RLS
        'Three (of them) were here, and two were there.' [subject argu-
        ment NP]

(5–33) *unu mž-taar=ru*   *saar-i–i*   *kuu-Ø.*
        that three-CLF.HUMAN=ACC take-THM-NRT come-IMP
        'Bring those three persons.' [Direct object argument NP]

(5–34) *sïn-tar*   *mž-taar=n*   *idjav-busï+munu=i*
        die-PST   three-CLF.HUMAN=DAT   meet-DES (+thing)=CNF
        '(I) wish I could see the three (who) died.' [argument NP]

(5–35) *kama=nu*   *mž-taar=nkai*   *munu=u*   *fii-ru.*
        that.place=GEN three-CLF.HUMAN thing=ACC give-IMP
        'Give things to the three persons there.' [Indirect object argu-
        ment NP]

(5–36) *ju-taar=kara*   *mž-taar=n=du*
        four-CLF.HUMAN=ABL   three-CLF.HUMAN=DAT=FOC
        nar-tar.
        become-PST
        '(The number of people) became three from (the original) four.'
        [peripheral argument NP and extended core argument NP]

(5–37) *kuma=n*   *t-tar=ra*   *mž-taar=du*
        this.place=DAT come-PST=TOP three-CLF.HUMAN=FOC
        a-tar.
        COP-PST
        '(The people who) came here was three (persons).' [Predicate

Morphology of nominals and adnominals 181

NP]

Depending on what is being counted, both numeral roots and classifier suffixes may take on different forms. For example, as illustrated in the examples above, humans are counted by the HUMAN classifier *-taa(r)* ('persons'), whereas, as in (5–38) and (5–39) below, inanimate nouns are counted by various classifiers such as the HOUSE classifier *-kjuu* or the GENERAL classifier *-cï*. Also, numeral roots are variable depending on the classifier suffix they carry. Thus 'three houses' in (5–38) and 'three things' in (5–39) differ both in the numeral root and the classifier suffix.

(5–38) *mž-kjuu=nu*   *jaa.*
        three-CLF.HOUSE=GEN   house
        'Three houses (or households)'
(5–39) *mii-cï=nu*   *macïgai*
        three-CLF.GENERAL=GEN error
        'Three errors'

As is shown in the examples above, the numeral form also differs depending on the classifier attached to it. In the case of a numeral for 'three', the basic form is mž-, which may be mii- when followed by the general classifier *-cï*. See TABLES 5–6 and 5–7 for more examples of classifiers and numerals.

In information questions, the numeral root is replaced by *ifï-* 'how many', as in:

(5–40) *ifï-taar=nu*   *pžtu=ga?*
        how.many-CLF.HUMAN=GEN   man=FOC
        'How many persons (are there)?'
(5–41) *ifï-kjuu=nu*   *jaa=ga?*
        how.many-CLF.HOUSE=GEN   house=FOC
        'How many houses (or households) (are there)?'
(5–42) *ifï-cï=nu*   *macïgai=ga?*
        how.many=CLF.GENERAL=GEN error=FOC
        'How many errors (are there)?'

Below are two major sets of numerals. The numeral set for general inanimate nouns (TABLE 5–6) is morphologically most transparent, and most of the numeral roots here are also used in cardinal counting in isolation.

182   Chapter 5

TABLE 5–6. Numerals for counting general inanimate nouns

Numbers	word form	morphological structure
1	*piti-cï*	NUM -CLF:GENERAL
2	*fitaa-cï*	
3	*mii-cï*	
4	*juu-cï*	
5	*icï-cï*	
6	*mm-cï*	
7	*nana-cï*	
8	*jaa-cï*	
9	*kukunu-cï*	
10	*tuu*	NUM
11 to 19	*tuu+piti-cï,* etc.	NUM ('10'+'1', etc.) -CLF:GENERAL
20+ (loans)	*nizjuu*	non-native number system (< Japanese)
How many	*ifï-cï*	NUM.WH-CLF.GENERAL

The basic numeral roots in the table above also participate in other numeral
+ classifier combinations as in TABLE 5–7, though the numeral roots of lower numbers (especially '1') tend to be irregular and suppletive. Note that in
TABLE 5–7 the numeral root for '1' is not the basic *pžtu-* but an irregular
tavkjaa.

TABLE 5–7. Numeral word set for counting humans

Numbers	human	morphological structure
1	*tavkjaa*	suppletive form
2	*fï-taar*[1]	NUM -CLF:HUMAN
3	*mž-taar*	
4	*ju-taar*	
5	*icï=nu pžtu*	*NUM + =GEN + pžtu* (with the minor exception for 'six')
6	*muju=nu pžtu*	
7	*nana=nu pžtu*	
8	*jaa=nu pžtu*	
9	*kukunu=nu pžtu*	
10	*tuu=nu pžtu*	
11 to 19	*tuu-piticï=nu pžtu*	NUM -CLF:GENERAL + =GEN + *pžtu*
20 (loans)	*nizjuu*	Non-native system (< Japanese)
How many	*ifï-taar*	NUM.WH-CLF.HUMAN

---

[1] Here, the numeral is underlyingly *fïta-,* with the second syllable deleted when followed by

Morphology of nominals and adnominals

5.2.4. Interrogatives

Interrogatives fall into six basic forms which are roots, and just two complex forms which are composed of a basic form plus other morpheme(s). The basic forms may function as NPs, and are thus nominals. On the other hand, complex forms are not straightforwardly classified as nominals.

5.2.4.1. Basic forms

The basic forms, as listed in TABLE 5–8 below, can all serve as NPs in any of the three functions.

TABLE 5–8. Basic forms of Interrogative

Form	Meaning
nau	what
taru	who
nza	where
nzi	which
icï	when
iccja	how much; to what extent

Unlike typical nominals such as nouns, it is not common for interrogatives to be modified by another NP or an adnominal (clause), but it is possible, as shown in (5–46) and (5–47).

(5–43) *nau=ju=ga*   *fau-tar=ga?*
  what=ACC=FOC   eat-PST=Q
  'What (did you) eat?' [Argument NP]

(5–44) *iccja=ga*   *a-tar=ga?*
  how.much=FOC   COP-PST=Q
  'How much was (it)?' [Predicate NP]

(5–45) *nza=nu*   *pžtu=ga*   *a-tar?*
  where=GEN   man=FOC   COP-PST
  'Which place's person was (he)?' [Modifier of NP]

(5–46) *vva=a*   *nza=nu*   *taru=ga?*
  2SG=TOP   where=GEN   who=Q
  'Who are you from whose family?' [modified by NP]

(5–47) *vva=a*   *iravcï=nu*   *nau=ju=ga*
  2SG=TOP   Irabu.language=GEN   what=ACC=FOC

-taar (*fïta-taar* > *fï-taar*) by hapalogy. This analysis was suggested by an anonymous examiner of the original thesis.

184   Chapter 5

>
> *nara-i+ur-Ø=ga?*
> learn-THM+PROG-NPST=Q
> 'What (element) in the Irabu language are you studying?' [modified by NP]

The interrogatives *icï* 'when' and *iccja* 'how much; to what extent' can also be used adverbially.

(5–48) *asii*   *mmja*   *icï=ga*   *fïï-kutu?*
         then   INTJ   when=FOC   come-OBL
         'Then, when will (you) come?'

(5–49) *vva=a*   *iccja=ga*   *kav-tar=ga?*
         2SG=TOP   how.much=FOC   buy-PST=Q
         'How much (did) you buy?'

It is not a straightforward matter to subclassify the numeral for *ifïcï* 'how many', as it exhibits characteristics of both numerals and interrogatives. On the one hand, it carries a classifier suffix just as numerals do; on the other hand, it marks an information question just as interrogatives do. Also, the major syntactic criteria for distinguishing nominal subclasses, i.e. in terms of the syntactic functions, do not work here. However, there is a subtle but consistent difference between numerals (including 'how many') and interrogatives: when used as subject, numerals all take nominative case *=ga* rather than *=nu*, while interrogatives take *=nu* rather than *=ga*. Thus in (5–51), *ifïtaar* 'how many (people)' takes *=ga*. However, it is much more common to use the numeral adverbially, as in (5–52), than as subject, as in (5–51).

(5–50) *taru=nu=ga*   *sïn-tar=ga?*
         who=NOM=FOC   die-PST=Q
         'Who died?'

(5–51) *ui=kara=a*   *ifï-taar=ga=ga*
         that=ABL=TOP   how.many-CLF.HUMAN=NOM=FOC
         sïn-tar=ga?
         die-PST=Q
         'Out of them, how many persons died?'

(5–52) *ui=kara=a*   *ifï-taar(=ga)*
         that=ABL=TOP   how.many-CLF.HUMAN(=FOC)
         sïn-tar=ga?
         die-PST=Q

Morphology of nominals and adnominals   185

'Out of them, how many persons died?'

5.2.4.2. Complex form: 'how'
'how' is expressed with *nau* 'what' followed by instrumental case =*sii*.
However, *nau=sii* is in most cases reduced to *nau=si*, and unlike an instrumental argument, *nau=si* can serve as head of a phrasal modifier NP,
meaning 'what kind of' (5–54):

(5–53) *sjensoo   uwar-i-i=kara   nausi=ga   nbjav-tar?*
        war   finish-THM-NRT=ABL   how=FOC   survive-PST
        'After the war finished, how did (you) survive?'
(5–54) *nausi=nu   munu=u=ga   kav-tar=ga?*
        how=GEN   thing=ACC=FOC   buy-PST=Q
        'What kind of thing did (you) buy?'

Since *nau=si(i)* has a conventional meaning 'how?' or 'what kind?', I describe it as a morpheme *nausi(i)*. Syntactically, *nausi(i)* directly modifies a
predicate (i.e. adverbial) or is the modifier of an NP. The latter characteristic at first appears to justify treating *nausi* as an adnominal, but given that it
carries the NP extension when functioning as the modifier of an NP, it is
actually a minimal NP, i.e. a nominal word.

5.2.4.3. Complex form: 'why/how'
The interrogative 'why' (or 'how') is expressed with a morphologically
complex construction centring on *nau* 'what': *nau=sï=tii* (what=do=QT
'(lit.) by doing what'). This construction functions adverbially. It is often
realised as a fused form *nautti or nauttee*. Based on this morphological unity and the conventional semantics I describe *nau=sï=tii* and its variants as
a single morpheme *nausïtii* (~*nauttii*) meaning 'why' or 'how'. They do not
function as NPs. Rather they only function adverbially, directly modifying
predicates. Thus they are exceptional 'interrogative adverbs'.

(5–55) *nautti=ga   par-tar=ga?*
        why=FOC   leave-PST=Q
        'Why did (you) leave?' or 'In what way did (you) leave?'

5.2.5. Indefinites
An indefinite functions as an argument NP, a predicate NP, or the modifier
of an NP. As shown in TABLE 5–9 below, indefinites all contain, at least historically, an interrogative. Indefinites derived from an interrogative + dubi-

186   Chapter 5

tative marker =*gagara* 'I wonder (how/what/why)' (§9.3.2). Thus, *nau=
gagara* 'something' is literally 'I wonder what'. Also, the indefinite for
'something' undergoes irregular phonological reduction whereby the interrogative *taru* 'who' is realised as *tau*. I treat each indefinite form as a single
morpheme based on its morphological unity, phonological irregularity, and
a high degree of lexicalisation.

TABLE 5–9. Indefinites (a comparison with interrogative forms)

Interrogatives		Indefinites	
Form	Meaning	Form	Meaning
nau	what	*naugagara*	something
taru	who	*taugagara*	someone
nza	where	*nzagagara*	somewhere
nzi	which	*nzigagara*	either
icï	when	*icïgagara*	sometime
iccja	how much; to what extent	*iccjagagara*	some; some extent

Unlike nouns, it is uncommon for these to be modified by another NP or
an adnominal (clause), but it is possible as shown in (5–59) and (5–60).

(5–56) *taugagara=nu=du*   *sïn-tar=ca*
        someone=NOM=FOC   die-PST=HS
        'Someone has died, they say.' [Argument NP]

(5–57) *taru? ss-a-n-Ø.*   *taugagara=dara!*
        who   know-THM-NEG-NPST   someone=CRTN
        '(You said) who? I don't know. (That's) someone, anyway.'
        [Predicate NP]

(5–58) *taugagara=nu*   *ffa.*
        someone=GEN   child
        'Someone's child' [Modifier of NP]

(5–59) *uma=nu*   *naugara=u*   *muc-i+kuu-Ø.*
        that.place=GEN   something=ACC   carry-THM+come-IMP
        'Bring the thing there.' [modified by NP]

(5–60) *ik-i-i=ja*   *mii-n-Ø*   *nzagagara=nkai*
        go-THM-NRT=TOP   EXP-NEG-NPST   somewhere=ALL
        ik-a-di.
        go-THM-INT
        '(I) will go to somewhere I have never been to.' [modified by
        adnominal clause]

Morphology of nominals and adnominals   187

5.2.6. Non-pronominal demonstrative nominals

5.2.6.1. Demonstrative locatives

Demonstrative locatives (TABLE 5–1) serve as an argument or a predicate NP, and the modifier of an NP. Unlike nouns, it is not common for a demonstrative locative to be modified by another NP or an adnominal (clause), but such examples occur, as in (5–64).

(5–61) *kuma=n=du*   ur-Ø=dooi,   *uja.*
        this.place=DAT=FOC   exist-NPST=EMP   father
        '(We're) in this place, daddy.' [Argument NP]

(5–62) *sïn-tar=ra*   *kuma=ru*   *a-tar=ru?*
        die-PST=TOP   this.place=FOC   COP-PST=FOC
        '(The place) (x) died was this place?' [Predicate NP]

(5–63) *kuma=nu*   *nii=u*   *tur-i.*
        this.place=GEN   root=ACC   take-IMP
        'Take (out) the root of this part.' [Modifier of NP]

(5–64) *ba=ga*   *ur-Ø*   *kuma=kara*   *massugu ifï-kutu.*
        1SG=NOM exist-NPST this.place=ABL   straight   go-OBL
        '(You) should go straight from this place (where) I am.'

5.2.6.2. Demonstrative manner words

Demonstrative manner words are the least typical nominals, in that their typical function is adverbial and their function as argument NPs is highly limited. According to my text database, where a demonstrative manner word functions as an argument NP, this NP is an instrumental NP, i.e. a peripheral argument, as shown in (5–68a). I found only one exception where a demonstrative manner word functions as direct object NP (5–68b). It is relatively common for demonstrative manner words to function as predicate NPs or as modifiers of NPs. I could not elicit or find in texts examples where a demonstrative manner word is modified by another NP or an adnominal (clause).

(5–65) *ai=du*   *asï-tar*   *kai=du*   *asï-tar=tii*
        that.way=FOC do-PST that.way=FOC   do-PST=QT
        ba=a   *ubui+u-Ø-m=mu.*
        1SG=TOP   remember+PROG-NPST-RLS=FOC
        'I cannot remember (things), (saying) "(I) did that way or did that way (i.e. did such and such things in such and such manner)"'. [adverbial]

(5–66) *ai=nu*   *kutu=u=baa*   *ss-a-n-Ø.*

188   Chapter 5

that.way=GEN   thing=ACC=TOP   know-THM-NEG-NPST
'I don't know things like that.' [modifier of an NP]

(5–67) *ai=du*   *a-tar=rju.*
that.way=FOC   COP-PST=EMP
'(It) was like that.' [predicate NP]

(5–68) a. *kai=sii*   *nbja-i-Ø*
that.way=INST   endure-THM-NRT
t-ta-m=dara.
come-PST-RLS=CRTN
'By that way, (I) have endured (i.e. have lived a severe life).'
[peripheral argument NP]

          b. *mmja nau=ju=ga*   *fau-tar=gagara*   *ai=mai*
INTJ what=ACC=FOC eat-PST=I.wonder thay.way=even
ss-i+u-Ø-m=mu.
know-THM+PROG-NPST-RLS=FOC
'Well, what would (they) eat, could I know even the way (they ate)?' [direct object argument NP]

It is also noted that the proximate from *kui* is not used in natural discourse. Here, the medial from *ai* is used. In elicitation, some speakers say *kui* is possible, but others say *kui* is ungrammatical.

5.3. The internal structure of the nominal word

The internal structure of the nominal word is schematically shown in (5–69):

(5–69)   Stem (-DIMinutive)(-PLural)(-APPRoximative)

The stem slot may be filled by a nominal root which is in itself a free form, a compound stem, or a class-changed stem (e.g. agent nominal; §8.5.2). The three affixes are all derivational: diminutive, plural, and approxima-tive. In principle, the restriction on derivational morphology depends not so much on the nominal subclass as on the semantic content of a stem. For example, the diminutive suffix *-gama* can mark either a noun or a demon-strative as long as it makes sense to encode 'tininess' or 'modesty', but cannot mark any nominal whose semantic content is incompatible with these notions. However, there does exist some interdependency between the subclass of nominals and derivational morphology. For example, the plural affix has different allomorphs for different nominal subclasses, as

Morphology of nominals and adnominals   189

shown in §5.3.2.

5.3.1. Diminutive *-gama*

The diminutive suffix is *-gama*. As is illustrated in the following examples, the diminutive suffix encodes a tiny entity (5–70), a modest degree (5–71), and so on, all of which concern the idea of 'a little bit of'. In relation to this semantic entailment, it can express a modest attitude on the part of the speaker (5–72), which is appropriate when one asks something to the hearer with politeness, or a derogative meaning, as in (5–73).

(5–70)   *ba=ga*   *ffa-gama=a*   *kanasï+munu.*
         1SG=GEN   child-DIM=TOP   lovely+thing
         'My little child is lovely'

(5–71)   *saki-gama=u=du*   *num-tar.*
         saki-DIM=ACC=FOC   drink -PST
         '(I) drank a bit of sake.'

(5–72)   s*aki-gama=u*   *tur-as-i.*
         saki-DIM=ACC   take-CAUS-IMP
         'Could you please pass me the sake?'

(5–73)   *uma=nu*   *zjunsja-gama*
         that.place=GEN   policeman-DIM
         'The bloody policeman (standing) there.'

5.3.2. Plural *-mmi/-ta*, etc.

There are several suffixes that mark plurality, depending on the lexical class of the root to which it is attached. For nouns, it is either *-mmi* or *-ta*. For pronouns it is *-ti* (first person), *-du* (second person; reflexive), or *-nukja* (third person; alternatively *-ntja*), as listed in §5.2.2.1.

The plural affix *-mmi* is a grammaticalised form of a common noun *mmi* 'crowd', and encodes plurality of animate referents. For non-human animate referents, the suffixing of *-mmi* is somewhat disfavoured and an analytic expression making use of the common noun *mmi* is more preferred, as illustrated in (5–75b–c).

(5–74)   *uma=n*   *pžtu-mmi=nu=du*   *ur-Ø.*
         that.place=DAT   man-PL=NOM=FOC   exist-NPST
         'There are people.'

(5–75)   a. *uma=n*   *tur-mmi=nu=du*   *ur-Ø.*
            that.place=DAT   bird-PL=NOM=FOC   exist-NPST
            'There are birds.'

190   Chapter 5

b. *uma=n*   *tur=nu*   *mmi=nu=du*
that.place=DAT   bird=GEN   crowd=NOM=FOC
ur-Ø.
exist-NPST
'There are a flock of birds in that place.'

c. *uma=n*   *tur=nu*   *mmi-as-i–i=du*
that.place=DAT   bird=NOM   crowd-VLZ-THM-NRT=FOC
ur-Ø.
PROG-NPST
'In that place birds are making a crowd.' [lit. In that place birds are doing crowd.]

-ta encodes associative plurality, translated as '(X and) his/her company'. Thus *-ta* can mark proper nouns, as in (5–76), while *-mmi* cannot (5–77).

(5–76)   *uma=n*   *zjunzi-ta=nu=du*   *ur-Ø.*
           that.place=DAT   Junji-PL=NOM=FOC   exist-NPST
           'There are Junji and his company.'

(5–77)   **uma=n*   *zjunzi-mmi=nu=du*   *ur-Ø.*
           that.place=DAT   man-PL=NOM=FOC   exist-NPST
           [Lit.]'There are several Junji's.'

In old-fashioned speech such as traditional song lyrics, it is not uncommon to find cases where *-ta* is followed by *-mmi*:

(5–78)   *mutui*   *kagi=nu*   *agu-ta-mmi*
           very   beautiful=GEN   friend-PL-PL
           'Very beautiful friends.'

The relative order is always *-ta* followed by *-mmi* as above, and there seems to be no difference in meaning between *agu-ta* 'friends; (specific) friend and his/her company' and *agu-ta-mmi*, or between other pairs in attested examples.

5.3.3. Approximative *-nagi*

The approximative suffix is *-nagi*. This suffix marks approximation, translated as 'something like; or else; or like', or 'and so on', which allows speaker to avoid an exact identification of the referent.

(5–79)   *pžtu-nagi=nu*   *u-tar.*

Morphology of nominals and adnominals   191

    man-APPR=NOM   exist-PST
    'There was a man or suchlike.'

(5–80)   *uma-nagi=u*   *sauc-cas-i.*
            that.place-APPR=ACC   cleaning-VLZ-IMP
            'Clean around there.'

(5–81)   *un-nagi=n=na*   *nau=mai*   *as-irai-t-tar.*
            that.time-APPR=DAT=TOP   what=even   do-POT-NEG-PST
            '(I) couldn't do anything in those days.'

5.4. Adnominals

Adnominals are distinct from nominals in that the former are restricted to functioning as the modifier of an NP. Also, they do not carry case, which is obligatory for nominals unless an NP functions as a predicate. The adnominal class is very small and closed. Adnominals never carry derivational affixes such as nominal derivational affixes (§5.3).

TABLE 5–10. Adnominals

SUBCLASS	FORM	GLOSS
Demonstratives	*ku-nu*	'this' (proximate)
	u-nu	'that' (medial)
	ka-nu	'that' (distal)
Others	*daizïna*	'great; awful'

5.4.1. Demonstrative adnominals

There is a class of demonstrative adnominals, functioning only as the modifier of NPs.

(5–82)   *kunu*   *pžtu=u*   *sinsii=tim=dooi.*
           this   man=TOP   teacher=HS=EMP
           'This man is a teacher, they say.'

The derivational suffix -*nu*, which derives an adnominal stem from a demonstrative root, may have developed from the genitive case marker =*nu*. Synchronically, however, it is not a clitic, in that it attaches to a bound stem rather than to a free word.

5.4.2. Other adnominals

I could identify only one adnominal that is not a demonstrative. This is a recent loan from Japanese adjective *daiji=na* (=*na* is an adnominal marker

192   Chapter 5

of Japanese, which has become part of the stem in Irabu *daizïna*). It functions as an intensifier, with either meaning of 'great' or 'awful'.

(5–83) *uri=a*   *daizïna*   *ss-ja=dooi.*
         3SG=TOP   great   know-NLZ=EMP
         'That (guy) is such a knowledgeable person.'

(5–84) *uri=a*   *daizïna*   *jana+pžtu=dooi*
         3SG=TOP   great   evil+man=EMP
         'That (guy) is such an evil person.'

Chapter 6
Verb morphology

This chapter sets out to describe the internal structure of verbs, focusing on both their inflectional and derivational morphology. The verb class is the only word class that shows inflection. The verb is thus unambiguously defined by inflection. In this respect, the copula is a verb, but it differs from other non-copula verbs in that it cannot head a verb phrase. It appears in a nominal predicate phrase (§7.2). A verb inflects word-finally. I call the portion of the verb word other than the inflection a stem. I call a minimal stem a root. However, a stem may be a compound and/or may be derived by affixation. A verb stem may be derived from another verb or from a property concept stem. The former process is described in this chapter, while the latter is described in Chapter 8.

6.1. Functional overview

6.1.1. Verb inflection and finiteness
A primary distinction is made between finite inflection, i.e. inflection that specifies tense and/or mood, and non-finite inflection, i.e. the inflection that specifies neither. Negative polarity is an inflectional category compatible with both inflection types.

Syntactically, finite verb forms can terminate a sentence, while non-finite verbs cannot terminate a sentence, always occurring subordinated, coordinated, or chained to a matrix clause (Chapter 11).

6.1.2. Tense, mood, negation, voice, and aspect
Typologically common predicate categories such as tense, mood-modality, negation, voice, and aspect, are encoded in various ways in Irabu, not necessarily in verb morphology.[1] Since these encodings often show complex interdependency and/or involve larger structures (phrases and clauses), they will be discussed more fully in Chapter 10 (the simple sentence). In what follows I outline the categories thus encoded as a basis for the subse-

---

[1] Irabu verbs do not have agreement morphology, i.e. are not inflected for person, number, etc., of subject.

194   Chapter 6

quent description of verb morphology.

6.1.2.1. Tense, mood-modality, and negation
Tense, mood, and negation are expressed by verb inflection. Two mood
categories are grammaticalised as verb inflection: realis and irrealis. A fuller discussion of mood occurs in §10.5.1, and it suffices here to note that
realis mood expresses the speaker's perceived certainty (e.g. on the basis
of actuality) and high information value (i.e. new information to the hearer), whereas irrealis mood expresses future intention or wish. There are
also forms that are unmarked for mood.

There are of course other kinds of non-grammaticalised modality (e.g.
uncertainty, guess, potentiality, necessity, hearsay evidentiality, etc.), which
are expressed by various non-inflectional strategies, e.g. through modal
markers such as =pazï 'maybe' (§9.3).

The tense system involves a two-way distinction between past and non-
past. Whereas all non-finite verbs are not tense-marked, many finite verbs
are marked with tense. There are a few finite verb forms that are not tense-
marked: these are intentional, optative, and imperative forms, which have
no formal opposition between past and non-past, simply carrying a mood
suffix attached to the stem.

Mood is also crucially implicated in encoding time reference. Thus a
non-past realis form implies immediate future time reference in which an
action or state of affairs is imminent (e.g. a situation obviously about to
occur in front of speaker, as in *Hai! uti-r-m=dooi!* 'Hey! The base is about
to drop!'), whereas the non-tense-marked finite forms, i.e. irrealis forms
such as *-di* (intentional) usually imply non-immediate future time reference, though this is not an inherent function of *-di*. Also, modal possibilities are dependent on tense in crucial ways. As is shown in FIGURE 6–1, the
realis mood form is only found in past tense (e.g. *ibi-ta-m* 'plant-PST-RLS:
(certainly) planted') and non-past tense that designates present or imminent
future time reference (e.g. *ibi-r-m* 'plant-NPST-RLS: be going to plant').
This asymmetry in the distribution of realis mood is a formal manifestation
of the semantic fact that past time reference and future time reference are
asymmetrical with regard to mood (Comrie 1985a; Chung and Timberlake

Time reference	Past >>>>>>>	Present to imminent future >>	Future >>>>>
TENSE	Past	Non-past	N/A
MOOD	{ Realis	{ Realis	
	Unmarked }	Unmarked }	Irrealis

FIGURE 6–1. Tense system and mood system: overview

Verb morphology 195

1985). Making a realis assertion with future time reference is much more difficult than making one with past or present/imminent future time reference.

Negative polarity is also inflectional, and is again intertwined with the tense/mood systems. In particular, negation is incompatible with the non-past realis. Thus *ibi-r-m* 'is going to plant' cannot be negated, whereas *ibi-r* (non-past unmarked) has a negative counterpart *ibi-n*. This can be seen as an instantiation of a typologically recurrent restriction on the compatibility of negation with realis (in fact, there are languages which treat all negative clauses as irrealis; Payne 1997: 245).

6.1.2.2. Voice
Three types of non-active voice (causative, passive, malefactive) are marked by derivational morphology on verbs (§6.4; §10.4). In Japanese linguistics, malefactive would alternatively be called 'adversative passive' (Shibatani 1990 for a review). However, if we restrict the term passive voice to a valency *decreasing* operation (Dixon and Aikhenvald 2000), it should not be treated as a type of passive in Irabu or in Japanese (see §10.4.3 for a fuller discussion).

6.1.2.3. Aspect
Aspect is marked by three different coding strategies: (1) aspectual auxiliary verb, as in *ibi-i=du ur-Ø* 'be planting' (plant-NRT=FOC PROG-NPST), (2) verb inflection, as in *ibi-tar* (perfective), etc., and (3) full reduplication of a verb root, as in *ibi+ibi* '(iteratively) plant; (habitually) plant'. Aspectual categories that are productively coded by one or more of these strategies are progressive, resultative, prospective 'complete something for some benefit', perfect, iterative, and habitual. Since aspect marking requires reference to a range of structures, from verb morphology to VP structure, it will be dealt with more extensively in §10.5.2 after all the relevant structures have been introduced.

6.1.3. Inflection and clause combining
Irabu verb inflection also encodes clausal subordination and clause chaining. These structures are described in Chapter 11. In what follows I only note their basic characteristics in relation to verb inflection.

A non-finite verb form called a converb is used mainly to mark adverbial or adsentential subordination. That is, a converb turns its clause into an adjunct constituent (adverbial or adsentential), retaining verbal features in its clause-internal syntax, as illustrated in the examples below (the comma or-

196   Chapter 6

thographically indicates a clause boundary).

(6–1) *aagu=u*   *cïcï-ccjaaki=du,*
       song=ACC   hear-SIM=FOC
       ninivv-as-i+u-tar.
       sleepiness-VLZ-THM+PROG-PST
       'While listening to a song, (he) got sleepy.' [adverbial adjunct]

(6–2) *uku+kazi=nu*   *fïï-tigaa,*   *mmna*   *jaa=nu*
       big+wind=NOM   come-CND   all   house=GEN
       naka=n   *ur-kutu.*
       inside=DAT   exist-OBL
       'If a big wind blows, everyone should be at home.' [adsentential
       adjunct]

A non-finite verb form called a narrative converb is used to construct
clause chaining (§11.3). In the following example, the first two clauses are
narrative converbal clauses that are chained to the matrix predicate *mii-tigaa*, which is itself an adsentential adjunct of the matrix that follows
(whose predicate is *atar=dara*).

(6–3) *utu=u*   *cïk-i-i,*   *puka=nkai*   *idi-i,*
       sound=ACC   hear-THM-NRT   outside=ALL   go.out-NRT
       mii-tigaa,   *mmja,*   *uma=nu=i,*
       look-CND   INTJ   that.place=GEN=CNF
       niwaa=nu   *piticï*   *kugani=nu*
       garden=GEN   full   gold=NOM
       unusjuku   *a-tar=ca.*
       that.much   exist-PST=HS
       '(He) heard the sound, went outside, and looked, so (there) was
       gold, that much, filling the whole garden.'

6.2. The structure of the verb word

The verb template is schematised as **Stem (THEMATIC)-INFLECTION**,
where the 'Stem' slot may be occupied by a simple root or a derived stem
extended by various derivational processes such as verb-verb compounding and derivational affixation (§6.4). The inflection part may be internally
complex, i.e. may consist of two or three inflectional affixes. Certain subclasses of stem carry a thematic vowel before certain inflectional affixes.
The presence or absence of thematic vowels is dependent on the stem

Verb morphology   197

class, and these are discussed in what follows.

6.2.1. Stem class

To describe inflection accurately, it is first necessary to introduce the major morphological classes of stem. These stem classes are termed Class 1 and Class 2. There are also certain irregular verb stems (see TABLE 6–1 below), which are dealt with in §6.3.5.

The two major stem classes are largely phonologically determined. Class 1 stems end in /i/ (e.g. *ibi-* 'plant'; *idi-* 'exit; come out'; *tumi-* 'search';

TABLE 6–1. Irabu verb classes

Class 1:	ending in /i/
Class 2:	largely C-final
Irregular:	Deictic directional roots 'come' (suppletive) Light verb root 'do' (Class 2-like) Negative verb root (Class 1-like) Existential verb root (Class 2-like) Copula verb root (Class 2-like)

TABLE 6–2. Frequently used class 1 stems and class 2 stems

Class 1		Class 2	
idi-	'go out; exit'	*asïb-*	'play'
ibi-	'plant'	*kat-*	'win'
mii-	'look'	*kak-*	'write'
nii-	'boil'	*kug-*	'paddle'
fii-	'give'	*nas-*	'give birth'
pazïmi-	'begin'	*muc-*	'lift'
nkai-	'welcome; bring'	*jum-*	'read'
tumi-	'search'	*sïn-*	'die'
pani-	'jump'	*niv-*	'sleep'
kui-	'exceed'	*až-*	'say'
bassi-	'forget'	*tur-*	'take'
karagi-	'turn over'	*fa-*	'eat'
kai-	'change'	*ff-*	'bite'
kangai-	'think'	*ss-*	'know'
tati-	'stand (sth)'	*cc-*	'put on'
katami-	'carry'	*mmm-*	'ripe'
mutagi-	'lift'	*vv-*	'sell'
sïdi-	'hatch'	*žž-*	'scold'
rri-	'put into'	*rr-*	'enter'

198   Chapter 6

nkai- 'welcome'; *rri-* 'put'; *kui-* 'exceed'; *mii-* 'look'; *fii-* 'give', etc.). Class
2 roots all end in /C/ except for certain cases that end in a vowel (e.g. *fa-*
'eat'; see §6.3.4.3).

Certain Class 2 roots consisting of a geminate onset without a nucleus
(//CC[V]//, where [V] is an unfilled nucleus) undergo different morphophonemic strategies to surface as a permissible syllable shape. See §2.7.3,
2.7.4, 2.7.5.

6.2.2. Thematic vowel (stem extension)

In order to carry certain inflectional affixes, Class 2 stems carry a thematic
vowel *-a* (or *-u* in certain lexical items; see §6.3.4.4) or *-i* to form a thematic stem. Otherwise they do not carry thematic vowels, so remain athematic
stems.[2] Class 1 stems are inherently athematic. The thematic vowels are
stem-extenders (Bickel and Nichols 2007), analogous to thematic segments
in Indo-European (Grundt 1978), Caucasian (Kibrik 1991), and certain
Oceanic languages (Lichtenberk 1983), occurring stem finally and marking
conjugational classes.

As an illustration of thematic stem formation, let us look at the Class 2
stem *tur-* 'write' and some of its inflection. Like all members of Class 2
members, *tur-* has three inflectional possibilities, depending on the inflectional affix that follows: (1) to remain an athematic stem, (2) to form a thematic stem with *-a*, and (3) to form a thematic stem with *-i*. The stem *tur-*
remains an athematic stem when carrying such an inflectional affix as the
conditional converb *-tigaa*, irrealis prohibitive *-na*, and past unmarked *-tar*.

(6–4)   a. *tur-tigaa*   b. *tur-na*   c. *tur-tar*
           take-CND   take-PRH   take-NPST
           'if (x) take'   '(you) don't take'   'took'

The stem *tur-* carries thematic *-a* when it further carries such inflectional
affixes as negative converb suffix *-da*, negative conditional converb suffix
-dakaa, and finite irrealis intentional suffix *-di*.

(6–5)   a. *tur-a-da*   b. *tur-a-dakaa*
           take-THM-NEG.NRT   take-THM-NEG.CND
           'not taking...'   'if (x) do not take'
        c. *tur-a-di*

---

[2] I will explain (in §6.2.3) the validity of the analysis where a thematic vowel belongs to the
stem, as opposed to the analysis where the segment belongs to part of the inflectional affix
that follows the stem.

take-THM-INT
'will take'

The stem *tur-* carries thematic *-i* before it further carries such inflectional affixes as narrative converb suffix *-i*, causal converb suffix *-ba*:

(6–6)   a. *tur-i-i*   b. *tur-i-ba*
          take-THM-NRT   take-THM-CSL
          '(x) take, and'   '(x) take, so that'

See §6.3.1 and §6.3.2 for an exhaustive list of inflectional affixes that do or do not require thematic stems.

On the other hand, a Class 1 stem is always athematic, i.e. does not carry a thematic vowel in any of these morphological environments:

(6–7)   a. *idi-tigaa*   b. *idi-rna*   c. *idi-tar*
          exit-CND   exit-IMP   exit-NPST
          'if (x) exit'   '(you) don't exit'   'exited'
(6–8)   a. *idi-da*   b. *idi-dakaa*   c. *idi-di*
          exit-NRT.NEG   exit-NEG.CND   exit-INT
          'not exiting...'   'if (x) do not put'   'will exit'
(6–9)   a. *idi-i*   b. *idi-ba*
          exit-NRT   exit-CSL
          '(x) exit, and'   '(x) exit, so that'

In summary, whether or not a thematic vowel can appear depends on the class of the verb stem, i.e. Class 1 (always athematic) or Class 2 (athematic or thematic), and in the latter class, whether thematic affix *-a* or *-i* is required is dependent on which inflectional affix follows.

6.2.3. Some notes on the thematic vowel analysis

Thematic vowels are stem extender affixes in the current description. However, there may be at least two alternatives in the treatment of what I regard as thematic vowels.

Analysis 1: to treat them as part of Class 2 stems (at the lexical level)
Analysis 2: to treat them as part of the suffix that follows.

This issue is worth discussing at some length in this grammar given that linguists working on Japonic languages often raise this issue (Kazama

200   Chapter 6

1992), and often suggest the solution (2).[3] Such an analysis would make
sense in Japanese, while it is definitely not in Irabu, as is shown in what
follows.

To begin with, Analysis 1 immediately turns out to be an ill analysis.
According to this analysis, a Class 2 minimal stem for 'write', for example,
should have three allomorphs *kafï*, *kaka*, and *kaki*. Thus there should not be
a stem form *kak-*.

(6–10)   Class 2 stem *kak-* 'write' [Analysis 1]
        a. *kaka-di*   b. *kaki-i*   c. *kafï-tar*
          write-INT   write-NRT   write-PST
          'will write'   'write, and...'   'wrote'

Here, it is noted that affixation of agent nominalizer suffix *-ja* to the stem
produces *kak-ja*. It is straightforward to consider that the stem is underlyingly *kak-* rather than one of *kaka*, *kaki*, or *kafï*. Thus thematic vowels
should not be included as part of Class 2 stems at the lexical level.

Turning to Analysis 2, it would be more advantageous than Analysis 1,
since we can dispense with the thematic-athematic stem distinction alto-
gether from the grammatical description. Compare (6–11) and (6–12)
below.

(6–11)   Class 2 stem *kak-* 'write' [Analysis 2]
        a. *kak-adi*   b. *kak-ii*
          write-INT   write-NRT
(6–12)   Class 1 stem *ibi-* 'plant' [either Analysis 1 or 2]
        a. *ibi-di*   b. *ibi-i*
          plant-INT   plant-NRT

However, we now have to postulate a host of allomorphy on the part of inflectional affixes. For example, even though Analysis 2 in (6–11) can dispense with the thematic-athematic stem distinction, we have allomorphy on
the part of the inflectional affix depending on whether it is attached to a
Class 2 stem (6–11) or a Class 1 stem (6–12).

The current thematic analysis resolves this allomorphy by analysing the
initial vowel of an inflectional affix in Analysis 2 (e.g. *-a* of *-adi*) as part of
the stem, i.e. as a thematic vowel, as illustrated in (6–13):

---

[3] This issue also seems to be cross-linguistically a recurrent topic. See, for example, Lichtenberk (1983) for his argument for thematic 'consonants' in Manam as stem extenders and not
as part of the subsequent affix or of the preceding root.

Verb morphology 201

(6–13)   Class 2 stem kak- 'write' [the current 'thematic vowel' analysis]
      a. *kak-a-di*   b. *kak-i-i*
      write-THM-INT   write-THM-NRT

However, in this analysis, we have to admit two types of stem, i.e. thematic stems and athematic stems. So, in terms of descriptive economy, we cannot really judge whether Analysis 2 or the thematic analysis is better.

The substantial reason for abandoning Analysis 2 and taking the current analysis concerns agglutinative Auxiliary Verb Construction, where a lexical verb stem and an auxiliary verb stem is serialised to form a single verb stem (§6.4.2.3). As will be noted in §6.4.2.3, there are three aspect markers *u(r)-* (progressive), *a(r)-* (resultative), and *uk-* (benefactive perfect) that are used as an auxiliary verb stem. They appear as an independent auxiliary verb word in a verb phrase (phrasal AVC, §7.1.4), as illustrated in (6–14a), or as the second stem in a single verb word (agglutinative AVC), as in (6–14b).

(6–14)   Class 1 stem *ibi-* 'plant'
      a. *ibi-i*   *u-tar.*   b. *ibi+u-tar.*
         plant-NRT   PROG-PST   plant-PROG-PST
         Lexical V   Aux V   [Lexical stem + Aux stem]$_V$
         '(x) was planting (something)'

As is clear from the above pair, the inflectional affix *-i* of the lexical verb in (a) example is deleted, and the lexical stem and the auxiliary stem is agglutinatively serialised to form (b) example.

Now, let us look at what happens in the same kind of word-phrase alternation when the lexical verb stem is a Class 2 stem.

(6–15)   a. *kak-i-i*   *u-tar.*
         write-THM-NRT   PROG-PST
         Lexical V   Aux V
         '(x) was writing'
      b. *kak-i+u-tar.*
         write-THM+PROG-PST
         [Lexical stem+Aux stem]$_V$

If we follow the current analysis, as is shown in (6–15) above, the alternation between (6–15a) and (6–15b) can be explained by the same rule as for (6–14a) and (6–14b): the inflectional affix *-i* of the lexical verb *kakii* is de-

202   Chapter 6

leted, and the lexical verb stem *kaki* (thematic) and the auxiliary verb stem
form a single stem.

This demonstrates that the thematic vowel *-i* cannot be attributed to the
property of inflectional affix. Here, if we maintained that the thematic vowel *-i* belonged to the progressive aspect root *u-*, then the overall structures
above would be as follows:

(6–16)   a. *kak-ii*   *u-tar.*   b. *kak+iu-tar.*
             write-NRT   PROG-PST   write+PROG-PST
             Lexical V   Aux V   [Lexical stem+Aux stem]$_V$
             '(x) was writing'

This analysis claims that the progressive aspect marker has two allomorphs, *iu(r)-* in an agglutinative AVC in which the first stem is Class 2 (as
in (6–16b)), and *u(r)-* elsewhere, as in (6–16a). However, such an analysis
is certainly ad-hoc with a multiple duplication of allomorphy both in inflectional affixes and in the three root aspect markers.

In sum, even though Analysis 2 and the thematic analysis are equally
plausible in terms of descriptive economy (i.e. the former opts for allomorphy on the part of the inflectional affix whereas the latter on the part of the
stem), the best way to describe the alternation between an agglutinative
AVC and a phrasal AVC is to adopt the thematic analysis.

6.3. Inflectional morphology

In this section I describe the formal aspects of finite and non-finite inflections, presenting a full list of inflectional paradigms with two representative stems: Class 1 *ibi-* 'plant' and Class 2 *tur-* 'take'. Following the basic
description of inflection, I note morphophonemic processes applicable to
certain subclasses of Class 2 stems.

6.3.1. Finite inflection

Finite inflection is the type of inflection which forms finite verbs, which
may terminate a sentence. Finite inflection marks tense and/or mood, and,
in certain forms, negative polarity.

TABLE 6–3 sets out the inflectional paradigm of finite verb forms (unmarked, realis, and irrealis forms). In the row for 'Structure', [Stem] is an
athematic stem, whereas [Stem(-a)] and [Stem(-i)] are a thematic stem with
-a and a thematic stem with *-i* respectively, if the stem is a Class 2 stem. If
the stem is a Class 1 stem, which is always athematic, the bracketed (-a) or

Verb morphology 203

(-i) is irrelevant. TABLE 6–4 and TABLE 6–5 illustrate each type of inflection with Class 1 stem *ibi-* 'plant' and Class 2 stem *tur-* 'take'. In addition to the paradigm below there are two 'secondary inflectional endings', described in §7.2.2.

TABLE 6–3. Finite inflection

(a) Unmarked form (inflected for tense)

		Class 1		Class 2	
	Structure	NPST	PST	NPST	PST
Affirmative	[Stem]-tense	*-r*	*-tar*	*-Ø*	*-tar*
Negative	[Stem(-a)]-neg-tense	*-n-Ø*	*-t-tar*	*-n-Ø*	*-t-tar*

Note: the negative suffix *-n* assimilates to *-t* when followed by *-tar*.

(b) Realis form (inflected for tense and mood)

		Class 1		Class 2	
	Structure	NPST	PST	NPST	PST
Affirmative	[Stem]-tense-mood	*-r-m*	*-ta-m*	*-Ø-m*	*-ta-m*
Negative	[Stem(-a)]-neg-tense-mood		*-t-ta-m*		*-t-ta-m*

Note: (1) *-ta-m* is formed by the past tense suffix *-tar*+the realis mood suffix *-m* with /r/ deleted by rule.

(2) there is no negative form for non-past realis.

(c) Irrealis form (inflected for mood)

	Structure	Class 1	Class 2
optative	[Stem(-a)]-mood	*-baa*	*-baa*
intentional	[Stem(-a)]-mood	*-di/-ju*	*-di/-Ø*
negative intentional	[Stem(-a)]-mood	*-djaan*	*-djaan*
imperative	[Stem(-i)]-mood	*-ru*	*-Ø*
prohibitive	[Stem]-mood	*-rna*	*-na*

Note: the intentional suffix has two variants in each stem class.

TABLE 6–4. Finite inflection of Class 1 *ibi-* 'plant' (stem is indicated by [ ])

(a) Unmarked form

	Structure	Non-past	Past
Affirmative	[Stem]-tense	*ibi-r* 'plant'	*ibi-tar* 'planted'
Negative	[Stem]-neg-tense	*ibi-n-Ø* 'not plant'	*ibi-t-tar* 'did not plant'

204 Chapter 6

(b) Realis form

	Structure	Non-past	Past
Affirmative	[Stem]-tense-mood	*ibi-r-m* 'plant'	*ibi-ta-m* 'planted'
Negative	[Stem]-neg-tense-mood		*ibi-t-ta-m* 'did not plant'

(c) Irrealis form

	Structure		
optative	[Stem]-mood	*ibi-baa*	'want to plant'
intentional	[Stem]-mood	*ibi-di or ib-ju*	'will plant'
negative intentional	[Stem]-mood	*ibi-djaan*	'won't plant'
imperative	[Stem]-mood	*ibi-ru*	'you plant'
prohibitive	[Stem]-mood	*ibi-rna*	'you do not plant'

Note: when the intentional suffix is -ju, the stem-final /i/ is deleted.

TABLE 6–5. Finite inflection of Class 2 tur- 'take' (stem is indicated by [ ])

(a) Unmarked form

	Structure	Non-past	Past
Affirmative	[Stem]-tense	*tur-Ø* 'take'	*tur-tar* 'took'
Negative	[Stem-a]-neg-tense	*tura-n-Ø* 'not take'	*tura-t-tar* 'did not take'

(b) Realis form

	Structure	Non-past	Past
Affirmative	[Stem]-tense-mood	*tur-Ø-m* 'take'	*tura-ta-m* 'took'
Negative	[Stem-a]-neg-tense-mood		*tura-t-ta-m* 'did not take'

(c) Irrealis form

	Structure		
optative	[Stem-a]-mood	*tura-baa*	'want to take'
intentional	[Stem-a]-mood	*tura-di*	'will take'
negative intentional	[Stem-a]-mood	*tura-djaan*	'won't take'
imperative	[Stem]-mood	*tur-i*	'you take'
prohibitive	[Stem]-mood	*tur-na*	'you do not take'

There is a gap in the inflectional paradigm above: the non-past realis form lacks a negative counterpart. This was noted in §6.1.2.1.

The irrealis intentional suffix for Class 1 stems is either -*ju* (only with a Class 1 stem) or -*di*, whereas that for Class 2 stem is either -*di* or -*Ø* (or the absence of -*di*). The suffix -*ju* causes truncation of the stem-final /i/, as shown in TABLE 6–4 (c) (*ibi-* + -*ju* > *ib-ju*). Other examples are: *mutagi-* 'lift' > *mutag-ju* 'will lift', *mii-* 'look' > *mi-ju* 'will look', *nkai-* 'welcome'

Verb morphology   205

> *nka-ju* 'will welcome'.

Below I list examples of affirmative finite verb forms. A full functional account is given in §10.5.1. In particular, unmarked forms have various uses, of which the major ones are listed below.

(6–17) Past realis (PST-RLS)
    nkjaan=na   *pav=mai*   *juu*   *u-ta-m.*
    old.times=TOP   snake=too   very   exist-PST-RLS
    'In those days (there) were a lot of snakes.' [direct experience;
    speaker is certain and is asserting that his/her statement is true.]

(6–18) Past unmarked (PST)
    a. *nkjaan=na*   *pav=mai*   *juu*   *u-tar?*
       old.times=TOP   snake=too   very   exist-PST
       'In old times (there) were a lot of snakes, weren't there?'
       [speaker is not certain that his/her statement is true.]

    b. *pav=nu=du*   *juu*   *u-tar.*
       snake=NOM=FOC   very   exist-PST
       '(It was) snakes (that) were plentiful.' [the statement is pre-
       supposed]

(6–19) Non-past realis (NPST-RLS)
    hai!   *uti-r-m=dooi!*
    INTJ   drop-NPST-RLS=EMP
    'Watch out! (the base) is going to drop!' [imminent future event
    that is certain to occur in speaker's presence]

(6–20) Non-past unmarked (NPST)
    a. *atu+fïni=a*   *sacï*   *nar-Ø.*
       late+boat=TOP   early   become-NPST
       'The boat departing late will arrive early.' [proverb: general
       truth atemporally applicable]

    b. *kunur=ra*   *maž=mai* *mm=mai*   *fau-Ø.*
       these.days=TOP   rice=too   potato=ACC=too   eat-NPST
       'Nowadays (one) eats both rice and potatoes.' [habitual]

    c. *upujuu=ja*   *pžsara=kara*   *fïï-Ø.*
       The Upujuu=TOP   Hirara=ABL   come-NPST
       'The Upujuu (ship) comes from Hirara.' [scheduled and reg-
       ularly occurring future event]

(6–21) Irrealis optative (OPT)
    ba=ga   *mmaga=u*   *mii-baa=i=ti,*
    1SG=GEN   grand.child=ACC   see-OPT=CNF=QT
    denwa   *asï-tar=ca.*

206   Chapter 6

        phone   do-PST=HS
        '(She) is said to have made a call and said "I want to see my
        grandchild."'
(6–22) Irrealis intentional (INT)
        ba=a   *aca*   *ik-a-di.*
        1SG=TOP   tomorrow   go-THM-INT
        'I will go tomorrow.'
(6–23) Irrealis imperative (IMP)
        pucci   *fa-i!*
        in.haste   eat-IMP
        'Eat in haste!'

6.3.2. Non-finite inflection

Non-finite inflection marks coordination or adverbial-adsentential subordination, with no tense or mood marking. The only exception to this is past
anterior *-tarjaa* 'did X, and then...' which can be considered to have derived from the finite unmarked inflectional affix *-tar*. Negative polarity is
systematically marked on narrative converbs, but only restrictively on other converbs.

The category of converb divides into (a) the narrative converb and (b)
other converbs. The narrative converb is distinct from the other converbs in
three major respects. First, as mentioned above, negative polarity is systematically marked for the narrative converb. Second, the former is integrated into the Auxiliary Verb Construction, functioning as the lexical verb
of the AVC (§7.1.2). Third, narrative converbs are highly contextual, with
no clear adverbial meaning (§6.3.2.1, §11.3).

6.3.2.1. Narrative converbs
TABLE 6–6 sets out the inflectional paradigm of narrative converbs. Although narrative converbs are non-finite, i.e. lacking tense and mood marking, they still mark polarity.

TABLE 6–6. Inflection of narrative converbs

	Class 1 *ibi-* 'plant' Stem-INFL	Class 2 *tur-* 'take' Stem(-THM)-INFL
medial 'do (sth), and...'	*[ibi]-i*	*[tur-i]-i*
negative medial 'not doing'	*[ibi]-da*	*[tur-a]-da*

The suffix *-i* has a variant, *-Ø*, which often occurs when the stem ends in /ii/

Verb morphology 207

or /ai/, as in *mii-Ø* (look-NRT) 'look:NRT' rather than *mii-i* and *fa-i-Ø* (eat-THM-NRT) 'eat:NRT' rather than *fa-i-i*. We do find *fa-i-i* in careful speech, but we never find **miii*, probably due to the impermissible syllable structure of this form ($*V_iV_iV_i$).

Below I list examples of narrative converbs. As illustrated in (a) examples and (b) examples below, a narrative converb may be used as a head of a chained medial clause (see §11.3 for a fuller account of clause chaining) or as a lexical verb of a complex VP (§7.1).

(6–24) Narrative converb (NRT)

a. *pisir=ru*   *fa-i-i,*   *sïgutu=u*   *as-i-i,*
lunch=ACC eat-THM-NRT work=ACC do-THM-NRT

ffa=u   *nkai-i=du,*   *jaa=n*   *ngi-tar.*
child=ACC bring-NRT=FOC house=DAT return-PST

'(I) ate lunch, worked, brought a child, and returned home.' [clause chaining]

b. *buuz=zu*   *nag-i-i=du*
sugar.cane=GEN   break.down-THM-NRT=FOC

ur-Ø.
PROG-NPST

'(He) is harvesting sugarcane.' [within VP structure]

(6–25) Negative narrative converb (NEG.NRT)

a. *suba=u=mai*   *misi-da,*   *kjoocïki*
side=ACC=even let.see-NEG.NRT standing.still

a-sïmi-tar.
do-CAUS-PST

'Not allowing (students) to look away, (the teacher) made (them) stand   still.' [clause chaining]

b. *uri=u=baa*   *ažž-a-da*   *ur-i.*
that=ACC=TOP say-THM-NEG.NRT PROG-IMP

'(I) kept unstating it.' [within VP structure]

6.3.2.2. Other converbs

TABLE 6–7 sets out the inflectional paradigm of the other converbs than the narrative converb.

In Class 1, the inflectional affixes of causal and conditional 1 are both *-ba*, but there may appear *ri* for causal converb *-ba*, securing the relevant distinction. This *ri* may be a structural analogue to the thematic *-i* stem of Class 2. The aversive converb *-zïm* may be followed by quotative marker *=tii* (§11.4.4.1).

208   Chapter 6

TABLE 6–7. Converb inflection: Comparison of Class 1 and Class 2

	Class 1 *ibi-* 'plant'	Class 2 *tur-* 'take'
conditional 1 (unproductive) 'if'	*[ibi]-ba*	*[tur-a]-ba*
negative conditional 1 'if not; unless'	*[ibi]-dakaa*	*[tur-a]-dakaa*
aversive 'lest'	*[ibi]-zïm(=ti(i))*	*[tur-a]-zïm(=ti(i))*
negative intentional conditional 'if will not'	*[ibi]-djaadakaa*	*[tur-a]-djaadakaa*
causal 'because; when; if'	*[ibi]-(ri)-ba*	*[tur-i]-ba*
circumstantial 'while'	*[ibi]-utui*	*[tur-i]-utui*
conditional 2 (productive) 'if; when'	*[ibi]-tigaa*	*[tur]-tigaa*
negative conditional 2 'if not... (it's OK)'	*[ibi]-gurai*	*[tur]-gurai*
simultaneous 'while'	*[ibi]-ccjaaki*	*[tur]-ccjaaki*
purposive 'in order that'	*[ibi]-ga*	*[tur]-ga*
continuous 'whenever'	*[ibi]-gakaazï*	*[tur]-gakaazï*
immediate anterior 'as soon as'	*[ibi]-tuu*	*[tur]-tuu*
past anterior 'did X, and then...'	*[ibi]-tarjaa*	*[tur]-tarjaa*

Below I list examples of converbs. A fuller account of converbs as head of subordinate clauses will be given in §11.4.1 and §11.4.2.

(6–26)   Conditional 1 (CND)
         kuma=n   *nci-ba=du,*   *zau-kar-Ø*
         this.place=DAT   put-CND=FOC   good-VLZ-NPST
         '(It's) fine if you put (it) here.'

(6–27)   Negative conditional 1 (NEG.CND)
         nnama   *par-a-dakaa,*   *junai=n*
         now   leave-THM-NEG.CND   night=DAT
         nar-Ø=dara.
         become-NPST=CRTN
         'If you don't go (back home) now, (it) will get dark.'

(6–28)   Aversive (AVR)
         kazam=nu   *par-ra-zïm,*   *tuu=ju*   *simi-ru.*
         fly=NOM   enter-THM-AVR   window=ACC   shut-IMP
         'Lest flies come in, shut the window.'

(6–29)   Negative intentional conditional (NEG.INT.CND)
         vva=ga   *ik-a-djaadakaa,*   *ban=mai*
         2SG=NOM   go-THM-NEG.INT.CND   1SG=too
         ik-a-djaan.
         go-THM-NEG.INT
         'If you will not go, I will not go either.'

(6–30)   Causal (CSL)
         ffa=nu   *nak-i-ba=du,*   *nivv-ai-n-Ø.*

Verb morphology   209

child=NOM   cry-THM-CSL=FOC   sleep-POT-NEG-NPST
'Because my child cries, I cannot sleep.'

(6–31)   Circumstantial (CRCM)

kunu   tugi=u=ba   tur-i-i   sïti-i,
this   spike=ACC=TOP   take-THM-NRT   do.away.with-NRT

uri=u   uju=u   fikas-i-utui=jaa,
3SG=ACC   hot.water=ACC   boil-THM-CRCM=ATN

ui=ga   naka=nkai   sa=tti   rri-ri-ba,
3SG=GEN   inside=ALL   ONM=QT   put-THM-CSL

japa-fi   nar-Ø=dara.
soft-AVLZ   become-NPST=CRTN

'You do away with these spikes, and, while boiling water, you
see, put it (the leaf whose spikes have been stripped off) into
the water; then it becomes softened.'

(6–32)   Conditional 2 (CND)

nkif=fu   tur-tigaa,
Caulerpa.lentillifera=ACC   take-CND

ukusu=nkai   cïk-i-i   ara-i.
marine.water=ALL   put-THM-NRT   wash-IMP

'If you get a Caulerpa lentillifera, put it into marine water and
wash (it).'

(6–33)   Negative conditional 2 (NEG.CND)

nnama   asï-gurai,   zjaubu=ju.
now   do-NEG.CND   fine=EMP

'If (you) don't do (it) now, (that's) fine.'

(6–34)   Simultaneous (SIM)

sïgutu=u   asï-ccjaaki=du,   ffa+murja=mai   asï-Ø.
work=ACC   do-SIM=FOC   child+sitting=too   do-NPST

'While (I) am working, (I) do baby-sitting as well.'

(6–35)   Purposive (PUR)

žžu   cïï-ga,   ik-a-di.
fish   catch-PUR   go-THM-INT

'Let's go to catch fish.'

(6–36)   Continuous (CNTN)

ba=ga   mii-gakaazï,   sauz=zu=bakaar=du
1SG=NOM   look-CNTN   cleaning=ACC=always=FOC

as-i+ur-Ø.
do-THM+PROG-NPST

'Every time I see (her), (she) is always doing house cleaning.'

(6–37)   Immediate anterior (ANT)

kunu	*ffa=a,*	*mma=n*	*katami-rai-tuu=du,*
this	child=TOP	mother=DAT	carry-PASS-ANT=FOC

nafi-Ø	*su=u*	*jami-r.*
cry-NPST	CMP=ACC	stop-NPST

'This child stops crying <u>as soon as it is carried by its mother</u>.'

(6–38) Past anterior (PST.ANT)

mii-tarjaa=du,	*mmja, naa=ga*	*tuzï*	*a-tar=ca.*
look-PST.ANT=FOC	INTJ RFL=GEN	wife	COP-PST=HS

'<u>(He) looked at (her), then</u> (he found that it) was his wife.'

6.3.3. Internal structure of inflectional endings

Some notes are necessary to justify the morphological analyses presented above.

6.3.3.1. Finite realis inflection as -(NEG)-TENSE-MOOD

A close look at the non-past realis/unmarked pairs in Classes 1 and 2 reveals that a realis form is formed by suffixing the mood suffix /m/ to an unmarked form. Thus, the Class 1 *ibi-r-m* 'plant-NPST-RLS' is analysable as the unmarked *ibi-r* + *-m*, and Class 2 *tur-Ø-m* 'take-NPST-RLS' is analysable as the unmarked *tur-Ø* + *-m*. From this observation, I have analysed that the past *-ta-m* can be analysed as *-tar* + *-m* (-PST + *-m*) with deletion of /r/. This synchronic analysis is diachronically supported, as the *-m* was once a nominaliser marker *=mo(no)*, which was a clitic, attached to the unmarked form (Karimata 1999).

TABLE 6–8. Morpheme boundaries in (non-) past realis and unmarked

Past	unmarked	*-tar*	
	realis	*-tar* + *-m* > *-ta-m*	
Non-past	unmarked	-r (Class 1)	-Ø (Class 2)
	realis	*-r* + *-m* > *-r-m*	*-Ø* + *-m* > *-Ø-m*

6.3.3.2. Finite inflection as -TENSE-MOOD[NEG]

It is impossible to extract a negative morpheme from the forms *-rna* (Class 1 prohibitive) or *-na* (Class 2 prohibitive) and *-djaan* (negative intentional). Clearly, in *-rna* and *-na* negative polarity is fused with mood, since *-na* (prohibitive) expresses negation by itself.

The form *-djaan* could be analysed as *-djaa* + *-n*, i.e. containing negative suffix *-n*, but there appears to be no justification for this analysis synchronically. I encountered just one attestation in my text corpus which suggests that *-djaa* and *-n* were originally separate morphemes.

Verb morphology 211

(6–39) vva=ga   nkai-djaadakaa,
       2SG=NOM   bring-NEG.INT.CND
       nau=h-u-di=ga?
       what=do-THM-INT=FOC
       'If you don't bring (him), what (would you) do?'

Here, -djaadakaa could be analysed into -djaa + -dakaa (negative conditional converb). In contemporary Irabu this is a completely fossilised expression, however, and I do not know whether any other combination of
[-djaa + another morpheme] is ever possible. As shown in TABLE 6–6, I
analyse -djaadakaa as a single negative intentional conditional converb
suffix.

6.3.4. Morphophonemics of Class 2 athematic stems

The underlying forms of Class 2 stems (i.e. Class 2 roots) end in stops,
fricatives, resonants, or in exceptional cases, vowels. They may undergo
(morpho-)phonemic processes in the formation of the athematic stem,
which has the same phonotactic constraint as holds for phonological
words, i.e. an athematic stem must end in a vowel or a resonant.

6.3.4.1. Stem-final stop lenition

As illustrated in TABLES 6–9, when appearing as athematic stems, Class 2
stems that underlyingly end in a stop undergo a morphophonemic adjustment, or what I call stem-final stop lenition ($b > v$, $t > c$, $k > f$, $g > v$).

TABLE 6–9. Stem-final stop lenition of Class 2 stems

a. Stem-final /b/

Example	tub- 'fly'	jurab- 'call'	asïb- 'play'
thematic -a	tub-a	jurab-a	asïb-a
thematic -i	tub-i	jurab-i	asïb-i
athematic	tuv	jurav	asïv

b. Stem-final /t/

Example	kat- 'win'	ut- 'smash'	mat- 'wait'
thematic -a	kat-a	ut-a	mat-a
thematic -i[4]	kac-i	uc-i	mac-i
athematic	kac(ï)	uc(ï)	mac(ï)

---

[4] Here, when the stem-final /t/ is followed by /i/, it alternates with /c/. /ci/ is phonetically [tʃi],
but note that in Irabu [tʃi] cannot be analysed as /ti/, as is the case in Japanese, since there is

212   Chapter 6

c. Stem-final /k/

Example	*kak-* 'write'	*nk-* 'pull out'	*fik-* 'wipe'
thematic *-a*	*kak-a*	*nk-a*	*fik-a*
thematic *-i*	*kak-i*	*nk-i*	*fik-i*
athematic	*kafï/kacï*	*nfï/ncï*	*fifï/ficï*

d. Stem-final /g/

Example	*tug-* 'burnish'	*kug-* 'paddle'	*nag-* 'bring down'
thematic *-a*	*tug-a*	*kug-a*	*nag-a*
thematic *-i*	*tug-i*	*kug-i*	*nag-i*
athematic	*tuv*	*kuv*	*nav*

For example, *tub-* 'fly' forms an athematic stem form *tuv-* when followed by conditional converb suffix *-tigaa*, yielding *tuv-tigaa* 'if fly'; in the same environment, *kat-* 'win' and *kak-* 'write' form athematic stems *kac-* and *kaf-*, but they additionally undergo the predictable /ï/ insertion, which occurs to fix ill formed phonotactic pattern, specifically a fricative coda C except for the permissible geminate $C_i.C_i$ (§2.7.3). Thus, we get *kacï-tigaa* 'if win' and *kafï-tigaa* 'if write' as a surface output. For stems ending in /k/ or /g/, a variant athematic stem form is observed, formed by turning /k/ and /g/ into /c/ and /z/ respectively. However, this is not common, and is primarily used to mark a class-changing derivation (verb stem > nominal stem: §6.3.4.5 below). For example, the underlying stem //kak-// 'write' is turned into two athematic stem forms, *kafï* or *kacï*. The former is noted above. The latter occurs in *kacï-tar* 'wrote' (write-PST), *kacï-tigaa* 'if write' (write-CND), and so on, but *kacï* is mainly used in forming a compound stem, especially of a compound noun (§6.3.4.5).

6.3.4.2. Class 2 stems ending in fricative and resonant
A Class 2 athematic stem ending in a fricative or a resonant does not undergo any peculiar morphophonemic processes. A Class 2 stem ending in a fricative simply undergoes predictable /ï/ insertion to avoid fricative-final C. For example, *nas-* 'bear; do' forms a thematic stem (*nas-a/nas-i*) or an athematic stem (*nasï-*, with predictable /ï/ insertion: *nasï-Ø* (non-past unmarked); *nasï-tam* (past realis), etc.).

A number of stems underlyingly consist of (or contain) gaminate //CC[V]//, where the CC indicates a geminate fricative or resonant, and [V] indicates an unfilled nucleus. In order to derive an athematic stem, fricative

---

[ti], which is phonemically analysed as /ti/. It is also noted that some speakers prefer to use /c/ throughout, as in *kac-a* and *kac-i*, *uc-a* and *uc-i*, *mac-a* and *mac-i*, and so on.'

Verb morphology 213

geminate stems and resonant geminate stems follow different steps. For a fricative geminate stem, it first undergoes the /ï/-insertion (e.g. //ff// 'bite' → /ffï/), which then undergoes the /ï/-spreading (/ffï/ → /fïï/). See §2.7.3 and §2.7.4 for the detailed analysis of these processes. For a resonant geminate stem, it undergoes the deletion of the second C, resulting in the moraic C being resyllabified as the coda (e.g. //ažž// 'say' → /až/), unless this deletion leads to the violation of the word minimality, as in cases of //žž// 'scold', //rr// 'enter', //vv// 'sell', etc. In the latter case, a simple resyllabification occurs, from //CC[V]// to /RR/. See §2.7.5 for a detailed account.

TABLE 6–10. Monomoraic stem and stem extension

Example	*ff-* 'bite'	*ss-* 'know'	*cc-* 'wear'	*kaff-* 'hide'	*vv-* 'sell'	*žž-* 'scold'	*rr-* 'enter'	*ažž-* 'say'
thematic -*a*	*ff-a*	*ss-a*	*cc-a*	*kaff-a*	*vv-a*	*žž-a*	*rr-a*	*ažž-a*
thematic -*i*	*ff-i*	*ss-i*	*cc-i*	*kaff-i*	*vv-i*	*žž-i*	*rr-i*	*ažž-i*
athematic	*fïï*	*sïï*	*cïï*	*kafïï*	*vv*	*žž*	*rr*	*až*

6.3.4.3. Class 2 stems that end in /v/
The Class 2 stems that end in /v/ delete the stem-final /v/ when followed by a thematic vowel, due to the synchronic constraint that /v/ never occur unless it is geminated.

If the stem occurs athematically, then it surfaces with /v/ as a coda. Exceptionally, *fav* 'eat' occurs as /fau/. Thus these Class 2 stems are in synchronic terms exceptional in that their thematic stems do not end in a consonant. Examples are *pa(v)-* 'creep', *fa(u)-* 'eat', *na(v)-* 'bind', and *ka(v)-* 'buy'. The stem *fau-* 'eat' is exceptional in that the athematic stem-final phoneme is a vowel rather than a consonant.

TABLE 6–11. Class 2 stems ending in historical **w* and their stem extension

Example	*fa(u)-* 'eat'	*na(v)-* 'bind'	*ka(v)-* 'buy'
thematic -*a*	*fa-a*	*na-a*	*ka-a*
thematic -*i*	*fa-i*	*na-i*	*ka-i*
athematic	*fau*	*nav*	*kav*

6.3.4.4. Class 2 stems with -*u* thematic vowel
Certain Class 2 stems that end in /v/ have -*u* thematic stems rather than -*a* thematic stems. TABLE 6–12 compares *tur-* 'take', a typical Class 2 stem that takes thematic -*a*, with other three stems that take thematic -*u*. These stems have the stem-final syllable structure /u(v)/. Thus, a thematic stem in -*u* can be regarded as an assimilation on the part of the thematic vowel.

214   Chapter 6

TABLE 6–12. Class 2 stem with -u thematic vowel

Example	*tur-* 'take'	*umu(v)-* 'think'	*juku(v)-* 'rest'	*su(v)-* 'follow'
thematic -*a*/-*u*	*tur-a*	*umu-u*	*juku-u*	*su-u*
thematic -*i*	*tur-i*	*umu-i*	*juku-i*	*su-i*
athematic	*tur*	*umuv*	*jukuv*	*suv*

6.3.4.5. Morphophonemic nominalisation

As noted in §3.6.2.1, in a compound nominal, the verb root (as a modifier) must be converted into a nominal stem. This nominalised stem form is identical with the athematic stem form as noted above, except if the root-final phoneme is /k/ or /g/, where the nominalised stem and the athematic stem differ, as shown in TABLE 6–13. Thus *kacï* as opposed to *kafï* is used as a nominal stem 'writing' which then combines with another nominal stem to form a compound nominal (*kacï+kata* 'the way of writing' (writing+way); *munu+kacï* '(the act of) writing' (thing+writing)).

TABLE 6–13. Nominalised stems and athematic stems

Root	*kak-*	*kug-*
	'write'	'paddle'
Nominalised stem	*kacï*	*kuzï*
Athematic stem	*kafï*	*kuv*

(6–40)   a. *kacï+kata*   (*kafï+kata)   b. *kuzï+kata*   (*kuv+kata)
              writing+way   paddling+way
              'writing method'   'paddling method'

A nominalised stem is also used as a V1 of a verb-verb compound (§6.4.2.1), as in *kacï+kai-r* 'rewrite (write+change-NPST)'. Unlike in compound nouns, however, the V1 here may alternatively be an athematic stem (thus *kafï+kai-r* is possible). Thus in Irabu, a first stem of a compound shows deverbalisation both in compound verbs and in compound nouns, even though it is more pervasive in compound nouns.

6.3.5. Irregular verbs

6.3.5.1. Deictic directional verb 'come'
In Japonic in general, the deictic directional verb expressing 'come' shows irregular inflection *par excellence*, with a number of stem forms. This also holds for Irabu, where there are four verb stems which are underlyingly distinct: (a) *kuu-*, (b) *cc-*, (c) *t-* and (d) *ff-*.

Verb morphology   215

TABLE 6–14. Deictic directional verb 'come' and its inflection

		Class 2 *tur-* 'take'	'come'
(a)	finite negative past realis	*tur-a-t-ta-m*	*kuu-t-ta-m*
	finite negative past unmarked	*tur-a-t-tar*	*kuu-t-tar*
	finite negative non-past unmarked	*tur-a-n-Ø*	*kuu-n-Ø*
	finite irrealis intentional	*tur-a-di*	*kuu-di*
	finite irrealis negative intentional	*tur-a-djaan*	*kuu-djaan*
	finite irrealis optative	*tur-a-baa*	*kuu-baa*
	conditional converb 1	*tur-a-ba*	*kuu-ba*
	negative conditional converb 1	*tur-a-dakaa*	*kuu-dakaa*
	aversive converb	*tur-a-zïm(=tii)*	*kuu-zïm(=tii)*
	negative medial	*tur-a-da*	*kuu-da*
	finite irrealis imperative	***tur-i***	***kuu***
(b)	narrative converb	*tur-i-i*	*cc-i-i*
(c)	finite past realis	*tur-ta-m*	*t-ta-m*
	finite past unmarked	*tur-tar*	*t-tar*
(d)	finite non-past realis	*tur-Ø-m*	*fïï-Ø-m*
	finite non-past unmarked	*tur-Ø*	*fïï-Ø*
	finite irrealis prohibitive	*tur-na*	*fïï-na*
	conditional converb 2	*tur-tigaa*	*fïï-tigaa*
	negative conditional converb 2	*tur-gurai*	*fïï-gurai*
	simultaneous converb	*tur-ccjaaki*	*fïï-ccjaaki*
	continuous converb	*tur-gakaazï*	*fïï-gakaazï*
	purpose converb	*tur-ga*	*fïï-ga*
	immediate anterior converb	*tur-tuu*	*fïï-tuu*
	causal converb	*tur-i-ba*	*ff-i-ba*

As shown in TABLE 6–14 above, these stems are parallel to Class 2 stems, where all finite and non-finite inflectional affixes are listed alongside those of the regular stem *tur* 'take'. Clearly, (a) *kuu-* exactly corresponds to the *-a* thematic stem, with one exception, shown in bold-face, i.e. the imperative, where *kuu-* corresponds to the imperative in Class 2 verbs. We see that (b) *cc-* corresponds to the *-i* thematic stem of Class 2 that carries the narrative converb suffix, (c) *t-* corresponds to the athematic stem of Class 2 that carries a finite past realis or unmarked suffix, and (d) *ff-* corresponds to the athematic stem of Class 2 that carries all other inflectional affixes.

6.3.5.2. Light verb *(a)s-* 'do'
The light verb 'do' is another major irregular verb in Japonic languages. In

216 Chapter 6

Irabu, however, it is not really irregular, but can be subsumed under Class 2. The only differences between a typical Class 2 and the light verb stem *(a)s-* (where /a/ may be dropped in the light verb constructions; see §3.2.3.2) are that the latter has a thematic stem in *-u* in place of a thematic stem in *-a*, and that the finite irrealis imperative form is either the irregular *assu* or the expected *as-i*, even though the latter is not common. The *-u* thematic stem *as-u* is alternatively *ah-u* in free variation (the latter is more common).

TABLE 6–15. Inflection of the light verb *(a)sï*

Example	*tur-* 'take'	*(a)s-* 'do'
thematic *-a*	*tur-a*	*(a)s-u/(a)h-u*
thematic *-i*	*tur-i*	*(a)s-i*
athematic	*tur*	*(a)s*
finite irrealis imperative	*tur-i*	*(a)ss-u/as-i*

6.3.5.3. Negative verb *njaa-* 'not exist'

The negative verb stem *njaa-* 'not exist' is like a Class 1 stem in that it lacks thematic stems, but shows a peculiar characteristic in its inflection. That is, even though the stem is already negative in meaning, it is morphologically negated in its inflected forms (I do not gloss the negative suffixes attached to *njaa-* as NEG henceforth): *njaa-n-Ø* 'not exist' (not.exist-NPST), *njaa-t-tar* 'did not exist' (not.exist-PST), *njaa-da* 'not existing' (not.exist-NRT). The inflectional possibilities of *njaa-* are also much more restricted than those of other regular verbs, since it only carries the negative inflections.[5]

TABLE 6–16. Negative verb inflection

	Class 1 *ibi-* 'plant'	Negative verb *njaa-*
finite negative past realis	*ibi-t-ta-m*	*njaa-t-ta-m*
finite negative past unmarked	*ibi-t-tar*	*njaa-t-tar*
finite negative non-past unmarked	*ibi-n-Ø*	*njaa-n-Ø*
negative conditional converb 1	*ibi-dakaa*	*njaa-dakaa*
negative conditional converb 2	*ibi-gurai*	*njaa-gurai*
aversive converb	*ibi-zïm(=tii)*	*njaa-zïm(=tii)*
negative medial	*ibi-da*	*njaa-da*

---

[5] The negative intentional conditional suffix cannot be carried by *njaa-* for another reason: the suffix only attaches to volitional verb stems.

Verb morphology 217

6.3.6. Existential verb, state verb, and copula verb

There are three etymologically related verb forms: the existential verb *ar* 'exist', the state verb *ar* 'be (in a state)' and the copula verb *ar*. These can be distinguished in several respects as summarised below.

TABLE 6–17. Existential verb, state verb, and copula verb

	Existential verb	State verb	Copula verb
Animacy-sensitive	+	-	-
Suppletive negation	+	+	-
VP internal	+	+	-
No allomorphy	+	+	-

6.3.6.1. Existential verb

An existential verb stem form varies depending on the animacy of the subject NP, i.e. an animate form *ur-* or an inanimate form *ar-*.[6] In terms of inflectional morphology, both stems are in most respects like a Class 2 stem but show some diachronically induced peculiarities.

TABLE 6–18. Existential verbs and their inflections

	Existential		*tur-* 'take'
thematic -*a*	*ur-a*	*ar-a*	*tur-a*
thematic -*i*	*ur-i*	*ar-i*	*tur-i*
athematic	*u(r)*	*a(r)*	*tur*
finite non-past realis	*u(r)-Ø-m*	*a(r)-Ø-m*	*tur-Ø-m*
finite non-past unmarked	*ur-Ø*	*ar-Ø*	*tur-Ø*
finite non-past prohibitive	*ur-na*	**ar-na*	*tur-na*
finite past realis	*u-ta-m*	*a-tam*	*tur-ta-m*
finite past unmarked	*u-tar*	*a-tar*	*tur-tar*
finite irrealis imperative	*ur-i*	*ar-i*	*tur-i*
conditional converb 2	*u-tigaa*	*a-tigaa*	*tur-tigaa*

In TABLE 6–18, the stem form of the finite past realis, finite past unmarked, and conditional converb 2 irregularly lacks stem-final /r/ in contrast with other athematic environments such as the finite prohibitive inflection and simultaneous converb inflection where the athematic stem carries /r/. It

---

[6] An anonymous reviewer pointed out an interesting phenomenon found in some Ryukyuan varieties, where the choice of the existential verb form is dependent on perceived self-control mobility rather than animacy. So, according to the reviewer, in these languages a typhoon, a ferry, a taxi, and so on, can take the form usually associated with animate subjects. This is also the case in Irabu, especially in the case of cars and ships.

218   Chapter 6

thus diverges from typical Class 2 stems where the stem-final consonant is retained in all environments. Also, in the finite non-past realis form, there is fluctuating variation between *u-Ø-m/a-Ø-m* and *ur-Ø-m/ar-Ø-m*. This suggests that in earlier Irabu /r/ was regularly present in other athematic stems as well (i.e. in finite past realis). I analyse that the underlying synchronic stem form as *ur-*, where /r/ is deleted by rule when followed by finite past realis, finite past unmarked, and conditional converb 2 suffixes.

The inanimate existential verb stem *ar-* is negated with the negative verb stem *njaa-*. Thus the negative forms of the inanimate existential verb are as shown in TABLE 6–16 (except for the prohibitive, which is semantically impermissible, though the expected form would be *ar-na).

(6–41)   A: *manzjuu=Ø=ja*   *a-Ø-m=mu?*
            papaya=Z=TOP   exist-NPST-RLS=Q
            'Is there any papaya?'
        B: *njaa-n-Ø.*
            not.exist-NPST
            'No, (there) isn't.'

6.3.6.2. Copula verb

The copula verb stem is identical in form to the inanimate existential verb stem *ar-* (§6.3.6.1), but differs from existential *ar-* in all four of the features listed in TABLE 6–17. First, it is not animacy-sensitive. Thus as illustrated in (6–42) below, the copula verb remains *ar-* whether the subject NP is animate or inanimate.

(6–42)   a. *kari=a*   *sinsii=du*   *a-tar.*
           3SG=TOP   teacher=FOC   COP-PST
           'He was a teacher.' [animate subject NP]
        b. *banti=ga*   *jaa=ja*   *imi+jaa=du*   *a-tar.*
           1PL=GEN   house=TOP   small+house=FOC   COP-PST
           'Our house was a small house.' [inanimate subject NP]

Second, the copula verb is negated by the regular morphological strategy using *-n* (finite non-past negative unmarked), *-ttam* (finite past negative realis), and so on.

(6–43)   *kari=a*   *sinsii=ja*   *ar-a-n-Ø.*
           3SG=TOP   teacher=TOP   COP-THM-NEG-NPST
           'He is not a teacher.'

Verb morphology   219

(6–44)   *sinsii*   *ar-a-dakaa,*   *vva=a*   *nau=ga?*
         teacher   COP-THM-NEG.CND   2SG=TOP   what=Q
         'If (you) are not a teacher, what (do) you (do)?'

(6–45)   *kari=a*   *sinsii=ja*   *ar-a-da,*   *siitu=dooi.*
         3SG=TOP   teacher=TOP   COP-NEG.NRT   student=EMP
         'He is not a teacher, but a student.'

Third, unlike any other verbs including the existential verb, the copula verb appears after an NP in a nominal predicate phrase (§3.1.1.2).

Fourth, the copula verb stem has an allomorph *jar-*, which is found either in main clauses with emphatic semantics, or in certain kinds of non-main clause. In the former case, a clause with *jar-* often contains the contrastive marker *=gami* (6–46). In the latter case, *jar-* is found in two converb inflections, the conditional converb 2 (6–47) and the causal converb (6–48), and in a coordinate clause with the 'but' conjunctive *=suga* (which may be *=ruga* as a result of assimilation) (6–49).

(6–46)   *kari=a*   *minku=gami=du*   *jar-Ø.*
         3SG=TOP   deaf=CNT=FOC   COP-NPST
         'He's a damn deaf (guy)!'

(6–47)   *midum*   *ja-tigaa,*   *kaami=ti*   *as-i.*
         female   COP-CND   Kaami=QT   do-IMP
         'If (the baby) is a girl, name her *Kaami*.'

(6–48)   *kiban+pžtu*   *ja-i-ba,*   *nau=mai*   *njaa-n-Ø.*
         poor+man   COP-THM-CSL   what=even   not.exist-NPST
         'Because (I) am a poor man, I have nothing.'

(6–49)   *kari=a*   *zau+midum*   *jar-Ø=ruga=du,*
         3SG=TOP   good+woman   COP-NPST=but=FOC
         apavcï+midum=dooi.
         talkative+woman=EMP
         'She's a good woman, but also a talkative woman.'

Compare (6–47) to (6–49) with the examples in which the inanimate existential verb appears in the same types of non-main clause, where no *jar-* allomorph is observed:

(6–50)   *zin=nu*   *a-tigaa,*   *zjautuu+jasïcï=nkai*   *asï-Ø.*
         money=NOM   exist-CND   great+house=ALL   do-NPST
         'If (there) were money, (I) would make (my house) a better one.'

220   Chapter 6

(6–51) *kari=a*   *taja=nu*   *a-i-ba,*
          3SG=TOP   strength=NOM   exist-THM-CSL
          nuuma=u=mai   *pžk-ai-r.*
          horse=ACC=even   pull-POT-NPST
          'Because he has (great) physical strength, (he) can even pull a
          horse.'

(6–52) *nkjaan=na*   *bannja=mai*   *a-tar=ruga,*
          old.times=TOP   field.hut=too   exist-PST=but
          nnama=gami=a   *mii-n-Ø=ni.*
          now=EMP=TOP   see-NEG-NPST=CNF
          'In older times (there) were field huts, but now (we) don't see
          them, eh?'

6.3.6.3. State verb

The state verb *ar-* 'be' differs from the existential verb *ar-* only in that the former is not animacy-sensitive, as in the case of the copula verb *ar-*. This is shown in the example below, where the verb stem *ar-* does not alternate with *ur-* as would be expected in the existential verb.

(6–53) a. *kari=a*   *taka-fi=du*   *ar-Ø.*
            3SG=TOP   high-AVLZ=FOC   be-NPST
            'He is (in a) tall (state).' [animate subject NP]
         b. *kanu   jama=a*   *taka-fi=du*   *ar-Ø.*
            that   mountain=TOP   high-AVLZ=FOC   be-NPST
            'That mountain is (in a) high (state).' [inanimate subject NP]

The state verb *ar-* and the existential verb *ar-* as opposed to the copula verb *ar-* shares the morphological characteristic whereby these are negated by suppletion (see §6.3.6.1 for the existential verb), whereas the copula verb *ar-* is negated by using the regular negative suffix *-n* (see §6.3.6.2).

(6–54) *kari=a*   *taka-fi=fa*   *njaa-n-Ø.*
          3SG=TOP   high-AVLZ=FOC   NEG-NPST
          'He is (in a) tall (state).' [the negative counterpart of (6–48a)]

Syntactically, the state verb *ar-Ø* 'be' takes the PC adverb (§8.3.2) *taka-fi* 'in a high state' as its complement, forming the state verb construction (§3.3.6.2).

Verb morphology   221

6.4. Derivational morphology

In this section I describe the internal structure of the stem. As is shown schematically in (6–55) below, there are three major portions of a stem: the primary stem ('Stem$_p$' slot below), the derivational affix chain, and a thematic vowel.

(6–55)   Primary stem   Derivational affix chain   Thematic vowel
         Stem$_p$ (-CAUS)(-PASS)(HON)   (-THM)

A primary stem may be derived by compounding or by a class-changing derivation (property concept stem > verb primary stem). The latter process is described in Chapter 8. A primary stem optionally carries a derivational affix chain that consists of voice affixes and honorific affixes in the order specified in (6–55). After all these derivations a thematic vowel optionally appears depending on the class of the entire stem and the inflectional affix that follows, as was described in §6.2.

In what follows I first describe derivational affixes, then primary stem formation for presentational purposes.

6.4.1. Derivational affixes

As shown in (6–55) above, derivational affixes are voice and honorific affixes. The 'PASS' slot is filled by the affix *-(r)ai*, which has a range of functions in addition to passive marking, i.e. malefactive marking and potential marking. I henceforth refer to this single form that fills the PASS slot as the passive affix, but I indicate its specific function in the interlinear gloss: passive (PASS), malefactive (MAL), and potential (POT).

It is not common for a verb to carry all three affixes, but elicitation confirmed that each affix shows the above ordering when they co-occur. When a derivational affix extends a stem, the class of the whole stem is determined by the final segment of the stem: as is illustrated in (6–56) and (6–57) below, there are two causative affixes *-as* (which only attaches to a Class 2 stem) and *-sïmi* (which only attaches to a Class 1 stem). Since a Class 1 is categorised as a stem ending in /i/ and a Class 2 is as a stem ending in a segment other than /i/, the stem with *-as* is a Class 2 stem, whereas the stem with *-sïmi* is a Class 1 stem. Thus in (6–56) below the stem *mii-* 'look' and the extended stem *mii-sïmi* both carry the non-past unmarked suffix *-r*, which demonstrates that both are Class 1 stems. Likewise, in (6–57) below the stem *nak-* 'cry' and the extended stem *nak-as* both show non-past unmarked zero affixation, which demonstrates that both are Class 2

222 Chapter 6

stems.

(6–56) Class 1 stem *mii-* 'look' + causative *-sïmi* → Class 1 stem *ibi-sïmi-*
    a. *mii-r*   b. *mii-sïmi-r*
       look-NPST   look-CAUS-NPST
       'look'   'make (someone) look'

(6–57) Class 2 stem *nak-* 'cry' + causative *-as* → Class 2 stem *nak-as-*
    a. *nafï-Ø*   b. *nak-asï-Ø*
       cry-NPST   write-CAUS-NPST
       'cry'   'make (someone) cry.'

Likewise, the passive-malefactive-potential affix *-(r)ai* creates a Class 1 stem. The honorific affix *-(s)ama(r)*, which does not end in /i/, does not derive a Class 2 stem.

(6–58) Class 2 stem *nak-* 'cry' + malefactive *-(r)ai* → Class 1 stem *nak-ai-*
    a. *nafï-Ø*   b. *nak-ai-r*
       cry-NPST   cry-MAL-NPST
       'cry.'   'is cried'

(6–59) Class 2 stem *nak-* 'cry' + honorific *-(s)ama(r)* → Class 2 stem
    nak-ama(r)
    a. *nafï-Ø*   b. *nak-amar-Ø*
       cry-NPST   cry-HON-NPST
       'cry'   'cry:HON'

6.4.1.1. Causative *-sïmi*, *-as*

The light verb *(a)s-* is a Class 2 stem, but the causative suffix that it carries is *-sïmi*. Also, when it occurs with the causative suffix, the affix-initial *s* is deleted (*(a)s-* + *-sïmi* > *(a)s-ïmi*).

(6–60) *uu-fï-Ø*   *nar-i-i*   *daizïna*
       big-VLZ-NRT   become-THM-NRT   very
       buuciri=jarruga   *vva=n=mai*
       mighty.one=but   2SG=DAT=too
       mii-sïmi-baa=i=ti.
       see-CAUS-NPST.OPT=CNF=QT
       '(He) has become a big boy, though (he's) a mighty boy, (I) want to let you see (him), you know.' [*mii-* is a Class 1 stem]

(6–61) *taru=nu=ga*   *nak-asï-tar=ga?*
       who=NOM=FOC   cry-CAUS-NPST=FOC

'Who has made (you) cry?' [*nak-* is a Class 2 stem]

(6–62) *nau=mai   a-sïmi-da*
    what=even   do-CAUS-NEG.NRT
    taigaku   s-ïmi-tar.
    withdrawal.of.school   do-CAUS-PST
    '(My parents) did not allow me to do anything, and made me withdraw from school.' [*(a)s-* is a Class 2 stem]

6.4.1.2. Passive-malefactive-potential *-(r)ai*

The passive suffix is *-(r)ai*. The bracketed /r/ is deleted when attaching to a Class 2 stem, as shown in (6–63) and (6–64). The examples below illustrate typical functions of the affix (see §10.4 for more detail).

(6–63) *ba=a   sinsii=n=du   žž-ai-tar.*
    1SG=TOP   teacher=DAT=FOC   scold-PASS-PST
    'I was scolded by the teacher.' [passive]

(6–64) *ba=a   jumunu=n   mm=mu=baa   fa-ai-tar.*
    1SG=TOP   rat=DAT   potato=ACC=TOP   eat-MAL-PST
    'I had my potatoes eaten by rats' [malefactive]

(6–65) *kuma=kara=a   fïni=u=baa*
    here=ABL=TOP   ship=ACC=TOP
    mii-rai-n.
    drink-POT-NPST-RLS=EMP
    '(I) can't see the ship from here.' [potential]

6.4.1.3. Honorific *-(s)ama(r)*

The honorific affix *-(s)ama(r)* appears after a voice affix when they co-occur. The initial /s/ is deleted when it is attached to a Class 2 stem. The final /r/ is deleted according to the rule that applies to the existential *ar* (§6.3.6.1), indicating that it was historically made up of the existential verb. Also, when *-(s)ama(r)* is attached to a Class 1 stem, the initial /s/ is frequently replaced by /h/ (*mii-samar-Ø ~ mii-hamar-Ø* 'look:HON' (look-HON-NPST)).

The honorific affix is losing productivity. Most of the attested examples of *-(s)ama(r)* are in fixed greeting expressions or in traditional song lyrics.

(6–66) *ganzuunar=ra   s-i-i*
    being.healthy=PRT   do-THM-NRT
    ur-amar-Ø-m=mu?
    PROG-HON-NPST-RLS=FOC

224   Chapter 6

'(Are) you healthy?' [a fixed greeting expression]

(6–67) *duju-ta=ga*   *kjuu=nu*   *ugunaar=ra*
        1PL.INCL-PL=GEN   today=GEN   gathering=TOP
        kan+ganasï=nu   *jurus-i-i*   *uk-amar-Ø.*
        god+beloved=NOM   allow-THM-NRT   PRF-HON-NPST
        'Today's gathering of ours, the god has allowed.' [in a tradition-
        al song]

Honorific *-(s)ama(r)* has an irregular form for the irrealis imperative: *-ci*
rather than expected *-i*. Furthermore, this imperative form is by far the most
well attested use of honorific *-(s)ama(r)*. Most younger speakers (in their
40's and younger) can only construct honorific forms with the fixed form
STEM-*(s)amaci*.

(6–68) *jurus-i-i*   *fii-sama-ci.*
        forgive-THM-NRT   BEN-HON-IMP
        'Please forgive me.'

(6–69) *zuu*   *nkjagi-sama-ci.*
        INTJ   eat.HON-HON-IMP
        'Now, please eat.'[7]

(6–70) *kuma=n*   *bžž-ama-ci.*
        this.place=DAT   sit-HON-IMP
        'Please be seated here.'

6.4.2. Primary stem

In this section I describe primary stem formation and related constructions.
Three major construction types are described here: (1) compound, (2) agglutinative serial verb construction (SVC) and auxiliary verb construction
(AVC), and (3) phrasal SVC and AVC. These are distinguished in terms of
whether a sequence of verb stems (V1 and V2) form a single primary stem
(whose boundary is schematically shown as [ ]), and whether the sequence
may occur as a complex stem of a word (indicated by '+') or as a phrase
(i.e. each stem appears as a word; a word boundary is indicated by # below).

---

[7] *nkjagi-* 'eat' (Class 1) is a lexical (suppletive) honorific form corresponding to non-honorif-
ic *faw-* 'eat' (thus *nkjagi-samaci* is double-marked for honorification). *nkjagi-* is the only form
that I identified as a lexical honorific form in Irabu.

Verb morphology 225

TABLE 6–19. verb-verb compound, agglutinative and phrasal SVC/AVC

Compounding	[V1+V2]
Agglutinative SVC/AVC	[V1]+[V2]
Phrasal SVC/AVC	[V1]#[V2]

Thus, a compound forms a single complex primary stem, whereas an agglutinative SVC/AVC forms a complex stem consisting of two primary stems. A complex phrase consists of two (or more) words. As will be described in what follows, some agglutinative AVCs are rearranged as phrasal AVCs.

In this section, our focus is on compounding and agglutinative SVC/AVC, as they constitute a stem within a verb. Phrase structure will be taken up in Chapter 7.

6.4.2.1. Compounds

Compounding two verb stems (V1 + V2) forms a single primary stem. As a single primary stem, the entire compound carries derivational affix(es) (if any) and an inflectional affix, and it is impossible for each component stem to carry these affixes independently. Although verb-verb compounds are largely compositional in meaning, it is collocational (i.e. the combination of V1 and V2 is not productive), and it is necessary for each V1+V2 to be listed as lexical items. Example (6–71) illustrates a semantically non-compositional compound, whereas (6–72) illustrates semantically compositional compounds.

(6–71) *panki+naur-Ø* (split+grow-NPST) 'bloom'
(6–72) a. *karagi+ukusï-Ø* (turn.over+get.up-NPST) 'turn up (window, etc.)'
     b. *kacï+kai-r* (write+change-NPST) 'rewrite'
     c. *tur+kai-r* (take+change-NPST) 'replace'
     d. *sïcï+bžžfï-Ø* (lay+crush-NPST) 'crush something by laying it'
     e. *usï+cïï-Ø* (push+crush-NPST) 'crush'
     f. *usï+tausï-Ø* (push+get.down-NPST) 'push down'
     g. *pžk-i+rri-r* (pull-THM+let.into) 'pull in'
     h. *pžfï+mudusï-Ø* (pull+return-NPST) 'draw back'
     i. *kurugi+uti-r* (turn.round+drop-NPST) 'tumble down'
     j. *tuv+uri-r* (jump+go.down-NPST) 'drop down'

From the examples above, it is possible to make several generalisations.

226   Chapter 6

First, if V1 is a Class 2 stem, the stem form must be an athematic stem
(§6.3.4) rather than a bare root. Morphophonemic nominalisation is also
common (§6.3.4.5), as seen in (6–72b) and (6–72d), where *kak-* 'write' and
sïk- 'lay' appear as *kacï-* and *sïcï-* (nominalised form) rather than *kafï-* and
sïfï- (athematic stem) respectively. In very limited cases, V1 is a thematic
-i, as in (6–72g). This synchronically exceptional form may have been
common in earlier Irabu, as there are many fossilised compounds where a
previous V1 stem can be considered to have been an *i* thematic stem: *muc-
jagar* 'pop up' (*muc-i* 'carry' + agar 'go up'), *tacjagar* 'stand up' (*tac-i*
'stand' + agar 'go up'), *pžkjagir* 'pull up' (*pžk-i* 'pull' + *agir* 'lift'), etc.
Here, */Ci+a/* (2 morae) is now reanalysed as /Cja/ (1 mora).

Second, there are some stems that often occur in the V1 slot and others
that often occur in the V2 slot. For example, *usï-* 'push' and *pžfï-* 'pull' are
well attested in the above examples as a V1 stem. Likewise, *kai-* 'change'
and *agar-* 'go up' are common as a V2 stem. However, *usï-* and *pžfï-* do not
freely combine with a large number of V2's; *kai-* and *agar-* do not freely
combine with a large number of V1's. This is in sharp contrast to agglutinative SVCs and AVCs described in the following sections, where V2 can
combine with almost any V1.

Third, most verbal compound stems form separate phonological words
in terms of (1) phonotactics and (2) the applicability of phonological rules.
The prosodic evidence is irrelevant here, since in each example above V1
is one foot, which means that V1+V2 is treated as a single domain for
rhythmic alternation (§2.9.4). With respect to (1) and (2), however, we see
a phonological word boundary between V1 and V2. For example, in (6–
72a) /ia/ occurs across the stem boundary, and it is pronounced as [i.a]
rather than [jaː], the latter of which would be obtained if /ia/ occurred in a
phonological word (§2.5.2). The same holds for (6–72i), where /iu/ is pronounced as [i.u] rather than [juː]. In (6–72j), V1 ends in a coda /v/, and V2
begins in a vowel. There is thus a /C.V/ sequence, which would induce the
geminate copy insertion rule (§2.7.2) to produce /C.CV/ if this sequence
occurs in a phonological word. However, it is not the case in (6–72j), indicating that each stem is treated as a separate phonological word.

6.4.2.2. Serial verb construction (SVC)

Irabu SVCs fall into two types. First, there are agglutinative SVCs, where
the component stems occur within a word rather than forming separate
grammatical words. They can be called 'one word constructions' in
Aikhenvald's (2006) typology of SVCs. Second, there are phrasal SVCs,
where the component stems occur as separate grammatical words (§7.1.3).

Verb morphology 227

In either case, Irabu SVCs are largely restricted to two-verb constructions.

There are two major differences between compound verbs and agglutinative SVCs in Irabu. First, V2 in an SVC never undergoes sequential voicing (§2.7.1), while V2 in a compound may do so (see, for example, (6–72d) *sïcï+bžžfï* 'crush something by laying it' where V2 is underlyingly *pžžk-* 'crush'). Second, unlike compounds, V1 and V2 in an SVC constitute separate primary stems. Since each stem is a primary stem, each can carry its own derivational affix as long as it is semantically appropriate. As a single word, however, the serialised stems carry a single inflectional affix.[8] Thus, as is shown in (6–73) below, whereas it is possible for V1+V2 as a whole to carry a causative suffix (6–73b), it is also possible for V1 *ibi-* 'plant' and V2 *pazïmi-* 'begin' to each carry the causative suffix *-sïmi*. These stems form a larger stem, which carries the past suffix *-tar*.[9]

(6–73)   a. *ibi+pazïmi-tar*   b. *ibi+pazïmi-sïmi-tar*
            plant+begin-PST   plant+begin-CAUS-PST
            'began planting'   'ordered someone to begin planting'

         c. *ibi-sïmi+pazïmi-sïmi-tar*
            plant-CAUS+begin-PASS-PST
            '(e.g. an owner) ordered (a servant leader) to make (servants) plant.'

As in shown in TABLE 6–2d, while V1 is almost unrestricted, V2 is chosen from a restricted set of verb stems that encode phases of actions (e.g. 'begin', 'stop', 'keep', etc.).

The verb *pati-* 'finish' and the verb *uwar-* 'finish' have different meanings. The former encodes exhaustivity, or a 'use up' situation, whereas the latter encodes completion of an action. Thus, *num+pati-r* means 'drink up', whereas *num+uwar-Ø* means 'finish drinking' with no entailment of an exhaustive use of what is drunk. Likewise, *kafï+pati-r* means 'write and use up paper', and so on, while *kafï+uwar-Ø* means 'finish writing', with no entailment of an exhaustive use of what is written on.

The last example, i.e. *maar-* 'wander', is exceptional in that it may alternatively appear as an independent word, as shown in (6–74), like aspectual

---

[8] In Irabu, inflection is per word, so the fact that inflection occurs after the series indicates that the whole SVC constitutes one word. However, even though the situation where inflection occurs after an entire series is typical of SVCs in a number of languages, it does not necessarily indicate that the series constitutes a single word, as in Kalam (Andrew Pawley, p.c.).

[9] In the case of a sequence of two primary stems, the 'stem' here would be called a 'verb theme', a higher-level unit consisting of primary stems (see Foley's 1991 description of Yimas for the notion verb theme).

228   Chapter 6

TABLE 6–20. V2 in agglutinative SVC

Form	Class	Gloss	Example	
pati-r	1	finish (or use up)	*ibi+pati-r*	'finish planting'
			num+pati-r	'finish drinking'
			tur+pati-r	'finish taking'
			kafï+pati-r	'finish writing'
uwar-Ø	2	finish	*ibi+uwar-Ø*	'finish planting'
			num+uwar-Ø	'finish drinking'
			tur+uwar-Ø	'finish taking'
			kafï+uwar-Ø	'finish writing'
pazïmi-r	1	begin	*ibi+pazïmi-r*	'begin planting'
			num+pazïmi-r	'begin drinking'
			tur+pazïmi-r	'begin taking'
			kafï+pazïmi-r	'begin writing'
cïzïki-r	1	keep	*ibi+cïzïki-r*	'keep planting'
			num+cïzïki-r	'keep drinking'
			tur+cïzïki-r	'keep taking'
			kafï+cïzïki-r	'keep writing'
maar-Ø	2	wander	*ibi+maar-Ø*	'plant here and there'
			num+maar-Ø	'drink here and there'
			tur+maar-Ø	'take here and there'
			kafï+maar-Ø	'write here and there'

auxiliary verbs (to be discussed below). Semantically, too, it is like an aspectual auxiliary verb in that it encodes iterative aspect rather than a phase
of action (initial phase, medial phase, and final phase).

   (6–74)   *ibi+maar-Ø*   →   *ibi-i*   *maar-Ø*
               plant+wander-NPST   plant-NRT   wander-NPST
               'plant here and there'

6.4.2.3. Auxiliary verb construction

The auxiliary verb construction (AVC) is defined as a 'mono-clausal structure minimally consisting of a lexical verb element that contributes lexical
content to the construction and an auxiliary verb element that contributes
some grammatical or functional content to the construction' (Anderson
2006: 7). In Irabu, there are two kinds of AVCs: agglutinative AVCs and
phrasal AVCs (§7.1.4). As shown schematically in TABLE 6–19, an agglutinative AVC is a one-word construction, where V1 (lexical verb) and V2
(auxiliary verb) form a single grammatical word, carrying a single inflec-

Verb morphology   229

tional affix. A phrasal AVC consists of two words, and each word is inflected (see §7.1.4).

Three aspectual auxiliary verbs, progressive *ur-*, resultative *ar-*, and prospective *ufi-* (§10.5.2), may form either an agglutinative AVC or a phrasal
AVC. Other auxiliary verbs only form a phrasal AVC. In (6–75) below, the
progressive auxiliary *ur-* can form an agglutinative AVC with the lexical
verb *ibi-* 'plant' (6–75a) or it can stand as an independent word, forming a
phrasal AVC with the lexical verb which is inflected for a narrative converb
form (the obligatory form for the lexical verb in a complex VP). In (6–76),
on the other hand, the perfect auxiliary verb *njaa-* never forms an agglutinative AVC with the lexical verb. The two verbs always form a phrasal
AVC.

(6–75)   Auxiliary 1   a. *ibi+ur-Ø* (plant+PROG-NPST)
                               'be planting'
                            b. *ibi-i ur-Ø* (plant-NRT PROG-NPST)
                               'be planting'
(6–76)   Auxiliary 2   *ibi-i njaa-n* (plant-NRT PRF-NPST)
                            'have planted'

The alternation between an agglutinative AVC and a phrasal AVC will
henceforth be called 'word-phrase alternation'. This alternation is in most
cases motivated by the focus marking on the lexical verb (V1 in agglutinative AVCs). Since the phonological host of a focus marker must be a
word(-plus) rather than a stem within a word, the lexical verb stem and the
auxiliary stem in an SVC must be kept separate syntactically. This requires
an agglutinative AVC to be turned into a phrasal AVC. However, when a
focus is on another element (an argument, a VP complement, or an adjunct), the lexical verb and the aspectual auxiliary are very often fused into
a single verb, as an agglutinative AVC.

(6–77)   a. *ba=a*   *tigami=u*
            1SG=TOP   letter=ACC
            kak-i-i=du   *u-tar.*
            write-THM-NRT=FOC   PROG-PST
            'I was writing a letter' [phrasal AVC]
         b. *ba=a*   *tigami=u=du*   *kak-i+u-tar.*
            1SG=TOP   letter=ACC=FOC   write-THM+PROG-PST
            'I was writing a letter.' [agglutinative AVC]
(6–78)   a. *ba=a*   *tigami=u*

230   Chapter 6

    1SG=TOP   letter=ACC

    <u>*kak-i-i=du*   *ar-Ø.*</u>

    write-THM-NRT=FOC   RSL-NPST

    'I have written a letter.' [phrasal AVC]

  b. *ba=a*   *tigami=u=du*   <u>*kak-i+ar-Ø.*</u>

    1SG=TOP   letter=ACC=FOC   write-THM+RSL-NPST

    'I have written a letter.' [agglutinative AVC]

(6–79) a. *ba=a*   *tigami=u*

    1SG=TOP   letter=ACC

    <u>*kak-i-i=du*   *ufi-kutu.*</u>

    write-THM-NRT=FOC   PROS-OBL

    'I am supposed to write a letter.' [phrasal AVC]

  b. *ba=a*   *tigami=u=du*   <u>*kak-i+ufi-kutu.*</u>

    1SG=TOP   letter=ACC=FOC   write-THM+PROS-OBL

    'I am supposed to write a letter.' [agglutinative AVC]

6.5. Citation form

In the rest of this grammar, I use a finite unmarked form for the citation form of a verb. Thus when we are talking of a verb designating 'look' without respect to its morphology, I represent the form by *miir* (mii-r: look-NPST), and when we are talking of a verb designating 'write', I represent the form by *kafi* (kafi-Ø: write-NPST).

Chapter 7

The predicate phrase

The predicate phrase is either verbal or nominal. A verbal predicate phrase consists of a verb phrase (VP) and its complement (if required; §3.1.1.1; §3.3.6.2). A VP consists of a verb word other than the copula. A nominal predicate phrase consists of a nominal phrase (NP) and a copula verb which is not expressed under certain conditions (§3.1.1.2). Bound markers may be attached to a predicate, sometimes intervening between elements of the phrase, as shown in (7–1) and (7–2) below, and/or sometimes after an entire predicate, as shown in (7–3) and (7–4) below.

(7–1) *ba=a*   *hon=nu*   *jum-i-i=du*   *ur-Ø.*
        1SG=TOP   book=ACC   read-THM-NRT=FOC   PROG-NPST
        'I am reading a book.'

(7–2) *kari=a*   *sinsii=du*   *a-tar.*
        3SG=TOP   teacher=FOC   COP-PST
        'He was a teacher.'

(7–3) *kari=a*   *mudur-i-i*   *t-tar =pazï*
        3SG=Z=TOP   return-THM-NRT   come-PST=maybe
        'He may have come back.'

(7–4) *kari=a*   *sinsii=pazï.*
        3SG=TOP   teacher=maybe
        'He may be a teacher.'

7.1. The structure of verbal predicate phrase

In this section I describe the internal structure of the verbal predicate phrase, which is schematically shown below:

(7–5) **(VP complement+) [lexical verb 1 (+auxiliary verb/lexical verb 2)]**$_{VP}$

Our focus in what follows is VP structure. See §3.1.1.1 and §3.3.6.2 for the description of VP complements.

232   Chapter 7

7.1.1. Verb inflection within a VP

When a VP is internally complex, the first verb (V1) is a non-finite, narrative converb form. The second verb (V2) is either a finite or a non-finite verb form, depending on whether the clause headed by the VP is independent or dependent. For example, the VP *purii ttar* in (7–6) has the structure V1$_{[narrative\ cvb]}$ + V2$_{[finite]}$, since the VP heads an independent clause. The VP *purii ccii* in (7–7), on the other hand, has the structure V1$_{[narrative\ cvb]}$ + V2$_{[narrative\ cvb]}$, since the VP heads a dependent clause that occupies a non-final slot in a clause chain (§11.3). The VP *purii ffiba* in (7–8) has the structure V1$_{[narrative\ cvb]}$ + V2$_{[causal\ cvb]}$, since the VP heads a dependent clause that functions as a causal adsentential clause (§11.4.1.3).

(7–6)   *pai=kara*   *mm=mu=du*   *pur-i-i*   *t-tar.*
        field=ABL   potato=ACC=FOC   dig-THM-NRT   come-PST
        'From the field (I) dug potatoes and came.' [head: finite verb]

(7–7)   *mm=mu*   *pur-i-i*   *cc-i-i,*   *fa-i.*
        potato=ACC   dig-THM-NRT   come-THM-NRT   eat-IMP
        '(You) dig potatoes and come, then eat (them).' [head: narrative converb]

(7–8)   *mm=mu*   *pur-i-i*   *ff-i-ba,*
        potato=ACC   dig-THM-NRT   come-THM-CSL
        mac-i+ur-i.
        wait-THM+PROG-IMP
        'Because (I) will dig potatoes and come, keep waiting.' [head: converb]

7.1.2. Lexical verb and auxiliary verb

In a VP the structural head and the semantic head do not necessarily coincide. Let us examine this mismatch step by step. To begin with, the headship of a VP that lacks a structural dependent is uncontroversial, since the structural head is filled by a lexical verb, which is also a semantic head, i.e. the 'primary information-bearing unit' (Croft 2003).

(7–9)   *ba=a*   *pisir=ru=baa*   *fau-ta-m=suga=du...*
        1SG=TOP   lunch=ACC=TOP   eat-PST-RLS=but=FOC
        'I ate lunch, but...'[1]

---
[1] The clitics =*suga* and =*du* are clause-level constituents and belong only phonologically to the VP.

The predicate phrase   233

On the other hand, in a complex VP where both the head slot and the dependent slot are filled, it is the verb filling the dependent slot that is morphologically marked for the dependency relation. Thus in (7–10) below, the structural dependent is marked by a special inflection, the narrative converb form. However, this structurally dependent verb may be the semantic head, i.e. the primary information-bearing unit. Thus the structural dependent *faii* 'eat' is fully lexical in meaning, whereas the second verb *ar* encodes resultative aspect. On the other hand, it is this second verb *ar* which has finite inflection, and functions as the structural head.

(7–10) *ba=a*   *pisir=ru=baa*   *fa-i-i=du*
        2SG=TOP   lunch=ACC=TOP   eat-THM-NRT=FOC
        ar-Ø.
        RSL-NPST
        a. Structural headship: Dependent   Head
        b. Semantic headship: Head   Dependent
        'I have eaten lunch.'

In this grammar an auxiliary verb is defined as a verb within an internally complex VP that fills the structural head slot but serves as a semantic dependent. In the example above, the auxiliary is the resultative aspectual marker *ar*. Thus 'auxiliary verb' labels the mismatch between structural and semantic headship. A lexical verb is defined as the verb that serves as semantic head, which may be either a structural head (e.g. *fautam* in (7–9)) or a structural dependent (e.g. *faii* in (7–10)).

7.1.3. Phrasal serial verb constructions
7.1.3.1. Definition
Those VPs in which V2 is also a lexical verb, with a double semantic head structure, are phrasal serial verb constructions (see §6.4.2.2 for agglutinative SVCs that constitute a verb stem). A phrasal SVC has structural asymmetry, where the first verb is non-finite (narrative converb form) and the second verb is finite (or non-finite, §7.1.1). An example of a phrasal SVC is:

(7–11) *agu=u*   *jurab-i-i*   *t-tar.*
        friend=ACC   call-THM-NRT   come-PST
        'I brought my friends' [lit. (I) called (my) friends and came back; motion]
(7–12) *tur-i-i,*   *mmja,*

234   Chapter 7

         take-THM-NRT   INTJ
         nak-i-i   *fau-ta-m=dara.*
         cry-THM-NRT   eat-PST-RLS=CRTN
         '(I) took (the dish), and ate (it) crying.'
(7–13)   *suu=ju*   *makas-i-i*   *tur-i.*
         vegetable=ACC   pull-THM-NRT   take-IMP
         'Pull the vegetable out.' [lit. Pull the vegetable and take (it).]

By contrast, a phrasal auxiliary verb construction (AVC), as illustrated in (7–10) above, has both semantic and structural asymmetry (see §6.4.2.1 for agglutinative AVCs). That is, V1 is the semantic head and V2 is the semantic dependent, whereas V1 is the structural dependent and V2 is the structural head.

TABLE 7–1. AVCs and SVCs

	AVC		SVC	
	V1	V2	V1	V2
Semantic head	*		*	*
Structural head		*		*

Since semantic headship is a notion of more/less rather than either/or kind, the double semantic heads in an SVC are not given absolutely equal status: V1 of an SVC may be more semantically prominent than V2, or vice versa, even though both verbs can still be seen as lexical verbs. For example, (7–11) above is a motion SVC, where the motion verb (V2) is less semantically prominent, since the argument structure is primarily determined by V1 (transitive). On the other hand, in (7–12) V2 is more semantically prominent than V1, since it is the V2 that determines the transitivity of the SVC as a whole, and V1 modifies V2 as a manner adverbial. In (7–13), it is difficult to judge whether V1 or V2 is semantically more prominent, as both A and O arguments are shared, and no modificational relationship is established between the two verbs. At any rate, in each of the examples, both verbs retain their lexical meaning.

On the other hand, V2 of an AVC is clearly a semantic dependent with much semantic bleaching. For example, the resultative aspectual auxiliary *ar* adds aspectual information to the event described by the lexical verb, and it does not retain its lexical meaning (*ar* '(inanimate subject) exist'). Cross-linguistically, an SVC is a typical diachronic source for AVCs (Payne 1997: 310; Anderson 2006: 11), and if either of the double semantic heads in an SVC has undergone a significant semantic bleaching or ab-

The predicate phrase   235

straction, the construction begins to be like an AVC. In Irabu, AVCs have
V2 as an auxiliary verb expressing aspectual and benefactive categories
(§7.1.4).

7.1.3.2. Typological characteristics of phrasal SVCs
The definition of an SVC given in the preceding section differs from that
suggested in Aikhenvald's (2006: 1), where she states that 'a serial verb
construction is a sequence of verbs which act together as a single predicate,
without any overt marker of coordination, subordination, or syntactic de-
pendency of any other sort' (emphasis mine).

This definition certainly excludes the Irabu VP (and other complex predicates in Japanese, Korean, and so-called Altaic languages), since the first
verb shows syntactic dependency (non-finite inflection). However, there
are enough functional-typological similarities for us to use the same term
for the Irabu case.[2] In general, SVCs often (but by no means must) exhibit
the following characteristics (Foley and Olson 1985; Givón 1990; Durie
1997; Pawley and Lane 1998; Aikhenvald 2006; *inter alia*), all of which are
shared by Irabu SVCs, as briefly noted in what follows:

(1) monoclausality
(2) argument sharing
(3) encoding of sequential events, manner, motions, etc.
(4) shared predicate categories ('operators' in Foley and Van Valin's
     1984 terms) such as tense and mood
(5) single intonational unit

(1) Monoclausality
A phrasal SVC is monoclausal, serving as a single predicate. If it occurs in
an independent clause, it consists of a narrative converb and a finite verb.
This analysis requires careful justification, as narrative converbs occur in
two structural contexts: as V1 within a VP, e.g. (7–14), and as the head of a
non-final clause in a chain (7–15).

(7–14) *agu=u*   *jurab-i-i*   *t-tar.*
        friend=ACC   call-THM-NRT   come-PST
        '(I) brought my friends' [lit. (I) called (my) friends and came
        back.]

---

[2] See also Payne (1997: 311) and Shibatani and Huang (2006) for a similar claim that non-finite marking on a verb within a series does not necessarily exclude the possibility to call the
construction an SVC, as such exclusion would entail a loss of generalisation.

236   Chapter 7

(7–15)   *agu=u*   *jurab-i-i,*   *t-tar.*
          friend=ACC   call-THM-NRT   come-PST
          '(I) called (my) friends, and (I) came back.'

There is a criterion for distinguishing between the two structures. A VP
is a tight syntactic knit, while two verbs in a clause chain are not. This is
easily tested by seeing whether it is possible to insert a word between the
two verbs in each case. The following example can only be interpreted as
two verbs in a clause chain, since the adverb *sugu(=du)* 'right away' intervenes between the first verb and the second verb.

(7–16)   *agu=u*   *jurab-i-i,*   *sugu=du*   *t-tar.*
          friend=ACC   call-THM-NRT   right.away=FOC   come-PST
          '(I) called (my) friends, and (I) came back right away.'

By contrast, if a VP is to be modified by an adverb, it must be placed before the whole VP (7–17).

(7–17)   *agu=u*   *sugu=du*   *jurab-i-i*   *t-tar.*
          friend=ACC   right.away=FOC   call-THM-NRT   come-PST
          'I brought my friends right away.'

There is a significant difference in semantics between (7–14) and (7–15)
above. In the monoclausal SVC (7–14), the act of calling a friend and the
act of coming (back) are directly related, thus the speaker actually brought
the friend, coming together with him. In Lord's (1974) terms, the second
verb is 'always in some sense a further development, result, or goal' of the
first verb. On the other hand, in the biclausal (7–15), it may be possible that
the speaker alone came back.

(2) Argument sharing
Both verbs in a VP (either an SVC or an AVC) must share a subject,
whereas two verbs in a chain may not. In (7–18) below the subject of the
VP is *ba=a* 'I', which is shared by both V1 and V2.

(7–18)   *ba=a*   *agu=u*   *jurab-i-i*   *t-tar.*
          1SG=TOP   friend=ACC   call-THM-NRT   come-PST
          'I brought my friends' [lit. I called (my) friends and came
          back.][3]

---

[3] It is important *not* to confuse semantic subject and grammatical subject (the latter of which
is what I mean by 'subject'). Of course, subject sharing is meant for the latter concept. (7–18)

The predicate phrase 237

In a clause chain like (7–19) below, a narrative converb inflection usually signals same-subject reference. Thus in (7–19) the second clause lacks an overt subject, but the subject in the second clause is interpreted as the same as that in the first.

(7–19) *ba=a*   *agu=u*   *jurab-i-i,*   *t-tar.*
         1SG=TOP   friend=ACC   call-THM-NRT   come-PST
         'I called (my) friends, and came.'

However, this same subject entailment is not an absolute rule. As is illustrated in (7–20) below, it is possible for each clause to have a different subject.

(7–20) *ba=ga*   *agu=u*   *jurab-i-i,*
         1SG=NOM   friend=ACC   call-THM-NRT
         kai=ga=du   *t-tar.*
         3SG=NOM=FOC   come-PST
         '(I) called (my) friends, and (among them) he came.'

(3) Encoding of sequential events, manner, motions, etc.
Phrasal SVCs encode sequential subevents (iconically ordered) that constitute a larger single event. The subevents are often iterative, as shown in (7–22) and (7–23), but may be manner (7–24) to (7–28), motion (7–29) and (7–30), and so on.

(7–21) *vvadu=ga*   *sïn-i-i*   *par-tigaa=dumma,*
         2PL=NOM   die-THM-NRT   leave-CND=EMP
         iravcï=mai   *njaa-n-Ø.*
         Irabu.language=too   not.exist-NPST
         'If your generation dies out, the Irabu language will also disappear.' [sequential events]
(7–22) *ami   fïï-Ø*   *atu=n=na*   *ssudur=nkai*
         rain   fall-NPST   after=DAT=TOP   ssudur=ALL
         ik-i-i,   *nuur+zuu=ju=mai*
         go-THM-NRT   nuur+plant=ACC=too

'I brought my friends' has the meaning 'I called my friends and *I and my friends* came back'. Here, one might argue that the semantic subject is *I and my friends*, and call into question the generalisation that subject sharing is obligatory. However, in terms of syntax, the subject must be 'I'. For example, if one says (7–18) with the reflexive pronoun, as in *unagaduu=sii* (RFL=INST) 'by oneself', the reflexive pronoun must refer to 'I', not 'I and my friends'. See §3.4.1 for reflexive control of subject.

238 Chapter 7

tur-i-i   *fau-Ø*.
pick-THM-NRT   eat-NPST
'After it rains (I) go to Ssudur (place name), and <u>pick and eat</u>
nuurzuu plant.' [sequential events: iterative]

(7–23) *kai*   *bazakar-i-i,*   *ff-a-Ø=tti*
like.that   show.claw-THM-NRT   bite-THM-INT=QT
as-i-i,   *uri=a*   *tur-i-i*   *rri-i...*
do-THM-NRT   3SG=TOP   take-THM-NRT   put.in-NRT
'(The crab) showed its claw, moving menacingly, (and I) <u>took it</u>
<u>and put it into</u> (the basket).' [sequential events: iterative]

(7–24) *nuuma=n*   *nuur-i-i*   *par-tar=ca*.
horse=DAT   ride-THM-NRT   leave-PST=HS
'(He) left riding on a horse.' [manner]

(7–25) *kata+bata=u=baa*   *jak-i-i*   *fau-Ø*.
half+body=ACC=TOP   burn-THM-NRT   eat-NPST
'(They) (would) burn and eat the half of the body.' [manner]

(7–26) *uri=u*   *nak-i-i=du*   *fau-tar*.
3SG=ACC   cry-THM-NRT=FOC   eat-PST
'(She) ate it crying.' [manner]

(7–27) *mma=a*   *naa=ga*   *ffa=u=baa*
mother=TOP   oneself=GEN   child=ACC=TOP
takara=ti=du   *umu-i+u-i-ba=i,*
treasure=QT=FOC   think-THM+PROG-THM-CSL=CNF
ffa=nu   *pana+dar=ru=mai*
child=GEN   nose+snot=ACC=even
jub-i-i   *tur-Ø*.
suck-THM-NRT   take-NPST
'A mother thinks that her baby is a treasure, you know, (she) can
<u>suck out</u> the snot of baby's snot.' [manner]

(7–28) *icu=u=baa,*   *mmja,*   *fïzï=sii*   *kir-Ø*.
thread=ACC=TOP   INTJ   mouth=INST   cut-NPST
mata,   *umacï=sii*   *jak-i-i*   *kir-Ø*.
and   fire=INST   burn-THM-NRT   cut-NPST
'(One) cuts threads with his mouth; also (one can) <u>cut (threads)</u>
<u>by burning</u> (them) with fire.' [manner]

(7–29) *uttussu=mai*
younger.brother=too
saar-i-i   *ifï-ta-m=dara*.
accompany-THM-NRT   go-PST-RLS=CRTN
'(I) <u>took</u> my younger brother, too (to some place).' [motion]

The predicate phrase   239

(7–30) *mm+pur-ja-gama=a*   *muc-i-i*   *ik-i-i,*
        potato+dig-NLZ-DIM=PRT   carry-THM-NRT   go-THM-NRT
        pžk-i-i   *cc-i-i...*
        pull-THM-NRT   come-THM-NRT
        '(people would) take (lit. carry go) a potato digger (to the field),
        and pull and bring (potatoes)...' [motion]

(4) Shared predicate categories
Since V1 of a phrasal SVC is a non-finite form, the specification of tense
and mood (finite inflectional categories) is dependent on V2, which can be
inflected for these categories. The scope of interrogation is also over an
entire SVC:

(7–31) *vva=a*   *unu*   *panas=su=baa*
        2SG=TOP   that   story=ACC=TOP
        cïk-as-i-i   *maar-tar=ru?*
        hear-CAUS-THM-NRT   wander-PST=Q
        'Did you visit hear and there exposing that talk?'
(7–32) *aa+gara=u=ru*
        foxtail.millet+hull=ACC=FOC
        tur-i-i   *sïti-r?*
        take-THM-NRT   do.away.with-NPST
        'Do (I have to) take and do away with the hulls of foxtail mil-
        let?'

On the other hand, the second verb in a clause chain can be independently
interrogated, with the truth value of the first clause being presupposed.

(7–33) *vva=a*   *uja=nu*   *sïn-i-i,*
        2SG=TOP   father=NOM   die-THM-NRT
        mjaaku=nkai=ja   *kuu-t-ta-m=mu?*
        Miyako=ALL=TOP   come-NEG-PST-RLS=Q
        'Didn't you come back$_{V2}$ to Miyako even when your father
        died$_{V1}$?'

Negation is more complicated. First, a narrative converb is inflected for
negative polarity, choosing either an affirmative form *-i* or a negative form
-da. Thus V1 can be independently negated within an SVC. This is also
true for an AVC.

240 Chapter 7

(7–34) *munu=u=mai*   *ažž-a-da*   *par-tar.*
thing=ACC=even   speak-THM-NEG.NRT   leave-PST
'(He) left without speaking anything.'

(7–35) *maasu=u=baa*   *maadaa*
salt=ACC=TOP   not.much
fa-a-da=du   *ur-Ø.*
eat-THM-NEG.NRT=FOC   PROG-NPST
'I am taking care not to eat too much salt.'

When V2 is negated with a finite inflection, either the scope is over an entire SVC, as illustrated in (7–36) below, or V1 is negated with contrastive meaning, as illustrated in (7–37) below. In the latter case, V1 is topic-marked, as the topic marking designates contrastive meaning.

(7–36) *banti=a*   *kiban-ka-ta=iba,*   *waa-nagi=a*
1PL=TOP   poor-VLZ-PST=so   pig-APPR=TOP
kurus-i-i   *fa-a-t-ta-m.*
kill-THM-NRT   eat-THM-NEG-PST-RLS
'We were poor, so did not kill and eat pigs.'

(7–37) *waa-nagi=a,*
pig-APPR=TOP
kuris-i-i=ja   *fa-a-t-tar=ruga,*
kill-THM-NRT=TOP   eat-THM-NEG-NPST=but
siis=su   *ka-i-i=du*   *fau-tar.*
meat=ACC   buy-THM-NRT=FOC   eat-PST
'(I) did not eat a pig by killing (one), but (I) bought and ate one.'
[i.e. I ate a pig not by killing but by buying its meat.]

(5) Single intonational unit
The verbs in a phrasal SVC or AVC undergo phrasal mapping of rhythmic alternation (§2.9.4), whereas two verbs in a clause chain do not. Thus in (7–38) below, the V1 of the SVC has one foot and therefore is treated as part of the phonological word (i.e. the entire SVC) for the purpose of the rhythmic alternation.

(7–38) *agu=u*   *jurab-i-i*   *t-tar.*
friend=ACC   call-THM-NRT   come-PST
'(I) brought (my) friends.' [lit. (I) called (my) friends and came back]
(aguu)   (jura)(bii)   (ttar)

| (H) | (H) (Ø) | (Ø) |

By contrast, if these same verbs are used in a clause chain, as illustrated in
(7–39) below, phrasal mapping does not occur, and each verb is treated as a
phonological word. There is also a clear intonational break (pause) between the first verb and the second verb in a chain in (7–39).

(7–39) *agu=u*   *jurab-i-i,*   *t-tar.*
        friend=ACC   call-THM-NRT   come-PST
        '(I) brought (my) friends.' [lit. (I) called (my) friends and came
        back]
        (aguu)   (jura)(bii)   (ttar)

| (H) | (H) (Ø) | (H) |

7.1.4. Phrasal auxiliary verb constructions

A phrasal AVC consists of a lexical verb (narrative converb inflection) and
an auxiliary verb (see also §6.4.2.3 for a summary of Irabu AVCs). Functionally, phrasal AVCs fall into two major types: aspectual AVCs (§7.1.4.1)
and benefactive AVCs (§7.1.4.2). The difference in function is carried by
the auxiliary verb. It is also reflected in certain syntactic differences, as will
be noted in what follows. As noted in §6.4.2.3, there is word-phrase alternation, where three aspectual auxiliaries (progressive *ur*, resultative *ar*, and
prospective *ufi*) may alternatively form an agglutinative AVC where V1 and
V2 constitute a single verb stem.

7.1.4.1. Aspectual AVCs

Aspectual AVCs express the basic aspectual distinctions of progressive, resultative, prospective ('do something for future benefit/purpose'), perfect,
and experiential ('have ever done; try doing'), by selecting an appropriate
aspect auxiliary verb (glossed PROG, RSL, PROS, PRF, and EXP respectively). A fuller functional account of aspect is provided in §10.5.2. Here it
is sufficient to note the following three structural characteristics.

First, all aspect auxiliary verbs represent grammaticalisations of their
lexical verb counterparts: progressive *ur* (< existential (for animate) *ur*),
resultative *ar* (< existential (for inanimate) *ar*), prospective *ufi* (< *ufi* 'put;
place'), perfect *njaan* (< negative stative *njaan* 'be non-existent'), and *miir*
(< *miir* 'look'). These auxiliary verbs are illustrated in the examples below.

(7–40)   Progressive
         ffa=nu   *nak-i-i=du*   *ur-Ø.*

child=NOM cry-THM-NRT=FOC PROG-NPST

'(My) child is crying.'

(7–41) Resultative

kuri=a *nak-i-i=du* *ar-Ø.*

3SG=TOP cry-THM-NRT=FOC RSL-NPST

'This (one) has cried (to the effect that he has a red-rimmed eyes)'

(7–42) Prospective

mm=mu=baa *piicja-gama*

potato=ACC=TOP little.amount-DIM

nukus-i-i=du *ufi-kutu.*

leave-THM-NRT=FOC PROS-OBL

'(We) have to keep a bit of potato (for dad who is absent).'

'Tomorrow (I) have to catch fish'

(7–43) Perfect

kari=a *sïn-i-i* *njaa-n.*

3SG=TOP die-THM-NRT PRF-NPST

'He has died.' [lit. He died, and is non-existent]

(7–44) Experiential

ku=nu *harigani=u* *umacï=sii* *nbas-i-i*

this=GEN wire=ACC fire=INST stretch-THM-NRT

mii-ru.

EXP-IMP

'Try stretching this wire with fire.'

Second, the auxiliary verbs that cannot form an agglutinative AVC, i.e. perfect *njaan* and experiential *miir*, are always contiguous with the lexical verb within an AVC, as illustrated in (7–43) and (7–44). That is, no focus marker or topic marker appears on the lexical verb.

Third, the perfect auxiliary is identical in form with the negative existential verb *njaan*. This can be seen in (7–43), where perfect aspectual AVC is literally 'died, and is non-existent'. However, the degree of semantic abstraction is such that the original semantic force does not necessarily hold. Thus in (7–45) below the auxiliary verb simply encodes a perfect event, and does not allow a literal interpretation '(I) read and that book is non-existent'.

(7–45) *hon=nu=baa* *jum-i-i* *njaa-n.*

book=ACC=TOP read-THM-NRT PRF-NPST

'As for the book, (I) have read (it).'

The predicate phrase   243

7.1.4.2. Benefactive AVCs
Benefactive AVCs express actions that are directed to a person for his/her
benefit.

(7–46) a. *ba=a*   *maccja=nkai=du*   *ifi-tar.*
           1SG=TOP   shop=ALL=FOC   go-PST
           'I went to a shop.'

        b. *ba=a*   *ui=ga*   *kaari=n*
           1SG=TOP   3SG=GEN   stead=DAT
           maccja=nkai=du   *ik-i-i*   *fii-tar.*
           shop=ALL=FOC   go-THM-NRT   BEN-PST
           'I went to a shop instead of him.'

        c. *kari=a*   *ba=ga*   *kaari=n*
           3SG=TOP   1SG=GEN   stead=DAT
           maccja=nkai=du   *ik-i-i*   *fii-tar.*
           shop=ALL=FOC   go-THM-NRT   BEN-PST
           'He went to a shop instead of me.'

The benefactive AVC is also observed in Japanese (Martin 1975). One interesting difference between Irabu and Japanese is that in Irabu the benefactive auxiliary is invariably *fii*, whereas in Japanese the choice of auxiliary depends on the deictic centre: (1) *ageru* '(speaker) do for someone's
benefit (from speaker's point of view)', (2) *kureru* '(non-speaker subject)
do for speaker's benefit', and (3) *morau* '(speaker) have something done
for speaker's benefit.' Note that (1) and (2) are encoded by *fii* in (7–46b)
and (7–46c) respectively. Also, (3) is expressed by (7–46c), where the deictic centre is the subject and not the speaker. To encode (3), Irabu also often
uses causative, as typical in Ryukyuan in general.

7.1.4.3. Auxiliary ellipsis
A past-tense progressive auxiliary verb may undergo ellipsis. This phenomenon is in most cases an avoidance of repetition of a previous utterance that contains the auxiliary, as illustrated in (7–47), though some examples cannot be seen as avoidance of repetition, as illustrated in (7–48)
where auxiliary ellipsis occurs without a previous mention of the auxiliary.

(7–47) A. *manjuu=gami=a*   *ar-i-i=ru*   *u-tar?*
           papaya=LMT=TOP   exist-THM-NRT=FOC   PROG-PST
           'Were (there) papayas (in those days)?'
        B. *ar-i-i=du.*

244 Chapter 7

exist-THM-NRT=FOC
'(There) were.'

(7–48) A. *ka=nu*   *buuciri+jarabi=a=da?*
          that=GEN   mighty+child=TOP=how.about
          'What has become of that mighty boy?'

       B. *kari=a*   *mmja*   *nak-i-i=du.*
          3SG=TOP   INTJ   cry-THM-NRT=FOC
          '(He) was crying.'

7.2. The structure of nominal predicate phrase

This section describes the structure of a predicate headed by an NP, or a nominal predicate. See §10.2.1 and §10.2.2 for the function of nominal predicates.

7.2.1. Basic structure

As mentioned in §3.1.1.2, a nominal predicate phrase consists of an NP as a predicate head, which may be focus-marked by the focus marker (see §9.5.2.1 for syntactic distribution of this marker), followed by a copula verb, which is obligatorily absent when certain conditions are met, i.e. in affirmative, in non-past tense, in absence of the focus marker on the NP, and in a main clause (see §3.1.1.2 for detail). Thus, in the following pair of examples, (7–49a) contains the copula verb *atar* as it is in past tense, whereas in (7–49b) it is absent, as the above-mentioned conditions are all met.

(7–49) a. *ba=a*   *sinsii=du*   *a-tar.*
            1SG=TOP   teacher=FOC   COP-PST
            'I was a teacher'

        b. *ba=a*   *sinsii.*
            1SG=TOP   teacher
            'I am a teacher.'

A predicate NP may be headed by a nominal word (Chapter 5) or an adjective word (Chapter 8), even though it is less common for an adjective to fill this syntactic slot (TABLE 8–8 of §8.3.4.1). The nominal word that heads a predicate NP may be any subclass of nominal, i.e. a noun, a pronoun, a numeral, an interrogative, an indefinite, a compound derived from a PC stem (§8.3.4).

The predicate phrase 245

(7–50) a. *kanu*   *pžtu=mai*   *irav+pžtu=dooi.*
       that   man=too   Irabu+man=EMP
       'That man (is) also a man from Irabu.' [nominal as head]
    b. *kama=nu*   *ngjamasï+ngjamasï=du*   *a-ta=iba.*
       that.place=NOM   RED+noisy=FOC   COP-PST=so
       'For that place was noisy.' [adjective as head]

In very limited cases, however, a predicate NP may also be headed by a verb that was historically composed of a verb followed by a formal noun, and this will be described in §7.2.2 below.

7.2.2. Secondary inflection

There are two bound forms, *kutu* 'thing' and *gumata* '?',[4] which can be used either as a bound nominal word or a finite inflectional affix. In the latter case, I call these 'secondary inflectional affixes'.

When used as a bound noun they head an NP modified by an adnominal clause, just like formal nouns (§4.2.1). In (7–51) and (7–52) below, the NPs take a copula verb.

(7–51)   *vva=ga*   *nkai-r*   *kutu=du*   *a-tar.*
         2SG=NOM   pick.up-NPST   thing=FOC   COP-PST
         '(It) was a you-pick-up (-your-child) case.' [i.e. You should have picked up your child.]
(7–52)   *vva=ga*   *nkai-r*   *gumata=du*   *a-tar.*
         2SG=NOM   pick.up-NPST   ?=FOC   COP-PST
         '(It) was a you-pick-up(-your-child) case.' [i.e. You were supposed to pick up your child.]

Note here that the preceding verbs that function as the predicates of the adnominal clauses are fully inflected (finite non-past unmarked), indicating that there is a grammatical word boundary between the verb and the secondary inflectional affix.

On the other hand, the same forms can be used as secondary inflectional affixes -*kutu* and -*gumata*. In this case, they are attached directly to the bare verb stem.

---

[4] Karimata (2003), in describing another Miyako Ryukyuan variety, Bora, notes that this form is a 'formal noun' i.e. a semantically abstract/empty nominal, which functions like a tense/mood formative that encodes definite future. As in the case of Bora, the lexical meaning of -*gumata* is unclear in Irabu as well.

246   Chapter 7

(7–53)   *vva=ga*   *nkai-kutu=du*   *a-tar.*
         2SG=NOM   pick.up-OBL=FOC   COP-PST
         '(It) was a you-pick-up(-your-child) case.' [i.e. You should have
         picked up your child.]

(7–54)   *vva=ga*   *nkai-gumata=du*   *a-tar.*
         2SG=NOM   pick.up-ANTC=FOC   COP-PST
         '(It) was a you-pick-up(-your-child) case.' [i.e. You were sup-
         posed to pick up your child.]

It is reasonable, then, to treat the head nouns of (7–51) and (7–52) as being
integrated into the finite verbal inflection paradigm in (7–53) and (7–54),
paradigmatically contrasting with other finite inflectional affixes (§6.3.1).
The secondary inflectional affixes -*kutu* and -*gumata* have irrealis modality
in this environment. Thus -*kutu* is best characterised as irrealis obligative/
potential (deontic or epistemic), and -*gumata* as irrealis anticipated future
(epistemic).

The finite verbs of secondary inflection only head a main clause predicate, but unlike other finite verbs they fill the NP slot of the nominal predicate phrase. Note that in (7–53) and (7–54) the verbs of secondary inflection are followed by a copula verb. Also, like NPs they are negated with a
copula verb:

(7–55)   *vva=a*   *nkai-kutu=u*   *ar-a-n-Ø.*
         2SG=TOP   pick.up-OBL=TOP   COP-THM-NEG-NPST
         '(It) isn't a you-pick-up(-your-child) case.' [i.e. You are not sup-
         posed to bring your child.]

(7–56)   *vva=ga*   *nkai-gumata=a*
         2SG=NOM   pick.up-NPST.ANTC=TOP
         ar-a-n-Ø.
         COP-THM-NEG-NPST
         '(It) isn't a you-pick-up(-your-child) case.' [i.e. You are not sup-
         posed to pick up your child.]

The secondary inflection phenomenon is an example of a grammaticalised structure occurring alongside its un-grammaticalised source structure,
a common situation cross-linguistically. In the case of -*gumata*, the degree
of grammaticalisation is greater, as it is seldom used in its un-grammaticalised source structure. The crucial fact in dealing with secondary inflection
is that the secondary inflectional affixes still show nominal features syntac-

tically, retaining their original syntactic function as head of NPs (as they carry a copula), even though they are inflectional affixes in terms of verb morphology.

Chapter 8

Property concepts, adjectives, and other derivational processes

This chapter focuses on (1) issues to do with' 'property concepts' ('high', 'good', 'white', etc.), including the description of the adjective class, and with (2) class-changing derivational processes. With regard to (1), there are four major word formation processes involving a given property concept stem (henceforth PC stem): adjective formation, nominal formation, verb formation, and adverb formation. With regard to (2), there are stem class-changing processes whereby a PC stem is derived from a verb stem, and a nominal stem is derived from a verb stem.

8.1. Property concept stems (PC stems)

A PC stem is a bound stem and requires suffixation, compounding, or reduplication to function as a grammatical word (a few exceptional free PC stems do exist; §8.1.2.2). An adjective is formed by reduplicating a PC stem (e.g. *taka-* 'high' > *takaa+taka*), and usually modifies the head nominal within an NP. The adjective class is fully described in §8.2. In addition to the adjective formation, there are three other ways to form a grammatical word from a PC stem: (1) a nominal compound (*taka+jama* 'high+mountain', *taka+munu* 'high(+thing)'), (2) a PC verb (*taka-ka-ta-m* 'was high-VLZ-PST-RLS'), and (3) a PC adverb (*taka-fi* 'high-ly'). Each constitutes a subclass of its respective word class. These are described in §8.3.

8.1.1. Property concept

Property concepts are cross-linguistically likely to be expressed as 'adjectives'. Dixon (1982) identifies the following semantic categories of property concepts: DIMENSION, AGE, VALUE, COLOUR, PHYSICAL PROPERTY, HUMAN PROPENSITY, and SPEED.

Many PC stems in Irabu are of these categories, but a number of PC stems belong to other categories such as Position, Difficulty, and Similarity (Dixon 2004: 5).

As indicated by '-' in TABLES 8–1 and 8–2 below, most PC stems are

250   Chapter 8

TABLE 8–1. Property concepts and Dixon's (1982) semantic types

DIMENSION	*uku-* 'big'	*naga-* 'long'	*taka-* 'tall'	*pžsu-* 'wide'
AGE	*mžž-* 'new'	*baka-* 'young'	*gaba-* 'old'	*jari-* 'old'
VALUE	*zau-* 'good'	*bar-* 'bad'	*kagi-* 'lovely'	*pinna-* 'odd'
COLOUR	*ffu* 'black'	*ssu* 'white'	*aka* 'red'	*au* 'blue'
PHYSICAL PROPERTY	*kupa-* 'hard'	*iv-* 'heavy'	*cuu-* 'strong'	*acï-* 'hot'
HUMAN PROPENSITY	*kuukacï* 'mean'	*pukarasï* 'happy'	*umukutu* 'clever'	*pazïkasï-* 'ashamed'
SPEED	*pjaa-* 'fast'	*niv-* 'slow'		

TABLE 8–2. Property concept roots and other semantic types

Position	*taka-* 'high'		*bžda-* 'low'	*tuu-* 'far'	*cïka-* 'near'
Difficulty	*mucïkasi-* 'difficult'				
Similarity	*junuguu* 'same'				

bound, except for a few free PC stems that may be zero-converted to nominal stems (see §8.1.2.2). For example, *junuguu* 'same' in TABLE 8–2 can stand alone if it is zero-converted to a nominal, and can function as head of an NP (either argument or predicate).

(8–1)   *ui=mai*   *sïn-i-i,*   *mmja,*   *junuguu=n=du*
        3SG=too   die-THM-NRT   INTJ   same=DAT=FOC
        nar-tar.
        become-PST
        'He also died, and became the same (as another guy who had died).'

(8–2)   *kui=tu*   *kui=tu=u*   *junuguu=du*   *jar-Ø.*
        this=ASC   this=ASC=TOP   same=FOC   COP-NPST
        'This and this are the same.'

8.1.2. Morphosyntax of the PC stem

A PC stem exhibits a number of morphosyntactic properties that distinguish it from other stem classes (nominal stems, verb stems, and adverb stems). I list them below, labelled (A), (B), and (C). (A) and (C) are borrowed from Motonaga (1978: 395).

(A) REDUPLICATION: a PC stem can be reduplicated. Unlike other kinds of reduplication such as verbal reduplication (§3.3.6.2; §10.5.2.6), PC

Property concepts, adjectives, and other derivational processes   251

stem reduplication involves a full reduplication *plus* lengthening of the stem-final phoneme by one mora. In some cases it is possible to consider that the reduplication expresses intensity by itself, but in others it is not. Rather, intensity is more regularly expressed by intonation and/or by the phonetic realisation of one-mora lengthening: the lengthening may be extra-long [:·] depending on the semantic intensity that speaker wishes to emphasise.[1]

(i) *taka-* 'high' > *takaa+taka*
(ii) *kuu-* 'hard' > *kuuu+kuu*
(ii) *kiban-* 'poor' > *kibann+kiban*

(B) DIRECT QUOTATION: with stem-final lengthening: a PC stem can be directly quoted by quotative marker *=ti(i)*, where the PC stem undergoes the lengthening that is identical to that in reduplication (A). The semantic effect of this is a quoted exclamation. This lengthened PC stem behaves partially like an interjection: even though it does not constitute an utterance, it is embedded into a matrix clause with the quotative marker *=ti(i)* (see §3.3.6.4 for the definition of interjections).

takaa=ti=nu   *pžtu*
high=QT=GEN   man
'a man who is like, "(how) tall!"'

(C) SPECIAL DERIVATIONAL AFFIXES: PC stems may have a distinct set of derivational affixes attached to them. These are the verbaliser *-ka(r)*, the state nominaliser *-sa*, and the adverbialiser *-fi*.

(i) *taka-ka-tar*	(ii) *taka-sa*	(iii) *taka-fi*
high-VLZ-PST	high-NLZ	high-AVLZ
'was high'	'highness; height'	'highly'

The following table shows how various PC stems satisfy each criterion. Also, the table lists nominal stems (k–m), which satisfy one or more of the criteria, showing that these are less prototypical nominal stems and more

---

[1] Karimata (2002: 61) pointed out this fact as a tendency that holds true for Miyako Ryukyuan varieties in general. He argues that when lengthening is sustained over two morae (he apparently considers that there is a phonemic contrast between monomoraic and bimoraic lengthening, which I do not agree with), reduplication is interpreted as intensifier.

252   Chapter 8

like PC stems, as Motonaga (1978) pointed out.

TABLE 8–3. PC stems and nominal stems: distinctive criteria

		(A)	(B)	(C) -sa	-fï	-ka(r)
a	*taka*- 'high'	*	*	*	*	*
b	*baka*- 'young'	*	*	*	*	*
c	*bar*- 'bad'	*	*	*	*	*
d	*cuu*- 'strong'	*	*	*	*	*
e	*pukarasï*- 'happy'	*	*	*	*	*
f	*niv*- 'slow'	*	*	*	*	*
g	*au* 'blue'	*	*	*	*	*
h	*aparagi* 'beautiful (person)'	*	*	*	*	*
i	*ujaki* 'rich'	*	*	*	*	*
j	*buuciri* 'mighty (person)'	*	*	*	*	*
k	*avva* 'oil'	*	*	?	*	*
l	*jarabi* 'child'	*	*			*
m	*gudun* 'dull person'	?	*			?

Note 1: The PC stems in (a–f) are taken from each column in TABLE 8–1. Others
          are taken from my own field note and Motonaga (1978: 395).
Note 2: * (attested)
          ? (grammaticality judgement varies among consultants)

The above table requires a number of comments. These correspond to the
three parts of the above table, i.e. (a–f), (g–j), and (k–m). For the descriptive purposes, I define a PC stem as a stem that is consistently judged by
consultants to satisfy all of (A), (B), and (C). Thus by my definition the
stems belonging to (a–j) in TABLE 8–3 are PC stems. As discussed below,
these PC stems fall into two subclasses: prototypical and less prototypical
PC stems, depending on whether they are bound stems. The PC stems listed in the table are representative sample stems. There are quite a large
number of PC stems in the Irabu lexicon (see, for example, Nakama 1992
for a large list of PC stems in Miyako Ryukyuan in general).

8.1.2.1. Prototypical PC stems: (a–f)
Among the three parts of TABLE 8–3, (a–f) are prototypical PC stems. They
satisfy all of (A) to (C), and are bound. All of these denote the seven semantic types of property concept suggested by Dixon (1982). See TABLE
8–1 above.
     Below I illustrate each prototypical PC stem (a) to (f) in terms of each of

Property concepts, adjectives, and other derivational processes   253

the morphosyntactic criteria (A) to (C).

(A) REDUPLICATION
      taka- 'high' > *takaa+taka* [takaː(˙)taka] '(very) tall'
      baka- 'young' > *bakaa+baka* [bakaː(˙)baka] '(very) young'
      bar- 'bad' > *barr+bar* [baɭː(˙)baɭ] '(very) bad'
      cuu- 'strong' > *cuuu+cuu* [tsuː(˙)tsuː] '(very) strong'
      pukarasï- 'happy' > *pukarasïï+pukarasï* [pukaɾasiː(˙)pukaɾasi] '(very)
      happy'
      niv- 'slow' > *nivv+niv* [niʋː(˙)niʋ] '(very) slow'

(B) DIRECT QUOTATION
      taka- 'tall'   >   *takaa=ti=nu*   *pžtu*
                                   tall=QT=GEN   man
                                   'a man who is like, "(how) tall!"'
      baka- 'young'   >   *bakaa=ti=nu*   *pžtu*
                                   young=QT=GEN   man
                                   'a man who is like, "(how) young!"'
      bar- 'bad'   >   *barr=ti=nu*   *pžtu*
                                   bad=QT=GEN   man
                                   'a man who is like, "(how) bad!"'
      cuu- 'strong'   >   *cuuu=ti=nu*   *pžtu*
                                   strong=QT=GEN   man
                                   'a man who is like, "(how) strong!"'
      pukarasï- 'happy'   >   *pukarasïï=ti=nu*   *cïmucï*
                                   happy=QT=GEN   feeling
                                   'a feeling like, "(how) happy!"'
      niv- 'slow'   >   *nivv=ti=nu*   *pžtu*
                                   slow=QT=GEN   man
                                   'a man who is like, "(how) slow!"'

(C) SPECIAL DERIVATIONAL AFFIXES
      taka- 'tall'   >   *taka-ka-ta-m* 'was tall'
                                   taka-sa 'height'
                                   taka-fï 'high:ADV'
      baka- 'young'   >   *baka-ka-ta-m* 'was young'
                                   baka-sa 'youth'
                                   baka-fï 'young:ADV'
      bar- 'bad'   >   *bar-ka-ta-m* 'was bad'
                                   bar-sa 'badness'

254   Chapter 8

                              bar-fï 'bad: ADV'

cuu- 'strong'   >   *cuu-ka-ta-m* 'was strong'

                              cuu-sa 'strength'

                              cuu-fï 'strongly'

pukarasï- 'happy' >   *pukarasï-ka-ta-m* 'was happy'

                              pukaras-sa 'happiness'

                              pukarasï-fï 'happily'

niv- 'slow'   >   *niv-ka-ta-m* 'was slow'

                              niv-sa 'slowness'

                              niv-fï 'slowly'

8.1.2.2. Less prototypical PC stems: (g–j)

Less prototypical PC stems also satisfy all of criteria (A), (B), and (C), though they show certain nominal features as noted below. Let us first confirm the fact that they satisfy the three relevant criteria.

(A) *auu+au* [auː(·)au] '(very) blue'

     aparagii+aparagi [apaɾaː(·)apaɾagi] '(very) beautiful'

     ujakii+ujaki [ujakiː(·)ujaki] '(very) rich'

     buucirii+buuciri [buːtʃiɾiː(·)buːtʃiɾi] '(very) mighty'

(B) *auu=ti=nu*   *tin*

     blue=QT=GEN   sky

     'the sky which is like, "(how) blue!"'

     aparagii=ti=nu   *pžtu*

     beautiful=QT=GEN   man

     'a man who is like, "(how) beautiful!"'

     ujakii=ti=nu   *pžtu*

     rich=QT=GEN   man

     'a man who is like, "(how) rich!"'

     buucirii=ti=nu   *pžtu*

     mighty=QT=GEN   man

     'a man who is like, "(how) mighty!"'

(C) *au-ka-ta-m* 'was blue'

     au-sa 'blueness'

     au-fï 'blue:ADV'

     aparagi-ka-ta-m 'was beautiful'

     aparagi-sa 'beautifulness'

     aparagi-fï 'beautifully'

Property concepts, adjectives, and other derivational processes   255

ujaki-ka-ta-m 'was rich'
ujaki-sa 'richness'
ujaki-fi 'richly'

buuciri-ka-ta-m 'was mighty'
buuciri-sa 'mightiness'
buuciri-fi 'mightily'

Even though PC stems (g–j) satisfy all of criteria (A), (B), and (C), they show the following nominal feature: they are free forms, and may function as an E argument of the verb 'become' by themselves (whereas prototypical PC stems (a–i) are bound). Thus, as is illustrated below, whereas a prototypical PC stem (a) *taka-* 'high' cannot appear alone, a PC stem (h) *aparagi* 'beautiful' may appear alone, as an E argument.

(8–3)   a. **taka=n=du*   *nar-tar.*
            high=DAT=FOC   become-PST
            '(She) became tall.'
        b. *aparagi=n=du*   *nar-tar.*
            beautiful=DAT=FOC   become-PST
            '(She) became beautiful.'

In order to function as an E argument of the verb 'become' a prototypical PC stem must be transformed into an adjective (§8.2) or a compound nominal (§8.3.4), as illustrated in (8–4) below, and to function as a VP complement of the verb 'become', it must be transformed into a PC adverb (§8.3.2), as illustrated in (8–5) below.

(8–4)   a. *takaa+taka=n=du*   *nar-tar.*
            RED+high=DAT=FOC   become-PST
            '(She) became tall.' [adjective: as head of an E argument]
        b. *taka+pžtu=n=du*   *nar-tar.*
            high+person=DAT=FOC   become-PST
            '(She) became a tall person.' [compound nominal: as head of
            an Eargument]
(8–5)   *taka-fi=du*   *nar-tar.*
        high-AVLZ=FOC   become-PST
        'became high' [PC adverb: as a VP complement]

See §3.4.1 for the syntactic characteristic of the verb 'become', which may

256 Chapter 8

be either an extended intransitive verb (when it takes an E argument NP),
or an intransitive verb (when it takes a VP complement).

Since *aparagi* is a PC stem, it may alternatively be a PC adverb form
(satisfying (C)) and function as a VP complement of the verb 'become'
rather than an E argument NP, as shown in (8–6).

(8–6) *aparagi-fï=du*   *nar-tar.*
       beautiful-AVLZ=FOC   become-PST
       'became beautiful.' [PC adverb: as a VP complement; cf. (8–3b)]

This multifunctional feature of less prototypical PC stems distinguishes
them from prototypical nominal stems, which cannot function as an input
stem of a PC adverb.

8.1.2.3. Less prototypical nominal stems: (k–m)

The stems belonging to this part are nominal stems rather than PC stems.
They can satisfy one or more of (A) to (C), but do not consistently satisfy
all of them. When these nominals occur in the structures of (A), (B), and
(C), they take on the meaning of property concepts:

(8–7) *avva* 'oil'   (A) *avvaa+avva* [avva:(·)avva]
                               '(very) oily'
                           (B) *avvaa=ti=nu*   *mssï*
                               oil=QT=GEN   miso.soup
                               'miso soup like "(how) oily!"'
                           (C) *avva-ka-tar* 'was oily'
                               ?*avva-sa* 'oiliness'
                               avva-fï 'oily:ADV'

(8–8) *jarabi* 'child'   (A) *jarabii+jarabi* [jaɾabi:(·)jaɾabi]
                               '(very) childish'
                           (B) *jarabii=ti=nu*   *pžtu*
                               child=QT=GEN   man
                               'a person who is like, "(how) childish!"'
                           (C) *jarabi-ka-tar* 'was childish'
                               *jarabi-sa
                               *jarabi-fï

(8–9) *gudun* 'dull person' (A) ?*gudunn+gudun*
                              (B) *gudunn=ti=nu*   *pžtu*
                                  dull=QT=GEN   person
                                  'a person who is like, "(how) dull!"'

Property concepts, adjectives, and other derivational processes   257

(C) *gudun-ka-tar* 'was dull'
    *gudun-sa
    *gudun-fi

Other nominal stems that behave similarly include *maifïga* 'wise child', *waacïna* 'selfish person', *katapa* 'handicapped person', and many others which belong to HUMAN PROPENSITY meaning. They are free forms, as in the case of nouns. However, they are not homogenous with regard to whether they can be used as arguments. Some are used both as arguments and predicate nominals, whereas others only opt for the latter.

For example, the stem *maifïga* cannot function as an argument unless it occurs as the modifying stem of a compound nominal, as in (8–10).

(8–10)   *maifïga+jarabi=a*   *nza=nkai*   *ik-a-ba=mai*
        wise+child=TOP   where=ALL   go-THM-CND=even
        žž-ai-n-Ø.
        scold-PASS-NEG-NPST
        'A wise person is never scolded wherever (s/he) goes.'

By contrast, the noun stem *katapa* 'handicapped person' may be used as an argument by itself, as in *katapa=nu=du ur* 'There is a handicapped (person)'.

8.1.3. Non-class-changing derivation by *-gi* 'seem; appear'

A PC stem, either prototypical or less prototypical, may be transformed into another PC stem by adding the suffix *-gi* 'seem; appear, -ish, somewhat'. A stem thus derived satisfies (A) to (C) in §8.1.2 above, and is uncontroversially a PC stem.

(8–11)   *taka-* 'tall' > *taka-gi* 'seem to be high'
        baka- 'young' > *baka-gi* 'seem to be young'
        bar- 'bad' > *bar-gi* 'seem to be bad'
        cuu- 'strong' > *cuu-gi* 'seem to be strong'
        pukarasï- 'happy' > *pukarasï-gi* 'seem to be happy'
        niv- 'slow' > *niv-gi* 'seem to be slow'
        au 'blue' > *au-gi* 'bluish'
        aparagi 'beautiful (person)' > *aparagi-gi* 'seem to be beautiful'
        ujaki 'rich (person)' > *ujaki-gi* 'seem to be rich'
        buuciri 'mighty (person)' > *buuciri-gi* 'seem to be mighty'

258   Chapter 8

(A) REDUPLICATION

taka-gii+taka-gi [takagi:(·)takagi] 'seem to be (very) high'
baka-gii+baka-gi [bakagi:(·)bakagi] 'seem to be (very) young'
bar-gii+bar-gi [baɭgi:(·)baɭgi] 'seem to be (very) bad'
cuu-gii+cuu-gi [tsu:gi:(·)tsu:gi] 'seem to be (very) strong'
pukarasï-gii+pukarasï-gi [pukaɾasɨgi:(·)pukaɾasɨgi] 'seem to be (very) happy'
niv-gii+niv-gi [niʋgi:(·)niʋgi] 'seem to be (very) slow'
au-gii+au-gi [augi:(·)augi] '(very) bluish'
aparagi-gii+aparagi-gi [apaɾagigi:(·)apaɾagigi] 'seem to be (very) beautiful'
ujaki-gii+ujaki-gi [ujakigi:(·)ujakigi] 'seem to be (very) rich'
buuciri-gii+buuciri-gi [bu:tʃiɾigi:(·)bu:tʃiɾigi] 'seem to be (very) mighty'

(B) DIRECT QUOTATION

taka-gii=ti=nu   *pžtu*
tall-seem=QT=GEN   man
'a man who seems like, "(how) tall!"'

baka-gii=ti=nu   *pžtu*
young-seem=QT=GEN   man
'a man who seems like, "(how) young!"'

bar-gii=ti=nu   *pžtu*
bad-seem=QT=GEN   man
'a man who seems like, "(how) bad!"'

cuu-gii=ti=nu   *pžtu*
strong-seem=QT=GEN   man
'a man who seems like, "(how) strong!"'

pukarasï-gii=ti=nu   *cïmucï*
happy-seem=QT=GEN   feeling
'a feeling that seems like, "(how) happy!"'

niv-gii=ti=nu   *pžtu*
slow-seem=QT=GEN   man
'a man who seems like, "(how) slow!"'

au-gii=ti=nu   *suu*
blue-seem=QT=GEN   vegetable
'a vegetable that seems like, "(how) bluish (green)!"'[2]

aparagi-gii=ti=nu   *pžtu*
beautiful-seem=QT=GEN man

---

[2] In Irabu, the semantic range of *au* includes 'green' as well as 'blue'.

Property concepts, adjectives, and other derivational processes   259

'a person who seems like, "(how) beautiful!"'

(C) SPECIAL DERIVATIONAL AFFIXES

taka-gi-ka-ta-m (high-seem-VLZ-PST-RLS) 'seemed high'

taka-gi-sa (high-seem-NLZ) 'a situation in which something seems high'

taka-gi-fï (high-seem-AVLZ) 'seem to be high:ADV'

baka-gi-ka-ta-m (young-seem-VLZ-PST-RLS) 'seemed to be young'

baka-gi-sa (young-seem-NLZ) 'a situation in which something seems young'

baka-gi-fï (young-seem-AVLZ) 'seem to be young:ADV'

bar-ka-ta-m (bad-seem-VLZ-PST-RLS) 'seemed bad'

bar-gi-sa (bad-seem-NLZ) 'a situation in which something seems bad'

bar-gi-fï (bad-seem-AVLZ) 'seem to be bad: ADV'

cuu-gi-ka-ta-m (strong-seem-VLZ-PST-RLS) 'seemed strong'

cuu-gi-sa (strong-seem-NLZ) 'a situation in which something seems strong'

cuu-gi-fï (strong-seem-AVLZ) 'seem to be strong:ADV'

pukarasï-gi-ka-ta-m (happy-seem-VLZ-PST-RLS) 'seemed happy'

pukarasï-gi-sa (happy-seem-NLZ) 'a situation in which something seems happy'

pukarasï-gi-fï (happy-seem-AVLZ) 'seem to be happy:ADV'

niv-gi-ka-ta-m (slow-seem-VLZ-PST-RLS) 'seemed slow'

niv-gi-sa (slow-seem-NLZ) 'a situation in which something seems slow'

niv-gi-fï (slow-seem-AVLZ) 'seem slow:ADV'

au-gi-ka-ta-m (blue-seem-VLZ-PST-RLS) 'seemed blueish'

?au-gi-sa (blue-seem-NLZ) 'a situation in which something seems blueish'

au-gi-fï 'seem blueish: ADV'

aparagi-gi-ka-ta-m (beautiful-seem-VLZ-PST-RLS) 'seemed beautiful'

?aparagi-gi-sa (beautiful-seem-NLZ) 'a situation in which someone seems beautiful'

aparagi-gi-fï (beautiful-seem-AVLZ) 'seem beautiful:ADV'

ujaki-gi-ka-ta-m (rich-seem-VLZ-PST-RLS) 'seemed rich'

?ujaki-gi-sa (rich-seem-NLZ) 'a situation in which someone seems rich'

ujaki-gi-fï (rich-seem-AVLZ) 'seem to be rich:ADV'

260   Chapter 8

buuciri-gi-ka-ta-m (mighty-seem-VLZ-PST-RLS) 'seemed rich'
?buuciri-gi-sa (mighty-seem-NLZ) 'a situation in which someone
seems mighty'
buuciri-gi-fi (mighty-seem-AVLZ) 'seem to be mighty:ADV'

8.2. The adjective class

8.2.1. Overview

This section outlines the morphological, semantic, and syntactic characteristics of adjectives.

8.2.1.1. Morphology
An adjective is a grammatical word created by reduplicating a PC stem,
lengthening the final segment of the first reduplicate.[3]

(8–12)   PC stem   >   Adjective
         taka- 'high'   *takaa+taka* 'high'
         kuu- 'hard'   *kuuu+kuu* 'hard'
         kiban 'poor'   *kibann+kiban* 'poor'

In addition, less prototypical nominal stems (§8.1.2.3) may be transformed
into an adjective word.

(8–13)   Nominal stem   >   Adjective
         avva 'oil'   *avvaa+avva* 'oily'
         jarabi 'child'   *jarabii+jarabi* 'childish'
         gudun 'dull (person)   *gudunn+gudun* 'dull'

It is easy to identify the adjective class morphologically. Even though
the reduplication strategy itself is also seen in verb stem reduplication (8–
14), which encodes iterative or habitual aspect (§10.5.2.6), a reduplicated
verbal form does not involve the lengthening of the final segment of the
reduplicate. Syntactically, a reduplicated verb stem fills the complement
slot of the light verb *(a)si* 'do', and is classified as a derived adverb
(§3.3.6.2).

(8–14)   *mii+mii*   *as-i+ur-Ø.*

---

[3] Unlike some of the Miyako varieties (such as the Nakachi dialect of Irabu and Hirara)
where laryngealisation is regularly heard in the duplicate, the reduplication in Irabu (Nagahama) does not involve laryngealisation.

Property concepts, adjectives, and other derivational processes 261

RED+look   do-THM+PROG-NPST
'(He) is staring.'

Thus the reduplicated form of PC stem and the reduplicated form of verb stem are unambiguously distinguished.

Another morphological characteristic of adjectives is that they do not inflect, nor do they carry derivational affixes with just a small number of exceptions. The diminutive suffix -*gama* may follow certain adjectives (e.g. *imii*+*imi-gama* 'small', *maruu*+*maru-gama* 'short', *ssuu*+*ssu-gama* 'a bit white'), belonging to the semantic categories of Dimension and Colour.

8.2.1.2. Semantics

As noted in §8.1.2, the reduplication strategy can itself encode intensity, but it is dependent on the degree of the phonetic lengthening, and its inherent connection to intensity is questionable. For example, an adjective may be modified by an intensifier such as *ati* 'very' without resulting in semantic redundancy.

(8–15)   *ati*   *takaa*+*taka=nu*   *pžtu=i.*
          very   RED+high=GEN   man=CNF
          '(He) is a very tall man, eh?'

Another fact that supports the analysis that reduplication is not necessarily connected to intensity is that, as noted in §8.2.1.1, certain adjectives may carry the diminutive suffix -*gama*, which designates a modest degree (§5.3.1), a concept contradictive to intensity.

In the example sentences I explicitly gloss an intensity meaning where it is evident from context, but otherwise do not gloss it.

8.2.1.3. Syntax

The adjective class does not have its own distinctive syntactic behaviour or its own phrase structure.[4] Rather, an adjective is 'parasitic' on both NP and VP structures, i.e. with a flexible ability to occur in either structure, though with a number of restrictions to be described in the following two sections. Thus there are a number of differences between an NP headed by an adjective and an NP headed by a nominal in terms of, for example, its argument

---

[4] By contrast, a Japanese 'uninflected adjective' (Backhouse 2004), or an attributive adjective, heads an adjective phrase with its phrasal extension =*na* (an adnominal inflection of the copula) as opposed to genitive =*no* as found in an NP in this language: *kirei=na hito* 'beautiful person' vs *okinawa=no hito* 'a person from Okinawa.'

262 Chapter 8

TABLE 8–4. Adjective in phrase structure

	As head of an NP (sorted by function)			In VP structure (sorted by slot)		
	Argument	Predicate head	NP modifier	A complex lex verb	VP aux	A minimal VP lex verb
Nominal	+	+	+	-	-	-
Adjective	(+)	+	+	+	-	-
Verb	-	-	-	+	+	+

function (the former usually functions as a modifier of a superordinate NP, whereas the latter has no such tendency). Crucially, the argument function of an NP headed by an adjective is highly limited and in certain respects questionable (see §8.2.2.1). When appearing in a VP, an adjective only fills the lexical verb slot of a complex VP, and never fills the auxiliary slot or the only available slot of a minimal VP.

As is clear from the table, it is easy to identify an adjective as opposed to a noun or a verb syntactically, since a noun *only* appears in an NP, and a verb *only* appears in a VP.

In addition to being able to appear in an NP and in a VP, an adjective may directly modify a predicate like an adverb. Adverbial modification is a common syntactic characteristic of adjectives in many languages (Dixon 2004: 11).

(8–16) *bždaa+bžda*   *pur-i.*
RED+low   dig-IMP
'Dig (to make the hole) deep.' [adverbial modification]

(8–17) *uku+daka=nu*   *takaa+taka*   *ma-i+ur-Ø.*
big+hawk=NOM   RED+high   fly-THM+PROG-NPST
'A big hawk is flying (very) high.' [adverbial modification]

In what follows I describe the adjective class in terms of phrase structure, first noting its characteristics in NPs, then in VPs.

8.2.2. Adjectives in NP structure

An adjective may head an NP. The NP may function as an E argument (see §3.5.3 for the notion of E argument) of the verb 'become' (8–18) on the analysis adopted here.

(8–18) *takaa+taka=n=du*   *nar-tar.*
RED+high=DAT=FOC   become-PST

Property concepts, adjectives, and other derivational processes   263

    '(He) became tall.' [E argument of the verb 'become']
  cf. *sinsii=n=du*   *nar-tar.*
       teacher=DAT=FOC   become-PST
       '(He) became a teacher.'

One might argue here that the E argument of the verb 'become' is not really an argument in the first place. The argument status is justified only by the fact that the NP carries dative case. Cross-linguistically, the theme NP that is governed by a verb designating 'become' is often analysed as a VP complement. For example, in describing English, Huddleston (1984) suggests that the complement of *become* as in *she became president* is part of a predicate, or a predicate complement. Huddleston points out that the predicate complement shows a number of peculiarities absent from, say, a direct object NP in transitive clauses such as *He shot the president*. The complement of *become* allows omission of the article and, unlike a direct object, cannot be passivised. Thus, even though I continue to regard the dative-marked NP as an E argument, there is an alternative descriptive solution whereby the NP is treated as a special type of VP complement (in such a case the problem would be that the complement exceptionally carries a case).

An NP headed by an adjective may also function as a predicate nominal (8–19) or the modifier of a superordinate NP (8–20). Since it heads the NP, the adjective carries case unless the NP functions as a predicate.

(8–19)   *uri=a*   *takaa+taka=du*   *a-tar.*
         3SG=TOP   RED+high=FOC   COP-PST
         'He was tall.' [head of a nominal predicate phrase]
         cf. *uri=a*   *sinsii=du*   *a-tar.*
            3SG=TOP   teacher=FOC   COP-PST
            'He was a teacher.'
(8–20)   *takaa+taka=nu*   *pžtu*
         RED+high=GEN   man
         'tall man' [modifier of a superordinate NP]
         cf. *irav=nu*   *pžtu*
            Irabu=GEN   man
            'A man from Irabu'

An NP headed by an adjective is different from an NP headed by a noun in three important respects: (1) its highly restricted ability to serve as an argument (i.e. its sole ability to serve as an E argument of the verb 'be-

264   Chapter 8

come'), (2) its skewed preference for the NP modifier function, and (3) its
ability to be modified by an adverb (like a verb) as well as by an adnominal
(like a nominal). We will see in §8.3.4 that (3) is shared by a compound
nominal derived from a PC stem, but an NP headed by an adjective is more
likely to be modified by an adverb than by an adnominal, whereas an NP
headed by a compound nominal derived from a PC stem shows no such
preference.

8.2.2.1. Highly restricted argument function
The argument function of an NP headed by an adjective is restricted to the
E argument of the verb 'become', carrying dative case.

(8–21)   *imii+imi=n=du*   *nar-tar.*
         RED+small=DAT=FOC   become-PST
         '(It) became small.' [Argument NP: complement of 'become'
         verb]
(8–22)   *umacï=sii*   *as-i+u-tigaa,*
         fire=INST   do-THM+PROG-CND
         ffuu+ffu=n=du   *nar-Ø.*
         RED+black=DAT=FOC   become-NPST
         'Burning with fire, (the paper) becomes black.'

Otherwise, an NP headed by an adjective cannot function as subject, direct
object, or any peripheral argument.

8.2.2.2. Skewed functional preference for the modifier NP function
The typical function of an NP headed by an adjective is to serve as modifier of a superordinate NP, attributively modifying the head noun, a function
which serves as a cross-linguistically recurrent, or probably the primary
criterion for identifying an adjective class (Schachter 1985; Hengeveld
1992; Bhat 1994; Wetzer 1996; Croft 2002, 2003; Dixon 2004).

(8–23)   *imii+imi=nu*   *mii-gama=nu*   *nar-Ø=dara.*
         RED+small=GEN   fruit-DIM=NOM   grow-NPST=CRTN
         'A small fruit grows.'
(8–24)   *nagaa+naga=nu*   *bau=ju*   *tur-as-i.*
         RED+long=GEN   stick=ACC   take-CAUS-IMP
         'Pass (me) a long stick.'

An NP headed by an adjective may also function as head of a nominal

Property concepts, adjectives, and other derivational processes   265

predicate phrase, but this function is much less common than the modifier function.

(8–25) *kanu*   *midum=ma*   *aparagii+aparagi=du*   *a-tar.*
        that   woman=TOP   RED+beautiful=FOC   COP-PST
        'That woman was very beautiful.' [predicate NP]

(8–26) *kuma=a,*   *mmja,*   *sïdasïï+sïdasï=dara=i?*
        this.place=TOP   INTJ   RED+cool=CRTN=CNF
        'It is very cool here, eh?' [predicate NP]

8.2.2.3. Modificational constraint

An NP headed by an adjective may be modified by an adverb, a characteristic not found in an NP headed by a nominal other than a compound nominal derived from a PC stem (§8.3.4). Whereas an NP headed by a compound nominal derived from a PC stem (8–27) may freely be modified by either an adnominal or an adverb, an NP headed by an adjective (8–28) is better modified by an adverb than by an adnominal, according to my consultants. Some consultants even reported that adnominal modification is 'incorrect'.

(8–27) a. *kuri=a*   *ati*   *kupa+munu=n=du*
           3SG=TOP   very   hard+thing=DAT=FOC
           nar-i+ur-Ø.
           become-THM+PROG-NPST
           'This has become a very hard thing.' [modified by the adverb
           ati 'very']

        b. *kuri=a*   *daizïna*   *kupa+munu=n=du*
           3SG=TOP   great   hard+thing=DAT=FOC
           nar-i+ur-Ø.
           become-THM+PROG-NPST
           'This has become a very hard thing.' [modified by the adnominal *daizïna* 'great']

(8–28) a. *kuri=a*   *ati*   *kupaa+kupa=n=du*
           3SG=TOP   very   RED+hard=DAT=FOC
           nar-i+ur-Ø.
           become-THM+PROG-NPST
           'This has become very stiff.'

        ?b. *kuri=a*   *daizïna*   *kupaa+kupa=n=du*
            3SG=TOP   great   RED+hard=DAT=FOC
            nar-i+ur-Ø.

266   Chapter 8

                        become-THM+PROG-NPST

8.2.3. Adjectives in VP structure

An adjective may appear in a VP, though this is much less common than
the use of an adjective to head an NP. For example, in my text count, of all
the tokens of adjectives (N = 328), the adjectives that appear in VP structure account for 8, whereas the adjectives that appear in NP structure account for 304, with the remaining 24 tokens accounting for other limited
syntactic functions such as adverbial function (see §8.1.2.3; see also Shimoji 2009 for a more detail). This usage-based fact tells us that the adjective class in Irabu is highly nominal in nature, showing a clear preference
to occur in NP structure.

When an adjective appears in a VP, there are two severe restrictions that
do not hold when a verb appears in a VP. First, an adjective only fills the
lexical verb slot of a complex VP (§3.1.1.1; §7.1.2). Second, the auxiliary
must be the progressive auxiliary (§7.1.4.1; §10.5.2.1).

(8–29) *hira,*   *kama=a*   *imii+imi=du*   *ur-Ø=ri.*
        INTJ   that.place=TOP   red+small=FOC   PROG-NPST=CNF
        'You see, that place is small, eh?'

(8–30) *cïnuu=ja*   *cïcï=nu*   *akaa+aka=du*
        yesterday=TOP   moon=NOM   RED+bright=FOC
        u-tar.
        PROG-PST
        'Yesterday, the moon was bright.'

(8–31) *kantja=a*   *jarabii+jarabi=du*   *ur-Ø=dara.*
        3PL=TOP   RED+child=FOC   PROG-NPST=CRTN
        'They are ? being childish, you see.' [lit. they are childish-ing,
        you see.]

There are a number of arguments for the analysis that the verb *ur* (or *utar*)
after an adjective cannot be regarded as the existential verb *ur* '(animate
subject) exists'. The existential verb *ur* only co-occurs with an animate
subject (e.g. *pžtu=nu=du ur* 'there is a <u>man</u>', *waa=nu=du ur* 'there is a
<u>pig</u>', but **jama=nu=du ur* 'there is a <u>mountain</u>'), whereas the auxiliary
verb *ur* has no such restriction. Examples (8–29) and (8–30) then clearly
show that *ur* is an auxiliary, and therefore we can say that the adjective fills
the main verb slot of a VP.

Another major argument for the analysis that the verb *ur* (or *utar*) after
an adjective cannot be regarded as the existential verb *ur* '(animate subject)

Property concepts, adjectives, and other derivational processes   267

exists' is that, as mentioned in §7.1.4.3, a past-tense progressive auxiliary (i.e. *utar*) may undergo ellipsis. This is also true in the construction of adjective + *utar*, as in (8–30), where the auxiliary may undergo ellipsis.

8.2.4. Adjectives derived from nominal stems

As noted in §8.2.1.1, an adjective may be derived from a certain set of nominal stems, wit the property concept meaning related to the input nominal stem (e.g. *jarabi* 'child' > *jarabii+jarabi* 'childish'). Even if the input stem of reduplication is a nominal stem, the output adjective word behaves exactly in the same way as other adjectives in terms of morphology (the lengthening of the final phoneme of the input stem) and syntax.

(8–32)   *jarabii+jarabi=n=du*   *nar-tar.*
         RED+child=DAT=FOC   become-PST
         '(He) became childish.'

(8–33)   *ati=du*   *jarabii+jarabi=nu*   *pžtu.*
         very=FOC   RED+child=GEN   man
         'very childish man' [dependent of an NP; modified by an adverb]

(8–34)   *jarabii+jarabi=du*   *a-tar.*
         RED+child=FOC   COP-PST
         '(He) was very childish.' [predicate]

(8–35)   *jarabii+jarabi*   *nafi-na.*
         RED+child   cry-PRH
         'Don't cry childishly.' [modifying like an adverb]

(8–36)   *jarabii+jarabi=du*   *ur-Ø.*
         RED+child=FOC   PROG-NPST
         '(He) is childish.' [VP lexical verb]

8.2.5. Summary

To sum up, adjectives constitute a distinct word class, distinguished from both nominals and verbs in terms of morphology and of syntax. Even though an adjective may head an NP, the NP headed by an adjective differs from the NP headed by a nominal in crucial ways: its argument function is very restricted, and it allows adverbial modification (a characteristic shared by a compound nominal derived from a PC stem). An adjective cannot serve as a minimal VP, even though it may serve like a lexical verb within a complex VP structure, with a severe restriction on the auxiliary that cooccurs.

8.3. Deriving nominals, verbs, and adverbs

In this section I describe how nominal, verbal, and adverbial stems are derived from PC stems. There are four derived forms: (1) state nominals, (2) compound nominals derived from a PC stem, (3) PC verbs, i.e. derived verbs whose primary stem is derived from a PC stem, and (4) PC adverbs, i.e. derived adverbs whose primary stem is derived from a PC stem. Except for type (1), where the derivations are typical nominal stems, derived stems of these classes which involve PC stems exhibit certain peculiarities in comparison to underived nominal, verb, and adverb stems. Thus it is necessary to recognise (2), (3), and (4) as subclasses of nominals, verbs, and adverbs respectively.

Assuming a morphosyntactic continuum from the verb class at one extreme to the nominal class at the other (following Wetzer 1996), the adjective class occurs in the middle, and we can situate the remaining subclasses of verb and nominal as shown in the figure below, where the double slashes segment each word class (the PC adverb does not find a place on the continuum, so is excluded here).

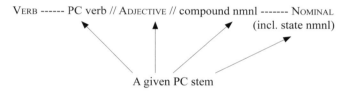

FIGURE 8–1. Wetzer's (1996) Noun-Verb continuum and its manifestation in Irabu

In what follows, I begin with the least controversial case, i.e. state nominalisation. Then I describe two subtler and inter-related cases, PC adverb derivation and PC verb derivation. Then I proceed to describe the most complicated case, the derivation of compound nominals.

8.3.1. State nominal derivation with -sa

The nominaliser -sa creates a stem that functions as head of an NP, and expresses a state nominalisation (Comrie and Thompson 1985), roughly translated as '-ness' or '-ity' in English. This NP has the full range of NP functions: an argument NP, a predicate NP, or a modifier of a superordinate NP. It does not allow adverbial modification, carrying an adnominal instead. Thus state nominalisation creates a (prototypical) nominal stem.

(8–37)   kai=ga   budur=nu   kagi-sa=nu=du

Property concepts, adjectives, and other derivational processes 269

> 3SG=GEN dance=GEN beautiful-NLZ=NOM=FOC
> *icïban.*
> No.1
> "Her dance is the most beautiful' [lit. 'The beauty of her dance is the best.'] [head of argument NP]

(8–38) *kantja=a*   *uccja=nu*   *cuu-sa=du*   *a-tar.*
3PL=TOP   that.much=GEN   strong-NLZ=FOC   COP-PST
'They were (with) that strength (i.e. they were strong that much).' [Head of predicate NP]

(8–39) *vva=ga*   *umukutu-sa=nu*   *ukagi=dara.*
2SG=GEN   wise-NLZ=GEN   advantage=CRTN
'(That's) your wisdom's advantage (i.e. I'm indebted to your wisdom).' [head of NP dependent]

Although it is not necessary to distinguish between an underived nominal and a state nominal in terms of major syntactic criteria, a state nominal has certain minor peculiarities. For example, when *-sa* attaches to *tuu-* 'far', it may express either the expected meaning of great distance or what would be more properly translated simply as 'far':

(8–40) *jaa=ja*   *tuu-sa=ru?*
house=TOP   far-NLZ=FOC
'Is your house far?' [lit. Is your house farness?]

Thus *tuu-sa* may behave semantically more like the English adjective 'far' than a state nominal. Interestingly, the adjective form *tuuu+tuu* is not preferred among native speakers (though they understand what it means), and this lexical gap must be related to the semantic peculiarity of *tuu-sa*. In terms of morphosyntax *tuu-sa* here is unambiguously a nominal word, since it only heads an NP. Also, as a nominal, it does not tolerate adverbial modification. Thus in the following examples, the state nominal *tuusa* can be modified by an adnominal (8–41a), but cannot be modified by an adverb (8–41b).

(8–41) a. *jaa=ja*   *daizïna*   *tuu-sa*
house=TOP   great   far-NLZ
ar-a-n-Ø=nu?
COP-THM-NEG-NPST=FOC
'Isn't your house that far?' [lit. 'isn't your house that farness?']

270   Chapter 8

*b. *jaa=ja*   *ati*   *tuu-sa*
   house=TOP   very   far-NLZ
   ar-a-n-Ø=nu?
   COP-THM-NEG-NPST=FOC

8.3.2. PC adverb with *-fï*

A PC adverb is derived from a PC stem by the adverbialiser *-fï*. The productive derivation of adverbs from PC stems compensates for the scarcity
of underived adverbs in the Irabu lexicon (§3.3.6.1). As shown in (8–42)
below, a PC adverb modifies a predicate verb as in the case of other adverbs, but this is not as common as the function noted in the following
paragraph.

(8–42)   *unu*   *tur=ra*   *taka-fï=du*   *tuv-tar.*
         that   bird=TOP   high-AVLZ=FOC   fly-PST
         'That bird flew high.'

Unlike underived adverbs (§3.3.6.1), a PC adverb more frequently
serves as a VP complement, either of the state verb *a(r)*, as in (8–43), or of
the verb 'become', as in (8–44) (see also §8.2.2.1, where this latter verb
may take an E argument rather than a VP complement). Note that in (8–
43), the state verb *ar* is not a copula, as its negative form is suppletive
njaan rather than morphological *ar-a-n* (§6.3.6.3).

(8–43)   a. *unu*   *jama=a*   *taka-fï=du*   *ar-Ø.*
            that   mountain=TOP   high-AVLZ=FOC   be-NPST
            'That mountain is high' [lit. That mountain exists in a high
            state]
         b. *unu*   *jama=a*   *taka-f=fa*
            that   mountain=TOP   high-AVLZ=TOP
            njaa-n-Ø.
            not.be-NEG-NPST
            'That mountain is not high' [*ar* is suppletively negated]
(8–44)   *nam=nu*   *taka-fï=du*   *nar-tar.*
         wave=NOM   high-AVLZ=FOC   become-PST
         'The wave became high.'

8.3.3. PC verb with *-ka(r)*

A PC verb consists of a verb stem derived from a PC stem by the verbaliser
suffix *-ka(r)* and an inflectional affix identical to one for other verbs. Thus

Property concepts, adjectives, and other derivational processes 271

it is uncontroversial to analyse the word form as a verb (see §3.3.3 for the definition of the verb). Even though a verb derived from a PC stem is a subclass of verb in terms of the definition of the verb class (i.e. inflection), it still exhibits a number of morphosyntactic differences that require us to distinguish between a PC verb and other verbs.

8.3.3.1. Diachronic account of -ka(r)

It is well known among Ryukyuan linguists (cf. Motonaga 1978; Nakama 1992; Uemura 1997) that the verbaliser -ka(r) developed from an analytic expression, specifically from *-ku (adverbialiser) and *ari (existential verb).[5] PC stems then acquired various affixation strategies, one of the earliest of which was an adverbialisation strategy (*-ku suffixation, regularly reflected by -fi suffixation in Irabu: *ku > /fi/). One important structure in which PC adverbs appeared was the state verb construction, as in (8–45a), which later fused to give rise to a single verb (8–45b), reflected as the -ka(r) verbaliser in Irabu.

(8–45) Old Japanese (diachronic development)
a. *taka-ku   ari-Ø.   >>>>>>   b. taka-kari-Ø
   high-AVLZ   exist-NPST   high-kari-NPST
   'is high'   'is high'

(8–46) Irabu (synchronic system)
a. taka-fi=du   ar-Ø.   b. taka-kar-Ø.
   high-AVLZ=FOC   exist-NPST   high-VLZ-NPST
   'is high'   'is high'

That is, the -ka(r) verbaliser developed from a situation, where an adverb and a verb were conjoined.

In Irabu, both the analytic structure (8–46a) and the fused structure (8–46b) co-exist in contemporary grammar. The analytic structure consists of a PC adverb and the state verb ar, where the PC adverb is the complement of the verb (state verb construction). The alternation between the two structures is motivated by focus and topic marking. Thus, as is illustrated in (8–46) above, if a PC stem is to be focused (or topicalised), it is adverbialised and the analytic (a) structure rather than originally fused (b) is selected. If a PC stem is not to be focused (or topicalised), the stem occurs within a sin-

---

[5] The proto-Japonic language originally lacked an adjective word class (which is not the case in Modern Japanese where there are two classes of adjectives, i.e. nominal or uninflected adjectives and verbal or inflected adjectives; Backhouse 2004), and PC stems were bare stem forms (Kasuga 1973, Yamazaki 1973, Nakama 1992).

272   Chapter 8

gle verb word, as in (b). This resembles word-phrase alternation (§6.4.2.3):

(8–47)   a. *tigami=u*   *kak-i-i=du*   *ur-Ø.*
            letter=ACC   write-THM-NRT=FOC   PROG-NPST
            '(I) am writing a letter.' [complex VP: a phrasal AVC]
        b. *tigami=u=du*   *kak-i+ur-Ø.*
            letter=ACC=FOC   write-THM+PROG-NPST
            '(I) am writing a letter.' [a verb word: an agglutinative AVC]

The diachronic relationship between (8–46a) and (8–46b) is that (8–46b) developed from an agglutinative stem sequence within a word (8–45b) whose source structure is a state verb construction (8–45a), reflected as (8–46a), in the same way that an agglutinative AVC (§6.4.2.3) developed from a phrasal AVC (§7.1.4). In both types of diachronically related structures, then, focus and topic marking reveals the historically older structure.

	Analytic (older structure)		Fused (new structure)
Grammaticalisation path		>>>>	
Word-phrase alternation	V1=FOC#V2		V1+V2
	V1=TOP#V2		V1+V2
The StVC-PC verb alternation	PC-*fi*=FOC#*a(r)*		PC stem-*ka(r)*
	PC-*fi*=TOP#*a(r)*		PC stem-*ka(r)*

8.3.3.2. The PC verb as a subclass of verb

As shown in TABLE 8–5 below, there are a number of morphosyntactic features shared between PC verbs and other verbs, including the definitional criterion, i.e. inflection. However, as the three rows on the right side indicate, there are two major and one minor differences between PC verbs and other verbs, which necessitate a distinction between them within the verb class. Each criterion is noted in order below.

TABLE 8–5. Verbs and PC verbs: distinctive criteria

	Inflection	Conjunction Clitics	NP modification	Complex VP	Negation	Verbal focus
Typical verbs	+	+	adnominal clause	+	suffixal	LVC
PC verbs	+	+	adnominal clause	(+)	suffixal or analytic	STVC

Note: LVC (Light Verb Construction); STVC (State verb construction)

Property concepts, adjectives, and other derivational processes 273

■ INFLECTION

A verb stem which is derived from a PC stem with *-ka(r)* carries a verb inflectional affix (with the morphophonemic pattern identical to the state verb *a(r)*). In the table below, I list two underived verb stems, i.e. the verb stem *tur-* 'take' (Class 2) and the state verb stem *a(r)-* for comparison. The symbol '?' indicates that the inflection in question is semantically impossible. As is clear from the table, there is a single set of inflectional affixes that applies to *tur-*, *a(r)-*, and *taka-ka(r)-*, with some morphophonemic adjustment on the part of the stem (which is identical in *a(r)-* and *taka-ka(r)-*). Thus, unlike Japanese, where an adjective and a verb have different sets of inflectional affixes (e.g. non-past inflection *-i* vs. *-(r)u*; Backhouse 1984), there is no ground on which to distinguish between a verb and a PC verb in terms of inflectional morphology.

TABLE 8–6. PC verb in terms of inflection (cf. §6.3.1, 6.3.2)

	tur- 'take'	Existential	*taka-ka(r)*
thematic *-a*	*tur-a*	*ar-a*	*taka-kar-a*
thematic *-i*	*tur-i*	*ar-i*	*taka-kar-i*
athematic	*tur*	*a(r)*	*taka-ka(r)*
finite past realis	*tur-ta-m*	*a-ta-m*	*taka-ka-ta-m*
finite past unmarked	*tur-tar*	*a-tar*	*taka-ka-tar*
finite non-past realis	*tur-Ø-m*	*a(r)-m*	*taka-ka(r)-m*
finite non-past unmarked	*tur-Ø*	*ar-Ø*	*taka-kar-Ø*
finite irrealis intentional	*tur-a-di*	*ar-a-di*	*taka-kar-a-di*
finite irrealis optative	*tur-a-baa*	*ar-a-baa*	*taka-kar-a-baa*
finite irrealis imperative	*tur-i*	*?ar-i*	*?taka-kar-i*
causal	*tu(r)-i-ba*	*a(r)-i-ba*	*taka-ka(r)-i-ba*
conditional 1	*tur-a-ba*	*ar-a-ba*	*taka-kar-a-ba*
conditional 2	*tur-tigaa*	*a-tigaa*	*taka-ka-tigaa*
negative conditional	*tur-a-dakaa*	*ar-a-dakaa*	*taka-kar-a-dakaa*
aversive (+ =*tii*)	*tur-a-zïm*	*ar-a-zïm*	*taka-kar-a-zïm*
negative intentional conditional converb	*tur-a-djaadakaa*	*ar-a-djaadakaa*	*taka-kar-a-djaadakaa*
simultaneous	*tur-ccjaaki*	*?ar-ccjaaki*	*?taka-kar-ccjaaki*
purposive	*tur-ga*	*?ar-ga*	*?taka-kar-ga*
continuous	*tur-gakaazï*	*ar-gakaazï*	*taka-kar-gakaazï*

274   Chapter 8

immediate anterior	*tur-tuu*	*?ar-tuu*	*?taka-kar-tuu*
medial	*tur-i-i*	*ar-i-i*	*taka-kar-i-i*
negative medial	*tur-a-da*	*ar-a-da*	*taka-kar-a-da*

■ CONJUNCTION MARKERS

There are a number of morphosyntactic features in which an ordinary verb
and a PC verb behave in the same way, all of which can be explained by
the fact that the verbaliser *-ka(r)* etymologically contains the state verb *ar*
(§8.3.3.1). One such feature is the conjunction marker attachment. A conjunction marker (§9.2) is a clitic that is attached only to a verb. When a
nominal predicate phrase is to be marked by this clitic, the copula verb is
obligatory as the phonological host of the clitic.

(8–48)   *uri=u=baa*   *cïfi-tar=ruga,*   *mmja,*   *bassi-i*
         3SG=ACC=TOP   hear-PST=but   INTJ   forget-NRT
         njaa-n.
         PRF-NPST
         '(I) heard about that, but, well, (I) have forgot.' [verb + *=suga*
         'but']

(8–49)   a. *kari=a*   *midum*   *jar-Ø=ruga,*   *taka+pžtu=dooi.*
            3SG=TOP   woman   COP-NPST=but   high+man=EMP
            'She is a woman, but (she) is a tall woman.'
         *b. *kari=a*   *midum=suga,*   *taka+pžtu=dooi.*
            3SG=TOP   woman=but   high+man=EMP

A PC verb behaves exactly like a verb in this regard, with the clitic directly
attaching to the PC verb.

(8–50)   a. *kari=a*   *aparagi-kar-Ø=ruga,*
            3SG=TOP   beautiful-VLZ-NPST=but
            jana+pžtu=dooi.
            bad.hearted+man=EM
            'She is beautiful, but (she) is evil-hearted.' man/person again

■ MODIFIER OF AN NP

In order to appear in the modifier slot of an NP, a verb must first head an
adnominal clause, which in turn fills the modifier slot. As noted in §4.1.2,
the head verb of an adnominal clause must inflect for the finite unmarked
form. This is true for PC verbs as well.

Property concepts, adjectives, and other derivational processes   275

(8–51) *sïn-tar*   *pžtu*
        die-PST   man
        'A man who died'

(8–52) *cuu-ka-tar*   *pžtu*s
        trong-VLZ-PST   man
        'A man who was strong'

■ COMPLEX VP

In a complex VP structure, both typical verbs and PC verbs may serve as a lexical verb (§7.1.2), with the same narrative converb inflection. However, there is a severe restriction on the auxiliary verb when a PC verb is the lexical verb: it must be the progressive auxiliary. Furthermore, not all PC verbs may serve as a lexical verb within a complex VP. There is a tendency for the PC verb within a complex VP to denote a HUMAN PROPENSITY (§8.1.1).

(8–53) *zau-kar-i-i*   *ur-i.*
        well.behaved-VLZ-THM-NRT   PROG-IMP
        'Be well behaved.' [i.e. 'behave yourself' e.g. in addressing a child]

(8–54) *ganzuu-kar-i-i*   *ur-ama-r-m=mu?*
        healthy-VLZ-THM-NRT   PROG-HON-NPST-RLS=FOC
        'Are you healthy?' [i.e. 'How are you?']

■ NEGATION

Whereas the negation of other verbs is consistently encoded by an inflectional suffix such as -*n*, the negation of a PC verb may be either morphological or analytical. Inflectional negation encodes *dynamic* rather than stative negation, and is used when a PC verb has an inchoative sense:

(8–55) a. *uri=a*   *ssu-kar-Ø.*
           that=TOP   white-VLZ-THM-NPST
           'That is white.' [affirmative: stative]

        b. *uri=a*   *ssu-kar-a-n-Ø.*
           that=TOP   white-VLZ-THM-NEG-NPST
           'That does not become whitened.' [negative: active]

        c. *uri=a*   *ssu-kar-a-t-tar.*
           that=TOP   white-VLZ-THM-NEG-PST
           'That did not become whitened.' [negative: active]

276   Chapter 8

Analytic negation encodes stative negation. It employs adverbialisation of
a PC stem (§8.3.2) and the negative verb *njaan* (§6.3.5.3).

(8–56)   a. *uri=a*   *ssu-kar-Ø*
            that=TOP   white-VLZ-THM-NPST
            'That is white.'
         b. *uri=a*   *ssu-f=fa*   *njaa-n-Ø.*
            that=TOP   white-AVLZ=TOP   NEG-NPST
            'That is not white.'

This syntactic asymmetry in the stative(afrm)-stative(neg) pair, shown
schematically in TABLE 8–7, reflects the diachronic fact that a PC verb was
originally an agglutinative stem sequence, in which PC stem + *-ku* and
*ari (existential verb) were fused to form a single word, as in (8–45b). As
was noted in §6.3.6, the state verb is suppletively negated by the negative
verb *njaan*, and this is reflected in the requirement that a PC verb requires
the verb *njaan* for stative negation.

TABLE 8–7. PC verbs and negation

	Morphosyntax	Semantics
Affirmative	PC verb	[be x]
Negative 1 (inflectional)	PC verb [+ negative inflection]	[not become x]
Negative 2 (analytic)	PC adverb + negative verb	[be not x]

■ VERBAL FOCUS
A final area in which a PC verb differs from a typical verb concerns verbal
focus, i.e. focus on the verb stem (§3.3.6.2). A verb may be analytically rearranged for the purpose of focus marking, so that a verb stem is converted
to an adverb, and the undocked inflectional affix instead docks on the light
verb *sï* 'do'.

(8–57)   *mii-tar*   >   *mii=du=sï-tar.*
         look-PST   look=FOC=do-PST
         'looked'   'did looking.'

A PC verb cannot employ this strategy. Instead, as noted in §8.3.3.1, the
analytic construction involving adverbialisation of a PC stem and the existential verb is obligatory.

(8–58)   *taka-ka-tar*   >   *taka-fï=du*   *a-tar.*

Property concepts, adjectives, and other derivational processes 277

high-VLZ-PST	high-AVLZ=FOC	exist-PST
'was high'	'was high' [lit. was in a high state]	

8.3.4. Compound nominals derived from PC stems

8.3.4.1. Overview

A PC stem and a nominal stem may be compounded to form a compound nominal. The head nominal may be unrestricted (8–59), or the noun *munu* 'thing', which may often lack a substantive meaning (8–60). The former compound will henceforth be referred to as a 'lexical head compound' and the latter as a 'dummy head compound'.

(8–59) Lexical head compounds
  a. *uku+pžtu*   b. *ssjana+pžtu*   c. *aparagi+pžtu*
     big+man   dirty+man   beautiful+man
     'big man'   'dirty man'   'beautiful man'
(8–60) Dummy head compounds
  a. *uku+munu*   b. *ssjana+munu*   c. *aparagi+munu*
     big(+thing)   dirty(+thing)   beautiful(+thing)
     'big (one)'   'dirty (one)'   'beautiful (one)'

Lexical head compounds appear in texts with no distributional bias for any particular syntactic slot (though a slight preference for the predicate function is observed), whereas dummy head compounds appear mostly as predicate NPs. Below are the results of a text count of nine long texts. I list the result of adjectives for comparison (the 4% for 'argument' function concerns the E argument function of the verb 'become').

TABLE 8–8. Nominals and adjectives: distribution in terms of NP function

	Argument	Predicate	Modifier of NP	Other
Non-compound nominal	52%	14%	22%	12%
Lexical head compound	34%	55%	11%	0%
Dummy head compound	19%	79%	2%	0%
Adjective	4%	12%	76%	8%

Diachronically, a dummy head compounding undoubtedly developed from a lexical head compounding. To make the discussion clear, let us assume two extreme cases in (8–61) below, where the head *munu* 'thing; man' of a compound nominal gradually underwent semantic abstraction. The semantic content of *munu* was completely lost (glossed Ø) in (8–61b).

278   Chapter 8

(8–61)   a. Lexical head   >>>>   b. Dummy head
            compounding   compounding
            uku+munu   *uku+munu*
            big+thing   big+ Ø
            'big thing'   'big'

The situation in (8–61b) is idealised and not consistently observed in Irabu.
Rather, in the synchronic system of Irabu the dummy head compound
structure is semantically situated somewhere between the two extremes, so
that the head *munu* is in most cases but not always a mere structural head.
There are still cases where *munu* literally means 'thing; man', and there is a
morphological attributive relationship obtaining between the PC stem and
the head.

(8–62)   *imi+munu=u*   ar-a-da,   *uku+munu=u*
          small+thing=TOP   COP-THM-NEG.NRT   big+thing=ACC
          tur-i.
          take-IMP
          'Don't take a small one: take a big one.'
(8–63)   *kanu   niv+munu-mmi=n   nk-ai-tar=ru=ti,   mmja.*
          those slow+man-PL=DAT   pass-POT-PST=FOC=QT   INTJ
          '"(Were you) passed over by those slow men?", said (the man).'

Note in (8–63) that the compound is marked by the plural suffix *-mmi*
(since *munu* literally means 'man'), which would never attach to a dummy
head compound where *munu* is semantically empty. Thus, even synchronically, lexical head compounding and dummy head compounding should
not be treated as two distinct types.

   In terms of the two cross-linguistically recurrent functions of PC words
(or adjectives if there is such a class in a language), i.e. attribution and
predication (Schachter 1985; Bhat 1994; Wetzer 1996; Dixon 2004), a distinction can be made in Irabu between *morphological attribution* in which a
PC stem directly modifies a nominal stem within a grammatical word (as in
compound nominals; (8–64a) below) and *syntactic attribution* in which an
adjective is derived from a PC stem and then the adjective word modifies
the head nominal word, as in (8–64b) below.

(8–64)   a. morphological attribution   b. syntactic attribution
            uku+jaa   *ukuu+uku=nu*   *jaa*
            big+house   RED+big=GEN   house

Property concepts, adjectives, and other derivational processes   279

'big house'   'big house'

It is possible for a nominal to be modified with both syntactic and morphological attribution, as in (8–65) and (8–66).

(8–65)   *ukuu+uku=nu*   *ssu+jaa.*
          RED+big=GEN   white+house
          Adjective   PC stem + nominal
          Syntactic attribution   Morphological attribution
          'big and white house' [lit. big white-house]

(8–66)   *ssuu+ssu=nu*   *uku+jaa*
          RED+white=GEN   big+house
          Adjective   PC stem + nominal
          Syntactic attribution   Morphological attribution
          'White and big house' [lit. white big-house]

See §8.4.2 for the functional difference between the two kinds of attribution illustrated in (8–64).

8.3.4.2. Lexical head compounds

Lexical head compounds have a fully lexical nominal stem (other than *munu* 'thing') as the head, modified by a PC stem (see §3.6.2.2 where I argued that the compound structure cannot be analysed as an NP). In what follows I note a syntactic difference between an ordinary nominal and a lexical head compound nominal. As shown in TABLE 8–9 below, like an adjective, the latter allows adverbial modification.

TABLE 8–9. Nominals and PC nominals

	Argument	Predicate	Modifier of NP	Modified by adverb
Ordinary nominals	+	+	+	-
Compound nominals				
Lexical head compound	+	+	+	+
Dummy head compound	+	+	(+)	+
Adjectives	(+)	+	+	+

Although a lexical head compound demonstrates a full range of NP functions, there is one conspicuous difference between it and an ordinary nominal: a lexical head compound allows both attributive and *adverbial* modification. Unlike an adjective, it shows no preference for either modifi-

280   Chapter 8

cation (§8.2.2.3).

(8–67) *kari=a*   *ati=du*   *taka+pžtu.*
        3SG=TOP   very=FOC   high+man
        'He is a very tall man.'
(8–68) *kari=a*   *daizïna*   *taka+pžtu.*
        3SG=TOP   great   high+man
        'He is a very tall man.'

Note that in (8–67) the focus marker is attached to the adverb *ati*, whereas
it is absent in (8–68). The focus marker *=du* can attach to an argument, an
adjunct, a VP complement, or a lexical verb within a complex VP (§9.5.2),
thus cannot attach to the modifier within an NP. Hence, in (8–67) *=du* cannot occur on the modifier of the NP, whereas in (8–68) *=du* may occur on
the adverb (which occurs outside an NP, serving as a predicate adjunct).

8.3.4.3. Dummy head compounds
In a dummy head compound the head nominal stem is the noun *munu*
'thing; man', as shown in (8–69b) below. This stem may often be semantically empty. In such a case, the head nominal stem is simply the structural
head of the compound, making the whole compound a nominal, but it is the
PC stem that serves as the semantic head. This mismatch in headship is
analogous to that found in the formal noun *su(u)* 'thing; man' (§4.2.1.8),
which is structurally an NP head but is semantically often not. The difference between *munu* and a formal noun is that the former is the structural
head of a single word, whereas the latter is the structural head of an NP.

(8–69) a. Lexical head compound   b. Dummy head compound
           uku+pžtu   *uku+munu*
           big+man   big(+thing)
           'big man'   'big (thing)'

Thus, unlike lexical head compounds, there is not usually an attributive relationship between the PC stem and the head *munu*, since the head is semantically empty.
    Dummy head compounds occur most often as predicate NPs. Also, like
lexical head compounds, they allow adverbial modification or adnominal
modification. This is true whether or not *munu* is semantically empty.

(8–70) a. *ba=a*   *ati=du*   *kuu+munu.*

Property concepts, adjectives, and other derivational processes   281

            1SG=TOP   very=FOC   hard+Ø
            'I feel very painful.'
        b. *ba=a*   *daizïna*   *kuu+munu.*
            1SG=TOP   great   hard+Ø
            'I feel very hard.'

(8–71)   a. *uri=a*   *ati*   *uku+munu=du*   *a-tar.*
            3SG=TOP   very   big+thing=FOC   COP-PST
            'It was a very big thing.'
        b. *uri=a*   *daizïna*   *uku+munu=du*   *a-tar.*
            3SG=TOP   great   big+thing=FOC   COP-PST
            'It was a very big thing.'

When *munu*, carrying its literal meaning 'thing', functions as semantic as well as structural head with its literal meaning, the dummy head compound may serve as argument, as shown in (8–72) below, or as modifier of an NP, as shown in (8–73) below, though the latter function is very rare (see TABLE 8–8).

(8–72)   a. *mmjahi*   <u>*uku+munu=u*</u>   *tur-i.*
            more   big+thing=ACC   take-IMP
            'Take a bigger one.'

(8–73)   <u>*buuciri+munu=nu*</u>   *uku+gui=ja*   *uturusï-ka-Ø-m.*
            mighty+man=GEN   big+voice=TOP   fearful-VLZ-NPST-RLS
            'The big voice of a mighty person is fearful.'

On the other hand, in my text data a dummy head compound in which *munu* is semantically empty *never* functions attributively, i.e. as the modifier of an NP. Such a modifier use is artificially constructed in (8–74), which most native speakers judged unnatural. As shown in §8.2.2.2, this kind of attributive function is normally taken over by an adjective, as shown in (8–75). Actually, the consultant corrected (8–74) as (8–75).

(8–74)   *?uku+munu=nu*   *pžtu.*
            big+Ø=GEN
            man [intended meaning] 'big man'

(8–75)   *ukuu+uku=nu*   *pžtu*
            RED+big=GEN   man
            'big man'

282   Chapter 8

TABLE 8–10. Dummy head compound and its syntactic function

	Argument NP	Predicate NP	Modifier of NP
Lexical head compound	+	+	+
Dummy head compound			
munu [+ lexical]	+	+	(+)
munu [- lexical]		+	

In summary, a dummy head compound is classified as a nominal, in that it only heads an NP. It demonstrates all the functions of NPs, even though this function depends on whether *munu* is semantically substantive or not. However, it is a subclass rather than a typical instance of the nominal class as it may additionally allow adverbial modification in addition to adnominal modification. Semantically, a dummy head compound is very much like an adjective especially when *munu* is semantically not substantive (e.g. (8–70)). However, they clearly differ in terms of syntax, since a dummy head compound (and a lexical head compound) never appears in VP structure.

As noted in the preceding paragraph, it is interesting that a similar adjectival meaning may be expressed by an adjective and a dummy head compound. What we are looking at in dummy head compounds may be an intermediate stage of the diachronic development from a lexical head compound to a true adjective. If we assume, as the typological literature suggests (Dixon 1982, 2004; Schachter 1985; Wetzer 1996; Croft 2002), that (a) attributive modification and (b) predicative modification are the two basic functions of the adjective class, then it turns out that the current Irabu system lacks an adjective class that regularly does the job of (b), since the existing adjective class mostly functions attributively (TABLE 8–8). There are three word forms that are likely to fill this functional gap in Irabu: compound nominals (dummy head compounds in particular) and PC verbs. As will be discussed in §8.4.1, PC verbs occur as predicates which are presupposed (i.e. not asserted), a situation which is not typical in adjectival predication where the subject is topic and the predicate is asserted. It is noteworthy that a dummy head compound mostly functions predicatively, and the predicate is asserted (§8.4.1). Now, the semantic change of *munu* may be interpreted as a change that creates the adjective specialised for predicative modification, which will emerge when the semantic content of *munu* has completely been lost and *munu* has been reanalysed as an 'adjectivalising suffix' that derives a predicative adjective.

Property concepts, adjectives, and other derivational processes   283

8.4. Adjective, compound nominal, and PC verb: functional account

The functions of words that include PC stems are summarised in TABLE 8–11 below. As described in §8.3.4, a dummy head compound mostly functions as a predicate NP, whereas an adjective mostly functions as modifier of an NP. A PC verb has an exclusive function of predication, either in a main clause or in a non-main clause, and the adnominal clause including the PC verb serves as modifier of an NP. In a lexical head compound nominal there is a morphological attributive relationship between the PC stem and the head nominal.

TABLE 8–11. PC nominals and PC verbs in terms of function

	Predication	Attribution	
		Syntactic	Morphological
Dummy head compound	*		
PC verb	*		
Adnominal clause including PC verb		*	
Adjective		*	
Lexical head compound			*

The table raises three questions. (1) When does a speaker encode a predication as a dummy head compound nominal and when as a PC verb? (2) When does a speaker encode an attribution as an adjective and when as a lexical head compound? (3) When does a speaker encode an attribution in an NP as an adnominal clause (whose predicate is a PC verb) and when as an adjective? These three questions are addressed below.

8.4.1. Dummy head compound vs PC verb: predicative function

There is a clear tendency for a dummy head compound nominal to occur as predicate in the pragmatically unmarked topic-comment structure. In this structure, there is a topic-marked NP, often subject, and the predicate is in the focus domain (i.e. carries new information). Conversely, there is a clear tendency for a PC verb to occur as predicate when the predicate is presupposed.

(8–76)   *kari=a*   *cuu+munu.*
         3SG=TOP   strong(+thing)
         'He is strong.' [unmarked topic-comment structure]

(8–77)   A. *nzi=nu=ga*   *cuu-kar-Ø?*

284   Chapter 8

         which=NOM=FOC   strong-VLZ-NPST
         'Which is strong(er)?'
    B. *kui=ga=du*   *cuu-kar-Ø.*
       this=NOM=FOC   strong-VLZ-NPST
       'This (guy) is strong(er).'

Another clear distributional tendency is that a dummy head compound is
much more likely to be used in a main clause than a PC verb. Given the
preference of a PC verb for presupposition, this distributional tendency
may be explained by the pragmatic status of subordinate clauses in general:
subordinate clauses tend to be presupposed, in the sense that the truth condition is not challenged by the addressee (Erteshik-Shir and Lappin 1979,
1983; Lewis 1979; Quirk et al. 1985; Lambrecht 1994).[6] See Koloskova
and Ohori (2008) for a similar claim with regard to the pragmatic status of
PC verbs in Hirara (a Miyako language related to Irabu) as being presupposed.

(8–78) *kuu-ka-tigaa,*   *mudur-i-i*   *kuu-Ø.*
        hard-VLZ-CND   return-THM-NRT   come-IMP
        'If (you feel things are) hard, come back.'

(8–79) *ujaki-kar-Ø*   *tukja=mai*   *a-tar=ruga,*
        rich-VLZ-NPST   time=too   exist-PST=but
        nnama=a   *hira*   *zin=mai*   *njaa-da*
        now=TOP   INTJ   money=too   not.exist-NEG.NRT
        ur-Ø.
        PROG-NPST
        '(There) was a time (I) was rich, but now, you see, (I) have no
        money.'

(8–80) *kunusjuku*   *kata-ka-i-ba=mai,*
        this.much   hard-VLZ-THM-CND=even
        nci+u-tigaa,   *japa-fi*   *nar-Ø=dara.*
        put+PROG-CND   soft-AVLZ   become-NPST=CRTN
        'Even if (it) is this hard, (it) will become softened if (you) put (it
        in water).'

───────────────

[6] For example, Erteshik-Shir and Lappin (1979) suggest what they call the 'lie-test': if an addressee, upon hearing a sentence, says 'that's not true', this statement is about the main clause
rather than the subordinate clause that is couched in the main clause. See Lambrecht (1994:
52) for more detailed discussion.

Property concepts, adjectives, and other derivational processes   285

8.4.2. Adjective vs lexical head compound: attributive function

An adjective modifies a nominal in NP structure (syntactic attribution), whereas a PC stem within a lexical head compound modifies a head nominal within the word (morphological attribution).

An adjective in attributive function almost always modifies a nominal that is newly introduced into discourse. This nominal tends to be referential.

(8–81) *nkjaan=du=i,*   *ujakii+ujaki=nu*   *pžtu=tu*
        old.times=FOC=CNF   RED+rich=GEN   man=ASC
        kibann+kiban=nu   *pžtu=tu*   *dusï*   *a-tar=ca.*
        RED+poor=GEN   man=ASC   friend   COP-PST=HS
        'Once upon a time, (there were) a rich man and a poor man, (and
        they) were friends.'

(8–82) *mii-tigaa,*   *ssuu+ssu=nu*   *mii-gama=nu*
        look-CND   RED+white=GEN   fruit-DIM=NOM
        a-ta=iba,
        exist-PST=so
        'When (I) looked, (there) was a white fruit, so...'

A PC stem within a lexical head compound is also an attributive modifier of the head nominal stem. Unlike the adjectival attribution noted above, the head nominal stem in a lexical head compounding is typically non-referential and the compound nominal is typically used as a predicate head of the proper inclusion expression, as in *uri=a taka+jama* (3SG=TOP high+mountain) 'this is a high mountain.' (see §10.2.1 for proper inclusion).

(8–83) *kari=a*   *maada=du*   *gaazuu+pžtu=dara=i.*
        3SG=TOP   very=FOC   selfish+man=CRTN=CNF
        'He's a very selfish man, eh?'

(8–84) *kuma=a*   *punicï+dukuma*   *ja-i-ba,*
        this.place=TOP   rocky+place   COP-THM-CSL
        nivv-ai-n-Ø.
        sleep-POT-NEG-NPST
        'This place is a rocky place, so (I) cannot sleep.'

8.4.3. Adnominal clause vs adjective: syntactic attributive function

As illustrated in (8–85) and (8–86) below, a PC verb may head an adnominal clause that fills the modifier slot of an NP. As the gloss indicates, the

286 Chapter 8

pragmatic implication here is always one of contrast. The modified nominal has already been invoked in the discourse. In (8–85) for example, the discourse is about whether a house that is white or a house that is black is better. See also (8–79) above, where a contrastive meaning is encoded by the PC verb *ujakikar* 'is rich (as opposed to poor)'.

(8–85) *ssu-kar-Ø*   *jaa=nu=du*   *masï.*
white-VLZ-NPST   house=NOM=FOC   better
'The house that is white (as opposed to black) is better.'

(8–86) *uu-kar-Ø*   *pžtu=mai*   *imi-kar-Ø*   *pžtu=mai*
big-VLZ-NPST   man=too   small-VLZ-NPST   man=too
uma=n   *davv-as-i-i=du*   *u-tar.*
that.place=DAT   crowd-VLZ-THM-NRT=FOC   exist-PST
'Bigger men and smaller men were both crowded there.'

On the other hand, as illustrated in (8–87) and (8–88) below, attribution by an adjective does not entail a contrast, since, as noted in §8.4.2, an NP containing an adjective introduces a new referent into discourse.

(8–87) *ssuu+ssu=nu*   *jaa=nu=du*   *ar-Ø.*
RED+white=GEN   house=NOM=FOC   exist-NPST
'(There) is a (very) white house.'

(8–88) *ukuu+uku=nu* *pžtu=tu* *imii+imi=nu*   *pžtu=tu*
RED+big=GEN   man=ASC RED+small=GEN   man=ASC
bafïtaa=sii=du   *u-tar.*
two=INST=FOC   exist-PST
'(There) were a (very) big man and a (very) small man together.'

8.5. Class-changing derivation

In this section I describe (1) noun-to-verb derivation, (2) verb-to-noun derivation and (3) verb-to-PC-stem derivation.

8.5.1. Noun-to-verb derivation (verbalisation)

This process is very limited in Irabu, since the light verb *(a)sï* 'do' functions as equivalents of verbalisation in other languages.[7] If one wants to derive a predicative expression from a noun *sauzï* 'cleaning', one uses it as

---

[7] Many scholars note that verbalisation is generally absent even in languages where nominalisation is productive (Hopper and Thompson 1984: 746).

Property concepts, adjectives, and other derivational processes   287

a direct object of the light verb *asï*.

(8–89) *sauz=zu*   *ah-u-di.*
        cleaning=ACC   do-THM-INT
        '(I) will do cleaning.'

In the following example, the direct object NP is marked as partitive, and the light verb is a phonologically independent, monomoraic form *=s*, which is cliticised to the preceding NP. Since the partitive almost always occurs in a narrative converbal clause, the light verb here also inflects as a narrative converb form *=sii*.

(8–90) *kansja=a=s-i-i,*   *par-tar=ca.*
        thanking=PRT=do-THM-NRT   leave-PST=HS
        '(He) left thanking'
(8–91) *kari=a*   *mmja*   *kiban-na=s-i-i=du*
        3SG=TOP   DSC   poor=PRT=do-THM-NRT=FOC
        u-tar.
        PROG-PST
        'He was poor.' [lit. He was doing poor]
(8–92) *agu=u=s-i-i*   *cyaa=mai=du*   *num-Ø.*
        friend=PRT=do-THM-NRT   tea=too=FOC   drink-NPST
        '(We) drink tea together.' [lit. (We) drink tea doing friends]
(8–93) *katana=a*   *juui=ja=s-i-i*
        knife=PRT   preparation=PRT=do-THM-NRT
        mac-i-u-tar.
        wait-THM-PROG-PST
        '(He) was waiting with a knife in his hand.' [lit. (He) was waiting preparing a knife]

The structure consisting of the direct object NP followed by partitive and the cliticised light verb occurs very frequently in Irabu discourse, and all have a modificational, circumstantial meaning as illustrated above.

There is an indication that the sequence *=a* and *=s* is being reanalysed as a single verbaliser *-as* that attaches to a noun stem and derives a verb stem [[noun]-as]$_{Vstem}$. That is, the direct object NP does not really function as such, since it may further carry a direct object NP as if the structure were a single transitive verb, as in (8–93). Note also that in (8–91), the 'object NP' is a PC stem rather than a noun. The partitive marker never attaches to a PC stem except for the light verb construction discussed here.

288   Chapter 8

Upshot is that we are looking at an ongoing grammaticalisation process whereby the source structure, which consists of the direct object NP followed by partitive and the light verb, is being reanalysed to give rise to the target structure, which consists of a noun stem (or a PC stem) and the verbaliser suffix -*as*. And the current situation is somewhere in between. In the present work, I treat the structure as a single morpheme, 'circumstantial verbaliser' -*as*, with an emphasis on the target structure. But readers should keep in mind that the characteristics of the source structure are not completely lost. For example, the allomorphy of the verbaliser -*as* is identical to that of the partitive =*a*: it is subject to the /j/-insertion if it is attached to the stem that ends in a long vowel/diphthong, as in (8–93), the geminate copy insertion rule if it is attached to the stem that ends in a consonant, as in (8–91), or the assimilation to /u/ if it is attached to the stem that ends in a short /u/, as in (8–92). Also, the derived verb stem is almost always inflected as a narrative converbal form just as with the verb form of the clause in which the partitive occurs.

8.5.2. Verb-to-noun derivation (nominalisation)

Verb-to-noun derivation derives nominals with the nominaliser -*ja* (see §2.8.3.2 for the morphophonemics of this suffix). The suffix is attached to a bare verb stem (rather than an athematic stem; §6.3.4). Thus in (8–94) below, for example, -*ja* is attached to *ss*- rather than its athematic stem form *sïï* (§6.3.4.2).

(8–94)   *kari=a*   *ss-ja=dooi.*
         3SG=TOP   know-NLZ=EMP
         'He is a person who knows a lot.'

(8–95)   *daizïna*   *sadur-ja=du*   *a-tar.*
         great   search-NLZ=FOC   COP-PST
         '(She) was a woman who chases men.' [lit. '(She) was such a (man) searcher.']

(8–96)   *sauz=zu=bakaar*   *as-i-i,*   *mmja,*
         cleaning=ACC=only   do-THM-NRT   INTJ
         vva=a   *daizïna*   *surumik-ja=i.*
         2SG=TOP   great   clean-NLZ=CNF
         'Doing cleaning all the time, you are a person obsessed with cleaning.'

When a transitive verb is nominalised, the underlying object appears as the first component of a compound stem, of which the verb stem is the second

Property concepts, adjectives, and other derivational processes   289

component.

(8–97) *site,*   *munu+kak-ja=n=ru*   *nar-tar=ru?*
        then   thing+write-NLZ=DAT=FOC   become-PST=FOC
        'Then, has (she) become a writer?'
(8–98) *vva=a*   *butu+muc-ja=ru?*
        2SG=TOP   husband+have-NLZ=FOC
        'Are you a husband-having man?'

As is shown in (8–99), *-ja* may in rare cases derive an instrumental nominal rather than a person nominal.

(8–99) *mm+pur-ja=u*   *muc-i+kuu-Ø.*
        potato-dig-NLZ=ACC   take-THM+come-IMP
        'Bring the potato-digger' [instrument nominaliser]

8.5.3. Verb-to-PC-stem derivation

A PC stem is productively derived from the athematic stem of a verb using one of three major derivational affixes: *-busï* 'wanting to', *-guri* 'difficult to', and *-jasï* 'easy to'. A derived PC stem satisfies (A), (B), and (C) in §8.1.2, as the three tables below illustrate.

TABLE 8–12. *mii-* 'look; see' + *-busï* 'want to' as a PC stem

Criteria		*mii-* 'look; see'	Gloss
(A) reduplication		*mii-busïï+mii-busï*	'(I) am wanting to see'
(B) direct quotation		*mii-busïï=ti=nu cïmucï*	'the feeling like, "(how much I am) wanting to see!"'
(C) special derivation	*-sa*	*mii-bus-sa*	'the degree to which (I) am wanting to see'
	-fï	*mii-busï-fï*	'wanting to see'
	-ka(r)	*mii-busï-ka-tar*	'(I) was wanting to see'

TABLE 8–13. *mii-* 'look; see' + *-busï* 'difficult to' as a PC stem

Criteria	*mii-* 'look; see'	Gloss
(A) reduplication	*mii-gurii+mii-guri*	'(it is) difficult to see'
(B) direct quotation	*mii-gurii=ti=nu munu*	'a thing which is like "(how) difficult to see (it is)!"'

290 Chapter 8

	(C) special derivation	-sa	mii-guri-sa	'the degree to which (it is) difficult to see'
		-fï	mii-guri-fï	'being difficult to see'
		-ka(r)	mii-guri-ka-tar	'was difficult to see'

TABLE 8–14. *mii-* 'look; see' + *-jasï* 'easy to' as a PC stem

Criteria			*mii-* 'look; see'	Gloss
(A) reduplication			*mii-jasïï+mii-jasï*	'(it is) easy to see'
(B) direct quotation			*mii-jasïï=ti=nu munu*	'a thing which is like "(how) easy to see (it is)!"'
(C) special derivation		-sa	*mii-jas-sa*	'the degree to which (it is) easy to see'
		-fï	*mii-jasï-fï*	'being easy to see'
		-ka(r)	*mii-jasï-ka-tar*	'was easy to see'

8.5.3.1. 'wanting to' *-busï*

A PC stem is derived from the athematic stem of a verb with the desiderative *-busï* 'wanting to'.

(8–100) *ba=a*   *vva=ga*   *ffa=u=baa*
           1SG=TOP   2SG=GEN   child=ACC=TOP
           mii-busï+munu=i.
           look-DES(+thing)=CNF
           'I want to see your child.'

(8–101) *ba=a*   *vva=ga*   *ffa=u=baa*
           1SG=TOP   2SG=GEN   child=ACC=TOP
           miibusïï+mii-busï=ti=du   *umu-i+ur-Ø.*
           RED+look-DES=QT=FOC   think-THM+PROG-NPST
           'I am thinking like "I want to see your child (very much)".'

(8–102) *kuri=u*   *ar-a-da,*   *kuri=u=du*
           3SG=ACC   COP-THM-NEG.NRT   3SG=ACC=FOC
           mii-busï-kar-Ø.
           look-DES-VLZ-NPST
           'Not this one, (I) want to see this one.'

(8–103) *uri=u=baa*   *mii-busï-f=fa*   *njaa-n-Ø.*
           3SG=ACC=TOP   look-DES-AVLZ=TOP   NEG-NPST
           '(I) don't want to see it.'

Property concepts, adjectives, and other derivational processes   291

8.5.3.2. 'difficult to' -*guri*

A PC stem is derived from the athematic stem of a verb with -*guri* 'difficult to'. As in the case of the derivation with -*busï* (§8.5.3.1), the derived PC stem with -*guri* may form an adjective, a state nominal, a compound nominal, a PC verb, or a PC adverb.

(8–104) *cïfïï-gurii+cïfïï-guri=nu*   *jaa*
          RED+make-difficult.to=GEN   house
          'a house that is difficult to make' [adjective]

(8–105) *ui=ga*   *cïfïï-guri-sa=nu=du*   *daizï.*
          3SG=GEN   make-difficult.to-NLZ=NOM=FOC   awful
          'Difficultness of (making) it is awful.' [state nominal]

(8–106) *uri=a*   *cïfïï-guri+munu=du*   *a-tar.*
          3SG=TOP   make-difficult.to(+thing)=FOC   COP-PST
          'It was (one) difficult to make.' [compound nominal]

(8–107) *uri=a*   *cïfïï-guri-ka-Ø-m=dooi.*
          that=TOP   make-difficult.to-VLZ-NPST-RLS=EMP
          'That is difficult to make.' [PC verb]

(8–108) *uri=a*   *cïfïï-guri-f=fa*   *njaa-n-Ø.*
          that=TOP   make-difficult.to-AVLZ=TOP   NEG-NPST
          'That is not difficult to make.' [PC adverb]

The syntactic valence (§3.5.1) of the verb stem may be either retained or decreased when the derived PC stem is further transformed into a word other than a state nominal (where the O of the verb stem surfaces as the modifier of the NP). When the valence is retained, the underlying O remains O ([O > O]); when the valence is decreased, the underlying O appears as an S (schematised as [O > S] below). The decreasing arrangement is more common. In (8–109a), the derived clause is headed by a nominal predicate phrase (whose head is a dummy head compound nominal), which still governs its direct object.

(8–109) a. *kantja=ga*   *jaa=ju=baa*   *daizïna*
              3PL=GEN   house=ACC=TOP   great
              cïfïï-guri+munu
              make-difficult.to(+thing)
              'Their house is very difficult-to-make(-house).' [O > O]

          b. *kantja=ga*   *jaa=ja*   *daizïna*
              3PL=GEN   house=TOP   great
              cïfïï-guri+munu

292   Chapter 8

make-difficult.to(+thing)
'Their house is very difficult-to-make(-house).' [O > S]

8.5.2.3. 'easy to' -*jasï*

A PC stem is derived from the athematic stem of a verb with -*jasï* 'easy to'.
The derived PC stem with -*jasï* may form an adjective, a state nominal, a
compound nominal, a PC verb, or a PC adverb.

(8–110)   *cïfïï-jasïï+cïfïï-jasï=nu*   *jaa*
          RED+make-easy.to=GEN   house
          'a house that is easy.to make' [adjective]
(8–111)   *ui=ga*   *cïfïï-jas-sa=nu=du*   *icïban*
          3SG=GEN   make-easy.to-NLZ=NOM=FOC   best
          'Easiness of (making) it is the best.' [state nominal]
(8–112)   *uri=a*   *cïfïï-jasï+munu=du*   *a-tar.*
          3SG=TOP   make-easy.to(+thing)=FOC   COP-PST
          'It was (one) easy to make.' [compound nominal]
(8–113)   *uri=a*   *cïfïï-jasï-ka-Ø-m=dooi.*
          that=TOP   make-easy.to-VLZ-NPST-RLS=EMP
          'That is easy to make.' [PC verb]
(8–114)   *uri=a*   *cïfïï-jasï-f=fa*   *njaa-n-Ø.*
          that=TOP   make-easy.to-AVLZ=TOP   NEG-NPST
          'That is not easy to make.' [PC adverb]

As in the case of -*guri* (§8.5.3.2), the syntactic valence of the verb stem
may be either retained or decreased when the derived PC stem is further
transformed into a word other than a state nominal. In (8–115a), the derived clause is headed by a nominal predicate phrase (whose head is a
dummy head compound nominal), which still governs its direct object.

(8–115)   a. *kantja=ga*   *jaa=ju=baa*   *daizïna*
             3PL=GEN   house=ACC=TOP   great
             cïfïï-guri+munu
             make-difficult.to(+thing)
             'Their house is very difficult-to-make(-house).' [O > O]
          b. *kantja=ga*   *jaa=ja*   *daizïna*
             3PL=GEN   house=TOP   great
             cïfïï-guri+munu
             make-difficult.to(+thing)
             'Their house is very difficult-to-make(-house).' [O > S]

Chapter 9

Bound markers

This chapter focuses on the syntactic distribution and the semantic-pragmatic function of various bound markers. Bound markers comprise (a) argument markers, (b) predicate markers and (c) discourse markers.

9.1. Overview of bound markers

Bound markers are all clitics (§3.2 for the distinction between clitics, words and affixes). As defined in §3.3, bound markers occur phrase- or clause-finally and encode various grammatical functions of the phrase or clause to which they syntactically attach. In what follows, all bound markers will be described in detail except for case markers, which have been collectively discussed in §4.3.

9.2. Conjunction markers

A conjunction marker typically marks coordination of a clause headed by a finite predicate without a dependency or embedding relationship to a matrix clause (§11.2). There are three conjunction markers: temporal =*kja(a)* 'when', 'But' conjunction =*suga*, and 'So' conjunction =*(ss)iba*.

9.2.1. Temporal =*kja(a)*

The conjunction marker =*kja(a)* is a temporal conjunction 'when' or 'while'. The bracketed phoneme is optional, though =*kja* is preferred when another clitic follows.

(9–1)	*uja=nu*	*sïn-Ø=kjaa=du*	*ffa-mmi=nu*
	parent=NOM	die-NPST=when=FOC	child-DIM=FOC
	av-Ø.		
	make.quarrel-NPST		
	'When a parent dies, the children quarrel.'		
(9–2)	*tida=nu*	*agar-Ø=kja=du*	
	sun=NOM	rise-NPST=when=FOC	
	fïm-i-i	*ik-i+u-tar.*	*miz=zu=baa.*

294   Chapter 9

        get-THM-NRT   go-THM+PROG-PST   water=ACC=TOP
        'When the sun rose (I) would go and get, (I mean) water.'

(9–3)   *ba=ga*   *munu=u*   *fa-i+ur-Ø=kjaa*
        1SG=NOM   thing=ACC   eat-THM+PROG-NPST=when
        maccja=nkai   *ik-i-i*   *kuu-Ø.*
        shop=ALL   go-THM-NRT   come-IMP
        'While I am eating, go to the shop and come back.'

In texts I found several examples in which *=kja(a)* apparently expressed 'until' rather than 'when' or 'while', as shown in (9–4).

(9–4)   *patarak-ai-r=kjaa,*   *sjuumun=nu*   *kacï+kai-Ø*
        work-POT-NPST=until   invoice=ACC   write+change-NRT
        ntsi-i   *par-i=tii*   *asï-tarjaa...*
        put-NRT   leave-IMP =QT   say-PST.CND
        'Until (I) am able to work, refresh (the due date of) the invoice and put it and come again, said (the man), then...'

However, a later elicitation revealed that this is a shortened version of *=kja=gami*, as in (9–5) below, where *=gami* (limitative case) expresses 'until'.

(9–5)   *kai=n*   *idjav=kja=gami=a,*   *munužž-a-da*
        3SG=DAT   meet=when=until=TOP   speak-THM-NEG.NRT
        ur-i.
        PROG-IMP
        'Keep silent until (you) see him.'

This may suggest that *=kja(a)* was a formal noun, since the *=gami* here can be considered a case marker expressing its case relation 'until; as far as'. If so, then *=kja* has almost lost its status as a formal noun in that it cannot carry any other case, and it is even possible for *=gami* to be unexpressed, as in (9–5).

9.2.2. 'So' conjunction *=(ss)iba*
The conjunction marker *=(ss)iba* expresses the 'so; therefore' causal relation. The initial /ss/ is present when *=(ss)iba* attaches to a host that ends in a CV, as in the finite irrealis intentional form (9–6).

(9–6)   *uku+nam=mu*   *jar-ah-a-di=ssiba,*

Bound markers   295

big+wave=ACC   send-CAUS-THM-INT=so
ur-i-i   *kuu-Ø=juu!*
descend-THM-NRT   come-IMP=UPDT
'(I) will cause a big wave, so come down with the wave!'

The initial /ss/ is deleted when attaching to the past unmarked suffix *-tar*
(9–7).

(9–7) *ubaa=ja*   *akjaada=mai*   *as-i+u-ta=iba,*
       old.woman=TOP   merchant=too   do-THM+PROG-PST=so
       uma+kuma   *maar-i+u-tar.*
       there+here   wander-THM+PROG-PST
       'The old woman was a merchant, so (she) visited here and there.'

In all other contexts only the first /s/ is deleted, i.e. we have the form *=siba*
(9–8). In very old speakers' speech, /s/ in *=siba* is subject to another
morphophonemic process in which it is assimilated to a preceding /n/ (see
(9–9) as opposed to (9–8)).

(9–8) *ba=a*   *ss-a-n-Ø=siba=gami=du*
       1SG=TOP   know-THM-NEG-NPST=LMT=FOC
       ažž-i+ur-Ø.
       say-THM+PROG-NPST
       'I don't know, so I am asking.'
(9–9) *uku+tagu*   *muc-ai-n-Ø=niba,*   *bakecï-gama=n*
       big+basin   carry-POT-NEG-NPST=so   bucket-DIM=DAT
       ir-i-i   *unu*   kuba-gama   *ka=tti.*
       put-THM-NRT   that   betel.palm-DIM   ONM=QT
       '(I) couldn't carry a big basin, so (I) put (water) in the betel palm,
       like this.'

9.2.3. 'But' conjunction *=suga*

The conjunction marker *=suga* expresses the adversative 'but' relation.
This clitic probably developed from *=su(u)* (formal noun 'man; thing') +
=ga (archaic conjunction 'but'?), but in the synchronic grammar of Irabu
=suga is a single morpheme that cannot be broken up. The initial /s/ is subject to the characteristic morphophonemic process of *=su(u)*: /s/ assimilates
to a preceding /r/ (§2.7.7.2), as illustrated in (9–12).

(9–10) *dzin=nu*   *ar-Ø*   *ujaki+munu-mmi=gami=a*

296   Chapter 9

money=NOM   exist-NPST   rich+man-PL=LMT=TOP
fa-i-Ø=du   *ufi-Ø=suga,*
eat-THM-NRT=FOC   PROS-NPST=but
banti=a   kuu+munu-gama=du   *a-ta=iba=du...*
1PL=TOP   poor+man-DIM=FOC   COP-PST=so=FOC
'Rich people who have money would eat (rice), but we were a
bit poor, so...'

(9–11) *imi-kar-Ø=kjaa=gami=a*
        small-VLZ-NPST=when=LMT=TOP
        ciff-a-n-Ø=suga=i,
        make-THM-NEG-NPST=but=CNF
        mmja   uu-fi-Ø   nar-i-i=kara=a
        INTJ   big-VLZ-NRT   become-THM-NRT=ABL=TOP
        mmja   pataki=mai   juu   a-tar.
        INTJ   field=too   very   exist-PST
        '(When) I was a kid (our family) did not plant (potatoes), but
        after becoming old (our family) had many fields.'

(9–12) *ba=a*   *ik-a-t-tar=ruga=du,*
        1SG=TOP   go-THM-NEG-PST=but=FOC
        ani=kara   *cïfi-tar.*
        elder.sister=ABL   hear-PST
        'I didn't go, but (I) heard from my elder sister.'

9.3. Modal markers

Modal markers function to encode non-grammaticalised modality, i.e. modality that is not encoded by verbal inflection (see §10.5.1 for the definition
of modality).

9.3.1. Dubitative *=bjaam*

The modal marker *=bjaam* expresses the speaker's doubtful attitude 'I
wonder if...', 'I doubt...', and so on. In (9–13) *=bjaam* is structurally attached to a nominal predicate, and in (9–14) it is attached to a verbal predicate.

(9–13) A. *kari=a*   *mmja   daizïna   nisïdu=dooi.*
            3SG=TOP   INTJ   awful   theft=EMP
            'He is an awful thief.'
        B. *ai=bjaam=mi.*
            that.way=I.doubt=CNF

'I wonder if (the fact is) that way.' [i.e. 'that's what you say.']

(9–14) *kan=nu=ru*   *ur-Ø=bjaam=ti,*
      crab=NOM=FOC   exist-NPST=I.wonder=QT
      muu=ju   *ujukasï-tigaa,* *bazakar-i-i=du*
      seaweed=ACC   shake-CND   raise.claw-THM-NRT=FOC
      u-tar.
      PROG-PST
      '(I thought) "I wonder if there is a crab," and when I shake sea-weed, (the crab) was raising its claw (to fight against my at-tack).'

As is illustrated in (9–14) above, *=bjaam* may be used in a self-question.

9.3.2. Dubitative 2 *=gagara*

The modal marker *=gagara* expresses the speaker's doubtful attitude 'I wonder how', 'I wonder what', and so on, always co-occurring with an interrogative such as *nau* 'what', *taru* 'who', *nza* 'where', *nausi* 'how', and so on. When it is directly attached to an interrogative, the resulting form is an indefinite nominal (Chapter 5).

The speech act of the sentence in which *=gagara* is found is not a question in the sense of invoking the hearer's verbal response (Sadock and Zwicky 1985), but an uncertain statement, or a self-question. Even though *=gagara* consisted originally of *=ga* (the focus marker of information question which is double-marked on a predicate; §9.5.2.2) and *=gara* (unknown morpheme), and this is still evidenced in its prosodic behaviour (see below), I treat it as a single morpheme, since *=ga* and *=gara* always appear together to function as a dubitative marker.

(9–15) *gui!*   *nau=nu=ga*   *ur-Ø=gagara=i?*
      Wow   what=NOM=FOC   exist-NPST=I.wonder=CNF
      'Wow, what is there....' [self-question]

(9–16) *taru=nu=ga*   *kuu+munu-mmi=u=mai*
      who=NOM=FOC   poor+man-PL=ACC=too
      mii-r=gagara=i?
      look.after=I.wonder=CNF
      '(I wonder) who would look after poor people as well?' [self-question]

As these examples show, *=gagara* is very often followed by the discourse

298 Chapter 9

marker =*i* (confirmative), which normally requests a verbal response from the hearer about what speaker says (§9.6.4). However, in a self-question =*i* is used as if there were an imaginary hearer in the monologue.

As noted in §2.9.2.2, the mora length of a morpheme makes a difference to this footing. A monomoraic morpheme is simply treated as part of the host on which default bimoraic footing operates, whereas a polymoraic morpheme always starts a foot. In this regard, =*gagara* behaves like =*ga* + =*gara*:

(9–17) *nau=ga=gara*
        a. (nauga)$_H$ (gara)$_L$
  *b. (nau)(gagara)

Here, the (b) pattern would be obtained if =*gagara* were treated prosodically as a single trimoraic morpheme. However, what we actually get is the (a) pattern in which =*gara* starts its own footing, and this induces a ternary foot on the part of its prosodic host, i.e. *nau* + =*ga,* the latter being treated as part of the host for footing purposes because it is monomoraic.

9.3.3. Hearsay =*ca* and =*tim(dara/dooi)*
The modal marker =*ca* functions to mark hearsay evidence. This is the default form that attaches to each sentence-final finite verb when one narrates a folktale story.

(9–18) *piicja-gama*   *num-a-di=ca.*
        small-DIM   drink-THM-INT=HS
        '(This guy says) "I'll drink a little bit".'
(9–19) *vva=ga*   *ujaku-mmi=a*   *kuma-nagi=n*
        2SG=GEN   relative-PL=TOP   this.place-APPR=DAT
        u-tar=ca.
        exist-PST=HS
        'Your relatives used to live here, they say.'
(9–20) *tooriike=tii=du=i,*   *ssibara,*   *maibara,*
        Tooriike=QT=FOC=CNF   back   front
        satu+bžtu=nu   *a-tar=ca.*
        neighbour+man=NOM   exist-PST=HS
        'In Tooriike (Trans-pond), (there) were neighbours facing each other.' [In a folktale story]

Another hearsay discourse marker =*tim(dara/dooi)* has two variants,

=*timdara* and =*timdooi*. These are analysable into =*tim* + =*dara* (certainty modal marker) and =*tim* + =*dooi* (emphatic modal marker) respectively, but no other element can intervene between =*tim* and =*dara*/=*dooi*, and =*tim* cannot appear alone. In terms of function, =*tim* expresses a situation in which the hearsay part of a proposition [x] in [x]=*tim* is already well integrated into an established knowledge of the speaker (that is, it expresses 'it is said that [x] holds true, and I am well aware that [x] is true.'). Thus =*tim* has a strong assertive sense even if the statement is not first-hand, and is often used when a speaker uses a second-hand message in an act of persuasion, warning or caution.

(9–21) *junai=n*   *maar-i+u-tigaa,*   *mmja*
        night=DAT   wander-THM+PROG-CND   INTJ
        mazïmunu=nu   *fïï-Ø=timdara.*
        evil.spirit=NOM   come-NPST=HS
        '(People say) If (one) wanders around in the night time, an evil
        spirit will come.' [connotation: 'so you shouldn't do that']

(9–22) A. *kanu*   *sjuu=ja*   *sïn-ta-m=dooi.*
           that   old.man=TOP   die-PST-RLS=EMP
           'That old man has died.'
        B. *ai=timdara.*
           that.way=HS
           '(I have already heard) that.' [connotation: 'I am already
           aware of it.']

Thus =*tim* is different from =*ca* in that the latter simply expresses '[x] is a hearsay fact', which is the default interpretation *not* integrated into speaker's knowledge. By using =*ca*, the speaker is not taking responsibility for the hearsay fact. On the other hand, =*tim* strongly expresses the speaker's certainty about the validity of the hearsay report. This is why it is followed by =*dara* or =*dooi*, which encode certainty and emphasis respectively.

(9–23) a. *kari=a*   *pžtarrjam=timdooi.*
           3SG=TOP   lazy.man=HS
           'He is said to be a lazy man.' [connotation: 'I can bet it, so
           you should   believe me']
        b. *kari=a*   *pžtarrjam=ca.*
           3SG=TOP   lazy.man=HS
           'He is said to be a lazy man.' [speaker may or may not be sure
           of the hearsay fact]

300   Chapter 9

9.3.4. Uncertainty =pazï

The modal marker =pazï expresses more or less uncertainty on the part of
the speaker.

(9–24) *ffufïgii,*   *ui=ga=du*   *juu*   *mma-ka-tar.*
        k.o.plant   that=NOM=FOC   very   tasty-VLZ-PST
        uri=a   *nnama=mai*   *nar-i-i=du*
        that=TOP   now=too   grow-THM-NRT=FOC
        ur-Ø=pazï=dooi.
        PROG-NPST=maybe=EMP
        'Ffufïgii, that was very tasty. (Trees) may bear that (fruit) still
        now.'

(9–25) *ss-a-n-Ø.*   *nnama=gami=a*   *pžsara=pazï.*
        know-THM-NEG-NPST   now=EMP=TOP   Hirara=maybe
        'I don't know. By now (she has arrived in) Hirara.'

The modal marker =pazï was probably a formal noun (see §4.2.1), that
had the structure adnominal clause + =pazï where the once adnominal
clause is now treated as a main clause predicate, and the modal use of
=pazï has derived from this construction. This is based on the fact that
=pazï shows some synchronic peculiarities in comparison with other modal markers: it can be followed by a copula, as shown in (9–26) below:

(9–26) *mmna*   *kuu-n-Ø=pazï=du*
        everyone   come-NEG-NPST=should.be=FOC
        a-ta=iba=du,   *sauc=cu=mai*
        COP-PST=so.that=FOC   cleaning=ACC=even
        ah-u-da   *unumama-as-i+u-tar.*
        do-THM-NEG.NRT   situation.as.it.is-VLZ-THM+PROG-PST
        '(I) thought that no one would come (in all probability), so that
        (I) did not clean (my house) and left everything as it was.'

9.3.5. Addressive assertive =su(u)da

This section and the next three (§9.3.6, §9.3.7, §9.3.8) describe markers
that are semantically more like discourse markers than typical modal
markers described so far, as they do not simply express a speaker's attitude
toward a proposition, but are addressee-oriented in one way or another.
Among these markers, the modal marker =su(u)da shows relatively clear
modal meaning. It encodes the speaker's assertion that his/her statement is
true, but with request for the hearer's confirmation that his/her statement is

actually true.

(9–27) A. *gama=nu*   *mii=tii=ja*   *nau=ju=ga*
            cave=GEN   place.around=QT=TOP   what=ACC=FOC
            až-Ø=ga?
            say-NPST=Q
            'What does (one) mean by "*gamanu mii*"?' [speaker A is not
            sure of the expression *gamanu mii*, though she knows that
            this expression is used in Irabu]

       B. *gama=nu*   *mii?*   *nau=ga*   *gama=nu*
            cave=GEN   place.around   what=FOC   cave=GEN
            mii?
            place.around
            '*gamanu mii*? What the hell is *gamanu mii*?'

       A. *gama=nu*   *mii=n*
            cave=GEN   place.around=DAT
            usum-i-i=ti=du   *duu=ja*
            hide-THM-NRT=QT=FOC   1PL=TOP
            až-Ø-m=suuda.
            say-NPST-RLS=AD.ASR
            'We say like, "hiding in *gamanu mii*", don't we?'

The marker *=su(u)da* can be traced back historically to *=su(u)* (formal
noun 'man; thing'; §4.2.1.8) + *=da* '?'. This is evidenced in the characteristic morphophonemics of *=su(u)*: as in the case of *=su(u)*, the initial /s/ of
=su(u)da is subject to the morphophonemic progressive assimilation (//r//
+ //su(u)da// > /rru(u)da/):

(9–28)   *vva=mai*   *asï-tar=ruda.*
         2SG=too   do-PST=AD.ASR
         'You did (it), too, don't you?'

Synchronically, however, the marker *=su(u)da* always occurs as a unit, and
no other element can intervene between *su(u)* and *da*. If its historical source
construction was an adnominal clause structure, i.e. [adnominal clause] +
formal noun *su(u)*, the host verb of *=su(u)da* should be the finite unmarked
form. However, it also appears after other inflected forms (see (9–27)), indicating that *=su(u)da* is no longer treated as a formal noun that is modified by an adnominal clause. Thus I treat it as a single modal marker.

     The modal marker *=su(u)da* shows one syntactic peculiarity that is not

302   Chapter 9

observed in other modal markers presented so far: its syntactic host is an
NP, but it cannot phonologically be attached to the last word-plus of an NP,
and requires the copula verb (*jar* rather than *ar*, which is the allomorph that
appears only in non-main clauses) as its phonological host. This constraint
is understandable given that =*su(u)da* was a formal noun (+ =*da*): *=*su(u)*
was a formal noun that was modified by an adnominal clause, which must
end in a verb.

(9–29) *kari=a*   *daizïna*   *buuciri*   *jar-Ø=ruuda.*
        3SG=TOP   awful   mighty.person   COP-NPST=AD.ASR
        'He's an awful mighty person, isn't he?'

9.3.6. Certainty =*dara*

The marker =*dara* expresses a modal meaning roughly characterised as
certainty about the speaker's statement. It is like a discourse marker in that
it almost always appears in dialogue rather than in monologue, indicating
that it has an addressee-oriented function. Since it expresses the speaker's
certainty, =*dara* never occurs in questions, only in statements, and in those
discourses in which a speaker reports an event or state that is based on his/
her direct experience.

(9–30) *unu*   *nubir+zuu-gama,*   *ui=ga=du*   *juu*
        that   k.o.plant+plant-DIM   that=NOM=FOC   very
        a-tar=dara.
        exist-PST=CRTN
        'The *nubir* plant, (there) were a plenty of them.'

(9–31) *kan=nu*   *idi-i*   *cc-i-i,*   *junai=n=ni,*
        crab=NOM   exit-NRT   come-THM-NRT   night=DAT=CNF
        jur,   *jur=rju,*   *jur*   *cc-i-i,*
        night   night=EMP   night   come-THM-NRT
        sugu   *kasakasakasa=tii*   *as-Ø=siba=du,*
        EMP   ONM=QT   do-NPST=so=FOC
        utu=u   *cïk-i-i,*   *banti=a*
        sound=ACC   hear-THM-NRT   1PL=TOP
        cc-i-i,   *uri=u*   *tu-i+fau-tar=dara.*
        come-THM-NRT   that=ACC   take-THM+eat-PST=CRTN
        'Crabs come out (of their nests), in the night, in the night (they)
        come with some noise like "*kasakasakasa*", so (we) listen for
        the sound, and we come and catch-and-eat them.'

Bound markers   303

Structurally, =*dara* is in a paradigmatic relation to the modal markers reviewed so far, except for the assertive =*su(u)da,* which may follow =*dara.* Here, =*su(u)da* is realised as the irregular form =*ssuda.* Alternatively, =*darassuda* might be treated as a single modal marker encoding a very strong assertion and certainty.

(9–32)   A. *kari=a*   *daizïna*   *munu+ss-ja=dooi.*
             3SG=TOP   great   thing+know-NLZ=EMP
             'She is such a knowledgeable person'
       B. *ai=dara=ssuda.*
             that.way=CRTN=AD.ASR
             'Exactly.'

9.3.7. Emphatic =*doo(i)*

The modal marker =*doo(i)* is an emphatic marker.[1] The parenthesized /i/ is usually present, but it is not uncommon to find examples in which it is absent. It may be historically decomposed into =*doo* + =*i* (discourse marker: confirmative), given that in many neighbouring varieties of Miyako Ryukyuan only =*doo* is used in the contexts in which =*dooi* would be used in Irabu.[2] In Irabu, =*dooi* may be further followed by =*i*, thus the /i/ found in =*dooi* does not function as a discourse marker any more.

(9–33)   *vvadu=ga*   *patarak-i+a-i-ba=du*   *kjuu=ja*
          2PL=NOM   work-THM+RSL-THM-CSL=FOC   today=TOP
          irav=va   *ar-Ø=dooi=i.*
          Irabu=TOP   exist-NPST=EMP=CNF
          'Because you have worked, today('s society), (I mean) Irabu, exists, doesn't it?'

When the finite intentional -*di* and =*doo(i)* co-occur, the complex form often appears as a fused form -*ttuu(i)*, where /i/ of -*di* is deleted and the resulting /dd/ geminate becomes a voiceless /tt/. The complex form can be analysed as -*t=tuu(i)*, encoding an immediate future intention.

---

[1] There are other markers that pertain to emphasis (§9.3.8, §9.4.6, and §9.6.1). Except for the information-updater (§9.6.1), I admit that it is rather inappropriate to regard all of them as 'emphatic' markers if the description is to be more precise. However, I am not at this stage in the position to be clear enough to assign more precise terms and descriptions, due to lack of substantial data. It is thus an important research topic to refine my description of these particular markers.

[2] For example, in Hirara (Nakama 1992) the form corresponding to Irabu =*doo(i)* is =*doo*. In Ikema, =*dooi* is observed (this was pointed out by an anonymous reviewer).

304   Chapter 9

(9–34) *ba=a*   *par-a-t=tuu.*
        1SG=TOP   leave-THM-INT=EMP
        'I'll go (right now).'
(9–35) *kuma=n*   *nci-t=tuui.*
        this.place=DAT   put-INT=EMP
        'I'll put (this) here (right now).'

A finite realis verb form very often co-occurs with *=dooi*. The realis
mood encodes strong certainty on the part of speaker and always carries
new information to hearer (i.e. encodes assertion as opposed to presupposition; §10.5.1.1). That is, when the realis form is used, (the speaker assumes
that) the hearer has a wrong assumption about, or is unaware of the truth of
the statement that the speaker expresses, and therefore the speaker naturally puts contrastive emphasis on his/her statement.

(9–36) *mma+munu*   *a-ta-m=dooi.*
        tasty+thing   COP-PST-RLS=EMP
        '(It) was delicious.' [connotation: 'although you might doubt
        it']
(9–37) *hai!*   *uti-r-m=dooi!*
        INTJ   drop-NPST-RLS=EMP
        'Watch out! (The vase behind you) is gonna drop!'
(9–38) *uma=nu*   *in=na*   *fïï-Ø-m=dooi.*
        that.place=GEN   dog=TOP   bite-NPST-RLS=EMP
        'The dog there will bite (people).' [connotation: 'so you
        shouldn't go there']

9.3.8. Reserved emphatic *=saa*

The modal marker *=saa* functions as an emphatic marker which also expresses a degree of reserve. It is often used by female speakers, and is often followed by the confirmative marker *=i*. Unlike *=dooi* (§9.3.7), *=saa=i*
cannot be followed by another *=i*, so *=saa=i* cannot be treated as a single
morpheme.

(9–39) *jarabi=a*   *mmja*   *panas=su=baa*
        child=TOP   INTJ   talk=ACC=TOP
        cïk-a-n-Ø=saa=i.
        hear-THM-NEG-NPST=R.EMP=CNF
        'Children (tend not to) listen to other's talk, you know.'
(9–40) *aunazï-nagi=mai*   *u-ta=iba=i,*   *ukuu+uku=nu*

ratsnake-APPR=too	exist-PST=so=CNF	RED+big=GEN

aunazï-nagi=mai.   *mii-rai-n-Ø=saa.*
ratsnake-APPR=too   see-POT-NEG-NPST=R.EMP
'(In those days) (there) were ratsnakes, so, you know, very big
ratsnakes. (But now) (we) cannot see (them).'

9.4. Limiter markers

A limiter marker quantifies or qualifies (e.g. emphasises) its syntactic host,
which is either the argument or adjunct. I have identified five limiter markers that function exclusively as such, and two case markers that additionally serve as limiters: =*mai* 'too', =*tjaaki* 'only', =*bakaar* 'always', =*cumma*
'no', =*dumma* (emphasis), =*kara* 'primarily; to begin with' (or ablative
case), =*gami* (contrastive/limitative case).

(9–41)   *pai=kara=gami=du*   *nau=ju=mai*   *muc-i-i*
         field=ABL=CNT=FOC   what=ACC=too   carry-THM-NRT
         cc-i-i   *as-i-i*   *fau-tar.*
         come-THM-NRT   do-THM-NRT   eat-PST
         '(I would) bring whatever (I need) from my field, and cooked
         and ate.'

Limiter markers may occur in sequence, as in (9–42), where *zinan* 'the second eldest son' is a subject argument with ellipted nominative case, to
which =*gami* (contrastive) and =*mai* ('too') are attached in sequence. Note
that =*gami* does not function here as a limitative case marker which would
mark a peripheral argument meaning 'until; as far as'.

(9–42)   *kantja=a*   *hira*   *zinan=gami=mai*
         3PL=TOP   INTJ   second.eldest.son=CNT=too
         jakusjo   *ja-i-ba.*
         city.hall   COP-THM-CSL
         'They are... well, (in their house) the second eldest son, too,
         (works at) city hall, so...'

9.4.1. 'Too' quantifier =*mai*

The marker =*mai* is a quantifier encoding 'too, also'. As this label suggests, =*mai* denotes that [x] in [x]=*mai* is a member of a set of referents.
The following example illustrates a typical use of =*mai*.

306   Chapter 9

(9–43)   *turuna=mai*   *fïkuna=mai*   *nubir=mai*
         k.o.plant=too   k.o.plant=too   k.o.plant=too
         im=nu   *suu=mai*   *juu*   *fau-tar=ruga=du*
         sea=GEN   weed=too   very   eat-PST=but=FOC
         nnama=a   *maada=a*   *mii-n-Ø=ni.*
         now=TOP   very=TOP   see-NEG-NPST=CNF
         '(We) used to eat *Turna, Fïkuna, Nubir,* and seaweeds very
         much, but now (we) don't often see (these vegetables and sea-
         weeds), do we?'

The marker *=mai* has the meaning 'even if' when it is attached to a
non-finite clause. In particular, *=mai* often combines with causal converbal
clauses and narrative converb clauses. *=mai* has a reduced form *=m* when it
is attached to causal converbal clauses, as is shown in (9–45) below.

(9–44)   *vva=ga*   *ažž-a-ba=mai*   *cïk-a-n-Ø.*
         2SG=NOM   say-THM-CND=even   listen-THM-NEG-NPST
         'Even if you say, (he) won't listen.'
(9–45)   *uma=n*   *nci-ba=m*   *zjaubu=ju.*
         that.place=DAT   put-CSL=even   alright=EMP
         'Even if (you) put (it) there, (that'll be) alright.' [i.e. you can put
         it there.]
(9–46)   *ffa=nu*   *nak-i-i=mai*   *puka=nkai=ja*
         child=NOM   cry-THM-NRT=even   outside=ALL=TOP
         id-ah-ai-r-m=mu?
         exit-CAUS-POT-NPST-RLS=Q
         'Even if the child cries, could (you) back (it) off outside? (no,
         you couldn't)'

9.4.2. 'Only' quantifier *=tjaaki*
The marker *=tjaaki* is a restrictive quantifier encoding 'only'.

(9–47)   *uri=u=tjaaki=du*   *žž-tar=dooi.*
         3SG=ACC=only=FOC   scold-PST=EMP
         '(I) scolded him only.'
(9–48)   *vva=tjaaki=a*   *ifï-na.*
         2SG=only=TOP   go-PRH
         'You alone don't go.'

The positioning of *=tjaaki* and the case marker, which should in principle precede =tjaaki (as shown in (9–47) above) can be reversed. Such flexible ordering is not common in Irabu clitic chains, but the fact that it occurs demonstrates an important difference between a clitic chain and an affix chain, as the latter must always follow the specified ordering within the word domain (see also §3.2.1.2 for the reorderability of clitics and words as opposed to affixes).

(9–49) ui=tjaaki=u=du   žž-tar=dooi.
        3SG=only=ACC=FOC   scold-PST=EMP
        '(I) scolded only him.'

9.4.3. 'Only' quantifier 2: =bakaar

The 'only' quantifier 2 =bakaar encodes 'only', but unlike the other 'only' quantifier as noted in §9.4.2, =bakaar entails negative meaning associated with 'only', as in 'only *x* monotonously'.

(9–50) jana+cïmuc-cas-i-i=du
        bad+spirit-VLZ-THM-NRT=FOC
        ju-kar-a-n-Ø   kutu=u=bakaar
        good-VLZ-THM-NEG-NPST   thing=ACC=only
        kangai+u-tar=ca.
        think+PROG-PST=HS
        'Having a bad spirit, (he) was always thinking only of things that are not good.'

(9–51) kai=n=bakaar   ffa+mur-ja   as-ïmi-i,
        3SG=DAT=only   child+baby.sit-NLZ   do-CAUS-NRT
        mmja,   nara=a   asïb-i-i
        INTJ   oneself=TOP   play-THM-NRT
        maar-i+ur-Ø.
        wander-THM+PROG-NPST
        '(The mother) tells only her to baby-sit, while she herself is going outside to have fun.'

9.4.4. 'Nothing' quantifier =cumma

This marker always appears in a negative sentence and negates the value of the argument to which it attaches. The argument must be headed by an interrogative nominal such as *taru* 'who' and *nau* 'what' (but not *nausi* 'how' or *naiti* 'how; why', as they are not nominals). According to my text database, this argument is always a direct object.

308   Chapter 9

(9–52)   *taru=u=cumma*   *ss-a-n-Ø.*
          who=ACC=nothing   know-THM-NEG-NPST
          '(I) don't know anyone.'

(9–53)   *nau=ju=cumma*   *as-irai-n-Ø=munu.*
          what=ACC=nothing   do-POT-NEG-NPST=for
          'For (I) cannot do anything.'

9.4.5. 'Primarily' qualifier =*kara*

The ablative case marker =*kara* (§4.3.8) can additionally function as a limiter marker encoding primacy, i.e. 'primarily, first, to begin with'.

(9–54)   *ba=a*   *bitur-i-i=du*   *ur-Ø.*
          1SG=TOP   be.full-THM-NRT=FOC   PROG-NPST
          ui=n=kara   *fii-ru.*
          3SG=DAT=first   give-IMP
          'I'm full. Give him (the food) first.'

The marker =*kara* is often attached to a non-finite clause, in particular to a narrative converb clause. Since a narrative converb is neutral with regard to the perfective/imperfective aspect distinction in verb morphology, the attachment of =*kara* helps explicate the telicity of an action by denoting the meaning 'after (doing something)'. Thus in (9–55) below, the (a) example is ambiguous in terms of the perfective/imperfective distinction, allowing either interpretation, whereas the (b) example with =*kara* only allows Interpretation 2.[3]

(9–55)   a. *nuuma=n*   *nuur-i-i=du*   *par-tar.*
            horse=DAT   ride-THM-NRT=FOC   leave-PST
           'Riding a horse, (he) left.' [Interpretation 1: imperfective]
           'After riding a horse, (he) left.' [Interpretation 2: perfective]
      b. *nuuma=n*   *nuur-i-i=kara=du*   *par-tar.*
            horse=DAT   ride-THM-NRT=after=FOC   leave-PST
           'After riding a horse, (he) left.' [Only Interpretation 2]

9.4.6. Emphatic qualifier =*dumma*

The emphatic qualifier marker =*dumma* attaches to arguments, usually indicating emphasis'. When it is attached to a subject argument, it does not

---

[3] There are other morphosyntactic means to explicate the perfective/imperfective distinction, one of which is non-canonical object marking (see §4.3.3).

Bound markers 309

(9–56) *ban=dumma*   *iravcï=mai*
1SG=EMP   Irabu.language=even
ss-a-n-fï   *nar-i+u-i-ba...*
know-THM-NEG-AVLZ   become-THM+PROG-THM-CSL
'I myself am becoming influent in Irabu, so...'

(9–57) *aagu=u=dumma*   *ss-ai=du*   *sï-Ø.*
song=ACC=EMP   know-POT=FOC   do-NPST
'(This woman) knows songs, too.'

Though not common, =*dumma* may attach to a non-finite subordinate clause, in particular to a conditional converbal clause. Here, =*dumma* may entail a 'lest' or 'just in case' meaning, as shown in (9–59).

(9–58) *saki=u*   *num-tigaa=dumma,*   *mecjakucja*
Sake=ACC   drink-CND=EMP   badly
as-i+u-tar.
do-THM+PROG-PST
'When/if he drank Sake, (he) went crazy.'

(9–59) *ui=ga*   *fau-tigaa=dumma,*   *nci+uk-i.*
3SG=NOM   eat-CND=lest   put+PROS-IMP
'Lest that (guy) should eat, put (it) aside.'

9.4.7. Contrastive =*gami*

The limitative case marker =*gami* (§4.3.9) can additionally function as a limiter encoding contrast. When =*gami* and a topic marker co-occur, the argument modified is interpreted as contrastive topic ('with respect to X (as opposed to Y)').

(9–60) A: *vva=mai*   *saada=n=ru*   *u-tar?*
2SG=too   Sawada=DAT=FOC   exist-PST
'You, too, were in Sawada?'

      B: *ban=gami=a*   *nagahama=n=du*
1SG=CNT=TOP   Nagahama=DAT=FOC
cc-i+u-tar=dara.
come-THM+PROG-PST=EMP
'I (as opposed to the others) had come to Nagahama (by then).'

(9–61) *mmja*   *nau=ju=ga*   *fau-tar=gagara*

310 Chapter 9

INTJ	what=ACC=FOC	eat-PST=I.wonder
ai=mai	*ss-i+u-Ø-m=mu?*	
thay.way=even	know-THM+PROG-NPST-RLS=Q	
zin=nu	*ar-Ø*	*ujaki+munu-mmi=gami=a*
money=NOM	exist-NPST	rich+man-PL=CNT=TOP
nau=mai	*fa-i-Ø=du*	*ufi-Ø=suga*
what=even	eat-THM-NRT=FOC	PRF-NPST=but
banti=a	*kuu+munu-gama=du*	*a-ta=iba.*
1PL=TOP	poor+man-DIM=FOC	COP-PST=so

'Well, what would (they) eat, could I know even the way (they)
ate)? Rich men who have much money would eat whatever
(they want), but we were not wealthy men, so...'

When =*gami* and the focus marker co-occur, the argument/adjunct modified is interpreted as being contrastively focused ('It is A, not B, that...').

(9–62) *pav*   *ar-a-da,*   *par=gami=du*
        snake   COP-THM-NEG.NRT   needle=CNT=FOC
        jar-Ø.
        COP-NPST
        '(I did) not say *pav*, but *par*.'

Thus, Irabu has the syntagmatic arrangement of two information-structure
markers: contrastive and topic/focus. This is related to the two conspicuous
facts about topic marking and focus marking in this language.

With respect to topic marking, zero topic marking of arguments is extremely limited in Irabu. Consider the topic marking in Japanese for comparison. In Japanese, especially in colloquial Japanese, topical arguments
are very often left unmarked, as in *ano hito ii hito da=ne* (that person good
person COP=SFP) 'That guy is a good person, eh?'. If the argument underlined here is overtly marked by the topic marker =*wa*, then it tends to carry
the tone of contrastive topic. That is, in Japanese there is a paradigmatic
arrangement of topic and contrastive topic marking: zero (topic) vs. =*wa*
(contrastive topic). In Irabu, it is very rare for a topic NP to be left unmarked. In Irabu, there is a syntagmatic arrangement of topic and contrastive topic marking: =*a* (topic) vs. =*gami=a* (=CNT=TOP).

As for focus marking, it is noted that the focus marker =*du* is used for
any kind of focus (contrastive focus, argument focus, and sentence-focus).
This functional ambiguity leads to the syntagmatic arrangement of the contrastive marker =*gami* followed by the focus marker =*du* to mark contras-

Bound markers 311

tive focus. Thus, there are motivations for the dedicated contrastive marker =*gami* independent of the focus and topic markers.

The marker =*gami* may be attached to a (non-)finite adverbial clause. Also, it may be attached to the (first) lexical verb of a VP which has developed historically from a non-finite adsentential clause. All the known examples involve =*gami* followed by focus marker =*du*.

(9–63) *vva=ga*   *ažž-i-ba=gami=du,*
        2SG=NOM   say-THM-CSL=CNT=FOC
        nak-i+ur-Ø=dara.
        cry-THM+PROG-NPST=CRTN
        'Because you say (it), (this kid) is crying.'

(9–64) *akjaada*   *as-i+ur-Ø=kja=gami=du*
        merchant   do-THM+PROG-NPST=when=CNT=FOC
        umakuma   *maar-i+u-ta=iba*
        here.there   wander-THM+PROG-PST=so
        ss-i+u-tar.
        know-THM+PROG-PST
        'When (she) was doing a merchant, she visited here and there, so (I) knew (her).'

(9–65) *ba=a*   *uri=u=baa*   *ss-i-i=gami=du*
        1SG=TOP   that=ACC=TOP   know-THM-NRT=CNT=FOC
        ur-Ø!
        PROG-NPST
        'I know that!'

9.5. Information-structure markers

Irabu has a rich inventory of topic and focus markers. There are two topic markers: =*ba(a)* is object topic marker, i.e. it only co-occurs with a direct object argument, whereas =*a* is used in other environments. There are three focus markers, each associated with a different kind of speech act: =*du* (statement), =*ru* (Yes-No question), and =*ga* (information question). There are distributional constraints on topic and focus markers in terms of inter-clausal syntax (e.g. a topic/focus marker cannot appear in a subordinate clause but may appear in a coordinate clause), and these will be discussed in Chapter 11.

As noted in §4.3.10, nominative case marking (=*ga*/=*nu*) and topic marking (=*a*) are in paradigmatic relation, i.e. they cannot co-occur. This is illustrated in (9–66).

312   Chapter 9

(9–66)   *kari=a*   *sinsii=du*   *a-tar.*
         3SG=TOP   teacher=FOC   COP-PST
         'He was a teacher.' [subject]

Otherwise the case marker and the topic marker are simply juxtaposed, showing a syntagmatic relation, as shown in (9–67) to (9–69). The paradigmatic relation holds between nominative *case* and the topic marker, and is not explained in terms of subject *grammatical relation*. Thus, in (9–68), the subject carries the dative case marker *=n* followed by the topic marker *=a*, just as in (9–67) where the dative case marker marks indirect object.

(9–67)   *kai=n=na*   *fii-rna.*
         3SG=DAT=TOP   give-PRH
         'Don't give (it) to him.' [indirect object]
(9–68)   *kai=n=na*   *as-irai-n-Ø.*
         3SG=DAT=TOP   do-POT-NEG-NPST
         'He can't do (that).' [dative subject construction; §3.5.2]
(9–69)   *pisir=ru=baa*   *fau-ta-m=mu?*
         lunch=ACC=TOP   eat-PST-RLS=Q
         'Have you eaten lunch?' [lit. (As for) lunch, have you eaten (it)?]

9.5.1. Topic markers
9.5.1.1. Object topic *=ba(a)*
Object topic *=ba(a)* marks direct object arguments only, and follows the accusative case marker. The parenthesised /a/ is optional. Although *=ba(a)* may encode either a general topic or a contrastive topic, it frequently encodes a contrastive topic. The general topic function is exemplified in (9–70), whereas the contrastive topic function is exemplified in (9–71) and (9–72). In (9–70), a discourse is initiated by the speaker's statement, and the discourse that follows is about 'the thing (I) let (you) have yesterday'. On the other hand, in (9–71), 'songs' is what the discourse is about, but it is contrasted with 'folktale stories' in the previous discourse. The same argument can be applied to (9–72).

(9–70)   *cïnuu*   *mut-asï-tar*   *munu=u=baa*
         yesterday   have-CAUS-PST   thing=ACC=TOP
         fau-ta-m=mu?
         eat-PST-RLS=Q
         '(Did you) eat the thing that (I) let (you) have yesterday?' [gen-

eral topic]

(9–71) [Context: The speaker asks a woman whether she knows folk-tale stories, and she said No. Then the speaker asks another question as follows:]

vva=a   aagu=u=baa   ss-i-i=ru
2SG=TOP   song=ACC=TOP   know-THM-CHN=FOC
ur-Ø?
PROG-NPST
'Do you know songs, then (as opposed to folktales)?' [contrastive]

(9–72) A. ba=a   kuri=u=du   nuzum-Ø.
         1SG=TOP   3SG=ACC=FOC   like-NPST
         'I like this (one).' [in presence of a range of things for choice]

       B. mmja   kuri=u=baa=da?
          INTJ   this=ACC=TOP=how.about
          'Well, (don't you like) this (one)?' [suggesting another one]

9.5.1.2. Non-object topic =a

The non-object topic marker =a marks syntactic constituents other than direct object. It marks a general topic, and contrastive topic may be marked by the combination of the contrastive =gami (§9.4.7) and the general topic =a. A constituent thus marked is not necessarily the subject. 'Setting NPs', i.e. spatial and temporal sentential adjuncts which are inherently topic-worthy (Foley and Van Valin 1984), are usually topic-marked.

(9–73) macïnaka=n=na   saada+pžtu=mai
       Shimoji.Island=DAT=TOP   Sawada+man=too
       finnaka+pitu=mai   nza+pžtu=mai   u-ta-m.
       Kuninaka+man=too   where+man=too   exist-PST-RLS
       pai=nu=du   a-ta=iba.
       field=NOM=FOC   exist-PST=so
       'In Shimoji Island (there) were people from Sawada, and people from Kuninaka, and people from anywhere. For (there) were (their) fields.' [general topic]

(9–74) nkjaan=na   pžtu=nu   juu=du
       old.times=TOP   man=NOM   very=FOC
       u-tar=rju.
       exist-PST=EMP
       'In old times (there) were many people.' [general topic]

314 Chapter 9

(9–75) *uma=n*   *jamatu+pžtu=nu=du*
that.place=DAT   main.land.Japan+man=NOM=FOC
ur-Ø=dara.   *kari=a*   *uku+biki+nisjai=dooi.*
exist-NPST=EMP   3SG=TOP   big+male+adolescence=EMP
'In that place (there) is a Japanese mainlander. He is a tall young guy.' [general topic]

(9–76) *ba=a*   *nnama=kara*   *ik-i-i*   *sugu*
1SG=TOP   now=ABL   go-THM-CHN   now
kari=u=baa   *kurus-a-di.*
3SG=ACC=TOP   kill-THM-INT
'I will go now and kill him right away.' [general topic]

In a complex predicate phrase (§3.1.1), the (first) lexical verb or the predicate NP is marked by the non-object topic marker when the predicate is negated. In some cases this can be interpreted as contrastive topic, as shown in (9–77) below.

(9–77) A. *vva=a*   *nauti=ga*   *tur-i-i*   *fau-tar=ga?*
2SG=TOP   why=FOC   take-THM-NRT   eat-PST=Q
'Why did you take and eat (that)?'

B. *fa-i-i=ja*   *ur-a-n-Ø=dooi.*
eat-THM-NRT=TOP   PROG-THM-NEG-NPST=EMP
'I didn't eat.' [lit. with respect to eating that, I didn't do it (though I took that); contrastive]

However, topic marking in negation is obligatory. It is ungrammatical for the topic marking to be absent, as in (9–78c) and (9–79c).

(9–78) a. *ba=a*   *bitur-i-i=du*   *ur-Ø.*
1SG=TOP   get.full-THM-NRT=FOC   PROG-NPST
'I am full.'

b. *ba=a*   *bitur-i-i=ja*
1SG=TOP   get.full-THM-NRT=TOP
ur-a-n-Ø.
PROG-THM-NEG-NPST
'I am not full.'

*c. *ba=a*   *bitur-i-i*   *ur-a-n-Ø.*
1SG=TOP   get.full-THM-NRT   PROG-THM-NEG-NPST
'I am not full.'

(9–79) a. *ba=a*   *sinsii=du*   *a-tar.*

Bound markers 315

      1SG=TOP   teacher=FOC   COP-PST
      'I was a teacher.'
  b. *ba=a*   *sinsii=ja*   *ar-a-t-tar.*
      1SG=TOP   teacher=TOP   COP-THM-NEG-PST
      'I was not a teacher.'
*c. *ba=a*   *sinsii*   *ar-a-t-tar.*
      1SG=TOP   teacher   COP-THM-NEG-PST
      'I was not a teacher.'

Thus topic marking in negative constructions no longer has a (contrastive) topic marking function. Rather it seems to provide double marking of negation both on the lexical part of a phrase and on the grammatical part (i.e. the auxiliary verb or the copula verb). I gloss such a use of topic marker as TOP, but it should be noted that it is not really 'topic'.

9.5.2. Focus markers

Irabu has a rich inventory of focus markers which are used depending on the sentence type: declarative focus =*du*, interrogative focus (=*ru* for yes-no, =*ga* for content questions).

9.5.2.1. Declarative focus =*du*

The declarative focus marker is =*du*. It only occurs in statements, not in questions or requests. The following elicited examples illustrate how =*du* can mark each of the arguments in an extended transitive clause which contains three (extended) core arguments plus a peripheral argument (instrumental). In (9–80) to (9–83) =*du* is added to a subject, instrument, goal and direct object argument, respectively :

(9–80) *agu=nu=du*   *sokutacï=sii*   *ucïnaa=nkai*
        friend=NOM=FOC   express=INST   Okinawa=ALL
        nimuc=cu   *ufïï-tar.*
        parcel=ACC   send-PST
        '(My) FRIEND sent a parcel to Okinawa by express.'
(9–81) *agu=nu*   *sokutacï=sii=du*   *ucïnaa=nkai*
        friend=NOM   express=INST=FOC   Okinawa=ALL
        nimuc=cu   *ufïï-tar.*
        parcel=ACC   send-PST
        '(My friend) sent a parcel to Okinawa BY EXPRESS.'
(9–82) *agu=nu*   *sokutacï=sii*   *ucïnaa=nkai=du*
        friend=NOM   express=INST   Okinawa=ALL=FOC

316 Chapter 9

nimuc=cu   *ufïï-tar.*
parcel=ACC   send-PST
'(My friend) sent a parcel TO OKINAWA by express.'

(9–83)   *agu=nu*   *sokutacï=sii*   *ucïnaa=nkai*
          friend=NOM   express=INST   Okinawa=ALL
          nimuc=cu=du   *ufïï-tar.*
          parcel=ACC=FOC   send-PST
          '(My friend) sent a PARCEL to Okinawa by express.'

9.5.2.2. Interrogative focus *=ru* and *=ga*

Interrogative focus is marked by *=ru* in yes-no questions and by *=ga* in information questions. Focus markers *=ru* and *=ga* are thus in effect question markers as well. Indeed, *=ru* and *=ga* may be 'double-marked', i.e. may redundantly appear twice, once on a focused constituent, and once on a sentence-final word-plus.

TABLE 9–1. Focus marking and speech act type (in simple sentences)

Form	*=du*	*=ru*	*=ga*
Speech act	Statement	Yes-No question	Information question
Double-marking	NO	YES	YES

(9–84)   *uri=u=ru*   *fau-tar(=ru)?*
          that=ACC=FOC   eat-PST(=Q)
          'Did (you) eat that?'

(9–85)   *nau=ju=ga*   *fau-tar(=ga)?*
          what=ACC=FOC   eat-PST(=Q)
          'What did you eat?'

As the examples below illustrate, I treat the double-marked sentence-final marker as a homophonous question marker (glossed as =Q) rather than a 'copied' focus marker. I do this because sentence-final *=ru*, but not focus-marking *=ru*, undergoes assimilation, whereby the initial //r// alternates with /m/ or /n/ if it is attached to a word-plus ending in /m/ or /n/ respectively.

(9–86)   *u-Ø-m=mu*   *mii-n-Ø=nu*
          exist-NPST-RLS=Q   see-NEG-NPST=Q
          ss-a-n-Ø.
          know-THM-NEG-NPST
          '(I) don't know (whether) (the person) is alive or not.'

Bound markers   317

This allomorphy is not observed in =*ru* functioning as a focus marker even
when the morphophonological environment is identical:

(9–87)   *uri=a*   *kam=ru*   *a-tar=ru?*
         3SG=TOP   god=FOC   COP-PST=Q
         'Was he a god?' [**kam=mu*]
(9–88)   *gama=nu*   *mii=n=ru*   *u-tar?*
         cave=GEN   inside=DAT=FOC   exist-PST
         '(Were they) inside of the cave?' [**mii=n=nu*]

The focus marker =*ru* or =*ga* marks a sentence as interrogative, and the
sentence-final question marker is redundant and may be omitted (as in (9–
89)). On the other hand, if there is no focus marker present, then the sentence-final question marker is the sole means of marking interrogative.
Such a situation occurs in yes-no questions.

(9–89)   *vva=a*   *pisir=ru=baa*   *fau-ta-m=mu?*
         2SG=TOP   lunch=ACC=TOP   eat-PST-RLS=Q
         'Have you eaten lunch?'

The question marker here might alternatively be analysed as a focus marker that focuses a predicate since the speaker's yes-no question asks whether
the addressee has eaten lunch or not. However, this would require us to admit a structural asymmetry between the declarative focus marker =*du* and
the interrogative marker =*ru*. As was noted in §9.1.2.4, =*du* never has
scope over an entire predicate even when the predicate as a whole is within
the focus domain, and there are a number of restrictions concerning the
predicate focus marking. By the same token I assume that =*ru* here does
not mark the predicate as being in focus.

9.6. Discourse markers

9.6.1. Information-updater =*ju(u)*
The information-updating discourse marker =*ju(u)*, where the bracketed /u/
is optionally deleted, has two related functions. It indicates that the clause
to which the marker is attached has a high information value in the sense
that the message encoded has a certain portion that contradicts the hearer's
assumption, or that the hearer failed to know. It often carries the tone of a
speaker's exasperation, especially if the wrong assumption or lack of the
knowledge on the part of the hearer comes from the hearer's responsibility.

318 Chapter 9

In (9–90), the speaker assumes that the hearer thinks that that guy arrived a while ago, and wants to correct the knowledge by using the information-updater =*ju*. If =*ju* is absent in the sentence, there is no such an implication, simply conveing the message 'that guy arrived just now'.

(9–90)　*uri=a*　　　　*nnama=du*　　*cïfï-tar=rju.*
　　　　3SG=TOP　　　now=FOC　　arrive-PST=UPDT
　　　　'That (guy) arrived just now.'

In (9–91), the speaker uses =*ju* since s/he believes the hearer to have a (wrong) assumption that 'this place' is not noisy and people can sleep well.

(9–91)　*kuma=a*　　　　*mmja*　　*ati*　　*ngjamasï-ka-i-ba,*
　　　　this.place=TOP　INTJ　　very　　noisy-VLZ-THM-CSL
　　　　nivv-ai-n-Ø=njuu!
　　　　sleep-POT-NEG-NPST=UPDT
　　　　'Because this place is very noisy, (I) cannot sleep!'

A similar example follows, where speaker B corrects speaker A's wrong understanding of what people are supposed to do with the 'water of luck'.

(9–92)　A. *karjuu=nu*　　*mizï=tii=ja*　　　*nausi=ga*　　*asï-Ø?*
　　　　　　luck=GEN　　　water=QT=TOP　　how=FOC　　do-NPST
　　　　　　uri=u=baa　　　　*ami-r?*
　　　　　　that=ACC=TOP　　　get.submerged-NPST
　　　　　　'What do you do with the water of luck (a bucket of holy
　　　　　　water)? Do you get submerged with it?'
　　　　B. *aran=dooi!*　　*zau=n*　　　*nci-kutu=ju!*
　　　　　　NEG=EMP　　　gate=DAT　　put-OBL=UPDT
　　　　　　'No way! (One is supposed to) put (it) at (one's) gate.'

In the following example, =*ju* is attached to a sentence which is a repeated message of speaker A. It is used since the message not only carries new information but is regarded by the speaker as something that the herarer should have received in the first dialogue.

(9–93)　A. *kuri=a*　　　　*nagahama+pžtu=ca.*
　　　　　　3SG=TOP　　　Nagahama+man=HS
　　　　　　'This (guy) is from Nagahama, according to him.'
　　　　B. *nau?*

Bound markers   319

what

'What?'

A. *gui!*   *nagahama+pžtu=juu!*

INTJ   Nagahama+man=UPDT

'Come on! (I said he's from) Nagahama!'

9.6.2. 'How about' =da

The discourse marker =*da* attaches to a topic-marked NP, functioning to present a new topic with the meaning 'how/what about [NP]?'

(9–94)   *kuma=a=da?*

        this.place=TOP=how.about

        'How about this place?'

The NP may be a clausal complement, as in (9–95).

(9–95)   A.   *akaudi=nu*   *mm=mai*   *pur-Ø,*

              premature=GEN   potato=too   dig-NPST

              nubir-zuu=ju   *pžk-i-i*

              Nubir-plant=ACC   pull.out-THM-NRT

              cc-i-i,   *nii+fau-Ø.*

              come-THM-NRT   boil+eat-NPST

              '(We) would dig early potatoes, pull and bring (home) *Nubir* plants, then boil and eat them.'

      B.   *mata*   *kaa=nkai*   *mizï*

              and   water.well=ALL   water

              fim-Ø=ma=da?

              get-NPST=TOP=how.about

              'And what about (going) to the well and getting water?'

Also, the topic marker must be the object topic marker =*ba(a)* if the NP functions as object of an (ellipted) predicate, as in (9–96).

(9–96)   *kuri=u=baa=da?*

        this=ACC=TOP=how.about

        'How about (doing) this?'

9.6.3. Confirmative =i

The confirmative discourse marker =*i* is similar to English tag marker 'eh?' in its basic function, requesting confirmation of what speaker says. How-

320   Chapter 9

ever, unlike 'eh?', =*i* may appear in a self-question, and may scope over almost any constituent of a clause, occurring iteratively in one utterance, which secures a constant attention and responsiveness on the part of the hearer.

(9–97)   *vva=ga*   *pataracï=dara=i?*
         2SG=GEN   work=CRTN=CNF
         '(That's) your work, eh?'

(9–98)   *nau=nu=ga*   *ur-Ø=gagara=i?*
         what=NOM=FOC   exist-NPST=CNF
         '(I wonder) what is there?' [self question]

(9–99)   *nkjaan=du=ca,*   *njkaan=du=i,*
         old.times=FOC=HS   old.times=FOC=CNF
         kam=nu=i,   *doobuc=cu=i,*
         god=NOM=CNF   animal=ACC=CNF
         icïmus=su=i,   *mmna*   *kam=nu*   *mai=n*
         living.thing=ACC=CNF   all   god=GEN   front=DAT
         zaa=nkai   *acïmar-Ø*   *tukja=nu*
         throne=ALL   gather-NPST   time=NOM
         a-tar=ca.
         exist-PST=HS
         'Once upon a time, (there) was a time when a god (ordered) animals, living things, all of them, (to) gather in front of his throne.'

9.6.4. Emotional =*ra(a)*, =*sja(a)*

The emotional discourse markers add a negative emotional nuance to the utterance, especially expressing such emotions as anger, feeling upset, and irritation. There is a clear distributional pattern whereby =*ra(a)* mostly appears in imperative clauses, whereas =*sja(a)* mostly appears in interrogative clauses.

(9–100) *vva=ga=du=ra*   *nara-as-i.*
         2SG=NOM=FOC=EMO   learn-CAUS-IMP
         'You teach (him).' [with an implication that the speaker feels unhappy about being asked to teach (him) a story]

(9–101) *ažž-i-i*   *mii-ru=raa!*
         say-THM-NRT   EXP-IMP=EMO
         'Just try speaking!'

(9–102) *agaii!*   *nau=ga=sja?!*

INTJ   what=FOC=EMO
'Shit! What the hell (are you saying)?!'

(9–103) *taru=ga=sjaa*   *vva=u*   *nuzum-Ø=ga?!*
         who=FOC=EMO   2SG=ACC   like-NPST=Q
         'Who ever would like you?!' [rhetorical question]

9.6.5. Question *=ru/=ga*

As described in §9.5.2.2, there are two question markers whose choice depends on the choice of focus marker with the focus marker that appears
within the same clause. Thus in a yes-no question sentence the question
marker is *=ru* (*=nu* or *=mu* depending on the final phoneme of the host; see
§9.5.2.2), whereas in an information question sentence it is *=ga*.

9.6.6. Question 2 *=e(e)*

The question marker *=e(e)* marks a yes-no question sentence, attaching to
any constituent that is utterance-final. While the short *=e* is always a distinct syllable nucleus optionally inducing the geminate copy insertion rule,
as in (9–104a), the long *=ee* may become the nucleus of a syllable in which
the final consonant of the preceding constituent is the onset, as in (9–105a),
optionally inducing an irregular resyllabification process and fused morphology, as in (9–105b).

(9–104) a. *vva=ga*   *cïfïï-tar=re?*
            2SG=NOM   make-PST=Q
            '(Did) you make (this)?' [/cï.fïï.tar.re/ CV.CVV.CVC.CV]
         b. *nau=sii=e?*
            what=INST=Q
            'By what (instrument do you make this)?' [/nau.sii.e/ CVV.
            CVV.V]

(9–105) a. *vva=ga*
            2SG=NOM
            cïfïï-tar=ee?
            make-PST=Q [/cï.fïï.ta.ree/ CV.CVV.CV.CVV]
         b. *nau=sjee?*
            what=INST.Q [/nau.sjee/ CVV.CGVV]

It is very difficult to analyse the functional difference between *=e* and
the question marker that was described in the preceding section, and this is
a future research topic. At this stage, it can be said that *=e* often carries emphasis:

322   Chapter 9

(9–106)   A. *nanahjakuman-en=timdooi.*
              seventy.thousand-yen=HS
              '(He earns) seventy thousand yen, I heard.'
          B. *ui=ga*   *uu-sa=e!?*
              that.way=GEN   many-NLZ=Q
              'That much!?'

Structurally it is easy to tell the difference, as *=e* never occurs with a focus marker, whereas *=ru/=ga* may do so, showing a formal concordance
with the focus marker within the clause.

Chapter 10

The simple sentence

In this chapter I describe various functional-typological phenomena centring on the simple sentence, many of which are morphosyntactically expressed across the different structures that have been described so far. These are: (1) major speech-act-related clause types (declarative, interrogative, and imperative), (2) expressions of proper inclusion, equation, state, location, and possession, (3) negation, (4) valency changing, and (5) tense-aspect-mood systems.

10.1. Speech acts and clause types

As summarised in TABLE 10–1, there are three clause types that are grammaticalised for three major speech acts, i.e. statement, question, and command (Lyons 1977; Givón 1984). The encoding devices are intonation, verb morphology, and focus marking.

TABLE 10–1. Speech act and focus marking

Speech act	Clause type	Focus marking	Verb inflection
STATEMENT	Declarative	=du	− Imperative
QUESTION	Interrogative	=ru (Yes-No type)	− Imperative
		=ga (Information type)	− Imperative
COMMAND	Imperative	None	+ Imperative

There are also mismatches between clause type and speech act, e.g. the interrogative clause type may express a (polite) command. These are described in §10.1.4.

10.1.1. Declarative clauses

A declarative clause may be syntactically distinguished from an interrogative clause by the choice of focus marker if a focus marker is present. The focus marker for declaratives is =du, as opposed to =ru or =ga for interrogatives.

(10–1)   *mm=mu=du*   *fau-tar.*

potato=ACC=FOC   eat-PST
'(I) ate potato.' [Declarative]

(10–2) *mm=mu=ru*   *fau-tar?*
potato=ACC=FOC   eat-PST
'Did (you) eat potato?' [Yes-No interrogative]

(10–3) *nau=ju=ga*   *fau-tar?*
what=ACC=FOC   eat-PST
'What did (you) eat?' [Wh-interrogative]

There is a prosodic feature that distinguishes declaratives from interrogatives and imperatives. In declarative clauses the prosodic pattern generated by the alternating rhythm (§2.9.3) is directly manifested:

(10–4) *vva=a*   *uri=u=mai*   *nii+ur-Ø*
2SG=TOP   that=ACC=too   boil+PROG-NPST
(vvaa)$_H$ (urir)$_H$ (mai)$_L$ (nii)$_H$ (ur)$_L$
'You are boiling that, too.' [Declarative]

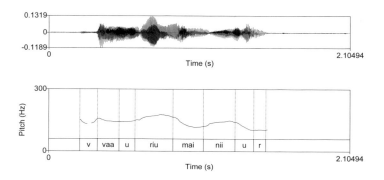

Interrogative clauses often carry a rising terminal contour superimposed on the rhythmic pattern. In (10–5) and in (10–6) the rising contour occurs somewhere around the final mora of the sentence-final word(-plus).[1]

(10–5) *vva=a*   *uri=u=mai*   *nii+ur-Ø?*
2SG=TOP   that=ACC=too   boil+PROG-NPST
'Are you boiling that, too?' [Interrogative: final rising contour]

---

[1] The pitch tracks here were extracted from the speech of a native speaker of Irabu (male, age = 67 in 2006), and processed with the software application *Praat*.

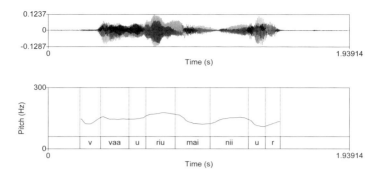

Note that in (10–6) below the word-plus ends in the question marker, and the rising contour occurs on the question marker rather than on the verb (as in (10–5)).

(10–6) *vva=a   uri=u=mai   nii+ur-Ø=ru?*
       2SG=TOP   that=ACC=too   boil+PROG-NPST=Q
       'Are you boiling that, too?' [Interrogative (with question marker): final rising contour]

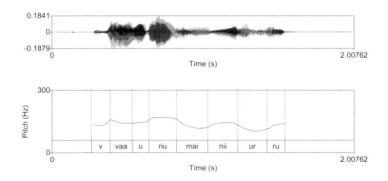

An imperative clause does not have the final rising contour observed in interrogative clauses. However, the final L-toned foot in imperatives is pronounced with a slightly higher and flatter contour than in declaratives.

(10–7) *vva=a   uri=u=mai   nii+ur-i.*
       2SG=TOP   that=ACC=too   boil+PROG-IMP
       'Keep boiling that, too.'

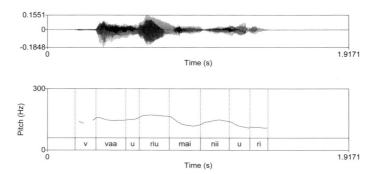

10.1.2. Interrogative clauses

An interrogative clause may be marked by focus marking on a clausal element (i.e. an argument, a VP complement, or an adjunct) and/or question marking on the clause-final word(-plus). There is no obligatory fronting of the interrogative word.

There are two subtypes of interrogative clause: Yes-No and Wh. An interrogative word (such as *taru* 'who') is obligatory in Wh interrogatives. In Yes-No interrogative clauses, the focus marker is =*ru*, as shown in (10–8) below, while in Wh interrogative clauses it is =*ga*, as is shown in (10–9). As illustrated in these examples, when a focus marker is present, a question marker is optional, and its form is identical to that of the focus marker in the same clause.

(10–8) *vva=ga=ru*   *uri=u*   *až-tar(=ru)?*
        2SG=NOM=FOC   that=ACC   say-PST(=Q)
        'Did you say that?'

(10–9) *vva=a*   *nau=ju=ga*   *až-tar(=ga)?*
        2SG=TOP   what=ACC=FOC   say-PST(=Q)
        'What did you say?'

As noted in §9.5.2.2, I treat these two (i.e. the focus marker and the question marker) as different morphemes based on the fact that the two forms show different allomorphic patterns, even though the focus marker may be the historical source of the question marker.

As is shown in (10–10), when a clause has no focus marker the question marker alone appears. This is the case in the yes-no type.

(10–10) *vva=a*   *uri=u*   *až-tar=ru?*
        2SG=TOP   that=ACC   say-PST=Q

The simple sentence   327

'Did you say that?'

10.1.3. Imperative clauses
An imperative clause is morphologically marked by the finite imperative
inflection (§6.3.1). The prohibitive is also a type of imperative, a negative
imperative.

(10–11)   a. *uma=n*   *bizi-ru.*
             that.place=DAT   sit-IMP
             'Sit there.'
          b. *uma=n=na*   *bizi-rna.*
             that.place=DAT=TOP   sit-PRH
             'Don't sit there.'

An imperative clause cannot co-occur with focus marking. Thus in the
examples of imperatives below, no focus marker appears in the sentence,
even where focus falls intonationally on a certain element in the sentence
(underlined).

(10–12)   *kai=ga*   *panasï*   *ar-a-da,*
          3SG=GEN   talk   COP-THM-NEG.NRT
          nnama=a   *ba=ga*   *panas=su*   *cïk-i.*
          now=TOP   1SG=GEN   talk=ACC   hear-IMP
          '(Do) not (listen to) his talk, now listen to my talk.'
(10–13)   *kui*   *ar-a-da,*   *uri=u*   *misi-ru.*
          3SG   COP-THM-NEG.NRT   3SG=ACC   show-IMP
          '(Do) not (show) this, show that.'

10.1.4. Mismatches or ambiguous cases
10.1.4.1. Polite command
An interrogative clause may function pragmatically as a polite command.

(10–14)   *zin=nu*   *kar-as-i-i*
          money=ACC   borrow-CAUS-THM-NRT
          fii-djaan=nu?
          BEN-NEG.INT=Q
          'Wouldn't you let me borrow money?

10.1.4.2. Rhetorical question
An interrogative clause may function pragmatically as a rhetorical ques-

328   Chapter 10

tion, which does not serve as a question but as a negative statement. In such cases, there is no rising contour characteristic of interrogative sentences.

(10–15)   *ba=a*   *ss-i+u-Ø-m=mu.*
          1SG=TOP   know-THM+PROG-NPST-RLS=Q
          'I don't know.' [lit. Would I know?]

A frequent use of rhetorical questions is one salient characteristic of Irabu discourse. In fact, rhetorical force is apparently very weak in most of the rhetorical questions (thus (10–15) above can be simply interpreted as 'I don't know', rather than the pragmatically highly rhetorical counterpart '(How) would I know?'). A similar example follows, where the speech of B is simply a response to that of A, with no special rhetorical force.

(10–16)   A. *ssagi=u=ba*   *ah-u-t-ta-m?*
              wedding=ACC=TOP   do-THM-NEG-PST-RLS
              '(Did you) not do a wedding?'
          B. *asï-Ø-m=mu.*
              do-NPST-RLS=Q
              'No, I didn't.' [lit. 'Would I do (that?)']

The use of rhetorical questions seems to be a mark of sophisticated speech style, and is particularly characteristic of older female speakers' speech.

The finite realis form (§6.3.1) is very often used as a predicate form of rhetorical questions, as illustrated in (10–15) and (10–16) above. We will return to this use of the finite realis form in §10.5.1.1.

10.1.4.3. Self question and clause types
A self question is formally marked by the modal marker *=bjaam* 'I wonder if...' (§9.3.1) or *=gagara* 'I wonder how/what/who...' (§9.3.2). A self question exhibits an intermediate characteristic between a question and a statement. On the one hand, it is not like a statement, in that it questions a proposition. On the other, it is not like a question in the sense of the act of requesting a verbal response, as it lacks an addressee. This intermediate status is reflected in the fact that a self question with the marker *=bjaam* (not *=gagara*) is encoded either by the declarative clause type or the interrogative clause type, in terms of focus marking. Thus in the following pair of examples, both (a) and (b) are equally possible.

The simple sentence   329

(10–17)   a.   *kanu*   *sjuu=ga=ru*   *asï-tar=bjaam=mi.*
             that   old.man=NOM=FOC   do-PST=I.wonder=CNF
             'I wonder if that old man did (it)...' [Interrogative sentence]
       b.   *kanu*   *sjuu=ga=du*   *asï-tar=bjaam=mi.*
             that   old.man=NOM=FOC   do-PST=I.wonder=CNF
             'I wonder if that old man did (it)...' [Declarative sentence]

10.2. Proper inclusion, equation, state, location, and possession

In this section I describe how proper inclusion (e.g. 'he is a student'), equation ('he is my father'), state (including property; 'he is tired'; 'he is tall'), location ('he is in school'), and possession ('he has a brother') are encoded. There is good reason to deal with these in the same section, as they are encoded in a similar or an identical way, as will be shown below.

10.2.1. Proper inclusion

Proper inclusion is encoded by either (a) a nominal predicate or (b) a verbal predicate where the predicate verb is the light verb *(a)sï* 'do' and the theme is encoded as an NP marked by the partitive. Examples (10–18) and (10–19) illustrate (a). Examples (10–20) to (10–22) illustrate (b).

(10–18)   *vva=a*   *jamatu+pžtu=ru?*
           2SG=TOP   mainland.Japan+man=Q
           'Are you a Japanese mainlander?'
(10–19)   *ba=a*   *zjunsja=du*   *a-ta=iba=du=i,*
           1SG=TOP   policeman=FOC   COP-PST=so=FOC=CNF
           mmna   *ss-i+ur-Ø.*   *banu=u=baa.*
           all   know-THM+PROG-NPST   1SG=ACC=TOP
           'I was a policeman, so, you know, everyone knows me.'
(10–20)   *agu=u*   *s-i-i,*   *umissi-ka-ta-m.*
           song=PRT   do-THM-NRT   fun-VLZ-PST-RLS
           'Being friends (each other), (everyday) was fun.' [lit. Doing friends...]
(10–21)   *biki+nisjai=ja*   *s-i-i,*
           male+young.man=PRT   do-THM-NRT
           umakuma   *maar-i+u-tar.*
           here.and.there   wander-THM+PROG-PST
           'Being a young man, (he) visited various places.'
(10–22)   *banti=ga*   *jarabi=a*   *s-i+ur-Ø=kjaa,*
           1PL=NOM   child=PRT   do-THM+PROG-NPST=when

330   Chapter 10

> *mmja,*   *eiga=mai*   *terebi=mai*
> INTJ   movie=even   television=even
> *njaa-ttar=ruda.*
> not.exist-PST=AD.ASR
> 'When I was a child, (there) was no movie (theatre), no TV,
> you know.' [lit. when I was doing a child...]

Note that in (10–20) and (10–21) the light verb heads a chained clause.
Also, in (10–22), the compound verb *siur* can be rearranged as a narrative
converb + an auxiliary (word-phrase alternation; §6.4.2.3), and the narrative converb in such a complex VP structure is historically derived from
the clause-chaining construction. Thus, all the examples of the light verb
construction encoding proper inclusion are (related to) a clause chaining
construction, which is the most typical environment for the partitive to occur (§4.3.3.1). The question raised here is whether the NPs marked by partitive case above are direct object NPs, as in the case of *tunuka-gama* in
(10–23) below. The NP in (10–23) satisfies one of the two criteria for direct object, i.e. (A) ability to be passivised, and (B) ability to be marked by
a special topic marker *=ba(a)* (§3.4.2). It can be marked by the object topic
marker *=ba(a)* (whereby partitive is replaced by accusative, as shown in
(10–23b)):

(10–23)   a. *tunuka-gama=a*   *nas-i-i...*
              egg-DIM=PRT   give.birth.to-THM-NRT
              'Giving birth to eggs...'
           b. *tunuka-gama=u=baa*   *nas-i-i...*
              egg-DIM=ACC=TOP   give.birth.to-THM-NRT
              'Giving birth to eggs...'

However, the NPs marked by the partitive in the light verb construction
do not satisfy either of the criteria for direct object. Thus, the NP marked
by the partitive in the light verb construction may be undergoing (or have
undergone) a diachronic reanalysis in which the NP is becoming less and
less like a direct object, and more and more like a predicate complement,
i.e. the complement of the light verb.

10.2.2. Equation

An equational expression is only encoded by a nominal predicate. Thus, in
Irabu one cannot say 'He is doing my father', meaning 'He is my father',
even when one can say 'He is doing a teacher' (as noted in §10.2.1.).

The simple sentence   331

(10–24) *kari=a*   *ba=ga*   *uja.*
         3SG=TOP   1SG=GEN   father
         'He is my father.'

(10–25) *kanu*   *sïma=a*   *ikima+zïma*   *jar-Ø=ruda.*
         that   island=TOP   Ikema+island   COP-NPST=AD.ASR
         'That island is Ikema Island.'

10.2.3. State

A state (including a property) is encoded by either a nominal predicate or a verbal predicate.

A property may be encoded by a PC stem (§8.1), from which an adjective, a (dummy) compound noun, a verb, or an adverb is derived.

(10–26) *ba=a*   *sabicïï+sabicï=du*   *a-tar.*
         1SG=TOP   RED+lonely=FOC   COP-PST
         'I was lonely.' [adjective]

(10–27) *sïdasï+kazi=nu=du*   *fïk-i+ur-Ø=ri?*
         cool+wind=NOM=FOC   blow-THM+PROG-NPST=CNF
         'A cool wind is blowing, eh?' [compound noun]

(10–28) *agaii=ti,*   *daizïna*   *pukarasï+munu=i=ti,*
         INTJ=QT   great   happy(+thing)=CNF=QT
         ai=du   *asï-Ø.*
         that.way=FOC   do-NPST
         '(I said) "Oh, (how) happy (I am)!", (I) did (i.e. said) like that.'
         [dummy compound noun]

(10–29) *kuma=ga=du*   *zau-kar-Ø.*
         this.place=NOM=FOC   good-VLZ-NPST
         'This place is good.' [verb]

(10–30) *jagami*   *uturusï-fï=du*   *ar-Ø=ri?*
         very   fearsome-AVLZ=FOC   be-NPST=CNF
         '(That) is very fearsome, eh?' [adverb]

Dynamic verbs may express states with the support of the progressive auxiliary (see §10.5.2.1 for progressive aspect), as illustrated in (10–31), or with non-finite inflections (§6.3.2) that encode states, such as simultaneous and circumstantial converb inflections, as illustrated in (10–32), and circumstantial converb inflection, as illustrated in (10–33). For narrative converbs, which do not morphologically mark the distinction between sequential (perfective) and non-sequential/descriptive (stative) functions, the presence of the partitive on the direct object NP in a narrative converbal

332   Chapter 10

clause is one indicator of stativity (§4.3.3.1).

(10–31)   *uku+gui=ja*   *s-i-i=du,*   *nnama=gami=a*
            big+voice=PRT   do-THM-NRT=FOC   now=EMP=TOP
            žž-i-i=du   *ur-Ø=pazï.*
            scold-THM-NRT=FOC   PROG-NPST=maybe
            'With the big voice, (I infer that he) is scolding (his child), perhaps.'

(10–32)   *cïcï-ccjaaki,*   *niniv=va*   *as-i+ur-Ø.*
            hear-SIM   snooze=PRT   do-THM+PROG-NPST
            'While listening, (she) is snoozing.'

(10–33)   *umac=cu*   *tacïgi-utui=du=i,*
            fire=ACC   burn-CRCM=FOC=CNF
            kam+nigai=mai   *asï-Ø.*
            god+prayer=too   do-NPST
            'Burning fire, (the shamans) do their prayers to gods.'

(10–34)   *miz=za*   *num-i-i=du*
            water=PRT   drink-THM-NRT=FOC
            juku-i+ur-Ø.
            take.rest-THM+PROG-NPST
            'Drinking water, (he) is taking rest.'

10.2.4. Location

A locational expression is encoded by a verbal predicate in which the lexical verb is an existential verb, and the location is encoded by a locative NP (which is dative-marked). Note that the verb form is either *ur* (for an animate subject) or *ar* (for an inanimate subject), and that the negative form of *ar* is the suppletive form *njaan* (§6.3.6.1).

(10–35)   *kanu*   *pžtu=u*   *mmja*   *nagoja=n=du*   *ur-Ø.*
            that   man=TOP   INTJ   Nagoya=DAT=FOC   exist-NPST
            'That person is, well, in Nagoya.' [animate subject NP]

(10–36)   *banti=ga*   *sïma=n=na*   *žžu=mai*   *kan=mai*
            1SG=GEN   island=DAT=TOP   fish=too   crab=too
            pinza=tii=mai   *juu*   *ur-Ø=ruga,*
            goat=QT=too   very   exist-NPST=but
            waa=mai,   *mmja,*   *mata*   *nau=nu=ga*
            pig=too   INTJ   and   what=NOM=FOC
            ur-Ø=gagara=i.
            exist-NPST=I.wonder=CNF

The simple sentence   333

'In our island, (there are) plenty of fish, crabs, goats, and so on, (and) pigs, too, and, well, what else is (there)?' [animate subject NP]

(10–37) *kama=nu*   *kujagaa-nagi=n*   *purkaa=nu,*
         that.place=GEN   Kuyagaa-APPR=DAT   well=NOM
         uku+purkaa=nu=du   *a-ta=iba=du...*
         big+well=NOM=FOC   exist-PST=so=FOC
         '(There) was a well, a big well around Kuyagaa (place name), so...'

As is shown in the following dialogue, in a series of conventionalised expressions such as (a) 'where do you live?' and the response to it, as in (b) 'I live in ....', the expression of (b) frequently involves the ellipsis of the existential verb.

(10–38) a. *vva=a*   *nza=n=ga*   *ur-Ø?*
             2SG=TOP   where=DAT=FOC   exist-NPST
             'Where are you (living)?'
         b. *ba=a*   *finnaka=n=du.*
             1SG=TOP   Kuninaka=DAT=FOC
             'I (live) in Kuninaka.'

10.2.5. Possession

A possessive expression ('I have a car') may be encoded by the existential verb construction that was described in §10.2.4. Thus Irabu demonstrates a cross-linguistically common isomorphism of existential, locative, and possessive expressions (Clark 1978). There are two major points to note with regard to existential expressions that are used to encode possession.

First, whether a possessive expression or a 'have' expression is chosen to express the existential verb construction depends on the relative animacy of the possessor and the possessed. In general, if both the possessor and the possessed are equal in animacy (e.g. both are humans, both are non-humans), the existential construction is used. For example, as illustrated in (10–39) below, such an expression as 'this house has big windows' is encoded literally as 'big windows exist in this house', using the existential pattern, since both the possessor and the possessed are non-humans. Likewise, when both the possessor and the possessed are humans, the existential pattern is used, and the existential verb must be *ur* rather than *ar* (10–40).

334   Chapter 10

(10–39)   *kunu   jaa=ja   ukuu+uku=nu   madu=nu=du*
          this   house=TOP   RED+big=GEN   window=NOM=FOC
          ar-Ø.
          exist-NPST
          'This house has big windows.' [lit. Big windows exist in this
          house.]

(10–40)   *ba=a   kjavdai=nu   tavkjaa   ur-Ø.*
          1SG=TOP   sibling=NOM   one.person   exist-NPST
          'I have one sibling.' [lit. One sibling is at me.]

The subject NP is directly followed by a topic marker. This occurs when
nominative case is replaced by a topic marker (§4.3.10).

In general, if the possessor is higher in animacy, one can use either a
'have' verb, such as *muc-* 'have' and *cïkana-* 'have (a domestic animal)', or
the existential expression, as shown in (10–41), but the choice also depends on the semantic type of the possessed. For example, abstract nouns
such as *taja* 'strength' cannot co-occur with a 'have' verb, but always require the existential verb (10–42).

(10–41)   a. *vvadu=u   jaa=ju=baa*
              2PL=TOP   house=ACC=TOP
              muc-i+ur-Ø=ru?
              have-THM+PROG-NPST=Q
              'Do you have a house?'
          b. *vvadu=u   jaa=ja   ar-i-i=ru   ur-Ø?*
              2PL=TOP   house=TOP   exist-THM-NRT   PROG-NPST
              'Do you have a house?' [lit. With respect to you, is there a
              house?]

(10–42)   *kari=a   taja=nu=du   ar-Ø.*
          3SG=TOP   strength=NOM=FOC   exist-NPST
          'He has strength.' [i.e. He is strong.]

The second major point about a possessive expression encoded by the
existential verb construction concerns subjecthood. The possessor NP can
be regarded as a subject since it triggers honorification and controls a reflexive pronoun (§3.4.1).

(10–43)   *sjuuganas=sa*   *umukutu=nu*   *ar-i-i*
          grandfather=TOP   wisdom=NOM   exist-THM-NRT
          Possessor   Possessed

The simple sentence 335

ur-ama-r.
PROG-HON-NPST
'Grandfather has wisdom.' [possessor as a trigger of honorification]

(10–44)   *kari=a*   *uja=kara*   *iži-tar*
         3SG$_i$=TOP   father=ABL   be.given-PST
         Possessor
         naa=ga   *pataki=nu=du*   *ar-Ø.*
         RFL$_i$=GEN   field=NOM=FOC   exist-NPST
                      Possessed
'He$_i$ has his$_i$ own field inherited from his father.' [possessor as a reflexive controler]

However, there are two qualifications that should be noted. First, whereas in an ordinary existential verb construction (as in locational expressions) the verb form is sensitive to the animacy of the subject NP, in the existential verb construction encoding a possessive expression the verb form is determined by the animacy of the possessed rather than the possessor, which indicates that the possessed takes on a subject property in this respect. For example, in (10–43) the existential verb form is *ar* (for an inanimate subject), even when the subject is animate. Second, the possessed nominal is marked by nominative, which is typically associated with a subject. The possessor NP is topic-marked, or may additionally be marked by dative, even though the syntactic test reveals that it is subject.

Thus it seems that a prototype approach better captures subjecthood in the existential verb construction here. For example, if we consider subject to be a grammatical relation that exhibits a cluster of several properties such as (1) reflexive control, (2) triggering of honorification, (3) the NP whose animacy determines the form of an existential verb, (4) morphological case marking as nominative, and (5) semantic status as an actor (i.e. potential initiator and/or controller of the action of the predicate; Foley and Van Valin 1984: 29), the possessed NP has two of them, i.e. (3) and (4), whereas the possessor has three of them, i.e. (1), (2), and (5). In this grammar, I have suggested a discrete and definitional view of subject in Irabu (§3.4.1), but there exist problematic cases, as shown here. In the discrete view, the possessed NP in the examples above is a non-subject NP (which cannot be characterised neatly), but in a prototype approach, it is a deficient subject NP, satisfying (3) and (4) above.

Interestingly, if the existential verb is negated, the possessed is marked by the partitive, a non-canonical direct object marker (§4.3.3.1).

336   Chapter 10

(10–45)   *ba=a*   *zin=na*   *njaa-n-Ø.*
                1SG=TOP   money=PRT   not.exist-NPST
                'I have no money'

(10–46)   *kuri=a*   *kan=na*   *njaan=ssiba,*   *nau=mai*
                3SG=TOP   sense=PRT   not.exist=so   what=even
                as-irai-n-Ø.
                do-POT-NEG-NPST
                'This (guy) has no good sense (i.e. is not ready-witted), so cannot do anything.'

However, the possessed NP cannot be justified as a direct object either, as it does not satisfy any of the criteria for direct object (i.e. an ability to be marked by object topic *=ba(a)*, or to be passivised; §3.4.2). Here, if we resort to a prototype approach, as in the case of subject, we can suggest several properties that characterise direct object: (1) an ability to be passivised, (2) an ability to be marked by *=ba(a)*, (3) an ability to be marked by accusative, and (4) semantic status as an undergoer (which does not perform, initiate, or control any situation but rather is affected by it in some way; Foley and Van Valin 1984: 29). The possessed NP shares (4) with (prototypical) direct objects. It is thus possible to analyse the possessed NP here as a grammatical role somewhere between a subject and a direct object NP, showing some subject properties and one direct object property.

10.3. Negation

Negation is encoded morphologically, lexically, or analytically, of which the first strategy is the most regularly employed in a wide range of predicates.

10.3.1. Inflectional negation

Inflectional negation uses the negative inflectional suffixes *-n, -ttar, -ttam, -djaan, -rna, -da,* and so on (§6.3.1, §6.3.2). Most verbs, without respect to whether the verb is a lexical verb or an auxiliary, are negated with this strategy, including copula verbs (§6.3.6.2). The exceptions to this are few and are noted in the following sections.

(10–47)   a. *ba=a*   *unu*   *midum=mu=du*   *nuzum-Ø.*
                  1SG=TOP   that   woman=ACC=FOC   want-NPST
                  'I want that woman.' [affirmative]
        b. *ba=a*   *unu*   *midum=mu=baa*

The simple sentence   337

                1SG=TOP   that   woman=ACC=TOP

                nuzum-a-n-Ø.

                want-THM-NEG-NPST

                'I don't want that woman.' [negative]

(10–48)   a. *ba=a*   *batafïsar-i-i=du*   *ur-Ø.*

                1SG=TOP   get.angry-THM-NRT=FOC   PROG-NPST

                'I am angry.' [affirmative]

          b. *ba=a*   *batafïsar-i-i=ja*

                1SG=TOP   get.angry-THM-NRT=TOP

                ur-a-n-Ø.

                PROG-THM-NEG-NPST

                'I am not angry.' [negative]

(10–49)   a. *ba=a*   *jamatu+pžtu.*

                1SG=TOP   mainland.Japan+man

                'I am a Japanese mainlander.' [affirmative]

          b. *ba=a*   *jamatu+pžtu=u*

                1SG=TOP   mainland.Japan+man=TOP

                ar-a-n-Ø.

                COP-THM-NEG-NPST

                'I am not a Japanese mainlander.' [negative]

10.3.2. Negation of existential and state verbs

The existential verb *ar* (for inanimate subject) and the state verb *ar* are negated by the lexical negative verb *njaan*.[2]

(10–50)   a. *uma=n*   *nagaa+naga=nu*   *bau=nu=du*

                that.place=DAT   RED+long=GEN   stick=NOM=FOC

                ar-Ø.

                exist-NPST

                '(There) is a long stick there.' [existential; affirmative]

          b. *uma=n=na*   *nagaa+naga=nu*   *bau=ja*

                that.place=DAT=TOP   RED+long=GEN   stick=TOP

                njaa-n-Ø.

                NEG-NPST

                '(There) is not a long stick there.' [negative]

(10–51)   a. *kari=a*   *aparagi-fï=du*   *ar-Ø.*

                3SG=TOP   handsome-AVLZ=FOC   be-NPST

                'He is (in a) handsome (state).' [state; affirmative]

---

[2] See §6.3.6 for the distinction between the existential verb and the state verb.

b. *kari=a*   *aparagi-f=fa*   *njaa-n-Ø.*
3SG=TOP   handsome-AVLZ=TOP   NEG-NPST
'He is not (in a) handsome (state).' [affirmative]

10.3.3. Negation of PC verb

A PC verb (§8.3.3) may be negated either inflectionally or analytically. The analytic negation consists of a PC adverb and the negative form of the state verb *ar*.

(10–52)   a. *ssu-kar-Ø.*
white-VLZ-NPST
'(That) is white.' [affirmative: stative]
b. *ssu-kar-a-n-Ø.*
white-VLZ-THM-NEG-NPST
'(That) does not become whitened'. [negative: dynamic]
c. *ssu-f=fa*   *njaa-n-Ø.*
white-AVLZ=TOP   NEG-NPST
'That is not white. [negative: stative]

As noted in §8.3.3.2, when a PC verb is inflectionally negated (with the same negative affix that is used for an ordinary verb), the negative form designates dynamic negation rather than stative negation.

10.4. Valency changing

In this section, I describe the ways in which semantic valence (which concerns the semantic arguments of the verb, or 'participants') and syntactic valence (which concerns core arguments, i.e. S/A and O) are (re-) arranged (see §3.5.1 for the notions of syntactic and semantic valence). In this valency changing process, an E argument, or a dative-marked argument that contributes to the semantic valence but does not contribute to the syntactic valence (§3.5.3), is also relevant, as the rearranged (demoted) core argument or a newly introduced participant may be encoded as an E argument.

Valency changing includes three morphological operations and one syntactic operation. The morphological operations are passive, causative, and malefactive. The syntactic operation is reflexive. There are also pairs of verb roots that contrast in inchoative versus causative meanings (e.g. *mui-* 'burn (intr)' vs. *muusï-* 'burn (tr)'), with no derivational relationship between the two, and these are noted in the section of causative.

10.4.1. Causative
10.4.1.1. Morphological causative

The morphological causative derives an (extended) transitive clause by the addition of a causative suffix (either *-asï* or *-sïmi*, depending on the class of the verb stem to which the causative suffix attaches; see §6.4.1.1).

(10–53) a. Class 1 *fii-* 'give'   > *fii-sïmi* 'make/let give'
                     mii- 'look'   > *mii-sïmi* 'make/let see'
                     idi- 'go out' > *idi-sïmi* 'make/let go out'
         b. Class 2 *fa-* 'eat'   > *fa-asï* 'make/let eat'
                     jum- 'read'   > *jum-asï* 'make/let read'
                     tur- 'take'   > *tur-asï* 'make/let take'

In terms of semantic valence, the morphological causative adds a causer to the existing proposition. In terms of syntactic valence, the causer is assigned the subject (S/A) status. If the underived clause is intransitive, the original agent, or the causee in the causative clause, is encoded either as a direct object (as in (10–54a)) or as an E argument (as in (10–54b)), depending on the degree of control of the causer over the causee. If the underived clause is transitive (as in (10–54c)) the causee is encoded regularly as an E argument, and the patient in the underived clause remains a direct object in the causativised clause.

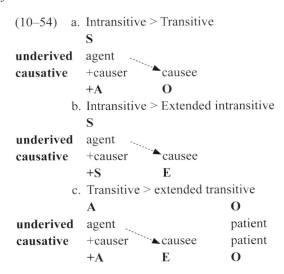

In the following pair of examples, the (a) example is an underived intransitive clause, from which the causativised transitive clause (b) is de-

340   Chapter 10

rived, illustrating (10–54a).

(10–55)   a. *ffa=nu*   *nafï-tar.*
             child=NOM   cry-PST
             'A child cried.' [underived]
          b. *uja=ga=du*   *ffa=u*   *nak-asï-tar.*
             father=NOM=FOC   child=ACC   cry-CAUS-PST
             'The father made the child cry.' [causative]

When the underived clause is intransitive, this type of causativisation is
typical. However, there is another type of causativisation, as schematised
in (10–54b) above, where the causee is encoded as an E argument. This is
illustrated in (10–56) below (the E argument is underlined).

(10–56)   *uja=a*   *tuu=ju*   *simi-i=du,*   *nara=a*
             father=TOP   door=ACC   shut-NRT=FOC   RFL=TOP
             puka=nkai   *ik-i-i,*   *ffa=n*
             outside=ALL   go-THM-NRT   child=DAT
             nak-asï-tar=ca.
             cry-CAUS-PST=HS
             'The father shut the door, and went outside, letting <u>the child
             cry</u> (without feeling ashamed).'

The semantic difference between (10–55b) and (10–56) is as follows.
Whereas in (10–55b) the causer has full control over the causee (i.e. the
causee is construed as a patient), in (10–56) the causer lets the causee cry,
thus the causee still exhibits an agentive characteristic.
    In the following pair of examples, the causative derivation is from a
transitive (a) to an extended transitive (b), illustrating (10–54c) above.

(10–57)   a. *unu*   *siitu=u*   *hon=nu=du*   *jum-tar.*
             that   pupil=TOP   book=ACC=FOC   read-PST
             'That pupil read a book.' [underived]
          b. *sinsii=ga*   *unu*   *siitu=n*   *hon=nu=du*
             teacher=NOM   that   pupil=DAT   book=ACC=FOC
             jum-asï-tar.
             read-CAUS-PST
             'The teacher had the pupil read the book.' [causative]

There are indications that a lexical extended transitive verb such as *fiir*

The simple sentence 341

'give' and *ufïï* 'send' cannot derive a causative, which would require four semantic and syntactic arguments. In free texts, such examples did not occur. In elicitation, some speakers did construct a four-place predicate clause with the instrumental NP encoding the causee, as shown in the (b) example below, derived from (a).

(10–58) a. *uttu=nu*   *uja=n*   *nimuc=cu=du*
younger.sibling=NOM   father=DAT   letter=ACC=FOC
ufïï-tar
send-PST
'The younger sibling sent the parcel to his/her father.'

     b. *ani=nu*   <u>*uttu=sii*</u>   *uja=n*
elder.sister=NOM   younger.sibling=INST   father=DAT
nimuc=cu=du   *uff-asï-tar.*
parcel=ACC=FOC   send-CAUS-PST
'The elder sister ordered <u>(her) younger sibling</u> to send the parcel to (their) father.'

However, a much more preferred alternative, according to the consultant who constructed this example, is to use either (a) a non-causative clause, or (b) an analytic expression:

(10–59) a. *ani=nu*   *uttu=sii*   *uja=n*
elder.sister=NOM   younger.sibling=INST   father=DAT
nimuc=cu=du   *ufïï-tar.*
parcel=ACC=FOC   send-PST
'The elder sister sent the parcel to (their) father by way of her younger sibling.' [cf. (10–58b)]

     b. *ani=nu*   *uttu=nkai*   *uja=n*
elder.sister=NOM   younger.sibling=ALL   father=DAT
nimuc=cu   *uff-i=ti=du*   *až-tar.*
parcel=ACC   send-IMP=QT=FOC   say-PST
'The elder sister said, "You send the parcel to daddy".'

Note that in (10–59a) the verb *ufïï-tar* does not carry the causative suffix *-as*. The causative meaning is inferred from the statement that the elder sister sent the parcel by way of the younger sibling, where the actual carrier is the younger sibling. In (10–59b), there are two verbs, one (*až-tar* 'said') governing the causer *ani* and the message quoted by *=ti* (*uja=n nimuc=cu uff-i* 'You send the parcel to daddy'), and the other (*uff-i* 'You

342   Chapter 10

send') governing the recipient *uja* and the gift *nimucï*.

In either example, burdening the verb *ufï* with the fourth argument, i.e.
the causer, is avoided. This means that Irabu verbs (like those in most
known languages) can govern up to three arguments, and thus no causative
derivation is possible from extended transitive verbs, as the introduced
causer cannot be governed by the verb that is already 'full'. This is why the
causee in (10–58b) is encoded by a peripheral argument (the instrumental
NP), which is not governed by (i.e. not part of the argument structure of)
the verb. The situation in (10–58b) is schematised as follows.

(10–60)   Extended transitive > Extended transitive + peripheral argu-
          ment

	A		E	O
underived	agent		recipient	patient
causative	+causer	╲ causee	recipient	patient
	+A	**peripheral**	E	O

Here, the causee occupies the lowest position of the hierarchy [A > O > E >
peripheral] that is not filled. This bears out Comrie's (1975) hierarchical
coding pattern of the original S/A in causatives (subject > direct object >
indirect object > oblique).

10.4.1.2. Lexical intransitive-transitive pairs
There are a small number of pairs of verbs where each pair consists of an
intransitive non-causative form (with an inchoative meaning), e.g. *idi-* 'go
out', and a transitive causative form, e.g. *idasï-* 'extract', sharing some part
of the root. If the other parts that differ (e.g. *idi̱-* vs. *idasï̱-*) could be analysed as inchoative and causative affixes respectively, these pairs of verbs
could be referred to as non-directed, equipollent alternations (i.e. there is
no basic-derived relationship) in terms of Haspelmath's (1993) typology of
causatives. However, since it is not possible to extract a single set of morphemes that express causation and inchoation, and since these pairs are
very limited in number and not productively created, I describe each verb
form simply as a a single root rather than a root + a causative suffix or a
root + an inchoative suffix. Below, the dot '.' is meant just to suggest a possible morpheme boundary in terms of the causative-inchoative contrast.

(10–61)   Inchoative   Causative
          id.i- 'go out'   vs.   *id.asï-* 'extract'
          maa.r- 'round'   vs.   *maa.sï-* 'round' [round something]

kak.ar- 'hang'	vs.	*kak.ir-* 'hang'
mu.i- 'burn'	vs.	*mu.usï-* 'burn'

The inchoative verbs here may also be causativised by the regular morphological means described in §10.4.1.1:

(10–62)	*idi-* 'go out'	>	*idi-sïmi* 'make/let go out'
	maar- 'round'	>	*maar-asï* 'make/let round'
	kakar- 'hang'	>	*kakar-asï* 'make/let hang'
	mui- 'burn'	>	*mui-sïmi* 'make/let burn'

The difference between the lexically causative forms of (10–61) and the morphologically derived causative forms of (10–62) is that with the former the causer has full control over the causee, a contrast also shown in an O argument vs an E argument in (10–54a–b). This difference in the degree of control shows up as a different arrangement of case for the causee. In (10–63) below, where the verb stem is a lexical causative form, the causee is encoded as an O argument (with accusative):

(10–63)	*kari=u*	*(isï=n*	*nuusi-i=du)*	*maasï-tar.*
	3SG=ACC	(chair=DAT	lift-NRT=FOC)	turn.round-PST
	'(I) turned round <u>him/her</u> (by lifting him/her on the chair).'			

In (10–64) below, on the other hand, the verb is morphologically causativised, and the causee is encoded as an E argument, deriving an extended intransitive clause.

(10–64)	*kai=n*	*(unagaduu=sii)*	*maar-asï-tar.*
	3SG=DAT	(oneself=INST)	round-CAUS-PST
	'(I) let <u>him/her</u> round (by him/herself)'		

10.4.1.3. Anticausative

The anticausative derives an inchoative verb (e.g. '(something spontaneously) break') from an underived causative verb that implies external causation (e.g. '(someone) break (something)') (Nedjalkov and Sil'nickij 1969; Haspelmath 1993: 91; Dixon and Aikhenvald 2000: 7–8). The derived anticausative form always implies a spontaneous event, and thus never allows a syntactic marking of an agent.

In Irabu, anticausative is not productive, and is strictly limited to a certain set of verbs. Even though it is possible to isolate an anticausative suf-

344   Chapter 10

fix -*i* (as is clear from the examples below), the suffix has no productivity
and shows some semantic irregularity.[3] I describe the putative anticausativ-
ised forms as roots rather than derived forms which is why I indicate the
possible morpheme boundary by a dot '.' rather than a hyphen '-'.

(10–65)   Inchoative verb   Anticausative verb
           bur- 'break (a stick, etc.)'   *bur.i-* 'break'
           bar- 'break (a glass, etc.)'   *bar.i-* 'break'
           tur- 'take (off)'   *tur.i-* 'get apart'

In the example below, the pair of *bur-* 'break' (inchoative) and *buri-* 'break'
(causative) is illustrated. Note that the former is a Class 2 verb, whereas the
latter is a Class 1 verb, which is reflected in the difference in the form of
the non-past unmarked suffix (§6.3.1).

(10–66)   a. *kii=nu*   *juda=u=du*   *bur-Ø.*
              tree=GEN   branch=ACC=FOC   break-NPST
              '(I) break a branch of a tree.'
           b. *kii=nu*   *juda=nu=du*   *buri-r.*
              tree=GEN   branch=NOM=FOC   break-NPST
              'A branch of a tree breaks.'

10.4.2. Passive

The passive derives an (extended) intransitive clause from a transitive clause
with the passive suffix -*(r)ai* (§6.4.1.2). The semantic valence of the verb remains the same, i.e. a passive agent is always implied, resulting in the semantic effect that the event is brought about by some external causer (see more
discussion below). In terms of syntactic valence, the passive agent NP is demoted, either by deletion (resulting in an intransitive clause) or to an E argument (resulting in an extended intransitive clause). The syntactic inclusion of
the agent depends on to what degree the agent is important in discourse.

(10–67)   Transitive > (extended) intransitive

	O	A
underived	patient	agent
passive	patient	(agent)
	S	(E)

---

[3] For example, it is possible to find such pairs as *rr-* 'enter' (inchoative) and *rri-* 'enter' (causative), where we see the opposite function of -*i*, deriving a causative form from an inchoative
form.

The simple sentence   345

In example (10–68) below the passive agent is not present, as the specification of the agent is not important in the discourse context.

(10–68) *katabata=a*   *fa-ai-i,*
         half.body=TOP   eat-PASS-NRT
         katabata=a   *jaa=nu*   *pana=n*
         half.body=TOP   house=GEN   roof=DAT
         nuus-irai+u-i-ba,   *nara=n=na*
         lift-PASS+PROG-THM-CSL   RFL=DAT=TOP
         kuu-rai-n-Ø.
         come-POT-NEG-NPST
         'A half of my body was eaten, and the other half of my body
         has been lifted on the roof of a house, so I cannot come
         (back).'

The part of the discourse from which the example was extracted is about a mermaid who was caught by two fishermen (i.e. the agents of the events described by the passivised clauses) and a god who wants to get her back to the sea world. The example is uttered by the mermaid, directed to the god, explaining her *current situation* from which she cannot come back to the sea world. (In this part and in the rest of the story the fishermen are not mentioned.)

Even though the specification of agent is pragmatically unimportant in the passive above, the event described here is not a spontaneous one, i.e. there is 'external causation' in the event described (Amberber 2000: 315). Thus it is easy to insert an agent NP in these examples, say, *pžtu=n* 'by a man'. This potentially added NP is regularly marked by dative case, thus we can refer to such an agent NP as an E argument. This semantic characteristic of passive is in sharp contrast to, say, the anticausative (§10.4.1.3) where an action occurs spontaneously and no agent is implied (thus the agent never appears as an NP). The anticausative is a clear example of the reduction of semantic valence, but the passive in Irabu does not reduce semantic valence.[4]

---

[4] This is a characteristic of Irabu that is distinct from Modern Japanese, where there are passives (in addition to the Irabu type passive) that decrease the semantic valency by not entailing the existence of an external causer. For example, in Modern Japanese we have such an example as *kikakukaigi no ato, ikutuka no aidea ga tamesareta* 'After the planning meeting, several ideas were tested.' Here, no external causer is implied, and it is difficult to add an appropriate agent NP to this sentence. In pre-Modern Japanese, however, most of the passive examples functioned to highlight a patient that is affected by an external causer, just like the passive in Irabu (Shiba 2005; Seino and Tanaka 2006: 326). Shiba states that in this latter

346   Chapter 10

One important characteristic of the patient NP is that it is in most cases a
human, who is either a speaker or an entity with whom the speaker feels
some 'empathy' (Kuno and Kaburaki 1977). Thus, the passive is likely to
take on a negative meaning in that the patient that the speaker feels empathy with is affected by the action of an external causer (that is, the proposition in which A acts on B is described like '*My* B is affected (by A)'). In the
example below, the passive subject has a third person referent, which is the
speaker's father, who is affected by the action of taking him away for the
defence army (against his and the speaker's will). The event is thus described with a negative meaning.

(10–69)   *banti=ga*   *uja=a*   *mmja*   *booeitai=nkai=ti*
          1PL=GEN   father=TOP   INTJ   defence.army=ALL=QT
          tur-ai-ta=iba.
          take-PASS-PST=so
          'Our father was taken (from us) for the defence army.'

In free texts it is possible to find cases where the passive subject is non-human, but such examples are not common, and the subjects were in most
cases seen as being possessed or related to the speaker in some way or another. One good example is (10–68) above where the subject in each passive clause is a body part of the speaker. Thus the relation 'My B is affected (by A)' holds true. Another example of non-human subject is as follows.

(10–70)   *pinza=u=du*   *cïkana-i+u-tar=ruga,*   *mmja,*
          goat=ACC=FOC   have-THM+PROG-PST=but   INTJ
          ba=ga   *ucïnaa=nkai*   *ik-i-i,*   *mata*
          1SG=NOM   Okinawa=ALL   go-THM-NRT   and
          mudur-i-i   *t-tar=dara.*   *assiba=du*

---

kind of passive, semantic valence remains the same, as the same event is described from the
perspective of the patient (see also Seino and Tanaka 2006).
    In other valency changing phenomena, such as applicative or applicative-like phenomena
(such as 'Ivan sowed wheat in the field' vs 'Ivan sowed the field with wheat'), it is often
pointed out that the number and the kind of semantic roles of the underived and the derived
verbs remain the same (which is to say, the semantic valency remains the same), though the
sentential meaning may be different, e.g. with respect to affectedness of the patient (Comrie
1985b: 314). In Comrie's terms, such valency changing processes are 'valency rearrangement' rather than 'valency decrease', and in the former, he notes that 'the rearrangement of
the arguments does entail differences in which arguments can optionally be omitted'.
    The passive of Irabu and in pre-Modern Japanese are thus a valency rearrangement opera-
tion, and the Modern Japanese passive may additionally function as a valency decrease operation.

The simple sentence 347

return-THM-NRT   come-PST=CRTN   so=FOC

uri=a   *mmja*   *kurus-ai-i...*

3SG=TOP   INTJ   kill-PASS-NRT

'(I) had a goat; I went to Okinawa and returned; and it had been killed...'

Though agentless passives are common, it is also common to find both in texts and in elicited data cases where the agent is explicitly stated with dative case, i.e. as an E argument. Interestingly, in elicitation, many speakers created a sentence with an agent when they were asked to create a passive clause without being provided any context, as illustrated in (10–71) and (10–72) below.

(10–71)   *uja=n*   *žž-ai-i=bakaar*

           parent=DAT   scold-PASS-NRT=only

           ur-Ø=ri=ti.

           PROG-NPST=CNF=QT

           '(I would say like) (You) are always scolded by (your) parents.'

(10–72)   *pžtu=n*   *mii-rai-rna.*

           man=DAT   look-PASS-PRH

           'Don't be witnessed (found out) by (any)one.'

10.4.3. Malefactive

Malefactivisation is a derivational process that uses the passive morphology (*-(r)ai* on the verb stem), but is distinct from passivisation in that it changes valency. However, certain semantic-pragmatic characteristics are shared between the malefactive and the passive, and the two can thus be subsumed under a single functional class encoded by the same morphology, as explained below.

In a malefactive clause, semantic valence *in*creases with the introduction of a malefactee, which is encoded as a subject. The original agent of the underived verb, which is a malefactor in the derived clause, is encoded either as an E argument or simply unstated, like a passive agent. Since malefactivisation simply adds the malefactee, malefactivisation may co-occur with both an intransitive verb and a transitive verb, deriving an extended subtype of each if the malefactor is stated, or simply rearranging the semantic roles and the syntactic arguments if the malefactor is unstated. Also, the syntactic status of the original O if any is not affected by the introduction of the malefactee, just like the causative.

(10–73) Intransitive > (Extended) intransitive

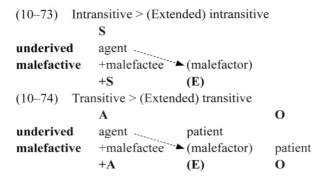

(10–74) Transitive > (Extended) transitive

Example (10–75a) below is an intransitive clause, from which an extended intransitive clause is derived by malefactivisation. In (10–75b), the depicted event consists of 'rain' (malefactor) and some other entity who is bothered by the fact that a rain falls (malefactee). This newly introduced malefactee appears as an S syntactically, whereas the malefactor is encoded as an E argument.

(10–75) a. *ami=nu=du   fïi.*
              rain=NOM=FOC   fall
              'Rain falls' [i.e. it rains]
         b. *ba=a   ami=n=du   ff-ai-r.*
              1SG=TOP   rain=DAT=FOC   fall-MAL-NPST
              'I am bothered by rain (that) falls.'

In (10–76) below, (a) is the underived intransitive clause, from which the malefactive clause (b) is derived. Here, unlike the example above, the malefactor is unstated. Thus what we get is still an intransitive clause, where the original agent is now demoted by deletion, and the newly introduced malefactee is encoded as an S.

(10–76) a. *tuzï=nu=du   ngi-tar.*
              wife=NOM=FOC   leave-PST
              'My wife left.'
         b. *ba=a   ngi-rai-tar.*
              1SG=TOP   leave-MAL-PST
              'I was bothered by the fact that (my wife) left.'

In (10–77) below, the (a) example is a transitive clause, from which an extended transitive (b) and a transitive clause (c) are derived. The original

The simple sentence   349

O remains O in either derived clause, and the newly introduced malefactee
is encoded as an A argument whereas the original A is demoted to an E argument (b) or deletion (c). In (c), the clause remains a transitive clause, but
the A argument is rearranged (agent > malefactee).

(10–77)   a. *taugagara=nu*   *jaa=ju=du*   *tur-tar.*
             someone=NOM   house=ACC=FOC   take-PST
             'Someone took a house (by force).'
          b. *kari=a*   *taugagara=n*   *jaa=ju=du*
             3SG=TOP   someone=DAT   house=ACC=FOC
             tur-ai-tar.
             take-MAL-PST
             'He was troubled (by the fact that) someone took his house
             (by force).'
          c. *uma=nu*   *pžtu=nu=du*   *mmja*
             that.place=GEN   man=NOM   INTJ
             ujaki+munu=u=s-i-i   *u-tar=ruga,*
             rich(+thing)=PRT=do-THM-NRT   PROG-PST=but
             jaa=ju=du   *tur-ai-tar=ca.*
             house=ACC=FOC   take-MAL-PST=HS
             'The man there was rich, but (he) was troubled (by someone
             who) took his house (by force).'

Compare (10–77c) above with the example below, which is a passive
clause derived from (10–77a). The original A is demoted to deletion, as in
the case of (10–77c), but here the original O is promoted to S, as shown in
(10–78) below.

(10–78)   *jaa=nu=du*   *tur-ai-tar.*
          house=NOM=FOC   take-PASS-PST
          'A house was taken by force'

In sum, malefactivisation exhibits characteristics that are similar to causativisation on the one hand and passivisation on the other. There are three
characteristics that are common in malefactivisation and causativisation:
(1) the introduction of a new role (increasing semantic valence), (2) the
coding of such a role as a syntactic subject, and (3) the retention of the
original O (if any) as O. On the other hand, malefactivisation is like passivisation in that (1') the patientive rather than agentive role (malefactee in
the case of a malefactive clause) is assigned the subject status, (2') the

350   Chapter 10

original subject may be deleted if it is unimportant in discourse (this is unlike a causee in a causativised clause, which must be stated as an E argument unless it is understood and zero pronominalised), and (3') there is a
negative meaning that an external causer brings about an action that affects
a patient.[5]

Thus, the suffix -(r)ai, which encodes either passivisation or malefactivisation, has a general function of focusing on the patient in an event, which
may be directly affected (as in passivisation) or indirectly affected (as in
malefactivisation) by an external causer (passive agent or malefactor).

It is noted that malefactivisation is not a frequently occurring voice phenomenon in Irabu, and that some speakers never use it and even say it is
unnatural. This might mean that malefactive is a result of language contact
with Japanese. A further research is needed.

10.4.4. Reflexive

Reflexivisation is not marked by verb morphology. Unlike English and
many other languages, where such concepts as 'wash', 'shave', and 'dress'
can be expressed by reflexives, they are never expressed in this way in Irabu. These verbs are always semantically bivalent, requiring an agent and a
non-reflexive theme. However, the theme in these verbs is often a body
part of the agent, and in this case the possessor (i.e. agent) may be simply
omitted or encoded by a reflexive pronoun na(r)a (§5.2.2.3).

(10–79)   kari=a   (naa=ga)   tii=ju=du
          3SG=TOP   (RFL=GEN)   hand=ACC=FOC
          ara-i+ur-Ø.
          wash-THM+PROG-NPST
          'He is washing (his) hand.'

If the possessor here is encoded by a third person demonstrative pronoun, it
implies that the possessor is different from the agent:

(10–80)   kari=a   kai=ga   tii=ju=du
          3SG=TOP   3SG=GEN   hand=ACC=FOC
          ara-i+ur-Ø.
          wash-THM+PROG-NPST

---

[5] In the elicitation data and the text data I could not find any example where a malefactive
form is used with a positive meaning as in the case of Japanese. But this might come from the
small size of my database rather than the true nature of malefactive.

The simple sentence   351

'He*i* is washing his*j* hand.' [e.g. a father helps his child wash hands]

It is not common to find in texts those examples where the agent and the patient/theme refer to exactly the same entity (rather than the whole-part relation as noted above). However, in elicitation, I was given the following examples with a reflexive pronoun replacing the patient/theme. In place of a reflexive pronoun, a lexical noun *duu* 'body' (which may also function as an equivalent of the first person inclusive form; §5.2.2.1) may be used.

(10–81) *pžtu=u=bakaar*   *mii-da,*   *duu=ju*
         man=ACC=always   look-NEG.NRT   body=ACC
         mii-ru.
         look-IMP
         'Stop looking always at others, but look at yourself' [i.e. take care of your own behaviour].
(10–82) *kari=a*   *nara=u=du*   *icïban=tii*
         3SG=TOP   RFL=ACC=FOC   No.1=QT
         umu-i+ur-Ø.
         think-THM+PROG-NPST
         'He is thinking himself to be the best.'

10.5. Tense, mood, and aspect

In this section I describe three predicate categories, tense, mood, and aspect.

10.5.1. Tense and mood

Tense and mood are expressed by inflectional affixes.[6] The tense system of Irabu is the binary system of past vs non-past. Tense is obligatorily marked on each finite verb form except for finite irrealis verbs. Finite irrealis verb forms only inflect for mood with future time reference being entailed. They are attemporal.

Non-finite verb forms heading subordinate or coordinate clauses depend on the finite verb of the matrix clause for tense specification. There is also relative tense, which occurs in finite verbs of adnominal clauses

---

[6] I follow Palmer (1986: 21–22) and Bybee and Fleischman (1995: 2) in defining moods as grammaticalised modalities (in the form of verb inflection), and modality as speaker's (subjective) attitudes and opinions (Bybee, Perkins, and Pagliuca 1994: 176). Modality consists of epistemic and deontic modalities (Palmer 1986; Payne 1997).

352 Chapter 10

(§10.5.1.4). As shown in FIGURE 10–1 below, specification of the time reference of non-past tense is dependent on the mood of the inflectional affix.

Time	past	<0>	definite future	indefinite future
Mood	unmarked	unmarked	realis	intentional
	realis			optative
				imperative
				anticipated future
				obligative/potential

Tense <<<PST>>>>><NON-PST>>>>>>>>>>>>>>> Attemporal

Note. <0>: 'here and now' deictic centre, habituals (including general truth)
definite future: imminent or well anticipated future
indefinite future: some time (no fixed time) in the future
Attemporal: finite irrealis inflection, which only encodes mood.

FIGURE 10–1. Interaction of tense and mood

The mood system of Irabu is characterised by the inflectional marking of reality status, whose highest-order categories are realis and irrealis (Elliot 2000; Payne 1997). There is also a verb form that is unmarked for these moods.

In what follows, I describe mood and the time reference that it entails in the tense system.

10.5.1.1. Realis mood

The realis mood inflection (see §6.3.1 for the morphological description) expresses both the semantic and the pragmatic stance of the speaker as summarised in (10–83).

(10–83) The realis mood inflection expresses (a) speaker's perceived certainty, and (b) high information value, in that the speaker indicates that his message is new information to the hearer as the hearer does not know, or has a wrong assumption about, the truth value of the proposition.[7]

---

[7] A number of studies of Miyako Ryukyuan have referred to the function of what I call finite realis verb forms (Uchima 1985; Uemura 1997; Karimata 1997; Nakama 1992; Izuyama 2002), but no conclusion or agreement has been reached. All authors agree that these forms express speaker's subjective judgement, as opposed to an unmarked or objective judgement which is said to be encoded by what I call finite unmarked forms. It is a matter of controversy exactly what these authors mean by 'subjective' and 'objective', but it is noted that these authors all tried to capture the mood system involving what I call realis forms and unmarked forms of Miyako Ryukyuan in terms of marked vs unmarked modal features. This is what I do in this grammar as well.

The simple sentence   353

As an initial approximation, the following dialogue illustrates (10–83a) and (10–83b). Here, speaker A has the assumption that 'this (woman)' is ignorant, which B thinks is wrong, as he is certain that 'this (woman)' is a wise person. Thus B corrects A's assumption by using the finite realis form.

(10–84)   A. *kuri=a*   *nau=mai*   *ss-a-n-Ø=pazï.*
              3SG=TOP   what=even   know-THM-NEG-NPST=maybe
              'This (woman) doesn't know anything, perhaps.'
          B. *gui!*   *kuri=a*   *nau=ju=mai*
              INTJ   3SG=TOP   what=ACC=even
              ss-i+u-Ø-m!
              know-THM+PROG-NPST-RLS
              'No way! She knows everything!'

Another example is given below, where speaker B warns speaker A not to buy things at supermarket x, as speaker B is quite certain that the goods sold at the supermarket are costly.

(10–85)   A. *mucïï=mai*   *njaa-n-Ø=niba.*   *x=n*
              rice.cake=too   not.exist-NPST=so   x=DAT
              ar=ru   *sï-Ø?*
              existing=FOC   do-NPST
              'I have run out of rice cakes, so (the supermarket) x sells some?'
          B. *ugui!*   *uma=a*   *taka-ka-Ø-m=ju!*
              INTJ   that.place=TOP   high-VLZ-NPST-RLS=EMP
              'Hey! they (sell) costly (things)!'

As illustrated in the above two examples, the non-past realis forms of stative predication encode the perceived certainty of the speaker towards the ongoing state. When a dynamic verb is inflected for the non-past realis form, as in (10–86) and (10–87) below, the verb expresses an imminent future event (see FIGURE 10–1). The speaker is aware that the event is going to happen in all probability, either because s/he has observed it to be imminent, or because the speaker has other reasons (e.g. a promise) to believe that the event will take place. On the other hand, the hearer is not aware of the imminent future. The speaker uses the realis form to call the hearer's attention to the occurrence of the event. Thus the realis form often entails a warning interpretation, as shown in (10–86), even though it is not always

354 Chapter 10

so, as shown in (10–87).

(10–86) *hai!*   *uti-r-m=dooi!*
INTJ   drop-NPST-RLS=EMP
'Watch out! (The base behind you) is going to drop!'

(10–87) *kaja,*   *kaja,*   *fïï-Ø-m!*
there   there   come-NPST-RLS
'(Hey don't you see) there, there, (the ship is) coming!'

Even though there is a natural correlation between speaker's certainty and speaker's direct experience/witness as a source of information (first hand evidentiality), this correlation is probabilistic rather than the norm. The following dialogue demonstrates this.

(10–88) A. *zau=n=du*   *mmna*   *mizï=nu*
gate=DAT=FOC   all   water=NOM
ar-i+u-i-ba=du.
exist-THM+PROG-THM-CSL=FOC
'There was (a bucket of) water at the entrance (of the house).'

B. *uma-nagi=n?*
that.place-APPR=DAT
'Over there?'

A. *uma-nagi=n=ju.*
that.place-APPR=DAT=EMP
'Yeah, over there.'

B. *taru=mai*   *sïn-ta-m=dara.*   *karjuu=nu*
who=too   die-PST-RLS=CRTN   luck=GEN
mizï=ti.
water=QT
'(Then it means that) <u>someone has died</u>. The water is holy water for keeping bad luck away.''

Here, speaker A is not familiar with Irabu culture, so that she does not know the symbolic meaning of a bucket of water in front of the gate of someone's house, so she reports what she saw to speaker B. Upon hearing the report, speaker B immediately understands what the bucket symbolises (i.e. she knows that this means someone's death, or a funeral). Speaker B then tells it to speaker A, relying on her established knowledge and providing new information to speaker A. Note that the speaker B does not see the

The simple sentence   355

bucket of water or the dead body. Thus the realis form is not a grammatical
marker of firsthand evidentiality or secondhand evidentiality.[8]

Several morphosyntactic correlates of (10–83a) and (10–83b) can be de-
tected. First, as illustrated in (10–85), (10–86), and (10–88) above, the realis form very often co-occurs with those markers that encode certainty (e.g.
=dara, §9.3.6) or emphasis (e.g. =dooi, §9.3.7; =ju, §9.6.1).

Second, because the realis form has the semantic characteristic of (10–
83a), it never co-occurs with the hearsay marker =ca (§9.3.3). This is understandable because a speaker uses =ca to indicate that s/he is not willing
to take the responsibility for the validity of the hearsay information. Thus if
a speaker were certain of a hearsay fact, s/he would not use =ca in the first
place. As noted in §9.3.3, when a speaker is certain of a hearsay fact, s/he
uses the other hearsay marker =tim(dooi/dara).

(10–89) jurav-na.   kari=a   daizïna   saki+fa-ja=timdooi.
         call-IMP   3SG=TOP   awful   Sake+eat-NLZ=HS
         'Don't invite (him): he is said to be an awful drunker.'
(10–90) junai=n   paka=nkai=nu   pžtu=nu.
         night=DAT   grave=ALL=GEN   man=NOM
         maar-i+ur-Ø=timdara
         wander-THM+PROG-NPST=HS
         'At night, men who are dead are walking around. (So return
         home before dark)' [speaking to children as if the speaker be-
         lieves that this rumour is true]

It is likely that this marker contains a historical remnant of realis mood
morpheme -m. That is, =tim may be traced back to quotative =ti + -m. One
piece of evidence is that, as noted in §9.3.3, =tim obligatorily co-occurs
with =dara (certainty marker) or =dooi (emphatic marker). This co-occurrence is naturally explained if we assume that =tim contained -m (see the

---

[8] In Weber's (1986: 137) description of Quechua, a distinction is made between evidentiality,
which concerns how the speaker came by the information, and validationality, which concerns
the speaker's attitude toward the information. The realis mood in Irabu then expresses validationality rather than evidentiality. The realis form of Irabu is very similar in function to 'finite
verbs' in Tungusic languages (Kazama 2005), which are alternatively called 'validational
forms' (Malchucov 2000). In Tungusic languages, the validational form (which, according to
Malchucov, has developed from a firsthand evidential form, which is still found in Udehe) is
highly restricted in use due to its marked modal feature, and only used when a speaker perceives certainty, and it is in most cases used in conversations, and in rhetorical questions
(Shinjiro Kazama, p.c.; Kazama 2005). All these generalisations precisely hold true in the realis form of Irabu.

356   Chapter 10

preceding paragraph). Historically, the realis morpheme *-m* is known to have derived from an epistemic marker *=*mo* or =*mono* (Uchima 1970). Given that it was originally a clitic, it is not surprising that it attached to a part-of-speech other than a verb (i.e. quotative marker =*ti*).

A third morphosyntactic correlate of the realis form is as follows: due to the pragmatic characteristic of (10–83b), the realis form never co-occurs with focus marking on an argument, a VP complement, or an adjunct (argument focus construction; §11.5.2.2) where the predicate is by definition presupposed. As will be discussed in §10.5.1.3, the predicate verb of the argument focus construction is typically a finite unmarked form, which is unmarked for the modal values (10–83a) or (10–83b).

Fourth, it is very rare for the realis form to be used in questions, which is evident considering that it marks speaker's certainty. However, as noted in §10.1.4.2, it is common for the realis form to be used in rhetorical questions, which pragmatically function as a negative statement. Example (10–91) illustrates this use of the realis form.

(10–91)   *uma=kara=a*   *fim-ai-r-m=mu.*
          that.place=ALL=TOP   get-POT-NPST-RLS=Q
          '(One) cannot get (water) from that place.' [lit. Could (one) get (water) from that place?]

If we consider that the realis form is used to encode speaker's perceived certainty about the *truth* of the proposition, the realis forms used in rhetorical questions are problematic, since these uses demonstrate the opposite function of the realis form: they mark the proposition as a *falsehood*. For example, in (10–91) above the speaker is certain of the untruth of the proposition 'one can get water from that place'. However, certainty and truth value should be mutually independent, as one can have certainty about what s/he thinks is false just as much as about what s/he thinks is true. Thus the realis form functions to express speaker's certainty, without respect to whether s/he regards a proposition as being true or false.

Finally, as briefly noted in §6.3.1, whereas the past realis inflection has both affirmative forms (consisting of the past tense *-ta* and the realis mood *-m*) and negative forms (consisting of the negative *-t*, the past *-ta,* and the realis mood *-m*), the non-past realis form lacks a negative counterpart. This asymmetry in negation is naturally explained by referring to the modal characteristic of realis: since it requires the speaker's perceived certainty, it is more difficult to use it with what will not occur (non-past tense) than with what did not actually occur (past tense). For example, the negation of

The simple sentence 357

(10–92a) is carried out by the unmarked inflection (10–92b), where no imminent future interpretation or definite future interpretation is inherently
expressed, and the speaker simply states that 'he will not come'.

(10–92) a. *kari=a*   *fïï-Ø-m.*
             3SG=TOP   come-NPST-RLS
             'He is coming' [imminent future] or
             'He is sure to come' [definite future]
         b. *kari=a*   *kuu-n-Ø.*
             3SG=TOP   come-NEG-NPST
             'He will not come.'

The independent evidence that (10–92b) is an unmarked form is that this
form can be used as the predicate of an adnominal clause, which must be
an unmarked form (§4.1.2).

(10–93) *kai=ga*   *kuu-n-Ø*   *pžž=ža*   *icï=ga?*
          3SG=NOM   come-NEG-NPST   day=TOP   when=Q
          'When is the day he will not come?'

In addition to the morphosyntactic correlates of the realis mood as noted
above, there is also a clear distributional characteristic of realis forms in
natural discourse. The text genres that are very likely to induce the use of
realis forms are conversations, and the text genres that are not likely to induce the use of realis forms are narratives, especially folktale stories and
procedural texts. This correlation between the text genres and the occurrence of realis forms can be easily explained from the pragmatic characteristic of realis forms: it is much more likely to occur in conversations than
in narratives since there is a hearer with a much more active role in the
conversational act than narration, and without a hearer who interacts ac-
tively with the speaker, (10–83b) would be irrelevant. An unmarked form
is typically used in place of a realis form in these narrative genres (see
§10.5.1.3).

10.5.1.2. Irrealis mood
The irrealis mood expresses that the proposition is weakly asserted as either possible, likely, or uncertain, or necessary, desired or undesired, but
the speaker is not ready to back up the assertion with evidence or other
strong grounds (Givón 1984; 1994: 268). Thus the irrealis mood clearly
contrasts with the realis mood in terms of speaker's certainty (10–83a), as

358   Chapter 10

it decidedly expresses the speaker's perception of uncertainty (cf. the unmarked form is neutral in this regard). Also, the irrealis mood does not express high information value as defined in (10–83b), in that it may be under the scope of presupposition. For example, in (10–94) below, the
predicate headed by the irrealis intentional form is presupposed.

(10–94)   *vva=a*   *nau=ju=ga*   *fa-a-di=ga?*
          2SG=TOP   what=ACC=FOC   eat-THM-INT=Q
          'What are you going to eat?'

As listed in FIGURE 10–1 (see also §6.3.1 for morphological detail), there
are five irrealis categories: intentional, optative, imperative, anticipated future *-gumata* and obligative/potential *-kutu*, the latter two being secondary
inflection (§7.2.2). These all entail future time reference, encoding future
intentions or wishes (see below).

The intentional form expresses (1) the speaker's future intention or (2)
the hortative, i.e. the mutual encouragement to do something.

(10–95)   *ba=ga*   *uma=n=na*   *nivv-a-di.*
          1SG=NOM   that.place=DAT=TOP   sleep-THM-INT
          '(As for) that place (where you are lying) I will sleep (in-
          stead).'
(10–96)   *pžtumi*   *ik-a-di.*
          together   go-THM-INT
          'Let's go together.'

The non-speaker participant's future intention may be expressed with the
intentional, but the use of the intentional is restricted to questions, quoted
speech, or constructions with a hearsay marker (Hayashi 2007).

(10–97)   *vva=a*   *kuu-di=ru?*
          2SG=TOP   come-INT=Q
          'Will you come?'
          cf. **vva=a*   *kuu-di.*
               2SG=TOP   come-INT
               'You will come.'
(10–98)   *kari=a*   *kuu-di=ca.*
          3SG=TOP   come-INT=HS
          '(According to him), he will come.'
          cf. **kari=a*   *kuu-di.*

The simple sentence   359

3SG=TOP   come-INT
'He will come'

The optative form expresses the speaker's wish ('want to') that is directed to future.

(10–99)   *nkifï?*   *ui=gami=a*   *mmja,*
          sea.grapes   3SG=EMP=TOP   INTJ
          fa-a-baa=tii=ja   *umu-u-n-Ø.*
          eat-THM-OPT=QT=TOP   think-THM-NEG-NPST
          'Sea grapes? Well, as for it (I) don't think like "(I) want to eat
          (them)."'
(10–100) *agaii,*   *ban=mai*   *ik-a-baa=i!*
          INTJ   1SG=too   go-THM-OPT=CNF
          'I want to go, too!'

The imperative mood expresses a command (see also §10.1.3). This is
also considered to be directed to some indefinite future time, in the sense
that the action will take place after the command is expressed.

(10–101) *kuma=n*   *ur-i.*
          this.place=DAT   exist-IMP
          'Stay here.'
(10–102) *munuž-na=ju,*   *ui=ga*   *taa=nkai*   *munuž-na!*
          speak-PRH=EMP   3SG=GEN   FIL=ALL   speak-PRH
          'Don't speak; don't speak to that creature!'[9]

The anticipated future form expresses an anticipated event at the moment of speech, as illustrated in (10–103), but it is not as imminent or evident as in the case of the non-past realis form, as illustrated in (10–104).

(10–103) *kari=a*   *aca=du*   *fïï-gumata.*
          3SG=TOP   tomorrow=FOC   come-ANTC
          'He will come tomorrow.'
(10–104) *kari=a*   *fïï-Ø-m.*
          3SG=TOP   come-NPST-RLS
          'He is coming' [e.g. when the speaker sees him approaching.]

---

[9] The noun *taa* is only used in this specific NP structure *ui=ga taa=nkai*. It can be replaced by
ui=nkai 'to him' but the complex NP expresses the speaker's irritation.

360 Chapter 10

Also, the degree of anticipation is lower than in the case of a habitual event, as illustrated in (10–105), where the verb is inflected for the non-past unmarked form (§10.5.1.3; §10.5.2.6).

(10–105) *kari=a*   *mainicï*   *fïï-Ø.*
          3SG=TOP   everyday   come-NPST
          'He comes everyday.' [e.g. referring to a paperboy who regularly brings newspapers]

The obligative/potential form expresses either speaker's obligation or the potentiality of the event described, thus demonstrating a cross-linguistically recurrent isomorphism of deontic and epistemic modalities.

(10–106) *uri=a*   *ba=ga*   *asï-kutu*   *ja-i-ba,*
          3SG=TOP   1SG=NOM   do-OBL   COP-THM-CSL
          vva=a   *zjaubu=ju.*
          2SG=TOP   all.right=EMP
          'As for it, I ought to (am supposed to) do (it), so you don't worry (about it).' [deontic reading]
(10–107) *siimai,*   *vva=a*   *mmja,*   *žž-ai-kutu.*
          INTJ   2SG=TOP   INTJ   scold-PASS-OBL
          'Keep me out of it... You will be scolded.' [epistemic]

Note that in (10–106) the verb is followed by the copula verb *jar*, an allomorph that appears only in subordinate clauses (§6.3.6.2). This is due to the historical fact that *-kutu* used to be a formal noun heading an NP with an adnominal clause (§7.2.2).

10.5.1.3. The verb form unmarked for mood
The finite unmarked form is unmarked for either realis or irrealis mood. This form is obligatorily required when a verb serves as a predicate head of an adnominal clause (§4.1.2).

When the finite unmarked form serves as head of a main clause predicate, it contrasts with realis forms and irrealis forms as a sentence-final predicate verb form. In past tense, where only the unmarked form and the realis form are available, the unmarked form is much more frequently used than the realis form. Due to the marked modal features of realis (§10.5.1.1), its use is very limited. On the other hand, in non-past tense, where there are several inflected forms available (realis form, unmarked form, and five irrealis forms), the use of the unmarked form is rather re-

The simple sentence   361

stricted, as future events are encoded by various irrealis forms depending
on the nature of the future expressed, i.e. intention, anticipation, wish, and
so on. In what follows I note the cases in which the unmarked form can be
or must be used over the realis form and the irrealis forms.

In contrast to the realis form, which always carries new information and
therefore never co-occurs with focus marking on the non-predicate element
(§10.5.1.1), the unmarked form (as well as the irrealis form) may co-occur
with focus marking, as it does not necessarily entail new information. In
past tense, therefore, the use of the unmarked form is obligatory in presence of the focus marker.

(10–108) *uri=a*   *mma-ka-ta-m.*
          3SG=TOP   tasty-VLZ-PST-RLS
          'That was TASTY.' [predicate focus]
(10–109) *ui=ga=du*   *mma-ka-tar.*
          3SG=NOM=FOC   tasty-VLZ-PST
          'THAT was tasty.' [argument focus]

In non-past tense and attemporal clauses, on the other hand, the verb form
that co-occurs with focus marking may be either an unmarked form or an
irrealis form, depending on the time reference. In short, the realis form is
excluded. See §11.5 for more detail on the interaction between focus marking and verb inflection, which is known as *kakarimusubi* in Japanese historical linguistics.

Another environment where the unmarked form is selected over the realis form is with markers that convey uncertainty on the part of the speaker.
Since the unmarked form does not express the speaker's perceived certainty, it can co-occur with the hearsay marker *=ca* (§9.3.3) and other markers
that convey speaker uncertainty, such as *=bjaam* 'I wonder' (§9.3.1) and
=pazï 'maybe' (§9.3.4). The realis form is not used in the presence of these
uncertainty markers.

(10–110) *kuri=a*   *sïtabutu=u*
          3SG=TOP   bedfellow=ACC
          muc-i+ur-Ø=bjaam=mi.
          have-THM+PROG-NPST=I.wonder=CNF
          'I wonder if this (woman) has a bedfellow.'
(10–111) *nnama=gami=a*   *cïk-i+ur-Ø=pazï.*
          now=EMP=TOP   arrive-THM+PROG-NPST=maybe
          '(She) may have arrived by now.'

362   Chapter 10

In fact, the unmarked form is the default form used in folktale stories, where =ca is typically used to end each sentence (see APPENDIX (1)).

One noteworthy feature of the unmarked form in terms of speaker's perceived certainty is that it can express the speaker's not yet established knowledge, i.e. newly learned information. The following pair of examples illustrates this. Example (10–112) is a restatement of (10–84B), where the realis form is used, since the speaker is certain of the stated proposition. The near-identical sentence (10–113), on the other hand, ends with the unmarked inflection, and indicates that the speaker has just now realised the fact expressed in the sentence, which is thus uttered with surprise.

(10–112) *gui!*   *kur=a*   *nau=ju=mai*
          INTJ   3SG=TOP   what=ACC=even
          ss-i+u-Ø-m!
          know-THM+PROG-NPST-RLS
          'No way! She knows everything!' [speaker is certain that she is wise]

(10–113) *gui!*   *kuri=a*   *nau=ju=mai*
          INTJ   3SG=TOP   what=ACC=eveb
          ss-i+ur-Ø!
          know-THM+PROG-NPST
          'Wow! She knows everything!' [speaker assumed that she was dull.]

Likewise, in the following example, the use of the unmarked form indicates newly learned information perceived with surprise.

(10–114) *vva=a*   *nagahama+pžtu=u=s-i+u-tar!*
          2SG=TOP   Nagahama+man=PRT=do-THM+PROG-PST
          '(Oh!) you were (from) Nagahama!' [speaker did not know this fact.]

The correlation between the unmarked form and newly learned information is explainable. In formulating a cross-linguistically valid epistemic scale of REALIS and IRREALIS modalities (as shown in FIGURE 10–2 below), Akatsuka (1985) situates newly learned information at the left edge of the domain of IRREALIS modality.

Newly learned information is like realis in that it designates a situation that speaker considers to hold true (schematised as 'exist x'), but it is nevertheless unlike REALIS since it is not integrated into the speaker's estab-

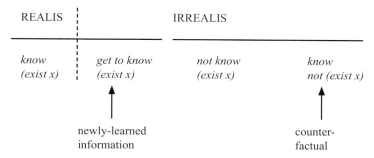

FIGURE 10–2. Akatsuka's (1985) epistemic scale

lished knowledge ('get to know (exist x)'). Akatsuka shows that in many languages this semantic scale is reflected in morphosyntactic distinctions. For example, the English conjunction *if* is characteristic of IRREALIS modality, but it may also be used in cases where the proposition is regarded as true but the speaker perceives the situation with a surprise, as in *if he's so happy to see me, I should have come earlier* (Akatsuka 1985: 630). In Irabu, newly learned information is encoded by the unmarked form rather than the realis form, thus supporting Akatsuka's claim that newly learned information is distinct from REALIS modality. But, in Irabu newly learned information is treated distinctly from the other part of IRREALIS modality, which is encoded by irrealis forms.[10]

Turning now to the environment where the unmarked form as opposed to the irrealis forms is selected in non-past tense, the unmarked form signifies habituality and general truth, or a state of affairs that holds true without respect to specific time reference. Also, when combined with the progressive aspect auxiliary, the unmarked verb form expresses present time reference.

---

[10] Akatsuka's other claim that counterfactuality cross-linguistically belongs to IRREALIS domain and therefore is expected to be coded by irrealis morphosyntax is not fully justified in Irabu. We observed in §10.5.1.1 that in Irabu the realis form can be used in rhetorical questions, which expresses counterfactuality in that the speaker knows that a proposition is false (thus it can be schematised as 'know not (exist x)' in the above FIGURE 10–2). The epistemic scale suggested by Akatsuka assumes that epistemic modality is more sensitive to truth value (schematised as '(exist x)' and 'not (exist x)') than speaker's perceived certainty (schematised as 'know' in FIGURE 10–2), since in the scale REALIS modality and counterfactuality are situated in the opposite margins even when they share the characteristic of speaker's certainty. This way of formulating epistemic modality is based on Western philosophical tradition (Givón 1994), and does not seem to be true in all languages. In Irabu, it seems rather that speaker's certainty is more important than truth value and can be encoded identically with the same form.

364   Chapter 10

(10–115)   *sjensoo=nu*   *tukja=n=na*   *nau=mai*
           war=GEN   time=DAT=TOP   what=even
           fau-Ø=i.
           eat-NPST=CNF
           'In warfare, (one) eats anything, right?'

(10–116)   *mii+jarabi-mmi=a,*   *mmja,*   *utedama=u=mai*
           female+child-PL=TOP   INTJ   juggling=ACC=too
           asï-Ø,   *maar=mai*   *vcï-Ø.*   *biki+jarabi-mmi=a,*
           do-NPST   ball=too   hit-NPST   male+child-PL=TOP
           mmja,   *tatimma=tii=mai,*   *mata*   *naugara=tii=mai*
           INTJ   stilt=QT=too   and   whatever=QT=too
           asï-Ø.
           do-NPST
           'Girls do juggling, and bounce balls; boys plays on stilts and
           so on.'

(10–117)   *atu+fini=a*   *sacï*   *nar-Ø.*
           late+boat=TOP   first   become-NPST
           'The boat (that started) late will become (the) first (that ar-
           rives).' [proverb: 'stay alert even when the game is on your
           side']

(10–118)   *žžu=u*   *cc-i-i=du*   *ur-Ø.*
           fish=ACC   catch-THM-NRT=FOC   PROG-NPST
           '(He) is catching fishes.' [i.e. he is fishing]

10.5.1.4. Relative tense
The tense in adnominal clauses is a relative as opposed to absolute tense
(Comrie 1985a). That is, the deictic centre of the tense of an adnominal
clause predicate (underlined below), is not the moment of speech but the
moment of the event described as a main clause predicate (double-under-
lined). Since the verb form of an adnominal clause must be a finite unmarked form, the tense marking is either past *-tar* or non-past *-r/-Ø* (Class
1/Class 2).

(10–119)   *unu*   *nak-i+ur-Ø*   *ffa=u=du*
           that   cry-THM+PROG-NPST   child=ACC=FOC
           <u>*mutagi-tar.*</u>
           lift-PST
           '(I) lifted the crying child.' [Relative clause]

(10–120)   <u>*žž-ai-i=bakaar*</u>   *ur-Ø*
           scold-PASS-NRT=only   PROG-NPST

The simple sentence   365

jarabi=du   *a-tar=ruga,*
child=FOC   COP-PST=but
nnama=gami=a   *zau+bikidum+nisjai=n*
now=EMP=TOP   good+male+young.guy=DAT
nar-i+ur-Ø.
become-THM+PROG-NPST
'(He) was a child who was always scolded, but now is a good young guy.'

(10–121)   *cc-i+u-tar*   *cïn=nu=du*
          wear-THM+PROG-PST   clothes=ACC=FOC
          nv-tar.
          take.off-PST
          '(She) took off the clothes she had worn (until the act of taking off)'

10.5.2. Aspect

Aspect is marked by (1) an auxiliary verb (§7.1.4.1), (2) finite unmarked inflection (§6.3.1), or (3) verbal reduplication (§3.3.6.2). There are five aspect auxiliaries, namely progressive, resultative, prospective, perfect, and experiential, of which the first three can be compounded with the lexical verb, depending on the focus marking on the lexical verb (word-phrase alternation; §6.4.2.3). The other two aspect auxiliaries always form a complex VP with the lexical verb, and no focus marking is allowed on this verb. Finite non-past unmarked inflection without any auxiliary construes an event as a habitual one, which holds true without respect to specific temporal location.[11] Verbal reduplication marks iterativity or habituality.

TABLE 10–2. Aspects and their coding strategies

	auxiliary	inflection	verbal reduplication
Progressive	+		
Resultative	+		
Prospective	+		
Perfect	+		
Experiential	+		
Habitual	+	+	+
Iterative			+

[11] On the other hand, finite non-past unmarked inflection without any auxiliary construes an event as a single whole, i.e. perfective in Comrie's (1976) terms.

366   Chapter 10

10.5.2.1. Progressive

Progressive aspect is expressed by the aspect auxiliary *ur*. This is a gram-maticalised form of the lexical verb *ur* '(animate referent) exist'. In Irabu, there are not many stative verb lexemes in the lexicon, so that many stative notions such as 'know', 'have', 'be ill', etc., are derived from punctual lex-emes (that express 'realise', 'lift', 'become ill', etc.) by the aspect auxilia-ry.

(10–122) *jarabi=nu*   *nak-i-i=du*   *ur-Ø.*
          child=NOM   cry-THM-NRT=FOC   PROG-NPST
          'A child is crying.'

(10–123) *pjaa=ja*   *aagu=u=mai*
          old.times=TOP   song=ACC=too
          ss-i-i=du   *u-tar=ruga=du,*
          know-THM-NRT=FOC   PROG-PST=but=FOC
          ui+pžtu=n   *nar-i-i=kara,*
          old+man=DAT   become-THM-NRT=after
          mmja,   *as-irai-n-Ø.*
          INTJ   do-POT-NEG-NPST
          'Previously (I) used to know songs, but (now I) have become an old man, (I) cannot sing.'

(10–124) *vva=a*   *tuz=za*   *muc-i-i=ru*
          2SG=TOP   wife=PRT   have-THM-NRT=FOC
          ur-Ø?
          PROG-NPST
          '(Do) you have a wife?'

(10–125) *ba=a*   *jam-i-i=du*   *ur-Ø=rju.*
          1SG=TOP   fall.ill-THM-NRT=FOC   PROG-NPST=EMP
          'I am ill.'

10.5.2.2. Resultative

Resultative aspect is expressed by resultative aspect auxiliary *ar*. This is a grammaticalised form of the lexical verb *ar* '(inanimate referent) exist'. Resultative aspect expresses that the action so marked has resulted in a cer-tain state, focusing on the current state rather than the action itself. The re-sultative auxiliary may co-occur either with an intransitive verb (10–126) or a transitive verb (10–127), though the latter is more typical.

(10–126) *vva=a*   *nautti=ga*   *nak-i+ar-Ø=ga?*
          2SG=TOP   why=FOC   cry-THM+RSL-NPST=Q

The simple sentence   367

'Why have you cried?'

(10–127)   *nakagus=su=baa*   *tur-i-i,*
            gut=ACC=TOP   take-THM-NRT
            ara-i-i=du   *ar-Ø.*
            wash-THM-NRT=FOC   RSL-NPST
            'As for the guts (of a pig), (I) have taken them out and cleaned
            them.'

In (10–128) and (10–129) below the patient is encoded as a subject. Thus resultative aspect seems to function like passivisation (§10.4.2). However, as shown in (10–130) and (10–131), as well as in (10–127) above, the clause may often remain the active voice, and the subject is very likely to be unexpressed.[12]

(10–128)   *mizï=nu=du*   *nci+ar-Ø.*
            water=NOM=FOC   put+RSL-NPST
            '(A bucket of) water has been put out.'

(10–129)   *ahaa*   *kuri=a*   *žž-ai-i*   *mmja*
            I.see   3SG=TOP   scold-PASS-NRT   INTJ
            nak-i-i=du   *ar-Ø=ri=tii*   *pazïmi=a*
            cry-THM-NRT=FOC   RSL-NPST=CNF=QT   first=TOP
            naugara   *umuv-tar=dara.*
            FIL   think-PST=EMP
            'I see, having been scolded this (boy) has cried (to the effect
            that he has a red-rimmed eyes); like this I thought.'

(10–130)   *buuz=zu=baa*   *ibi-i=du*   *ar-Ø.*
            sugarcane=ACC=TOP   plant-NRT=FOC   RSL-NPST
            'As for the sugarcane, (it) has been planted.'

(10–131)   *daizina*   *surumik-ja*   *ja-i-ba,*
            great   clean-NLZ   COP-THM-CSL
            jaa=ju=mai   *zjautuu=n*   *ssabi-i=du*
            house=ACC=too   satisfaction=DAT   clean-NRT=FOC
            ar-Ø.
            RSL-NPST
            '(She) is a person who likes cleanness, so the house has also

---

[12] Martin (1975) refers to the corresponding auxiliary *aru* in Japanese as 'intransitivizing resultative', as in Japanese the resultative auxiliary derives an intransitive clause where the subject encodes the patient. In this regard, then, the Irabu resultative auxiliary *ar* is different from the Japanese counterpart.

368   Chapter 10

been cleaned to satisfaction (lit. (she) has also cleaned the
house to satisfaction).'

10.5.2.3. Prospective

Prospective aspect is so named because it encodes the implicit prospect of
an event/state resulting from the event that is deliberately done in advance
and is encoded by prospective aspect. In the following example, the predicate is encoded with the prospective auxiliary *ufï*, which is a grammaticalised form of the lexical verb *ufï* 'put'.

(10–132)   *ba=a*   *zin=nu*   *tami-i=du*
           1SG=TOP   money=ACC   save-NRT=FOC
           uk-a-di.
           PROS-THM-INT
           'I will save money (for some future event).'

The preliminary event is construed either as a single whole (i.e. perfective event) or as an ongoing process (imperfective, as shown above). In the
following example, the predicate marked with the prospective auxiliary
designates a perfective action that will have been completed by the time
one eats dinner.

(10–133)   *kan=mai*   *žžu=mai*   *banti=ga*   *tumi-i=du*
           crab=too   fish=too   1PL=NOM   search-NRT=FOC
           ufï-kutu.
           PROS-OBL
           'We will search for crabs and fish (for dinner).'

In the following example, the predicate marked with the prospective auxiliary (a compound verb) designates an imperfective event preliminary for
the future event (i.e. the arrival of the parcel).

(10–134)   *vva=a*   *par-i.*   *ba=ga*
           2SG=TOP   leave-IMP   1SG=NOM
           mac-i+uk-a-di.
           wait-THM+PROS-THM-INT
           'You leave. I will wait (for the parcel to come).'

As schematically shown in Figures 10–3 and 10–4, prospective aspect
and resultative aspect (§10.5.2.2) have parallel aspectual-temporal struc-

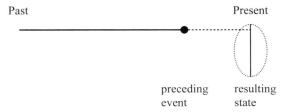

FIGURE 10–3. Resultative aspect

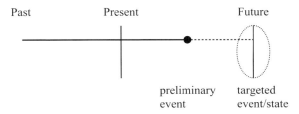

FIGURE 10–4. Prospective aspect

tures, in that in both aspects the state/event resulting from the event marked with the aspect auxiliary is relevant.

Both of the following examples are concerned with certain states/events resulting from preceding events encoded with the respective auxiliaries, but contrast in the time of the preceding event.

(10–135) a. *tigami=u=baa*   *kak-i+ar-Ø.*
            letter=ACC=TOP   write-THM+RSL-NPST
            'As for the letter, it has been written.'
         b. *tigami=u=du*   *kak-i+ufi-Ø.*
            letter=ACC=FOC   write-THM+PROS-NPST
            '(I) will write a letter (e.g. before sending it in afternoon)'

Since both aspects are more or less concerned with the state/event resulting from a preceding event, their aspectual meaning may entail an evidential meaning, i.e. inferential evidentiality. That is, these aspects trace the preceding event encoded by the auxiliary from the resulting state. This evidential extension of perfect/resultative aspect is common cross-linguistically (Comrie 1976: 110; Bybee, Perkins, and Pagliuca 1994: 95–97). In the following example, the resultative aspect marking expresses that one

370   Chapter 10

can infer what happened from the present state of the child.[13]

(10–136)   *mii-tarjaa=du*   *naugara*   *ahaa,*   *kuri=a*
           look-PST.ANT=FOC   FIL   INTJ   3SG=TOP
           jam-i-i=du   *ar-Ø=ri=tii.*
           fall.ill-THM-NRT=FOC   RSL-NPST=CNF=QT
           '(I) looked (at the child), then (I thought) "hmmm, this guy
           has come down with illness."' [resultative aspect implying
           inferential evidence]

The prospective aspect also has inferential entailment. However, the resulting event/state is the present state rather than a future event/state, a present
state which has resulted from the past event, In this respect it is just like
resultative aspect in the aspectual-temporal structure (see FIGURE 10–3).
Also, the 'preliminary' event is not really preliminary, as it is not volitional. There are simply two related events, and the speaker is focusing on the
resulting event/state, from which he infers the preceding ('preliminary')
event. In example (10–137), the use of the prospective aspect auxiliary expresses that there is a present state (i.e. that the ground is wet), from which
the speaker infers that it rained some time before the moment of speech.

(10–137)   *ami=nu=du*   *ff-i+ufi-Ø=i.*
           rain=NOM=FOC   fall-THM+PROS-NPST=CNF
           '(Considering the fact that the ground is wet) it has rained.'

In example (10–138), the use of the prospective aspect auxiliary expresses
that there is a present state (that they are absent in the place they should
be), from which the speaker infers that they have already died.

(10–138)   *kantja=a*   *ur-a-t-ta=iba,*
           3PL=TOP   exist-THM-NEG-PST=so
           sïn-i+ufi-Ø=pazï=i=ti.
           die-THM+PROS-NPST=maybe=CNF=QT
           'They weren't (at the place where we promised to meet), so
           (I) thought "(they) have died."'

---

[13] The inferential evidential entailment of resultative aspect has already been reported in the
description of Ishigaki (a Southern Ryukyuan language spoken on Ishigaki Island) by Miyara
(1995: 163–164), where he notes that the resultative *eer* may be used in such cases as where
the speaker sees the ground wet and infers that it rained.

The simple sentence   371

Likewise, in the following example, the prospective auxiliary expresses that there is a certain resulting state (i.e. that his shoes are in the entrance) that the speaker actually sees, from which he infers that he has come back home by the time of speech.

(10–139)   *cc-i-i=du*   *ufi-Ø=pazï.*
           come-THM-NRT   PROS-NPST=maybe
           '(He) has come (back), perhaps.' [looking at his shoes in the entrance.]

10.5.2.4. Perfect

Perfect aspect is expressed by the perfect aspect auxiliary *njaan*. This is a grammaticalised form of the lexical verb *njaan* 'not exist'. The perfect auxiliary expresses a currently relevant state brought about by the past event. To demonstrate the current relevance inherent to perfect aspect, let us consider the following pair of examples where the (a) example ends with a lexical verb inflected for past unmarked and the (b) example ends with the perfect auxiliary.

(10–140)   a. *uri=u=baa*   *cïfi-tar.*
              3SG=ACC=TOP   hear-PST
              '(I) heard about that.'
           b. *uri=u=baa*   *cïk-i-i*   *njaa-n.*
              3SG=ACC=TOP   hear-THM-NRT   PRF-NPST
              '(I) have heard about that.'

Here, the (a) example may be followed by such an expression as 'but I had forgotten it, whereas the (b) cannot. This is because in the (b) example the past event 'I heard about that' has current relevance.

The perfect auxiliary often pragmatically entails the speaker's regret about the resulting state.

(10–141)   *ju-taa*   *u-tar=ruga,*
           four-CLF.HUMAN   exist-PST=but
           tavkjaa=ja   *sïn-i-i*   *njaa-n.*
           one.person=TOP   die-THM-NRT   PRF-NPST
           'There were four (children), but one has died.'
(10–142)   *jurus-i-i*   *fii-hama-ci.*   *unu*
           forgive-THM-NRT   BEN-HON-IMP   that
           zin=nu=baa

372   Chapter 10

                money=ACC=TOP

cïka-i-i	*njaa-n=ti=du*	*až-tar=ca.*
spend-THM-NRT	PRF-NPST=QT=FOC	say-PST=HS

                '(He) said, "Please forgive me; (I) have spent that money."'

10.5.2.5. Experiential

Experiential aspect is expressed by experiential aspect auxiliary *miir*, which is a grammaticalised form of the lexical verb *miir* 'look'. Experiential aspect designates an action roughly translated as 'try V-ing'. In its negative form, the verb *miin* designates the lack of experience 'have never V-en' as exemplified in (5–60) in Chapter 5.

(10–143)   *nzi,*   *ažž-i-i*   *mii-ru.*
                INTJ   say-THM-NRT   EXP-IMP
                'OK, try speaking.'

(10–144)   *ik-ai-r*   *tukuma=gami*   *ik-i-i*   *mii-di.*
                go-POT-NPST   place=LMT   go-THM-NRT   EXP-INT
                'I will try going as far as I can go.'

(10–145)   *mii-Ø*   *mii-tarjaa=du,*   *uku+bav=nu*
                look-NRT   EXP-PST.ANT=FOC   big+snake=NOM
                u-tar=ca.
                exist-PST=HS
                'When (she) had a look (inside), there was a big snake.'

The semantic bleaching of the auxiliary verb *miir* in the above examples is clear. First, in all the examples above, the auxiliary does not mean 'look'. Note that in (10–145) it co-occurs with the lexical verb *miir*, which would result in redundancy if the auxiliary also meant 'look'. Second, the argument structure of the predicate is determined solely by the lexical verb.

10.5.2.6. Habitual and iterative

Habitual aspect describes a situation which is characteristic of an extended period of time, and is viewed as a characteristic feature of a whole period (Comrie 1976: 28). Habitual aspect is expressed by progressive auxiliary (10–146) or finite non-past unmarked inflection without auxiliary (see (10–115) to (10–117) above). It may also be expressed by verbal reduplication *asï+asï* 'do', as illustrated in (10–147) and (10–148) below.

(10–146)   *imi-kar-Ø=kja=gami=a,*   *mmja,*
                small-VLZ-NPST=when=EMP=TOP   INTJ

The simple sentence

juu	*pinza=nu*	*fïsa=u=mai*	*kar-i-i=du*
often	goat=GEN	grass=ACC=too	cut-THM-NRT=FOC

u-tar.
PROG-PST

'When (I) was small, (I) used to gather grass for goats.'

(10–147)   *ssagi=ti*   *asï-tigaa,*   *midum=mu*
          wedding.ceremony=QT   do-CND   woman=ACC

          bikidum=nu   *mai=nkai*   *saar-i-i*   *ik-i-i,*
          man=GEN   front=ALL   take-THM-NRT   go-THM-NRT

          budur=mai   *aagu=mai*   *asï+asï.*
          dance=too   song=too   RED+do

          'When it comes to a wedding ceremony, (people) take a bride to the house of the groom, and do dances and songs.'

(10–148)   *kari=a*   *saada+pžtu*   *ja-i-ba=i,*
          3SG=TOP   Sawada+man   COP-THM-CSL=CNF

          sagu=u   *s-i-i,*   *nau*   *sï-tarjaa,*
          melody=ACC   do-THM-NRT   what   do-PST.ANT

          ika   *sï-tarjaa=tii*   *asï+asï.*
          ECHO   do-PST.ANT=QT   RED+do

          'She is from Sawada, so (she) has a characteristic speech melody, doing (i.e. saying) like "if you do such and such...."'

Iterative aspect is encoded by verbal reduplication. Unlike the case of habitual aspect, verb stem reduplication is not restricted to *asï* 'do'. It is also very common for the reduplicated form to be framed in a specific construction where A=topic B+B LV (A is inflected for narrative converb, B+B is a reduplicated verb form, and LV is a light verb *asï*). Here, the actions encoded by A and B are iterated.

(10–149)   *uki-i=ja*   *kair+kair=s-i-i=du*
          stand-NRT=TOP   RED+turn.over=do-THM-NRT=FOC

          ifï-tar=ca.
          go-PST=HS

          '(He) went standing up and turning over and over.'

(10–150)   *pur-i-i=ja*   *tur+tur*   *as-i-i=du*
          dig-THM-NRT=TOP   RED+take   do-THM-NRT=FOC

          ur-Ø.
          PROG-NPST

          '(They) are digging and taking (potatoes).'

(10–151)   *nak-i-i=ja*   *fau+fau,*   *nak-i-i=ja*

cry-THM-NRT=TOP RED+eat cry-THM-NRT=TOP
fau+fau as-i-ba=gami=du, mmna *barav-tar.*
RED+eat do-THM-CSL=EMP=FOC all laugh-PST
'(The girl) was crying and eating repeatedly, so everyone laughed (at her).'

Chapter 11

The complex sentence

This chapter describes complex clause structures, noting three major clause linkage types: (1) coordination, (2) clause chaining, and (3) subordination. I also describe the syntactic characteristics of focus constructions (§11.5), as focus marking and complex clause structures are inter-related.

11.1. Overview of complex clause structures

Coordination falls into symmetrical coordination (where the first clause and the second clause are conjoined by a conjunction word: §3.3.6.3) and asymmetrical coordination (where the first clause is marked by a conjunction marker; §9.2). Clause chaining consists of a series of non-finite, medial clauses, which are typically narrative converbal clauses (§6.3.2.2), terminated by a finite clause. Subordination falls into adsentential subordination (where the subordinate clause functions as a sentential adjunct), adverbial subordination (where the subordinate clause functions as a predicate adjunct), adnominal subordination (where the subordinate clause functions as an adnominal), and complementation (where the subordinate clause functions as an argument).

TABLE 11–1. Irabu clause linking types

Linking type	Subtype
Coordination	Symmetrical
	Asymmetrical
Clause chaining	
Subordination	Adsentential
	Adverbial
	Adnominal
	Complement

11.2. Coordination

Coordination links two main clauses either by a conjunction word (§3.3.6.3) or by a conjunction marker (§9.2) attached to the first clause.

376   Chapter 11

11.2.1. Symmetrical coordination

In symmetrical coordination, two (or more) main clauses are linked by a free conjunction word such as *mata* 'and' (see §3.3.6.3 for a full list of conjunctions). Both clauses in the coordinate construction are fully independent, i.e. both clauses have a form that can be used independently, may be inflected for any finite form (§6.3.1), and are independently specified for speech act (declarative, interrogative, or imperative; §10.1). Also, there is an intonational break between the two clauses. Thus I insert a period '.' rather than comma ',' between the linked clauses.

(11–1) *nkjaan=na*   *budur-nagi=mai*
        old.times=TOP   dance-APPR=too
        umissi-ka-ta-m.
        interesting-VLZ-PST-RLS
        assuga,   *nnama=a*   *mii-n-Ø=ni.*
        but   now=TOP   see-NEG-NPST=CNF
        'In old days dances were fun; but now (we) don't see (dances), eh?'

(11–2) *buuc=cu=mai*   *ibir-tigaa*   *ibi-ru.*
        sugarcane=ACC=too   plant-CND   plant-IMP
        mata, nngi=nu   *paa=mai tur-tigaa   tur-i.*
        and   sweet.potato=GEN   leaf=too take-CND   take-IMP
        'Plant sugarcane if you want; and take sweet potato leaves if you want.'

11.2.2. Asymmetrical coordination

In asymmetrical coordination, the first clause is marked by a conjunction marker. This clause is inflected for a finite form like the second, but there is a severe restriction on the finite inflection of the first clause. As summarised in TABLE 11–2 below, the restriction varies depending on the type of clitic that is attached to the clause. The clause marked by the temporal conjunction *=kja* (§9.2.1) is not a coordinate clause but an adsentential subordinate clause, and is excluded from the table below (and the verb form must be a finite unmarked form).

TABLE 11–2. Conjunction marker and finite inflection

	Unmarked		Realis		Irrealis		
	PST	NPST	PST	NPST	INT	OPT	IMP
=(ss)iba 'so'	+	-	-	-	+	-	-
=suga 'but'	+	+	-	+	-	-	-

The complex sentence   377

The following examples illustrate the use of =(ss)iba 'so' (see §9.2.2 for
the morphophonemics of this marker) with the unmarked past inflection
and the irrealis intentional inflection.

(11–3)   [aur   nana-cï   jaacï=nu
         still   seven-CLF.GENERAL   eight-CLF.GENRAL=GEN
         munu=n   azïki-i=du   pai=nkai=mai
         man=DAT   trust-NRT=FOC   field=ALL=too
         par-ta=iba],   nau=ja   h-u-da
         leave-PST=so   what=PRT   do-THM-NEG.NRT
         u-Ø-m=bjaam=mi.
         PROG-NPST-RLS=I.wonder=CNF
         '(I) have trusted (the baby) to a child of only seven or eight
         years old and left for the field, so I wonder if (the child) is not
         doing something bad.'

(11–4)   [kuma=n   nci-di=ssiba],
         this.place=DAT   put-NPST.INT=so
         muc-i+par-i=juu=i.
         have-THM+leave-IMP=EMP=CNF
         '(I) will put (this bag) here, so take (it) away, OK?'

The following examples illustrate the use of =suga 'but' (See §9.2.3 for the
morphophonemics of this marker) with the unmarked inflection and the realis inflection.

(11–5)   [mž-taa   u-tar=ruga],   tavkjaa=ja
         three-CLF.HUMAN   exist-PST=but   one.person=TOP
         sïn-i-i...
         die-THM-NRT
         '(There) were three (children), but one died, and...'

(11–6)   [mmi-gama=nu   kama=n   zjaa=tti
         sea-DIM=GEN   that.place=DAT   ONM=QT
         akaras-i+ur-Ø=ruga],
         light-THM+PROG-NPST=but
         kuri=a   kuma=nkai=mai   akaras-i-i
         3SG=TOP   this.place=ALL=too   light-THM-NRT
         ur-Ø=bjaam=mi.
         PROG-NPST=I.wonder=CNF
         '(The evil spirit) is lighting up over there beyond the sea, but
         this (one) is perhaps trying to light up this place too, I wonder.'

378   Chapter 11

(11–7) *[kari=a   fïï-Ø-m=suga],   nnama*
        3SG=TOP   come-NPST-RLS=but   now
        ar-a-n-Ø=dooi.
        COP-THM-NEG-NPST=EMP
        'He will come, but (it) is not now.'

The first clause in an asymmetrical coordinate clause construction is dependent, in that it is usually followed by another, non-cliticised clause, as
illustrated in the examples above. This kind of structure is actually canoni-
cal in elicitation. Thus it is like an adverbial or adsentential subordinate
clause, where the first clause is dependent and the second clause is independent. However, it is very common in texts (especially in conversational
texts) for the first clause in an asymmetrical coordination construction to
terminate a sentence (nearly 65% of all the attested asymmetrical coordination), demonstrating a construction like insubordination (or 'incoordina-
tion'). Furthermore, the sentence-terminating coordinate clause is very often marked by the focus marker *=du*.

(11–8) *unukja=ga   mmja   unu   kuusjuu=n=mai*
        3PL=NOM   INTJ   that   bombardment=DAT=too
        tavkjaa=ja   sïn-i-i,   mmja,
        one.person=TOP   die-THM-NRT   INTJ
        mž-taar   a-tar=ruga=du.
        three-CLF.HUMAN   COP-PST=but=FOC
        'They (my child), among them one died in the bombardment;
        (they) were three (brothers), though.'

There is usually a major intonational break between the sentence-terminating coordinate clause and a clause that follows.
    As illustrated in (11–9) below, the sentence-terminating coordinate
clause may contain a focus marker within itself.

(11–9) *kazi=a   fik-i-i=du   ur-Ø=ruga=du.*
        wind=TOP   blow-THM-NRT=FOC   PROG-NPST=but=FOC
        'The wind is blowing, though.'

The above examples suggest that the sentence-final 'focus marker' does
not really function as a focus marker, as the declarative focus marker never
occurs sentence-finally in other contexts and the focus marker in principle
appears only once in a sentence. It is unclear at this stage, however, what

The complex sentence   379

function this sentence-final marker has.

11.3. Clause chaining

Cross-linguistically, clause chaining has been defined as 'the use of non-finite forms not headed by a conjunction with temporal or circumstantial
meaning' (Myhill and Hibiya 1988: 363). This definition is morphological
and functional. There are also syntactic criteria that identify clause chaining as opposed to other clause linking strategies such as adsentential subordination and coordination (§11.6). See also §7.1.3.2 for the related and important issue of the distinction between clause chaining (a narrative
converbal clause as a medial clause + a finite clause as the final clause of
the chain) and a phrasal SVC (a narrative converb + a finite verb as a single complex predicate).

A clause chain consists of one or more non-finite clauses, or medial
clauses, and one finite clause that terminates the chain, or the final clause.
A medial clause is a converbal clause, especially the narrative converbal
clause, the conditional converbal clause and the causal converbal clause.
Above all, the narrative converbal clause is the major bulk of the medial
clause chain. The final clause must be a finite clause.

The following example illustrates a typical clause chain, in this case
consisting of seven chained non-finite clauses (each of which is numbered
a, b, c...g.) and a finite final clause (h).

(11–10)   a. *unu*   *cïmi=u=kara*   *guusï=tii*   *uri=a*
             that   claw=ACC=first   ONM=QT   3SG=PRT
             tur-i-i,
             take-THM-NRT
          b. *birafï=nkai*   *rri-i,*
             basket=ALL   put-NRT
          c. *fïtaa-cï,*   *fïtaa-cï,*
             two-CLF.GENERAL   two-CLF.GENERAL
             kai   *badzakar-i-i,*
             that.way   raise.claw-THM-NRT
          d. *ff-a-Ø=ti*   *as-i-i,*
             bite-THM-NPST.INT=QT   do-THM-NRT
          e. *uri=a*   *tur-i-i,*
             3SG=PRT   take-THM-NRT
          f. *rri-i,*
             put-NRT

380   Chapter 11

g. *mata*   *kuzïmi-gama=u=mai*   *bur-i-i,*
   and   small.claw-DIM=ACC=too   break-THM-NRT

h. *ai=sii=du*   *fau-tar.*
   that.way=INST   eat-PST

'(I) take the claws (of the crabs)[a], put them into a Birafu (small basket)[b]; (crabs) raise their claws, two (claws)[c], trying to bite me[d], (I) catch them[e], put (them) into (the Birafu) [f]; and (in so doing I) also break the small claws[g]; (I) ate (crabs) in this way[h].'

As illustrated above, chained medial clauses encode temporally sequential, narrative events (or 'foreground' in Hopper's 1979 terms) or temporally non-sequential, modificational events/states ('background'). For example, the foreground clauses in (11–10) are [a], [b], [e], and [f], which are surrounded by background clauses that describe each event, e.g. [d] describes the circumstantial event of [c], and these two clauses describe the background for the sequential events [a] and [b].

A narrative converb is a contextual converb, conflating the perfective-narrative function and the imperfective-modificational function. From the discourse-functional perspective, the two semantic (aspectual) functions are broadly understood as foregrounding and backgrounding respectively (Hopper 1979). Foregrounded clauses constitute a main story line, depicting perfective events in temporal sequence. Backgrounded clauses modify the main story line. The distinction between the two is crucial in tracking the information flow of discourse, but the narrative converb conflates the distinction.[1] There are several means to make this distinction explicit. These are (1) same or switch subject reference tracking, (2) limiter marker attachment, and (3) partitive marking.

First, when the subject of a following clause is the same as that of the medial clause in question, the foreground function is usually entailed (e.g. (a) and (b), (e) and (f)). This is not exceptionless, as illustrated in (11–10) where the (g) clause has the same subject as (h), but they overlap temporally. On the other hand, if the subject is switched, the two clauses are not normally temporally sequential, but are contrasted with each other. For example, in (11–10), the (c) clause has a different subject 'crab', and it serves as a background clause for the preceding sequential events (a) and (b).

Second, the limiter marker =*kara* (§9.4.5) expresses 'after', marking the

---

[1] This conflation of foreground and background functions is a typical feature of clause chaining in Asian languages (Central, South, and East Asian languages) in general (Bickel 1998).

The complex sentence   381

foreground use of the medial clause to which it is attached, as shown in
(11–12).

(11–11)   *[nuuma=n   nuur-i-i]=du*   *par-tar.*
          horse =DAT   ride-THM-NRT=FOC   leave-PST
          a. '(He) rode a horse, and left.'
          b. '(He) left riding a horse.'
(11–12)   *[nuuma=n   nuur-i-i]=kara=du*   *par-tar.*
          horse =DAT   ride-THM-NRT=after=FOC   leave-PST
          a. '(He) rode a horse, and left.'
        *b. '(He) left riding a horse.'

Third, the partitive =*a* helps distinguish the backgrounded narrative converbal clauses from the foregrounded ones, since it is largely restricted to
narrative converbal clauses whose aspect is imperfective (see §4.3.3).
Thus, in the following example, only interpretation (b) is allowed.

(11–13)   *[bura=a   mak-i-i]=du*   *ifi-tar.*
          sleeve=PRT   turn.up-THM-NRT=FOC   go-PST
        *a. '(He) turned up his sleeves, and went.'
          b. '(He) went with his sleeves turned up.'

In (11–10) above, it can be seen that both the (a) clause and the (e)
clause contain the partitive, even when each of them is logically sequential
with (b) and (f) respectively. However, they entail iterativity, i.e. (a)-(b) are
iteratively carried out, so are (e)-(f). Thus the presence of the partitive in a
sequential clause does affect the interpretation of sequential clauses, implying some temporal overlap rather than a perfective sequence.

11.4. Subordination

Subordination embeds a clause within the main clause, making the subordinate clause function as a constituent of the main clause, i.e. an argument,
an adnominal, or an adjunct. The latter is either a predicate adjunct (adverb) or a sentential adjunct.

The distinction between adsentential and adverbial clauses is justified on
the basis of whether the clause is under main clause illocutionary force, as
will be discussed in §11.6.3.

382   Chapter 11

11.4.1. Adsentential subordination

An adsentential subordinate clause is a sentential adjunct of the main clause. It functions as a spatial-temporal setter, providing a topic or framework for subsequent discourse described by the main clause ('sentence margin' in Thompson and Longacre's 1985: 236 terms; see also Bickel 1998: 384). It usually occurs at the left margin of a sentence, as illustrated in (11–14) below, but it may also be nested within the main clause, as in (11–15). This nesting structure often occurs when the subject of the main clause is a topic (cf. internal topic marking is disallowed in a subordinate clause; §11.6.2).

(11–14)   *[saki=u*   *num-tigaa],*   *ba=a*   *sugu=du*
          Sake=ACC   drink-CND   1SG=TOP   right.away=FOC
          niv-Ø.
          sleep-NPST
          '[When I drink Sake], I sleep easily.'

(11–15)   *ba=a*   *[saki=u*   *num-tigaa],*   *sugu=du*
          1SG=TOP   Sake=ACC   drink-CND   right.away=FOC
          niv-Ø.
          sleep-NPST
          '[When I drink Sake], I sleep easily.'

Both finite and non-finite clauses serve as an adsentential clause. The finite adsentential clause is a clause with the temporal conjunction marker *=kja* 'when; while' (§9.2.1). Also, the adnominal clause with a formal noun such as *tukja* 'when', *mai* 'before', *atu* 'after', *jau* 'state', and *tami* 'purpose' (§4.2.1) functions like a finite adsentential clause, even though it is syntactically not a sentential adjunct, but occurs within an NP (adnominal clause + head noun). See §4.2.1 for these formal noun constructions, which are not dealt with in what follows. The non-finite adsentential clause is a converbal clause (§6.3.2.2). Many but not all converbal clauses are adsentential clauses, including: the (negative) conditional clause 'if (not)', the causal clause 'because; so', the continuous clause 'whenever', the immediate anterior clause 'as soon as', and the aversive clause 'lest'.

11.4.1.1. Temporal clauses with *=kja* 'when/while'
A temporal adsentential clause is a finite clause designating 'when/while' marked by the temporal conjunction marker *=kja* 'when' (§9.2.1).

(11–16)   *[ba=ga*   *jarabi=a*   *s-i+ur-Ø=kjaa],*

The complex sentence   383

1SG=NOM   child=PRT   do-THM+PROG-NPST=while

ffa+mur-ja=mai   *asï-Ø.*

child+sit-NLZ=too   do-NPST

'[When I was a child], (I) would do a baby sitter.'

In the above example, the main clause ends in an unmarked non-past form, which encodes habitual aspect (§10.5.2.6).

11.4.1.2. Conditional clause

A conditional clause is a clause encoding the 'if' relation or the 'when' relation. This clause is headed by one of five conditional converbs, *-ba, -ti-gaa* 'if; when' and *-dakaa* 'if not' and *-djaadakaa* 'if will not' (§6.3.2.2).

The conditional form *-ba* 'if; when' is restricted to fixed expressions such as the following:

(11–17)   *[vva=ga   kak-a-ba]=du,   zau-kar-Ø.*
          2SG=NOM   write-THM-CND=FOC   good-VLZ-NPST
          'If you write, (that) will be good.' [fixed expression: Stem-*ba(=du) zaukar* 'Why not ...'?]

(11–18)   *[ba=ga   kak-a-ba]=mai,   zjaubu=ru?*
          1SG=NOM   write-THM-CND=even   alright=FOC
          'Even if I write, (is that) alright?' [fixed expression: Stem-*ba=mai zjaubu* 'It is OK to...']

Conditional 'if, then' is more commonly expressed by *-tigaa*.

(11–19)   *[zin=nu   a-tigaa],   kav-Ø=suga.*
          money=NOM   exist-CND   buy-NPST=but
          '[If (there) is money], I would buy, though.' [adsentential subordination]

The negative conditional form *-dakaa* encodes 'if not; unless'.

(11–20)   *[zin=nu   para-a-dakaa],*
          money=ACC   pay-THM-NEG.CND
          idah-a-n-Ø=dooi.
          let.go.out-THM-NEG-NPST=EMP
          '[If (you) don't pay money], I will not let you out.'

The negative conditional intentional form *-djaadakaa* encodes 'if not'

384   Chapter 11

with an intentional meaning.

(11–21)   *[zin=nu   para-a-djaadakaa],*
          money=ACC   pay-THM-NEG.CND.INT
          idah-a-n-Ø=dooi.
          let.go.out-THM-NEG-NPST=EMP
          '[If (you) won't pay money], I will not let you out.'

11.4.1.3. Causal clause with converb 'because; if/when'
A causal clause is a clause encoding 'because' or 'if/when'.[2] This clause is
headed by the causal converb *-ba*.

(11–22)   *[ffa=nu   mmja   mainicï   nak-i-ba]=du*
          child=NOM   INTJ   everyday   cry-THM-CSL=FOC
          nivv-ai-n-Ø=saa.
          sleep-POT-NEG-NPST=R.EMP
          '[Because (my) child cries everyday], (I) cannot sleep.'
(11–23)   *[unu   mc=cu   ik-i-ba]=du   kujagaa=nkai idi-r.*
          that   road=ACC   go-THM-CSL   Kujagaa=ALL exit-NPST
          '[If (you) go through that road], (you) will get to Kuyagaa.'

11.4.1.4. Continuous clause *-gakaazï* 'whenever'
A continuous clause is headed by a continuous converb with *-gakaazï*
'whenever'. All the collected examples in my texts indicate that a continuous clause encodes exasperation on the part of the speaker.

(11–24)   *[kari=u   jurav-gakaazï],   saki-gama=u*
          3SG=ACC   call-CNTN   Sake-DIM=ACC
          muc-i+kuu-Ø=ti=du   *asï-Ø.*
          carry-THM+come-IMP=QT=FOC   do-NPST
          '[Whenever (we) call him], (he) says "bring Sake, please."'

11.4.1.5. Immediate anterior clause with *-tuu* 'as soon as'
An immediate anterior clause is headed by an anterior converb with *-tuu*
'as soon as'.

---

[2] This semantic conflation of causal and temporal meaning in one subordinating morpheme is
common cross-linguistically. Thompson and Longacre (1985: 181) state that this is because
two events which are mentioned together as being simultaneous or adjacent in time are often
inferred to be causally related.

The complex sentence   385

(11–25)   [Context: in the past a pupil had to wear a 'vernacular board'
           around his/her neck when the teacher heard him/her using Ira-
           bu rather than Japanese.]
           asi,   *[unu*   *sinsii=ga*   *par-tuu]=du,*   *mmja,*
           then   that   teacher=NOM   leave-PST=FOC   INTJ
           nubui=n   *kaki+ar-Ø*   *munu=u=baa*
           neck=DAT   hang+RSL-NPST   thing=ACC=TOP
           tur+tur.
           RED+take
           'Then, [as soon as the teacher left], (the students) would take
           off the thing (the vernacular board) from the neck.'

11.4.1.6. Aversive clause with *-zïm* 'lest'
An aversive clause is headed by an aversive converb with *-zïm* 'lest'.

(11–26)   *[kuma=n*   *nivv-i-i*   *njaa-zïm],*
           this.place=DAT   sleep-THM-NRT   PRF-AVR
           naugara   *ah-u-di.*
           something   do-THM-INT
           '[Lest (we) should fall asleep here], let's do something.'

11.4.2. Adverbial subordination

Adverbial subordination embeds a clause within the main clause as a predicate adjunct, i.e. as an adverb (§3.3.6.1). An Irabu adverbial clause modifies the main clause predicate as a manner modifier or a purpose modifier,
and is encoded by a converbal clause. Just as there are very few underived
adverbs in Irabu (§3.3.6.1), only two converbal clause types are used for
adverbial subordination, i.e. (1) a simultaneous clause, and (2) a purpose
clause, and (2) is being reanalysed as a monoclausal element, i.e. a phrasal
SVC.

11.4.2.1. Simultaneous clause with *-ccjaaki* 'while'
A simultaneous clause is headed by a simultaneous converb with *-ccjaaki*
'while'.

(11–27)   *[tatimma*   *asï-ccjaaki]=du*   *tii=ju*   *kai+kai*
           stilt   do-SIM=FOC   hand=ACC   RED+change
           as-i+ur-Ø.
           do-THM+PROG-NPST
           '(He) is taking his hands off the stilt several times [while doing

386   Chapter 11

           stilts].'
(11–28)   *[nacï-ccjaaki]*,   *cc-i+u-tar*
           cry-SIM   wear-THM+PROG-PST
           cïn=nu=baa   *nug-i-i...*
           clothes=ACC=TOP   take.off-THM-NRT
           'She took off her clothes [while crying].'

11.4.2.2. Purpose clause with *-ga* '(go) in order to'
A purpose clause is headed by a purposive converb with *-ga* 'in order to'.

(11–29)   *nnama=kara*   *[ssjugacï=nu*   *sïki+munu*
           now=ABL   Obon.festival=GEN   offering+thing
           kav-ga],   *ifï-kutu.*
           buy-PUR   go-OBL
           '(I) have to go [to buy things for offering in the Obon festi-
           val].'
(11–30)   *[sinsii=ju*   *jurav-ga]*,   *ik-a-di.*
           teacher=ACC   call-PUR   go-THM-INT
           'Let's go [to call the teacher].'

The direct object of the purposive converb is usually not case-marked, as in
(11–29), but the accusative marking is not ungrammatical, as in (11–30).
   This converb only co-occurs with directional verbs such as *ifï* 'go', *fïï*
'come', and *mudur* 'return', and so on, and no word can intervene between
the two. It is thus like a phrasal SVC (§7.1.3), and I describe it as an intermediate case between a biclausal construction (adverbial clause + main
clause) and a phrasal SVC (I thus do not indicate the clausal boundary with
',' as in the case of other converbal clauses). For example, among the five
criteria I suggested in §7.1.3.2 for the distinction between a biclausal construction and a phrasal SVC, which are restated in (11–31) below, the purposive converbal construction satisfies four, the exception being (e).

(11–31)   a. monoclausality: nothing can intervene between the two
              verbs
           b. argument sharing
           c. encoding of sequential events, manner, motions, etc.
           d. shared predicate categories such as tense, mood, negation,
              etc.
           e. single intonational unit

The complex sentence   387

With respect to (a), the purposive converb and the main clause verb form a tight syntactic unit, and nothing can intervene between them. With respect to (b), the two verbs together require the same subject. With respect to (c), it is fairly common cross-linguistically for an SVC to encode purpose (Foley and Olson 1985; Aikhenvald 2006). With respect to (d), predicate categories such as tense, negation and interrogative hold/have scope over an entire purposive construction. However, this feature is seen in Irabu subordination in general (§11.6.3). Finally, (e) distinguishes a purposive construction from a phrasal SVC. As noted in §2.9.4, rhythmic alternation maps onto an entire phrase if the first member of a phrase has one mora only. Thus the phrasal SVC in (11–32) shows the prosodic pattern (a) rather than (b) (/H/ represents High tone, and /Ø/ toneless). However, in a purposive construction in (11–33), the attested prosodic pattern is (b) even when the first member (i.e. the purposive converb) has one mora. Thus prosodically the construction is not a phrase.

(11–32)	*jak-i-i*	*fau-tar.*
	burn-THM-NRT	eat-PST
	'burned and ate.'	
	a. (H)	(Ø)(Ø)
	*b. (H)	(H)(Ø)
(11–33)	*kav-ga*	*ifi-kutu.*
	buy-PUR	go-OBL
	'go to buy'	
	*a. (H)	(Ø)(Ø)
	b. (H)	(H)(Ø)

11.4.3. Adnominal subordination

11.4.3.1. Overview

An adnominal clause functions like an adnominal word (§3.3.2), so that it directly fills the modifier slot of an NP without carrying case, occurring prenominally. No relativiser is required, but the predicate verb of the adnominal clause must have the finite unmarked form (inflecting only for tense; §6.3.1; §10.5.1.3). In the relativisation of the argument of the adnominal clause, the 'gap' strategy (Keenan 1985) marks the position relativised. Any argument, core, extended core, or peripheral, can be relativised. Furthermore, an NP that cannot be seen as an argument of the adnominal clause can establish a modifying semantic relationship with the adnominal clause, where pragmatic inference determines how the adnomi-

388 Chapter 11

nal clause narrows down the reference without the head noun playing any role in the adnominal clause. In this latter case it is more appropriate to call the modificational relationship simple attribution rather than relativisation.[3] In what follows I first describe relativisation, followed by simple attribution.

11.4.3.2. The NP that can be relativised

In relativisation, the underlying adnominal clause contains an NP coreferential with the head NP that it modifies. This coreferential NP is left out of the surface adnominal clause, leaving a gap. In the following example, the adnominal clause is shown in brackets.

(11–34) *[kuu-ttar]*   *pžtu=u=baa*
come-NEG.PST man=ACC=TOP
žž-a-dakaa   *nar-a-n-Ø.*
scold-THM-NEG.CND become-THM-NEG-NPST
'(I) have to scold those men [(who) did not come].' [subject]

(11–34) above and the following set of examples suggest that in Irabu one can relativise any argument on the so-called Accessibility Hierarchy (Keenan and Comrie 1977): subject > direct object > indirect object > possessor.

(11–35) *[žži-tar]* *munu=gami=a* *ukaasa* *ar-Ø.*
obtain-PST thing=EMP=TOP plenty exist-NPST
'(There) are a plenty of things [(I) obtained (from him)].' [direct object]

(11–36) *kuri=a*   *[vva=ga*   *unusjuku*
3SG=TOP   2SG=NOM   so.much
iravc=cu   *naraasï-tar]* *pžtu=dara.*
Irabu=ACC   teach-PST   man=CRTN
'This (guy) is the man (to whom) you taught Irabu a lot.' [E argument: indirect object]

(11–37) *[vva=ga*   *nar-a-baa=ti*
2SG=NOM   become-THM-NPST.OPT=QT
umu-i+ur-Ø]

---

[3] The encoding of relativisation and simple attribution with the same structure is found in Japonic adnominal clauses in general. Teramura (1993) refers to this distinction between relativisation and simple attribution as 'internal' and 'external' relationships respectively, noting whether the NP relativised can be considered to be underlyingly an internal member (i.e. an argument) to the adnominal clause.

think-THM+PROG-NPST

munu=u   *nau=ga?*

thing=TOP   what=Q

'What is the thing [you think you want to become]?' [E argument: the argument of the 'become' verb]

(11–38)   *[muzï*   *kar-Ø]*   *juurja=n=na*

         barley   harvest-NPST   season=DAT=TOP

         muzi=nu   *puu-gama*   *ff-i-i*

         barley=GEN   spike-DIM   bite-THM-NRT

         cc-i-i...

         come-THM-NRT

         'In the season (when) [(one) harvests barley], (I) will bring barleys holding them in my mouth, and...' [peripheral argument: temporal]

(11–39)   *banti=ga*   *zidai=n=na,*   *munu=u*   *cïfïï-Ø=ti*

         1PL=GEN   time=DAT=TOP   thing=ACC   make-NPST=QT

         asï-tigaa,   *[munu=u*   *jafï-Ø]*   *konro=mai*

         do-CND   thing=ACC   burn-NPST   grill=even

         njaa-t-ta=iba...

         not.exist-PST=so

         'In our times, when it comes to cooking, (there) was no grill [with which one burns things], so...' [peripheral argument: instrumental]

(11–40)   *nau=ti=ga*   *až-tar=gagara,*   *unu,*

         what=QT=FOC   say-PST=I.wonder   INTJ

         [ffa=nu   *jamatu+jumi=a*   *s-i+ur-Ø]*

         child=NOM   mainland.Japan+wife   do-THM+PROG-NPST

         sjuu...

         old.man

         'How can I say, well, the old man [(whose) child is a wife of a Japanese mainlander]...' [possessor]

11.4.3.3. Relativisation of an NP from a complement clause

If the underlying adnominal clause contains a sentential complement (introduced by quotative =*ti(i)*), it is still possible for an NP within the complement to be relativised. For example, from the underlying clause (11–41a), the NP *pžtu* (subject of the complement clause) can be relativised, as shown in (11–41b).[4]

---

[4] The (b) examples are taken from texts, and the corresponding (a) examples were constructed by the present author and checked by native consultants.

390   Chapter 11

(11–41) a. *ba=a* *[pžtu=nu* *icïgu* *togucinupama=n*
     1SG=TOP man=NOM always Toguchi.beach=DAT
     bizi+ur-Ø]=ti=du   *až-tar.*
     sit+PROG-NPST=QT=FOC say-PST
     'I said [that a man is always sitting on Toguchi beach]'.

    b. *[ba=ga*   *[icïgu*   *togucinupama=n*
     1SG=NOM always Toguchi.beach=DAT
     bizi+ur-Ø]=ti *až-tar]*$_{adnm}$ *pžtu*
     sit+PROG-NPST=QT say-PST man
     'The man [(who) I said is always sitting on Toguchi beach].'

11.4.3.4. Relativisation of an NP from an adjunct clause

The NP in an adjunct clause (an adverbial clause or an adsentential clause; §11.4.1, §11.4.2) may be relativised, even though this is not common in natural discourse. Thus from the structure $[C_{ad}[C_{main}]]$, the NP in C_{ad} (adjunct clause) can be relativised, giving rise to an NP $[C_{ad}[C_{main}]]_{adnm} N_{nead}$. The relativisation of core arguments is the most common, but a peripheral argument may also be relativised. In (11–42) the relativisation of the direct object NP in an adverbial clause (simultaneous converbal clause) is illustrated. (11–42a) is an underlying clause, from which (11–42b) is derived.

(11–42) a. *ba=a* *[pžtu=u* *macï-ccjaaki]=du* *sïgutu=u*
     1SG=TOP man=ACC wait-SIM=FOC work=ACC
     as-i+u-tar.
     do-THM+PROG-PST
     'I was doing work [while waiting for a man].'

    b. *[ba=ga*   *[macï-ccjaaki]* *sïgutu=u*
     1SG=TOP wait-SIM   work=ACC
     as-i+u-tar]$_{adnm}$ *pžtu.*
     do-THM+PROG-PST man
     'The man [(whom) I was doing work [while waiting for]].'

(11–43) below illustrates the relativisation of the locative NP in a conditional adsentential clause.

(11–43) a. *[kunu* *jaa=n*   *sïmav-tigaa],*
     this   house=DAT live-CND
     ngjamasï-gi-ka-Ø-m.
     noisy-seem-VLZ-NPST-RLS
     '[If I live in this house], (it) should be noisy, it seems.'

The complex sentence   391

b. *[[sïmav-tigaa],   ngjamasï-gi-kar-Ø]ₐₐₙₘ   jaa.*
live-CND   noisy-seem-VLZ-NPST   house
'A house [in which [if I live], it should be noisy].'

11.4.3.5. Relativisation of an NP from other kinds of complex clause
It is impossible for an NP within a coordinate clause (§11.2) to be relativised. When the NP in a clause chain (§11.3) is relativised, the relativised
NP must belong in the final main clause, not in a chained clause. In (11–
44a) below, the topic-marked subject belongs in the main clause. It may be
relativised, deriving (11–44b).

(11–44)   a. *hikooki=a   [bakudan=nu   utus-i-i],*
plane=TOP   bomb=ACC   drop-THM-NRT
[sïn-as-i-i],
die-CAUS-THM-NRT
[kizjuu=ju   vc-i-i],   par-tar.
machinegun=ACC   shoot-THM-NRT   leave-PST
'The plane [dropped bombs], [killed (people)], [fired machineguns, and] left.'
b. *[[bakudan=nu   utus-i-i],   [sïn-as-i-i],*
bomb=ACC   drop-THM-NRT   die-CAUS-THM-NRT
[kizjuu=ju   vc-i-i],   par-tar]ₐₐₙₘ
machinegun=ACC   shoot-THM-NRT   leave-PST
hikooki.
plane
'The plane [(that) [dropped bombs], [killed (people)], [fired
machineguns, and] left].'

(11–45) and (11–46) below further illustrate the restriction of relativisation
in clause chaining. In (11–45) below, from the underlying clause (11–45a),
the E argument NP of the final main clause is relativised to derive (11–
45b).

(11–45)   a. *uja=a   [ffa=u   nas-i-i],*
parent=TOP   child=ACC   give.birth-THM-NRT
pžtu=n=du   azïki-tar.
man=DAT=FOC   trust-PST
'The parent (mother) [gave birth to a child, and] entrusted it
to a man.'
b. *[uja=nu   [ffa=u   nas-i-i],*

parent=NOM	child=ACC	give.birth-THM-NRT
*azïki-tar]*adnm	*pžtu*	
trust-PST	man	

'the man [to whom the parent (mother) [gave birth to a child and] entrusted it]'.

If the final clause here is turned into a chained clause, as shown in (11–46) below, then the relativisation of the same E argument NP becomes impossible.

(11–46) a.

uja=a	*[ffa=u*	*nas-i-i],*
parent=TOP	child=ACC	give.birth-THM-NRT
[pžtu=n	*azïki-i],*	*par-tar.*
man=DAT	trust-NRT	leave-PST

'The parent (mother) [gave birth to a child], [entrusted it to a man, and] left.'

b.

*[uja=ga	*[ffa=u*	*nas-i-i],*
parent=NOM	child=ACC	give.birth-THM-NRT
[azïki-i],	*par-tar]*adnm	*pžtu*
trust-NRT	leave-PST	man

[Intended meaning] 'a man [with whom the parent (mother) [gave birth to a child], [entrusted it, and] left].'

If the structure of the last medial clause and the final clause (i.e. *azïkii, par-tar*) in (11–46a) is rearranged as a monoclausal constituent, i.e. a phrasal SVC, with single phrasal prosody (§7.1.3.2 (5)), *azïkii partar* is treated as the main clause predicate VP governing *uja* 'a parent' (A argument), *ffa* 'child' (zero pronominalised O argument) and *pžtu* 'man' (E argument). In this structure, it is possible for the E argument to be relativised, as it belongs in the main clause.

(11–47)

[uja=nu	*[ffa=u*	*nas-i-i],*
parent=NOM	child=ACC	give.birth-THM-NRT
azïki-i	*par-tar]*adnm	*pžtru*
trust-NRT	leave-PST	man

'a man [to whom a parent, [after giving birth to a child], entrusted it]'

11.4.3.6. Simple attribution
In simple attribution, the NP modified by an adnominal clause does not

The complex sentence   393

function as an argument in the underlying adnominal clause. Thus in (11–48) below the relativised NP *kaagi* 'smell', which serves as head of the subject NP of the main clause, cannot be analysed as an argument of the adnominal clause, which has a complete set of arguments, i.e. (ellipted) A and O *žžu* 'fish'.

(11–48)   *[žžu=u   jafi-Ø]   kaagi=nu=du   fïï-Ø.*
          fish=ACC   burn-NPST   smell=NOM=FOC   come-NPST
          'A smell [that (occurs when one) burns fish comes].'

Likewise, the NP in (11–49) below is not seen as a core or peripheral argument of the adnominal clause.

(11–49)   *[vva=ga   budur-tar]   kagi-sa=a   mmja*
          2SG=NOM   dance-PST   beautiful-NLZ=TOP   INTJ
          icïban.
          best
          'The beauty [with which you danced] is, well, the best.'

Further examples follow, which demonstrate that in principle any head noun and any clause can establish the modificational relationship as long as pragmatic inference can permit this. In (11–50), the head noun *kui* 'voice' and the adnominal clause *sïtabutu=nu ur* 'there is a bedfellow' establish a modificational relationship, even though the head noun has no role in the adnominal clause. By pragmatic inference the hearer knows that this adnominal clause narrows down the type of voice heard over the telephone.

(11–50)   *hai,   kuri=a   mmja   [sïtabutu=nu   ur-Ø]*
          Hey   3SG=TOP   well   bed.fellow=NOM   exist-NPST
          kui=dooi=tii.
          voice=EMP=QT
          'Hey, this (voice of her that is heard over telephone) sounds like a voice which is heard when her bedfellow is at her place.' [i.e. This voice is so upset that this probably indicates that her bedfellow is at her place now.]

In (11–51a) below, the interpretation is that the head noun has a role in the adnominal clause (as a patient subject), whereas in (11–51b) the interpretation is that the head noun has no role.

394   Chapter 11

(11–51)   a. *[cuu-fï   sïgu-rai-tar]   mipana*
             strong-AVLZ   hit-PASS-PST   face
             'The face that was terribly hit.'
          b. *[cuu-fï   sïgu-rai-tar]   mipana*
             strong-AVLZ   hit-PASS-PST   face
             'The face that (indicates that he) was terribly hit.' [e.g. when
             you are looking at a person with a bitter face, you infer
             that this person must have been teriibly beaten.]

11.4.4. Complementation

Complementation is the 'syntactic situation that arises when a notional
sentence or predication is an argument of a predicate' (Noonan 1985:42).
Complementation involves two syntactic constructions: quotative construction (§11.4.4.1) and adnominal clause + formal noun (§11.4.4.2).

   A complement clause functioning as the object of speech act verbs such
as *až* 'say', *cïfï* 'hear', and *tanum* 'ask', and cognitive verbs such as *umuv*
'think' is introduced by the quotative *=ti(i)*. Otherwise, no special complementiser morpheme exists in Irabu. Rather, there is a grammaticalisation
path from an adnominal clause structure towards a complement clause
structure, and a formal noun (*su(u)* 'thing; man', *kutu* 'fact', and *munu*
'thing') heading an adnominal clause functions like a complementiser.
Thus, this latter type of complementation is actually a subtype of adnominal clause structure, but functions as a complement clause.

11.4.4.1. Quotative complement

A quotative clause is a type of finite complement clause, functioning as an
object complement of speech act verbs such as *až* 'say', *asï* 'do' (which has
the senses 'do' and 'say'), *panasï* 'speak', etc., and cognitive verbs such as
umuv 'think', *kangair* 'think', *sïï* 'know', etc.

(11–52)   *[kjuu=ja   ueno=nkai=du   ik-i-i*
          today=TOP   Ueno=ALL=FOC   go-THM-NRT
          t-tar=tii]=du   asï+asï.
          come-PST=QT=FOC   RED+do
          '(She) goes like, ["Today (I) went to Ueno"].'
(11–53)   *[uri=u   fa-a-baa=tii]=ja*
          3SG=ACC   eat-THM-NPST.OPT=QT=TOP
          umu-u-n-Ø.
          think-THM-NEG-NPST
          '(I) don't think like, ["(I) want to eat it"].'

The complex sentence   395

Unlike other subordinate clauses, a quotative clause can contain a topic marker and/or focus marker independently of the main clause in which it is embedded, as it is direct quotation. In (11–54) below, the quotative clause contains the topic marker =*ja* and the focus marker =*du*. Note that the quotative clause itself is marked by the focus marker =*du*, which belongs in the main clause.

(11–54)   *[kuri=a   nau=n=mai=du*
          3SG=TOP   what=DAT=too=FOC
          nar-i+ufi-Ø=tii]   *umu-i-ba=du,*
          become-THM+PROS-NPST=QT   think-THM-CSL=FOC
          puka=nkai=ja   *ik-ah-a-n-Ø=dooi.*
          outside=ALL=TOP   go-CAUS-THM-NEG-NPST=EMP
          '(It is) because (I) think like, ["This (guy)'s gonna become (troubled by) whatever trouble"], (that) (I) do not let you go out.' [object complement]

11.4.4.2. Adnominal clause structure functioning like a complement
Two formal nouns, *su(u)* 'thing; man' (§4.2.1.8) and *kutu* 'fact' (§4.2.1.4), function like an English complementiser 'that', and the modifying adnominal clause functions like a complement clause. The formal nouns are glossed COMP below.

In (11–55a) below, the NP consisting of the adnominal clause and the formal noun *su(u)* (which is realised as *ruu* as a result of assimilation) functions as a direct object. As an NP, it carries case, just like other NPs as illustrated in (11–55b).

(11–55)   a. *[fau-tar=ruu]=ju=mai*   *bassi-i=du*
          eat-PST=COMP=ACC=even   forget-NRT=FOC
          ar-Ø.
          RSL-NPST
          '(He) has even forgot [the fact that (he) ate].' [object complement]
          b. *[uri]=u=mai*   *basi-i=du*   *ar-Ø.*
          3SG=ACC=even   forget-NRT=FOC   RSL-NPST
          '(He) has forgot even [that].' [object NP]

There are two important differences between a formal noun construction and a quotative clause construction. First, whereas the former carries case when functioning as an argument just like an argument NP, the quotative clause does not carry case in the same environment. Second, whereas quotation embeds a fully finite, fully independent clause of any speech act type (i.e. declarative, interrogative, or imperative; §10.1) into a main clause, an NP consisting of an adnominal clause and a formal noun is subject to severe restrictions, just like other adnominal clauses (§11.4.3.1): (1) the adnominal clause is a finite unmarked form; (2) the adnominal clause cannot contain its own topic and focus, as a general restriction on subordination; (3) the adnominal clause cannot have an independent interrogative/imperative force, again as a general restriction on subordination. In (11–56) below, the quotative clause is headed by a finite realis verb, contains the topic marker =*a*, and is an interrogative clause.

(11–56) *[vva=a*   *kuu-ka-ta-m=mu=tii]*   *až-tar.*
         2SG=TOP   hard-VLZ-PST-RLS=Q=QT   say-PST
         '(I) said, ["Did you feel painful?"]'

By contrast, the predicate of the adnominal clause in (11–57) below is a finite unmarked verb, the clause does not contain the topic marker, and the clause cannot be an interrogative or imperative clause.

(11–57) *[vva=ga*   *kuu-ka-tar=ru]=u=baa*
         2SG=NOM   hard-VLZ-PST=COMP=ACC=TOP
         ss-i+ur-Ø.
         know-THM+PROG-NPST
         '(I) know that you felt painful.'

11.5. Focus construction (*kakarimusubi*)

This section describes the focus construction. Focus marking is discussed in this chapter because it is associated with complex clause structures (e.g. a focus marker may be attached to an adsentential clause, and so on.).

11.5.1. A brief note on *kakarimusubi*

The focus construction in Irabu and other Ryukyuan varieties and in Old Japanese is known as *kakarimusubi* (literally 'marking and predication') in Japanese linguistics (see Hendriks 1998 and Shinzato and Serafim 2003 for a historical account of Japonic *kakarimusubi*, and Karimata 1999 and Uchima 1985 for Ryukyuan *kakarimusubi*). *Kakarimusubi* is characterised by two features: focus marking and verbal concordance, as discussed below.

As a simple approximation, a standard Japonic *kakarimusubi* is a con-

The complex sentence   397

cord phenomenon where the use of a focus marker triggers the use of a
specific verb form, e.g. adnominal form or *Rentaikei*, instead of the expected finite, or *Shushikei* (based on Shinzato and Serafim 2003: 189). Pragmatically, the focus marking on an argument (or another non-predicate element such as an adverb) entails the presupposed status of the predicate.

Whereas a standard Japonic *kakarimusubi* is a 'positive' concordance
phenomenon where the use of a focus marker *requires* the use of a specific
verb form, Irabu *kakarimusubi* is a 'negative' concordance phenomenon,
where the use of a focus marker *blocks* the use of a specific verb form, the
finite realis form (§6.3.1), due to the pragmatic characteristic that this verb
form marks an assertion carrying new information (§10.5.1.1, §10.5.1.3).[5]
That is, the finite realis form marks predicate focus, thus this form cannot
co-occur with the focus marking on the argument (argument focus, where
the predicate is presupposed).

(11–58)   *ba=ga=du*   *mii-tar/-di/*-ta-m*
          1SG=NOM=FOC   do-PST/-INT/*-PST-RLS
          'I saw/will see/*(surely) saw.' [predicate is presupposed]

In argument focus structure, the predicate verb form is a finite form other
than the realis form, i.e. an unmarked form (§10.5.1.3) or an irrealis form
(§10.5.1.2). Thus Irabu *kakarimusubi* can be explained in terms of the
pragmatic function of the verb form, rather than in terms of a mere syntactic concordance, as in the case of a standard Japonic *kakarimusubi*.

In what follows I describe focus marking in terms of (a) the domain or
scope of focus and (b) the function of focus in information-structure. With
regard to (a), the distinction is made between Sentence-Focus (§11.5.2.1),
which scopes over the entire sentence (a.k.a. broad focus), Argument Focus
(§11.5.2.2), which scopes over the specific constituent (argument or adjunct) of a sentence, and Predicate Focus (§11.5.2.3), which scopes over
the predicate. With regard to (b), the distinction is made between WH Focus (§11.5.2.4), which focuses on the unspecified portion of the proposition
and Contrastive Focus (§11.5.2.5), which, by focusing on an element in a
proposition, strongly evokes alternatives to the focused element in the
mind of the addressee.

---

[5] On the other hand, *kakarimusubi* in other Miyako Ryukyuan varieties may be referred to as
'no concordance' phenomenon, since the use of a focus marker does not restrict the choice of
verb form, i.e. any verb inflection is possible (Uchima 1985).

398   Chapter 11

11.5.2. Focus marking
11.5.2.1. Sentence-Focus
A glance at just a few example sentences listed in the present work reveals that focus marking is almost obligatory in every sentence in Irabu. In fact, focus marking is obligatory even in the Sentence-Focus environment, where the entire sentence is within the scope of the focus domain and no particular focus is put on an a constituent of the sentence. The focus marking occurs on the left-most constituent in the SF context. In the following example, where B's response to the question raised by A is all-new in terms of information-structure (hence SF), but the focus marking still occurs on the left-most constituent.

(11–59)   A: *nautti=ga*   *vva=a*   *cïmudi+ur-Ø?*
              why=FOC   2SG=TOP   get.angry+PROG-NPST
              'Why are you angry?'
          B: *agu=ga=du*   *uttu=u*
              friend=NOM=FOC   younger.sibling=ACC
              nak-asï-tar=rju.
              cry-CAUS-PST=UPDT
              'My friend made my brother cry.'
(11–60)   B: *uttu=u=du*   *agu=ga*
              younger.sibling=ACC=FOC   friend=NOM
              nak-asï-tar=rju.
              cry-CAUS-PST=UPDT
              'My friend made my brother cry.'

11.5.2.2. Argument Focus
In Argument Focus, the focus marker *=du* has scope over an argument or an adjunct, whether it be phrasal or clausal. Since the focus marker has scope over the whole argument, it never occurs within a complex NP. Thus the modifier, whether it is an NP, an adnominal word, or an adnominal clause, cannot be focus-marked. In (11–61) below, the pragmatically focused element in B's speech is the modifier NP *ucïnaa=nu* of the superordinate peripheral argument NP (ablative-marked), but the focus marker does not mark the modifier NP but the entire peripheral argument NP (indicated by square brackets) that contains the modifier NP.

(11–61)   A. *pžsara=nu*   *kuukoo=ru?* *ucïnaa=nu*   *kuukoo=ru?*
              Hirara=GEN   airport=Q   Okinawa=GEN   airport=Q
              '(Are you leaving from) the airport in Hirara, or the one in

The complex sentence   399

Okinawa?'

B. *[ucïnaa=nu*   *kuukoo=kara]=du*   *ifï-kutu.*
   Okinawa=GEN   airport=ABL=FOC   go-OBL
   'I am supposed to go [from the airport in HIRARA].'

A complement clause may be focus-marked if it is an argument of the main clause.

(11–62)   *[nnama=kara*   *ik-i-i,*   *kurus-a-di=tii]=du*
            now=ABL   go-THM-NRT   kill-THM-INT=QT=FOC
            až-tar=ca.
            say-PST=HS
            '(He) said, ["(I) will go now, and kill (him)"].'

(11–63)   *[cïn=nu*   *mima-i+u-tar=ruu=ju]=du*
            clothes=ACC   tidy-THM+PROG-PST=COMP=ACC=FOC
            juu   *ubui+ur-Ø.*
            clearly   remember+PROG-NPST
            '(I) remember [that (he) would tidy up my clothes].'

An (sentential) adjunct, an adsentential clause (11–64) or an adverbial clause (11–65) may be focus-marked.

(11–64)   *[vva=ga*   *mii-n-Ø=kja]=du,*
            2SG=NOM   look-NEG-NPST=when=FOC
            bara-i+ur-Ø=pazï.
            laugh-THM+PROG-NPST=maybe
            '(It is) [when you are not aware] (that) (they) are laughing, perhaps.'

(11–65)   *[aagu=u*   *asï-ccjaaki]=du,*   *icï+muju*
            song=ACC   do-SIM=FOC   five+six
            ark-i+u-tar.
            walk-THM+PROG-PST
            '(It was) [while singing a song] (that) the five or six (people) were walking.'

A chained medial clause or a series of chained medial clauses may also be focus-marked, indicating that the whole medial chain is treated as a single constituent.

(11–66)   *unusjuku*   *num-i-i,*   *bjuu-i-i=du,*

so.much   drink-THM-NRT   get.drunk-THM-NRT=FOC

aagu=mai   *až-tar.*

song=too   say-PST

'(I) drank so much, got drunk, and then sang a song, too.' [medial clause as adsentential clause]

According to my text data, the focus-marked clause in a clause chain is always the last medial clause in a chain, as illustrated above. This suggests that an entire medial clausal chain (M_1, M_2, M_3...M_n) is focus-marked, as opposed to the final clause (F). Thus the clause structure of (11–66) is schematised as $[[[M_1], M_2]_{=FOC} F]$.

An asymmetrical coordinate clause is not focus-marked. This means that an asymmetrical coordinate clause and a following clause cannot establish a single presupposition-focus information structure. Seemingly focus-marked asymmetrical coordinate clauses are in most cases sentence-terminating coordinate clauses (§11.2.2), and as noted in §11.2.2, this focus marker does not function as such, as there is no clause that governs it. The very few attested examples where an asymmetrical coordinate clause seems to be marked by the focus marker and further followed by another clause, such as (11–67), turn out to be bisentential in several respects.

(11–67)   *kazi=a*   *fik-i-i=du*

         wind=TOP   blow-THM-NRT=FOC

         ur-Ø=ruga=du.   *kunkuriito*

         PROG-NPST=but=FOC   Concrete

         ja-i-ba=du,   *maadaa*

         COP-THM-CSL=FOC   not.very

         ss-ai-n-Ø=dara.

         know-POT-NEG-NPST=CRTN

         'The wind does blow, but (the house you are living in is made of) concrete, so (you) can't recognise (the fact that the wind blows outside).'

First, there is a major intonation break between the first clause and the second, as in the case of symmetrical coordination (§11.2.1) and a sentence-terminating asymmetrical coordinate clause (§11.2.2). Second, if we consider that the asymmetrical coordinate clause is dependent on the second clause (which is internally complex, consisting of an adsentential causal clause and the main clause), then the main clause governs two focus

The complex sentence   401

markers, one on the coordinate clause and the other on the adsentential clause. This would be a serious exception to the general constraint that the focus marker appears once only in a sentence (see the first paragraph of this section). It is thus more plausible to consider that the coordinate clause here is a sentence-terminating one, and the second clause commences a new sentence.

11.5.2.3. Predicate Focus

If the predicate is focused, the focus is basically put on the left-most element of the predicate phrase, but the focus may be put on the direct object NP if the predicate takes the direct object. In the following example, the question by A induces Predicate Focus, and the response of B puts the focus marker =du after the lexical verb of the aspectual AVC.

(11–68)   A. *vva=a*   *nau=ju=ga*   *as-i+ur-Ø?*
              2SG=TOP   what=ACC=FOC   do-THM+PROG-NPST
              'What are you doing?'
          B. *ba=a*   *juku-i-i=du*   *ur-Ø.*
              1SG=TOP   take.rest-THM-NRT=FOC   PROG-NPST
              'I am taking a rest.'

If the aspectual AVC is transitive, either the lexical verb or the direct object NP is focus marked. Thus the response to (11–68A) would be either of the following:

(11–69)   B. *ba=a*   *tigami=u*   *kak-i-i=du*
              1SG=TOP   letter=ACC   write-THM-NRT=FOC
              ur-Ø.
              PROG-NPST
              'I am writing a letter' [phrasal AVC]
(11–70)   B. *ba=a*   *tigami=u=du*   *kak-i+ur-Ø.*
              1SG=TOP   letter=ACC=FOC   write-THM+PROG-NPST
              'I was writing a letter.' [agglutinative AVC]

Note here that the presence of focus marking lead to the phrasal AVC and its absence leads to the agglutinative AVC, showing the word-phrase alternation pattern (§6.4.2.3).

If the predicate consists of a single word, and if the speaker wants to put focus on it, three possible strategy are available. First, he simply uses a modal or discourse marker that pertains to emphasis, such as the emphatic

402   Chapter 11

marker =*dooi* (§9.3.7), the certainty marker =*dara* (§9.3.6) and the information-updater =*ju* (§9.6.1). Second, in a very limited environment, the
speaker uses the realis mood to mark the focus on the predicate
(§10.5.1.1), even though the realis mood marking is more than simple focus marking, integrated into the mood system of this language and carries
the tone of warning, rhetorical question, etc. There is a third strategy,
whereby the focus marking divides the word into two parts, turning the single word predicate to a phrase.

(11–71)   *ba=a*   *jukuv=du=sï-Ø.*
          1SG=TOP   take.rest=FOC=do-NPST
          'I take a rest.'

This process is the zero conversion of the verb stem to an independent
word that functions as the VP complement of the light verb construction
(§3.3.6.2). That is, this phrase consists of the light verb *sï* (§6.3.5.2) and its
complement *jukuv*, which is a zero-converted adverb that now functions as
the complement of the light verb.

   The exact function of the third strategy as against the first strategy is still
unclear. The attested examples of my corpus and my elicitation data suggest that this zero-converted light verb construction does not function as a
mere verbal focus construction, expressing a general-habitual meaning. A
further research is needed to fully clarify the function of this third strategy.

11.5.2.4. WH Focus

Let us now turn to the functional aspects of focus marking. WH Focus is
marked by the dedicated WH focus marker =*ga* (§9.5.2.2). The WH focus
marker =*ga* is used for embedded WH questions as well, as the following
examples illustrates.

(11–72)   *[taru=nu=ga*   *sïn-tar=gagara]*
          who=NOM=FOC   die-PST=DUB
          ss-a-n-Ø.
          know-THM-NEG-NPST
          '(I) don't know who died.'

(11–73)   *[taru=nu=ga*   *sïn-tar=tii]=ja*
          who=NOM=FOC   die-PST=QT=TOP
          ss-i+ur-Ø.
          know-THM-PROG-NPST
          '(I) know who died.'

The complex sentence 403

In (11–72), the embedding marker is the dubitative marker =*gagara* (§9.3.2), which may also be used as the modal marker that closes off the independent sentence. In (11–73), the embedding marker is the quotative marker =*tii* (§11.4.4.1). Note that this difference comes from the certainty with which the speaker has with respect to the answer of the WH question being embedded. According to Kinuhata (2016), the Irabu-Nakachi dialect of Irabu employs different focus markers (=ga/=du) as well as different embedding markers (=*gara*/=*tii*) depending on whether the speaker knows the answer of the embedded WH question, in such a way that =*du* (declarative focus marker) and =*tii* (quotative embedding marker) are used if the speaker is certain about the answer of the WH question embedded whereas =*ga* (interrogative focus marker) and =*gara* (dubitative marker) are used if the speaker is uncertain about it. In the Nagahama dialect of Irabu, which the present work is concerned with, such an alternation of focus marking is not observed, and there is only the alternation of the embedding marker as illustrated above.

11.5.2.5. Contrastive Focus
Contrastive Focus is illustrated below, where the declarative focus marker =*du* or the interrogative focus marker =*ru* may be used depending on the sentence type.

(11–74) *kaami*   *ar-a-da,*   *zjunzi=u=du*
        Kaami   COP-THM-NEG.NRT   Junji=ACC=FOC
        jurab-i+ur-Ø.
        call-THM+PROG-NPST
        '(I) am calling Junji, not Kaami.'
(11–75) *kaami*   *ar-a-da,*   *zjunzi=u=ru*
        Kaami   COP-THM-NEG.NRT   Junji=ACC=FOC
        jurab-i+ur-Ø?
        call-THM+PROG-NPST
        '(Are you) calling Junji, not Kaami?'

Contrastive Focus may be explicitly marked by the contrastive marker =*gami*. As mentioned in §9.5.1, this additional marking is helpful since the focus marker =*du* is used both in Sentence-Focus and in Contrastive Focus, conflating the two functions.

404   Chapter 11

11.6. Degree of dependency: Coordination, clause chaining, adsentential and adverbial subordination

In this section I describe criteria for distinguishing between coordination, clause chaining, adsentential and adverbial subordination. As summarised in TABLE 11–3 below, there are four criteria: (1) focus marking, (2) restriction on clause-internal topic marking, (3) dependency with respect to main clause illocutionary scope, and (4) relativisation of an NP from inside the clause.[6]

TABLE 11–3. Coordination and subordination: distinction

Linkage type	Subtype	Focus marking	Restriction on clause-internal topic marking	under the scope of main clause illocutionary force	Relativisation of an NP from inside the clause
Coordination	Sym	-	-	-	-
	Asym	-	-	-	-
Clause chaining		+	±	±	-
Subordination	Ads	+	+	±	+
	Adv	+	+	+	+

The major criterion for distinguishing between coordination and other linkage types is focus marking. Coordination and clause chaining on one hand and subordination on the other are distinguished by the restriction on relativisation. These and other criteria are discussed in the sections below.

11.6.1. Focus marking

As noted in §11.5.2, an adsentential clause, an adverbial clause, and a chained clause (or a series of chained clauses) may be focus-marked, while coordinate clauses may not, assuming that the sentence-final focus marker in asymmetrical coordination is not functioning as such (§11.5.2).

The most relevant theoretical question here is whether focussability of a clause reveals the embedded status of the clause. This is relevant especially

---

[6] Criteria (1) and (3) are due to Foley and Van Valin (1984), Bickel (1993) and Bisang (1995). Criterion (3) is known as 'operator dependency' in the literature, which concerns whether a clause is dependent on the main clause for specification of clausal categories, or 'operators', such as tense, negation, and illocutionary force. Foley and Van Valin (1984) assume a three-way distinction of clause linking types, or 'nexus' types with the two criteria (1) and (3): (A) coordination (-embedded, -dependent), (B) subordination (+embedded, +dependent), and (C) co-subordination (-embedded, +dependent).

The complex sentence   405

in the study of clause chaining, which is standardly defined as clausal 'co-subordination' (Foley and Van Valin 1984), where a clause is dependent but not embedded (see Footnote 6 of this chapter). However, if we assume that focussability indicates embeddedness (as in Haspelmath 1995: 15), Irabu clause chaining would be an embedding structure, as in the case of adsentential and adverbial subordination.

I do not take focussability as a feature of embeddedness, and I argue against the analysis that chained clauses in Irabu are embedded. This argument rests on two observations. First, a chained clause cannot be seen as a constituent of a superordinate clause. This is in sharp contrast to complements, which serve as (fill the structural slot of) argument NPs, adjunct clauses, which serve as (sentential or predicate) adjuncts, or adnominal clauses, which serve as adnominal words. Second, whereas clear embedded processes such as complementation and adverbial/adsentential/adnominal subordination are not freely recursive (due to the extralinguistic factor of information-processing), clause chaining is almost unrestricted with regard to recursiveness.

I take focussibility as a feature of dependency. That is, a focused element cannot be independently a focus but must always entail the presence of a presupposed element. This is a dependency at the level of information structure.

11.6.2. Restricted clause-internal topic marking

A coordinate clause may contain a topic marker. In (11–76), two independent clauses are conjoined by a conjunction word (§3.3.6.3), demonstrating symmetrical coordination. Each clause contains the topic marker =a (§9.5).

(11–76) *pinza=a*   *mcï=kara=du*   *par-tar=ca.*
        goat=TOP   road=ABL=FOC   leave-PST=HS
        mata   *unta=a*   *kaa=kara=du*   *par-tar=ca.*
        and   frog=TOP   river=ABL=FOC   leave-PST=HS
        'The goat left along the road; the frog left along the river.'

Example (11–77) demonstrates asymmetrical coordination, where the first clause is marked by a conjunction marker (§9.2). Again, each clause contains the topic marker =a.

(11–77) *kari=a*   *nnama=kara=du*   *fïï-Ø=suga,*
        3SG=TOP   now=ABL=FOC   come-NPST=but

406   Chapter 11

vva=a	*sugu=du*	*ifï-kutu?*
2SG=TOP	right.away=FOC	go-OBL

'He is going to come soon, but are you going now?'

An adsentential or adverbial subordinate clause, on the other hand, does not accommodate topic marking. In the following example, therefore, the topic-marked subject NP belongs in the main clause, not in the adsentential clause.

(11–78)
pžtu=u	*[sïn-tigaa],*	*nza=nkai=ga*	*ifï-kutu*
man=TOP	die-CND	where=ALL=FOC	go-OBL

'Where does a man go when (he) dies?'

Since the topic-marked NP belongs in the main clause, when the converbal clause is extraposed to the left margin of the sentence, we get the following structure:

(11–79)
[sïn-tigaa],	*pžtu=u*	*nza=nkai=ga*	*ifï-kutu?*
die-CND	man=TOP	where=ALL=FOC	go-OBL

'Where does a man go when (he) dies?'

In (11–80) below, the nominative-marked NP belongs in the converbal clause. This is evidenced in the fact that it is impossible for the NP to be transposed to the medial position, as in (11–81), where the strict verb-final order within a subordinate clause is violated.

(11–80)
[pžtu=nu	*sïn-tigaa],*	*nza=nkai=ga*	*ifï-kutu?*
man=NOM	die-CND	where=ALL=FOC	go-OBL

'Where does a man go when (he) dies?'

(11–81)
*[sïn-tigaa,	*pžtu=nu]*	*nza=nkai=ga*	*ifï-kutu?*
die-CND	man=NOM	where=ALL=FOC	go-OBL

'Where does a man go when (he) dies?'

A chained clause may contain the topic marker =a only if the clause is backgrounded. Pragmatically, when the topic marker =a appears in a chained clause, it is always interpreted as marking a contrastive topic.

(11–82)
bikidum=ma	*samsin-gama=mai*	*pžk-i-i,*
male=TOP	Samsin-DIM=too	play-THM-NRT
midum=ma	*aagu-gama=u=mai*	*až-Ø.*

The complex sentence   407

female=TOP   song-DIM=ACC=too   say-NPST
'Men play the *Samsin* guitar, whereas women sing songs.'

By contrast, when a chained clause functions as a foreground clause encoding a sequential event (see §11.3), it cannot contain the topic marker.

11.6.3. Main clause illocutionary scope

An adverbial clause is under the scope of the illocutionary force (interrogative force, imperative force, mood, negation, etc.) of the main clause
(demonstrating 'conjunct scope' in Bickel's 1993 terms), whereas a coordinate clause is not (demonstrating 'disjunct scope'). An adsentential clause
and a chained clause may be either under the scope of the main clause illocutionary force or independent of it.

Let us take negation and interrogative force as examples of the main
clause illocutionary force, as these represent the narrowest and broadest
scopes of various illocutionary forces in Irabu respectively. As summarised
in TABLE 11–4 below, a coordinate clause a chained clause, and an adsentential clause are independent of the scope of the main clause negator
whereas an adverbial clause is always under the scope of the main clause
negator. With respect to interrogative force, a chained clause and an adsentential clause may be under the scope of the main clause interrogator.

TABLE 11–4. Main clause illocutionary force

	Coordination	Chaining	Adsentential	Adverbial
Negation	-	-	-	+
interrogative	-	±	±	+

11.6.3.1. The scope of negation
A coordinate clause, either symmetrical or asymmetrical, is independent of
the scope of the main clause negator, as both clauses are finite, inflecting
for negative polarity. Likewise, a medial clause in a clause chain, which is
headed by a narrative converb, is also independently inflected for negation
(-*i* for affirmative and -*da* for negative). If the medial clause in a chain is in
the affirmative, the main clause negator does not negate the medial clause:

(11–83)   *nak-i-i,*   *fa-a-t-ta-m.*
          cry-THM-NRT   eat-THM-NEG-PST-RLS
          'Crying over, (she) didn't eat.'

Here, if this construction is rearranged as a phrasal SVC (§7.1.3), by mak-

408   Chapter 11

ing the whole construction pronounced with a single unit of prosody
(phrasal mapping of rhythmic alternation; §2.9.4), the main clause negator
scopes over the entire SVC:

(11–84)   nak-i-i(=ja)   fa-a-t-ta-m.
          cry-THM-NRT(=TOP)   eat-THM-NEG-PST-RLS
          '(She) did not eat crying.' or
          '(She) ate in some way but not while crying' (contrastive)

Here, the topic marker =a may appear as a (contrastive) negative marker
within a VP (§9.5.1.2).
   An adsentential clause is independent of the scope of the main clause
negator, as in (11–85).

(11–85)   batafïsari-ka-i-ba,   puka=nkai
          angry-VLZ-THM-CSL   outside=ALL
          idi-t-ta-m=dooi.
          go.out-NEG-PST-RLS=EMP
          'Because (I) was angry, (I) didn't go out.'

An adverbial subordinate clause such as the simultaneous converb is under the scope of the main clause negator. In (11–86a), the negative scope is
over an entire sentence. In (11–86b), the negative scope is on the converbal
clause. Here, the topic marker indicates contrastiveness.

(11–86)   a. [nacï-ccjaaki]   munužž-a-t-ta-m.
             cry-SIM   speak-THM-NEG-PST-RLS
             '(He) did not speak crying.' [i.e. It wasn't the case that he
             spoke eating]
          b. [nacï-ccjaaki=a]   munužž-a-t-ta-m.
             cry-SIM=TOP   speak-THM-NEG-PST-RLS
             '(He) did not speak crying.' [i.e. He spoke in some occasion,
             but not while eating]

11.6.3.2. The scope of interrogation
A coordinate clause, either symmetrical or asymmetrical, is independent of
the main clause interrogator (here the question clitic =ru; §9.6.6).

(11–87)   ba=a   fa-a-n-Ø=suga,   vva=a
          1SG=TOP   eat-THM-NEG-NPST=but   2SG=TOP

The complex sentence   409

fa-a-di=ru?
eat-THM-INT=Q
'I don't eat (it), but will you eat (it)?'

A chained clause may be within the scope of the main clause interrogator, as in (11–88a), or outside it, as in (11–88b) (see also §7.1.3.2 (4)). Furthermore, the medial clause alone may be within the scope of interrogation, with a contrastive meaning, as in (11–88c). In this case, the medial clause is often focus-marked.

(11–88)   *ucïnaa=nkai*   *ik-i-i(=ru),*   *kaimunu*
          Okinawa=ALL   go-THM-NRT(=FOC)   shopping
          asï-ta-m=mu?
          do-PST-RLS=Q
          a. 'Did (you) go to Okinawa and go shopping?'
          b. '(You) went to Okinawa, and did (you) go shopping?'
          c. 'Did (you) go to Okinawa (rather than to Hirara) and went shopping?'

An adsentential clause may also be either within the scope of the main clause interrogator or independent of it. However, unlike a medial clause, when an adsentential clause is within the scope of the main clause interrogator, the interrogative scope is not over the entire sentence (as in the case of (11–88a) above), but over the adsentential clause only, with a contrastive meaning (11–89b). In this latter case, the focus marker appears.

(11–89)   *ucïnaa=nkai*   *ifï-tigaa(=ru),*   *kaimunu*
          Okinawa=ALL   go-THM-NRT(=FOC)   shopping
          ah-u-di=ru?
          do-THM-INT=Q
          a. 'If you go to Okinawa, will you go shopping?'
          b. 'Will (you) go shopping if you go to Okinawa (rather than to Hirara)?'

An adverbial clause is always under the scope of the main clause interrogator, either with a sentential scope (11–90a) or with a narrower scope on the adverbial clause only (11–90b).

(11–90)   *munu=u*   *vv-ccjaaki(=ru),*   *fa-i+u-tar=ru?*
          thing=ACC   sell-SIM(=FOC)   eat-THM+PROG-PST=Q

410 Chapter 11

   a. 'Were (you) eating while selling things?'

   b. '(Was it) while selling things (that) you were eating?'

11.6.4. Restrictions on relativisation

As noted in §11.4.3.3 to §11.4.3.5, whereas it is possible for an NP in an adsentential clause and an adverbial clause to be relativised, it is impossible for an NP in a chained clause or in a coordinate clause.

Appendix

In what follows I list two narrative texts produced by two native speakers of Irabu, and transcribed by the present author with the help of one native speaker of Irabu.

(1) *Junaitama, a mermaid of Tooriike*, a folktale explaining how Tooriike on Shimoji Island (MAP 2 in §1.1) was created. This text was narrated by a female speaker living in Nagahama (age: 92 in 2007).

(2) *Vernacular plate*, a narrative describing the speaker's schooldays, when pupils would be punished when they used Irabu instead of Japanese, the standard language of Japan. The pupils who used Irabu had to wear a plate from their neck, and the plate was called a vernacular plate. This text was narrated by a female speaker living in Nagahama (age: 67 in 2007).

To keep confidentiality secured, these texts sometimes contain XX, which substitutes person names, place names, etc. When a text contains sentences of Japanese, I indicate it by square brackets. Loan words from Japanese and other languages are not particularly indicated, and phonemically represented with Irabu orthography (§2.2). Each Irabu sentence is numbered, but when a sentence is so long that it is reasonable to break it down into two parts for translation purposes, I did so and numbered accordingly.

(1) *Junaitama, a mermaid of Tooriike*

01. *tooriike=tii=du=i,   ssibara,   maibara,*
    Tooriike=QT=FOC=CNF   back   front
    satu+bžtu=nu   a-tar=ca.   fita-kiv.
    neighbour+person=NOM   exist-PST=HS   two-CLF.HOUSE
    'In (what is now called) Tooriike,[1] there were two neighbouring houses, back (north) and front (south).'

---

[1] *Tooriike* is literally "trans-pond", which consists of two neighbouring ponds. These ponds developed from underground caverns. *Tooriike* is situated on Shimoji, and there are numerous legends and folktales about it.

412 Appendix

02. *fita-kiv*   *ar-i-utui=du,*
two-CLF.HOUSE   exist-THM-CRCM=FOC
pžtu-kiv=ga   *im=nu*   *acca*   *ja-i-ba,*
one-CLF.HOUSE=NOM   sea=GEN   side   COP-THM-CSL
unukja=a,
3PL=TOP
'Of the two houses, one was beside the sea, so…'

03. *pžtu-kiv=nu*   *pžtu=nu*
one-CLF.HOUSE=GEN   man=NOM
ssibara=ru   *a-tar=ru*   *maibara=ru*   *a-tar=ru*
back=FOC   COP-PST=Q   front=FOC   COP-PST=Q
mmja   *ss-a-n-Ø=suga,*
INTJ   know-THM-NEG-NPST=but
'The man from one of the houses — I'm not sure whether (the house) was of the backside or of the frontside — …'

04. *pžtu-kiv=nu…*   *fita-kiv=kara*
one-CLF.HOUSE=NOM   two-CLF.HOUSE=ABL
pžtu-kiv=nu   *pžtu=nu*   *junai,*   *ningjo,*
one-CLF.HOUSE   man=NOM   junai   mermaid
junaitama=u   *tu-i+cc-i-i,*
Junaitama=ACC   catch-THM+come-THM-NRT
'(The man from) one house of the two houses caught and brought *junai*, I mean, a mermaid, *Junaitama*…'

05. *kurus-i-i,*   *mmja*   *uri=a*   *žžu*   *ja-i-ba,*
kill-THM-NRT   INTJ   3SG=TOP   fish   COP-THM-CSL
kurus-i-i,   *kata+bata=u=baa*   *jak-i-i*
kill-THM-NRT   half+body=ACC=TOP   burn-THM-NRT
fa-i-Ø,   *kata+bata=u=baa*   *jaa=nu*   *pana=n*
eat-THM-NRT   half+body=ACC=TOP   house=GEN   lift-NRT
nuusi-i,   *pus-i+a-tar=ca.*
roof=DAT   dry-THM+RSL-PST=HS
'and killed it, as it is a fish; (he) killed and burned and ate half of the body (of *Junaitama*), and laid the other half on the roof of his house.'

06. *aidu,*   *rjuukjuu…*   *rjuuguu=nu*   *kam=nu*
then   Ryukyu   sea.world=GEN   god=NOM
junaitama,   *junaitama=tii*   *ass-i-ba=du,*

Junaitama   Junaitama=QT   say-THM-CSL=FOC

'Then, the god of Ryukyu, no, Ryugu (sea world) said calling "Junai-tama! Junaimata!", so…'

07. *nara=a*   *mmja*   *kurus-ai-Ø=du,*   *kata+bata*
     RFL=TOP   INTJ   kill-PASS-NRT=FOC   half+body

     fa-ai-i,   *kata+bata=a*   *jaa=nu*   *pana=n*
     eat-PASS-NRT   half+body=TOP   house=GEN   roof=DAT

     nuusi-rai+u-i-ba,   *nara=n=na*
     lift-PASS+PROG-THM-CSL   RFL=DAT=TOP

     kuu-rai-n-Ø=tii   *až-tar=ca.*
     come-POT-NEG-NPST=QT   say-PST=HS

     '(Junaitama) said, "I have been killed, and half of my body was eaten, and the other half has been laid on the roof, so I cannot come back (to the sea world)."'

08. *unu*   *rjuukjuu…*   *rjuuguu=nu*   *kam=nu=du*   *mmja,*
     that   Ryukyu   sea.world=GEN   god=NOM=FOC   INTJ

     ui+saar-Ø=tii   *cc-i-i,*   *jurab-i-ba,*
     3SG+take-NPST=QT   come-THM-NRT   call-THM-CSL

     'The god of Ryukyu, no, Ryugu, called (Junaitama) to take her back home, so…'

09. *nara=a*   *kata+bata*   *fa-ai-i,*
     RFL=TOP   half+body   eat-PASS-NRT

     kata+bata=a   *jaa=nu*   *pana=n*   *nuus-i-i=du,*
     half+body=TOP   house=GEN   roof=DAT   lift-THM-NRT=FOC

     nara=u=baa   *pus-i-i*   *nci+ar-Ø=tii*
     RFL=ACC=TOP   dry-THM-NRT   put+RSL-NPST=QT

     až-tarjaa,
     say-PST.ANT

     '(Junaitama) said, "I have had my half eaten; as for the other half, (the man) has laid it on the roof of his house and dried", so…'

10. *ttigaa,*   *uku+nam=mu*   *jar-ah-a-di=ssiba,*
     then   big+wave=ACC   create-CAUS-THM-INT=so

     uri-i   *kuu-Ø=juu=tii*   *až-tarjaa,*
     come.down-NRT   come-IMP=EMP=QT   say-PST.ANT

     '(The god) said, "Then I will let there be a big wave, so come down riding on it", so…'

414   Appendix

11.   *nndi=ti*   *asï-tarjaa,*
      yes=QT   say-PST.ANT
      '(Junaitama) said, "I see", so…'

12.   *uku+nam=mu*   *baa=tti*   *jar-asï-tarjaa,*
      big+wave=ACC   ONM=QT   create-CAUS-PST.ANT
      tuduk-a-n-Ø=niba,   *mata*   *mme+pžtu+nam*
      reach-THM-NEG-NPST=so   and   another+one+wave
      ookii   *uku+nam=mu*   *baa=tti*   *jar-asï-tarjaa,*
      big   big+wave=ACC   ONM=QT   create-CAUS-PST.ANT
      zazaa=ttii   *uri-i,*   *mmja*   *uri=a*
      ONM=QT   come.down-NRT   INTJ   3SG=TOP
      mmja   *par-tar=ca.*
      INTJ   leave-PST=HS
      '(The god) created a big wave, but it did not reach, and (he) created
      another big wave, so that (Junaitama) came down riding on the wave,
      and left (for the sea world).'

13.   *aidu*   *uma=nu*   *ssibara*   *maibara=a*   *mmja*
      thus   that.place=GEN   back   front=TOP   INTJ
      doofi=ti   *uti-i=i,*   *tooriike=n*
      ONM=QT   collapse-NRT=CNF   Tooriike=DAT
      nar-tar=ca.
      become-PST=HS
      'Thus, the place around the backside and the frontside collapsed, and
      became what we now call *Tooriike*.'

(2) *The vernacular plate*

01.   *banti=ga*   *sïma=n=na*   *hoogen=nu...*
      1PL=GEN   island=DAT=TOP   vernacular=ACC
      hjoozjungo   *cïkav-Ø*   *pžtu=nu=du*   *mii-da,*
      standard.language   use-NPST   man=NOM=FOC   see-NEG.NRT
      mmna   *sinsii-taa=nkai=mai*   *hoogen=nu*
      all   teacher-PL=ALL=even   vernacular=ACC
      cïka-i+u-tar=dara=i.
      use-THM+PROG-PST=CRTN=CNF
      'In our island, (we) do not see people who use a vernacular… no, the
      standard language (Japanese); everyone would use the vernacular
      even (when speaking) to teachers.'

Appendix   415

02. *mmja,*   *juubinkjokucjoo=nu*   *ffa=nu*   *unukja=a...*
INTJ   postmaster=GEN   child=NOM   3PL=TOP
untja=a   *mmja,*   *sokai=ja*   *s-i-i,*
3PL=TOP   INTJ   evacuation=PRT   do-THM-NRT
ik-i-i   *sï-tjaaki,*   *mudur-i+cc-i-i,*
go-THM-NRT   do-CRCM   return-THM+come-THM-NRT
hjoozjungo   *cïka-i+u-tar=dara.*
standard.language   use-THM+PROG-PST=CRTN
'Well, (there was) a child of a postmaster; they...they evacuated (to escape from the bombard, as it was in the middle of the Second World War), and spent sometime for a while; when they returned, they ended up with speaking the standard language.'

03. *untja*   *pžtu-kiv=du*   *mmja*
3PL   one-CLF.HOUSE=FOC   INTJ
hjoozjungo=u=baa   *cïka-i+ufi-Ø=pazï.*
standard.language=ACC=TOP   use-THM+PROS-NPST=maybe
'They alone were speaking the standard language, I suppose.'

04. *mmna*   *hoogen=na*   *s-i-i.*
all   vernacular=PRT   do-THM-NRT
'Everyone (else) spoke the vernacular.'

05. *aidu,*   *hoogen+fida=a,*   *konsjuu=no*   *reikoo=wa*
then   vernacular+board=TOP   this.week=GEN   goal=TOP
hjoozjungo=o   *cuka-i-masjoo=tii=du*
standard.language=ACC   use-THM-POL.NPST.HRT=QT=FOC
kokuban=Ø   *kak-ai+u-tar.*
blackboard=DAT   write-PASS+PROG-PST
'With regard to the vernacular plate, (a message) was written on the blackboard saying, "This week's goal is this: let us use the standard language ".'

06. *mmja,*   *hjoozjungo=u*   *cïka-a-n-Ø*
INTJ   standard.language=ACC   use-THM-NEG-NPST
pžtu=u,   *akaa+aka=nu*   *ica=u=baa=i,*
person=TOP   RED+red=GEN   board=ACC=TOP=CNF
hoogen+fida=tii=du   *až-tar.*
vernacular+plate=QT=FOC   say-PST
'Well, (for) those who do not speak the standard language, (there was)

a red board, which was called a vernacular plate.'

07. *asi,*   *uri=u=i,*   *nubui=n*   *pak-as-i-i*
then   3SG=ACC=CNF   neck=DAT   wear-CAUS-THM-NRT
maar-tar.
wander-PST
'Then (the teacher) made them wear it.'

08. *uri=a*   *kaki-sïmi-i=du*   *hoogen=nu*
3SG=PRT   wear-CAUS-NRT=FOC   vernacular=ACC
cïkav-tigaa=ju, *batafïsari-ka-i-ba,*   *unu* *juubin=nu*
use-CND=EMP be.angry-VLZ-THM-CSL that post.office=GEN
XX, *banti=tu* *piti-cï*   *tusïsïta* *ja-i-ba,*
XX   1PL=ASC one-CLF.GENERAL junior   COP-THM-CSL
'(The teacher) would make (pupils) wear it, if (they) used the vernacular; (this made us) angry; now XX (person name), the postmaster's (daughter), was one year junior to us…'

09. *uri=u=ba*   *cïmcc-i-i,*   *hoogen=nu*   *cïka-i!*
3SG=ACC=TOP   pinch-THM-NRT vernacular=ACC use-IMP
vva   *hoogen=nu*   *cïka-i,*   *nande* *vva*   *tavkjaa*
2SG   vernacular=ACC use-IMP why   2SG   one.person
uri=u   *kaki-n-Ø=ga=ti*   *ažž-i-ba,*
3SG=ACC wear-NEG-NPST=Q=QT   say-THM-CSL
'(I) pinched her (so that she would utter the vernacular involuntarily), saying "use the vernacular! You use the vernacular! How come you alone don't wear it (the plate)?"…'

10. *site,*   *watasi=ni=wa*   *i-e-nai=noni=ti*
for   1SG=DAT=TOP   say-POT-NEG.NPST=so=QT
ažž-i-ba,   *ažž-i,*   *ažž-i,*   *vva=mai*
say-THM-CSL   say-IMP   say-IMP   PL=too
hoogen=na   *ažž-i=tii*   *až-tar.*
vernacular=PRT say-IMP=QT say-PST
'So (she) said, "For I cannot speak (the vernacular) anyway", (so I) said "Say (it)! Say (it)! You speak the vernacular (like us)!".'

Bibliography

Abraham, Werner. 1997. The interdependence of case, aspect and speci!city in the history of German: the case of the verbal genitive. In Ans van Kemenade & Nigel Vincent, eds., *Parameters of morphosyntactic change,* 29–61. Cambridge: Cambridge University Press.

Aikhenvald, Alexandra Y. 2006. Serial verb constructions in typological perspective. In Aikhenvald, Alexandra Y., and R.M.W. Dixon, eds., *Serial verb constructions: A cross-linguistic typology*, 1–68. Oxford: Oxford University Press.

Aissen, Judith. 2003. Differential object marking: iconicity vs. economy. *Natural Language & Linguistic Theory* 21: 435–483.

Akatsuka, Noriko. 1985. Conditionals and the epistemic scale. *Language* 61 (3): 625–639.

Amberber, Mengistu. 2000. Valency-changing devices and valency-encoding devices in Amharic. In Dixon, R.M.W, and Alexandra Y. Aikhenvald, eds., *Changing valency: case studies in transitivity,* 312–332, Cambridge: Cambridge University Press.

Anderson, Gregory D.S. 2006. *Auxiliary verb constructions.* Oxford; New York: Oxford University Press.

Aoi, Hayato. 2010. Minami Ryukyu hogen ni okeru "shitasaki boin" no choonteki tokucho. *Journal of the Phonetic Society of Japan* 14:2.

Aoi, Hayato. 2012. Miyako Tarama hogen ni okeru "nakajita boin" no onseiteki kaishaku. *Journal of the Linguistic Society of Japan* 142.

Asato, Susumu. 1999. *Okinawajin wa doko kara kitaka.* Okinawa: Boodaainku.

Backhouse, A.E. 2004. Inflected and uninflected adjectives in Japanese. In Dixon, R.M.W., and Alexandra Y. Aikhenvald, eds., *Adjective classes,* 50–73, Cambridge: Cambridge University Press.

Bhat, D.N.S. 1994. *The adjectival category.* Amsterdam/Philadelphia: John Benjamin Publishing Company.

Bhat, D.N.S. 2004. *Pronouns.* Oxford: Oxford University Press.

Bickel, Balthasar. 1993. Belhare subordination and the theory of topic. In Ebert, K. H, ed., *Studies in clause linkage,* 23–55, Zürich: ASAS Press.

418   Bibliography

Bickel, Balthasar. 1998. Review article: Converbs in cross-linguistic perspective. *Linguistic Typology* 2(3): 81–397.

Bickel, Balthasar, and Johanna Nichols. 2007. Inflectional morphology. In Shopen, Timothy, ed., *Language typology and syntactic description* (3), 2nd edition, 169–240, Cambridge: Cambridge University Press.

Bisang, Walter. 1995. Verb serialization and converbs - differences and similarities. In König, Ekkehard, and Martin Haspelmath, eds., *Converbs in cross-linguistic perspective*, 137–188, Berlin: Mouton de Gruyter.

Bybee, Joan, Revere Perkins, and William Pagliuca. 1994. *The evolution of grammar: Tense, aspect, and modality in the languages of the world.* Chicago; London: University of Chicago Press.

Bybee, Joan, and Suzanne Fleischman. 1995. Issues in mood and modality. In Bybee, Joan, and Suzanne Fleischman, eds., *Modality in grammar and discourse,* 1–14, Amsterdam: John Benjamins.

Chung, Sandra, and Alan Timberlake. 1985. Tense, aspect, and mood. In Shopen, Timothy, ed., *Language typology and syntactic description* (1), 202–258, Cambridge: Cambridge University Press.

Clark, Eve V. 1978. Existential, locative, and possessive construction. In Greenberg, Joseph H, ed., *Universals of human language* (4), 85–126, Stanford: Stanford University Press.

Comrie, Bernard. 1975. Causatives and universal grammar. *Transactions of the Philological Society* 1974: 1–32.

Comrie, Bernard. 1976. *Aspect.* Cambridge: Cambridge University Press.

Comrie, Bernard. 1981. *Language universals and linguistic typology: syntax and morphology.* Oxford: Blackwell.

Comrie, Bernard. 1985a. *Tense.* Cambridge: Cambridge University Press.

Comrie, Bernard. 1985b. Causative verb formation and other verb-deriving morphology. In Shopen, Timothy, ed., *Language typology and syntactic description* (3), 309–348, Cambridge: Cambridge University Press.

Comrie, Bernard, and Sandra A. Thompson. 1985. Lexical nominalization. In Shopen, Timothy, ed., *Language typology and syntactic description* (3), 349–398, Cambridge: Cambridge University Press.

Croft, William. 2002. *Radical construction grammar: syntactic theory in typological perspective.* Oxford: Oxford University Press.

Croft, William. 2003. *Typology and universals.* 2nd edition. Cambridge: Cambridge University Press.

Dixon, R.M.W. 1982. *Where have all the adjectives gone? and other essays in semantics and syntax.* Berlin: Mouton.

Dixon, R.M.W. 1994. *Ergativity.* Cambridge: Cambridge University Press.

Dixon, R.M.W. 2004. Adjective classes in typological perspective. In Dixon, R.M.W., and Alexandra Y. Aikhenvald, eds., *Adjective classes,* 1–49, Cambridge: Cambridge University Press.

Dixon, R.M.W., and Alexandra Y. Aikhenvald. 2000. Introduction. In Dixon, R.M.W., and Alexandra Y. Aikhenvald, eds., *Changing valency: case studies in transitivity,* 1–29, Cambridge: Cambridge University Press.

Elliott, Jennifer R. 2000. Realis and irrealis: Forms and concepts of the grammaticalisation of reality. *Linguistic Typology* 4:55–90.

Erickson, Blaine. 2003. Old Japanese and Proto-Japonic word structure. In Vovin, Alexander, and Toshiki Osada, eds., *Nihongokeitooron no genzai,* 493–510, Kyooto: Kokusainihonbunkasentaa.

Erteshik-Shir, Nomi, and Shalom Lappin. 1979. Dominance and the Functional Explanation of Island Phenomena. *Theoretical Linguistics* 6: 41–85.

Erteshik-Shir, Nomi, and Shalom Lappin. 1983. Under Stress: a Functional Explanation of English Sentence Stress. *Journal of Linguistics* 19: 419–453.

Filimonova, Elena. 2005. *Clusivity: Typology and case studies of the inclusive–exclusive distinction.* Amsterdam/New York: John Benjamin.

Fischer, Susann. 2003. Partitive vs. genitive in Russian and Polish: An empirical study on case alternation in the object domain. In Susann Fischer, Ruben van de Vijver & Ralf Vogel, eds., *Experimental studies in linguistics,* 123–137, Potsdam: Institut für Linguistik.

Foley, William A. 1986. *The Papuan Languages of New Guinea.* Cambridge University Press.

Foley, William A. 1991. *The Yimas language of New Guinea.* Stanford; California: Stanford University Press.

Foley, William A, and Robert Van Valin Jr. 1984. *Functional syntax and universal grammar.* Cambridge: Cambridge University Press.

Foley, William A, and Micheal Olson. 1985. Clausehood and verb serialization. In Nichols, Johanna, and Anthony C. Woodbury, eds., *Grammar inside and outside the clause,* 17–60, Cambridge: Cambridge University Press.

Givón, Talmy. 1984. Syntax. *A functional-typological introduction* (1). Amsterdam; Philadelphia: John Benjamins.

Givón, Talmy. 1990. Verb serialization in Tok Pisin and Kalam: a comparative study of temporal packaging. In Verhaar, J.M.W, ed., *Melanesian Pidgin and Tok Pisin*, 19–55, Amsterdam: Benjamins.

Givón, Talmy. 1994. Irrealis and the subjunctive. *Studies in language* 18 (2): 265–337.

Greenberg, J. H. 1988. The first person inclusive dual as an ambiguous category. *Studies in Language* 12: 1–18.

Grimes, Barbara F. ed. 1996. *Ethnologue: languages of the world* (13th edition). Dallas: Summer Institute of Linguistics, Inc. [on line] http://www.sil.org/ethnologue/ethnologue.html.

Grundt, Alice Wyland. 1978. The functional role of the Indo-European theme vowel. *Pacific Coast Philology* 13: 29–35.

Haiman, John. 1987. On Some Origins of Medial Verb Morphology in Papuan Languages. *Studies in Language* 11: 347–364.

Haspelmath, Martin. 1993. More on the typology of inchoative/causative verb alternations. In Comrie, Bernard, and Maria Polinsky, eds., *Causatives and transitivity*, 87–120, Amsterdam: John Benjamins.

Haspelmath, Martin. 1995. The converb as a cross-linguistically valid category. In Haspelmath, Martin. and Ekkehard König, eds., *Converbs in crosslinguistic perspective*, 1–55, Berlin: Mouton de Gruyter.

Hayashi, Yuka. 2010. Ikema. In Shimoji, Michinori, and Thomas Pellard, eds., *An introduction to Ryukyuan languages,* Tokyo:ILCAA.

Hayashi, Yuka. 2013. Minami Ryukyu Miyakogo Ikema hoogen no bunpoo [A grammar of the Ikema dialect of the Miyako language of the Ryukyu]. Kyoto: Kyoto University.

Hendriks, Peter. 1998. Kakari particle and the merger of the predicative and attributive forms in the Japanese verbal system. *Japanese and Korean Linguistics* 7: 197–210.

Hengeveld, Kees. 1992. *Non-verbal predication: theory, typology, diachrony.* Berlin and New York: Mouton de Gruyter.

Hirayama, Teruo. 1964. Ryuukyuu miyakohoogen no kenkyuu. *Kokugogaku* 56: 61–73.

Hirayama, Teruo. 1967. *Ryuukyuu sakishima hoogen no soogooteki kenkyuu* (with Ichiroo Ooshima and Masachie Nakamoto). Tokyo: Oohuusha.

Hirayama, Teruo, Ichiro Oshima, and Masachie Nakamoto. 1966. *Ryuukyuuhoogen no soogooteki kenkyuu.* Tokyo: Meijishoin.

De Hoop, Helen. 1992. *Case configuration and noun phrase interpretation.* Groningen: Univeristy of Groningen dissertation.

De Hoop, Helen & Andrej Malchukov. 2008. Case-marking strategies. *Linguistic Inquiry* 39: 565–587.

Hopper, Paul J, and Sandra A. Thompson. 1980. Transitivity in grammar and discourse. *Language* 56 (2): 251–299.

Hopper, Paul J. 1979. Aspect and foregrounding in discourse. In Givón, Talmy, ed., *Discourse and syntax*, 213–241, New York: Acedemic Press.

Hopper, Paul J, and Sandra A. Thompson. 1984. The discourse basis for lexical categories in Universal grammar. *Language* 60 (4): 703–752.

Hosei Daigaku Okinawa Bunka Kenkyujo. 1977. Miyako Oogamijima. *Ryuukyuu no hoogen* 3.

Huddleston, Rodney. 1984. *Introduction to the grammar of English*. Cambridge: Cambridge University Press.

Hyman, Larry M. 2001. Privative tone in Bantu. In Kaji, Shigeki, ed., *Proceedings of the symposium of cross-linguistic studies of tonal phenomena: tonogenesis, Japanese accentology, and other topics*, 237–259, Tokyo: ILCAA.

Hyman, Larry M. 2006. Word prosodic typology. *Phonology* 23: 225–257.

Ito, Junko, and Armin Mester. 2003. *Japanese Morphophonemics: Markedness and Word Structure*. Cambridge: MIT Press.

Izuyama, Atsuko. 2002. A study on the grammar of Miyako Hirara dialect of Luchuan. In Sanada, Shinji, ed., *Grammatical Aspects of Endangered Dialects in Japan* (1), 35–97, Tokyo: ELPR.

Jarosz, Aleksandra. 2015. Nikolay Nevskiy's Miyakoan dictionary: reconstruction from the manuscript and its ethnolinguistic analysis. Unpublished PhD thesis, the Adam Mickiewicz University

Kanaseki, Takeo. 1976. *Nipponminzoku no kigen*. Tokyo: Hooseidaigakushuppankyoku.

Karimata, Shigehisa. 1982. Miyakojimahoogen no foneemu ni tsuite. *Ryuukyuu no gengo to bunka*.

Karimata, Shigehisa. 1986. Miyakohoogen no chuuzetsuboin o megutte. *Okinawabunka* 22 (2): 73–83.

Karimata, Shigehisa. 1997 [1992]. Miyakohoogen. In Kamei, Takashi, Rokuroo Koono, and Eiichi Chino, eds., *Nipponrettoo no gengo* (Gengogakudaijiten special selection), 388–403, Tokyo: Sanseidoo.

Karimata, Shigehisa. 1999. Miyakoshohoogen dooshi "shuushikei" no seiritsu ni tsuite. *Nihon tooyoobunkaronsjuu* 5: 27–51.

Karimata, Shigehisa. 2002. Notes on adjectives in Miyako dialects of the Ryukyuan language. In Karimata, Shigehisa, Toshiko Tsuhako, Shinichi Kajiku, and Shunzo Takahashi, eds., *Preliminary research on endangered Ryukyuan language*, 44–69, Tokyo: ELPR.

Karimata, Shigehisa. 2003. Okinawaken Miyakogun Gusukubechoo Borahoogen. Hoogen ni okeru dooshi no bunpookategorii no ruikeiteki

Bibliography

kenkyuu (research project of Mayumi Kudoo).

Karimata, Shigehisa. 2004. Kikigengo to shite no Ryuukyuugo no bunpoo-kenkyuu no kadai. *Nihon tooyoobunnkaronshuu* 10: 57–77.

Karimata, Shigehisa. 2005. Miyako Hirarahoogen no phoneme. *Nihon Tooyoobunkaronsjuu* 11: 67–113.

Kasuga, Kazuo. 1973. Keiyooshi no hassei. In Suzuki, Kazuhiko, and Oki Hayashi, eds., *Hinshibetsu Nihonbunpookooza* (4), Tokyo: Meijishoin.

Kawada, Takuya, Yuka Hayashi, Shoichi Iwasaki, and Tsuyoshi Ono. 2008. Ryuukyuugo Miyako Ikemahoogen ni okeru *mmya* no danwakinoo. Shibasaki, Reijiroo, ed., *Gengobunka no kurosuroodo*, 111–130, Okinawa: Bunshin'insatsu.

Kazama, Shinjiroo. 1997. Tsunguusushogo ni okeru bubunkaku. Miyaoka, Osahito, and Jiroo Tsumagari, eds. *Kankitataiheiyoo no gengo*, 103–120, Kyoto: Kyootodaigaku.

Kazama, Shinjiro. 2005. Naanaigo no gimonshi ni yoru hangohyoogen ni tsuite. In Tsumagari, Jiroo, ed., *Kankitataiheiyoo no gengo* (12), 129–163, Hokkaido: Hokkaidoodaigakudaigakuin bungakuken-kyuuka.

Kazama, Shinjiro. 2015. Nihongo (hanashi kotoba) wa juzokubu hyojigata no gengo nanoka? *Kokuritsu kokugo kenkyujo ronshu* 9: 51–80.

Keenan, Edward L. 1985. Relative clauses. In Shopen, Timothy, ed., *Language typology and syntactic description* (2), 141–170, Cambridge: Cambridge University Press.

Keenan, Edward L, and Bernard Comrie. 1977. Noun phrase accessibility and universal grammar. *Linguistic Inquiry* 8: 63–99.

Kibe, Nobuko. ed. 2012. *Shometsu kiki hogen no chosa hozon no tame no sogoteki kenkyu: minami ryukyu miyako hogen chosa hokokusho.* Tokyo: NINJAL.

Kibrik, Aleksandr E. 1991. Organizing principles for nominal paradigms in Daghestanian languages: comparative and typological observations. In Plank, Frans, ed., *Paradigms: the economy of inflection,* 255–274, Amsterdam: John Benjamins Publishing Company.

Kinuhata, Tomohide. 2016. Minamiryuukyuu miyakogo no gimonshi gimon kakarimusubi: Irabushuuraku hoogen o chuushin ni. *Gengo Kenkyuu* 149. 19–42.

Kinuhata, Tomohide and Yuka Hayashi. 2014. Ryukyu Miyako Karimata Hogen no onin to bunpo. *Ryukyu no Hogen* 38.

Kiparsky, Paul. 1998. Partitive case and aspect. In Miriam Butt & Wilhelm Geuder, eds., *The projection of arguments*, 265–307. Stanford:

Bibliography   423

CSLI Publications.

Koloskova, Yulia. 2007. Ryukyugo Miyako hogen no chokusetsu mo-kutekigo no hyoshiki to tadosei. In Mie Tsunoda, Kan Sasaki & Toru Shionoya, eds., *Tadosei no tsugengogakuteki kenkyu*, 283–294. Tokyo: Kurosio Publishers.

Koloskova, Yulia, and Toshio Ohori. 2008. Pragmatic factors in the development of a switch-adjective language: a case study of the Miyako-Hirara dialect of Ryukyuan. *Studies in language* 32 (3): 610–636.

Krifka, Manfred. 1992. Thematic relations as links between nominal reference and temporal constitution. In Ivan A. Sag & Anna Szabolcsi, eds., *Lexical matters,* 29–53. Stanford: CSLI Publications.

Kubozono, Haruo. 1993. *The organization of Japanese prosody.* Tokyo: Kuroshio Publishers.

Kuno, Susumu, and Etsuko Kaburaki. 1977. Empathy and syntax. *Linguistic Inquiry* 8: 627–672.

Kuribayashi, Yu. 1989. Accusative marking and noun-verb constructions in Turkish. *Gengo kenkyuu* 95: 94–119.

Lambrecht, Knud. 1994. *Information structure and sentence form: topic, focus, and the mental representations of discourse referents.* Cambridge: Cambridge University Press.

Langacker, Ronald. 1987. *Foundations of cognitive grammar*, volume I: Theoretical prerequisites. Stanford: Stanford University Press.

Lawrence, Wayne P. 2008. Yonagunijimahoogen no keitootekiichi. *Ryuukyuu no hoogen* 32: 59–68.

Lawrence, Wayne P. 2012. Southern Ryukyuan. In Tranter, Nicholas, ed., *Languages of Japan and Korea*, London: Routledge.

Leben, William R. 1997. Tonal feet and the adaptation of English borrowings into Hausa. *Studies in African Linguistics* 25: 139–154.

Leben, William R. 2002. Tonal feet. In Gut, Ulrike, and Dafydd Gibbon, eds., Proceedings, typology of African prosodic systems (Bielefeld Occasional Papers in Typology 1): 27–40.

Leben, William R. 2003. Tonal feet as tonal domains. In Mugane, John, ed., *Trends in African Linguistics 5: Linguistic typology and representation of African languages*, 129–138. Africa World Press.

Lewis, David. 1979. Scorekeeping in a Language Game. *Journal of Philosophical Logic* 8:339–359.

Lichtenberk Frantisek. 1983. *A grammar of Manam.* Hawaii: University of Hawaii Press.

Lord, Carol. 1974. Causative constructions in Yoruba. *Studies in African*

Linguistics 5: 195–204.

Lyons, John. 1977. *Semantics*. 2 volumes. Cambridge: Cambridge University Press.

Malchukov, Andrej. N. 2000. Perfect, evidentiality and related categories in Tungusic languages. In Johanson, Lars. and Bo Utas, eds., *Evidentials: Turkic, Iranian and neighbouring languages*, 441–470, Berlin; New York: Mouton de Gruyter.

Malchukov, Andrej L, and Helen de Hoop. 2011. Tense, aspect, and mood based differential case marking. *Lingua* 121. 35–47.

Martin, Samuel E. 1975. *A Reference Grammar of Japanese*. Yale University Press.

McCarthy, John J, and Alan S. Prince. 1995. Prosodic morphology. In Goldsmith, John A. (ed., *The handbook of phonological theory*, 319–366. UK: Blackwell).

Miyara, Shinsho. 1995. *Minamiryuukyuu Yaeyama Ishigakihoogen no bunpoo*. Tokyo: Kuroshioshuppan.

Motonaga, Moriyasu. 1978. Miyako Hirarahoogen no keiyoosi. In Inoue, Fumio, Koichi Shinozaki, Takashi Kobayashi, and Takuichiro Onishi, eds., *Ryuukyuuhoogen koo* 7, 351–359. Tokyo: Yumani Shoboo.

Motonaga, Moriyasu. 1982. Irabuhoogen no kenkyuu. *Ryuukyuu no gengo to bunka* 1982: 13–32.

Myhill, John, and Junko Hibiya. 1988. The discourse function of clause-chaining. In Haiman John, and Sandra A. Thompson, eds., *Clause combining in grammar and discourse*, 361–398, Amsterdam: John Benjamins.

Nakama, Mitsunari. 1983. Ryuukyuu Miyako Nagahama hoogen no on'in. *Ryuudai kokugo* 2: 198–218.

Nakama, Mitsunari. 1992. *Ryuukyuuhoogen no kosoo*. Tokyo: Daiichishoboo.

Nakasone, Seizen. 1976. Miyako oyobi Okinawahontoo no keigohoo. "irassharu" o chuushin to shite. Kyuugakkairengoo Okinawachoosaiinkai, ed., *Okinawa: shizen, bunka, shakai*, Tokyo: Koobundoo.

Nakasone, Seizen. n.d (a). Miyako Irabuchoo Nagahama, Taramason Shiokawa no hoogen. Nakasone Seizen Gengoshiryoo [93802040].

Nakasone, Seizen. n.d (b). Miyako Irabuchoo Sawadahoogen no on'in. Nakasone Seizen Gengoshiryoo [93802043].

Nakasone, Seizen. n.d (c). Miyakohoogen no dooshi no katsuyoo (Miyako Irabu Nagahama). Nakasone Seizen Gengoshiryoo [93802049].

Nakasone, Seizen. n.d (d). Miyakohoogen no keiyooshi. Nakasone Seizen Gengoshiryoo [93802055].

Bibliography 425

Nakasone, Seizen. n.d (e). Miyakohoogen choosanooto 1. Nakasone Seizen Gengoshiryoo [96400235].

Nakasone, Seizen. n.d (f). Miyakohoogen choosanooto 2. Nakasone Seizen Gengoshiryoo [96400236].

Nakasone, Seizen. n.d (g). Hoogenchoosanisshi (Miyako, Yaeyama). Nakasone Seizen Gengoshiryoo [96400236].

Nakasone, Seizen. n.d (h). Kisogoihyoo (Miyako, Yaeyama). Nakasone Seizen Gengoshiryoo [93802027].

Nedjalkov, Vladimir P, and Georgij G. Sil'nickij. 1969. Tipologija morfologičeskogo i leksičeskogo kauzativov. In Xolodovič, Aleksandr A, ed., *Tipologija kauzativnyz konstrukcij*, 20–50, Leningrad: Nauka.

Nevski, Nikolai A. 1971. *Tsuki to hushi* (edited by Masao Oka). Tookyoo: Heibonsha.

Nevski, Nikolai A. 1998. *Miyako no fookuroa* (translated by L. L. Gromkovskaya and Shigehisa Karimata).

Noonan, Micheal. 1985. Complementation. In Shopen, Timothy, ed., *Language typology and syntactic description*, 42–140, Cambridge: Cambridge University Press.

Oi, Kotaro. 1984. *Ikemajimashishi*. Ikema: Ikemajimashishihakkooiinkai.

Osada, Toshiki. 2003. Hajimeni. In Vovin, Alexander, and Toshiki Osada, eds., *Nihongokeitooron no genzai*, 3–14, Kyoto: Kokusainihonbunkasentaa.

Palmer, Frank R. 1986. *Mood and modality*. Cambridge: Cambridge University Press.

Pawley, Andrew, and Jonathan Lane. 1998. From event sequence to grammar: serial verb sonstructions in Kalam. In Blake, Barry J., Anna Siewierska and Jae Jung Song, eds., *Case, typology, and grammar: in honor of Barry J.Blake,* 201–227, Amsterdam: John Benjamins Publishing Company.

Payne, Thomas E. 1997. *Describing morphosyntax.* Cambridge: Cambridge University Press.

Pellard, Thomas. 2007. Miyako syohoogen no on'in no mondaiten. Paper read at the second workshop on Ryukyuan languages, held at Kyoto University (available on-line at the author's website): http://perso. orange.fr/japonica999/Miyakoonin20070909.pdf

Pellard, Thomas. 2009. Ōgami—Éléments de description d'un parler du Sud des Ryūkyū. Ph.D. thesis, École des hautes études en sciences sociales

Pellard, Thomas. 2015. The linguistic archeology of the Ryukyu islands. In

Heinrich, Patrick, Miyara, Shinsho and Shimoji, Michinori, eds., *Handbook of the Ryukyuan languages: History, structure, and use*, De Gruyter Mouton.

Quirk, Randolph, Sidney Greenbaum, Geoffrey Leech, and Jan Svartvik. 1985. *A Comprehensive Grammar of the English Language*. London: Longman.

Ryuukyuudaigaku hoogenkenkyuu kurabu. 2005. Irabu. Unpublished material.

Sadock, Jerrold M., and Arnold M. Zwicky. 1985. Speech act distinctions in syntax. In Shopen, Timothy. ed., *Language typology and syntactic description,* 155–196, Cambridge: Cambridge University Press.

Sato, Yamato. 1989. Hukugoogo ni okeru akusentokisoku to rendakukisoku. In Sugito, Miyoko, ed., *Nihongo no onsei on'in,* 233–265, Tokyo: Meijishoin.

Sawaki, Motoei. 2000. Controversial topics on Miyako dialect. *Onsei Kenkyuu* 4: 36–41.

Schachter, Paul. 1985. Parts-of-speech systems. In Shopen, Timothy, ed., *Language typology and syntactic description* (1), 3–61, Cambridge: Cambridge University Press.

Schachter, Paul, and Timothy Shopen. 2007. Parts-of-speech systems. In Shopen, Timothy, ed., *Language typology and syntactic description* (1), 2nd edition, 1–60, Cambridge: Cambridge University Press.

Seino, Tomoaki, and Shin Tanaka. 2006. The "passive" voice in Japanese and German: argument reduction versus argument extension. *Linguistics* 44 (2): 319–342.

Selkirk, Elisabeth. 1984. *Phonology and syntax: the relation between sound and structure.* Cambridge, MA: MIT Press.

Serafim, Leon A. 2003. When and from where did the Japonic language enter the Ryukyus? - A critical comparison of language, archaeology, and history. In Vovin, Alexander, and Toshiki Osada, eds., Nihongokeitooron no genzai, 463–476, Kyoto: Kokusainihonbunkasentaa.

Shiba, Ayako. 2005. Hutatsu no ukemi: hidooshashuyakuka to datsutadooka. *Nihongobunpoo* 5 (2).

Shibata, Takeshi. 1972. Nagahamahoogen. In NHK, ed., *Zenkokugoogenshiryoo* (11).Tokyo: NHK.

Shibatani, Masayoshi. 1990. *The languages of Japan.* Cambridge: Cambridge University Press.

Shibatani, Masayoshi, and Lillian M. Huang. 2006. Serial verb constructions in Formosan languages. The 3rd Oxford-Kobe Seminar in

Linguistics: The Linguistics of endangered Languages, Kobe, Japan.

Shimajiri, Soichi. 1983. Ryuukyuu Miyakohoogen no joshi: Noharahoogen no ga to u o chuushin ni. *Ryuudaikokugo* 2.

Shimoji, Kazuaki. 1979. *Miyakoguntoogojiten*. Yoneko Shimoji (privately-printed book).

Shimoji, Michinori. 2006. Minamiryuukyuu Miyako Irabujimahoogen. In Nakayama, Toshihide, and Fuyuki Ebata, eds., *Bunpoo o egaku* 1, 85–117. Tokyo: ILCAA.

Shimoji, Michinori. 2007. Irabu phonology. *Shigen* 3: 35–83.

Shimoji, Michinori. 2008a. Irabujimahoogen no dooshikussetsukeitairon. *Ryuukyuu no hoogen* 32: 69–114.

Shimoji, Michinori. 2008b. Ajiagatahukudooshi no danwakinoo to keitaitoogoron. In Shibasaki, Reijiroo, ed., *Gengobunka no kurosuroodo*, 85–110, Okinawa: Bunshin'insatsu.

Shimoji, Michinori. 2008c. Descriptive units and categories in Irabu. *Shigen* 4: 25–55.

Shimoji, Michinori. 2009a. The adjective class in Irabu Ryukyuan. *Studies in the Japanese Language* 5 (3): 33–50.

Shimoji, Michinori. 2009b. Foot and rhythmic structure in Irabu Ryukyuan. *Journal of Linguistic Society of Japan* 135.

Shimoji, Michinori. 2011. Irabu Ryukyuan. In Yamakoshi, Yasuhiro, ed., *Grammatical sketches from the field*, Tokyo: ILCAA.

Shinzato, Rumiko. 2013. Nominalization in Okinawan: from a diachronic and comparative perspective. In Yap, Foong. H. and Janick Wrona, eds., *Nominalization with and without copula in East Asian and Neighboring Languages*. The Netherlands: John Benjamins Publishing Company.

Shinzato, Rumiko, and Leon A. Serafim. 2003. Kakari musubi in comparative perspective: Old Japanese ka/ya and Okinawan -ga/-i. *Japanese/Korean Linguistics* 11: 189–202.

Silverstein, Michael. 1976. Hierarchy of features and ergativity. In Dixon, R.M.W., ed., *Grammatical categories in Australian languages*, 112–171, Canberra: Australian Institute of Aboriginal Studies.

Takubo, Yukinori. 2015. Issues in the verbal morphophonemics of Ikema Ryukyuan. Paper presented at Oninron Forum 2015.

Teramura, Hideo. 1993. *Teramura Hideo ronbunshuu* (1). Tokyo: Kuroshioshuppan.

Thompson, Sandra A. 1988. A discourse approach to the category "adjective". In Hawkins, John, ed., *Explaining language universals*, 167–

210, Oxford: Blackwell.

Thompson, Sandra A., and Robert E. Longacre. 1985. Adverbial clauses. In Shopen, Timothy, ed., *Language typology and syntactic description* (2), 171–234, Cambridge: Cambridge University Press.

Tomihama, Sadayoshi. 2013. *Miyako Irabu hogen jiten.* Naha: Okinawa Times.

Uchima, Chokujin. 1970. Ryuukyuuhoogen dooshikatsuyoo no kijutsu. In Hirayama Teruo Hakushi Kanreki Kinenkai, ed., *Hoogenkenkyuu no mondaiten.* Tookyoo: Meijishoin.

Uchima, Chokujin. 1985. Kakarimusubi no kakari no yowamari: Ryuukyuuhoogen no kakarimusubi o chuushin ni. *Okinawabunkak-enkyuu* 11: 223–244.

Uemura, Yukio.1997 [1992]. Soosetsu. In Kamei, Takashi, Rokuro Kono, and Eiichi Chino, eds., *Nipponrettoo no gengo* (Gengogakudaijiten special selection), 311–354, Tokyo: Sanseidoo.

Weber, David J. 1986. Information perspective, profile and patterns in Quechua. In Chafe, Wallace, and Johanna Nichols, eds., *Evidentiality: the linguistic encoding of epistemology,* 137–55, New York: Ablex.

Wetzer, Harrie. 1996. *The typology of adjectival predication.* Berlin and New York: Mouton.

Yamazaki, Hajime. 1973. Keiyooshi no hattatsu. In Suzuki, Kazuhiko, and Ooki Hayashi, eds., *Hinshibetsu Nihonbunpookooza* (4), Tokyo: Meijishoin.

Zwicky, Arnold M. 1977. *On clitics.* Indiana University Linguistic Club.

Subject Index

A

ablative   30, 83–84, 88, 138, 140, 162–163, 165, 305, 308, 398

accent   6–7, 51

accusative   11, 40, 44, 86, 112–113, 121, 138–140, 143–145, 148–151, 153, 166–168, 173, 312, 330, 336, 343, 386

adjective   10, 96–99, 102, 121–122, 124–125, 127–129, 191, 244–245, 249, 255, 260–267, 269, 271, 273, 278–279, 281–283, 285–286, 291–292, 331

adnominal clause   79, 86, 95, 118, 125–126, 130–137, 155, 168, 172, 186, 245, 272, 274, 283, 300–302, 357, 360, 364, 382, 387–389, 392–396, 398, 405

adnominal form (*rentaikei*), *see* unmarked form

adnominal word   81–82, 97–98, 102–103, 120, 124, 169–170, 180, 183, 185, 187, 191, 261, 264–265, 268–269, 280, 351, 357, 375, 381

adverb   10, 57, 77, 102–105, 122, 127, 172, 220, 236, 249–250, 255–256, 260, 262, 264–271, 276, 279–280, 291–292, 331, 338, 385, 397, 402

adverbial clause   87, 132, 147, 311, 381, 385–386, 390, 399, 404, 407, 409–410

affricate   16

alignment   138

allative   44, 110, 113, 115, 138–140, 154, 157–162

anaphora   143, 180

animacy   138, 142, 217–218, 220, 333–335

anticausative   343–345

apposition   125, 130, 136

approximant   9, 15

approximative   188, 190

argument structure   76, 111–112, 116–117, 234, 324, 372

aspect   11–12, 76, 105, 137–138, 144, 146–150, 152, 193, 195, 201–202, 228, 233, 241, 260, 308, 323, 331, 351, 363, 365–373, 381, 383

associative   83, 85, 138, 140, 163–164

auxiliary verb construction (AVC)   85, 92, 150, 201–202, 206, 224–226, 228–229, 234–236, 239–243, 272, 401

auxiliary verb   69, 75–76, 81, 85, 92–93, 150, 161, 195, 201–202, 228–229, 231–235, 241–243, 262, 266–267, 275, 315, 330–331, 336, 363, 365–372

B

bound marker   10, 75, 89, 91–92, 96, 102–103, 124, 293

C

case-marking   137, 167

causative   61, 65, 110, 115, 117, 158–159, 195, 221–222, 227, 243, 338–344, 347

central vowel   8, 39

clause-chaining   6, 70, 113, 195–196, 207, 330, 375, 379–380, 391, 404–

405

Clitic Group 91

clitic 13–14, 25, 35, 39, 48, 57, 75, 79–83, 86–92, 94, 134, 164, 191, 210, 274, 293, 295, 307, 356, 376, 408

coda 18–26, 28, 39, 43, 52–55, 212–213, 226

complementation 375, 394, 405

compound 4, 10, 14, 30, 37–38, 41, 71–73, 79, 87, 93, 118, 120–121, 175, 188, 193, 196, 212, 214, 224–227, 244, 249, 255, 257, 264–268, 277–285, 288, 291–292, 330–331, 368

conjugation 7, 198

conjunction 78, 81, 83, 85, 94–95, 100, 102, 106, 132, 274, 293–295, 363, 375–376, 379, 382, 405

consonant cluster 18, 22–23, 25–26, 30, 45

consonant inventory 15–16

converb 25, 42, 61, 113, 149–151, 195–196, 198–199, 206–207, 211–212, 215–219, 229, 232–233, 235, 237, 239, 241, 273, 275, 287, 306, 308, 330–331, 373, 379–380, 384–387, 407–408

coordination 100, 206, 235, 293, 375–379, 400, 404–405

copula verb 75–78, 94–95, 100–101, 164, 193, 197, 217–220, 231, 244–247, 261, 270, 274, 300, 302, 315, 336, 360

copular sentence, *see* predicate nominal

core argument 111–113, 117, 124, 137–138, 141, 163, 166–167, 315, 338, 390

D

dative 25, 44, 53, 110, 112–115, 117, 132–133, 138–140, 154–159, 161, 173, 263–264, 312, 332, 335, 338, 345, 347

declarative 315, 317, 323–324, 328, 378, 403

demonstrative 97, 142, 151, 169–173, 176, 187, 191, 350

dependency 11, 13, 79–81, 86–89, 92, 100, 130, 137, 233, 235, 293, 404–405

derivation 43, 212, 221, 257, 268, 270, 286, 288–291, 340, 342

diminutive 87, 129, 188–189, 261

diphthong 5, 24, 27, 44, 48, 52, 54, 288

dual 11, 175–176

E

epenthetic 16, 39

evidentiality 194, 354–355, 369

exclusive 11, 173–174, 176–177

existential verb 137, 150, 197, 217–220, 223, 242, 266, 271, 276, 332–335, 337

extended core argument 111, 113, 138, 154, 180, 315

extension 111, 123–124, 136, 169–170, 185, 198, 213, 261, 369

F

focus 11, 78, 86, 93, 99–100, 102–103, 105–106, 124, 136, 167, 229, 242, 244, 271–272, 276, 280, 283, 297, 310–311, 315–317, 321–323, 326–328, 356, 361, 365, 375, 378, 395–405, 409

foot 9–10, 13, 17, 52, 58–63, 66–70, 72–73, 88–91, 134, 226, 240, 298, 325

formal noun 45, 95, 130, 136, 164, 245, 280, 294–295, 300–302, 360, 382, 394–396

fricative 15–16, 18, 21, 27–28, 37, 39, 41–43, 51, 212–213

Subject Index

G

geminate 18, 20, 23, 26–30, 36, 38–40, 42–44, 46, 51, 54, 72, 198, 212–213, 226, 288, 303, 321

genitive 11, 79, 98, 103, 123–129, 136, 138, 140–142, 150, 172–175, 177, 180, 191, 261

glide 16, 22, 47, 49

grammatical relation 75, 108–111, 117, 312, 335

grammaticalisation 92–93, 130, 134, 246, 288, 394

H

honorific 8, 108, 142, 221–224

I

imperative 106, 144, 194, 206, 215–216, 224, 320, 325, 327, 352, 359, 396, 407

inclusive 11, 173–177, 351

inflection 11, 76, 105, 113, 150, 193–198, 202–204, 206, 208, 210, 214–217, 227, 232–233, 235, 237, 240–241, 245–246, 261, 271–273, 275–276, 296, 323, 327, 331, 351–352, 356–358, 361–362, 365, 372, 376–377, 397

information-structure 85, 99, 102, 124, 138, 166, 310–311, 397–398

instrumental 116–117, 138, 140, 157, 162, 175, 185, 187, 315, 341–342, 389

insubordination 378

interjection 8, 10, 81, 96, 103, 107–108, 251

intonation 57, 90, 235, 240–241, 251, 323, 327, 376, 378, 386, 400

K

kakarimusubi 11, 361, 396–397

kinship term 128, 138, 142

L

language contact 350

limitative 138, 140, 165, 294, 305, 309

limiter 3, 85, 99, 102–103, 124, 140, 165–167, 305, 309, 380

long vowel 5, 16, 24, 27, 34–35, 44, 49–52, 54, 288

M

malefactive 195, 221–223, 338, 347–350

minimal contrast 17, 35, 48

modality 100–101, 193–194, 246, 296, 351, 362–363

mood 8, 11–12, 25, 97, 193–195, 202–204, 206, 210, 235, 239, 245, 304, 323, 351–352, 355–360, 386, 402, 407

mora 13, 32–36, 38, 44, 51–63, 66, 68, 73, 88–92, 98, 122, 127, 213, 226, 251, 287, 298, 324, 387

N

nasal 15, 19–20, 22, 26, 28, 31, 33, 35–36, 43–46, 61, 84, 156, 173–174

negation 78, 193–195, 210, 217, 239, 272, 275–276, 314–315, 323, 336–338, 356, 386–387, 404, 407

nominal word class 96

nominalisation 29, 48, 55, 135, 210, 214, 226, 251, 268, 286, 288–289, 350, 392

nominative 11, 35, 94, 109, 112–113, 128–129, 138, 140–142, 166–168, 172–174, 177, 180, 184, 305, 311–312, 334–335, 406

nucleus 9, 19–20, 23, 27, 39, 42–43, 51, 198, 212, 321

number 11, 124–125, 172–173, 175–176, 182, 193

numeral 124–125, 143, 175, 179–182, 184, 244

O

onomatopoeic word 107–108
onset 9, 15–16, 18–28, 30–32, 37, 39, 41–42, 46, 49, 51, 66, 73, 135, 198, 321

P

part of speech, *see* word class
particle, *see* bound marker
partitive 11, 110, 112–113, 138–140, 143–146, 148–153, 287–288, 329–331, 335, 380–381
passive 61, 65–66, 109, 111, 154, 156, 195, 221–223, 338, 344–347, 349–350
peripheral argument (adjunct) 75, 111, 116–117, 137–138, 140, 154, 162, 164–165, 180, 187–188, 264, 305, 315, 342, 389–390, 393, 398
person 11, 35, 48–50, 53, 89–90, 94, 142, 156, 172–179, 189, 193, 346, 350, 351
phoneme inventory 15–16, 47, 49
phonotactics 15–16, 18, 20, 22, 24–26, 31–32, 35, 38–39, 41, 45, 73, 87, 211–212, 226
pitch 9–10, 52–53, 55–57, 90–92, 324
plurality 11, 61, 80, 83–85, 87, 89, 170, 173–177, 188–190, 278
potential modality 194, 246, 352, 358, 360
potential voice 112, 221–223
predicate nominal (nominal predicate) 75, 77–78, 94–95, 97, 100–101, 103, 123–124, 169, 193, 219, 231, 244, 246, 257, 263, 274, 291–292, 296, 329–331
pronoun 11, 35, 53, 68, 89–90, 94, 96–97, 124, 128, 138, 142, 145, 156, 169–170, 172–180, 187, 189, 237, 244, 334, 350–351, 392
proper name 56, 128, 138, 142, 145

property concept stem (PC stem) 6, 98, 104–105, 119, 122, 127, 129, 193, 221, 249–252, 254–257, 260–261, 264–265, 267–268, 270–273, 276–280, 283, 285–292, 331
property concept 6, 10, 125, 127, 137, 193, 221, 249–250, 252, 256, 267
prosody 6, 8–10, 14, 17, 24, 26, 35, 51–54, 56–57, 62–63, 66–67, 69–72, 87–89, 92, 134, 226, 297–298, 324, 387, 392, 408

Q

quantifier 99, 103, 124, 140, 179, 305–307
question 16–17, 31, 181, 184, 297–298, 302, 311, 315–317, 320–321, 323, 325–328, 355–356, 358, 363, 402–404, 408
quotation 127, 179, 251, 289–290, 395–396

R

reduplication 6, 10, 14, 75, 97, 104, 117, 121–122, 129, 171, 195, 250–251, 260–261, 267, 289–290, 365, 373
referentiality 133, 144–145, 148, 153, 285
reflexive 68, 109, 172, 177–179, 237, 335, 350–351
relative clause, *see* adnominal clause
rendaku, *see* sequential voicing
rentai form, *see* unmarked form
resonant 9, 15, 17–21, 23–26, 28–31, 33, 35–37, 43, 46, 211–213
rhythm 10, 12, 62, 67, 72–73, 134, 324

S

sequential voicing (*rendaku*) 37–38, 41–42, 71, 73, 120–121, 227 serial verb construction (SVC) 72, 76, 224–230, 233–237, 239–240, 379, 385–387, 392, 407–408

short vowel 35, 40, 49–51

speech act 12, 175, 297, 311, 316, 323, 376, 394, 396

stop 15, 19–21, 28–29, 43, 211

subordination 11, 100, 195, 235, 375, 382, 385, 387, 396, 404–405

suppletion 220

syllabic consonant (nucleic resonant) 9, 19–20

syllable 7, 13–26, 28, 30–37, 41–43, 46, 49, 53–57, 67, 71, 73, 122, 182, 198, 207, 213, 321

T

tap 9, 15

tense 8, 11–12, 78, 97, 193–195, 202–204, 206, 235, 239, 243–245, 267, 323, 351–352, 356, 360–361, 363–364, 386–387, 404

thematic vowel 72, 196, 198–202, 213–214, 221

tone 6, 9–10, 12–13, 17, 51–59, 62, 64, 66–67, 69–70, 87–91, 310, 317,
387, 402

topic 11, 38–39, 44, 99–100, 102–104, 109, 112–115, 138, 152–153, 166, 173, 240, 242, 271–272, 282–283, 309–315, 319, 330, 334–336, 373, 382, 391, 395–396, 404–408

U

unmarked form 126, 205, 210, 230, 274, 301, 352, 356–357, 360–363, 376, 387, 396–397

V

verb serialisation, *see* serial verb construction

W

word class 96–97, 169, 193, 268, 271

word minimality 24, 27, 32, 35, 43, 58, 71, 73, 88–89, 118, 213

word order 10

Z

zero case (ellipsis) 79, 124, 137–138, 167–168

Language Index

Altaic 235

Amami 4

Austronesian 11, 177

Bora 245

Chinese 128

English 129, 131, 134, 163–164, 263, 268, 319, 363, 395

Finnish 11, 148, 151

Gusukube 144

Hirara 7–8, 57, 144, 152–153, 260,
284, 303

Ikema 3–8, 42, 144, 150, 152, 303

Irabu-Nakachi 4–5, 403

Ishigaki 370

Japanese 2–4, 10–11, 14, 17, 37, 56, 97, 104, 133, 137–138, 167, 182, 191–192, 195, 200, 211, 235, 243, 261, 271, 273, 310, 345–346, 350, 361, 367, 411

Japonic 2–3, 11, 36, 128, 177, 199,

214–215, 271, 388, 396–397
Karimata 152
Korean 235
Kuninaka 4–5, 12
Miyako 2–4, 6–9, 25, 57, 144, 152–153, 167, 173, 245, 251–252, 260, 284, 303, 352, 397
Nagahama 4–6, 12, 260, 403, 411
Northern Ryukyuan 2–3, 133
Ogami 7
Okinawan 4

Phillipine language 128
pre-Modern Japanese 271, 345–346, 396
Russian 150
Sarahama 4–6
Sawada 4–6, 12
Southern Ryukyuan 2–4, 7, 370
Tarama 3
Tungusic 355
Yaeyama 3

Studies in the Humanities

The Faculty of Humanities, Kyushu University, as a center of research in and education on the Humanities, has set up a fund to publish the results of its academic research under the series title *Studies in the Humanities*, to promote its research activities and share the outcomes with a wide audience.

Already published in the series:

1　王昭君から文成公主へ——中国古代の国際結婚——
　　藤野月子（九州大学大学院人文科学研究院・専門研究員）

2　水の女——トポスへの船路——
　　小黒康正（九州大学大学院人文科学研究院・教授）

3　小林方言とトルコ語のプロソディー
　　　　　　——一型アクセント言語の共通点——
　　佐藤久美子（長崎外国語大学外国語学部・講師）

4　背表紙キャサリン・アーンショー
　　　　　　——イギリス小説における自己と外部——
　　鵜飼信光（九州大学大学院人文科学研究院・准教授）

5　朝鮮中近世の公文書と国家——変革期の任命文書をめぐって——
　　川西裕也（日本学術振興会特別研究員 PD）　〈第4回三島海雲学術賞受賞〉

6　始めから考える——ハイデッガーとニーチェ——
　　菊地惠善（九州大学大学院人文科学研究院・教授）

7　日本の出版物流通システム——取次と書店の関係から読み解く—
　　秦　洋二（流通科学大学商学部・准教授）　〈第7回地理空間学会賞学術
　
8　御津の浜松一言抄——『浜松中納言物語』を最終巻から読み解
　　辛島正雄（九州大学大学院人文科学研究院・教授）

9　南宋の文人と出版文化——王十朋と陸游をめぐって——
　　甲斐雄一（日本学術振興会特別研究員 PD）

10　戦争と平和，そして革命の時代のインタナショ
　　山内昭人（九州大学大学院人文科学研究院・教授）

11　On Weak-Phases: An Extension of Feature-
　　Tomonori Otsuka (Lecturer of English Linguistics, Kyus

12　A Grammar of Irabu, A Southern Ryuky
　　Michinori Shimoji (Associate Professor of Linguist

Studies in the Humanities

The Faculty of Humanities, Kyushu University, as a center of research in and education on the Humanities, has set up a fund to publish the results of its academic research under the series title *Studies in the Humanities*, to promote its research activities and share the outcomes with a wide audience.

Already published in the series:

1 王昭君から文成公主へ――中国古代の国際結婚――
藤野月子（九州大学大学院人文科学研究院・専門研究員）

2 水の女――トポスへの船路――
小黒康正（九州大学大学院人文科学研究院・教授）

3 小林方言とトルコ語のプロソディー
――一型アクセント言語の共通点――
佐藤久美子（長崎外国語大学外国語学部・講師）

4 背表紙キャサリン・アーンショー
――イギリス小説における自己と外部――
鵜飼信光（九州大学大学院人文科学研究院・准教授）

5 朝鮮中近世の公文書と国家――変革期の任命文書をめぐって――
川西裕也（日本学術振興会特別研究員PD）　〈第4回三島海雲学術賞受賞〉

6 始めから考える――ハイデッガーとニーチェ――
菊地惠善（九州大学大学院人文科学研究院・教授）

7 日本の出版物流通システム――取次と書店の関係から読み解く――
秦　洋二（流通科学大学商学部・准教授）　〈第7回地理空間学会賞学術賞受賞〉

8 御津の浜松一言抄――『浜松中納言物語』を最終巻から読み解く――
辛島正雄（九州大学大学院人文科学研究院・教授）

9 南宋の文人と出版文化――王十朋と陸游をめぐって――
甲斐雄一（日本学術振興会特別研究員PD）

10 戦争と平和，そして革命の時代のインタナショナル
山内昭人（九州大学大学院人文科学研究院・教授）

11 On Weak-Phases: An Extension of Feature-Inheritance
Tomonori Otsuka（Lecturer of English Linguistics, Kyushu Kyoritsu University）

12 A Grammar of Irabu, A Southern Ryukyuan Language
Michinori Shimoji（Associate Professor of Linguistics, Kyushu University）

（著者の所属等は刊行時のもの）